D1321210

Agricultural Economics and Rural Sociology

The Contemporary Core Literature

A volume in the series

The Literature of the Agricultural Sciences

WALLACE C. OLSEN, Series Editor

AGRICULTURAL ECONOMICS AND RURAL SOCIOLOGY

The Contemporary Core Literature

Wallace C. Olsen

With Contributions by

Margot A. Bellamy *and*

Bernard F. Stanton

Cornell University Press

ITHACA AND LONDON

This book was typeset from disks supplied by the staff of the
Core Literature Project, Albert R. Mann Library, Cornell University.
Gwen Urey and Sharon Van De Mark prepared the machine-readable text.

First published 1991 by Cornell University Press.

International Standard Book Number 0-8014-2677-4
Library of Congress Catalog Card Number 91-55261
Printed in the United States of America
Librarians: Library of Congress cataloging information appears on the last page of the book.

♾ The paper in this book meets the minimum requirements of the American National Standard for Information Sciences—Permanence of Paper for Printed Library Materials, ANSI Z39.48-1984.

Dedicated to agricultural pioneers
Hulda A. Olsen, homesteader, and
I. T. Littleton, pathfinder in the literature
of agricultural economics

Contents

Preface

This book grew out of my long-standing desire to analyze the literature of the agricultural sciences. The project became feasible with the advent of sophisticated machine-readable bibliographic records in large quantity and the software to study trends and changes. Online bibliographic utilities, locally mounted computer tapes, and compact disks with hundreds of thousands of citations make advanced analysis economically possible. Agricultural economics and rural sociology are appropriately the first subjects explored because they traditionally encompass basic agricultural precepts, policy formulation and the philosophy of agriculture. This subject area is the first in a projected series of volumes examining the literature of the agricultural sciences.

One aim in undertaking the work was to provide assistance to persons engaged in several areas of library and literature collection management. The timing is apropos because of the increased importance attached to evaluating academic collections and the prospect of being able to store full texts electronically. Also, dramatic changes have occurred in the agricultural world as a result of internationalization, self-sufficiency, and competition. The 1980s appear to have been a watershed in world agriculture as well as in its literature. The growth of literature concerned with international agricultural development is accelerating. Academic institutions and research organizations in the Third World are beginning to have an increased local or regional impact, but many of these institutions lack the financial or other capabilities to provide the necessary literature resources to support this dramatic change. Because journals, monographs and reports are difficult to access in many Third World countries, the Rockefeller Foundation has underwritten the systematic study of the literature to determine what is of paramount value to developing countries. Hence, the work was conceived as a project to assist academic institutions in both the developed and the developing countries. With this framework in mind, the management of

Cornell University's Albert R. Mann Library established the following goals:

(1) Analysis of the literature aims to provide better tools for evaluating and determining the strengths and weaknesses of academic collections, in terms of both instructional and research literature;
(2) The evaluation and analysis system should assist in establishing rankings of specific titles for historical preservation; and
(3) Several useful scholarly products would result, including a critical review of the literature of the disciplines of the agricultural sciences and, most important, listings of the currently most valuable monographs, journals, and report series. Also to be provided, as a portion of the total study, are evaluation tools and title compilations for agricultural literature important to the Third World. A final undertaking will be the storage, page by page, of the core literature on compact disks for Third World use.[1]

I began work on the project in 1988, prior to receiving external financing. After thirteen months, and with the advent of Rockefeller and other funding, support personnel were added. The analysis of citations in books and journals is highly labor intensive, requiring concentration on details. Near the end of the second year, a larger staff was assembled and the scope of the project increased to cover examination of older, historically important literature as well as that of current value. When study of a new subject area begins, a steering committee of scientists in that discipline and experienced librarians is brought together to set the subject parameters and agree upon the course of action. The Core Literature Project staff of the Mann Library is then responsible for locating the literature and interacting with scholars and evaluators. This staff analyzes citations, data and trends, formulates conclusions, and does the primary writing, all of which is critically reviewed by steering committee members and others.

The other six volumes planned are:

Agricultural Engineering;
Animal Science and Health;
Soil Science;
Crop Improvement and Protection;
Food Science and Human Nutrition; and
Forestry and Silviculture.

The nature and scope of each agricultural subject, rather than any overall format, will determine the contents of each volume.

United States and world agricultural scholars and literature collectors will find assistance here in evaluating their collection strengths, in measuring

[1]Jan K. Olsen, Strategic Issues in Information: With Special Reference to Developing Countries, in *IAALD Quarterly Bulletin* XXXIV, 3 (1989).

their journal literature holdings, and in making decisions for preservation of historically pertinent literature. Agricultural economists and rural sociologists will find quantitative and qualitative data on the literature of their fields.

Acknowledgments

The staff of Mann Library, Cornell University, has been patient with my many requests and very helpful in locating hard-to-find items of literature. The Library's director has been untiring in her support of this book and the work of the Core Literature Project. Gwen Urey provided valuable service in solving early difficulties, counseling me, assisting with statistical decisions, and managing the computerized input and organization of files. Sharon Van De Mark has contined this extensive support in a cheerful and speedy manner. The patience of both was tried and not found wanting. This work is heavily indebted to the support of the Rockefeller Foundation.

The errors and oversights in the text are those of the author. Many more avenues of investigation should have been pursued, but not all roads could be taken. Many questions remain to be answered by other researchers.

WALLACE C. OLSEN

Ithaca, New York

Agricultural Economics and Rural Sociology

The Contemporary Core Literature

1. Trends and Development of Agricultural Economics and Rural Sociology in the United States

BERNARD F. STANTON

Department of Agricultural Economics Cornell University

The academic disciplines known as agricultural economics and rural sociology in the 1990s had their origins in the ferment of the late nineteenth and early twentieth centuries. The years from 1865 to 1900 were difficult ones in rural America. The new lands brought into production west of the Mississippi and the new agricultural technologies adopted in the recently settled Midwest meant that agricultural supply persistently outpaced domestic and international demand. Farm prices were low; farmers were restive and politically active. The Granger and Populist movements and the Greenback party owed much of their strength to farmers and other rural people looking for better conditions for themselves and their families. It was in this environment that the first studies of enterprise costs and returns were made, the first agricultural surveys were completed, and the American Country Life Movement was initiated at the turn of the century.

A. Early Years, 1900–1920

Agricultural supply and demand came more nearly into balance in the first two decades of the twentieth century. State and federal funding for colleges of agriculture and agricultural experiment stations made possible the first serious investigations of farm business activity at a variety of locations across the country. Resources for a few studies of rural society were also provided in this way.

Agronomists interested in the economics of farming and economists con-

The outline for this chapter benefited from the suggestions and comments of Dr. Olaf Larson, Department of Rural Sociology, Cornell University, but does not reflect the considered views of a rural sociologist.

cerned about the agricultural economy joined forces to form the American Farm Management Association in 1910, and the American Association of Agricultural Economists was established by members of the American Economics Association in 1917. In 1919 the two separate associations joined forces to create the American Farm Economic Association (American Agricultural Economics Association after 1968) and began publication of the *Journal of Farm Economics* (*American Journal of Agricultural Economics* after 1968).

Within the U.S. Department of Agriculture (USDA), several groups worked on economic issues and rural social policy from 1902 onward. The Bureau of Agricultural Economics (BAE) was established July 1, 1922. The Division of Farm Population and Rural Life within the BAE was a national center for work on demography and rural sociology. Early research in agricultural economics centered on farm management and ways to improve farm profitability. Land use patterns, distribution of federal lands, and conservation were also investigated, and the first studies of commodity prices and market institutions began. The foundation of the two disciplines as they are known today were well established before 1920.

The leaders in the field wrote the first textbooks during these years. Henry C. Taylor was the first to use the expression "agricultural economics" in the title of his classic text, *An Introduction to the Study of Agricultural Economics*.[1] Another important work was *Principles of Rural Economics*,[2] by T.N. Carver, a Harvard professor of economics influential in the beginnings of both rural sociology and agricultural economics. Also a major figure was Liberty Hyde Bailey, whom President Theodore Roosevelt appointed chairman of the Country Life Commission. Bailey's book *The Country Life Movement*[3] provides a sense of the concerns of the time to improve the lot of rural people. In 1913 John M. Gillette's *Constructive Rural Sociology*,[4] the first text in rural sociology, appeared, as did George F. Warren's *Farm Management*,[5] the best-selling textbook of the period. Thomas F. Hunt, another central influence and author of the important *How to Choose a Farm*,[6] taught agronomy and farm management at the University of Illinois and Pennsylvania State, Cornell, and Ohio State universities, and was a dean at the University of California. Taylor dedicated his book,

1. Henry C. Taylor, *An Introduction to the Study of Agricultural Economics* (New York: Macmillan, 1905).
2. T. N. Carver, *Principles of Rural Economics* (New York: Ginn, 1911).
3. Liberty Hyde Bailey, *The Country Life Movement* (New York: Macmillan, 1911).
4. John M. Gillette, *Constructive Rural Sociology* (New York: Sturgis and Walton, 1913).
5. George F. Warren, *Farm Management* (New York: Macmillan, 1913).
6. Thomas F. Hunt, *How to Choose a Farm* (New York: Macmillan, 1913).

The Story of Agricultural Economics,[7] to Hunt, "who opened the door for agricultural economics in the land-grant colleges."

B. The Agricultural Depression of the 1920s

The period of World War I was a time of relatively high prices for farm products. Land prices rose; rural America prospered. The agricultural adjustments following World War I proved more difficult than had been imagined. The capacity for increased production encouraged by the war effort was in place, but there was no money in international markets to buy the added output from American farms. Farm prices fell, but the prices of such farm inputs as machinery and fertilizer rose. The real value of farm land fell every year for fourteen consecutive years starting in 1920. The bust that followed the war boom was traumatic. Farm foreclosures and sales for taxes became common. While much of the rest of the country was doing well, the rural economy was in depression.

Some farm leaders proposed cooperatives and cooperative marketing as one way to control supplies of individual crops voluntarily, but these efforts failed. Studies of cooperatives, encouraged by the Capper-Volstead Act (1922), and research on commodity markets were given substantial attention by agricultural economists. Price analysis and the first statistical studies of demand and supply were completed. Elmes Working's famous article, "What Do Statistical Demand Curves Show?," in the 1927 *Quarterly Journal of Economics*,[8] reflected the substantial efforts to understand more fully the underlying relationships responsible for the economic circumstances observed in the 1920s.

Major studies of land use to discover why some land was forced out of production while other soils were used intensively were given priority. The incidence of farm foreclosures and bank failures spurred investigations of agricultural credit and finance. The Purnell Act of 1925 provided federal funds for studies of marketing, public policy alternatives, and sociological investigations. The federal government's first efforts to assist farmers in controlling supplies came with the creation of the Federal Farm Board and the authorization to purchase and store surplus commodities. The USDA and colleges began to develop price series and index numbers of production

7. Henry C. Taylor and Anne Dewees Taylor, *The Story of Agricultural Economics in the United States, 1840–1932: Men—Services—Ideas* (Ames, Iowa: Iowa State College Press, 1952).

8. Elmer J. Working, "What Do Statistical Demand Curves Show?" *Quarterly Journal of Economics* 41 (1927): 212–35.

to insure that all actors in agricultural markets had access to current and historical information. Agricultural outlook efforts stemmed from this period.

One of the most influential figures during this period and in subsequent decades was John D. Black, University of Minnesota, who moved to Harvard University in the late 1920s. His book *Introduction to Production Economics*[9] had a major impact on both economics and agricultural economics. Leadership in land economics centered around Richard T. Ely, of the University of Wisconsin and the Institute of Land and Public Utility Economics (founded in 1920). *Land Economics*, a new journal launched in 1925, is still recognized internationally.

W. J. Spillman, first director of the USDA's Office of Farm Management in 1902, produced a book of lasting interest with Emil Lang, *The Law of Diminishing Returns*.[10] This was one of the first formulations of Alexander Mitscherlich's procedures to estimate mathematical production functions. The importance of cooperatives in agricultural marketing as a field of study was suggested in 1923 by O. B. Jesness, in *The Cooperative Marketing of Farm Products*.[11] The first International Conference of Agricultural Economists hosted in 1929 at Dartington Hall, England, by Leonard Elmhirst fostered international interactions among agricultural economists. Out of this meeting grew the International Association of Agricultural Economists, with Elmhirst as founder president.

C. The 1930s and the Great Depression

Few times in the history of the United States were more trying than the depth of the Great Depression, 1932–34. Franklin Roosevelt's New Deal and government intervention in agriculture were accepted in part because much of the U.S. economic system had essentially collapsed. These were years of great experimentation. Much of what is accepted today in public policy with respect to agriculture had its origins in these years. Henry A. Wallace, secretary of agriculture for President Franklin Roosevelt, encouraged a wide range of study and research at the state and federal level. The Bureau of Agricultural Economics, USDA, fostered a remarkable amount

9. John D. Black, *Introduction to Production Economics* (New York: Henry Holt, 1926).

10. W. J. Spillman and Emil Lang, *The Law of Diminishing Returns* (Yonkers on Hudson: World Book, 1924).

11. O. B. Jesness, *The Cooperative Marketing of Farm Products* (Philadelphia: J. B. Lippincott, 1923).

of substantive interaction, inviting anyone who had ideas to try to solve the many problems of agriculture and rural America.

During the Depression agricultural policy emerged as an important area for study in agricultural economics; research and extension concentrated on marketing, price analysis, and finance. Land use policy, particularly the plight of sharecroppers and those forced off their land, received special attention. Data handling and statistics made major advances. Ezekiel's *Methods of Correlation Analysis*[12] was influential, as was the advent of IBM equipment and desk calculators.

Rural sociology emerged as a separate discipline in the social sciences with the formation of the Rural Sociological Society in 1937 and its national journal, *Rural Sociology*, in 1936. A separate "rural" section in the American Sociological Society had existed since 1921. In the land-grant colleges, the growth of rural sociology accelerated in the 1930s; most professionals in this field were members of university departments of sociology or agricultural economics.

Charles J. Galpin, head of the Division of Farm Population and Rural Life, BAE, 1919–34, played a major role in encouraging the establishment of rural sociology in the land-grant colleges and universities. The number of full-time rural social scientists was small, so cooperative work between staffs at the USDA and the land-grant colleges was common. Carl C. Taylor, division head from 1935 to 1952, was a leader in rural sociology and actively promoted the use of rural sociology in government policies and programs.

The combination of droughts in 1934 and 1936, lack of markets for U.S. agricultural commodities, and no jobs outside agriculture for rural people focused substantial public attention on the plight of rural Americans. The government invested federal funds in roads and bridges, the rural electrification system, public works and buildings, and conservation efforts on individual farms. Rural social scientists were involved in these special programs' administration, research, and outreach. Other agricultural academic disciplines began to recognize the extent of contributions from rural social scientists.

The New Deal years saw a number of new agencies created, along with a wide range of federal programs. The Soil Conservation Service, the Tennessee Valley Authority, the Resettlement Administration (today's Farmers' Home Administration), and the Rural Electrification Administration remain vital in the 1990s. Collection of data received new impetus as a requirement

12. Mordecai Ezekiel, *Methods of Correlation Analysis* (New York: Wiley, 1930).

for administering these programs and to evaluate their impact on individuals and rural society. Demand for the products of rural social scientists rose.

D. The 1940s and World War II

The second great war of the twentieth century ended the days of surplus agricultural production and put new emphasis on labor efficiency, work simplification, and capital-labor substitution. The great exodus of U.S. workers out of agriculture to industry, the replacement of animal power with tractors and trucks, and the adoption of new technology came with a rush. Crisis leads to rapid change. Agricultural production was encouraged and supported. Planning efforts required by the war gave new emphasis to macroeconomics, W. W. Leontief's input-output models, and aggregate analysis procedures.

The ferment of the immediate postwar years caused a new awareness of the international dimension, both in problems to be solved and in the consciousness of those who had spent time outside the United States during World War II. The need for professionals in the rural social sciences was now much greater than the supply. Graduate education was encouraged by federal assistance and the rapid expansion of research, extension, and agricultural business activity. T. W. Schultz's book *Agriculture in an Unstable Economy*[13] reflected what had been learned from experience with New Deal programs and the problems that agriculture had to face in the postwar years. Agricultural policy became a major area for study and scholarship. Debate ensued over government intervention and methods. The Marshall Plan and efforts to rebuild agriculture in both the developed world of Europe and Japan and the less developed countries of Asia and South America created a new focus for work and expanded the opportunities for rural sociologists and farm economists.

E. The 1950s and 1960s

As the U.S. economy grew steadily during the 1950s and 1960s its importance rose in international trade and commerce. A quiet revolution occurred in U.S. agriculture as the number of farms fell from 5.4 million in 1950 to 2.7 million in 1969. Half of the farms went out of business or were combined into larger units in a span of twenty years. Displaced farmers

13. T. W. Schultz, *Agriculture in an Unstable Economy* (New York: McGraw-Hill, 1945).

moved into industrial or service positions. Tractor power, mechanization, and new technology increased labor productivity very rapidly. Supplies of agricultural products outstripped aggregate demand. In the 1950s and 1960s the central concern was agricultural surpluses and methods to control them effectively.

This was also a time of major growth in funding for agricultural research, teaching, and extension at both state and federal levels. The public university system expanded rapidly. Enrollments in graduate schools soared; aggregate demand for qualified teachers and researchers exceeded supply. Increasingly, students from around the world came to the United States for graduate study in the agricultural sciences, including agricultural economics and rural sociology.

Agricultural development in the Third World became an area for serious study with the advent of U.S. Public Law 480 which provided the use of U.S. farm surpluses both as a source of humanitarian aid as well as a way to support agricultural development in less developed countries. P.L. 480 allowed Third World countries to buy U.S. surpluses in their local currencies which had to be spent by the U.S. in those developing countries. Funding was provided for university projects overseas working to rebuild and develop agricultural research and educational institutions. Agricultural economists and rural sociologists were major participants in these programs. A flow of studies and research papers resulted, describing the various processes of development, difficulties encountered, and proposed solutions. J. W. Mellor's *Economics of Agricultural Development*[14] was one of the first classic texts, widely used and translated into a number of foreign languages.

International trade and commodity analyses commanded increased attention. This was a natural counterpart to international aid programs and efforts to move large quantities of food and feed grains into both soft and hard currency markets. The formation of the European Economic Community (EEC) and its Common Agricultural Policy focused even more attention on methods of protection to support U.S. agriculture and ways to assure access to overseas markets. Trade and aid were very much at the center of policy discussions in the United States.

Production economics also entered the spotlight. Earl O. Heady's *Economics of Agricultural Production and Resource Use*[15] influenced the education and research of agricultural economists around the world. Interdis-

14. John W. Mellor, *The Economics of Agricultural Development* (Ithaca, N.Y.: Cornell University Press, 1966).

15. Earl O. Heady, *Economics of Agricultural Production and Resource Use* (New York: Prentice Hall, 1952).

ciplinary studies involving agronomists, animal scientists, and agricultural economists became much more common; this pattern of cooperative work on field experiments and their analysis began to appear in overseas settings as well.

The 1950s and 1960s marked a rapid upsurge in the use of statistics, quantitative methods, and econometrics. Linear programming burst on the scene as a useful tool in solving a variety of problems from least cost rations for livestock to plant location to optimal distribution systems. Fred Waugh, Karl Fox, and Marc Nerlove made striking contributions in the developing field of econometrics in the Bureau of Agricultural Economics, USDA.[16] Availability of high-speed computing facilities encouraged a strong shift toward more statistics and quantitative methods in graduate programs in the rural social sciences.

The concept of "agribusiness" was developed and popularized early in this period, with its emphasis on the interrelationships among input suppliers, farmers, processors and food manufacturers, and food retailers. Marketing research expanded rapidly with substantial funding from both state and federal sources. Increasingly, marketing research projects were partially funded or carried out in cooperation with large agricultural cooperatives or with corporations that had interests in the food and agricultural sector. Experimental designs for market testing, which are now almost universally used in industry, were pioneered by agricultural economists and biometricians.

Rural poverty and the needs of the institutions serving rural America were highlighted in the report of President Lyndon Johnson's National Advisory Commission on Rural Poverty, *The People Left Behind.*[17] Community surveys and studies included significant inputs from local groups, as they investigated differentials between rural and urban incomes, services, and facilities. Rural development efforts received new emphasis. Methodology for input-output analysis at the county or regional level was developed.

Rural sociology began to include social-psychological approaches as workers addressed such issues as the adoption and diffusion of farm practices, the career choices of rural youth, and protest movements by farmers. Methodological sophistication advanced in terms of sample design and anal-

16. a. Frederick V. Waugh, *Selected Writings on Agricultural Policy and Economic Analysis*, edited by Martin E. Abel and James P. Houck (Minneapolis: University of Minnesota Press, 1984). b. Karl A. Fox, *Econometric Analysis for Public Policy* (Ames, Iowa: Iowa State College Press, 1958). (Reprinted in 1977.) c. Marc Nerlove, *The Dynamics of Supply: Estimation of Farmers' Response to Price* (Baltimore: Johns Hopkins University Press, 1958). (Reprinted in 1978 by AMS Press.)

17. United States National Advisory Commission on Rural Poverty, *The People Left Behind* (Washington, D.C.: U.S. Government Printing Office, 1967).

ysis, including scaling. Funding of regional research at agricultural experiment stations encouraged analysis of changing demographics in rural areas and comparative rural social systems.

Rural social scientists were actively involved in the study and analysis of federal food stamp programs, surplus commodity distributions, and the expansion of school milk and lunch programs. Working with nutritionists, sociologists examined the impact of these federal programs on the health and well-being of participants, and they identified people at risk. The Women, Infants and Children (WIC) program and school breakfasts were just two results of the new cooperation between nutritionists, rural sociologists, and agricultural economists.

These decades witnessed growth in the numbers of professionals and rising academic recognition for agricultural economists and rural sociologists. The numbers of universities giving graduate degrees in these fields increased; opportunities for research and study across disciplines grew; international exchange of scholars became much more common. The first World Congress of Rural Sociology was held in 1964. The International Association of Agricultural Economists now included members from all continents, with meetings held beyond the borders of Europe and North America.

F. International Disciplines—The 1970s and 1980s

After more than twenty years of concerns about excess capacity in American agriculture and a series of federal programs to limit planted acreage, in the early 1970s demand caught up with supply. Prices fluctuated widely. Acreage restrictions were removed and world attention was directed to potential *shortages* of food, not surpluses. By the mid-1980s, surpluses of grain and export crops were a central problem for world agriculture; the bust that follows a boom had occurred in commercial agriculture in both Europe and North America. Government intervention was more substantial than ever in farming in most of the richer countries of the world.

In this setting, international market forces came to the fore, because they increasingly determined how domestic policy would be constructed. In turn, domestic policies had a strong impact on international competitiveness. Macroeconomic policy, world trade, and international finance demanded greater attention. In the 1980s, the United States ceased to be the world's largest creditor and became the world's largest debtor. The international dimensions of the rural social sciences were now a regular component of the work of most professionals, no longer the province of the specialists in trade and development.

With increasingly powerful quantitative tools and advances in computer technology, econometrics and sociometrics were integral parts of most research programs and projects. Agricultural journals included more algebra and mathematics; most professionals around the world had access to sophisticated computing procedures. Model building and simulation studies became common. Less and less research funding went to the collection of primary data, while more analytical efforts were expended on secondary data and national data-gathering. Mail questionnaires and telephone interviews replaced personal interviews as the costs of field studies became prohibitive. Systems analysis, much talked about in earlier decades, became more nearly a reality, although the complexity of the real world defied the ability of research workers to capture the true subtleties in a set of properly specified equations.

Natural resource economics grew in both academic rigor and influence as society began to recognize the pressing problems of the environment. Efforts in integrated pest management, and, more important the identification of pollutants in the biosphere and a growing awareness of their deleterious effects emerged in the 1970s and 1980s. Common property resources such as fisheries, scenery, wildlife, and recreations facilities gained attention as workers evaluated alternative approaches to their uses and devised policies for their maintenance and enhancement. Global warming and ground-water pollution necessitated cooperative work across disciplines in the biological and social sciences.

The changing structure of agriculture and its associated social systems demanded sophisticated study. Researchers tried to project the impact of advances in biotechnology to agricultural productivity, and in turn, to changes in the numbers and sizes of farms. Part-time farming in developed societies, the integration of off-farm jobs with agricultural enterprises, and the role of women in agriculture in developed and less developed societies became important research topics.

The food and fiber system in which production agriculture is a critical component has gained more attention, too, especially in aggregate and sector analyses. The relationships between input suppliers and the farm sector, as well as the interface between food processors and manufacturers and the complex of food retailers and food service suppliers, have drawn increased consideration. Food safety and risk tolerances are also prominent public policy issues.

International capital markets, along with national and local systems providing financial services to agriculture and the food industry, came under scrutiny in the 1980s. Restructuring of the Cooperative Farm Credit System was in part a result of a farm financial crisis in many parts of the United

States. Priority has been given to research on issues in agricultural finance, from efficient ways to restructure debt on farms to structural change within the banking system itself. Also significant are the informal credit markets in less developed countries, and the problems of servicing international debt.

The number of professional journals in the rural social sciences expanded rapidly in these two decades, as specializations within agricultural economics established their own quarterly periodicals. Regional journals reflected the research problems and approaches to solutions in different parts of the United States and other countries. Emphasis on refereed journal publication in the assessment of research productivity has become an international phenomenon.

G. Concluding Comments

This brief overview of the development of thought and academic work in rural sociology and agricultural economics is necessarily limited; only a few books and major figures are mentioned here, with an emphasis on the changing setting within these two developing fields and on some of the major strands of activity as they grow in importance. For a more complete understanding of rural sociology trends, the reader is referred to three significant sources written between 1957 and 1988.[18] At the start of the 1990s, the rural social sciences are fully integrated academic fields in the land-grant universities. Professionals from these disciplines actively participate in policy formation and administration. Increasingly, we have come to recognize our global interdependence as we study individual problems and pursue their solutions. Future work must take into account important interrelationships, with the assistance of scientists in other disciplines, if we are to understand and contribute to the solution of real world problems.

18. See Edmund de Schweinitz Brunner, *The Growth of a Science: A Half-Century of Rural Sociological Research in the United States* (New York: Harper Brothers, 1957); Lowry Nelson, *Rural Sociology: Its Origin and Growth in the United States* (Minneapolis: University of Minnesota Press, 1969); a series of articles by John S. Holik and Edward W. Hassinger on the Rural Sociological Society, prepared in connection with the society's fiftieth anniversary, which appeared in the *Rural Sociologist* during 1986–88.

2. Characteristics of Agricultural Economics Literature

The Swedish agronomist, Joosep Nou, in a six-hundred-page scholarly history of European agricultural economics, divides the development of the field into three periods: (1) the Encyclopedic Stage, covering the eighteenth century and characterized by a lack of scientific treatment; (2) the Agronomic Stage, from the last decades of the eighteenth century into the last quarter of the nineteenth, characterized by the acceptance of agronomy as a discipline; and (3) the Economic Stage, which began to take shape in the 1880s. "The United States," he wrote, "was the first country in which agricultural business economics was converted from an agricultural into an economic subject."[1] He summarized the geographic influences and shifts:

> During the 200-year history of agricultural business economics the geographical basis of this development has shifted several times. In the pre-scientific period (the 18th century) the most important contributions were made in Great Britain and France. England was beyond question the leading country in the technique and economy of agriculture. During the 19th century the centre of priority was in the German-speaking countries, although an independent tradition was built up in Russia in the second half of the century. An important development also took place in Italy. At the beginning of the 20th century the German-speaking countries still predominated, but America (the United States) began to compete for the leading position.[2]

The emergence of agricultural economics from economics and agronomy did not take place in academic institutions until the first decade of this century. The first departments, which were in the United States, concentrated on farm management or used the history of agriculture as the learning

1. Joosep Nou, *Studies in the Development of Agricultural Economics in Europe* (Uppsala, Sweden: Almquist and Wiksells, 1967), vol. 33, no. 1, *Lantbruks-Hogskolans Annaler* (Annals of the Agricultural College of Sweden), p. 501.

2. *Ibid.*, p. 503.

device. Henry C. Taylor, who is credited with the first comprehensive U.S. textbook in 1905, notes in a later work that "at Cornell, Illinois, Michigan, Minnesota, Ohio, and Wisconsin are found the roots which seem to account for most of the early growth of agricultural economics in the United States."[3]

The consolidation of farm management, agricultural economics, estimates, and statistics within the U.S. government took place in 1922 with the establishment of the Bureau of Agricultural Economics.[4] The BAE began its own library immediately. Bibliographers and those interested in the early history of agricultural economics in the United States should be familiar with Henry and Anne Taylor's story of agricultural economics through 1932. The authors make numerous references to early studies, laws, and other literature basic to American agriculture. As with growing disciplines, the literature increased with specialization.

Rural sociology at many academic institutions today remains as an adjunct to agricultural economics, although this is not universally true. The relationship between sociology and rural sociology is the same as that between economics and agricultural economics. In both cases, methodologies and principles have come from the parent disciplines, but have been adapted or expanded to the needs of the subdisciplines. The relationship of economics and sociology to agricultural economics and rural sociology is critical in a bibliographic study such as this. The analyses in later chapters clearly show the core of economic and sociology literature on which the agricultural aspects are based. It is not possible to study or characterize the literature of agricultural economics and rural sociology without the inclusion of portions of the literature of economics and sociology.

A study to determine the reliance on or subject dispersion of general economics citations in the agricultural economics literature was accomplished through an analysis of the citations in the 1970–79 articles appearing in the *American Journal of Agricultural Economics* and the *Indian Journal of Agricultural Economics*.[5] The most important distinction, that between economics and agricultural economics, was not made. The 7,701 citations were classified by their major subjects in broad areas, and the largest grouping was the social sciences (68%) while 27.2% was assigned to the applied sciences including agriculture and economics. The investigator's subject scheme placed articles that are clearly in agricultural eco-

3. Henry C. Taylor and Anne Dewees Taylor, *The Story of Agricultural Economics in the United States, 1840–1932: Men—Services—Ideas* (Ames, Iowa: Iowa State College Press, 1952), p. 79.

4. *Ibid.*, pp. 604–6.

5. M. Mahapatra and S. K. Musib, "Subject Dispersion Studies in Agricultural Economics," *Libri* 34 (1984): 341–49.

nomics into the social sciences. Sociology accounted for 5.0% of all of the citations, closely followed by statistics and managerial sciences.

A. Agricultural Economics and Rural Sociology in These Studies

Agricultural economists working in production, commerce, organizations, or academia, or for governments, often find themselves operating in a mix of subject matters. They may be called upon to aid in the economics of apple propagation, storage, or sales, or to model the economics of rural community services or tourism. In the same manner, the rural sociologist has wide-ranging problems to solve. The immense divergence of knowledge and skills is mirrored in the literature. Agricultural economics is an integral segment of the other sciences of agriculture. Therefore, determining the subject inclusiveness in these fields is basic to a bibliographic study.

This kind of subject breakdown shown in Table 1 is used by those who index articles, pamphlets, and books. Categories have been worked out for agricultural economics and rural sociology by all three of the major indexers of agricultural literature. One of these, CAB International, groups similar or related subjects in order to make browsing and retrieval possible. CAB International provides three printed indexes covering the categories cited in Table 1: *Rural Development Abstracts; Rural Extension, Education, and Training Abstracts*; and *World Agricultural Economics and Rural Sociology Abstracts*. Similar categories had been used since 1980 by the two other major indexes, the National Agricultural Library, USDA, and the Food and Agricultural Organization in their respective databases, AGRICOLA and AGRIS.

All the subjects in Table 1 are included in the analyses in this book. There are some variations, however, which must be noted.

(1) Agricultural administration and legislation are generally included in the teaching and research of agricultural economics departments in academia, and most of the literature concerning these topics appears in agricultural economics journals and monographs. These are given different category locations in the three indexing systems. These topics are included in this monograph as aspects of agricultural economics and rural sociology.
(2) Education in agriculture is included, but not education for specific subdisciplines, except for rural sociology and agricultural economics.
(3) Agricultural communications is also included.
(4) Statistical methods for agriculture are included, although the emphasis is on those appropriate to the social sciences.
(5) All statistics of agriculture, agricultural history, and economic analyses are included except when concerned with only one or two commodities. The economics of broad areas, such as food services, are included.

(6) Agricultural international development and related economic development literature are included.

Decisions about the scope of the fields in this study were guided by citations in the published literature of agricultural economics and rural sociology. We accomplished such demarcation by using landmark or overview monographs and one journal in each field; the citations and the subjects covered in these works set the parameters of the study. Therefore, comparisons with standard hierarchical subject schemes are limited. Shifts in the scope of agricultural economics and rural sociology are evident from comparisons with past analyses of this literature.[6]

Table 1. CABI Abstracts' agricultural economics and rural sociology categories

0R00	General agricultural economics including research
0R05	Agricultural policy (developed countries)
0R06-19	Agricultural development (developing countries)
0R20	Supply, demand, and prices
0R30-39	Marketing and distribution
0R40	International trade
0R45	Finance and credit
0R50-79	Farm economics (land, labor, capital, management)
0R80	Types of farming
0R81	Cooperatives and collectives
0R84-88	Education, extension, and research
0R89-99	Rural sociology
1R	Rural extension, education, and training
2R	Rural development

Source: Summarized from *CABI Abstracts Online Manual* (Wallingford, Eng.: CAB International, 1989).

Studies have examined the place of agricultural economics and rural sociology within the total field of agriculture through printed indexes and databases. An early study found that 9.2% of all entries in the *Bibliography of Agriculture* in 1975 referred to agricultural economics and rural sociology.[7] Later, AGRIS reported 11.6% and 9.4% devoted to agricultural economics, rural sociology and agricultural administration in 1978 and 1979, respectively.[8] A recent examination of AGRICOLA and CABI Ab-

6. H. Buntrock, "A Statistical Analysis of Literature in Agricultural Economics and Rural Sociology," *Quarterly Bulletin of the International Association of Agricultural Librarians and Documentalists* 16(1) (1972): 15–28.

7. T. I. Sheinina, "The *Bibliography of Agriculture* as an Information Source for World Agricultural Literature," *Quarterly Bulletin of the International Association of Agricultural Librarians and Documentalists*, 23(3–4) (1978): 46–48.

8. Abe Leibowitz, "AGRIS since the First Technical Consultation," *Agricultural Libraries Information Notes* 6(9/10) (1980): 5–7.

stracts for the imprint years 1984–87 found 7.9% and 7.6% of the total files dedicated to agricultural economics and rural sociology, respectively. This analysis was done by the author using subject category codes to search the two online databases mounted by Dialog, Inc.

B. Language Concentrations

Several potential methods exist to measure the languages used in agricultural sciences literature, but these methods prove unreliable or lacking in detail when examined closely. The first hurdle is the lack of a single authorative source for identifying all the agricultural literature. Among the problems are (1) lack of reporting of items published by countries or publishers; (2) differences in definitions, such as how a serial publication differs from a monograph; and (3) inability of one or more agents to collect and catalog all the material published. An examination of numerous records and sources makes it clear that the indexing services offer the most readily available compilations of the literature. Nevertheless, the universe of agricultural literature is estimated to be 5–10% greater than what is represented in the databases of the indexing services. Idiosyncrasies in definitions and the methods of counting make greater precision very expensive and difficult.

The three large databases that concentrate on agriculture, AGRICOLA, AGRIS, and CABI Abstracts, all aim to cover the world literature of the agricultural sciences in all subject areas. AGRICOLA and CABI Abstracts databases, however, are selective in coverage, on the basis of the nature, subject, and value of the individual pieces or articles of literature. The database AGRIS is a cooperative enterprise accepting citations from food and agricultural organizations around the world, and therefore it is more representative of all the literature of agriculture, rather than only that which is deemed of greatest importance. The USDA's National Agricultural Library, which compiles AGRICOLA, indexes worldwide literature but contributes only U.S. imprints to the AGRIS database. In 1988–89, 59.4% of AGRICOLA was loaded into AGRIS during an eight-month period.[9] The 40.6% of imprints removed in the transfer are non-U.S. imprints in any language, since these citations are supplied to AGRIS by its participating indexing centers around the world. One can conclude that about 60% of

9. Personal communication with Martha Feldman, National Agricultural Library, August 1989. During the eight-month period AGRICOLA averaged 9,011 citations per month, of which an average of 5,358 went to AGRIS.

Table 2. Languages of major agricultural databases (in percent)

	AGRICOLA			AGRIS			CABI Abstracts	
Languages	1968–77[a]	1983[b]	1984–87[c]	1975–80[d]	1983[b]	1975–87[e]	1983[b]	1984–87[c]
English	61	71	87	55	60	57	68	70
Russian	9	10	3	2	3	2	6	6
German	8	4	3	7	6	7	6	6
French	4	3	2	8	5	8	4	4
Spanish	3	1	1	10	7	8	2	2
Japanese	2	2	1	3[f]	2	5	2	2
Italian	11	1	.2	4	4	4	2	2
Portuguese	1	1	NA	2	2	2	1	NA
All others	11	7	2.8	9	11	7	10	8[f]

Sources:

[a]"Language Distribution in AGRIS and AGRICOLA," *Agricultural Libraries Information Notes* 6(9/10) (1980): 7. More detailed data is provided about AGRICOLA in *ALIN* 3(5) (1977): 6–7.

[b]Norbert Deselaers, "The Necessity for Closer Cooperation among Secondary Agricultural Information Services: An Analysis of AGRICOLA, AGRIS and CAB," *Quarterly Bulletin of the International Association of Agricultural Librarians and Documentalists* 31(1) (1986): 19–26.

[c]Results of searches of CABI and AGRICOLA for imprint years 1984–87, done, respectively, on the DIALOG and BRS online systems; and the AGRICOLA compact disks issued by Silver Platter.

[d]H. Buntrock, "A Statistical Analysis of Literature in Agricultural Economics and Rural Sociology," *Quarterly Bulletin of the International Association of Agricultural Librarians and Documentalists* 16(1) (1972): 22.

[e]"Languages in the AGRIS Database," *Quarterly Bulletin of the International Association of Agricultural Librarians and Documentalists* 32(4) (1987): 228 (as quoted from *AIDS* [Newsletter of AGRIS]).

[f]Extrapolated.

AGRICOLA citations are to U.S. publications of journals, books, and gray or fugitive literature.

In its effort to serve the member nations of the Food and Agricultural Organization, AGRIS includes all of the literature it can get into citation format. This methodological difference is evident in the language coverage of its database when contrasted with the other two databases. The long-standing difference in English coverage reflects a greater quantity of non-English language gray literature than with the other services. Additional language details are provided in Appendix A.

The swings and variations in percentages result from decisions concerning indexing coverage, variations in processing, and the nonparticipation of some countries in the AGRIS cooperative. The shift to English is evident. The AGRIS database may continue to show a much lower percentage of

Table 3. Languages in agricultural economics and rural sociology, as shown in two studies (in percent)

Languages	1984–87 study[a] AGRICOLA	1984–87 study[a] CABI Abstracts	1969 primary journals study (N = 2,112 journals)[b]
English	87.6	64.1	39.8
German	2.4	8.0	16.3
French	2.5	5.8	9.1
Russian	2.2	2.9	3.5
Spanish	.8	2.3	3.3
Japanese	.7	.2	1.0
Italian			3.1
All others	3.8	16.8	23.9

Sources:

[a]Results of searches of CABI and AGRICOLA for imprint years 1984–87, done, respectively, on the DIALOG and BRS online systems; and the AGRICOLA compact disks issued by Silver Platter.

[b]H. Buntrock, "A Statistical Analysis of Literature in Agricultural Economics and Rural Sociology," *Quarterly Bulletin of the International Association of Agricultural Librarians and Documentalists* 16(1) (1972): 15–28.

English-language sources since nationalism and a greater quantity of extension literature influence this file but are of little significance in the other two databases. Within agricultural economics and rural sociology literature, the language patterns differ somewhat from all of agricultural literature, as illustrated in Table 3.

The top five languages (English, Russian, German, French, and Spanish) remain relatively the same in agricultural economics and rural sociology literature. Comparison with Buntrock's twenty year old study of citations in 2,112 agricultural economics and rural sociology journals shows a decided shift to English (Table 3). The comparison between journal citations and *all* citations is realistic because journal articles constitute about 75% of all entries in AGRICOLA and CABI Abstracts. The German- and French-language literature appears stronger in agricultural economics and rural sociology than in all of agriculture, particularly with CABI Abstracts, which probably is a continuation of the influence of these languages from earlier years.

Several possible conclusions arise from these data, together with empirical evidence in language and publishing shifts:

(1) English continues to grow in importance in agriculture as well as in the primary literature of agricultural economics and rural sociology.

(2) The greatest change in agricultural economics and rural sociology languages is the drop in German and French.
(3) The CABI database continues to cover French and German extensively, while AGRICOLA covers much less of these and other non-English languages.
(4) The other languages in Table 3 also appear to be less well covered by the current databases. In addition to a shift to English, the change is partially the result of the exclusion of unusual language materials which are often so site-specific that they have little application beyond the country of publication.

C. Format of Publication

Counting all the pieces of literature that come to the attention of a creator of large citation databases or to libraries that catalog and store the physical pieces is a prodigious task. Extending that concept into sorting, counting, and recording the thousands of articles within the 2,000 active agricultural economics and rural sociology journals becomes an even more impressive accomplishment. In both these efforts, the most accessible data come from the agricultural indexing services. Concentration in the three major agricultural databases is summarized in Table 4.

Table 4. Type of publication as shown in major agricultural databases (in percent)

	AGRICOLA	AGRIS	CABI Abstracts	Average
Journal articles or book chapters	85	74	80	79.6
Government reports and documents	5	14	10	9.7
Monographs, theses, proceedings, maps	10	12	10	10.7

Source: Martha E. Williams and Carolyn G. Robins, eds. and compilers, *Agricultural Databases Directory* (Washington, D.C.: U.S. Dept. of Agriculture, National Agricultural Library, Oct. 1985), *Bibliographies and Literature of Agriculture*, no. 42, pp. 6–7, 29–30.

The twenty-year history of the AGRICOLA database shows a decided shift to a concentration on journal articles. Not until the last few years has that database included chapters from books; these items are still few in number. A study of the 1975 issues of the *Bibliography of Agriculture*, the printed counterpart of AGRICOLA, found that 75% of the entries were journal articles, 7% were government reports and documents, and the remainder in the last category.[10] Slight variations are common among all of

10. Sheinina, op. cit.

the databases because of processing or management policies. Agriculture follows the general pattern of science publishing in which 80–90% of the citations are to journal literature. Because of experiment station bulletins and extension and outreach literature not common to other science disciplines, the percentage of journal literature is somewhat lower in agriculture. Table 5 shows agricultural economics and rural sociology publications by type for 1969 and 1984–87.

Table 5. Agricultural economics and rural sociology publications by type (in percent)

	Buntrock[a] study of 1969 data	1984–87 Study[b]		
		AGRICOLA	CABI Abstracts	Average
Journal articles	80	81.4	72.1	77.8
Government reports or documents	13	18.6[c]	27.9[c]	22.2[c]
Monographs, theses, proceedings	7			

[a]H. Buntrock, "A Statistical Analysis of Literature in Agricultural Economics and Rural Sociology," *Quarterly Bulletin of the International Association of Agricultural Librarians and Documentalists* 16(1) (1972): 25.

[b]Results of searches of CABI and AGRICOLA for imprint years 1984–87, done, respectively, on the DIALOG and BRS online systems; and the AGRICOLA compact disks issued by Silver Platter.

[c]These figures represent the combined total of reports, documents, monographs, theses and proceedings.

In an earlier, extensive study of the writings of U.S. agricultural economists, the results were distinctly different from those in Table 5. The literature studied was published in 1961, 1962, or 1963, and was gathered by contacting the authors for references, not the indexing or publishing sources. Here is the breakdown by type of publication, when grouped to match the categories in Table 5:[11]

Journal and informational or trade periodical articles	31.4%
Government reports or documents	3.5
Monographs, theses, proceedings	39.0
Miscellaneous documents	6.1

Methodology and the people polled account for a small portion of the differences. The time period has a great influence, since the types of publica-

11. I. T. Littleton, *The Bibliographic Organization and Use of the Literature of Agricultural Economics* (Ph.D. Thesis, University of Illinois, 1968), p. 44. A briefer form of the thesis appeared as *The Literature of Agricultural Economics: Its Bibliographic Organization and Use*. (Raleigh, N.C.: North Carolina Agricultural Experiment Station, 1969), *Technical Bulletin* no. 191.

tions identified in this study by Littleton have not been as prevalent recently.

The dramatic growth in journal publishing denotes a change in the basic literature from 1950 to 1990. The trend has been to scholarly journal and monograph publishing with fewer manuals, how-to books, and instructional workbooks being registered in scholarly writings. In addition, today's bibliographic databases do not index or list the traditional trade or application literature thoroughly or systematically. It must be remembered that these professions have advanced to a point of research and scholarship that obviates the need for basic application referencing. The database creators have followed this pattern and now lean toward the literature most appropriate for the profession. As in the past, the report literature commonly issued by agricultural experiment stations, college departments, and government agencies today is a greater percentage in agricultural economics and rural sociology than for the total field of agriculture.

3. The Role of CAB International's *World Agricultural Economics and Rural Sociology Abstracts* in Meeting the Information Needs of Agricultural Economists

MARGOT A. BELLAMY

CAB International

This chapter is concerned principally with the role played by *World Agricultural Economics and Rural Sociology Abstracts* (*WAERSA*) as a major force in providing international bibliographic services in agricultural economics and rural sociology, both before and since its incorporation in the Commonwealth Agricultural Bureaux (CAB), now CAB International (CABI).

WAERSA's main mission has been to serve the information needs of the international agricultural economics profession. After years of deliberation, it was entrusted with this role in the late 1950s by two major professional organizations, the International Association of Agricultural Economists and the International Association of Agricultural Librarians and Documentalists. The evolution of *WAERSA* should be seen against the background of the history of efforts, international and national, to provide information services to agricultural economics; the changing interests and compositions of its own clientele; the changing parameters of the subject itself; developments in agricultural information provision worldwide; and the advent of information technology.

A. Origins of Agricultural Economics Information Services

It is significant that the roots of bibliographic information services in agricultural economics can be traced back within the three organizations,

For comment and analysis of the history and evolution of agricultural economics information, the author has drawn heavily on the writings of the late Dr. S. von Frauendorfer, *WAERSA*'s first editor. The author acknowledges with gratitude the assistance of Janice Osborn, of CAB International, in the compilation of statistics.

which are regarded today as the leaders in agricultural information provision worldwide: the United Nations Food and Agricultural Organization (FAO), the USDA's National Agricultural Library (NAL), and CAB International.

There was a considerable time lag in the appearance of agricultural economics on the documentation scene, however, which allowed the biological and technological branches of agricultural science to gain an incontestable lead. This slow rate of development is considered by Frauendorfer to be partly attributable to the rather late crystallization of the economic and social aspects of agriculture, as had been the case with economic theory, into a generally recognized and autonomous field of knowledge.[1] Research therefore developed slowly, and in the early twentieth century there was such a small body of definable literature that the more general bibliographic and indexing services that already existed were considered adequate to the needs of scholars and others interested in the field.

Another difficulty identified by Frauendorfer as impeding the initiation of a specific abstracting service for the agricultural economics field (unlike the physical scientific branches of agriculture) was the lack of a clear-cut borderline between *scientific* and *non-scientific* studies, in the sense that "opinions, attitudes and sometimes critical statements regarding controversial questions are so interwoven with results of genuine research and factual information that it is often difficult to determine whether a book or article should be classified as a scientific study or not." Moreover, others believed that the controversial nature of some writings on agricultural policy and rural social organization, particularly in terms of politics and ideology, might discourage official bodies from involvement in an abstracting service. Although Frauendorfer clearly feels that these difficulties disappear "wherever the competent information service is strictly unbiased and publishes simple factual summaries of the papers' contents," it is worth noting that this fear of possible inability to convey an objective view of the subject matter pervaded discussions of abstracting services for agricultural economics, even among agricultural economists, for several decades. The difficulties associated with maintaining objectivity is still probably the main difference between the physical and social science disciplines linked to agriculture.[2]

Attitudes and conditions changed, however, as more and more progressive agriculturalists realized that their work had economic implications, and farming was recognized as being a way of life, with accompanying social

1. S. von Frauendorfer, preface to preliminary edition of *WAERSA* (July 1958). S. von Frauendorfer, *The Story of Abstracting in Agricultural Economics* (Offprint, full context unknown).

2. S. von Frauendorfer, *The Story of Abstracting in Agricultural Economics.*

and economic problems. Perhaps the earliest international manifestation of this change occurred when separate sections for economic and social questions as well as statistics were established within the International Institute of Agriculture (1905). This organization, established by an intergovernmental convention, was the first official international body dealing with agriculture. It had a keen interest in documentation activities from its inception. Yet it was nearly thirty years before this interest was translated into reality. The Institute's *International Bibliography of Agricultural Economics*, was printed as a regular supplement to the journal *Berichte über Landwirtschaft* from 1932 to 1938, with funds provided by the German government. Beginning in 1938–39, the *Bibliography* was issued quarterly by the International Institute itself, in a trilingual edition, under the title *Bibliographie Internationale d'Agriculture*. The initiator and first editor (until 1943) was S. von Frauendorfer. This bibliographic service was mainly due to the initiative of the then librarian of USDA, Claribel R. Barnett. The bibliography continued until 1946, the year in which the International Institute was dissolved and absorbed by the newly founded Food and Agriculture Organization of the United Nations.

For various reasons, largely concerned with the scope and magnitude of its new responsibilities, FAO did not consider reviving publication of the bibliography, and although it actively supported all later discussions and efforts to set up an abstract journal, it was unable to take a lead. It was not until the late 1960s that FAO reentered the field of international agricultural documentation.

Although FAO's predecessor could boast the first international information service, the first bibliographic journal specializing in agricultural economics was the mimeographed house organ of the former Bureau of Agricultural Economics of the USDA in Washington, D.C., which started in 1923 as *Library Supplement* to *BAE News*. It was later (in 1927) transferred and expanded into a regular journal called *Agricultural Economics Literature*, edited by the BAE's librarian Mary G. Lacy. This journal continued until 1942 when the USDA Library (now the National Agricultural Library) centralized the previously independent bibliographic efforts of the Agriculture Department's individual bureaus and offices into the *Bibliography of Agriculture*. This was designed as a title-only service, although there have been intermittent efforts since the 1940s to provide abstracts as well as titles for the agricultural economics section of the literature, both in published form and online, with funding from the American Agricultural Economics Association. Then, as now, the main emphasis was on U.S. and Canadian sources.

B. Enter the International Association of Agricultural Librarians and Documentalists, and the International Association of Agricultural Economists

During the 1940s and 1950s much discussion surrounded the need for an abstracting service in agricultural economics. Proposals to develop a Bureau of Agricultural Economics on the same pattern as those already set for the physical agricultural sciences were considered seriously by the Imperial (later Commonwealth) Agricultural Bureaux (CAB) from 1943 onward, the subject first having been very briefly mentioned within the organization in the late 1920s.[3]

After World War II, the expanding profession of agricultural economics was left with no abstracting service, at a time of postwar food supply problems, modernization, and rehabilitation of agriculture. Help was at hand, following the inauguration, in 1955 of the International Association of Agricultural Librarians and Documentalists (IAALD) at an international meeting in Ghent, Belgium. The director of USDA's NAL, Foster G. Morhardt, was elected president of this new association. Rather than expand the *Bibliography of Agriculture* to include abstracts for agricultural economics publications, and after exploratory discussions, a formal proposal was submitted to IAALD's 1957 executive committee suggesting that IAALD take the lead in starting an abstract journal. S. von Frauendorfer, IAALD vice-president, was asked to make plans to set up an editorial office. The IAALD began negotiations with the International Conference (now Association) of Agricultural Economists (IAAE). It was decided jointly to launch an abstract journal as an experimental cooperative venture. Funds were raised in the United States: the Council of Economic and Cultural Affairs (now the Agricultural Development Council) and the Ford Foundation made grants for periods of three and five years, respectively. A test issue of the new journal *World Agricultural Economics and Rural Sociology Abstracts* was produced in July 1958, and 1,400 copies were circulated for comment (on layout, content, classification, and so on) to leading agricultural economists worldwide. The tenth International Conference of Agricultural Economists, held in Mysore, India, in 1958, welcomed the experiment and strongly recommended support for the journal. It was therefore decided to produce a quarterly, based on voluntary contributions of abstracts from a panel of agricultural economists from all over the world. The first issue of *WAERSA* appeared in 1959, with a total of 1,444 abstracts.

3. Imperial Agricultural Bureaux, *Memoranda* (relating to setting up of bureaus following the 1928 Review Conference, 1930).

C. The Vienna Years

The editorial office for the new journal was set up in Vienna in the Austrian Ministry of Agriculture's new Agrarwirtschaftsinstitut. The institute's library was an excellent source of material, supplemented by the voluntary contributions from the IAAE's international panel. S. von Frauendorfer became the managing editor. The treasurer of IAALD, T. P. Loosjes in Wageningen, Netherlands, dealt with the journal's finances and found a publisher (North-Holland, Amsterdam). An editorial board of fifteen members was established, with the president and vice-president of IAALD as members *ex officio*. The board met during the conferences of IAAE (1958, Mysore, India; 1961, Cuernavaca, Mexico; 1964, Lyons, France).

In spite of operating at very low cost, the journal soon faced financial difficulties, because of the limited duration of the various grants and the rising printing and production costs, due to the rapidly growing size of the journal. The *WAERSA* nearly doubled in size in its first six years. The executive council of CAB, which had closely followed *WAERSA*'s development, decided after consultation with its contributing countries to approve a grant to *WAERSA* of £1,000 in each of the years 1959–60, 1960–61 and 1962–63. This was increased to £2,000 in 1963–64 and a grant was also received from the Gulbenkian Foundation, Lisbon. But by 1964, the situation reached a critical point. The Ford Foundation grant had expired and S. von Frauendorfer was due to retire. When, in 1963, CAB was approached to increase its grant to £5,000, it decided to give the whole question of *WAERSA*'s future, and CAB's role in this, more serious consideration.

D. The Transition to CAB

The inclusion of *WAERSA* in CAB's range of abstract journals, and the transition of the editorial office to a fully fledged bureau, can be traced back to the Imperial Agricultural Research Conference of 1928. The first forum in which the question was discussed in any depth was the Hankey report of 1943, which declared that

> From a perusal of the subjects which a bureau in this subject would be expected to cover, we are of the opinion that it would fit more appropriately into an organisation whose chief function is economic intelligence. . . . We do not recommend the inclusion of agricultural economics among the subjects to be covered by this group of scientific bureaux but special care should be taken to "establish and maintain contact between the bureaux and any organisation

which, in the post war period, may be set up for the supply of economic information in relation to agriculture."[4]

The possible establishment of a Bureau of Agricultural Economics was featured on the agenda of quinquennial review conferences of CAB for the next twenty years. To judge from some of the correspondence, the agricultural economists themselves may have contributed to the protracted nature of the debate, as there appears to have been disagreement among some of the eminent people consulted in the early stages about the scope of the subject, the relevance of work in one country to the interests of another, and dubious likelihood of being able to write "objective" abstracts of a literature containing elements that could reflect political or other value judgments.

Finally, however, an agreement to an annual subvention was easily approved when CAB was approached for funds in the 1960s. During and between succeeding CAB review conferences, the subject of a bureau continued to be debated, and the Agricultural Economics Research Institute at Oxford, under succeeding directors, participated very actively in discussions and the international consultation process. The CAB's 1950 review conference recommended that a bureau be set up in association with the University of Oxford, and CAB approved the funds. Correspondence of the time indicates difficulties in finding suitable accommodations for the bureau as the main reason that this recommendation was not followed through.

In the meantime, international discussion and correspondence continued about the value of setting up an abstracting service and its subject scope. In Oxford itself, the *Digest of Agricultural Economics* was established to cover literature of the United Kingdom. The *Digest* was able to provide abstracts, in a shorter form, for *WAERSA* in Vienna. Proposals that CAB should take over the *Digest*, with some expansion of coverage, were not accepted at the 1960 CAB Review Conference, although the continuation of the grant to produce *WAERSA* was endorsed.

The CAB's Interim Review Conference in June 1963 appointed a special committee, under the Sir Norman Wright, chairman of the British Association for the Advancement of Science, to consider, whether CAB should assume any further responsibility for *WAERSA*. The committee had the benefit of an exhaustive memorandum prepared by Professor Edgar Thomas of the University of Reading, as well as discussions with L. K. Elmhirst, chairman of the Dartington Hall Trustees (and founder president of IAAE),

4. *Report by a Committee on the Imperial Agricultural Bureaux*, The Rt. Hon. Lord Hankey, GCB, GCMG, CVO, FRS, Chairman (London; His Majesty's Stationery Office, 1943).

and J. O. Jones, director of the Institute of Agrarian Affairs, Oxford, which produced the *Digest*. It was agreed that CAB should "agree in principle to the production of an abstract journal subject to the negotiation of satisfactory terms with other interested parties."

The recommendations were summarized as follows: (1) CAB should accept responsibility for *WAERSA* in collaboration with the journal's present sponsors; (2) as an interim measure, funds should be provided from the general reserve to cover the cost of producing *WAERSA* at Oxford on as economical a basis as possible, having due regard to the need to expand and improve it; and (3) the 1965 Review Conference should consider whether a Bureau of Agricultural Economics should be established and, if so, where it should be located. It is worth pointing out that, in spite of the clear "Commonwealth" orientation of CAB's membership, the composition and mandate of its review conferences, and its obvious responsibilities toward its member countries, there was no question that the proposed agricultural economics abstract journal should be limited to the Commonwealth in either its coverage or its clientele.

In 1964, the *WAERSA* editorial office moved to Oxford, into accommodations secured by the Dartington Hall Trustees. The 1965 Review Conference approved the formation of a Commonwealth Bureau of Agricultural Economics, with the production of *WAERSA* as its main task. The location was still in some doubt, because of a proposal to have the bureau established in India. This was resolved late in 1966, and Oxford, where the editorial office had already been established, was confirmed as the location, with J. O. Jones as the editor. Oxford proved an ideal choice; its advantages were enhanced when in 1970 the Dartington Hall Trustees invested in a center to house the Oxford University Agricultural Economics Institute, the Commonwealth Bureau of Agricultural Economics, and the Institute of Agrarian Affairs, the editorial office for the IAAE's triennial conferences. An important element in this was a joint library. Thus, *WAERSA* was firmly established in a congenial academic environment. Its international connections (IAAE, IAALD) were retained and strengthened, the editorial board continued to meet at triennial IAAE conferences, and its standing committee of three or four representatives who could easily meet in Oxford continued to review progress.

E. Sources

The sources of literature for *WAERSA* have always been diverse, dispersed through many disciplines. There is clearly a "core" literature (its nature is defined in detail elsewhere in this volume) but one of the main difficulties for the conscientious editor of an abstract journal in the field is to identify and maintain regular access to all material of potential interest. And, while the volume of literature in science and technology increased fivefold between 1960 and 1980, in economics and sociology there was a tenfold increase.

Access to the core literature, and some of the periphery, has been facilitated by close connections with excellent libraries, and by donations from individuals, institutions, and publishers all over the world, through the network of correspondents and abstractors originally established through *WAERSA*'s Vienna office, and constant vigilance on the part of abstractors in identifying literature in a whole range of catalogs, bibliographies, and library accessions lists. About 60% of *WAERSA*'s coverage is serial literature, including both journals and numbered reports in series. The number of serials cited increased from 646 in 1964 to nearly 1,300 in 1989. The list of potentially relevant serials numbers about 5,000, however, indicating the wide range of literature to which access is needed to ensure coverage. Other documents include books, conference proceedings, reports of published theses, and a considerable amount of fugitive or grey literature.

Since the late 1970s, the Bureau has expanded its direct acquisition of original documents, and reduced its reliance on other secondary sources, and there has been a drastic reduction in the contributions of foreign correspondents. In 1967 (volume 9) *WAERSA* had correspondents in thirty-two countries and three international organizations, contributing 1,395 of the total 4,455 abstracts. At the time, only about half of the literature was accessible at Oxford in its original form.[5] In 1989 the figures for foreign correspondents were five and one, respectively; together with freelance abstractors in the United Kingdom largely covering foreign language material supplied by the bureau, foreign correspondents contribute about 10% of the total number of abstracts. But these trends in no way indicate a diminution in geographical scope or range of subject. The literature of many countries is now acquired directly from the source. Links with the International Association of Agricultural Economists, which originally provided the foreign correspondents, now result in direct dispatches of the original literature. Geographical coverage is thus fully international, although some regions and countries are better covered than others. The largest proportion of the literature, with the exception of India, comes from developed countries, including Korea and Japan. Coverage of literature from South America and

5. J. O. Jones, "Information and Communication: The Services of the Commonwealth Bureau of Agricultural Economics," *Journal of Agricultural Economics* 20 (1969): 25–44.

Southeast Asia is not as broad as would be desirable. Regrettably, the dearth of publications from many developing countries in Africa is largely the result of those nations' inadequate funds for publishing and limited access to recent literature as a basis for research work.

In terms of language, there has been a marked shift toward publication in English. In 1984, for example, 57% of total coverage was in English; the percentage was 67.5% in 1989. German (10%), French (8%), and Russian (5%) are the other main languages; virtually all material published in Spain, Portugal, Latin America, and Japan appears in its original language. Although many publications do include English summaries, these are frequently ambiguous, and language skills are needed to read the original document.

F. Subject Scope

Not only is the literature of agricultural economics spread throughout the social sciences; the interests of those working in agricultural economics and related disciplines have also broadened. The early *WAERSA* was almost totally concerned with farming and the economic and social problems of the farm population; this emphasis was reflected in the early titles of some of the main primary journals, for example, *Farm Economist* and *Journal of Farm Economics*. As agricultural economists gradually became more concerned with world issues of supply and trade, and as Third World agricultural development gained ground as a subject interest, so too did the wider issues of land and agrarian reform, income distribution, and the Green Revolution. It became clear that the problems of rural areas worldwide could not be dealt with in terms of farming alone, so the subject coverage spilled over into regional development of rural areas, conflicts over use of agricultural land, effects of modern agriculture on the environment, and the development of tourism and recreational activities as an alternative source of employment and as a competing use for rural areas. New economic groupings (such as the European Communities) stimulated a wealth of literature, and created a host of new problems and policies (such as surpluses, common markets, trade conflicts) for agricultural economists. And the wealth of analytical techniques made available by the development of econometrics and the advent of computers is clearly reflected in the literature. These developments are well documented by U.S. and British economists.[6]

6. L. R. Martin, ed. *Survey of Agricultural Economics Literature*, 3 vols. (Minneapolis: University of Minnesota Press, 1977–81); K. E. Hunt, "The Concern of Agricultural Economists in Great Britain since the 1920s," *Journal of Agricultural Economics* 27(3) (1976): 285–96.

Meanwhile, the subjects of farm management and economics, macroeconomics, and development were rapidly expanding. Initially, *WAERSA* was able to accommodate most of these trends, with slight shifts in subject headings and classification. The new interest in nonagricultural problems of rural areas, however, and the increasing awareness of Third World economics and social problems, launched three new abstracting journals in the 1970s. *Rural Development Abstracts* is concerned with the economic and social problems of the rural poor in developing countries. *Rural Extension, Education and Training Abstracts* (1978–89) was aimed at the needs of teachers and trainers in rural education and extension services. *Leisure, Recreation and Tourism Abstracts*, which began as a journal about recreation as an alternative rural land use, is now the world's main abstract journal in its field. Today, the Bureau of Agricultural Economics publishes 14,000 abstracts, 7,400 of these in *WAERSA*.

By the late 1980s, new subjects in *WAERSA* included food policy; the food industry and related issues, for which separate subject classifications have been created; biotechnology, for which *WAERSA* covers policy, social, and ethical aspects, as well as the economics of some of the products; the funding and organization of agricultural research, including national agricultural research systems; farming systems; and environmental issues. This last area is expected to gather momentum during the 1990s. Agribusiness, too, is of increasing interest, and is considered well covered in *WAERSA*, particularly for North American material.[7]

Some of these changes in subject scope and emphasis are reflected in the journal classification and contents lists, particularly in the 1959 and 1989 examples shown in Table 6. Changes in the volume of literature are reflected in the numbers of abstracts published (Table 7).

G. Indexing

The Bureau of Agricultural Economics, CAB International, is responsible for three indexing/abstracting publications that publish 14,000 abstracts per year from 12,000 records. Most of this 2,000 record overlap is between *WAERSA* and *Rural Development Abstracts*. The online files, of course, show 12,000-records with duplicate coding for subject access.

The *WAERSA* contains an author index as well as subject/geographical indexes in each issue; a cumulative annual index is published early in the following year as a separate volume; since 1988 this includes a list of the serials cited in that year. The controlled vocabulary was originally derived

7. M. Ojala, "The Dollar Sign: Finding Agribusiness Information," *Database* 11(3) (1988): 84–88.

Table 6. Subject classifications of *WAERSA*

Volume 1, 1959

- Agricultural Conditions
- Bibliography
- Agricultural History
- Biographies
- Agricultural Geography
- Agricultural Education and Research
- Extension. Advisory Work
- Agricultural Administration
- Agricultural Legislation
- International Organizations
- Rural Sociology
- Agricultural Policy
- Land Tenure
- Agrarian Collectivism
- Production and Productivity
- Consumption and Nutrition
- Agricultural Credit
- Insurance
- Taxation
- Tenancy
- Farm Organization and Management
- Farm Profits
- Farm Accounting
- Farm Labour
- Co-operation
- Agricultural Marketing and Prices
- Common European Market
- Agricultural Statistics
- Grain Crops
- Root Crops
- Cotton
- Pastures
- Horticultural Crops
- Viticulture
- Tropical Crops
- Other Agricultural Products
- Farm Buildings
- Mechanization
- Land Development, Reclamation
- Fertilizer Economy
- Feeding Stuffs
- Domestic Animals
- Meat
- Dairy Products

Volume 31, 1989

Agricultural Economics
- General
- Theory and Methodology

Agricultural Policy
- World, Continents and Regions
- Agricultural Development
- Theory
- Land and Natural Resources
  - Policy
  - Land Use and Environment
  - Survey and Census Methods
- Regional Agricultural Policy
- Structural Policy and Agrarian Reform
- Infrastructure Policy
- Employment Policy
- Income Policy
- Input Industries
  - General
  - Fertilizers and Chemicals
  - Tractors and Farm Machinery
  - Petroleum and Other Fuels
- Transport and Storage
- Packing, Processing, etc.
- Wholesaling
- Retailing
- Consumers

International Trade[a]
- Theory
- World, by Continents or Regions

Finance and Credit Policy[a]
- Theory
- World, by Continents or Regions

Farm Economics[a]
- General
- Land
  - Valuation
  - Ownership and Tenure
  - Farm Structure and Layout
  - Improvement, Irrigation, etc.
- Labour
  - Wages and Systems of Payment
- Farm Organization
  - Management
  - Records and Accounts
  - Planning Techniques
- Types of Farming
  - Mixed Farming
  - Ancillary Farm Enterprises

Cooperatives and Collectives[a]
- Theory
- World, and by Continents or Regions

Education, Extension and Research
- General
- Education and Training
- Advisory and Information Services
- Agricultural Research
  - Policy and Planning
  - Theory
  - World, and by Continents or Regions
- Farming Systems Research
  - Theory

Biotechnology
Veterinary and Pharmaceutical

Supply, Demand and Prices[a]
Theory
World, Continental and Regional

Food Policy
Food Aid
Food Industry
Nutrition

Marketing and Distribution
Market Regulations
Market Concentration, Integration, Competition
Quality Control

Productivity and Work Study
Farm Capital and Insurance
Building and Equipment
Machinery and Tools
Livestock
Permanent Crops
Other Inputs
Fuel and Power
Fertilizers
Concentrates and Feed Mixes
Plant Protection
Veterinary Products
Seeds and Plants
Farm Inputs
Farm Services

World, and by Continents or Regions

Rural Sociology
General
Demography and Settlement
Rural/Urban Relations and Migration
Rural Communities
Social Stratification
Rural Families
Behaviour and Attitudes
Adoption of Innovations
Conflict and Political Movements
Leadership
Cultural Factors

[a]Also includes these subcategories: Livestock and Livestock Products, Field Crops and Products, Other Crops and Products

from a list of subject headings generated in the bureau. The next stage was its incorporation into a multilingual thesaurus developed within the European Communities, and into CAB's own multidisciplinary thesaurus. The third edition published in 1990 is also used by the USDA's National Agricultural Library to index AGRICOLA, and is likely to form the core of a major effort toward a multilingual agricultural thesaurus.[8]

Table 7. Number of abstracts published in *WAERSA*, 1959–89

Year	Abstracts published
1959	1,444
1964	3,522
1969	4,351
1974	6,144
1979	7,127
1984	7,476
1989	7,387

8. CAB International, *CAB Thesaurus*—1990 ed., 2 vols. (1207p.) (Wallingford, Eng.: CAB International, 1990).

H. Quality

From the point of view of the abstractor, the social sciences literature, including much of the literature of agricultural economics, is handicapped by its verbosity and lack of impartiality (especially in terms of political ideology). Moreover, it generally lacks the clarity and discipline of presentation usually found in the physical science literature. These shortcomings hamper the ability to produce a concise abstract and to present an objective view of the aims, content, and conclusions of many papers. They can also slow down timely coverage of the literature. A further handicap is the general dearth of author abstracts in the social sciences literature, particularly in the political sciences. It is encouraging, however, that a recent survey of its members by the Anthropology and Sociology Section of the Association of College and Research Libraries found *WAERSA* to be of high quality, with informative abstracts, a high degree of timeliness, and well indexed.[9]

I. Clientele

The subscribers' list of *WAERSA* shows that the published journal can be found in universities, government departments, research organizations, international agencies, and a few private firms. The geographical spread shows the main usage in Europe, North America, India, and Japan. Some countries receive copies on a quota system linked to their membership in CAB International. Sadly, developing countries, particularly those in Africa, have fewer subscriptions. The number of paid subscriptions worldwide peaked in the mid-1970s at about 1,200. The list of subscribers tends to mask the actual users, however who may include policymakers, academics, students, consultants, and business people. At least one consultant known to the *WAERSA* editor never starts a new project without consulting *WAERSA* first; this philosophy is now committed to print.[10]

J. Developments and Expansion

In 1965 the word "database" in relation to agricultural bibliographic information had not been coined but *WAERSA* had, in effect, become part of

9. Ann Wood, "World Agricultural Economics and Rural Sociology Abstracts . . . ," *ANSS Currents: The Newsletter of the ACRL Anthropology and Sociology Section* 4(1) (May 1989): 6–7.
10. P. Bowbrick, *Practical Economic for the Real Economist* (London: Graham and Trotman, 1988).

CAB's stable of abstract journals and, thus, of its future database. Then, as now, CAB journals were produced using a common format, with the individual bureaus taking responsibility for content, accuracy, and editorial standards. Production methods for *WAERSA* in the 1960s in Oxford continued much as they had in Vienna, using conventional printing and publishing, with all stages of production completed manually.

This all changed in 1972 with the introduction of CAB's first computerized production system. This affected the bureaus' production methods: all journal classification systems evolved into a set of sequencing codes, indexing received set punctuation norms, and weekly batches of typed input forms were dispatched for further processing to the central CAB Systems Department. Although these changes provided a central database, enabling the production of magnetic tapes, and the inclusion of the CAB Abstracts file on database host systems such as DIALOG, it was not until 1982 that a new system brought direct data entry down to the bureau level, with data transmitted weekly to the mainframe computer at CAB headquarters. Standardized bibliographic control and general editorial standards and conventions were introduced throughout CAB. Each individual bureau retained responsibility for quality and subject content, but was expected to adhere to the controlled vocabulary contained in the thesaurus, and to bibliographic and other standards established at the headquarters.

K. *WAERSA* Online

Since *World Agricultural Economics and Rural Sociology Abstracts* first appeared in 1958, well over 200,000 abstracts have been published. From 1973 on, with the adoption of computer-aided phototypesetting, more that 120,000 *WAERSA* records have been entered into the CAB Abstracts database. *WAERSA* may be searched online either as a subfile of the CAB Abstracts database or in one of the special economics databases that cover *WAERSA*, *Rural Extension, Education and Training Abstracts (REETA)*; and *Rural Development Abstracts (RDA)* (Table 8).

Where access is through the CABI Abstracts database, the search should be confined to the *WAERSA* subfile. Table 8 shows the file/subfile names and codes for *WAERSA* on each of the online hosts. Once the file/subfile has been selected, the search can encompass subject keywords, authors' names, and individual words and phrases from the titles and abstracts. The list of keywords used for indexing may be found in the *CAB Thesaurus*. Records of economic interest from other sections of the CABI Abstracts database are also coded for the *WAERSA* subfile.

Table 8. Online hosts, CABI Abstracts subfile names and codes

Host	Subfile	Economics Database
BRS	OR.HC	ECON
CAN/OLE	OR,J	—
DIALOG	SF=OR	—
DIMDI	SU=OR	CAB ECONOMICS
ESA/IRS	AJ=OR	—
JICST	CN:OR&	—
Tsukuba	SJ 'World Agricultural Economics and Rural Sociology	—

Comment on *WAERSA* online is generally favorable, even among North American users, who are more familiar with AGRICOLA.[11] A study carried out in France for the European Communities on the coverage by several databases of nine specific topics in the agricultural economics field found CAB Abstracts (*WAERSA*) the most favorable database for the questions treated, in terms of both numbers and quality of references, as well as wide geographical coverage and level of informativeness.[12]

The advent of CABI Abstracts on CD-ROM, and the facility thereby to download smaller packages of information to personal computers will, it is hoped, encourage more potential users of the kind of information *WAERSA* offers to select their own profiles from the database in floppy disk or SDI format. It will also bring database access much more realistically within the reach of users in developing countries.

L. Centralization

In 1985 the decision was made to centralize all the CAB bureaus. The site chosen was at Wallingford, England, midway between Oxford and

11. (a) S. Harvey, *CAB/CAIN Evaluation Report, a Comparative Study of Two Agricultural Databases in a Computerized Current Awareness Service* (Wageningen, The Netherlands: PUDOC, 1979) (also *British Library R & D Report* no. 5483). (b) J. A. Seiss and J. B. Braden, "Online Databases Relevant to Agricultural Economists," *American Journal of Agricultural Economics* 64(4) (1982): 761–67. (c) R. A. Dahlgran, "Agricultural Economists in the Information Age: Awareness, Usage, and Attitudes towards Electronic Bibliographic Databases," *American Journal of Agricultural Economics* 69 (1987): 166–73.

12. M. A. Farget, "Un test de performance de diverses bases de données documentaire pour l'économie agricole," *Economie Rurale* 160 (1984): 37–39.

Reading. In the transitional phase, there was much concern about the effect of this move on the linkages between bureaus and the centers of excellence with which they had become associated. As the Bureau of Agricultural Economics faced this new challenge, the Oxford Institute of Agricultural Economics also entered a new phase, merging with the Institute of Commonwealth Studies into the new International Development Centre. One of the key elements contributed by the bureau, an enormous share of the library resources, continues to be held at Oxford, and by agreement this arrangement will continue.

The Bureau of Agricultural Economics moved to the new headquarters at Wallingford in June 1987, and has become fully integrated into CAB's activities. Centralization has made production, operations and communication more efficient, and encourages a greater degree of collaboration between bureaus and awareness of the subject scope of the rest of the database. Centralization has also begun to stimulate abstractors to produce abstracts for the database, rather than for an individual journal, making sure that the essential elements to aid retrieval by users of both media are retained.

As mentioned earlier, a central accessions system acquires and documents all literature that arrives for abstracting. This database lists some 14,000 journal and other numbered titles in serials as well as books, annual reports, newsletters, and the like. Its strengths lie in its elimination of duplicates, its ability to claim missing and overdue issues, and its standardization of titles. The serials list generated is forming part of a joint CABI/NAL/FAO serials list.[13] A new system planned for the 1990s will combine the accessions, data entry, and other systems to minimize handling of all data connected with database and journal production.

While direct daily contact with other agricultural economists may have been lost, the bureau has gained from having access to other CABI professional staff and linguists. They, in their turn, have gained some insight into the role of economics in agriculture. Close links have been formed with Reading University, and the Oxford links have been retained. *WAERSA* still has an editorial advisory board that includes representatives of its founders and of the International Rural Sociology Association. And there is still a constant stream of literature and correspondence arriving from contacts forged during the 1960s.

13. *International Union List of Agricultural Serials: National Agricultural Library of the U.S. Department of Agriculture, Commission of the European Communities, Food and Agriculture Organization of the United Nations, CAB International*. Wallingford, Oxon, UK: CAB International, 1990.

In January 1991, the Bureau made another transition, to become the Economics Department of the newly formed Division of Natural Resources, Forestry and Economics within CAB International's Information Services. This brings together some 20 information professionals from a wide range of disciplines, and among other advantages gives some cohesion to the group's overall responsibility for coverage of environmental issues in *CAB Abstracts*.

M. Future Development

In 1983, I wrote an article speculating that desk-top fingertip access to bibliographic information services and statistical databanks for agricultural economists would someday be accomplished with the same facility as they process personal data.[14] This dream has now become reality, and not for just the fortunate sophisticated users in the developed world. The ability to produce all the world's major agricultural databases on CD-ROM, and to download them into tapes and floppy disks, makes it possible for any professional, from any discipline, to make information needs known and to obtain a product to fit these needs. The task that remains is to ensure that information providers and users combine forces and communicate with one another to identify the kinds of packages that best suit their demands. More studies of the information requirements of agricultural economists like those of Littleton, Seiss and Braden, and Dahlgran to help bridge the gap are sorely needed.[15] And a crystal ball, aided by judicious foresight, is needed to predict the subjects that will be of most interest at the beginning of the twenty-first century.

14. Margot A. Bellamy, "The Evolution of Information Sources and the Use of Information Technology in Agricultural Economics," *Journal of Agricultural Economics* 35 (1984): 31–38.

15. (a) I. T. Littleton, "The Bibliographic Organization and Use of the Literature of Agricultural Economics" (Ph.D. Thesis; University of Illinois, 1968). A brief form of the thesis appeared as *The Literature of Agricultural Economics: Its Bibliographic Organization and Use* (Raleigh, N.C.: North Carolina Agricultural Experiment Station, 1969), *Technical Bulletin* No. 191. (b) J. A. Seiss and J. B. Braden, "Online Databases Relevant to Agricultural Economists," *American Journal of Agricultural Economics* 64(4) (1982). (c) R. A. Dahlgran, "Agricultural Economists in the Information Age: Awareness, Usage, and Attitudes towards Electronic Bibliographic Databases," *American Journal of Agricultural Economics* 69 (1987): 166–73.

4. Citation Analysis

Beginning in the 1950s, the counting and analysis of citations appearing as references in journals and books grew dramatically. A great deal of the interest has been generated by *Science Citation Index* and the *Social Sciences Citation Index*, which index the citations in articles that appear in approximately 5,500 science journals.[1] Since the 1950s, this bibliometric technique has been used in a variety of applications within the publishing, library, and information areas. It has also proven useful in measuring research and education productivity, determining the quality of a scientist's work, and as indicators of social and economic growth. So fast have the applications grown that a journal, *Scientometrics*, was begun in 1978 using citation information as the major tool in the measurement of science.[2]

A. Bibliometric Techniques

Citation counts and analyses were used informally in libraries and as bibliographic evaluations in the first quarter of the twentieth century. The first published results appeared in 1917, when comparative anatomy articles and books published from 1543 to 1860 were counted by number of publications and by country.[3] An earlier term synonymous with bibliometrics, "statistical bibliography," was coined in 1923 by E. W. Hulme.[4] The word "bibliometrics" was introduced by A. Pritchard in 1969 and defined as "the

1. Institute for Scientific Information, compiler and publisher. *Science Citation Index* 1961– . *Social Sciences Citation Index* 1977– . Philadelphia: Institute for Scientific Information.

2. *Scientometrics* 1– , Sept. 1978– . (Amsterdam: Elsevier; Budapest: Akademiai Kiado)

3. F. J. Coles and Nellie B. Eales, "The History of Comparative Anatomy," *Science Progress* 11 (1917): 578–96.

4. E. W. Hulme, *Statistical Bibliography in Relation to the Growth of Modern Civilization* (London: Grafton, 1923).

application of mathematics and statistical methods to books and other media of communication."[5] Three Hungarian researchers offered this review in 1985:

> Bibliometrics considers books, periodicals, etc. as formal and tangible documents, its major purpose being the quantitative analysis of library collections and services with a view to improving scientific documentation, information and communication activities. Scientometrics analyses the quantitative aspects of the generation, propagation and utilization of scientific information, in order to contribute to a better understanding of the mechanisms of scientific research as a social activity.[6]

Scientometricians might take issue with this definition of scientometrics since today's applications go far beyond scientific research. An historical and literature review written in 1977 by Narin and Moll provides useful definitions, explanation of techniques, and excellent short overview of bibliometrics.[7] The validity of bibliometric techniques is challenged regularly, but as Narin and Moll pointed out, numerous studies have tested bibliometrics. They offer a few illustrations:

> K. E. Clark correlated a variety of bibliometric measures with other measures used to select a panel of eminent psychologists and found that citation measures were especially significant in indicating eminence. . . . Bayer and Folger found that citation measures correlate positively with the quality of a scientist's graduate education.
>
> Cole and Cole (1967), sociologists, found that citation data correlated highly with survey data in determining the quality of a scientist's work.
>
> Solomon, another sociologist, compared the correlations in studies ranking graduate programs in sociology with a set of productivity indexes compiled from published books and major articles.
>
> Bush et al. compared citation rankings of journals in economics with a study of expert opinions to obtain similar rankings, and found that the two rankings were "remarkably close."
>
> Martino, in an article advocating use of citation data for research and development . . . management, reviewed a number of studies correlating citation frequency with quality of research and reported a study of work evaluation by the Air Force Office of Scientific Research. He concluded that citation patterns

5. Alan Pritchard, "Statistical Bibliography or Bibliometrics," *Journal of Documentation* 25(4) (1969): 348–49.

6. Tibor Braun, Wolfgang Glanzel, and Andras Schubert, *Scientometrics Indicators: A 32-Country Comparative Evaluation of Publishing Performance and Citation Impact* (Singapore and Philadelphia: World Scientific, 1985), 5–6.

7. Francis Narin and Joy K. Moll, "Bibliometrics," *Annual Review of Information Science and Technology* 12 (1977): 35–58.

correlate with the quality of work. . . . Virgo compared peer review evaluation of pairs of scientific papers with an evaluation of the same papers using citation data. She found that citation data was able to consistently mirror the judges' opinions.

Cohen-Shanin found that peer judgments of the innovative quality of research papers in plant physiology correlated very highly with rates of citations to these papers.

Despite the mass of evidence validating bibliometric analysis, negative reactions persist, based more on subjective fear and emotion than fact.[8]

The wide influence of citation analysis is reflected by a meeting of the United Nations Advisory Committee on Science and Technology for Development held in Austria in 1984. The topic was science and technology indicators for development. Three of the twelve discussion papers emphasize the use of citations as reliable indicators. One chapter in the published proceedings is devoted entirely to problems in using literature-based science and technology indicators in developing countries.[9] An overview of the conference notes: "New science is almost always published in one form or another, thus enabling us to use the number and quality of these publications as indicators. Indeed, such bibliometric indicators are among the best developed in the field."[10]

The limitations of bibliometric methods, analyses, and applications must be carefully handled within different disciplines, by databases used, and by time periods. Both Narin and Moll and *Scientometrics Indicators* detailed areas of caution and possible invalidity. The definitive work on citation indexing is by Eugene Garfield, the creator of *Science Citation Index* and related indexes.[11] Some recent articles discuss the value and limitations of citation analysis.[12] As with any statistical analysis, experience has revealed some problems, most of which have been overcome by checks, double checks, and statistical techniques. The most common faults are these:

(1) Variations between disciplines in citing habits can have an influence on outcomes and in trying to relate one subject area to another. It is a proven truism, however, that most scientists do not cite irrelevant or useless papers.

8. Ibid., p. 43.

9. Hiroko Morita-Lou, ed., *Science and Technology Indicators for Development* (Boulder, Colo., and London: Westview Press, 1985).

10. Ibid., pp. 117–22.

11. Eugene Garfield, *Citation Indexing: Its Theory and Application in Science, Technology, and Humanities* (Philadelphia: ISI Press, 1979).

12. (a) Alexander Sandison, "Thinking about Citation Analysis," *Journal of Documentation* 45(1) (March 1989): 59–64. (b) D. Lindsey, "Using Citation Counts as a Measure of Quality in Science: Measuring What's Measurable Rather Than What's Valid," *Scientometrics* 15 (1989): 190–203. (c) Terrence A. Brooks, "Literature Core Zones Adjusted by Impact Factors," *Journal of Information Science* 16 (1990): 51–57.

(2) The purpose of the citation anlaysis must be known and the most representative literature chosen to match it. An esoteric subject cannot measure a total field. The influence of prestige journals must be recognized. The predominance of basic texts such as those supporting methodologies and statistical techniques also must be dealt with. Several possible skews from these under- or overmeasurements must be accommodated.

(3) Sweeping conclusions cannot be made without adequate statistical validity; relationships must be taken into account. Efforts to use citations analysis to evaluate individuals or departments of universities have often not made the necessary adjustments for the local circumstances such as full-time equivalencies among departments, and literature impact factors. It is the old statistical story of avoiding comparing apples and oranges.

(4) The nature of scholarship brings some complications. Citation analysis is overly representative of popular scientific trends. It is not sensitive to ethical considerations. Important scientific works are sometimes overlooked by colleagues because they do not fit the standard or accepted theories at that time. In like manner, applied scientists tend not to be cited as readily as theoreticians or researchers, although this is not as great a problem in the agricultural sciences where most work is application-oriented. Linguistics, geography, and access to literature are also influential and can result in skews. These latter complications were somewhat reduced as English became the publishing language, and with the internationalization of social and economic actions.

These four potential problems can be eliminated or minimized through a variety of techniques, some statistical, some empirical. An extensive knowledge of the literature of the field can obviate false starts and misdirection. A running bibliography on quantitative studies of science is carried by *Scientometrics*. Approximately 80% of the 274 references in the 1988 update by Schubert refer to bibliometric studies.[13]

B. Use of Citation Analysis in the Agricultural Sciences

Bibliometric techniques are most widely used in the agricultural sciences to analyze indexes, library collections, databases, journal primacy, and for related applications for indexing and libraries. Such studies are cited in this chapter and will be further explored in later chapters. This section examines uses of citation analysis in the agricultural sciences *not* aimed at indexing or library operations.

One of the most extensive and widely accepted uses of citation analysis in the agricultural sciences has been to measure research productivity. An enterprising example is the work of Robert E. Evenson, the eminent Yale

13. A. Schubert, "Quantitative Studies of Science: A Current Bibliography, No. 11," *Scientometrics* 13(3–4) (1988): 139–72.

University economist, and his co-authors. Their studies were published in the mid-1970s supported largely by funds from the World Bank and the Agricultural Development Council. Evenson and Kislev studied research and productivity in wheat and maize using scientific publications as the major output indicator and by consulting *Plant Breeding Abstracts* as their counting tool. They explained their use of citations:

> The use of "paper counts" as measures of research can, of course, be subject to criticism. In its defense we offer a few points. (1) The large number of papers published assure a substantial degree of regularity. (2) Most results of research work are published, though the publication system is, perhaps, biased in favor of the countries in which the professional journals are edited. (3) There is a "floor" to the quality of articles accepted by journals of international standing, and further screening by the abstracting journals helps to secure homogeneity. (4) Published papers represent research output, while manpower and expenditures are inputs. (5) This is the only way to get measures of crop-specific research.[14]

Later work by Evenson and Kislev,[15] and Boyce and Evenson,[16] employed input parameters such as scientist-years, crop input costs by country, and extension investments. These were correlated with scientific publications as a major output, but also with crop production and sales values. Boyce and Evenson found that "these reviews show quite clearly that agricultural research investment has yielded a high rate of return in almost all situations. Indeed, the estimated rates of return reveal that investment levels have been far below optimal. The evidence regarding extension investment, on the other hand, tends to show relatively normal rates of return."[17] The work of Boyce, Evenson, and Kislev was very influential in justifying agricultural research budgets in the late 1970s in the United States and internationally. Comments continue about this work, the most recent being concerned with the utility of the international publication data.[18]

Another use of publication or citation data is in the evaluation of individuals and organizations. One of the most extensive efforts was that of

14. Robert E. Evenson and Yoav Kislev, "Research and Productivity in Wheat and Maize," *Journal of Political Economy* 81(6) (1973): 1311.

15. Robert E. Evenson and Yoav Kislev, *Agricultural Research and Productivity* (New Haven, Conn., and London: Yale University Press, 1975).

16. James K. Boyce and Robert E. Evenson, *National and International Agricultural Research & Extension Programs* (New York: Agricultural Development Council, 1975).

17. Ibid., p. 101.

18. T. Hastings, "A Note on the Utility of International Publication Data," *Scientometrics* 3(5) (1981): 389–95.

the Agricultural Research Service of the USDA in the 1960s.[19] The purpose of this elaborate investigation was to determine the validity of using the quantity of publications by a scientist as one of several measures in an individual's performance evaluation. Correlations were made in almost every conceivable manner. The study found that the quality determination of publications when made by in-house peers, external peers, and the scientists themselves, came out remarkably close. Also, quantity was a valid measurement when the prestige of the journals was taken into account, when the time period was no less than two years, and when a differential was made for the years since the scientist received the last advanced degree. A recent assessment of the use of bibliometric indicators in the natural and life sciences covers data collection and applicability.[20]

C. Economics, Sociology, and Agricultural Economics

Citation analysis has been extensively applied in both general economics and sociology. Emphasis in sociology has been in two areas: (1) measurement of the quality of sociological research, institutions, or academic departments; and (2) determination of the value, ranking, or use of sociological journals. In most cases, the studies have been specific to local sites or journal titles. The literature is extensive and not summarized here, although references to some of the major studies are provided.[21]

19. Byron T. Shaw, *The Use of Quality and Quantity of Publications as Criteria for Evaluating Scientists* (Washington, D.C.: USDA, Agricultural Research Service, 1967), *USDA Miscellaneous Publ.* no. 1041.

20. H. F. Moed, *The Use of Bibliometric Indicators for the Assessment of Research Performance in the Life Sciences: Aspects of Data Collection, Reliability, Validity and Applicability* (Leiden: DSWO Press, 1989), also published as a thesis, Leiden, 1989.

21. (a) James C. Baughman, "A Structural Analysis of the Literature of Sociology," *Library Quarterly* 44 (1974): 293–308. (b) R. N. Broadus, "A Citation Study for Sociology," *American Sociologist* 1 (1967): 19–20. (c) R. N. Broadus, "An Analysis of Literature Cited in the *American Sociological Review*," *American Sociological Review*, 17 (1952): 355–56. (d) Jonathan Cole, "The Social Structure of Science" (Ph.D. diss., Columbia University, 1969). (e) Stephen Cole, "Professional Standing and the Reception of Scientific Papers," *American Journal of Sociology* 76 (1970): 286–306. (f) Stephen Cole and Jonathan Cole, "Scientific Output and Recognition: A Study in the Operation of the Reward System in Science," *American Sociological Review* 32 (1967): 377–90. (g) Stephen Cole and Jonathan Cole, "Visibility and the Structural Bases of Awareness of Scientific Research," *American Sociological Review* 33 (1967): 397–413. (h) Stephen Cole and Jonathan Cole, "Measuring the Quality of Sociological Research: Problems in the use of the *Science Citation Index*," *American Sociologist* 6 (1971): 23–29. (i) Diana Crane, "Scientists at Major and Minor Universities: A Study of Productivity and Recognition," *American Sociological Review*, 30 (1965): 699–714. (j) Norval D. Glenn, "American Sociologists' Evaluations of Sixty-three Journals," *American Sociologist* 6 (1971): 298–303. (k) Warren O. Hagstrom, "Inputs, Outputs, and the Prestige of University Science Departments," *Sociology of Education* 44(4) (1971): 375–97. (l) Irving Louis Horowitz, "Trans-Action: A Decade of Critical Social Science Journalism," *Inter-*

The use of bibliometric techniques in economics is understandable considering the profession's heavy reliance on published literature. Economics is one of the few disciplines that has a well-respected journal dedicated to its literature. The *Journal of Economic Literature* (JEL), publishes some original economics articles, numerous literature reviews, book reviews, lists of books and reports, and provides awareness service on the contents of current journals important to economists. Both *JEL* and *American Eco nomic Review* are published by the American Economics Association. A brief history of the association's publications was prepared for the one-hundredth anniversary of the association by A. W. Coats, a historically minded economist from the University of Nottingham and Duke University, Durham, N.C.[22]

Economists are interested in determining which economic journals wield the greatest impact; they have published such studies using bibliometric techniques. Most recent and historically worthwhile is the work of Liebowitz and Palmer, who used journal citation counts with adjustments for the number of pages or size of a journal, and its age.[23] Some of these data are compared with agricultural economics journals in a later chapter. The same authors employed these techniques to evaluate earlier document assessments.[24] Similarly, journal citations and publication patterns have been used to measure the relative output of academic economics departments in the southern United States.[25] The literature is diverse and extensive.[26]

---

national Social Science Journal 25 (1973): 169–89. (m) Nan Lin and Carnot E. Nelson, "Bibliographic Reference Patterns in Core Journals, 1965–1966," *American Sociologist* 4 (1969): 47–50. (n) William William A. Satariano, "Journal Use in Sociology: Citation Analysis versus Readership Patterns," *Library Quarterly* 48(3) (1978): 293–300. (o) Warren E. Solomon, "Correlates of Prestige Ranking of Graduate Programs in Sociology," *American Sociologist* 7(5) (1972): 13–14.

22. A. W. Coats, "The American Economic Association's Publications: An Historical Perspective," *Journal of Economic Literature* 7(1) (1969). 57–68.

23. S. J. Liebowitz and J. P. Palmer, "Assessing the Relative Impacts of Economics Journals," *Journal of Economic Literature* 22 (1984): 77–88

24. S. J. Liebowitz and J. P. Palmer, "Assessing Assessments of Economics Departments," *Quarterly Review of Economics and Business* 28(2) (1988): 88–113.

25. Albert W. Niemi, Jr., "Journal Publication Performance During 1970–1974: The Relative Output of Southern Economics Departments," *Southern Economic Journal* 42(1) (1975): 97–106.

26. (a) Bradley B. Billings and George J. Viksnins, "The Relative Quality of Economics Journals: An Alternative Rating System," *Western Economics Journal* 10(4) (1972): 467–69. (b) Winston C. Bush, Paul W. Hamelman, and Robert J. Staaf, "A Quality Index for Economic Journals," *Review of Economics and Statistics* 56(1) (1974): 123–25. (c) A. W. Coats, "The Role of Scholarly Journals in the History of Economics: An Essay," *Journal of Economic Literature* 9(1) (1974): 29–44. (d) P. Davis and G. Papanek, "Faculty Rating of Major Economics Departments by Citations," *American Economic Review* 74 (1984): 225–30. (e) Robert G. Hawkins, Lawrence S. Ritter, and Ingo Walter, "What Economists Think of Their Journals," *Journal of Political Economics* 81(4) (1973): 1017–32. (f) Timothy D. Hogan, "Rankings of Ph.D. Programs in Economics and the Relative Publishing Performance of Their Ph.D.'s: The Experience of the 1960s," *Western Economic Journal* (December 1973): 429–50. (g) William J. Moore, "The Relative Qual-

Rulon D. Pope recently analyzed the literature citations appearing in the *Journal of Economic Literature* for two distinct years, 1974 and 1984. The *JEL* runs the title-pages of the journals as they are issued and is very diligent in this current awareness assistance. Pope used the articles of those recent or forthcoming journals for his study which employed a very elaborate subject classification scheme. He attempted to show which areas of economics had expanded in the literature over the ten-year period and then used this information as a guide to predict the likely direction of agricultural economics in the future.[27]

As with economics, agricultural economics has used citation analysis to answer two questions: (1) How do the agricultural economics departments in the United States rank? (2) What does the *American Journal of Agricultural Economics (AJAE)* publish and who are the authors? Several articles since 1968 have examined these and related questions.

The earliest article analyzed the contents of the *Journal of Farm Economics*, which changed its name in 1968 to *American Journal of Agricultural Economics* with continuous volume numbering. Of particular historical interest is the extensive review of the first thirty-five years (1919–53) of the *Journal of Farm Economics*, which provides counts and analysis of types of articles, division of the 2,849 contributions into subject categories, breakdown into four time periods, identification of organizational sources, rankings of the most heavily contributing nineteen academic institutions, and the most prolific individual authors. Two non-land-grant universities are represented with heavy faculty writing for the *Journal*: Harvard and Stanford. John D. Black of Harvard is cited as having provided twice as many papers as the next most active writer, Geoffrey Shepherd.[28] John D. Black's books are heavily represented in the core listings in later chapters of this book. Besides this worthwhile article, particularly valuable for its subject categorization, two other articles about the *American Journal of*

---

ity of Economics Journals: A Suggested Rating System," *Western Economic Journal* (June 1972): 159–69. (h) William J. Moore, "The Relative Quality of Graduate Programs in Economics, 1958–1972: Who Published and Who Perished," *Western Economic Journal* (March 1973): 1–23. (i) John J. Siegfried, "The Publishing of Economic Papers and Its Impact on Graduate Faculty Ratings, 1960–69," *Journal of Economic Literature* (March 1972): 31–49. (j) Jack W. Skeels and Ryland A. Taylor, "The Relative Quality of Economics Journals: An Alternature Rating System," *Western Economic Journal* (December 1972): 470–73.

27. Rulon D. Pope, "Developments in Economics of Importance to Agricultural Economics," in *Agriculture and Rural Areas Approaching the Twenty-First Century*, ed. R. J. Hildreth, Kathryn L. Lipton, Kenneth C. Clayton, and Carl C. O'Connor (Ames, Iowa: Iowa State University Press, 1988), pp. 238–56.

28. Carl J. Arnold and Raleigh Barlowe, "*The Journal of Farm Economics*—Its First 35 Years," *Journal of Farm Economics* 36 (1954): 441–52.

Agricultural Economics deal with the frequency of invited papers, and the concentration of number of papers by a few individuals.[29] Other useful observations appeared in 1963 and 1955.[30]

Most later evaluations revolve around the institutional affiliations of contributors to *American Journal of Agricultural Economics*. Holland and Redman provided an update to the *Journal of Farm Economics* thirty-five-year study for the 1953–72 period. They also categorized the articles into ten subject categories by three time periods, and within each category they identified the five most active land-grant institutions. The University of Illinois, Purdue University, and the University of Wisconsin ranked at the top in two categories each.[31] This article, which usefully identified the USDA scientists as a distinct group, was extended and commented on by Finley.[32] The *American Journal of Agricultural Economics* for the 1973–83 period was analyzed by Simpson and Steele, and author contributions were analyzed by geographic location of the American Agricultural Economics Association membership in 1972.[33]

In 1977, Opaluch and Just corrected the earlier deficiency of analyzing only one journal by examining eleven primary journals in addition to the *American Journal of Agricultural Economics*. Using the membership directory of the American Agricultural Economics Association to identify authors of articles in the twelve journals, their aim was to show the university affiliation of the authors; other organizational affiliations were excluded.[34] Their large examination was further extended by a 1986 study based on counts of citations to works of agricultural economists in the *Social Sciences Citation Index* (SSCI). Their work updates many of the tabulations and

29. (a) John Moore, "Frequency of Invited Papers," *Journal of Farm Economics* 45 (1963): 219–20. (b) James Nielson and Harold M. Riley, "Concentration of Authorship in the *JFE*?" *Journal of Farm Economics* 45 (1963): 885–87.

30. (a) Alan R. Bird, "Frequency of Invited Papers by Land Grant Institutions," *Journal of Farm Economics* 45 (1963): 662–63. (b) R. L. Kohls, "*Journal of Farm Economics Content*—A Further Comment," *Journal of Farm Economics* 37 (1955): 114–15.

31. David W. Holland and John C. Redman, "Institutional Affiliation of Authors of Contributions to the *American Journal of Agricultural Economics* 1953–1972," *American Journal of Agricultural Economics* 56 (1974): 784–90. Table 7 data, p. 789.

32. Robert M. Finley, "Institutional Affiliation of Authors of Contributions to the *American Journal of Agricultural Economics* 1953–72: Comment," *American Journal of Agricultural Economics* 57 (1975): 522–24.

33. (a) J. R. Simpson and J. T. Steele, "Institutional Affiliation of Authors of Contributors to the *American Journal of Agricultural Economics*, 1973–83," *American Journal of Agricultural Economics* 67 (1985): 325–27. (b) John C. Redman, "Locational Distribution of AAEA Membership and Journal Contributions," *American Journal of Agricultural Economics* 54 (1972): 145–46.

34. James Opaluch and Richard E. Just, "Institutional Affiliation of Authors of Contributions in Agricultural Economics, 1968–72," *American Journal of Agricultural Economics* 59 (1977): 400–403.

Table 9. Rankings by citation studies of institutional affiliations of U.S. academic agricultural economics authors

	SSCI[a], 1980–84		*AJAE*[b], 1980–83		12 major journals[c] 1968–72		*AJAE*[d] 1953–72
			Average pages		Average pages		Total pages
Institution	Total citations	Research,[e] FTE, and experience	All	Teaching & research	Faculty A	Faculty B	Ranking
Univ. of California, Berkeley	1	1	1	1	1	1	6
Stanford Univ.	2	2					
Univ. of Minnesota	3	6	6	8	2	2	5
Iowa State	4	4	4	4	10	10	1
Univ. of Illinois	5	9	10	10	12	12	8
Univ. of Wisconsin	6	7	12	15	6	5	4
Cornell	7	10	9	13	9	7	10
Oklahoma State	8	14	2	2	5	5	14
Texas A & M	9	16	13	9			18
Michigan State	10	8	15	12	11	11	2
Purdue	11	22	5	6	7	7	3
Univ. of Maryland	12	5					
Univ. of California, Davis	13	19	3	7	3	3	9

Montana State	14	3	14	14			
Univ. of Florida	15	20	11	11	4	4	19
North Carolina State	16	10	8	3			7
Oregon State			17	19	7	9	15
Virginia Polytechnic			7	5			

AJAE = American Journal of Agricultural Economics

Sources:

[a]Richard P. Beilock, Leo C. Polopolus, and Mario Correal, "Ranking of Agricultural Economics Departments by Citations," *American Journal of Agricultural Economics* 68 (1986): 595–604.

[b]J. R. Simpson and J. T. Steele, "Institutional Affiliation of Authors of Contributors to the *American Journal of Agricultural Economics*, 1973–83," *American Journal of Agricultural Economics* 67 (1985): 325–27. The two columns distinguish between teaching and research faculty only, and the total faculty which includes some extension and other responsibilities. The study includes averages for 1973–79 which are not shown in this table.

[c]James Opaluch and Richard E. Just, "Institutional Affiliation of Authors of Contributions in Agricultural Economics, 1968–72," *American Journal of Agricultural Economics* 59 (1977): 400–403. The membership directory of the American Agricultural Economics Association was used. In addition to the *AJAE*, the journals were *American Economic Review, Econometrica, Journal of Political Economy, International Economic Review, Economic Journal, Quarterly Journal of Economics, Review of Economics and Statistics, Review of Economic Studies, Journal of the American Statistical Association, European Economic Review, Economica*, and *Journal of Economic Theory*. Faculty Group A is teaching & research; B is A plus extension faculty.

[d]David W. Holland and John C. Redman, "Institutional Affiliation of Authors of Contributions to the *American Journal of Agricultural Economics*—1953–1972," *American Journal of Agricultural Economics* 56 (1974): 784–90. Table 7 data p. 789. This extensive study has perspective because of the time span. It also includes nonacademic contributions by USDA and other government agencies, business firms, and foreign sources. Data were provided on invited and noninvited papers, which were combined. In 1968–72, the study found that academics accounted for 70.3% of all articles of which the land-grants constituted 60.7%.

[e]The *SSCI* counts citations to an author's works. The second column resolves part-time, extension, and years of experience, thereby putting institutions on a more nearly equal basis. This technique is used in two of the other studies also. FTE = Full-Time Equivalancies.

analysis of earlier studies, but is also significant for including authors from non-land-grant institutions, which places Stanford University as second-ranked behind the University of California, Berkeley.[35]

Table 9 displays the data from four citation studies. Institutional affiliation was determined by membership or other directories, or by using the affiliation noted in the journals. The *SSCI* study used a large cumulative database, thereby giving retrospective credit to an author at the current location only. The other studies are based on page counts of articles. Blank spaces indicate that the institution ranked lower than the last number shown, except in the case of Stanford University in the last three studies where it was not included because the analyses dealt with land-grant universities only.

On the basis of writings, there are some impressive newcomers in agricultural economics, particularly the University of California at Davis, the University of Maryland, and Montana State University. The Berkeley campus of the University of California is outstanding with its small faculty of eighteen; Stanford has thirteen. Both have far fewer faculty than other leading institutions.[36] Only when gross page counts are used for ranking in the last study does Berkeley fall out of the top. The consistent rankings of Berkeley, Minnesota, Iowa State, Illinois, Wisconsin, Cornell, Oklahoma State, Michigan State, and Purdue place them as long-term, strong agricultural economics institutions.

The subject analysis by Holland and Redman of articles in the *American Journal of Agricultural Economics,* 1953-72, is of special interest.[37] Although their purpose probably was to show the emphases within the *AJAE*, the changes exemplified by counts in the first and last periods are reflective of the changes within agricultural economics. (See Table 10.) The *AJAE*, the most important journal in agricultural economics, has had consistently high editorial standards and attempts to reflect current questions and interests in a scholarly manner. Therefore, the data represent shifts in academic subject concentrations.

35. Richard P. Beilock, Leo C. Polopolus, and Mario Correal, "Ranking of Agricultural Economics Departments by Citations," *American Journal of Agricultural Economics* 68 (1986): 595–604.

36. (a) Wyn F. Owen and Douglas A. Ruby, eds., *Guide to Graduate Study in Economics, Agricultural Economics, Public Administration, and Doctoral Programs in Business Administration in the United States and Canada,* 8th ed. (Boulder, Colo.: Economics Institute, 1989). (b) USDA Cooperative State Research Service, *1990–91 Directory of Professional Workers in State Agricultural Experiment Stations and Other Cooperating State Institutions*. (Washington, D.C.: USDA, 1990 [*USDA Agricultural Handbook* no. 305]).

37. David W. Holland and John C. Redman, "Institutional Affiliation of Authors of Contributions to the *American Journal of Agricultural Economics*—1953–1972," *American Journal of Agricultural Economics* 56 (1974): 784–90, Table 7 data, p. 789.

Table 10. Subject concentrations of *AJAE*, 1953–85 (in percent)

Subject	Distribution of page counts[a]		Articles[b]
	1953–62	1968–72	1961–85
Production	22.3	17.7	16.1
Commodities (supply, demand, prices)	15.3	9.1	7.8
Foreign trade, developments, economics	10.4	12.5	14.3
Teaching, research, extension methods	10.2	9.8	11.4
Agricultural policy	9.6	7.4	6.6
Domestic development (human, labor, income, sociology)	8.6	15.4	12.3
Marketing, storage, & distribution	8.5	10.3	15.0
Resource economies (land, water, environment)	7.0	9.5	7.9
General agricultural economics	5.5	5.1	3.4
Farm finance, capital, credit	2.7	3.3	5.3

[a]David W. Holland and John C. Redman, "Institutional Affiliation of Authors of Contributions to the American Journal of Agricultural Economics—1953–1972," American Journal of Agricultural Economics 56 (1974): 784–90, Table 7 data, p. 789.

[b]Catherine Halbrendt, C. M. Gempesaw II, Roger Glendenning, and Melvin Blase, "Focus and Trends of the American Journal of Agricultural Economics: 1961–1985," Paper presented at 1988 Annual Meeting of the American Agricultural Economics Association, Knoxville, Tenn. Data from Table 1.

The article tabulations for Table 10 were done for five time periods of five years each so that comparisons could be made over a twenty-five-year period: the 1961–85 figures were computed for the entire period. Two subjects were divided into four in the article tabulation and were recombined to coincide with the earlier page-count study. On a long-term basis, the changes do not seem of great significance, except for the continued downturn of production, an upturn of foreign trade and development, and marketing.

The publication output of academics has long been used as a determinant of faculty salaries. Several articles have applied these value systems to agricultural economists. A 1982 study used different devices and methods to establish the influence of the determinants. Publications were given a weight of 5 for any book; 2 for an article in *AJAE*; 1 for publication in national, regional, foreign, and international journals; and ⅓ for experiment station and extension publications. The authors note: "Although any weighting scheme can be considered arbitrary, the weights reflect the procedures and empirical findings of previous studies on economics faculty salaries."[38]

38. Josef M. Broder and Rod F. Ziemer, "Determinants of Agricultural Economics Faculty Salaries," *American Journal of Agricultural Economics* 62 (1982): 301.

The same authors, along with a colleague, compared regional publication output by U.S. agricultural economists.[39] These techniques and their applications are the basis for the analyses to attain the core literature in the following chapters.

39. Rod F. Ziemer, Josef M. Broder, and Stan R. Spurlock, "A Regional Comparison of Publication Output of Academic Agricultural Economists," *North Central Journal of Agricultural Economics* 2 (1980): 167–70.

5. Citation Analysis for Creation of Core Lists

Since the 1970s, numerous well-documented studies have analyzed scientific literature, its meaning and uses. In addition to the valuable Narin and Moll[1] article previously mentioned, a 1985 article with 203 references to science publication studies attests to these efforts.[2] Readers may also wish to delve into citation applications and related publishing practices as an influence in information systems.[3]

Of particular value in analyzing literature by counting citations is the work and publications of the Institute for Scientific Information (ISI). *Science Citation Index* and the *Social Sciences Citation Index*[4] are valuable print and online tools, along with the ISI's annual *Journal Citation Reports*.[5] A summary of the techniques and applications are provided by the indexes' creator, Eugene Garfield.[6]

Any meaningful literature pattern requires a structured citation database from which data, correlations, and conclusions can be devolved. This study began with attempts to use the immense ISI databases and publications to analyze the literature of agricultural economics and rural sociology. It soon became clear, however, that the ISI database and publications scantily cover agricultural economics and rural sociology. The references that do

1. Francis Narin and Joy K. Moll, "Bibliometrics," *Annual Review of Information Science and Technology* 12 (1977): 35–58.

2. F. Vlachy, "Citation Histories of Scientific Publications; The Date Sources," *Scientometrics* 7(3–6) (1985): 505–28.

3. See Kenneth S. Warren, ed., *Selectivity in Information Systems: Survival of the Fittest* (New York: Praeger, 1985).

4. *Science Citation Index* (1961 to date) and *Social Sciences Citation Index* (1977 to date), are compiled and issued by the Institute for Scientific Information, Philadelphia.

5. *Journal Citation Reports* are annual companion volumes to the *Science Citatation Index* and the *Social Sciences Citation Index*, all issued by the Institute for Scientific Information, Philadelphia. Numerous tabulations and counts are provided on a year's citation indexing.

6. Eugene Garfield, *Citation Indexing: Its Theory and Application in Science, Technology and Humanities* (Philadelphia: ISI Press, 1979). His *Essays of an Information Scientist* also published by ISI Press (1977+), currently in ten volumes, summarizes years of analyses from the databases.

exist are usually limited to economics and general agriculture. Some useful data concerning journal literature will be shown later.

A common complaint about the ISI databases is that they concentrate on the research literature of a discipline. The citations at the ends of journal articles reflect the point of view of individual researchers. The citations may or may not represent the range of literature that would be used by an educator or applications practitioner, particularly in the agricultural sciences. It was necessary to establish another path for identification of titles, and for quantifying what we wanted to know. Findings then had to be related to other studies or databases when valid and possible.

A. Aim and Methods

The primary aim of this study is to determine the core literature of agricultural economics and rural sociology since the 1950s which still has impact in academic teaching and research today. A further aim was to determine the relative rank and merits of the titles for both the worldwide academic community, including developing or Third World countries. An additional purpose sought to identify the pertinent literature from earlier periods, which is older heritage literature.

Bibliographic databases in agriculture and those of ISI provide an immense current record but retrospective capabilities are restricted. Alternative and often-used methods had to be employed.

The literature of agricultural economics is prolific. A variety of specialty abstracting tools, such as *Sociological Abstracts*, exist. These, however, present some of the same problems as other indexes or databases. Older literature studies offer some help, but they concern themselves with journals only and our aim was to examine all formats. Some core lists have been developed, but they have restricted scope and subject matter, or else, they are too vast and not adequately restrictive. One aspect missing from nearly every compilation was qualitative and professional evaluation. This logically lead to literature reviews, selective readings brought together in books, reserve readings used in academic libraries as adjuncts to the classroom, and landmark reviews of agricultural economics and rural sociology. This "overview" literature proved most nearly to meet the aims of the project as a valid method to establish our base. Overview literature incorporates a twofold quality factor; the works are classics on their own, and are also peer-reviewed.

B. The Overview Literature

Agricultural economics is closely allied with or is a subset of economics. Economic literature characteristics carry over into academic agricultural economics and rural sociology. The amount of overview literature, particularly literature reviews, is great in both disciplines.

The American Farm Economic Association, predecessor to the current American Agricultural Economics Association, commissioned literature reviews and selected readings volumes as early as 1949. The provision of current-awareness by both associations provides a wealth of valuable review literature which served as building blocks in the compilation of monograph and journal lists.

This study aimed to identify the most-cited literature of the recent past which is appropriate for the educational process and initial research effort. The intellectual aim could also be characterized as that associated with advanced undergraduate and graduate work. Source volumes that best suited this aim had to be chosen. To avoid skews we chose historically important works; literature reviews covering broad periods of times, or monographs with this perspective; works or portions of works representative of all subject areas of agricultural economics and rural sociology today and in the past twenty years; and avoided the literature that is primarily research-oriented. The decisions on the approach and the titles were made in consultation with agricultural economists and rural sociologists at Cornell University.

The following source titles were used for the extraction of titles and for counts on journal titles and books. The citations they yielded are the basis for the analysis in this and the next two chapters.

Peer-Reviewed or Evaluated Publications used to Compile Monograph and Journal Data (Source Documents)

Lee R. Martin, ed. *A Survey of Agricultural Economics Literature*, 3 vols. Minneapolis: University of Minnesota Press for the American Agricultural Economics Association, 1977–81. Fourth volume forthcoming in 1992.

1989

Randolph Barker. Unpublished 1989 reference list of 1486 citations to agricultural development in Asia, loaned by the compiler.

Carl K. Eicher and Doyle C. Baker. "Research on Agricultural Development in Sub-Saharan Africa: A Critical Survey." June 1989. Forthcoming in *A Survey of Agricultural Economics Literature*, ed. Lee R. Martin, vol. 4 (due 1992).

1988

G. Antonelli and A. Quadrio-Curzio, eds. *The Agro-Technological System towards 2000: A European Perspective*. Amsterdam and New York: North-Holland, 1988. 297p.

David L. Brown, et al. *Rural Economic Development in the 1980's: Prospects for the Future*. Washington, D.C.: U.S. Dept. of Agriculture, 1988. 399p. (*USDA Rural Development Research Report*, no. 69).

R. J. Hildreth, Kathryn L. Lipton, Kenneth E. Clayton, and Carl C. O'Connor, eds. *Agriculture and Rural Areas Approaching the Twenty-first Century: Challenges for Agricultural Economics*. Ames, Iowa: Iowa State University Press, 1988. 565p.

John W. Mellor and Mohinder S. Mudahar. "References for Agriculture in Economic Development: Theories, Findings, and Challenges in an Asian Context." 1988. Forthcoming in *A Survey of Agricultural Economics Literature*, ed. Lee Martin, Vol. 4.

G. Edward Schuh and Antonio Brandão. "References for the Literature on Agricultural Development in Latin America." 1988. Forthcoming in *A Survey of Agricultural Economics Literature*, ed. Lee Martin, Vol. 4.

1985

Edward Tower, compiler. *Agricultural Economics, Agriculture in Economic Development, and Health Economics*. Durham, N.C.: Eno River Press, 1985. 184p. (Economics Reading Lists, Course Outlines, Exams, Puzzles and Problems; vol. 22).

1984

Carl K. Eicher and John M. Staatz, eds. *Agricultural Development in the Third World*. Baltimore and London: Johns Hopkins University Press, 1984. 491p.

1982

Don A. Dillman and Daryl J. Hobbs, eds. *Rural Society in the U.S.: Issues for the 1980's*. Boulder, Colo.: Westview Press, 1982. 437p.

1979

Tan Bock Thiam and Shao-Er Ong, eds. *Readings in Asian Farm Management*. Singapore: Singapore University Press, 1979. 350p.

1975

Committee on Economics Teaching Material for Asian Universities. *The Economics of Agriculture*. New York: John Wiley and Sons, 1975. 245p. (Economics Theory and Practice in the Asian Setting, vol. 3).

1974

E. A. R. Bush. *Agriculture: A Bibliographical Guide*. London: MacDonald, 1974. 2 vols., 1571p. Monographs in appropriate subjects were extracted from vol. 1, pp. 27–32; 39–49; 51–61; 65–67; 70–71; 208–15.

1971

Markets in the United States, 1950–1971: A Bibliography of Economics Studies. St. Paul, Minn.: Minnesota Agricultural Experiment Station, 1971. (*Miscellaneous Report* no. 103).

1970

Bruce F. Johnston. "Agriculture and Structural Transformation in Developing Countries: A Survey of Research." *Journal of Economic Literature* 8(2) (1970): 369–404.

1969

Karl S. Fox and D. Gale Johnson, selectors. *Readings in the Economics of Agriculture*. Selected by a Committee of the American Economics Association. Homewood, Ill.: Richard D. Irwin, 1969. 517p., 27 articles.

1967

Joosep Nou. "Studies in the Development of Agricultural Economics in Europe." *Lantbruks-Högskolans Annaler* (Annals of the Agricultural College of Sweden) 33(1) (1967): 3–611.

1966
J. Price Gittinger. *The Literature of Agricultural Planning*. Washington, D.C.: National Planning Association, 1966. 135p. (Center for Development Planning, Planning Methods Series no. 4).
1954
Frederick V. Waugh, ed. *Readings on Agricultural Marketing*. Ames, Iowa: Iowa State College Press, 1954. 456p. (Assembled and published under the sponsorship of the American Farm Economic Association).
1953
Murray R. Benedict. *Farm Policies of the United States, 1790–1950: A Study of Their Origins and Developments*. New York: Twentieth Century Fund, 1953. 548p.
1949
O. B. Jesness, ed. *Readings on Agricultural Policy*. Philadelphia and Toronto: Blakiston, 1949. 470p. (Assembled and published under the sponsorship of the American Farm Economic Association).

Particular note must be taken of *A Survey of Agricultural Economics Literature*, edited by Lee R. Martin, upon commission of the American Agricultural Economics Association. The volumes, each near 500 pages, have these titles:

Vol.1, *Traditional Fields of Agricultural Economics, 1940s to 1970s*. 2,255 citations.
Vol.2, *Quantitative Methods in Agricultural Economics, 1940s to 1970s*. 2,156 citations.
Vol.3, *Economics of Welfare, Rural Development, and Natural Resources in Agriculture, 1940s to 1970s*. 3,755 citations.
Vol.4, Due in 1992: *Agriculture in Economic Development*. This volume primarily concerns Third World countries. 4,248 known citations.

The Martin work is an immense long-range literature review which is still ongoing. The three published volumes contain 8,166 citations, of which approximately 68% are duplicate citations to the same journal or book. The reference lists to three of the chapters to be included in volume 4 were obtained from the authors. Citations in these chapters totaled 4,248. Although the three chapters have been submitted to the editor, some citations may be removed in the review process. The total Martin works have 12,414 citations concerned with agricultural economics from an American point of view, along with the primary literature of economic agriculture in the developing countries. The other sixteen overview volumes yielded the remaining citations so that in total 19,000 were examined. The counts, titles, and data shaped the initial core lists in monographs and journals.

An effort was made to provide a full scope of agricultural economics by utilizing different points of view and different time periods. The chosen overview monographs were published from 1949 through 1990. Some emphasis was given to the most recent and authoritative overviews in the broad areas of agricultural economics and rural sociology.

C. Compilation and Counting

Every citation or reference in the twenty-two titles was examined and entered into lists or counts. The three Martin-edited volumes were done first, yielding approximately 2,500 monograph titles and 129 journal titles. Detailed information was extracted from sixteen of the volumes. In this process, 16,529 citations were examined and categorized and counted by journal title, publisher, date of publication, and type of publication. Before examining those results, the methods and definitions must be understood. Distinctions between journals, serial works, and monographs are necessary. Series issues, short works, and books were treated as monographs when they were cited as distinct works with an author or editor, when a title was distinctive regardless of a series, and when the item was complete. Therefore, a work complete in itself as are all titles in the *USDA Agricultural Handbook* series was counted as a monograph in all cases. The same was true of proceedings volumes when sub-titled with distinctive titles, which was the case with most cited proceedings. Those with no distinct title or special subject focus and which reoccurred regularly were counted as journals or serials. Journals follow the pattern of having several articles on different and specific subjects in one issue, and are traditionally cited as being "in" a title.

Chapters in books were counted as monographs. The definitions worked well since they followed the citation patterns and thinking of agricultural authors.

A count was kept for each book and journal title, whether cited as a part, article, or chapter or the whole. The results are counts on the number of times each journal was cited, and each book or book chapter referenced. As more overview works were tallied, the numbers of new monographic and journal titles fell off sharply. Towards the end of the compilation, less than 3% of the citations in the volumes being examined yielded new titles.

By this method, a journal list of 520 titles was compiled. Over 80 were cited fewer than ten times in a total citation pool of 19,000. The monographs totaled nearly 5,000 individual titles. At the point of determining how much data could be utilized from computerized databases and the possibility for misinformation, the conclusion was reached to submit the tallied monograph list to evaluation by scientists in the discipline. This process is described in Chapter 7. Their votes on specific titles were added to the accumulated totals from the overview volumes so that a ranking system was accomplished.

D. Results of the Overview Compilations

Analysis of sixteen of the volumes or reference list (p. 55) provides data which casts some light on the use of literature in agricultural economics and rural sociology. The Early works in Table 11 are all *Readings in . . .* volumes, which contain journal articles reprinted as valuable literature for action or learning. The percentage of citations to journals in these three early works is far greater than that of all of the other overviews. This literature can be categorized as nontheoretical, or action literature, that is, intended to aid in solving rather immediate problems. It is probably a fair conclusion that such literature is less frequent on a percentage basis today, or has such a short life that it is downplayed in the scholarly literature. The second total summary in Table 11 removes the influence of these early works to measure their overall influence. Similarly, the Martin citations in the three published volumes, half of all in Table 11, were removed to indicate their influence.

The results in the three totals remain relatively the same. Journals are cited in a range from 41.8 to 43.5%; monographs from 54.8 to 56.6%. This solidly indicates that agricultural economics literature for instruction and research more heavily relies on monographic materials.

Perhaps not as surprising is the decided lean toward monographs in the Third World literature. The five works analyzed vary widely in their percentage of journal literature, from 32.4% to 44.4%. Reasons for the ten-point spread are not clear. Possible influences are regional or continental coverage in three of the works, state of agricultural economic development, scholarly writing limitations, or the authors' differing assessments of which literature is most pertinent.

Data were collected on the publishers of the monographs. Figure 1 displays the kinds of publishers of the monographs cited in the first three volumes edited by Martin. The government category includes state, province, country, and international bodies, including the FAO and other United Nations agencies. Independent publishers are institutes, international centers, societies, and associations that are not part of a government or university, for example, the Brookings Institution and the international agricultural research centers. University organizations and presses account for nearly 50% of monographic publishing: this group includes publications of

Table 11. Citations to journals, monographs, and dissertations in sixteen overview works

	Journals	Monographs	Dissertations	Total
Early works				
Jesness (1949)	135	48		183
Waugh (1954)	133	79		212
Fox & Johnson (1969)	337	198		535
	605	321		926
	65.3%	34.7%		
Martin works				
Vol. 1 (1977)	921	1,309	25	2,255
Vol. 2 (1977)	1,179	939	38	2,156
Vol. 3 (1981)	1,625	2,051	79	3,755
	3,725	4,299	142	8,166
	45.6%	52.7%	1.7%	
Late agricultural economics works				
Antonelli & Quadrio-Curzio (1988)	62	167	1	230
Tower (1985)	380	371	2	753
	442	538	3	983
	45.0%	54.7%	.3%	
Rural sociology works				
Dillman & Hobbs (1982)	251	508	14	773
Hildreth et al. (1988)	362	367	13	742
Brown et al. (1988)	108	151	1	260
	721	1,026	28	1,775
	40.6%	57.8%	1.6%	
Third World works				
Eicher & Staatz (1984)	222	452	11	685
Mellor & Mudahar (1988)	671	838	2	1,511
Schuh & Brandao (1988)	362	558	77	997
Barker (1989)	636	848	2	1,486
Eicher & Baker (1989)	575	1,156	43	1,774
	2,466	3,852	135	6,453
	38.2%	59.7%	2.1%	
Total of all citations	7,959	10,036	308	18,303
	43.5%	54.8%	1.7%	
Total excluding early works (1949–69)	7,354	9,715	308	17,377
	42.3%	55.9%	1.8%	
Total excluding Martin works (1976–81)	4,234	5,737	166	10,137
	41.8%	56.6%	1.6%	

departments, campus institutes, experiment stations, and extension services. Extension publications are not represented in the final core list of monographs, and their overall publishing influence is almost nonexistent. Commercial publishing ranges from 9.5 to 21%.

The three early works (Jesness, Waugh, Fox and Johnson) cover a major

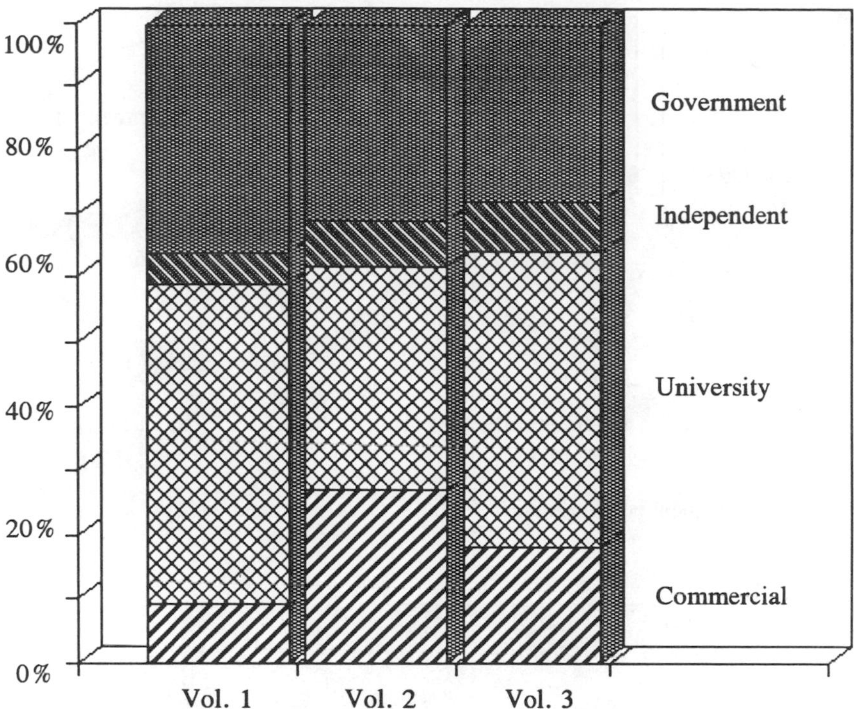

Figure 1. Publishers of monographs cited in Martin, vols. 1–3.

portion of the same time period as the three Martin volumes represented in Figure 1. The publishing patterns are somewhat different, however: see Figure 2. Although the university publishing remained the same, the citation patterns for government and commercial publishing changed placed in importance. The Martin works deal heavily with government intervention programs in the United States, which accounts for the dramatic change. The pattern of reduced commercial involvement of the more recent Martin volumes seems to be changing back to more commercial publishing judging from the core list of monographs identified in Chapter 7.

A similar analysis was made of the citations concerned with developing agricultural economies as represented in the Third World works, displayed in Figure 3. The similarity of publishing patterns in all five volumes is fairly conclusive. The increase of independent publishing organizations from the Eicher and Staatz list (1984) to the Barker list (1989) probably will be accentuated in the future. The independent group includes reports, monographs, and other nonjournal publications of the international agricultural centers around the world. Their influence has increased at the ex-

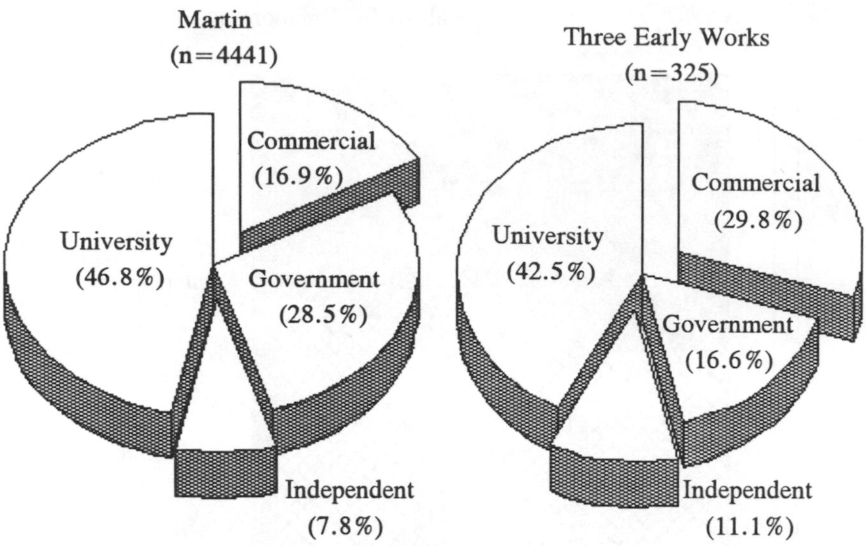

Figure 2. Monograph publishers cited in Martin (vols. 1–3) and the early works.

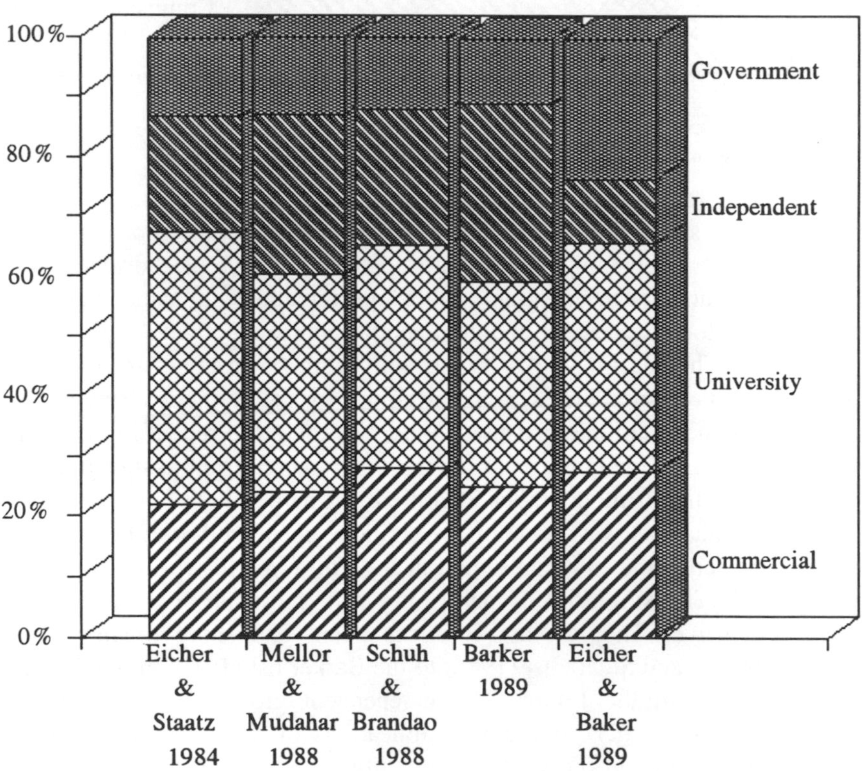

Figure 3. Publishers of cited works concerned with developing agricultural economies.

pense of all the other publishers. University publications are half as important here as in the three Martin volumes.

Figure 4 combines the categories in Table 11 and adds a sixth, a composite of all the 9,145 monographs and dissertations. These groupings provide graphic illustrations of the publishing characteristics of different types of agricultural economics and rural sociology literature. The university publications stand out, being nearly double the nearest competitor, commercial presses, in nearly every category.

Upon examination of university publications, the data show a 3:1 ratio of university press citations to those for university institutes and departments. Of some significance is the 21.7% of rural sociology citations to government documents or publications, and 28.5% in the three Martin volumes. Government publishing is much lower with the other groups, ranging from 11.3% to 16.6%. Except for the Third World works, all of the more recent books show a more nearly equal split between commercial and university presses. This change is partially the result of a determined attitude of many governments to reduce their publishing, and also by policies such as that of the World Bank, which has arranged to have its longer and more substantial monographs published by Johns Hopkins University Press or Oxford University Press. This World Bank policy was implemented in the late 1970s.

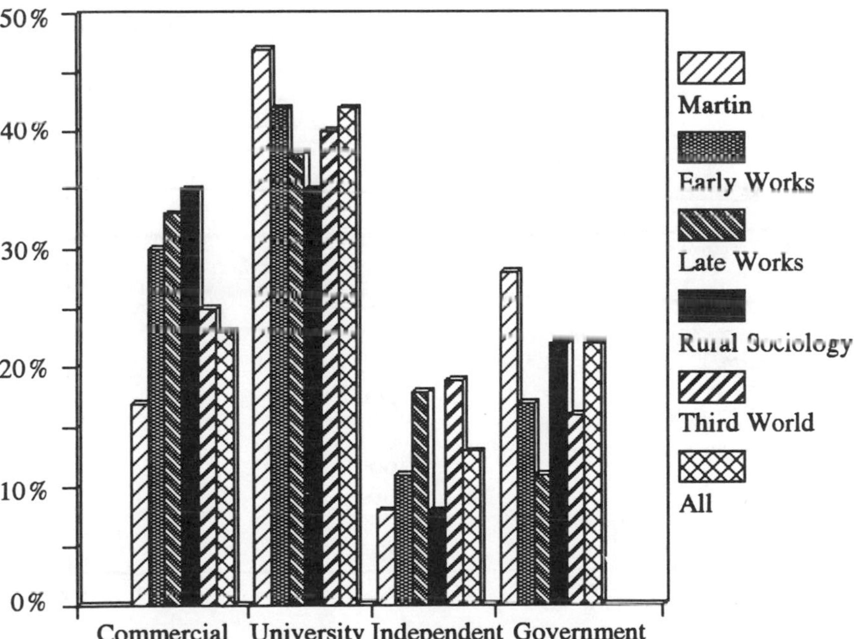

Figure 4. Publishers of cited monographs from six categories.

E. How Old Is the Cited Literature?

Since the mid-1960s, studies have been assessing the obsolesence of the literature of a discipline. Although this may be accomplished a variety of ways, the most common and easily computed is to establish the "half-life" by way of citation analysis. The half-life of literature is the median date of the analyzed citations. This measure is achieved by keeping records on the date of the citations and finding the median age of the total population, counting back from the date of the citing document. The result gives us clues to how the literature of a discipline is used and viewed by its scientists. A journal, for example, with a very short half-life of two years probably is a popular journal or magazine handling very current and topical subjects. The journal *Choices*, begun in 1986 by the American Agricultural Economics Association, will probably demonstrate a very short half-life when it has been around long enough to be cited for a valid length of time.

Half-lives were computed on the journal and monograph citations in the sixteen volumes identified in Table 11, and are displayed in Figure 5. These

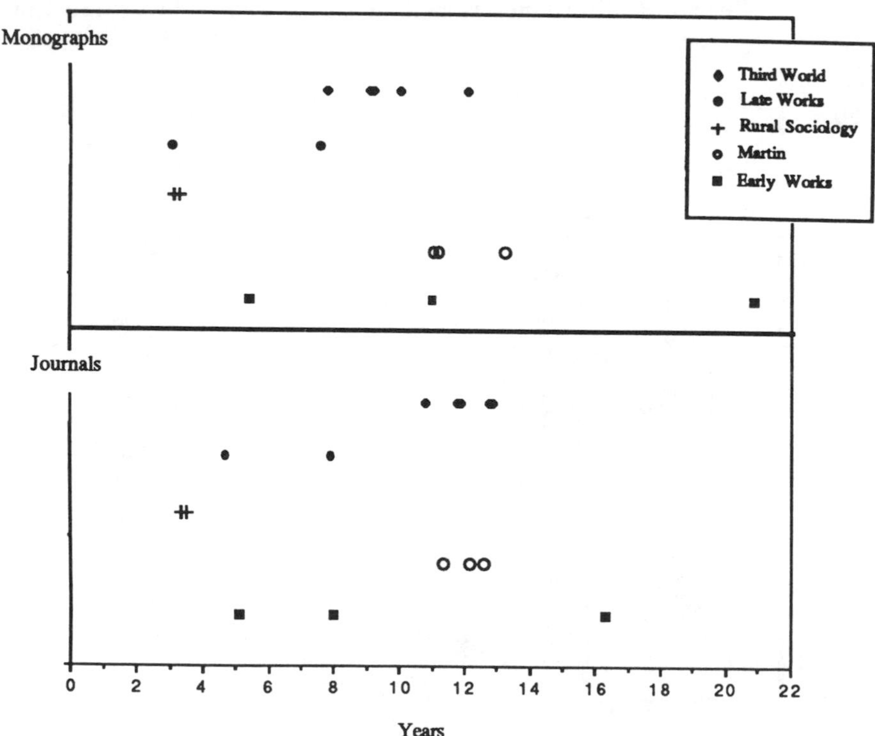

Figure 5. Half lives of cited works.

data should be read in the following manner: The computations on journals and monographs cited in the late agricultural economics works identified in Table 11 are shown in Figure 5 as round black dots. There are two volumes analyzed in this category, hence two dots each for monographs and journals. The half-life of the cited monographs ranged from about two to eight years. The half-life of the cited journals ranged from nearly four years to eight. It is clear from this analysis that rural sociology writings (the plus signs [+] in the figure) today cite very recent journal and monograph literature compared to the other literature groupings.

F. What Is Cited in the *American Journal of Agricultural Economics*?

The most heavily used and cited journal in agricultural economics was examined for frequency counts, titles of journals, and other data for 1978, which had 156 articles, and for 1987, which had 140 articles. (See Table 12.)

There are no clearly perceivable trends from these comparisons. The 8.4% spread in citations to journals in the *AJAE* over ten years may be a beginning trend, suggesting a switch to more journal references than to monographs. Additional analysis from the years between and later might confirm this. One surprising difference is the increased percentage of dis-

Table 12. Comparisons of cited items in *AJAE*

	1978		1987		Ranges of overview citations from monographs, Table 11
Journals	814 =	44.8%	871 =	53.2%	41.8 - 43.5%
Monographs	937 =	51.6	726 =	44.4	54.8 - 56.6
Dissertations	66 =	3.6	40 =	2.4	1.6 - 1.8
	1,817		1,637		
Monograph publishers					
Commercial presses		23.3%		26.0%	23.3%[a]
University presses	11.6		16.6		
Univ. departments, institutes	22.6		19.0		
		34.2		35.6	42.5
Independent organizations		12.5		13.2	12.7
Governments		30.0		25.2	21.6

[a]Composite data shown in Figure 4.

Table 13. Place of publication of monographs cited in *AJAE* in 1978 and 1987 (in percent)

	1978	1987
United States	84.6	78.9
United Kingdom	3.1	6.2
Canada	4.8	6.4
Netherlands	2.1	2.0
All Others[a]	5.4	6.6

[a]All others were nineteen countries in 1978, thirteen in 1987.

sertations in the *AJAE*. This probably is the result of publishing immediate research results in the journal literature, research often tied to or associated with past or current theses.

The numbers of citations to monographs issued by several governments in many departments and bureaus were counted as represented in Table 13. In 1978 the U.S. government accounted for 23.3% of all the citations, and for 25.1% in 1987. *Journal Citation Reports* of the Institute for Scientific Information notes the numbers of citations in the *AJAE* for 1978 and 1987. Our counts page by page do not match those reported in *Journal Citation Reports*; ISI counted 1,713 to our 1,817 (for 1978) and 1,742 to our 1,637 in 1987. The numbers in *Journal Citation Reports* make clear why the ISI citation indexes have so little application in agricultural economics. Of the 1,713 citations they register from *AJAE* in 1978, 1,191 are below threshold reporting level and therefore lumped into an "other" category rather than being shown title by title with counts. This dispersion of citations over numerous titles, an estimated 70% of them to monographs, is repeated in 1978 where 951 of the total 1,742 citations are in the "other" category.

6. Current Primary Journals and Serials

Libraries and evaluators of productivity have attempted to obtain firm figures on the world's production of journals and serials for many years. The best conclusions have ranged widely. Complications in what would appear to be a routine task involve precisely defining a serial and deciding whether to count it as a periodic publication or as a monograph, and dealing with the inconclusiveness and complexity of information in numerous catalogs and listings, as well as language and time difficulties. Cost-effectiveness seems to preclude obtaining complete answers.

There have been some valiant attempts at determining firm figures for scientific and technical journals and serials. One of the most authoritative and highly cited was done at the U.S. Library of Congress.[1] Gottschalk and Desmond estimated that there were 35,000 science and technology serials in publication in 1961, a figure used as a base for many later comparisons. The study excluded organizational house organs, proceedings of international organizations, and technical report series estimated at 17,000–19,000 additional titles. The ranking of countries of publication was: (1) United States (6,200 titles); (2) East and West Germany (3,050); (3 & 4) France and Japan (2,800 each); and (5 & 6) the Soviet Union and the United Kingdom (2,200 each). These seven countries accounted for 55% of all titles. The study divided science and technology into four categories: Natural and Physical Sciences, Medicine, Agriculture, and Technology. Agricultural serials as a percentage of all titles of each of the six heaviest producers of serials were as follows:

Japan	23%	Germany	16%
United States	23%	Soviet Union	16%
France	18%	United Kingdom	15%

1. Charles M. Gottschalk and Winifred F. Desmond, "Worldwide Census of Scientific and Technical Serials," *American Documentation* 14 (1963): 188–94.

The estimate for U.S. agricultural serials was 1,500. Agricultural titles worldwide were estimated to be about 18.5% of all scientific and technical journals, which would set the total agricultural serials near 6,500. No doubt the numbers have changed since the 1960s, but no equally authoritative work is known. From the publishing trends observed in earlier chapters and in the analyses for this book, the total world production of scientific and technological titles appears to have leveled off at a rate slightly above 35,000, using the same definitions and delimitations.

Literature on the modern scientific journal is extensive; the limited data on early works concentrate on Europe and the United States. The reader is referred to two publications for details on history, economics of journal publication, refereeing, format and content, and analyses of the journal literature.[2]

A. Agricultural Journals and Serials

Complex methods may be used to ascertain the extent of journal and serial publishing in the world. These include the use of current lists of journals prepared by commercial firms, lists in selected subdisciplines of agriculture, catalogs of holdings of large research libraries, compilations of indexing and abstracting services, and estimates by researchers.

While the Gottschalk and Desmond study on scientific and technical journals was under way at the Library of Congress, an elaborate registration of agricultural journal titles was being edited at Oxford University by D. H. Boalch for the International Association of Agricultural Librarians and Documentalists. This remarkable two-volume work, compiled with the assistance of IAALD librarians around the world, stood as the most definitive agricultural serial compilation in authoritative bibliographic form until recently.[3] Volume 1 (1965) lists 12,427 active journals and serials; volume 2 (1967) is the subject classification assigned to each title, plus a quadrilingual index by subject and place of origin of the titles. In 1976, the National Agricultural Library published a list of its current journals and serial receipts totaling about 19,000 titles.[4] This NAL list, as with all figures from

2. (a) A. J. Meadows, ed., *The Scientific Journal* (London: Aslib, 1979), Aslib Reader Series, vol. 2, for a 300-page compilation of writings, primarily from journals. (b) Bernard Houghton, *Scientific Periodicals: Their Historical Development, Characteristics and Control* (London: Clive Bingley, 1975).

3. D. H. Boalch, ed., *Current Agricultural Serials: A World List of Serials in Agriculture and Related Subjects (excluding Forestry and Fisheries) Current in 1964*. 2 vols. (Oxford: International Association of Agricultural Librarians and Documentalists, 1965–67).

4. National Agricultural Library, *Serials Currently Received at the National Agricultural Library, 1975: A Keyword Index* (Beltsville, Md.: National Agricultural Library, June 1976).

libraries and indexing services, probably includes 10–15% inactive or deceased titles in the count, although this is slightly offset by new titles. A decade later (1988) the CAB International listed 9,576 titles in its serials checklist.[5] A union list of serials held by Canada Agriculture libraries in 1977 lists an estimated 16,914 current titles.[6] The 1988 *Annual Report* of the National Agricultural Library states that 9,000 serials are received by purchase and 18,000 by gift or exchange.[7] This whopping 27,000 figure is probably inflated by inactive or dead titles, and is rather unlikely given the 19,000 count about a decade earlier. Mann Library, Cornell University, lists its current serial titles at 9,933, acknowledging the probability of 10% being discontinued or dead.[8]

In all these examples, the scope of coverage of agriculture by institution or by abstracting service is nearly identical. The major allowance necessary is in the veterinary field where NAL and Mann Library, Cornell, do not collect worldwide. Two of the best sources for the numbers of active agricultural serials are the CAB International list of 9,576, and the *Aglinet Union List of Serials*, which cited 6,837 in 1979, and 3,497 in its second edition in 1985.[9] The preface to the second edition indicates that titles commonly held by libraries, such as *Science* and *Nature*, were not retained in the latest edition. The Aglinet list uses the indexing input data from the AGRIS system along with select local listings, not indexed in AGRIS.

In 1990 an extensive listing of journals and serials was compiled and published through the joint efforts of the National Agricultural Library (USDA), Commission of the European Communities, Food and Agriculture Organization, and CAB International. This *International Union List of Agricultural Serials*[10] is a compilation of titles indexed in the three major bibliographic databases with some augmentation from other records. The compendium lists 11,567 publications, all believed to be current in 1989 when final editing was done. This compilation undoubtedly is missing a quantity of serial publications that are not indexed or analyzed in one of the biblio-

5. The *CAB International Serials Checklist*. (Wallingford, Eng.: CAB International, 1988), has 511 pages and an estimated 43.2 titles per 280 pages = 9,576 estimated titles.

6. Headquarters Library, Ottawa, *Union List of Serials in Canada Department of Agriculture Libraries. Repertoire collectif des publications en serie des bibliotheques du Ministere de l'agriculture du Canada*, 2nd ed. (Ottawa: Canada Dept. of Agriculture, 1977) 745p. 22.5 operative titles per page × 745 pages = estimated 16,914 titles.

7. *National Agricultural Library Annual Report for 1988* (Beltsville, Md.: National Agricultural Library, August 1989), p. 1.

8. Data supplied by William Kara, Acquisitions, Albert R. Mann Library, Cornell University, October 1989.

9. *Aglinet Union List of Serials* (Rome: Food and Agriculture Organization, David Lubin Memorial Library, 1979, 2nd ed., 1985).

10. *International Union List of Agricultural Serials* (Wallingford, Eng.: CAB International, 1990), 767p.

graphic databases, but is the most authoritative count and listing of current journals and serials published in the agricultural sciences.

Hence, recent figures range from a high of 27,000 to 11,567. How can there be such disparity? Several factors are at play, as was already mentioned, and it must be emphasized that we are citing selected titles for indexing versus all titles collected by a research library. The indexing databases exclude select types of publications, for example ephemeral material of the action or extension genre which often have very local application only, or whose contents are duplicative. Also, it is difficult to index a brief or lengthy compilation of agricultural statistics, so indexing services often ignore these publications, while most libraries collect those of international, continental, or national significance. Numerous other reasons exist.

Boalch's 1964 total of 12,427 titles, excluding forestry and fisheries, tends to give validity to the 16,914 Canada Agriculture union list, and the 19,000 current serials of NAL in 1975. In the indexing arena, Deselaers found 6,742 unique titles indexed in 1986 among the three agricultural databases (AGRICOLA, AGRIS, and CABI Abstracts).[11] This is very different than the 11,567 announced in 1990.[12] Conclusions from these data may be risky, but it is fairly clear that about two-thirds of the journal or serial titles are routinely covered by the indexing services. Given the nature of much of the short-lived agricultural literature, and the costs of indexing, listing, and printing, this may be understandable, if not desirable.

B. Agricultural Economics and Rural Sociology Journals and Serials

The breadth of interest and research needs in agricultural economics complicates any comparisons or determination of the universe of journals and serials. There are, however, some readily available data that will help set a range. A good source of this information is the Library of the Giannini Foundation for Agricultural Economics at the University of California at Berkeley. The Giannini Library has a stellar collection, which is a close match to the subject scope of this study, as well as to the definitions outlined in Chapter 2. The only variation, which is inconsequential, is the concentration on graduate school and research materials, along with the absence of general agricultural literature, which is held in a separate campus library. The current serials received at the library number approx-

11. Norbert Deselaers, "The Necessity for Closer Cooperation Among Secondary Agricultural Information Services: An Analysis of AGRICOLA, AGRIS and CAB," *Quarterly Bulletin of the International Association of Agricultural Librarians and Documentalists* 31(1) (1986): 20.

12. *International Union List of Agricultural Serials* (Wallingford, Eng.: CAB International, 1990) p. vi.

imately 3,000, with the probability that nearly 10% have ceased, putting the final figure near 2,800. This includes annual reports and working papers.[13]

The managing editor of *WAERSA* and related CABI indexes indicated in Chapter 3 that 5,000 journals or serials are scanned for relevant citations, including numerous titles in general economics and sociology. These two figures probably indicate that the agricultural economics and rural sociology worldwide serial literature is about 4,000 titles. In each of its three abstracting tools (*WAERSA*; *Rural Development Abstracts*; and *Rural Extension, Education and Training Abstracts*) for 1988, CAB International supplied the specific series or journal titles from which citations were taken. The numbers of titles are 902 unique journal titles, 450 unique serial titles, 37 unique newsletters, making a total of 1,389 unique titles indexed in 1988. This means that only 36% of the 5,000 titles scanned in 1988 yielded items appropriate for the agricultural economics and rural sociology databases of CABI.

These numbers highlight the diversity of literature that research faculties need, literature that is rarely cited or used and often concerns local circumstances only. This situation is the bane of any research library that is called upon to provide immense collection coverage.

An interesting historical source is the listing of periodicals and serials received in the library of the USDA Bureau of Agricultural Economics in 1932–34.[14] The compilation represents titles from nearly all areas of the world and includes numerous governments, languages, and serials. It delineates a remarkable library collection in agricultural economics and rural sociology. The two-volume compilation lists 2,102 separate titles, or approximately half of today's estimate for this literature. Of these, almost exactly half, 1,101, are journal titles, the other half being newsletters and numbered series of reports and monographs.

From this vast and varied universe, the primary journals and serials had to be extracted. As previously noted, references in the overview volumes (Chapter 5) did not cite a span of years for numbered publications in series, but cited them as individual monographic pieces. Listings in this study follow the same pattern. Numbered serials were noted and counted in over half of the overview volumes to determine which were the most cited. These data appear later in this chapter, and series titles are excluded from the journal analyses.

13. Personal communication with Grace Dote, Librarian, Giannini Foundation Library, University of California, Berkeley. October 25, 1989.

14. Vajen E. Hitz, compiler, *Periodicals Received Currently in the Library of the U.S. Bureau of Agricultural Economics* (Washington, D.C.: U.S. Dept. of Agriculture, 1932), and *Supplement*, December 1934.

Methodologies described in Chapter 5 were applied to journals and serials, as with monographs. Counts of times cited and select other data were kept on approximately 450 journal and serial titles. Over 40% of these were cited two or fewer times, demonstrating the scattering of the literature. Details were kept on specific journals in sixteen volumes, and the 1978 and 1987 issues of the *American Journal of Agricultural Economics*. Table 14 displays this information.

The remarkable showing of the *Journal of Farm Economics (JFE)*, twenty years after its change to *AJAE*, leaves little dispute that the American Agricultural Economics Association's publications are the leaders. This is reinforced by the *AJAE*'s rank as the primary journal in the Third World literature also. Outstanding, continuous performance is maintained by numerous articles per year, nearly 1,300 pages of print annually, high standards of editing, and a wide range of pertinent subjects. It can be used as a valid barometer of growth, changes, and emphases in agricultural economics. The journals were cited nearly exactly the same number of times under the two titles *JFE* and *AJAE*: it was the leader historically as well as currently. Both titles were cited 3.4 times more than *American Economic Review*, its closest competitor; and 4.8 times more than *Journal of Political Economy*, which ranked fourth.

Because of the predominance of the *American Journal of Agricultural Economics*, a tally was made of the journals cited in it from 1978 *through* 1988 using the *Science Citation Index Journal Citation Reports* for each year. The *Reports* tabulate the number of citations to all sources each year, and names the journals cited with counts for each. The citations to journals that were listed (excluding citations to monographs) totaled 7,780 in the eleven-year period, out of a total of 18,718 citations in *AJAE*. The titles were named even if they had only five or six citations to them a year. All of the remaining lower frequency journals, plus monographic serials and monographs make up an "All Other" category, which is nearly always greater than the number identified by specific journal title. Table 15 provides data on the 7,780 citations in the *AJAE*.

In Table 15, no rankings were given from Table 14 unless a title tallied over thirty citations. Table 15 shows remarkable similarities to Table 14 when the reasons for the low show of some titles from Table 14 are understood. The *Journal of Econometrics* is relatively new and not represented in the greater time period and more comprehensive evaluation of Table 14. The other titles in Table 15 without rankings from Table 14 are all heavily U.S. oriented, or they represent the increased concern with management and statistical techniques. Those missing titles from Table 14 that ranked fourteenth or above and which are not represented in Table 15 are all con-

Table 14. Ranking of top journals by citation counts [a]

	A All citations (N = 9,644)	= B General literature (N = 5,493)	+ C AJAE[b] 1978 & 1988 (N = 1,685)	+ D Third World (N = 2,466)
Journal of Farm Economics	1	1	5	7&8
American Journal of Agricultural Economics	2	2	1	1
American Economic Review (incl. Papers & Proceedings)	3	3	4	4
Journal of Political Economy	4	4	3	7&8
Agricultural Economic Research	5	5	6	—
Economic Development & Cultural Change	6	15	23	2
Econometrica	7	10	2	—
Food Research Institute Studies	8	25	16&17	3
Journal of the American Statistical Association	9	6	9	—
Quarterly Journal of Economics	10	8	10	12
Review of Economics & Statistics	11	9	7	16
Rural Sociology	12	7	—	—
Economic Journal	13	11	11	9
Indian Journal of Agricultural Economics	14	—	—	5
Land Economics	15&16	12	12	—
World Development	15&16	29	—	6
Water Resources Research	17	13	25	
Canadian Journal of Agricultural Economics	18&19	16	8	—
Southern Economics Journal	18&19	11	—	—
Journal of Economic Literature	20&21	17	24	21
Review of Economic Studies	20&21	19	14	22

[a]"All Citations" category (Column A) is an arithmetic sum of the citations from the other three categories. The "General" column includes the three-volume Martin work, Fox and Johnson, Waugh, Jesness, Antonelli and Quadrio-Curzio, Tower, Dillman and Hobbs, Hildreth, et al., and Brown (all cited in the list in Chapter 5). The *AJAE* data are from the 1978 and 1988 issues; the Third World data are from four volumes in Table 11 (excluding Barker).

[b]The *AJAE* superseded the *Journal of Farm Economics* in 1968, and the two could be considered one title. Even though the *JFE* was deceased ten or twenty years when the *AJAE* articles were published, it continued to rank very high. Titles beyond the twenty-fifth rank in each group are not shown; the dash (—) is no indication that a title was not cited, it just did not rank high enough.

Table 15. Journal rankings from citations in the *AJAE*, 1978–88, from *SCI Journal Citation Reports* and comparison to Table 14

	Ranking *AJAE* citings	Ranking from Table 14
American Journal of Agricultural Economics	1	2
American Economic Review	2	3
Econometrica	3	7
Journal of Political Economy	4	4
Journal of Farm Economics	5	1
Review of Economics and Statistics	6	11
Journal of the American Statistical Association	7	9
Review of Economic Studies	8	20&21
Quarterly Journal of Economics	9	10
International Economic Review	10&11	29
Southern Journal of Agricultural Economics	10&11	18&19
Journal of Econometrics	12	—
Economic Journal	13	13
Western Journal of Agricultural Economics	14	—
Journal of Law and Economics	15	—
Land Economics	16	—
Canadian Journal of Agricultural Economics	17	18&19
African Economic Research	18	—
Journal of Economic Theory	19	31
Bell Journal of Economic & Management Science	20	—
Management Science	21	27
Journal of Finance	22	—
Journal of Economic Literature	23	20&21
Food Research Institute Studies	24	8
Southern Economic Journal	25	18&19

cerned with international agricultural development, or one with rural sociology. Clearly, a core collection will include all of the titles in both tables.

In 1989 the fifty journals most cited by the twenty-seven core economics journals used for input to the *Social Sciences Citation Index* were analyzed, using 1986 data.[15] The similarities between these data and the agricultural economics journals in Table 15 attest to the close tie with the field of economics. Seventeen of the twenty-five titles in Table 14 are in the fifty most-cited journals by *SSCI* reports. The remaining eight are logical omissions since they deal with agricultural economics only, such as the *Southern*

15. Arthur M. Diamond, Jr., "The Core Journals of Economics," *Current Contents: Agriculture, Biology and Environmental Sciences* 20(1) (January 2, 1989). This is part 1; the second part is in *Current Contents* 20(2) (January 9, 1989): 3–8.

Journal of Agricultural Economics, and two have not been published for some time. One of the latter, the *Bell Journal* . . . is cited in the *SSCI* in its successor name, *Rand Journal of Economics*. Agricultural economists have not taken to the Rand publication or cited it often.

The 7,780 citations to known journals obtained from the *SCI Journal Citation Reports*, 1978–1988 (Table 15), are displayed in Figure 6. The *American Journal of Agriculture Economics*, with 2,950 citations to it far outranks the next journal, *American Economic Review*. The curve ends as a nearly flat line of numerous titles with very little difference between them.

The scattering of titles valuable for the Third World in Table 14 after the eleventh title, marks the line between the literatures of developed and developing countries. There is agreement on the primary titles, since these eleven Third World titles are among the top sixteen in the total sample; diversity comes beginning with the seventeenth.

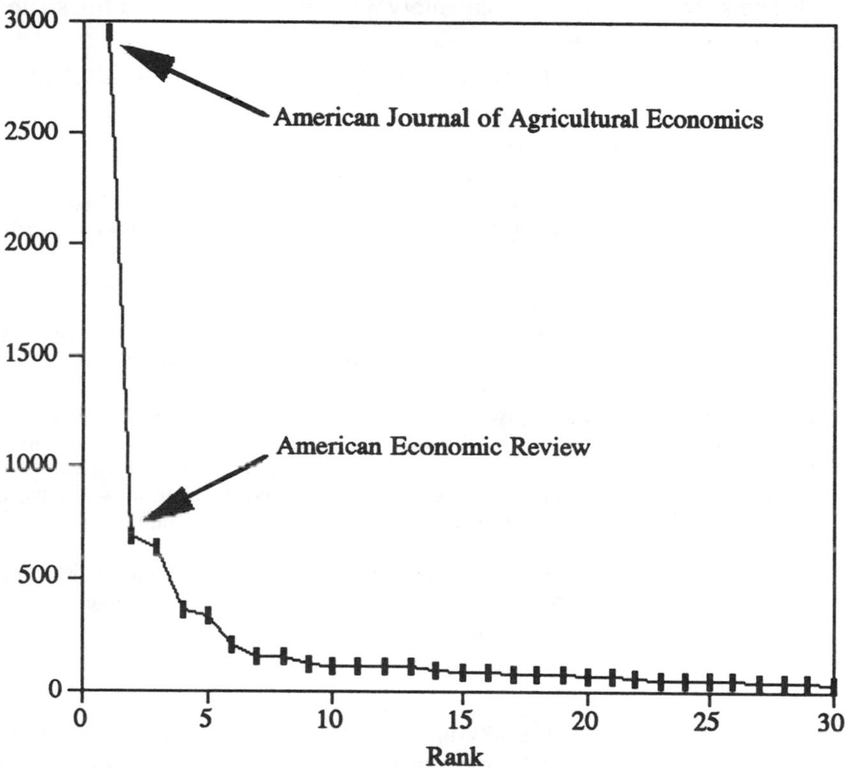

Figure 6. Citations to selected journals (Source: SCI Journal Citations Reports, 1978–88).

Table 16 ranks the most-cited journals in Third World agricultural development from the same four source documents as represented in the last column in Table 14, also identified as Third World in Table 11.

Table 16, Category A, includes titles that appear in three or all four citing source documents. Categories B and C are ranked within their own categories only; and no title is given if it was not cited 15 or more times.

Primary Journals in Agricultural Economics and Rural Sociology

The multitude of records examined, analyzed, counted, and weighted have resulted in a primary list of journals. The listings are a direct output from the 18,000 citations analyzed, the evaluations of other research studies mentioned in Chapters 2 and 5, correlations with data from the ISI databases and reports, and weighing from previously recommended core titles, such as those made by academicians for course work. The threshold levels and skews excluded approximately 83% of the 520 journal titles cited in the studies.

These points must be kept in mind in using this compilation.

(1) Only currently published journals are listed. Therefore, recently deceased titles are not included, nor are those where the journal changed its name recently and no data under a newer title were created. An exception was made for the *FAO Quarterly Bulletin of Statistics*, a continuation of the highly cited *FAO Monthly Bulletin of Statistics*.
(2) One can observe a citing bias toward those journals which have been around long enough to be cited widely. Only heavily cited titles have been listed with two exceptions: the current-issues-oriented and highly popular *Choices*, founded in 1986 by the American Agricultural Economics Association, and *World Bank Economic Review* begun the same year. Neither has enough history to place it near the top.
(3) Librarians must not construe this list as showing all that they need in their libraries. An analysis of the appropriate literature for all of South America, as an example, would be a distinctly different list. This list of Core Journals is appropriate for a research library with worldwide interests, and Third World interests when those titles are included. Country or state-specific materials that did not rate highly are not listed.
(4) The list contains journal and periodical material only, by the standard definition used in scholarship. Therefore, monographic series such as numbered reports, bulletins, and working papers are handled separately later in this chapter and in Chapter 8.

This work has consistently attempted to study the literature patterns in general agricultural economics and rural sociology literature for developed countries and those of the Third World. As noted earlier in this chapter, there is great similarity in ranking between the two groups, particularly

Table 16. Most cited journals in analysis of Third World literature

Category A	
1.	American Journal of Agricultural Economics
2.	Economic Development and Cultural Change
3.	Food Research Institute Studies
4.	American Economic Review (incl. Papers & Proceedings)
5.	Indian Journal of Agricultural Economics
6.	World Development
7–8.	Journal of Farm Economy
	Journal of Political Economy
9.	Economic and Political Weekly
10–11.	Economic Journal
	Journal of Development Studies
12.	Quarterly Journal of Economics
13.	Journal of Development Economics
14.	Food Policy
15.	Oxford Economic Papers
16.	Review of Economics and Statistics
17.	Pakistan Development Review
18.	Journal of Economic Literature
19.	Manchester School of Economics & Social Studies
20.	Review of Economic Studies
21.	International Development Review
22–24.	Foreign Affairs
	Journal of Economic History
	Science
Category B	Cited in two source lists
25.	Pesquisa e Planejamento Economica
26.	Bangladesh Development Studies
Category C	Cited in one source list only
27.	Journal of Agricultural Economics (UK)
28.	Journal of Modern African Studies
29–30.	Agricultural Situation in India
	East African Journal of Rural Development
31.	Experimental Agriculture
32.	L'Agronomie Tropicale
33.	Latin American Research Review
34.	Bulletin of Indonesian Economic Studies
35.	Agricultural Systems
36–37.	Oxford Bulletin of Economics and Statistics
	Revista Brasiliera de Economica
38–39.	East African Economic Review
	Economics Weekly

through the twentieth ranked item in each. In the list that follows, all of the developed country titles are Core Journals if they have a rank of 1 or 2 in the developed countries column. These are journals that ranked high in Third World journal counts, but which were statistically insignificant in the developed countries counts. The merged list demonstrates high and low correlations between the two groups. The no. 1's in the developed country list column denote those titles which rated nearest the top in the counts; the 2's constitute the next lower level. The Core List of journals constitutes 16% of all of the titles recorded in analysis, current or deceased, but the list accounts for just over 50% of all the journal citations. There are thirty journals with top ranking in the developed country list. The subject sweep of journals is truly amazing and defies realistic characterization. Aspects of social, biological, mechanical, botanical, tropical, and all variations on these were evident, from industrial and labor relations in India to jojoba growing in Spain. The diversity of experiences and needs of scientists in this field are astounding.

A minimum of bibliographic detail is provided, but enough to make some observations about the nature, publishers, ages, and probable reasons for the high rankings.

Currently Published Core Journals for Agricultural Economics and Rural Sociology

	Developed countries list	Primary Third World
Africa Research Bulletin. Economic Series. Vol. 22 (1985)+ Exeter, England, Africa Research Ltd. Monthly. (Continues Africa Research Bulletin Economic, Financial, and Technical series.)		X
Agrarian Development Studies. No. 1 (1965)+. Ashford, Kent; Wye College (University of London) Department of Agricultural Economics. Irregular.	2	X
Agrarokonomische Studien (Agricultural Economic Studies). (1981)+ Kiel, West Germany, Wissenschlaftsverlag Vauk, issued by Institut fur Landwirtschaftliche Betriebs-und Arbeitslehre der Christian Albrechts. Irregular.	2	
Agrarwirtschaft. Vol. 1. (1952)+ Hannover, A. Strothe. Monthly.	2	
Agribusiness: An International Journal. Vol. 1. (1985)+ New York: Wiley. Quarterly.	2	
Agricultural Administration and Extension. Vol. 1 (1974)+. Barking, Essex, England, Elsevier Applied Science Publishers. 3 vols/year.	1	X

	Developed countries list	Primary Third World
Agricultural Finance Review. Vol. 1 (1938)+ Ithaca, NY, Dept. of Agricultural Economics, Cornell University. Annual. Volumes through No. 42 (1982) were issued by the U.S. Dept. of Agriculture.	2	
Agricultural Situation in India. (1948)+ New Delhi, India, Directorate of Economics and Statistics. Monthly.	2	X
Agricultural Systems. Vol. 1 (1976)+ Barking, Essex, England, Elsevier Applied Science Publ. Quarterly.	1	X
Agri-Finance. Vol. 1. (1959)+. Skokie, IL, Century Communications. 7/year.	2	
Agri-Marketing. Vol. 1 (1972)+ Skokie, IL. Century Communication Inc. Quarterly.	2	
American Economic Review. Vol 1. (1911)+. Nashville, Tenn., American Economics Association. 5 no./year (Quarterly 1911– 6 no./year 1985–).	1	X
American Journal of Agricultural Economics. Vol. 50 (1968)+. Lexington, KY, American Agricultural Economics Association. (Formerly Journal of Farm Economics). Quarterly.	1	X
American Sociological Review. Vol 1. (1936)+. Albany, NY, American Sociological Association. Bimonthly.	2	
Annals of Economic and Social Measurement. New York, National Bureau of Economic Research. Vol 1. (1972)+. Quarterly (irregular).	1	X
Appropriate Technology. Vol. 1 (1974)+ London, Intermediate Technology Publ. Quarterly.		X
Australian Journal of Agricultural Economics. Vol. 1 (1957)+. Sydney, Australian Agricultural Economics Society. 3 no./year.	2	
Bangladesh Development Studies. Vol. 1 (1973)+ Bangladesh, Bangladesh Institute of Development Economics. (vol 1–2 as Bangladesh Economic Review). Quarterly.	2	X
Bangladesh Journal of Agricultural Economics. Vol. 1 (1978)+ Mymensing, Bureau of Socioeconomic Research and Training, Bangladesh Agricultural University. Semi annual.	2	X
Brookings Papers on Economic Activity No. 1+ (1970)+. Washington, D.C., Brookings Institution. 3 no./year issued as vols. 1–3/year.	1	X
Bulletin of Indonesian Economic Studies. Vol. 1 (1965)+ Canberra, Research School of Pacific Studies, Australian National University, Dept. of Economics. 3 no./year.	2	X
Canadian Journal of Agricultural Economics. Vol. 1 (1952)+. Ottawa, Canadian Agricultural Economics and Farm Management Society. 3 times/year plus 2 special issues (semiannual 1952–68).	1	
Choices, Vol. 1 (1986)+. Ames, Iowa, American Agricultural Economic Association; Washington, D.C., distributed by Dunnington Communication. Quarterly.	2	
Demography. Vol. 1 (1964)+ Chicago, IL; Population Association of America. Quarterly.	2	X

	Developed countries list	Primary Third World
The Developing Economies. Vol. 1 (1963) + Tokyo, Japan, Institute of Asian Economic Affairs. Quarterly (Semiannual 1963–1966).	1	X
Development and Change. Vol. 1 (1969) + The Hague, Mouton. Quarterly (3 issues/year 1969–1974).	2	X
Developments in Agricultural Economics. Vol. 1 (1983) +. Amsterdam, New York, Elsevier Scientific Publ. Irregular.	2	X
Eastern African Economic Review. Vol. 1 (1969) + Nairobi, Oxford University Press and Kenyatta Literature Bureau.	2	X
Econometrica. Vol. 1 (1933) + Bristol, England, The Econometric Society. Bi-monthly.	1	X
Economic and Political Weekly. Vol. 1 (1966) + Bombay, Sameeksha Trust. Weekly.		X
Economic Development and Cultural Change. Vol. 1. (1952) +. Chicago, University of Chicago Press, edited by the Research Center on Economic Development & Cultural Change. Quarterly (5 no./year 1952–74).	1	X
Economic Journal. Vol. 1 (1891) + London, Cambridge University Press, Issued by the Royal Economic Society. Quarterly.	1	X
Economica. New series. Vol. 1 (1934) + London School of Economics and Political Science.	2	
European Economic Review. Vol. 1 (1969) + Amsterdam, The Netherlands, North Holland Publ. Co., Sponsored by the Association Scientifique Europeenne D'Economie Appliquee. Bi-monthly (4 no./year 1969–1979, 9 no./year 1980–1985).	2	
European Review of Agricultural Economics. Vol. 1 (1973) + The Hague, Mouton. 4 issues/year.	2	X
Experimental Agriculture. Vol. 1 (1965) + London, New York, Cambridge University Press. Quarterly.	2	X
F.A.O. Quarterly Bulletin of Statistic. Vol. 1 (1988) + Rome, Food and Agriculture Organization of the United Nations. (Supersedes F.A.O. Monthly Bulletin of Statistics.)	1	X
Food Policy. Vol. 1 (1975) + Guildford, England; IPC Science and Technology Press. Quarterly.	2	X
Food Research Institute Studies. Vol. 1 (1960) + Stanford, CA, Food Research Institute, Stanford University. Irregular.	1	X
Foreign Affairs. Vol. 1 (1922) + New York, Council on Foreign Relations. 5 issues/year (Quarterly 1922–1978).	2	
Foreign Agricultural Trade of the United States (FATUS) Jan. (1972) + Washington, D.C., USDA, Economic Research Service. 8 vols./year.	2	
Foreign Agriculture. Vol. 1 (1963) + Washington, D.C., USDA, Foreign Agricultural Service. Weekly.	1	X
IDS Bulletin. Vol. 7. no. 1 (Apr. 1975) + Brighton, East Sussex: Institute of Development Studies.	2	X
Indian Journal of Agricultural Economics. Vol. 1 (1946) + Bombay, Indian Society of Agricultural Economics. Semiannual 1946–, Quarterly, 1962–.	2	X

	Developed countries list	Primary Third World
International Economic Review. Vol. 1 (1960) + Philadelphia, Wharton School of Finance and Commerce, University of Pennsylvania. (1960–70 vols. issued by Kansai Economic Federation) 3 no./year.	1	X
International Labour Review. Vol. 1 (1921) + . Geneva, International Labour Office. Irregular. Bimonthly, May 1979.	2	
JASA. Journal of the American Statistical Association. Vol. 1 (1888) + Washington, American Statistical Association. Quarterly.	1	X
Journal of Agricultural Economics. Vol. 1 (1928) + . Reading, England, Agricultural Economics Society. 3 no./year.	1	X
Journal of Agricultural Economics Research. Vol. 39 (1987) + Washington, D.C., USDA Economics Research Service. (Vol. 1–39 1949–1987 as Agricultural Economics Research) Quarterly.	1	X
Journal of Developing Areas. (1966) + Macomb, Ill.; Western Illinois University. Quarterly.	2	X
Journal of Development Economics. (1974) + Amsterdam, Netherlands; Elsevier Science Publ. Quarterly.	1	X
Journal of Development Studies. Vol. 1 (1964) + London, F. Cass. Quarterly.	2	X
Journal of Econometrics. Vol. 1 (1973) + Amsterdam, The Netherlands, North-Holland Publ. 9 no./year.	2	
Journal of Economic History. Vol. 1 (1941) + New York, Published for the Economic History Association by New York University. Quarterly (Semiannual 1941–50).	1	X
Journal of Economic Literature. Vol. 1 (1963) + Nashville, Tenn.; American Economic Association. Quarterly.	1	X
Journal of Economic Theory. Vol. 1 (1969) + New York, Academic Press. Bi-monthly.	2	X
Journal of Finance. Vol. 1 (1946) + Chicago, American Finance Association. 5 no./year.	2	
Journal of Law and Economics. Vol. 1 (1958) + Chicago, University of Chicago Law School, University of Chicago Press. Semi-annual.	2	X
Journal of Political Economy. Vol. 1 (1892) + Chicago, University of Chicago Press. Bimonthly (Quarterly 1892–1905 Monthly 1906–1923).	1	X
Journal of Rural Economics and Development. Vol. 9(1974/75) + Ibadan, Department of Agricultural Economics, University of Ibadan. (Continues Bulletin of Rural Economics and Sociology) Semiannual.		X
Journal of Rural Studies. Vol. 1 (1985) + Oxford, New York, Pergamon Press. Quarterly.	2	X
Land Economics. Vol. 24 (1948) + . Madison, Wisconsin, University of Wisconsin Press. (Continues Journal of Land and Public Utility Economics) Quarterly.	1	X

	Developed countries list	Primary Third World
Management Science. Vol. 1 (1954)+ Providence, RI, Institute of Management Sciences. Monthly.	2	
Manchester School of Economic and Social Studies. Vol. 1 (1930)+ Manchester, England, University of Manchester, Dept. of Economics. 4 no./year since 1976 (Semi-annual, irregular, 3 issues/year, 1930–1976).	2	X
North Central Journal of Agricultural Economics. Vol. 1 (1979)+ Urbana, Ill., University of Illinois, Department of Agricultural Economics. Semiannual.	2	
Outlook on Agriculture. Vol. 1 (1956)+ Elmsford, NY; Pergamon Press. Quarterly.	2	X
Oxford Bulletin of Economics and Statistics. Vol. 35 (1973)+ Oxford, Basil Blackwell issued by Oxford University Institute of Economics and Statistics. (Continues Bulletin of the Institute of Economics and Statistics).	2	X
Oxford Economic Papers. No. 1 (1938)+ Oxford, England, Oxford University Press. Quarterly.	2	X
Pakistan Development Review. Vol. 1 (1961)+ Islamabad, issued by Pakistan Institute of Development Economics. Quarterly.		X
Pesquisa e Planejamento Economico. Vol. 1 (1971)+ Rio de Janeiro, Instituto de Planejamento Econmico e Social. Publ. irregularly.		X
Philippine Agricultural Economics Review. Vol. 1 (1978)+ Quezon City, Philippines, Bureau of Agricultural Economics. Irregular.	2	X
Population and Development Review. Vol. 1 (1975)+ New York, Population Council. Quarterly.	2	X
Quarterly Journal of Economics. Vol. 1 (1886)+ Cambridge, Mass., Harvard University. Quarterly.	1	X
Review of Economic Studies. Vol. 1 (1933)+ Edinburgh, issued by the London School of Economics and Political Science; 1958+ by the Economic Study Society. 3 no./year.	1	X
Review of Economics and Statistics. Vol. 1 (1919)+ Amsterdam, The Netherlands, Published for Harvard University by North-Holland Publ. Co. Quarterly. (Frequency varies 1919–1948).	1	X
Review of Marketing and Agricultural Economics (1932)+ Sydney, New South Wales. Department of Agriculture, Division of Marketing and Economics. Quarterly.	2	
Rural Africana. No. 1 (1967)+ East Lansing, Mich., African Studies Center, Michigan State University. 3 times per year.		X
Rural Development Studies. No. 4 (1975)+ Uppsala, Swedish University of Agricultural Sciences, International Rural Development Centre.	2	X
Rural Sociology. Vol. 1 (1936)+ Urbana, University of Illinois, Rural Sociological Society. Quarterly.	1	X
Science. Vol. 1 (1883)+ Washington, D.C., American Association for the Advancement of Science. Weekly.	2	X

	Developed countries list	Primary Third World
Sociologia Ruralis. (Journal of the European Society for Rural Sociology) Vol. 1 (1960)+ Assen, The Netherlands, Van Gorcum. Quarterly.	2	X
Sociological Review. Vol. 1–44 (1908–1952); New Series Vol. 1 (1953)+ London, England, published for the University of Kelle by Routledge and Kegan Paul.	2	X
Southern Economic Journal. Vol. 1 (1933)+ Chapel Hill, N.C., Southern Economic Association. Twice Monthly.	1	
Southern Journal of Agricultural Economics. Vol. 1 (1969)+ Lexington, KY, Southern Agricultural Economics Association. Semiannual.	2	
Water Resources Research. Vol. 1 (1965)+ Washington, American Geophysical Union. Quarterly.	2	
West African Journal of Agricultural Economics. Vol. 1 (1972)+ Nigeria.	2	X
Western Journal of Agricultural Economics. Vol. 1 (1977)+ College Station, Texas, Western Agricultural Economics Association. Semiannual.	1	
World Bank Economic Review. Vol. 1 (1986)+. Washington, D. C.; The World Bank. Three times per year.	2	X
World Development. 1973+ Oxford & N.Y., Pergamon Press, Inc. Monthly.	2	X

The core journals identified in the list have these characteristics:

Publishers		Place of Publication	
Associations, societies, or independent institutes	35.6%	United States	45.0%
Commercially published	26.6	United Kingdom	20.0
University published	27.8	Netherlands	7.8

The long-entrenched journals continue to be very important: 28.9% started before 1950. About 40% were begun in the 1950s and 1960s. Surprisingly, eight of them began in the 1980s. The general economics journals account for 18.9% of all the titles. If these are combined with political economy and all types of general sociology, the percentage jumps to 33.3%. This certainly reaffirms the heritage of the disciplines of agricultural economics and rural sociology.

C. Small Monographs in Numbered Series

As reported earlier, those publications which are relatively short, on a subject complete in an issue, and in a numbered series, were counted and reported as monographs in Chapter 5. These scholarly or statistical publications are usually written by a single individual and most commonly published by governments, state experiment stations, institutes, or academic departments. Examples are:

Asian Development Bank *Staff Paper.*
FAO *Agricultural Planning Study.*
Giannini Foundation of Agricultural Economics *Research Report.*
IDS *Discussion Paper.*
Idaho Agricultural Experiment Station *Research Bulletin.*
Overseas Development Institute Pastoral Network *Paper.*
USDA *Agricultural Economic Report.*
World Bank *Agriculture and Rural Development Department Report (ARU)*

These less formal, relatively brief, easily produced, and limitedly distributed publications are exceedingly important in the field of economics as well as agricultural economics. Their heavy influence has not yet spread widely in rural sociology.

A study was made of select volumes of the peer-reviewed or evaluated volumes itemized in Chapter 5. For the sake of comparison, the citations on Third World agricultural development and rural sociology were tabulated separately. Included in the Third World group were the works of Eicher and Baker (1989), Mellor and Mudahar (1988), Schuh and Brandão (1988), the Barker list (1989), and *The Economics of Agriculture* compiled by the Committee on Economics Teaching Material for Asian Universities (1975). These included 4,782 citations of which 60% were references to monographs or numbered monographs in series, such as the titles just listed above. The remaining 40% were journal and dissertation citations. Of the 4,782 citations, 505 were in this numbered monographic series group. In these series counts, no commercial or university press titles were included either in a numbered or unnumbered series. Therefore, the sample is reports or separately issued papers generally under seventy-five pages, issued primarily by academic departments, colleges, or government agencies. This type of literature constituted 10.6% of all citations.

Using the same definitions and counting methods, six general titles (eight volumes) were tabulated for the same data. Comparisons are made in Table 17.

The titles in the general literature are those of Martin, vols. 1–3 (1977–81), Antonelli and Quadrio-Curzio (1988); Brown et al. (1988); Dillman and Hobbs (1982); Hildreth et al. (1988); and Tower (1985). The three Martin volumes constitute slightly over half of the 11,048 citations in the general literature sample. Note must be made that the Martin volumes con-

Table 17. Numbered monograph series

	Citations in sample	Numbered monograph citations	%
Third World volumes	4,782	505	10.6
General literature	11,048	1,666	15.1

stitute an extensive literature review with emphasis on agricultural economics and rural sociology in the United States. Given this knowledge, the reason for heavier concentration (15.1%) on this literature of reports and working documents becomes clear: the federal and state documents are the influential factors, which is confirmed by examination of the citations. The 11–15% spread conclusively indicates a significant influence by this type of literature in agricultural economics and rural sociology scholarship. Analysis of the agencies issuing these cited publications is provided in Table 18.

Table 18. Agencies in both lists issuing numbered series publications (in percent)

	Third World % of 505	General literature % of 1,666
World Bank	16.0	0.36
International Food Policy Research Institute	11.9	0.06
Michigan State University	11.9	3.3
United Nations (incl. FAO)	8.1	1.7
Cornell University	7.5	1.5
U.S. Dept. of Agriculture	2.9	39.4
University of Wisconsin	1.2	2.5
University of California & Giannini Foundation	.59	4.3
Iowa State University	.19	2.3
Purdue University	.19	2.2
U.S. Congress	.19	3.5
University of Illinois	.19	1.9
University of Minnesota	.19	2.5

Table 18, which includes only organizations cited in both samples, indicates that 48% of Third World citing is concentrated with these thirteen institutions; 65% for the general literature. With the Third World, the scattering is great with 181 separate series titles published by 131 organizations. Of the 181 titles, 85 were cited only once. The following list demonstrates the geographic and organizational dispersion even when citing only every fifth title. In the general literature, 275 titles were issued by 178 organizations such as the USDA and the University of Wisconsin. Within the general literature sample, which deals extensively with U.S. agricultural economics and rural sociology, one university, North Carolina State, has a higher percentage (5.3) of citations than other universities, but it is not represented in Table 18 because it was cited in the general literature *only*. The USDA titles cited most often were *Marketing Research Report* (153 times); *Agricultural Economic Report* (119); *ERS* Series (68); and *Foreign Agricultural Economic Report* (56). The USDA had thirty-three separate titles scattered among its alphabetic agencies. When the USDA citations are added to others from the federal government, the U.S. government percentage rises to 44.1%. The U.S. agencies are influential in this type of publication, and they issue a vast number of series which appear to be used by scholars.

Every Fifth Title Listed in Third World Compilation

AID. Project Eval. Rpt.
Asian Dev. Bank. Econ. Staff Paper.
Bangladesh ARC. Agric., Econs. & Rural Soc. Sciences Papers.
Centro Inter-Americana de Reforma Agraria. Materiales de Ensenanza para Reforma Agraria
CIDA (Mexico). Trajabo.
CIMMYT (Mexico). Report.
Cornell Univ. Dept. of Ag. Econ. Occasional Paper.
Cornell Univ. International Agric. Mimeo.
FAO Agric. Credit Case Studies. Working Paper.
Illinois Univ. Agric. Econs. Staff Paper. New Series E.
Indonesia. Agro-Economic Survey. Occasional Paper.
ICRISAT (India). Occasional Paper.
Int. Labour Org. World Employment Res. Programme. Working Paper.
International Monetary Fund. Paper.
Iowa St. Univ. Int. Studies in Econs. Monograph.
Land Tenure Center (Univ. of Wisc.). Paper.
Mich St. Univ. African Rural Economy Paper.
Mich. St. Univ. Dept. of Ag. Econs. Rural Devel. Working Paper.
Overseas Dev. Institute. Pastoral Network Paper.
Rand Corp. Memorandum (RM).
SAREC (Stockholm) Report.
U. S. Dept. of Agric. For. Agric. Econ. Report.
Univ. Catolica del Peru. Cisepa. Docum. de Trabajo.
Univ. of Calif. Dept. of Agr. & Resource Economics. Working Paper.
Univ. of Nairobi. IDS Occasional Paper.
UNRISD. Report.
WARDA. Seminar Series.
World Bank. PPR. Working Paper.
World Bank. Report.
Wye College. Occas. Paper.

Universities are fond of creating quantities of numbered series of publications. Michigan State University provides this exemplary array of titles:

Agricultural Economics Report.
DAE/ARE. International Development Paper
DAE/ARE. Paper
DAE/ARE. Rural Development Working Paper
DAE/ARE. Staff Paper
DAE/ARE. Working Paper
MSU African Rural Economy Paper
MSU Consortium for the Study of Nigerian Rural Dev. Rpt.
MSU International Agriculture Research Report

The most frequently cited series titles culled from these extensive studies are provided in the following list. The asterisks indicate series that are heavily cited in Third World lists. Keep in mind that a few individual titles in these series which were heavily cited and evaluated are included in the monograph listings in Chapter 7. Approximately 10–15% of the 19,000 citations examined fall into this monographic series; only a handful have made their way to the Core Monographic Literature in the chapter following.

Primary Numbered Reports Series

	Heavily Cited in Third World Lists
Ahmado Bello Univ. IAR Samaru Miscellaneous Paper. = T	*
Agrarstatistisches Jahrbuch . . . Yearbook of Agricultural Statistics. Brussels, European Economic Community	
Australia. Bureau of Agricultural Economics. Occasional Papers.	
Brazil. Ministerio da Agricultura. Colecao Analise e Pesquisa. = T	*
CGIAR Study Paper.	*
Calif. Univ. Agric. Exp. Station. Bulletin	
Cambridge University Agricultural Economics Branch. Occasional Paper.	
Canada. Agricultural Economics Research Council. Research Report.	
Center for Agricultural and Rural Development, Iowa State University. International Development Series.	
Center for Agricultural and Rural Development, Iowa State University. CARD Report.	
CDC. International Development Paper. University of Kentucky, Center for Developmental Change.	
Commonwealth Scientific and Industrial Research Organization. Division of Land Use Research. Research Report.	
Connecticut Agricultural Exp. Station. Bulletin	
Cornell University. Agricultural Economics Staff Paper.	

	Heavily Cited in Third World Lists
Cornell University. Agricultural Exp. Station. Bulletin	
Cornell University. Dept. of Agricultural Economics. Occasional Paper.	
Cornell University. Dept. of Agricultural Economics. AE Research.	
Cornell University. International Agricultural Development Bulletin.	*
Current Population Reports. (U.S. Census Bureau)	
Delhi. University. Agricultural Economics Research Centre. Research Study.	*
Development Study. University of Reading, Dept. of Agricultural Economics and Management	
FAO Agricultural Development Paper.	*
FAO Agricultural Planning Studies.	*
FAO Commodity Policy Studies.	
FAO Commodity Review and Outlook.	
FAO Economic and Social Development Series. = T	*
FAO Food and Nutrition Series. = T	*
FAO Trade Yearbook.	
FAO Yearbook of Food and Agricultural Statistics. = T	*
Florida Agr. Exp. Station. Bulletin.	
Georgia Agricultural Exp. Station. Bulletin	*
Ghana. Univ. ISSER. Technical Publication Series. = T	*
Giannini Foundation of Agricultural Economics. Research Report.	
Giannini Foundation of Agricultural Economics. Mimeo Reports.	
Gottinger Schriften zur Agrarokonomie (Gottingen Reports on Agricultural Economics). Gottingen University, Institut fur Agrarokonomie.	
Guelph University School of Agricultural Economics and Ext. Education. AAEA Series.	
Harvard Institute for International Development. Discussion Paper.	*
Hitotsubashi Univ. Inst. of Economic Research. Research Series.	*
IFDC Technical Bulletin. = T	*
Illinois University. Agricultural Economics Staff Paper. New Series E.	
Illinois University. Agricultural Experimental Station. AAER.	
Illinois University. Agricultural Experimental Station. Bulletin.	
Instituo de Economia Agricola. Informacoes Economicas. Sao Paulo, Brazil	
International Crops Research Institute for the Semi-Arid Tropics. Occasional Paper-Economic Program. Hyderabad, India. = T	*
International Food Policy Research Institute. Occasional Paper. = T	
International Food Policy Research Institute. Research Report.	*
International Food Policy Research Institute. Working Paper. = T	*
International Studies in Economics.	
Iowa Agricultural Exp. Station. Research Bulletin	
Iowa Agricultural Exp. Station. Special Report	

	Heavily Cited in Third World Lists
IRRI. Research Paper. = T	*
Kansas Agricultural Exp. Station. Technical Bulletin	
Kentucky Agricultural Exp. Station. Bulletin.	
Land Tenure Center. Paper. (University of Wisconsin) = T	*
Land Tenure Center. Research Paper. (University of Wisconsin)	
Landbow-Economisch Mededelingen (Agricultural Economics Report). The Hague, Landbow-Economisch Instituut.	
Maryland Agric. Exp. Station. Misc. Publication.	
Michigan State University. Agric. Exp. Station. Research Report.	
Michigan State University. Agric. Exp. Station. Technical Bulletin.	
Michigan State University. Department of Agricultural Economics. Agricultural Economics Report.	*
Michigan State University. Dept. of Agric. Economics. ARE Paper.	
Michigan State University. Dept. of Agric. Economics. ARE Working Paper.	
Michigan State University. Dept. of Agric. Economics. International Development Paper. = T	*
Michigan State University. Dept. of Agric. Economics. Rural Development Working Paper.	*
Michigan State University. Institute of International Agriculture. Research Report. = T	*
Minnesota Agric. Exp. Station. Bulletin.	
Minnesota Agric. Exp. Station. Technical Bulletin.	
Minnesota. University. Department of Agricultural and Applied Economics. Staff Paper Series.	
Missouri Agric. Exp. Station. Bulletin	
Missouri Agric. Exp. Station. Research Bulletin	
Nairobi. University. IDS Occasional Paper. = T	*
National Research Institute of Agricultural Economics (Japan). Nogyo Sogo Kenkyujo (Annual Report).	
Nebraska Agric. Exp. Station. Special Bulletin.	
Nebraska University. Department of Agricultural Economics. Report.	
New Hampshire Agric. Exp. Station. Bulletin	
Norges Landbrukshogskole, Institutt for Landbruksokonomi (University of Norway, Department of Agricultural Economics) Melding (Report).	
North Carolina State University. Agric. Exp. Station. A.E. Information Series.	
North Carolina State University. Agricultural Policy Institute. API Series.	
North Carolina State University. Department of Economics and Business. Economics Research Report.	
Ohio Agricultural Res. and Dev. Center. Research Bulletin.	
Ohio State University. Department of Agricultural Economics and Rural Sociology. ESS.	

	Heavily Cited in Third World Lists
Ohio State University. Department of Agricultural Economics and Rural Sociology. Occasional Paper	
Oklahoma State University. Agricultural Exp. Station. Bulletin.	
Oklahoma State University. Department of Agricultural Economics. AE Paper.	
Oregon Agricultural Exp. Station. Special Report	
Organisation for Economic Cooperation and Development. Policy Reports.	*
ORSTOM. Memoires. = T	*
Overseas Development Institute. Pastoral Network Paper. = T	*
Pennsylvania Agricultural Exp. Station Bulletin	
Pennsylvania State University. Department of Agricultural Economics and Rural Sociology. A.E. & R.S.	
Philippines. Bureau of Agricultural Economics. Economics Research Report.	
PIDS. Working Paper. = T	*
Purdue Agricultural Exp. Station. Bulletin	
Purdue Agricultural Exp. Station. Research Bulletin	
Recherches d'Economie et de Sociologie Rurales. Paris, Institute National de la Recherche Agronomique.	
Rural Education Yearbook	
Studien zur Agrarwritschaft	*
Sydney. University. Department of Agricultural Economics. Research Report.	
Texas Agricultural Exp. Station. Bulletin	
United Nations Statistical Yearbook = T	*
U.S. Dept. of Agriculture:	
Agricultural Economic Report = T	
Agricultural Handbook	
Agricultural Information Bulletin	
Agricultural Statistics	
Foreign Agricultural Economic Report	
Market Research Report	
Miscellaneous Publication	
Statistical Bulletin	
Technical Bulletin	
U.S. Dept. of Agriculture. Agric. Marketing Service. AMS Series.	
U.S. Dept. of Agriculture. Agric. Research Service. ARS Series.	
U.S. Dept. of Agriculture. Econ. Research Service. ERS Series.	
U.S. Dept. of Agriculture. Econ. Research Service. ERS Series. ERS Foreign. = T	*
Virginia Agricultural Exp. Station. Bulletin	
Washington State Agric. Exp. Station. Bulletin	
West Virginia. Agricultural Exp. Station. Bulletin	
Western Agricultural Economics Association. Proceedings . . . (Annual)	
Wisconsin. University. Department of Agricultural Economics. Ag. Econ.	

	Heavily Cited in Third World Lists
World Bank:	
Country Policy Discussion Paper = T	
Report Series = T	
Staff Occasional Paper	
Staff Working Paper	*
World Develoment Report (Annual) World Bank = T	*
World Food Programme Studies. Rome, FAO.	
Year Book of Agricultural Cooperation. London, Horace Plunkett Foundation. = T	*

T = Recommended for support of Third World agricultural economics and rural sociology.

In mid-1990, the World Bank began publishing *MADIA Discussion Papers* with eleven initial titles ranging from twenty to seventy-nine pages. This will be a valuable series. MADIA is an acronym for *Managing Agricultural Development in Africa*.

7. Core Lists of Primary Monographs

One of the aims of the investigations in this book sought to identify those monographs cited most heavily in the academic and research literature of agricultural economics and rural sociology. A spread of twenty-five years in publishing was used to determine the journals and monographs of greatest value, which gave an historical and current prospective on the literature. As a result, it was possible to provide gradations of value and to select primary works for the developed and the Third World.

A. Compilation and Review

The methods outlined in Chapter 5 were applied to all of the twenty-four overview evaluated publications listed in that chapter. Every citation in these volumes was examined for new titles of monographs and journals and recorded in appropriate lists. Similarly, each time a chapter or the book itself was cited, a count was made of each. In this process, approximately 4,500 distinctive monographs were identified from 11,000 monographic citations, which served as the beginning core. Approximately 2,000 of these titles fell out of the compilation or review process near the end of the evaluation. Certain materials were excluded:

(1) Short monographs, fifty pages or fewer which were cited only once and evaluated by reviewers as unimportant.
(2) Country, state, or provincial documents of brief pagination, with a highly specialized focus, often statistical in nature or a report.
(3) Difficult-to-read language materials *when* focused on all of agriculture rather than on this discipline.
(4) Select esoteric works, particularly with limited geographic scope.
(5) Select geographic materials when not in a national or international context which got cited only once, or was deemed unimportant by the reviewers.

(6) References to *early* mathematical, economic or statistical techniques because these working tools are primarily the core of other disciplines with slight application to agriculture. References to such materials published in the last thirty years were retained. Numerous early works of this type were kept in the lists based on the number of times cited or their high ratings.
(7) Early editions when a later one was cited, although both the earliest and latest are given in most cases in the final listings.

The initial list of monographs, about 2,500 titles, was evaluated locally in order to test the reviewing methods. Some titles were removed following the criteria just outlined. At this point additional overview volumes were added to the list. In the review process, lists of a similar nature or references to them were solicited from reviewers. Although no lengthy lists were recommended, nearly 100 more recent titles were proposed.

At the initiation of this work, the decision was made to compile and count citations, but to pass the results through another qualitative screen. For this purpose, economists and sociologists were asked to evaluate the titles. After the lists had been reviewed twice at Cornell University and the philosophy and purpose of the project clearly set, the resulting lists were sent to reviewers. These evaluators were chosen on the basis of their years of academic and research work, particularly teaching, standings in their specialties, and a broad understanding of world agricultural economics or rural sociology. Their first review clearly indicated that we should think in terms of two or more aims for these lists. One aim concerned the case, strongly made, to distinguish Third World materials from the total compilation. Although this offered a potential skew, in the second iteration a division was made on the basis of the evaluations where a distinctive line could be drawn between the reviewers' evaluations when they came from a developed or a developing country. Approximately 39% of the titles which rated poorly when voted upon by developed world reviewers but fared better with Third World reviewers, were removed from the developed countries list. But all the titles were kept in the Third World list, thus providing the opportunity for Third World reviewers to choose between all the best literature in the context of the best literature for the Third World. This process worked well, so two lists were run concurrently aimed at two different clientele: researchers, academicians, and students in developed countries, and in developing countries. The two resulting lists in this chapter have 44.8% duplication of titles across both. This means that 543 monographs are core publications for both groups.

Instructions to the reviewers included basic criteria for inclusion of a title, methods of scoring, aim of the final product, and counsel on the relationship of historically significant with currently valuable titles. The review process went on for over a year. Each individual's ranking was tabulated and used in the final ordering of the lists.

Reviewers of Monograph Lists

Dr. Bernard F. Stanton, Department of Agricultural Economics, Cornell University, offered extensive consultation and assistance in several literature studies performed by the Mann Library. He was helpful in the choice of source publications used in the compilation of a monograph list and for analysis. He also served as a reviewer of select lists as they progressed. Dr. Randy Barker, Department of Agricultural Economics, Cornell University, organized several of his colleagues at Cornell to evaluate lists. This aided the review process substantially.

The following people conscientiously and systematically reviewed lists, many offered additional title suggestions and other recommendations.

Burhanuddin Abdul Salam, Markets and Pricing, Palm Oil Research Institute of Malaysia

Dale W Adams, Agricultural Economics and Rural Sociology, Ohio State University

Chew Tek Ann, Agricultural Economics, Universiti Pertanian Malaysia

Mohd. Ariff Hussein, Faculty of Economics and Managment, Universiti Pertanian Malaysia

George Banta, International Development Research Center, Ottawa, Canada.

Mohd. Yusof bin Shahabuddin, Applied Economics and Statistics, Rubber Research Institute of Malaysia

David Blandford, Agricultural Economics, Cornell University

David L. Brown, Rural Sociology, Cornell University

Emery N. Castle, Economics, Oregon State University

James A. Christenson, Rural Sociology, University of Kentucky

Carl K. Eicher, International Agriculture, Michigan State University

Cornelia Flora, Sociology, Anthropology and Social Work, Kansas State University

Olan D. Forker, Agricultural Economics, Cornell University

Maritza Hee Houng, Coordinator of Review Process, Central Agricultural Experiment Station, Trinidad and Tobago

Richard A. King, Agricultural Economics, North Carolina State University

Steven C. Kyle, Agricultural Economics, Cornell University

Olaf F. Larson, Rural Sociology, Cornell University

John K. Lynam, Rockefeller Foundation

A. F. Mabawonku, Agricultural Economics, University of Ibadan

Prabhu L. Pingali, Agricultural Economics, International Rice Research Institute
Kenneth L. Robinson, Agricultural Economics, Cornell University
Syed Salim Agha, Coordinator of Review Process, Universiti Pertanian Malaysia
William G. Tomek, Agricultural Economics, Cornell University
Zahra Yaacob, Librarian, Yayasan Sabah, East Malaysia

Some problems were encountered in this evaluation process, although reviewers were inventive with their solutions. When a reviewer lacked knowledge of a title, author, or other data on which to make a decision, the title was passed over. In at least two evaluations in the Third World, problems were solved by committee decisions. One Third World evaluator scored all titles of the topmost value reflecting the attitude that everything was needed and, therefore, valuable. This evaluation was disqualified. The developed countries list was divided late in the review process into nine subject groupings and then distributed to specialists for those subjects. In some cases, people scored one or more lists depending upon their backgrounds and knowledge. There was some difficulty in getting the caliber of person needed to agree to score the list on a timely basis. Twelve such refusals were tendered all on the basis of lack of time; several offered to do the evaluation if a stipend could be attached. The reviewing was a prodigious task, and the project officers are very pleased to have had so much cooperation and assistance from reviewers. The return of valid evaluations was 90%.

B. The Developed Countries List of Monographs

The end of the Second World War fostered a dramatic revolution in agricultural economics and rural sociology which had begun in the late 1930s. Upon examination of the literature and in consultation with colleagues at Cornell University, 1950 was set as a fairly clear breaking point for currently valuable monographic literature. The resulting developed country list should have application, or serve as a minimum collection, in all academic institutions in the developed world where advanced agricultural economics and rural sociology are taught or practiced.

Some adjustments in the basic list of monographs had to be made since the bulk of the overview volumes were published prior to 1985 thereby excluding much recently published material. This was overcome by introducing approximately 300 titles from current bibliographic sources in the review process. Some of these titles have made an impact, and thus made it to this final listing, but most have not. This was reversed with Third World literature since three of the reference source documents were compiled in the last four years, were up to date, and are awaiting publication in 1992. The result should be a balanced list based over time. The principle that the current or recent builds on the past is true in this discipline as well as others.

An analysis of the final compilation was made to ascertain to what degree specialties in agricultural economics and rural sociology are represented. Categorization of the titles, into such groups as farm finance or international agricultural finance, was painstakingly done. The results were compared to the original structure and emphases in the Martin three-volume work. There can be no authoritative basis for determining positive subject correlations since the slight variations noted probably demonstrated the shifts in emphasis and publishing of the last ten years. The most discernible variation in this regard is the area of international agricultural development which is the area of greatest growth and development in all of agricultural economics.

Weighting the Monograph List

Several devices were used to rank the titles from the data. Numeric scores were assigned to these elements for each title and computed. The data used are these:

(1) Counts were kept each time a monograph or a chapter of a monograph was cited for all citations in the list of overview Peer-Evaluated publications cited in Chapter 5. These counts were coded into the monograph lists as they progressed through review and evaluation. The initial citing that placed each in the list was not computed in the final evaluation; only the later counts that ranged from none to sixty-five were used. This citation analysis element was given the weight of 2 per citing.

(2) Rankings of reviewers were also coded into the monograph lists for each of the three evaluative levels provided in the review. These were graded 3, 2, or 1 and were multiplied by the number of recomendations in each category.

(3) Books that have won awards or have been specially cited were identified from two sources. One is the Classics Award voted by the fellows of the American Agricultural Economics Association (AAEA) within the past few years—the winners are undergoing literature reviews again in the *AJAE* (Appendix B). The second source of awards are those for "Quality publications" granted by the American Agricultural Economics Association since 1964 and reported in the proceedings of their annual meetings. Both groups totaling seventy-one titles appear in this Core List or in the Historically Significant List in the following chapter. These are identified at the end of its citation by "AAEA Classic" statement or "Q." Most of the Q awards went to brief monographs in series. Only a few book titles were added by this process. Each

of these two designations was given a weight of 3. Works reprinted since 1979 were also weighted with 3.

The equation for this computation is:

$$((\#) \times 2) + (\#3\times3 + \#2\times2 + \#1\times1) + (\mathrm{AAEA}\times3) + (\mathrm{Q}\times3) + (\mathrm{Rpnt}\times3)$$

The accrued values clustered into three logical ranges. The fewest titles are in the first ranke and are the most important core books. The last group has the least range of scores and the greatest number of titles. The identifications on the developed countries list are

First rank = top ranking—18%
Second rank = middle ranking—40%
Third rank = bottom ranking—42%

Readers are reminded that all titles in the two monograph lists are highly ranked monographs valuable for instruction or research today. The ranking is provided to aid in making decisions for purchase, preservation, or collection assessments.

The Top Twenty World Monographs

The top twenty titles in the monographic tabulation fell at a numerically clear dividing line, and are displayed in rank order below. Some interesting data are observed from this list. The point distance between the first ranked (Martin) and the second ranked (Wharton) is one-quarter of the full range of points from the top of the list to the last of 1,420 items: Martin's *Survey of Agricultural Economics Literature* stands out far ahead of all other titles. Since 1977 it is the only monograph that is consistently cited in the *American Journal of Agricultural Economics* articles according to the *Science Citation Index Journal Citation Reports*. The reasons are clear when we remember that this is a recent authoritative work summarizing the status and literature of agricultural economics and rural sociology. Researchers writing since its appearance need only to cite one or more of the chapters in the volumes to cover historical and substantive knowledge without extensive referencing. The forty-four authors of the sixteen parts covered the waterfront very well in the three volumes. Undoubtedly, Volume 4, on international and Third World agricultural economic development, will boost the importance of this publication.

Developed Countries Twenty Top-Ranked Monographs

1. Lee R. Martin, ed. *A Survey of Agricultural Economics Literature*. 3 vols. Minneapolis: University of Minnesota Press for the American Agricultural Economics Association, 1977–1981. (Vol. 4 due in 1992).
2. Clifton R. Wharton, ed. *Subsistence Agriculture and Economic Development*. Chicago: University of Chicago; Aldine Publ., 1969. 481p.
3. Herman M. Southworth and Bruce F. Johnston, eds. *Agricultural Development and Economic Growth*. Ithaca, N.Y.: Cornell University Press, 1967, reprinted 1979. 608p. Quality Award of AAEA.
4. Lloyd G. Reynolds, ed. *Agriculture in Development Theory*. New Haven, Conn.: Yale University Press, 1975. 510p.
5. Yujiro Hayami and Vernon W. Ruttan. *Agricultural Development: An International Perspective*. Baltimore: Johns Hopkins University Press, 1971. 367p. (Revised and expanded in 1985, 506p.). AAEA Classic and Quality Publication Award.

6–7–8. Hans P. Binswanger and Vernon W. Ruttan. *Induced Innovation: Technology, Institutions, and Development*. Baltimore: Johns Hopkins University Press, 1978. 423p. Quality Publication Award of AAEA.
Carl K. Eicher and John M. Staatz, eds. *Agricultural Development in the Third World*. Baltimore: Johns Hopkins University Press, 1984. 491p.
Theodore W. Schultz. *Transforming Traditional Agriculture*. New Haven, Conn.: Yale University Press, 1964. 212p. (Reprinted by Arno Press, 1976). AAEA Classic.

9. Thomas M. Arndt, Dana G. Dalrymple, and Vernon Ruttan, eds. *Resource Allocation and Productivity in National and International Agricultural Research*. Minneapolis: University of Minnesota Press, 1977. 617p.
10. John W. Mellor. *Economics of Agricultural Development*. Ithaca, N.Y.: Cornell University Press, 1970. 418p. Quality Publication Award of AAEA.
11. Vernon W. Ruttan. *Agricultural Research Policy*. Minneapolis: University of Minnesota Press, 1982. 369p.
12. Carl K. Eicher and L. W. Witt, eds. *Agriculture in Economic Development*. New York: McGraw-Hill, 1964. 415p.
13. I. Adelman and Erik Thorbecke, eds. *The Theory and Design of Economic Development*. Baltimore: Johns Hopkins University Press, 1967. 427p.
14. Theodore W. Schultz. *Agriculture in an Unstable Economy*. New York: McGraw-Hill, 1945. 299p. AAEA Classic.
15. Don Paarlberg. *Farm and Food Policy: Issues of the 1980s*. Lincoln: University of Nebraska Press, 1980. 338p.
16. C. Peter Timmer, Walter P. Falcon, and Scott R. Pearson. *Food Policy Analysis*. Baltimore: Johns Hopkins University Press, 1983. 301p. Quality Publication Award of AAEA.

17–18–19. James K. Boyce and Robert E. Evenson. *National and International Agricultural Research and Extension Programs*. New York: Agricultural Development Council, 1975. 229p.
Earl O. Heady. *Economics of Agricultural Production and Resource Use*. New York: Prentice-Hall, 1952. 850p. AAEA Classic and Quality Publication Award.
John W. Mellor. *The New Economics of Growth: A Strategy for India and the Developing World*. Ithaca, N.Y.: Cornell University Press, 1976. 335p.

20. James A. Roumasset, Jean-Marc Boussard, and Inderjit Singh, eds. *Uncertainty and Agricultural Development*. Laguna, Philippines: Southeast Asian Regional Center for Graduate Study and Research in Agriculture: and New York: Agricultural Development Council, 1979. 453p.

The point range between the second and twentieth ranked volumes is also about one-quarter of the total range for the full list. Therefore, the top twenty items constitute 45% of the numerical scoring range for the 1,420 citations.

Some interesting points and questions are evident in the top twenty. University press books make up 75% of these titles with Johns Hopkins (four), Cornell (three), and the University of Minnesota (three) having the most. The three commercial books published in 1945, 1952, and 1964 are among the four oldest on the list. Does this indicate today's scholars' unwillingness to publish with commercial presses, or the commercial presses unwillingness to take a financial risk? All three of these early commercial books were voted Classics by the Fellows of the American Agricultural Economics Association (See Appendix B). Eight of the twenty titles have been designated AAEA Classics or have won the Quality Publication Award of the AAEA: two of the eight are in both categories.

The more recent titles appear to be multiauthored or edited works, often resulting from conferences or small workshops to which papers were invited. The top four titles are edited works. In fact, 40% of the titles are of multiple authorship or multiple editorship. Wrongly or not, the editors of these volumes tend to get credit for the parts inside the covers, as well as the total volume. Of the twelve volumes not edited, nearly half have multiple authors. It appears that agricultural economics and rural sociology have turned to collaborations, and generally shorter, more discrete pieces of work.

The chronological breakdown is:

one from the 1940s,
one from the 1950s,
five from the 1960s,
nine from the 1970s, and
four from the 1980s, none later than 1984.

The most common name in the list is Vernon Ruttan whose *Agricultural Research Policy* is included along with three additional co-edited works. One of these is an AAEA Classic and two won Quality Publication Awards. Two other names are each in the list twice, Ted W. Schultz, the eminent Nobel laureate, and John W. Mellor. These scholars authored both of their works alone. A third Schultz title, *Distortions of Agricultural Incentives*, ranks twenty-fourth. All of the top twenty authors are well known in agricultural economics.

The refocusing of agricultural economics on international trade and development is clear, with five of the twenty titles on these subjects, all written since 1975.

Agricultural Economics and Rural Sociology Core List of Monographs for Developed Countries, 1950–88, 1420 titles

A

Third — Abramovitz, M., ed. Capital Formation and Economic Growth. Princeton; Princeton University Press for National Bureau of Economic Research, 1959. 677p.

Third — Abt, Clark, ed. The Evaluation of Social Programs. Beverly Hills, Calif.; Sage, 1976. 503p.

Third — Acharya, S. S. Green Revolution: Impact on Farm Employment and Incomes. Jaipur, India; Sanghi Prakashan, 1982. 156p.

First rank — Ackerman, Joseph, Marion Clawson, and Marshall Harris, eds. Land Economics Research: Papers Presented at a Symposium, Lincoln, Nebraska, June 1961. Resources for the Future, 1961, distributed by Baltimore; Johns Hopkins University Press. 270p. (Reprinted by AMS Press, Inc., 1962.)

Second — Adams, Dale W., Douglas H. Graham, and J.D. Von Pischke, eds. Undermining Rural Development with Cheap Credit. Boulder, Colo.; Westview Press, 1984. 318p.

First rank — Adelman, I. and E. Thorbecke, eds. The Theory and Design of Economic Development. Baltimore; Johns Hopkins University Press, 1967. 427p.

First rank — Adelman, I. and C. T. Morris. Economic Growth and Social Equity in Developing Countries. Stanford; Stanford University Press, 1973. 257p.

First rank — Agarwala, A. N. and S. P. Singh, eds. The Economics of Underdevelopment. New York; Holt-Rinehart, 1961. 510p.

Second — Agrawal, R. C. and E. O. Heady. Operations Research Methods for Agricultural Decisions. Ames; Iowa State University Press, 1972. 303p.

Second — Agriculture Stability and Growth: Toward a Cooperative Approach. Port Washington, New York; Associated Faculty Press, 1984. 240p.

Second — Ahmed, Iftikhar, and Vernon W. Ruttan, eds. Generation and Diffusion of Agricultural Innovations: the Role of Institutional Factors. Aldershot, Hants, Eng. and Brookfield, Vermont; Gower Publishing Co., 1988. 471p.

Third — Ahmed, Raisuddin and M. Hossain. Infrastructure and Development of a Rural Economy: A Case Study of Bangladesh. Washington, D.C., International Food Policy Research Institute; and Dacca, Bangladesh, Bangladesh Institute of Development Studies, 1987.

Second — Ahsan, Syed M. Agricultural Insurance: A New Policy for Developing Countries. Brookfield, Vermont; Gower Publishing Co., 1985. 262p.

Second — Akoto, O. A. Public Policy and Agricultural Development in Africa. Brookfield, Vermont; Gower Publishing Co, 1988.

Second — Alavi, Hamza, and Teodor Shanin, eds. Introduction to the Sociology of "Developing Societies." New York; Monthly Review Press, 1982. 474p.

Second — Alberts, Tom. Agrarian Reform and Rural Poverty: A Case Study of Peru. Boulder, Colo.; Westview Press, 1983. 306p.

Second — Alexander, M., ed. Agricultural Policy: A Limiting Factor in the Development Process. Washington, D.C.; Inter-American Development Bank, 1975. 507p.

Third — Alexandratos, Nikos, ed. World Agriculture: Towards 2000: An FAO study. New York; New York University Press, 1988. 338p.

Third — Allen, David M. and Foster B. Cady. Analyzing Experimental Data by Regression. Belmont, Calif.; Lifetime Learning Publ., 1982. 394p.

Third — Allen, G. R. Agricultural Marketing Policy. Oxford University Press, 1959. 336p.

Third — Amacher, Ryan C., Robert D. Tollison, and Thomas D. Willett, eds. The Economic Approach to Public Policy. Ithaca, N.Y.; Cornell University Press, 1976. 528p.

Second — Amin, Samir. Unequal Development: An Essay on the Social Formations of Peripheral Capitalism. New York; Monthly Review Press, 1976. 440p. (Transl. of Le Developpement Inegal; Paris; Les Editions de Minuit, 1973.)

Second — Amin, Samir. Accumulation on a World Scale: A Critique of the Theory of Underdevelopment. 2 vols. New York; Monthly Review Press, 1974. 666p. (Transl. from French by B. Pearce.)

First rank — Anderson, C. Arnold and M. J. Bowman, eds. Education and Economic Development. Chicago. Ill.; Aldine Press, 1965. 436p.

Second — Anderson, Jock R., John L. Dillon, and J. Brian Hardaker. Agricultural Decision Analysis. Ames; Iowa State University Press, 1977. 344p.

Third — Anderson, Kym and Rodney Tyers. Distortions in World Food Markets. Cambridge, Eng.; Cambridge University Press, 1988.

Second — Anderson, Kym, Y. Hayami, and others. The Political Economy of Agricultural Protection: East Asia in International Perspective. Sydney, Australia and Boston; George Allen and Unwin, 1986. 185p.

Third — Andreou, Paris. Contemporary Issues in Agricultural and Economic Development of Developing Nations: Selected Reading in the Economic Development of Poor Countries. Nairobi; East African Lit. Bureau, 1977. 340p.

Second — Andrews, Frank M. and Stephen B. Withey. Social Indicator of Well-Being: Americans' Perceptions of Life Quality. New York; Plenum Press, 1976. 455p.

Second — Anschel, Kurt R., Russell H. Brannon, and Eldon D. Smith, eds. Agricultural Cooperatives and Markets in Developing Countries. New York; Praeger, 1969. 373p.

Third — Antonelli, G. and A. Quadrio-Curzio, eds. The Agro-Technological System Towards 2000: A European Perspective. Amsterdam and New York; North Holland, 1988. 297p.

Second — Aoki, Masanao. Optimal Control and System Theory in Dynamic Economic Analysis; A System-Theoretic Approach. New York; American Elsevier, 1975. 400p.

First rank — Arndt, Thomas M., Dana G. Dalrymple, and Vernon Ruttan, eds. Resource Allocation and Productivity in National and International Agricultural Research. Minneapolis; University of Minnesota Press, 1977. 617p.

Third — Arnot, Marie, Lee J. Cary, and Mary Jean Houde. The Volunteer Organization Handbook. Blacksburg, Va.; Center for Volunteer Development, Cooperative Extension Service, Virginia Polytechnic Inst. and State University, 1985. 182p.

First rank — Arrow, Kenneth J. Social Choice and Individual Values. 2d ed. New Haven, Conn.; Yale University Press, 1963. Reprinted in 1970. 124p. (1st ed., New York; John Wiley and Sons, 1951. 99p.)

Third — Asian Development Bank. Agriculture in Asia: Its Performance and Prospects; The Role of ADB in Its Development. Manila, Philippines; Asian Development Bank, 1985.

Third — Asian Development Bank. Rural Asia—Challenge and Opportunity. New York; Praeger, 1977, 1978. 489p.

Third — Asian Productivity Organization. Farm Credit in Selected Asian Countries: Report of a Study Mission Conducted in Japan, Aug.-Sept. 1984. Tokyo; Asian Productivity Organization, 1985. 197p.

Third — Asian Productivity Organization. Farm Mechanization in Asia. Tokyo; Asian Prod. Organization, 1983. 510 p.

Third — Asian Productivity Organization. Productivity Measurement and Analysis: Asian Agriculture. Tokyo; Asian Prod. Organization, 1987. 834 p.

Second — Askari, Hossein, and John T. Cummings. Agricultural Supply Response: A Survey of the Econometric Evidence. New York; Praeger, 1976. 443p.

Third — Astori, Danilo. La Agricultura en una Estrategia de Desarrollo Economico. Montevideo, Uruguay; Ediciones de la Banda Oriental, 1969. 132p.

Second — Atkinson, Anthony B. The Economics of Inequality. 2d ed. Oxford and New York; Oxford University Press, 1983. 330p. (1st ed., Oxford; Clarendon Press, 1975. 295p.)

Third — Attwood, D. W. and B. S. Baviskar, eds. Co-operatives and Rural Development. Oxford University Press, 1988. 320 p.

Second — Austin, James E. Agroindustrial Project Analysis. Baltimore; Johns Hopkins University Press, 1981. 213p.

Third — Austin, James E., and Gustavo Esteva, eds. Food Policy in Mexico: The Search for Self-Sufficiency. Ithaca, N.Y.; Cornell University Press, 1987. 383p.

Third — Australian Bureau of Agricultural Economics. Rural Industry in Australia. 3d ed. Canberra; Australian Government Publ. Service, 1983. 126p.

B

Second — Baden, John, ed. The Vanishing Farmland Crisis: Critical Views of the Movement to Preserve Agricultural Land. Lawrence; University Press of Kansas, 1984. 184p.

Second — Bagchi, Amiya. The Political Economy of Underdevelopment. Cambridge and New York; Cambridge University Press, 1982. 280p.

Second — Bairoch, Paul and Maurice Levy-Leboyer. Disparities in Economic Development Since the Industrial Revolution. New York; St. Martin's Press, 1981. 428p.

Third — Bairoch, Paul. The Economic Development of the Third World Since 1900. Transl. by Cynthia Postan of 4th French edition. Berkeley; University of California Press, 1975, 1977. 260p.

Second — Balassa, Bela. Trade Prospects for Developing Countries. Homewood, Ill.; Richard D. Irwin, 1964. 450p.

First rank — Balassa, Bela. The Structure of Protection in Developing Countries. Baltimore; Johns Hopkins University Press, for the World Bank, 1971. 375p.

Second — Ball, A. Gordon, and Earl O. Heady, eds. Size, Structure and Future of Farms. Ames; Iowa State University Press, 1972. 404p.

Third — Bansil, P. C. Agricultural Problems of India. 2d rev. and enlarged ed. New Delhi, India; Vikas Publ., 1975. 608p.

First rank	Baran, P.A. The Political Economy of Growth. 2d ed. New York; Monthly Review Press, 1962. 308p. (1st ed., 1957, 308p.)
Second	Bardach, Eugene, and Robert A. Kagan, eds. Social Regulations: Strategies for Reform. San Francisco; Institute for Contemporary Studies, 1982. 420p.
Second	Bardhan, Pranab K. Interlocking Factor Markets. London and Delhi; Macmillan, 1984.
Second	Bardhan, Pranab K. The Political Economy of Development in India. Oxford and New York; Basil Blackwell, 1984. 118p.
First rank	Bardhan, Pranab K. Land, Labor, and Rural Poverty: Essays in Development Economics. New York; Columbia University Press, 1984. 252p.
Second	Barger, Harold, and Hans H. Landsberg. American Agriculture, 1899–1939: A Study of Output, Employment, and Productivity. Ayer Company Publishers, Inc., 1975. 440p. (National Bureau of Economic Research Ser.) (Reprint of 1942 ed.)
Third	Barker, J. W. Agricultural Marketing. Oxford University Press, 1981. 226p.
Third	Barker, Jonathan, ed. The Politics of Agriculture in Tropical Africa. Beverly Hills, Calif.; Sage Publications, 1984. 320p.
First rank	Barker, Randolph, and Robert W. Herdt. The Rice Economy of Asia. Washington, D.C.; Resources for the Future. Baltimore: Johns Hopkins University Press, 1985. 324p. Q
Second	Barker, Randolph and Radha P. Sinha, eds. Thc Chinese Agricultural Economy. Boulder, Colo.; Westview Press, 1982. 266p.
First rank	Barkley, P.W., and D.W. Seckler. Economic Growth and Environmental Decay: The Solution Becomes the Problem. New York; Harcourt Brace Jovanovich, 1972. 193p.
First rank	Barlett, Peggy F. Agricultural Choice and Change: Decision Making in a Costa Rican Community. New Brunswick, N.J.; Rutgers University Press, 1982. 196p.
Second	Barlowe, Raleigh. Land Resource Economics: The Economics of Real Estate. 4th ed. Englewood Cliffs, N.J.; Prentice-Hall, 1986. 559p. (1958, 585p.)
Third	Barnard, C. S. and J. S. Nix. Farm Planning and Control. Cambridge University Press, 1979. 600p. (1st ed., 1973, 549p.)
Third	Barnes, Douglas F. Electric Power for Rural Growth: How Electricity Affects Rural Life in Developing Countries. Boulder, Colo.; Westview Press, 1988. 236p.
Second	Barnett, Harold J., and Chandler Morse. Scarcity and Growth: The Economics of Natural Resource Availability. Baltimore; Johns Hopkins University Press for Resources for the Future, 1963. 288p.
Second	Barnum, Howard N., and Lyn A. Squire. A Model of an Agricultural Household: Theory and Evidence. Baltimore; Johns Hopkins University Press, 1980. 120p.
Second	Barraclough, Solon L. Agrarian Structure in Latin America. Cambridge, Mass.; Lexington Books, 1973. 351p.
First rank	Barry, Peter J., ed. Risk Management in Agriculture. Ames; Iowa State University Press, 1984. 282p.
Second	Barry, Peter J., John A. Hopkin and C. B. Baker. Financial Management in Agriculture. 4th ed. Danville, Ill.; Interstate, 1988. 500p. (1st ed., 1973, 459p.)

Third	Bartsch, William H. Employment and Technology Choice in Asian Agriculture. New York; Praeger, 1977. 125p.
Third	Bassis, Michael S., Richard Gelles, and Ann Levine. Sociology, An Introduction. 3d ed. New York; Random House, 1987, 1988. 608p.
Third	Batchelor, J. Operations Research: An Annotated Bibliography. St. Louis; St. Louis University Press, 1959–1964. 4 vols.
Third	Bates, Robert H., and M. F. Lofchie, eds. Agricultural Development in Africa: Issues of Public Policy. New York; Praeger, 1980. 451p.
Third	Bates, Robert H. Essays on the Political Economy of Rural Africa. Cambridge University Press, 1983. 178p.
Second	Bates, Robert H. Markets and States in Tropical Africa: the Political Basis of Agricultural Policies. Berkeley; University of California Press, 1981. 178p.
Third	Bathrick, David D. Agricultural Credit for Small Farm Development. Boulder, Colo.; Westview Press, 1981. 170p.
First rank	Batie, Sandra S., and Robert G. Healy. The Future of American Agriculture as a Strategic Resource. Washington D.C.; The Conservation Foundation, 1980. 291p. Q
Second	Batten, Thomas R. Communities and Their Development. London; Oxford University Press, 1957. 248p. (Reprinted by Westport, Conn.; Greenwood Press, 1980.)
Third	Batten, Thomas R. with M. Batten. The Non-Directive Approach in Group and Community Work. London; Oxford University Press, 1967. 148p. (Also 1975 ed.)
Third	Bauer, P. T. West African Trade: A Study of Competition, Oligopoly and Monopoly in a Changing Economy. Cambridge University Press, 1954. 450p. (Reprinted, with a new preface, by London; Routledge and Kegan Paul, 1963; and New York; A. M. Kelley, 1967.)
Third	Baum, E.L., H.G. Diesslin, and E.O. Heady, eds. Capital and Credit Needs in a Changing Agriculture. Ames; Iowa State University Press, 1961. 406p.
First rank	Baum, Kenneth H. and Lyle P. Schertz. Modeling Farm Decisions for Policy Analysis. Boulder, Colo.; Westview Press, 1983. 418p.
Second	Baumol, W. J. Economic Theory and Operations Analysis. Third ed. Englewood Cliffs, N.J.; Prentice-Hall, 1972. 626p.
Third	Bayliss-Smith, Tim, and Sudhir Wanmali, eds. Understanding Green Revolutions: Agrarian Change and Development Planning in South Asia. Cambridge University Press, 1984. 384p.
Second	Beal, George M., Ronald Powers, and E. Walter Coward, eds. Sociological Perspectives of Domestic Development. Ames; Iowa State University Press, 1971. 309p.
First rank	Beattie, Bruce B., and C. Robert Taylor. The Economics of Production. New York; Wiley, 1985. 258p.
Second	Beaulieu, Lionel J., ed. The Rural South in Crisis: Challenges for the Future. Boulder, Colo.; Westview Press, 1988. 384p.
Second	Beaumont, P., and Keith McLachlan, eds. Agricultural Development in the Middle East. Chichester, Eng. and New York; John Wiley and Sons, 1985. 349p.
First rank	Becker, G. S. Human Capital: A Theoretical and Empirical Analysis, with Special Reference to Education. 2d ed. Chicago, University of Chicago Press, 1975, 1980. 268p. (1st ed., New York; Columbia University Press for National Bureau of Economic Research, 1964. 187p.)

Third	Becker, G. S. A Treatise on the Family. Cambridge; Harvard University Press, 1982. 288p.
Second	Behrman, Jere R. Development, the International Economic Order and Commodity Agreements. Reading, Mass.; Addison-Wesley Publ. Co., 1978. 152p.
Third	Beierlein, James G., Kenneth C. Schneeberger, and Donald D. Osburn. Principles of Agribusiness Management. Englewood Cliffs, N.J.; Prentice-Hall, 1986. 441p.
Third	Bellah, R., R. Madsen, W. M. Sullivan, A. Swidler, and S. M. Tipton. Habits of the Heart: Individualism and Commitment in American Life. Berkeley; University of California Press, and New York; Harper and Row, 1985. 355p.
Third	Bellman, Richard, and Stuart E. Dreyfus. Applied Dynamic Programming. Princeton; Princeton University Press, 1962. 363p.
Third	Belsley, David A., E. Kuh, and Roy Welsch. Regression Diagnostics: Identifying Influential Data and Sources of Collinearity. New York; Wiley, 1980, 292p.
Second	Bender, Thomas. Community and Social Change in America. New Brunswick, N.J.; Rutgers University Press, 1978. 159p.
Second	Benedict, M. R. Farm Policies of the United States, 1790–1950. New York; Twentieth Century Fund, 1953. 548p. AAEA Classic.
Second	Bennett, J. L., ed. Building Decision Support Systems. Reading, Mass.; Addison-Wesley, 1983. 277p.
Second	Benor, D., J. Q. Harrison and Michael Baxter. Agricultural Extension: The Training and Visit System. 2d ed. Washington, D.C.; World Bank, 1984. 85p. (1st ed., Benor and Harrison, 1977. 85p.)
Third	Berardi, Gigi M., ed. World Food, Population, and Development. Totowa, N.J.; Rowman and Allanheld, 1985. 346 p.
Second	Berardi, Gigi M. and Charles C. Geisler, eds. The Social Consequences and Challenges of New Agricultural Technologies. Boulder, Colo.; Westview Press, 1984. 376p.
Second	Berg, A. D. Malnutrition: What Can Be Done? Lessons from World Bank Experience. Baltimore; Johns Hopkins University Press for the World Bank, 1987. 139p.
First rank	Berg, A. D., N. S. Scrimshaw, and D. L. Call, eds. Nutrition, National Development, and Planning. Cambridge, Mass.; MIT Press, 1973. 401p.
Third	Berger, Peter L. and John Neuhaus. To Empower People. Washington, D.C.; American Enterprise Institute for Public Policy Research, 1977. 45p.
Third	Bergmann, Theodor. The Development Models of India, the Soviet Union and China. Assen; Van Gorcum, 1977. 255p. (Publications of European Society for Rural Sociology Ser.: No. 1).
Third	Bernstein, Gail Lee. Haruko's World: A Japanese Farm Woman and Her Community. Stanford; Stanford University Press, 1983. 199p.
Second	Berry, R. Albert, and William R. Cline. Agrarian Structure and Productivity in Developing Countries. Baltimore, Md.; Johns Hopkins University Press, 1979. 248p.
Second	Berry, R. Albert, and R. Soligo, eds. Economic Policy and Income Distribution in Colombia. Boulder, Colo.; Westview Press, 1980. 269p.
Second	Berry, Wendell. The Unsettling of America: Culture and Agriculture. San Francisco; Sierra Club Books, 1977. 228p. (Reprinted in 1986.)

Third | Beteille, Andre. Studies in Agrarian Social Structure. Oxford University Press, 1974. 206p.

Second | Bhaduri, Amit. The Economic Structure of Backward Agriculture. London and New York; Academic Press, Inc., 1983. 151p.

Third | Bhagwati, J. N. and P. Desai. India: Planning for Industrialization: Industrialization and Trade Policies Since 1951. London; Oxford University Press for the OECD Development Centre, 1970. 537p.

Third | Bhagwati, J. N., R. W. Jones, R. A. Mundell, and J. Vanek, eds. Trade Balance of Payments and Growth; Papers in International Economics in Memory of C. P. Kindleberger. Amsterdam; North-Holland Publ., 1971. 532p.

Third | Bhattacharjee, Jyotiprasad, ed. Studies in Indian Agricultural Economics. Ayer Company Publishers, Inc., 1976. 326p. (Reprint of Bombay; Indian Society of Agric. Econ., 1958.)

Third | Bhatia, B.M. Indian Agriculture: A Policy Perspective. Beverly Hills, Calif.; Sage Publ., 1988. 192 p.

Third | Bhattacharya, S.N. Indian Rural Economics. New Delhi; Metropolitan, 1984. 467p.

Third | Biddle, William W. and Loureice J. Biddle. The Community Development Process: The Rediscovery of Local Initiative. New York; Holt, Rinehart and Winston, 1965. 334p.

Third | Biddle, William W. and Loureice J. Biddle. Encouraging Community Development: A Training Guide for Local Workers. New York; Holt, Rinehart and Winston, 1968. 224p.

Third | Biebuyck, D., ed. African Agrarian Systems. Oxford University Press, 1963. 407p.

Second | Bieri, J., and A. de Janvry. Empirical Analysis of Demand under Consumer Budgeting. Berkeley; University of California, 1972. 60p. (Giannini Foundation Monograph 30)

Second | Bingen, R. James. Food Production and Rural Development in the Sahel: Lessons from Mali's Operation Riz-Segou. Boulder, Colo.; Westview Press, 1985. 167p.

First rank | Binswanger, Hans P. The Economics of Tractors in South Asia: An Analytical Review. New York; Agricultural Development Council; and Hyderabad, India; International Crops Research Institute for the Semi-Arid Tropics, 1978. 96p.

First rank | Binswanger, Hans P., Robert E. Evenson, Cecilia A. Florencio, and Benjamin N.F. White, eds. Rural Household Studies in Asia. Singapore; Singapore University Press, 1980. 369p.

First rank | Binswanger, Hans P., and Mark R. Rosenzweig. Contractual Arrangements, Employment and Wages in Rural Labor Markets in Asia. New Haven; Yale University Press, 1984. 330p.

First rank | Binswanger, Hans P., and Vernon W. Ruttan. Induced Innovation: Technology, Institutions, and Development. Baltimore; Johns Hopkins University Press, 1978. 423p. Q

First rank | Binswanger, Hans P., and P. L. Scandizzo. Patterns of Agricultural Protection. Washington, D.C.; World Bank, 1983 (Report ARU15).

Second | Bishop, C., and W. D. Toussaint. Introduction to Agricultural Economic Analysis. New York; Wiley, 1958. 258p.

Third | Biswas, Asit K., D. K. Zuo, J. E. Nickum, and C. M. Liu. Long Distance Water Transfer: A Chinese Case Study and International Experiences. Dun Laoghaire, Ireland; Tycooly International Publ., 1983. 417p.

Second Black, John D. Economics for Agriculture: Selected Writings. Edited by Jesse P. Cavin. Cambridge, Mass.; Harvard University Press, 1959. 719p.

Second Blackie, M. J., and Dent, J. B., eds. Information Systems for Agriculture. London; Applied Science Publ., 1979. 176p.

Second Blakely, Edward J., ed. Community Development Research: Concepts, Issues and Strategies. N.Y.; Human Sciences Press, 1979. 224 p.

Second Blakeslee, L. L., E. O. Heady, and C. F. Framingham. World Food Production, Demand and Trade. Ames; Iowa State University Press, 1973. 417p. Q

Second Blalock, Hubert M., Jr. Conceptualization and Measurement in the Social Sciences. Beverly Hills, Calif.; Sage Publications, 1982. 284p.

Second Blalock, Hubert M., Jr. Theory Construction: From Verbal to Mathematical Formulations. Englewood Cliffs, N.J.; Prentice-Hall, 1969. 180p.

Third Blanckenburg, Peter von and Hans-Diedrich Cremer, eds. Handbuch der Landwirtschaft und Ernahrung in den Entwicklungslandern. (Handbook for Agriculture and Food in Developing Countries.) Stuttgart; E. Ulmer, 1982–1989. 4 vols.

Third Blase, Melvin G.,ed. Institutions in Agricultural Development. Ames; Iowa State University Press, 1971. 247p.

Third Blaug, Mark. Economic Theory in Retrospect. Homewood, Ill.; R.D. Irwin, 1962. 633p. (3d ed. New York; Cambridge University Press, 1978. 756p.)

Third Blaug, Mark. The Methodology of Economics. New York; Cambridge University Press, 1980. 296p.

Third Bliss, C. J. and N. H. Stern. Palanpur: The Economy of an Indian Village. Oxford and New York; Oxford University Press, 1982. 340p.

Third Blohm, G. Angewandte Landwirtschaftliche Betriebslehre. (Applied Agricultural Management.) Stuttgart; E. Ulmer, 1959. 360p.

Third Bloom, Gordon F. Productivity in the Food Industry: Problems and Potential. Cambridge, Mass.; MIT Press, 1972. 314p.

Third Bochlje, Michael D., and Vernon R. Eidman. Farm Management. New York; John Wiley and Sons, Inc., 1984. 806p.

Second Bogue, Donald J. Principles of Demography. New York; John Wiley and Sons, 1969. 917p.

Third Bonanno, Alessandro. Small Farms: Persistence with Legitimation. Boulder, Colo.; Westview Press, 1987. 228p.

Third Booth, A. and R. M. Sundrum. Labour Absorption in Agriculture: Theoretical Analysis and Empirical Investigations. New York; Oxford University Press, 1985. 327p.

Third Borch, K., and J. Mossin, eds. Risk and Uncertainty. New York; Stockton Press, 1986. 455p.

Second Bose, Nirmal Kumar. Multidimensional Systems Theory: Progress, Directions and Open Problems in Multidimensional Systems. Dordrecht, Holland and Boston; Reidel Publishing Company; Hingham, Mass.; Kluwer Academic Publishers, 1985. 264p.

Third Boserup, Ester. Population and Technological Change: A Study of Long-term Trends. Chicago; University of Chicago Press, 1981. 255p.

First rank Boserup, Ester. Conditions of Agricultural Growth: The Economics of Agrarian Change Under Population Pressure. Chicago; Aldine Publ. Co., 1965. 124p.

First rank Boulding, Kenneth E. Beyond Economics: Essays on Society, Religion, and Ethics. Ann Arbor; University of Michigan Press, 1968. 302p.

First rank Boulding, Kenneth E. Evolutionary Economics. Beverly Hills, Calif.; Sage Publishing, 1981. 200p.

Second Bowen, H. R. The State of the Nation and the Agenda for Higher Education. San Francisco; Jossey-Bass, 1982. 212p.

Third Bowles, Samuel and Herbert Gintis. Schooling in Capitalist America. New York; Basic Books, 1976. 340p.

First rank Box, G. E. P., and G. M. Jenkins. Time Series Analysis, Forecasting and Control. San Francisco; Holden-Day, 1970. 553p. (Revised ed. 1976, 575p.)

Third Boyce, James K. Agrarian Impasse in Bengal: Institutional Constraints to Technological Change. Oxfordshire; Oxford University Press, 1986. 308p.

First rank Boyce, James K., and Robert E. Evenson. National and International Agricultural Research and Extension Programs. New York; Agricultural Development Council, Inc., 1975. 229p.

Third Brada, Josef C., and Kar-Eugen Wadekin, eds. Socialist Agriculture in Crisis: Organizational Response to Failing Performance. Boulder, Colo.; Westview Press, 1987. 450p.

Third Bradnock, R.W., and M. Walker. Agricultural Change in South Asia. London; John Murray, 1984. 64p.

Second Brake, J.R., ed. Emerging and Projected Trends Likely to Influence the Structure of Midwest Agriculture, 1970–1985. Iowa City; University of Iowa, 1970. 126p. (Iowa Agricultural Law Center, Monograph 11)

Second Brandow, George E. Interrelations Among Demands for Control of Market Supply. University Park; Pennsylvania Agric. Experiment Station, 1961. 124p. (Penna. State Agric. Exp. Station Bull. No. 380) An Interregional Publication for the State Agricultural Experiment Stations. Q

Third Branson, Robert E., and Douglas G. Norvell. Introduction to Agricultural Marketing. New York; McGraw-Hill Book Company, 1983. 544p.

Third Bray, Francesca. The Rice Economies: Technology and Development in Asian Societies. Oxford and New York; Blackwell, 1986. 254p.

Second Braybrooke, D., and C.E. Lindblom. A Strategy of Decision: Policy Evaluation as a Social Process. New York; Free Press, 1963. 268p. (Paper ed. 1970.)

Second Breimyer, H.F. Economics of the Product Markets of Agriculture. Ames; Iowa State University Press, 1976. 208p.

First rank Bressler, Raymond G., Jr., and R. A. King. Markets, Prices, and Interregional Trade. New York; Wiley, 1970. 426p. (Reprinted Raleigh, N.C.; Norman-Weathers Print. Co., 1978.)

Third Briggs, V.M., Jr. Chicanos and Rural Poverty. Baltimore; Johns Hopkins University Press, 1973. 81p.

Third Brody, A., and A. P. Carter, eds. Input-Output Techniques. Amsterdam; North Holland, 1972. 600p.

First rank Bromley, D. W. ed. Natural Resource Economics: Policy Problems and Contemporary Analysis. Hingham, Mass.; Kluwer-Nijhoff, 1986. 234p.

Second Brower, David J., and Daniel S. Carol, eds. Managing Land-Use Conflicts: Case Studies in Special Area Management. Durham, N. C.; Duke University Press, 1987. 368p.

Second Brown, David L., et al., eds. Rural Economic Development in the 1980's:

Preparing for the Future. Washington, D.C.; U.S. Department of Agriculture, 1988. 399p. (U.S.D.A. Economic Research Service, Rural Development Research Report No. 69.)

First rank — Brown, David L., and John M. Wardwell, eds. New Directions in Urban-Rural Migration: The Population Turnaround in Rural America. Academic Press, Inc., 1980. 412p.

Second — Brown, Lester R. Man, Land and Food: Looking Ahead at World Food Needs. New York; Ayer Company Publ., Inc., 1976. 153pp. (Reprint of 1963 ed.)

First rank — Brown, Lester R. Seeds of Change: The Green Revolution and Development in the 1970's. New York; Praeger for the Organization of Economic Cooperation and Development, 1970. 205p.

Second — Brown, Murray. On the Theory and Measurement of Technical Change. Cambridge; At the University Press, 1968. 214p.

Second — Brown, Murray, ed. The Theory and Empirical Analysis of Production. New York; Columbia University Press, for the National Bureau of Economic Research, 1967. 515p.

Second — Browne, William P. and Don F. Hadwiger. World Food Policies: Toward Agricultural Interdependence. Boulder, Colo.; Lynne Rienner Publ., 1986. 222p.

Third — Browning, Frank. The Vanishing Land: The Corporate Theft of America. New York; Harper and Row, 1975. 119p.

Second — Brunner, Edmund. The Growth of a Science—A Half Century of Rural Sociological Research in the United States. New York; Harper and Brothers, 1957. 171p.

Third — Buckett, M. Introduction to Farm Organization and Management. 2d ed. Oxford and New York; Pergamon Press, Inc., 1988. 338p. (1st ed., 1981, 280p.)

Second — Buckwell, Allan, David Harvey, Kenneth Thomson, and Kevin Parton. The Costs of the Common Agricultural Policy. London; Croom Helm, 1982. 184p.

Third — Budd, E.C., ed. Inequality and Poverty. New York; Norton, 1967. 217p.

Third — Burbach, Roger, and Patricia Flynn. Agribusiness in the Americas. New York; Monthly Review Press; North American Congress on Latin America, 1980. 314p.

Second — Burch, William R., Neil Cheek, and Lee Taylor, eds. Social Behavior, Natural Resources, and the Environment. New York; Harper and Row, 1972. 374p.

Second — Burdge, Rabel J., R. Hogan, C. Srihakim, and J. Donnermeyer. A Social Science Bibliography of Leisure and Recreation Research. Lexington, KY; Dept. of Sociology, University of Kentucky, 1975.

Second — Burmeister, Larry L. Research, Realpolitik, and Development in Korea: The State and the Green Revolution. Boulder, Colo.; Westview Press, 1988. 200p.

Third — Burns, James MacGregor. Leadership. New York; Harper and Row, 1978. 530p.

Third — Burns, Jim, J. McInerhey, and A. Swinbank, eds. The Food Industry: Economics and Policies. London; Heinemann, 1983. 307p.

Third — Burton, John E., Jr., and David L. Rogers. A Model for Evaluating Development Programs. Ames; Iowa State University, North Central Regional Center for Rural Development, 1976.

Third Busch, Lawrence, and William B. Lacy. Science, Agriculture, and the Politics of Research. Boulder, Colo.; Westview Press, 1983. 303p.

Second Buse, R. C., and D. W. Bromley. Applied Economics: Resource Allocation in Rural America. Ames; Iowa State University Press, 1975. 623p.

Second Butler, Lorna M., and Robert E. Howell. Coping With Growth. Corvallis; Western Rural Development Center, Oregon State University, 1980.

First rank Buttel, Frederick H., and Howard Newby, eds. The Rural Sociology of the Advanced Societies: Critical Perspectives. Montclair, N.J.; Allanheld, Osmun and Co., 1980. 529p.

Third Butterwick, M., and E. N. Rolfe. Food, Farming, and the Common Market. London; Oxford University Press, 1968. 259p.

C

Second Cairncross, A.K. Factors in Economic Development. London; Allen and Unwin, 1962. 346p.

Second Caldwell, Bruce. Beyond Positivism: Economic Methodology in the Twentieth Century. London and Boston; Allen and Unwin, 1982. 277p.

Third Caldwell, John C. African Rural-Urban Migration: The Movement to Ghana's Towns. New York; Columbia University Press, 1969. 257p.

Third Caliendo, M. A. Nutrition and the World Food Crisis. New York; Macmillan, 1979. 368p.

Second Calkins, Peter H., and Dennis D. Dipietre. Farm Business Management: Decisions in a Changing Environment. New York; Macmillan Publ. Co.; and London; Collier Macmillan Publ., 1983. 442p.

Second Campbell, Angus, P. Converse, and W. Rodgers. The Quality of American Life: Perceptions, Evaluations, and Satisfactions. New York; Russell Sage Foundation, 1976. 583p.

Second Campbell, Keith O. Food for the Future: How Agriculture Can Meet the Challenge. Lincoln; University of Nebraska Press, 1979. 178p.

Second Cancian, Frank. Change and Uncertainty in a Peasant Community: The Maya Corn Farmers of Zinacantan. Stanford, Calif.; Stanford University Press, 1972. 208p.

Third Capalbo, Susan M. and John M. Antle, eds. Agricultural Productivity: Measurement and Explanation. Washington, D. C.; Resources for the Future; Distributed by Baltimore; Johns Hopkins University Press. 1988. 404p.

Third Cardiff, John. Farming and the Computer. Seattle, Wash.; Group Four Publ., Inc., 1985. 231p.

Second Carlson, Sune. A Study on the Pure Theory of Production. Clifton, N.J.; Augustus M. Kelley, 1956. 128p. (Reprint of 1939 ed.)

Third Carr, Marilyn, ed. The AT Reader: Theory and Practice in Appropriate Technology. Croton-on-Hudson, New York; Intermediate Technology Development Group of North America, 1985. 486 p.

Second Carrier, Else H. Water and Grass: Study in the Pastoral Economy of Southern Europe. New York; AMS Press, Inc., 1980. 434p. (Reprint of 1932 ed.)

Third Carruthers, I. D., ed. Aid for the Development of Irrigation. Paris; Organization for Economic Cooperation and Development, 1983. 166p.

Third Carruthers. I. D., and C. Clark. The Economics of Irrigation. 3d ed.; Liverpool Univ. Press, 1981. 300p.

First rank Carson, Rachel. Silent Spring. Greenwich, Conn; Fawcett; and Boston;

Houghton-Mifflin, 1962. 368p. (Reprinted by New York; Ballantine Books, 1982.)

Second Carter, A. P., and A. Brody, eds. Applications of Input-Output Analysis. Amsterdam; North-Holland, 1972. 2 vols.

Second Carter, Harold O., George M. Briggs, John R. Goss, Maurice L. Peterson, David W. Robinson, Seymour D. Van Gundy, Pran Vohra, and James G. Youde. A Hungry World: The Challenge to Agriculture. Berkeley; University of California-Davis; Division of Agricultural Sciences, 1974. 303p. Q

Second Casavant, Kenneth, and Craig Infanger. Economics and Agricultural Management: An Introduction. Reston, Virg.; Reston Publishing Co., 1984. 290p.

Second Casley, Dennis J. Data Collection in Developing Countries. 2d ed. Oxford and New York; Clarendon Press, 1987. 225p. (1st ed., 1981, 244p.)

Third Casley, Dennis J. and Kumar Krishna. Project Monitoring and Evaluation in Agriculture. Baltimore; Johns Hopkins University Press, 1987. 159p.

Third Castells, Manuel. The City and the Grassroots. Berkeley; University of California Press, 1983. 450p.

Second Castle, Emery N., and K. Hemmi, eds. U.S.-Japanese Agricultural Trade Relations. Baltimore; Johns Hopkins University Press; and Washington, D.C.; Resources for the Future, 1982. 436p.

Second Castle, Emery N., Manning H. Becker, and A. Gene Nelson. Farm Business Management. 3d ed. Macmillan Publ. Co., Inc., 1986. 456p.

Third Caudill, Harry M. My Land is Dying. New York; E. P. Dutton and Co., 1971. 144 p.

Second Caudill, Harry M. Night Comes to the Cumberlands: A Biography of a Depressed Area. Boston; Little, Brown, 1962. 394p.

Second Caves, Richard E. American Industry: Structure, Conduct, Performance. 6th ed. Englewood Cliffs, N.J.; Prentice-Hall, 1987. 124p. (1st ed., 1964, 120p.)

Third Cernea, M. M., ed. Putting People First: Sociological Variables in Rural Development. New York; Oxford University Press for the World Bank, 1985. 430p.

Second Chakravarty, S. Capital and Development Planning. Cambridge, Mass.; MIT Press, 1969. 344p.

Third Chambers, Jonathan D., and G. E. Mingay. The Agricultural Revolution, 1750–1880. London; B. T. Batsford, 1966. 222p.

Third Chambers, Robert. Rural Development: Putting the Last First, London and New York; Longman, 1983. 246p.

Third Chao, Kang. Man and Land in Chinese History: An Economic Analysis. Stanford, Calif.; Stanford University Press, 1984. 268p.

Third Chao, Kang. Agricultural Production in Communist China, 1945–1965. Madison; University of Wisconsin Press, 1970. 374p.

Third Chapman, Duane. Energy Resources and Energy Corporations. Ithaca, N.Y.; Cornell University Press, 1983. 365p.

First rank Chayanov, A. V. On the Theory of Peasant Economy. (Translation of his Peasant Farm Organization; Moscow; Cooperative Publ. House, 1925.) Transl. D. Thorner, B. Kerblay, and R. E. F. Smith, with a forword by Teodor Shanin. Homewood, Ill.; Richard D. Irwin, 1966. 317p. (Reprinted by Madison; University of Wisconsin Press, 1986.)

Third	Chazan, Naomi, and Timothy M. Shaw, eds. Coping with Africa's Food Crisis. Boulder, Colo.; L. Reinner, 1988. 250p.
Third	Checkoway, Barry, ed. Strategic Perspectives on Planning Practice. Lexington, Mass.; Lexington Books, 1986. 278p.
Second	Cheek, Neil H., and William R. Burch, Jr. The Social Organization of Leisure in Human Society. New York; Harper and Row, 1976. 283p.
Third	Chekki, Dan A., ed. Community Development: Theory and Method of Planned Change. New Delhi, India; Vikas Press, 1979. 258p.
Second	Chenery, Hollis, ed. Studies in Development Planning. Cambridge, Mass.; Harvard University Press, 1971. 422p.
First rank	Chenery, Hollis, et al. Redistribution With Growth: Policies to Improve Income Distribution in Developing Countries in the Context of Economic Growth. Oxford, Eng.; published for World Bank and Institute of Development Studies, University of Sussex, by Oxford University Press, 1974. 304p.
Third	Chenery, Hollis. Transitional Growth and World Industrialization; Nobel Symposium on the International Allocation of Economic Activity. Stockholm, 1976.
First rank	Chenery, Hollis. Structural Change and Development Policy. Oxford University Press for the World Bank, 1979. 526p.
Second	Chenery, Hollis, and T. N. Srinivasa, eds. Handbook of Development Economics. Amsterdam and New York; North-Holland Publ., 1988–89. 2 vols. (Handbooks in Economics, Vol. 9)
Second	Chenery, Hollis, and M. Syrquin. Patterns of Development, 1950–1970. London; Oxford University Press for the World Bank, 1975. 234p.
First rank	Cheung, Steven N. Theory of Share Tenancy: With Special Application to Asian Agriculture and the First Phase of Taiwan Land Reform. University of Chicago Press, 1969. 188p.
First rank	Chisholm, Anthony H., and Rodney Tyers, eds. Food Security: Theory, Policy and Perspectives from Asia and the Pacific Rim. Lexington, Mass.; Lexington Books, 1982. 359p.
Second	Chou, Marilyn, et al. World Food Prospects and Agriculture Potential. New York; Praeger Publ., 1977. 336p.
Third	Christ, C., et al., eds. Measurement in Economics: Studies in Mathematical Economics and Econometrics in Memory of Yehuda Greenfeld. Stanford, Calif.; Stanford University Press, 1963. 319p.
First rank	Christenson, James A., and Jerry W. Robinson, Jr., eds. Community Development in America. Ames; Iowa State University Press, 1980. 245p.
Second	Christenson, James A., and Jerry W. Robinson, Jr., eds. Community Development in Perspective. Ames; Iowa State University Press, 1989. 398p.
Second	Churchman, C. W. The Systems Approach. New York; Dell Publ. Co., 1968. (Revised and updated in 1979, 243p.)
Second	Ciriacy-Wantrup, S. V. Resource Conservation: Economics and Policies. 3d ed. Berkeley; University of California Press, 1968. 395p. (1st ed., 1952.) AAEA Classic
Third	Clairmonte, Frederick, and John Cavanagh. The World in Their Web: Dynamics of Textile Multinationals. London; Zed Pr.; and Westport, Conn; L. Hill, 1981. 278p.
First rank	Clark, Colin. The Conditions of Economic Progress. London; Macmillan, 3d ed., 1957. 720p. (1st ed., 1940. 504p.)

Second Clark, Colin, and M. Haswell. The Economics of Subsistence Agriculture. 4th ed. London; Macmillan; New York; St. Martin's Press, 1970. 267p. (1st ed., 1964. 218p.)

Second Clark, Colin W. Bioeconomic Modelling and Fisheries Management. New York; Wiley, 1985. 291p.

Third Clark, Kenneth, and Jeanette Hopkins. A Relevant War Against Poverty: A Study of Community Action Programs and Observable Social Change. New York; Harper and Row, 1969. 275p.

Second Clark, T.N. ed. Community Structure and Decision-Making: Comparative Analyses. San Francisco; Chandler, 1968. 498p.

Second Clawson, Marion. America's Land and Its Uses. Baltimore; Johns Hopkins University Press for Resources for the Future, 1972. 166p.

Second Clawson, Marion. Policy Directions for U. S. Agriculture: Long Range Choices in Farming and Rural Living. Baltimore; John Hopkins University Press, 1968. 398p.

Second Clawson, Marion, and J. L. Knetsch. Economics of Outdoor Recreation. Baltimore; Johns Hopkins University Press for Resources for the Future, 1966. 328p. (Reprinted in 1971.)

Third Clay, E.J., and B. B. Schaffer, eds. Room for Manoeuvre: An Exploration of Public Policy Planning in Agricultural and Rural Development. Rutherford, N.J.; Fairleigh Dickinson University Press, 1984. 209p.

Third Cleave, John H. African Farmers: Labor Use in the Development of Smallholder Agriculture. New York; Praeger Publishers, 1974. 253p.

Third Cline, W. R. Economic Consequences of a Land Reform in Brazil. Amsterdam; North-Holland Publ, 1970. 213p.

Third Cline, W.R., and A. Berry. Farm Size, Productivity and Technical Change. Washington,D.C.; International Bank for Rural Development, 1976.

Second Cobia, David W., ed. Cooperatives in Agriculture. Englewood Cliffs, N.J.; Prentice Hall, 1989. 445p.

Third Cochrane, J. L., and M. Zelany, eds. Multiple Criteria Decision Making. Columbia; University of South Carolina Press, 1973. 816p.

First rank Cochrane, Willard W. The Development of American Agriculture: An Historical Analysis. Minneapolis; University of Minnesota Press, 1979. 464p. Q

First rank Cochrane, Willard W. Farm Prices, Myth and Reality. Minneapolis; University of Minnesota Press, 1958. 189p. AAEA Classic

Second Cochrane, Willard W. The World Food Problem, A Guardedly Optimistic View. New York; Thomas Y. Crowell Company, Inc., 1969. 331p.

Second Cochrane, Willard W., and Mary E. Ryan. American Farm Policy 1948–1973. Minneapolis; University of Minnesota Press, 1976. 431p. Q

Second Cohen, Morris R., and Ernest Nagel. An Introduction to Logic and Scientific Method. New York; Harcourt, Brace and Co., 1934. 467p. (Reissued 1962)

Third Cohen, Ronald, ed. Satisfying Africa's Food Needs: Food Production and Commercialization in African Agriculture. Boulder, Colo.; Lynne Rienner Publ., 1988. 244p.

Second Coleman, James S. Community Conflict. New York; Free Press, 1957. 28p.

Third Collins, Joseph, Frances M. Lappe, and Nick Allen. Nicaragua: What Difference Could a Revolution Make?. Grove Press, 1986. 192p.

Second Collins, N.R., and L.E. Preston. Concentration and Price-Cost Margins in Manufacturing Industries. Berkeley; University of California Press, 1968. 163p.

Third Collins, Randall. Conflict Sociology: Toward an Explanatory Science. New York; Academic Press, 1975. 584 p.

Second Collinson, M.P. Farm Management in Peasant Agriculture: A Handbook for Rural Development Planning in Africa. New York; Praeger, 1972. 444p. (Reprinted Boulder, Colo.; Westview Press, 1983, 454p.)

Third Colyer, Dale, and George Irwin. Beef, Pork and Feed Grains in the Cornbelt: Supply Response and Resource Adjustments. Columbia; Missouri Agr. Experiment Station, 1967. 113p. (Missouri Agricultural Experiment Station Research Bulletin No. 921) (North Central Regional Publ.) Q

Third Commins, S. K., M. F. Lofchie, and R. Payne. Africa's Agrarian Crisis: The Roots of Famine. Boulder, Colo.; L. Rienner Publishing, 1986. 237p.

First rank Commons, J. R. The Legal Foundations of Capitalism. New York; Macmillan, 1924. 394p. (Reissued: Madison; Univ. of Wisconsin Press, 1959.)

First rank Commons, J.R. Institutional Economics: Its Place in Political Economy. New York; Macmillan, 1934. 921p. (Reissued: Madison; Univ. of Wisconsin Press, 1959.)

Third Comstock, Gary, ed. Is There A Moral Obligation to Save the Family Farm? 1st ed. Ames; Iowa State University Press, 1987. 427p.

Third Connor, John, M., Richard T. Rogers, Bruce W. Marion, and Willard F. Mueller. The Food Manufacturing Industries: Structure, Strategies, Performance and Policies. Lexington, Mass.; Lexington Books, 1985. 474p. Q

Third Conover, W. J. Practical Nonparametric Statistics. 2d ed. New York; Wiley, 1980. 493 p.

Third Cook, Paul and C. Kirkpatrick, eds. Privatisation in Less Developed Countries. Brighton, Eng.; Wheatsheaf Book; and New York; St. Martin's Press, 1988. 315p.

Third Coombs, P.H., and M. Ahmed. Attacking Rural Poverty; How Nonformal Education Can Help. International Council for Educational Development for the World Bank. Baltimore; Johns Hopkins University Press, 1974. 292p.

Second Coppedge, R.O., and C.G. Davis, eds. Rural Poverty and the Policy Crisis. Ames; Iowa State University Press, 1977. 220p.

Second Cosby, Arthur B. and William G. Howard. Residential Preferences in America: The Growing Desire for Rural Life. Washington, D.C.; Economics, Statistics, and Cooperatives Service, USDA, 1976. (Rural Development Seminar Series)

Third Cosby, Arthur B., and Ivan Charner, eds. Education and Work in Rural America: The Social Content of Early Career Decision and Achievement. College Station, Texas, Department of Rural Sociology, Texas A & M University, 1978. 219p.

Second Coward, E. Walter, Jr., ed. Irrigation and Agricultural Development in Asia: Perspectives from the Social Sciences. Ithaca, N.Y.; Cornell University Press, 1980. 369p.

Second Coward, Raymond T. and William M. Smith, Jr., eds. The Family in Rural Society. Boulder, Colo.; Westview Press, 1981. 238p.

Third	Cowling, K., David Metcalf and A. J. Rayner. Resource Structure of Agriculture: An Economic Analysis. New York, Oxford; Pergamon Press, Incorporated, 1970. 248p.
Third	Cox, Fred M., John L. Erlich, Jack Rothman, and John E. Tropman, eds. Strategies of Community Organization: A Book of Readings. 3d ed. Itasca, Ill.; Peacock, 1979. 526p. (1st ed., 1974, 393p.)
Second	Cramer, Gail L. and Clarence W. Jensen. Agricultural Economics and Agribusiness. 4th ed. New York; John Wiley and Sons, Inc., 1988. 461p. (1st ed., 1979. 440p.) Q
Second	Crosson, Pierre R. Economic Growth in Malaysia: Projections of Gross National Product and of Production, Consumption, and Net Imports of Agricultural Commodities. Washington, D.C.; National Planning Association, Center for Development Planning, 1966. 188p.
First rank	Crosson, Pierre R., ed. The Cropland Crisis—Myth or Reality? Baltimore; Johns Hopkins University Press for Resources for the Future, 1982. 276p.
Second	Crosson, Pierre R. Productivity Effects of Cropland Erosion in the United States. Washington, D.C.; Resources for the Future, 1983. 103p. Q
First rank	Crosson, Pierre R., and S. Brubaker. Resource and Environmental Effects of U. S. Agriculture. Washington, D.C.; Resources for the Future, 1982. 255p.
Second	Crosson, Pierre R., and Kenneth D. Frederick. The World Food Situation: Resource and Environmental Issues in the Developing Countries and the United States. Washington, D.C.; Resources for the Future, Inc., 1977. 230p.
Third	Cruz de Schlesinger, L. and L. J. Ruiz. Mercadeo de Arroz en Colombia. Bogotá; Centro de Estudios sobre Desarrollo Económico, 1967.
Second	Csaki, Csaba. Simulation and Systems Analysis in Agriculture. (Translation of his Szimeilacio Alkalmazasa a Mezogazdasagban, revised and enlarged.) Amsterdam and New York; Elsevier Science Publ. Co., 1985. 262p.
Second	Cukierman, A. Inflation, Stagflation, Relative Prices, and Imperfect Information. New York; Cambridge University Press, 1984. 202p.
Third	Cullen, Matthew, and Sharon Woolery, eds. Second World Congress on Land Policy. Boston, Mass.; Oelgeschager, Gunn and Hain, Inc. in association with Lincoln Institute of Land Policy, 1985. 320p.
Second	Currie, J. M. The Economic Theory of Agricultural Land Tenure. Cambridge University Press, 1981. 194p.
Third	Curtis, Donald, Michael Hubbard, and Andrew Shepherd. Preventing Famine: Policies and Prospects for Africa. London and New York; Routledge, 1988. 250p.
Second	Cyert, R. M., and J. G. March. A Behavioral Theory of the Firm. Englewood Cliffs, N.J.; Prentice-Hall, 1963. 332p.

D

Third	Dahl, Dale C., and J. M. Hammond. Market and Price Analysis: The Agricultural Industries. New York; McGraw-Hill, 1977. 323p.
Third	Dahl, Robert A. After the Revolution: Authority in a Good Society. New Haven; Yale University Press, 1970. 171p.
Third	Dahl, Robert A., and Charles E. Lindblom. Politics, Economics and Welfare: Planning and Politico-Economic Systems Resolved into Basic So-

cial Processes. Chicago; University of Chicago Press, 1953. 557p. (Reprinted in 1976.)

Second Dahlberg, Kenneth A. Beyond the Green Revolution: The Ecology and Politics of Global Agricultural Development. New York; Plenum Press, 1979. 256p.

Third Dalrymple, Dana G. Development and Spread of High-Yielding Wheat Varieties in Developing Countries. Washington, D.C.; Bureau of Science and Technology, Agency for International Development, 1986. 99p.

Third Dalton, George, ed. Economic Development and Social Change: The Modernization of Village Communities. New York; Natural History Press, 1971. 664p. (American Museum Sourcebooks in Anthropology)

First rank Dams, T. and K. Hunt, eds. Decision Making and Agriculture. Oxford; Agricultural Economic Institute for International Association of Agricultural Economists; Lincoln; University of Nebraska Press, 1977. 603p.

Third Danbom, David B. The Resisted Revolution: Urban America and the Industrialization of Agriculture, 1900–1930. Ames; Iowa State University Press, 1979. 195p.

Third Danda, Ajit K., ed. Studies on Rural Development: Experiences and Issues. New Delhi; Inter-India Publications, 1984. 107p.

Third Daniel, Cletus E. Bitter Harvest: A History of California Farmworkers, 1870–1941. Ithaca, N.Y.; Cornell University Press, 1981. 368p.

Third Darrow, K., K. Keller, and R. Pam. Appropriate Technology Sourcebook: For Tools and Techniques That Use Local Skills, Local Resources and Renewable Sources of Energy, Vol. 2. Stanford, Calif; Volunteers in Asia, 1981.

Third Dasgupta, Ajit K. Agriculture and Economic Development in India. New Dehli; Associated Publishing House, 1973. 117p.

Third Dauber, Roslyn, and Melinda Cain, eds. Women and Technological Change In Developing Countries. Boulder, Colo.; Westview Press for American Association for the Advancement of Science, 1981. 266p.

Second Davidson, Donald A. Land Evaluation. Van Nostrand Reinhold Co., Inc., 1986. 400p.

Third Davidson, J.R., and H.W. Ottoson, eds. Transportation Problems and Policies in the Trans-Missouri West. Lincoln; University of Nebraska Press, 1967. 377p.

Second Davis, L. E. and D. C. North. Institutional Change and American Economic Growth. Cambridge; Cambridge University Press, 1971. 282p.

Third Davis, Ted J., and Isabella A. Schirmer, eds. Sustainability Issues in Agricultural Development: Proceedings of the Seventh Agricultural Sector Symposium. Washington, D.C.; World Bank, 1987. 382p.

Third Dawson, Andrew H. The Land Problem in the Developed Economy. New York; St. Martin's Press, 1984. 280p.

Third Dawson, O. L. Communist China's Agriculture: Its Development and Future Potential. New York; Praeger Publ., 1970. 326p.

First rank Day, R. H., and A. Cigno, eds. Modelling Economic Change: The Recursive Programming Approach. Amsterdam; North-Holland Publ. Co.; and New York; Elsevier, 1978. 447p.

Second Day, R. H., and T. Groves, eds. Adaptive Economic Models: Proceedings of a Symposium Conducted by the Mathematical Research Center. New York; Academic Press, 1975. 581p.

Second De Datta, S. K., et al. A Handbook on the Methodology for an Integrated

Experiment: Survey on Rice Yield Constraints. Los Banos; International Rice Research Institute, 1978. 59p.

Third — de Haen, Hartwig, Glenn L. Johnson, and Stefan Tangermann, eds. Agriculture and International Relations: Analysis and Policy; Essays in Memory of Theodor Heidhus. New York; St. Martin's Press, 1985. 306p.

First rank — de Janvry, Alain. The Agrarian Question and Reformism in Latin America. Baltimore; Johns Hopkins University Press, 1981. 311p.

First rank — de Janvry, Alain, and Jean-Jacques Dethier. Technological Innovation in Agriculture: The Political Economy of Its Rate and Basis. Washington, D.C.; World Bank, 1985. 90 p. (CGIAR Study Paper no. 1)

Second — de Janvry, Alain, and K. Subbarao. Agricultural Price Policy and Income Distribution in India. Dehli; Oxford University Press, 1986. 113p.

Third — De Wilde, John C. Agriculture, Marketing and Pricing in Sub-Saharan Africa. Los Angeles, Calif.; African Studies Association, 1984. 129p.

Third — De Wilde, John C. Experiences with Agricultural Development in Tropical Africa. Vol. 1. The Synthesis. Vol. 2. The Case Studies. Baltimore; Johns Hopkins University Press, 1967. 264p.

Second — Dean, Gerald W., and Norman R. Collins. World Trade in Fresh Oranges: An Analysis of the Effect of European Economic Community Tariff Policies. Berkeley; University of California, Division of Agricultural Sciences, 1967. 70p. (Giannini Foundation Monograph 18) Q

Second — Dean, J. Managerial Economics. Englewood Cliffs, N. J.; Prentice-Hall, 1951. 621p.

Second — Deaton, Angus and John Muellbauer. Economics and Consumer Behavior. Cambridge University Press, 1980. 450p. (Reprinted with corrections in 1983.)

Second — Deaton, Brady J. Industrialization of Rural Areas: Recent Trends and the Social and Economic Consequences. Blacksburg, Va.; Dept. of Agric. Economics, Virginia Polytechnic Institute and State University.

Third — Debertin, David L. Agricultural Production Economics. New York; Macmillan, 1986. 366p.

Third — Dejene, Alemneh. Peasants, Agrarian Socialism and Rural Development in Ethiopia. Boulder, Colo.; Westview, 1986. 140p.

Third — Dent, J. B., S. R. Harrison, and K. B. Woodford. Farm Planning with Linear Programming: Concepts and Practice. Butterworth, 1986. 209p.

Third — Dernberger, R. F., ed. China's Development Experience in Comparative Perspective. Cambridge, Mass.; Harvard University Press, 1980. 341p.

Third — Desai, A.R., ed. Agrarian Struggles in India after Independence. Oxford University Press, 1986. 653p.

Third — Desai, Meghnad J., S. H. Rudolph, and A. Rudra, eds. Agrarian Power and Agricultural Productivity in South Asia. Berkeley; University of California Press, 1984. 384p.

Third — Dewan, M. L. Agriculture and Rural Development in India: A Case Study on the Dignity of Labour. New Delhi, India; Concept, 1982. 240p.

Second — Dewey, J. Logic: The Theory of Inquiry. New York; Holt, 1938. 546p.

First rank — Dillman, Don A., and Daryl J. Hobbs, eds. Rural Society in the U.S.: Issues for the 1980's. Boulder, Colo.; Westview Press, 1982. 437p. (Rural Studies Series of the Rural Sociological Society)

First rank — Dillman, Don A. Mail and Telephone Surveys: The Total Design Method. New York; Wiley Interscience Publ., 1978. 325p.

First rank — Dillon, John L, and Jock R. Anderson. The Analysis of Response in Crop and Livestock Production. 3d ed. Oxford and New York; Pergamon Press, 1990. 251p. (1st and 2d eds. by Dillon, 1968 and 1977. 135p. and 213p.)

First rank Di Marco, L. E., ed. International Economics and Development: Essays in Honor of Raul Prebisch. New York; Academic Press, 1972. 515p.

Third Dinham, Barbara, and Colin Hines. Agribusiness in Africa. London; Earth Resources Research, 1983. 224p. (Reprinted by Trenton, N.J.; Africa World Press, 1984).

Third Dixey, Roger N., ed. International Explorations of Agricultural Economics: A Tribute to the Inspiration of Leonard Knight Elmhirst. Ames; Iowa State University Press, 1964. 306p.

Second Dobb, Maurice H. Papers on Capitalism, Development, and Planning. New York; International Publishers; and London; Routledge and K. Paul, 1967. 274p.

Third Dobb, Maurice H. Theories of Value and Distribution since Adam Smith: Ideology and Economic Theory. Cambridge, Eng.; Cambridge University Press, 1973. 295 p.

Third Dobyns, H.F., P.L. Doughty and H.D. Lasswell, eds. Peasants, Power and Applied Social Change: Vicos as a Model. Beverly Hills, California; Sage Publications, 1971. 237p.

Second Doll, John P., V. J. Rhodes, and J. G. West. Economics of Agricultural Production, Markets, and Policy. Homewood, Ill.; Richard D. Irwin, 1968. 557p.

Second Doll, John P., and Frank Orazem. Production Economics: Theory with Applications. 2d ed. New York; Wiley, 1984. 470p.

First rank Domar, E.D. Essays in the Theory of Economic Growth. New York; Oxford University Press, 1957. 272p.

First rank Donald, Gordon, ed.. Credit for Small Farmers in Developing Countries. Boulder, Colo.; Westview Press, 1976. 286p.

Third Dore, R.P. Land Reform in Japan. London, New York: Oxford University Press, 1959. 510p. (American edition: New York; Schocken Books, 1985)

Third Dorfman, Robert, and N.S. Dorfman, eds. Economics of the Environment: Selected Readings. New York; Norton, 1977. 494p. (1st ed., 1972)

First rank Dorfman, Robert, P. A. Samuelson, and R. Solow. Linear Programming and Economic Analysis. New York; McGraw-Hill, 1958. 525p. (Reprinted by New York; Dover Publ., 1987.)

Second Dorfman, Robert. Prices and Markets. Englewood Cliffs, N.J.; Prentice-Hall, 1967. 152p. (3d ed., 1978, 264p.)

First rank Dorner, Peter, ed. Cooperative and Commune: Group Farming in the Economic Development of Agriculture. Madison; University of Wisconsin Press, 1977. 392p.

First rank Dorner, Peter, ed. Land Reform in Latin America: Issues and Cases. Madison, Wisc.; Land Tenure Center, University of Wisconsin, 1971. 276p.

Second Dorner, Peter. Land Reform and Economic Development. Harmondsworth; Penguin Books, 1972. 167p.

Second Douglas, J. Sholto and Robert A. Hart. Forest Farming: Towards a Solution to Problems of World Hunger and Conservation. 2d ed. London; Intermediate Technology Publ., 1984. 207p. (1st ed., London; Watkins, 1976. 197p.)

First rank Douglass, Gordon K., ed. Agricultural Sustainability in a Changing World Order. Boulder, Colo.; Westview Press, 1984. 282p.

Second Dovring, Folke. Land Economics. Boston, Mass.; Breton Publ., 1987. 532p.

Second Downey, W. David and Trocke, John K. Agribusiness Management. McGraw-Hill Book Co., 1980. 480p.

First rank Downs, A. An Economic Theory of Democracy. New York; Harper and Bros, 1957. 310p.

Third Doyle, Jack. Altered Harvest: Agriculture, Genetics, and the Fate of the World's Food Supply. New York, N.Y.; Viking, 1985. 502p.

Third Dregne, Harold E., ed. Arid Lands in Transition. Washington, D.C.; American Association for the Advancement of Science, 1970. 524p. (Publication No. 90 of the American Association for the Advancement of Science)

Second Duft, Kenneth D. Principles of Management in Agribusiness. Reston, Va.; Reston Publ. Co., 1979. 470p.

Third Duggan, William R. An Economic Analysis of Southern African Agriculture. New York; Praeger, 1986. 259 p.

Second Duncan, G. J. Years of Poverty, Years of Plenty: The Changing Economics Fortunes of American Workers and Families. Ann Arbor; University of Michigan, Inst. for Social Research, 1984. 184p.

Second Duncan, Kenneth, Ian Rutledge and Colin Harding, eds. Land and Labour in Latin America: Essays on the Development of Agrarian Capitalism in the Nineteenth and Twentieth Centuries. Cambridge University Press, 1977. 535p.

Third Duncan, Marvin, compilor. Western Water Resources: Coming Problems and the Policy Alternatives. Boulder, Colo.; Westview Press, 1980. 324p.

Third Dunn, E S., Jr. Social Information Processing and Statistical Systems—Change and Reform. New York; Wiley, 1974. 246p.

Second Dunn, P. D. Appropriate Technology: Technology with a Human Face. New York; Schocken Books, 1979. 220p.

Third Dutt, Romesh C. Famines and Land Assessments in India. Repr. of 1900 edition. Delhi; B.R. Publ. Corp., 1986. 322p.

E

Third Eashvaraiah, P. Political Dimension of Land Reforms in India. New Dehli; Ashish, 1985. 136p.

Second Easter, K. W., ed. Irrigation Investment Technology and Management Strategies for Development. Boulder, Colo.; Westview Press, 1986. 270p.

Third Eckholm, Erik. The Dispossessed of the Earth: Land Reform and Sustainable Development. Washington, D.C.; Worldwatch Institute, 1979. 48p.

Third Eder, James. Who Shall Succeed?: Agricultural Development and Social Inequality on a Philippine Frontier. Cambridge University Press, 1982. 256p.

Third Edwards, Allen and Dorothy Jones. Community and Community Development. The Hague, Netherlands; Mouton and Co., 1976. 326p.

Third Edwards, Edgar O., ed. Employment in Developing Nations: Report on a Ford Foundation Study. New York; Columbia University Press, 1974. 428p.

Third Egbert, A. C. Agricultural Sector Planning Models: A Selected Summary and Critique. Washington, D.C.; World Bank, 1978. 59p. (World Bank Staff Working Paper, No. 297.)

Third	Eicher, Carl K., and Doyle C. Baker. Research on Agricultural Development in Sub-Saharan Africa: A Critical Survey. East Lansing; Michigan State University, Dept. of Agricultural Economics, 1982. 335p. (A revision of this work is in progress and will appear in 1992 in vol. 4 of the Lee Martin series: A Survey of Agricultural Economics Literature.)
First rank	Eicher, Carl K., and John M. Staatz, eds. Agricultural Development in the Third World. Baltimore; Johns Hopkins University Press, 1984. 491p.
First rank	Eicher, Carl K., and L. W. Witt, eds. Agriculture in Economic Development. New York; McGraw-Hill, 1964. 415p.
Third	Eisenmenger, R.W. The Dynamics of Growth in New England's Economy, 1870–1964. Middletown, Conn.; Wesleyan University Press, 1967. 201p.
Second	El Ghonemy, M.R., et al. Studies on Agrarian Reform and Rural Poverty. Rome; Food and Agriculture Organization of the United Nations, 1984. 104p.
Third	Ellickson, Robert C., and A. Dan Tarlock. Land Use Controls. Boston; Little, Brown and Co., 1981. 1239p.
Third	Ellis, H. S. and H. C. Wallich, eds. El Desarrollo Economico y America Latina (Economic Development and Latin America). Mexico, BA; Fondo de Cultura Economica, 1960, 1961. English edition—New York; St. Martin's Press, 1961.
Second	Elo, I. J. and Beale, C. L. Natural Resources and Rural Poverty: An Overview. Washington, D.C.; National Center for Food and Agricultural Policy, and Resources for the Future, 1983. various pagings.
Second	Elz, Dieter. Agricultural Marketing Strategy and Pricing Policy. Washington, D.C.; World Bank, 1987. 148p.
First rank	Emerson, R. D., ed. Seasonal Agricultural Labor Markets in the United States. Ames; Iowa State University Press, 1984. 564p.
Third	Enke, S. Economics for Development. Englewood Cliffs, N.J.; Prentice-Hall, 1963. 616p.
Third	Epp, Donald J. and John W. Malone, Jr. Introduction to Agricultural Economics. New York; Macmillan Publ. Co., 1981. 354p.
Third	Esman, Milton J. and Norman T. Uphoff. Local Organization: Intermediaries in Rural Development. Ithaca; Cornell University Press, 1984. 391 p.
Third	Espenshade, Thomas J. and George J. Stolinitz, eds. Technological Prospects and Population Trends. Boulder, Colo; Westview Press, 1987. 211p. (AAAS Selected Symposium No. 103)
Third	Etienne, Gilbert. Food and Poverty: India's Half Won Battle. New Delhi and Newbury Park, Calif.; Sage Publ., 1988. 272p.
Third	Etienne, Gilbert. Rural Development in Asia: Meetings with Peasants. Transl. by Arati Sharma. Rev. ed. New Delhi and Beverly Hills, Calif.; Sage Publications, 1985. 276p.
Third	Evans, H. H., ed. Land Use Allocation: Processes, People, Politics, Professionals. Society of American Foresters, 1981. 298p. (SAF Convention Proceedings Ser.)
Third	Evans, Michael K., and L. R. Klein. The Wharton Econometric Forecasting Model. Philadelphia; University of Pennsylvania Press, 1968. 182p. (Studies in Quantitative Economics, No. 2)
Second	Evenson, Robert Eugene and Yoav Kislev. Agricultural Research and Productivity. New Haven, Conn.; Yale University Press, 1975. 204p.

Third — Ezekiel, Mordecai, and Karl A. Fox. Methods of Correlation and Regression Analysis: Linear and Curvilinear. 3d ed. New York; Wiley, 1959. 548p. AAEA Classic (First published in 1930 as Methods of Correlation and Analysis)

F

Second — Farris, Paul., ed. Future Frontiers in Agricultural Marketing Research. Ames; Iowa State University Press, 1983. 342p.

Second — Fear, Frank A. and Harry K. Schwarzweller, eds. Research in Rural Sociology and Development: Focus on Community, Vol. 2. Greenwich, Conn.; JAI Press, 1985.

Third — Fecer, Gershon. Adoption of Agricultural Innovations in Developing Countries: A Survey. Washington, D.C.; World Bank, 1982. 62p.

Third — Feder, Gershon, et al. Land Policies and Farm Productivity in Thailand. Baltimore; Johns Hopkins University Press, 1988. 165p.

Second — Feeney, David A. The Political Economy of Productivity: Thai Agricultural Development, 1880–1975. Vancouver; University of British Columbia Press, 1981. 238p.

Second — Fennell, Rosemary. The Common Agricultural Policy of the European Community. 2d ed. Oxford; Blackwell Scientific Publications, 1988. 227p. (1st ed. Montclair, N.J.; Allanheld, Osmun, 1979. 243p.)

Third — Ferguson, Charles E. Microeconomic Theory. Homewood, Ill.; R.D. Irwin, 1961. 439p. Later editions written with J. P. Gould. (6th ed., 1986, by Gould and Edward Lazear. 640p.)

Third — Fienberg, S., and A. Zellner. Studies in Bayesian Econometrics and Statistics in Honor of L. J. Savage. Amsterdam; North-Holland, 1975. 676p.

Second — Fienup, D. F. and Riley, H. M. Training Agricultural Economists for Work in International Development. New York; Agricultural Development Council, 1980. 137p.

Third — Finney, Essex E., Jr., ed. Handbook of Transportation and Marketing in Agriculture, Vol. II: Field Crops. Boca Raton, Fla.; CRC Press, 1981. 520p.

Third — Fischer, C. and Associates, eds. Networks and Places: Social Relations in the Urban Setting. New York; Free Press, 1977. 229p.

Third — Fischer, Lewis A. and Phillip E. Uren. The New Hungarian Agriculture. Montreal; McGill-Queen's University Press, 1973. 138p.

Second — Fischer, Stanley, ed. Rational Expectations and Economic Policy. Chicago; University of Chicago Press, 1980. 293p.

Third — Fisher, J. L., and N. Potter. World Prospects for Natural Resources: Some Projections of Demand and Indicators of Supply to the Year 2000. Baltimore; Johns Hopkins University Press, 1964. 73p.

Third — Fisher, Ronald A. The Design of Experiments. 9th ed. New York; Hafner Press, 1971. 248p.

Third — Fishman, G. S. Spectral Methods in Econometrics. Cambridge; Harvard University Press, 1969. 212p.

Second — Fitchen, Janet. Poverty in Rural America: A Case Study. Boulder, Colo.; Westview Press, 1981. 257p.

Third — Fleiss, Joseph L. Statistical Methods for Rates and Proportions. 2d ed. New York; John Wiley and Sons, 1981. 321 p.

Second — Fomby, T., R. C. Hill, and S. R. Johnson. Advanced Econometric Methods. New York; Springer Verlag, 1984. 624p.

Third Food and Agriculture Organization. African Agriculture: The Next 25 Years. Rome; Food and Agriculture Organization, 1986. 5 vols.

Third Food and Agriculture Organization. Agricultural Price Policies: Issues and Proposals. Rome; FAO, 1987. 210p. (FAO Economic and Social Development Series, no. 42.)

Third Food and Agriculture Organization. Bibliography of Food Consumption Surveys. Rome; Food and Agriculture Organization, 1987. 49p. (FAO Food and Nutrition Paper, No. 18, Revision 2)

Second Food and Agriculture Organization. Development Strategies for the Rural Poor. Rome; FAO, 1984. 117p.

Second Food and Agriculture Organization. Economic Accounts for Agriculture: Production and Capital Formation. Rome; 2d issue, 1979. 319p.

Third Food and Agriculture Organization. The Fifth World Food Survey. Rome; Food and Agriculture Organization, 1987. 75p.

Third Food and Agriculture Organization. Food Balance Sheets: 1979–1981 Average. Rome; FAO, 1984. 272p.

Second Food and Agricultural Organization. Provisional Indicative World Plan for Agricultural Development. Rome; FAO, 1970. 3 vols.

Third Food and Agriculture Organization. Review of Food Consumption Surveys 1977: Household Food Consumption By Economic Groups. Rome; FAO, 1979. 2 vols. (FAO Food and Nutrition Paper)

Third Food and Agriculture Organization. World Food Security: Selected Themes and Issues. Rome; FAO, 1985. 108p.

Third Food and Agricultural Organization. Technical Advisory Committee. Sustainable Agricultural Production: Implications for International Agricultural Research. Rome; Food and Agriculture Organization, TAC Secretariat, 1988.

Third Ford, Thomas R., ed. Rural U. S. A: Persistence and Change. Ames; Iowa State University Press, 1978. 255p.

Third Forster, D. Lynn, and Bernard L. Erven. Foundations for Managing the Farm Business. Columbus, Ohio; Grid Publ., 1981. 351p.

Third Fortmann, Louise, and John W. Bruce, eds. Whose Trees? Proprietary Dimensions of Forestry. Boulder, Colo.; Westview Press, 1988. 341p.

Second Fortmann, Louise, and James Riddell. Trees and Tenure: An Annotated Bibliography for Agroforesters and Others. Madison; University of Wisconsin, Land Tenure Center, 1985. 135p.

Second Foster, George M. Traditional Societies and Technological Change. New York; Harper and Row, 1973. 286p.

Second Fox, Karl A., J. K. Sengupta, and E. Thorbecke. The Theory of Quantitative Economic Policy with Applications to Economic Growth and Stabilization. 2d ed. Amsterdam; North-Holland; and New York; American Elsevier, 1973. 517p. (1st ed., Amsterdam; North-Holland, 1966. 517p.) (Studies in Mathematical and Managerial Economics, vol. 5)

Second Fox, Karl A. and Don G. Miles, eds. Systems Economics: Concepts, Models, and Multidisciplinary Perspectives. Ames, Iowa; Iowa State University Press, 1987. 252p.

First rank Fox, Karl A. Econometric Analysis for Public Policy. Ames; Iowa State College Press, 1958. 288p. (Reissued 1977) Q

Third Francioni, Manuel J. El Credito en la Produccion Agraria. Buenos Aires; El Ateneo, 1944. 430p.

Third Francisco, Ronald A., B. A. Laird, and R. D. Laird, eds. Political Economy of Collectivized Agriculture: A Comparative Study of Communist and Non-Communist Systems. Pergamon Press, Inc., 1979. 256p.

Second — Frankel, Francine R. India's Green Revolution: Economic Gains and Political Costs. Princeton University Press, 1971. 232p.

Second — Frederick, K.D. and J.C. Hanson. Water for Western Agriculture. Washington, D.C.; Resources for the Future; and Baltimore; Johns Hopkins University Press, 1982. 241p.

Third — Freivalds, John, ed. Successful Agribusiness Management. Aldershot, Hants, Eng.; Brookfield, Vermont; Gower Publishing Co., 1985. 245p.

Third — Frey, William H. and Alden Speare, Jr. Regional and Metropolitan Growth and Decline in the United States. New York; Russell Sage Foundation; For the National Committee for Research on the 1980 Census, 1988. 586p. (The Population of the United States in the 1980s: A Census Monograph Series.)

First rank — Friedman, M. A Theory of the Consumption Function. Princeton; Princeton University Press, 1957. 243p.

Third — Friedman, Robert, and William Schweke, eds. Expanding the Opportunity to Produce: Revitalizing the American Economy through New Enterprise Development: A Policy Reader. Washington, D.C.; The Corporation for Enterprise Development, 1981. 549p.

Third — Friedmann, D. J., and H. C. Farnsworth. The West German Grain Economy and the Common Market, 1925–1975. Stanford University, Food Research Institute, 1966. 134p.

Second — Fusfeld, Daniel R. Age of the Economist. Glenview, Ill.; Scott, Foresman, 1966. 147p. (4th ed. 1982.)

Third — Furtado, Celso. Analise do Modelo Brasileiro (Analysis of the Brazilian "Model"). 7th ed. Rio de Janeiro; Civilizacao Brasileria, 1982. 122p. (1st ed., 1972)

Third — Futrell, Gene A., ed. Marketing for Farmers. 2d ed. St. Louis, Missouri; Doane Information Services, 1987. 306p. (1st ed., St. Louis, Mo.: Doane-Western, 1982. 288p.)

G

Third — Gabriel, Stephen C., Dean W. Hughes, Michael D. Boehlje, and Peter J. Barry. Financing the Agricultural Sector: Future Challenges and Policy Alternatives. Boulder, Colo.; Westview Press, 1985. 200p.

Second — Galbraith, John K. American Capitalism: The Concept of Countervailing Power. Rev. ed. Cambridge; Houghton Mifflin, 1956. 208p.

Second — Galbraith, John K. Economic Development. Cambridge; Harvard University Press, 1964. 109p.

First rank — Galbraith, John K. The New Industrial State. 4th ed. Boston; Houghton Mifflin, 1985. 438p. (1st ed. 1967, 430p.) AAEA Classic

Second — Galbraith, John K. The Nature of Mass Poverty. Cambridge; Harvard University Press, 1979. 150p.

First rank — Galeski, Boguslaw and Eugene Wilkening, eds. Family Farming in Europe and America. Boulder, Colo.; Westview Press, 1987. 350p.

Third — Garcia-Zama, Jean Claude. Public Participation in Development Planning and Management: Cases from Africa and Asia. Boulder, Colo.; Westview Press, 1985. 264p.

First rank — Gardner, Bruce L. The Governing of Agriculture. Lawrence; Regents Press of Kansas, 1981. 148p.

Second Gardner, Bruce L. Optimal Stockpiling of Grain. Lexington, Mass.; Lexington Books, 1979. 175p. Q

First rank Gardner, Bruce L., ed. U.S. Agricultural Policy: The 1985 Farm Legislation. Washington D.C.; American Enterprises Institute for Public Policy Research, 1985. 385p.

Second Garfinkel, I., and R.H. Haveman. Earnings Capacity, Poverty, and Inequality. New York; Academic Press, 1977. 118p.

Second Gass, Saul I. Linear Programming: Methods and Applications. 5th ed. N.Y.; McGraw-Hill, 1985. 532 p.

Third Gasson, Ruth M. The Economics of Part-time Farming. Harlow, Essex, Eng.; Longman Scientific and Technical; New York; copublished in the U. S. with J. Wiley, 1988. 188p.

First rank George, P. S., and G. A. King. Consumer Demand for Food Commodities in the United States with Projections for 1980. Berkeley; University of California, Agricultural Experiment Station, 1971. 161p. (Giannini Foundation Monograph 26) Q

Second Gersovitz, Mark, Carlos F. Diaz-Alajandro, Gustav Ranis and Mark Rosenzweig. The Theory and Experience of Economic Development: Essays in Honor of Sir W. Arthur Lewis. London; George Allen and Unwin, 1982. 403p.

Third Ghai, Dharam and Smith Lawrence. Agricultural Prices, Policy and Equity in Sub-Saharan Africa. Boulder, Colo.; Lynne Rienner, 1987. 174p.

Third Ghai, Dharam P. and Samir Radwan, eds. Agrarian Policies and Rural Poverty in Africa. Geneva; International Labour Office, 1982. 311p.

Second Ghai, Dharam, Azizur R. Khan, Eddy Lee, and Samir Radwan, eds. Agrarian Systems and Rural Development. New York; Holmes and Meier Publ., Inc., 1979. 375p.

Second Ghatak, Subrata, and Ken Ingersent. Agriculture and Economic Development. Baltimore; Johns Hopkins University Press, 1984. 380p.

Third Ghose, Ajit Kumar, ed. Agrarian Reform in Contemporary Developing Countries. London; Croom Helm, and New York: St. Martin's Press, 1983. 364p.

Third Ghosh, Pradip K., ed. Development Policy and Planning: A Third World Perspective. Westport, Conn.; Greenwood Press, 1984. 626p. (International Development Resource Books, No. 8)

Second Ghosh, Pradip K., ed. Health, Food and Nutrition in Third World Development. Westport, Conn.; Greenwood Press, 1984. 617p. (International Development Resource Books, No. 6)

Third Ghosh, Pradip K., ed. Multi-National Corporations and Third World Development. Westport, Conn.; Greenwood Press, 1984. 437p. (International Development Resource Books, No. 11)

Third Ghosh, Tushar K. Operation Barga and Land Reforms: An Indian Experiment. Delhi, India; B. R. Publ. Corp., 1986. 200p. (Distributed by Apt Bks.)

Third Giersch, H. International Economic Development and Resource Transfer; Workshop 1978. Tubingen; J.C.B. Mohr, 1979. 619p.

Third Gilford, Dorothy M., Glenn L. Nelson, and Linda Ingram, eds. Rural America in Passage: Statistics for Policy. Panel on Statistics for Rural Development Policy, Committee on National Statistics, Assembly of Behavioral and Socal Sciences, National Research Council. Washington, D. C.; National Academy Press, 1981. 592p.

Third	Gillis, Peter and Thomas R. Roach. Lost Initiatives: Canada's Forest Industries, Forest Policy and Forest Conservation. Westport, Conn.; Greenwood Press, 1986. 339p.
Third	Gilmore, Richard. A Poor Harvest: The Clash of Policies and Interests in the Grain Trade. New York; Longman, 1982. 303p.
First rank	Gittinger, J. Price. Economic Analysis of Agricultural Projects. 2d ed. Baltimore; Johns Hopkins University Press for the International Bank for Reconstruction and Development, 1982. 505p.
Second	Gittinger, J. Price, Joanne Leslie and C. Hoisington. Food Policy: Integrating Supply, Distribution, and Consumption. Baltimore; Johns Hopkins University Press, 1987. 567p.
Second	Glaeser, Bernhard, ed. The Green Revolution Revisited. London; Allen Unwin; and New York; St. Martin's Press, 1987. 224p.
Third	Glaser, E. M., H. H. Abelson, and K. N. Garrison. Putting Knowledge to Use: Facilitating the Diffusion of Knowledge and the Implementation of Planned Change. San Francisco; Jossey-Bass, 1983. 636p.
Third	Glenn, John C. Livestock Production in North Africa and the Middle East: Problems and Perspectives. Washington, D.C.; World Bank, 1988. 44p. (World Bank Discussion Paper 39)
Third	Godelier, Maurice. Rationality and Irrationality in Economics. New York; Monthly Review Press, 1975. 326p.
Third	Gold, Gerald. Modern Commodity Futures Trading. 7th rev. ed. New York; Commodity Research Bureau, 1975. 312p. (1st ed., 1959)
Third	Goldberg, Ray A. Agribusiness Coordination: A Systems Approach to the Wheat, Soybean and Florida Orange Economics. Harvard University, Graduate School of Business Administration, 1968. 256p.
Second	Goldberg, Ray A., ed. Research in Domestic and International Agribusiness Management; Research Annual. Vol. 1 (1980) Vol. 9 (1988). Greenwich, Conn.; JAI Press, Incorporated.
Third	Goldenberg, S. Thinking Sociologically. Belmont, Calif.; Wadsworth Publishing Co., 1987. 241p.
First rank	Goldschmidt, Walter R. As You Sow: Three Studies in the Social Consequences of Agribusiness. Glencoe, Ill.; Free Press, 1947. 288p. (Revised ed. Montclair, N.J.; Allanheld, Osmun, 1978. 505p.)
Third	Gomez, O. Hernando and Eduardo D. Wiesner, eds. Lecturas Sobre Desarrollo Economico Colombiano en Honor de Alvaro Lopez Toro. Bogota, Colombia; Fundacion para la Educacion Superior y el Desarrollo, 1974. 624p.
Third	Gonzales, Juan L., Jr. Mexican-American Farm Workers: The California Agricultural Industry. New York; Praeger, 1985. 240p.
Third	Gonzales-Vega, C. The Rural Banking System of the Philippines and CB-IBRD Agricultural Credit Program. Washington, D. C.; World Bank, 1975. 338p. (Operations Evaluation Report: Agricultural Credit Programs Background Paper; 2a)
Third	Goodman, David and Michael Redclift. From Peasant to Proletarian: Capitalist Developments and Agrarian Transitions. New York; St. Martin's Press, Inc., 1982. 244p.
Second	Goreux, Louis-Marie, and A.S. Manne. Multi-Level Planning: Case Studies in Mexico. New York; American Elsevier, 1973. 556p.
Third	Gossling, W. F. Productivity Trends in a Sectoral Macroeconomic Model: A Study of American Agriculture and Supporting Industries, 1919–1964. London; Input-Output Publ. Co., 1972. 296p.

Third	Graaf, J. de V. The Economics of Coffee. Wageningen, The Netherlands; PUDOC, 1986. 294p.
Second	Graaf, J. de V. Theoretical Welfare Economics. London; Cambridge University Press, 1967. 178p.
Third	Graham, Norman A., and Keith L. Edwards. The Caribbean Basin to the Year 2000; Demographic, Economic, and Resource-Use Trends in Seventeen Countries: A Compendium of Statistics and Projections. Boulder, Colo.; Westview Press, 1984. 166p.
Third	Gramlich, Edward M. Benefit-Cost Analysis of Government Programs. Englewood Cliffs, N.J.; Prentice-Hall, 1981. 273p.
Third	Granger, C. W. J., and M. Hatanaka. Spectral Analysis of Economic Time Series. Princeton; Princeton University Press, 1964. 299p.
Third	Gray, Jack and Gordon White, eds. China's New Development Strategy. London; Academic Press, 1982. 341p.
Second	Greenshields, Bruce L., and M.A. Bellamy. Rural Development: Growth and Equity. Oxford; International Association of Agricultural Economists; and Aldershot, Hampshire and Brookfield, Vermont; Gower Publishing Co., 1983. 312p.
Third	Griffen, James M. Energy Economics and Policy. 2d ed. Orlando; Academic Press College Division, 1986. 398p. (1st ed., New York; Academic Press, 1980. 370p.)
First rank	Griffin, Keith. The Political Economy of Agrarian Change: An Essay on the Green Revolution. 2d ed. London; Macmillan, 1979. 268p. (1st ed., Cambridge, Mass.; Harvard University Press, 1974. 264p.)
Third	Grigg, David. Agricultural Systems of the World: An Evolutionary Approach. Cambridge University Press, 1974. 358p.
Second	Grigg, David. Dynamics of Agricultural Change. New York; St. Martin's Press, 1982. 260p.
Second	Grigg, David. Introduction to Agricultural Geography. London and Dover, New Hamp.; Hutchinson Education, 1984. 204p.
First rank	Griliches, Zvi, and Intriligator, M., eds. Handbook of Econometrics. Amsterdam and New York; North Holland Publ., 1983–86. 3 vols. (Handbooks in Economics, Bk. 2)
Third	Grindle, Merilee S. State and Countryside: Development Policy and Agrarian Politics in Latin America. Baltimore, Md.; Johns Hopkins University Press, 1985. 255 p.
Third	Grindle, Merilee S., ed. Politics and Policy Implementation in the Third World. Princeton; Princeton University Press, 1980. 310p.
Second	Gruchy, A. G. Contemporary Economic Thought: The Contributions of Neo-Institutional Economics. Clifton, N.J.; August M. Kelley, 1972, 1974; and London; Macmillan, 1973. 360p.
Second	Gudeman, Stephen. The Demise of a Rural Economy: From Subsistence to Capitalism in a Latin American Village. London and Boston; Routledge and K. Paul, 1978. 176p.
Third	Guillet, D. Agrarian Reform and Peasant Economy in Southern Peru. Columbia; University Missouri Press, 1979. 227p.
Third	Gupta, Avijit. Ecology and Development in the Third World. London, New York; Routledge, 1988. 80p. (Routledge Introductions to Development).
Third	Gusfield, Joseph. Community: A Critical Response. Oxford; Basil Blackwell, and New York; Harper and Row, 1975. 120p. (Reprinted New York; Harper Colophon, 1978)

Third Gutkind, P. C. W. and I. Wallerstein, eds. The Political Economy of Contemporary Africa. 2d ed. Beverly Hills, California; Sage Publ., 1985. 344p. (1st ed. 1976, 318p.)

Third Gutiérrez, A. N. and R. Hertford. Una Evaluación de la Intervención del gobierno en el Mercadeo de Arroz en Colombia. Cali, Colombia; Centro Internacional de Agricultura Tropical, 1974. (CIAT Technical Pamphlet No. 4)

H

Second Hadwiger, Don F. Public Policy and Agricultural Technology: Adversity Despite Achievement. New York; Macmillan, 1987. 300p.

First rank Hadwiger, Don F. The Politics of Agricultural Research. Lincoln; University of Nebraska Press, 1982. 230p.

First rank Hadwiger, Don F. and W. P. Browne, eds. The New Politics of Food. Lexington, Mass.; Lexington Books, 1978. 267p.

Third Haefele, E.T. Representative Government and Environmental Management. Baltimore; Johns Hopkins University Press for Resources for the Future, 1973. 188p.

Second Hagen, E.E. The Economics of Development. 3d ed. Homewood, Ill.; R.D. Irwin; and Georgetown, Ont.; Irwin Dorsey, 1980. 412p. (1st ed., Homewood, Ill.; R.D. Irwin, 1968. 536p.)

Second Hagen, E.E. On the Theory of Social Change: How Economic Growth Begins. Homewood, Ill.; Dorsey Press, 1962. 557p.

Third Hägerstrand, T. Innovation Diffusion As a Spatial Process. Postscript and translation by A Pred. Chicago; University of Chicago Press, 1967. (Originally published in 1953.) 334p.

Third Hahn, David, James Beirlein, Michael Woolverton, and James Niles. Casebook for Agribusiness. Reston, Vir.; Reston Publ. Co., Inc., 1985.

Second Halcrow, Harold G. Agricultural Policy Analysis. New York; McGraw-Hill Book Co., 1984. 564p. Q

Second Halcrow, Harold G. Agricultural Policy of the United States. New York; McGraw-Hill, 1953. 458p.

First rank Halcrow, Harold G. Economics of Agriculture. New York; McGraw-Hill Book Co., 1980. 383p. Q

Second Halcrow, Harold G. Food Policy for America. New York; McGraw-Hill Book Co., 1977. 564p. Q

Second Halcrow, Harold G., Earl O. Heady, and Melvin L. Cotner, eds. Soil Conservation Policies, Institutions, and Incentives. Ankeny, Iowa; Soil Conservation Society of America for North Central Research Committee, 1982. 330p.

Second Halter, A. N., and G. W. Dean. Decisions under Uncertainty with Research Applications. Cincinnati; South-West Publishing, 1971. 266p.

Third Hammig, M. and H. Harris, Jr. Farm and Food Policy; Critical Issues for Southern Agriculture. Clemson, SC; Clemson University Press, 1983. 268p.

Third Handley, J.E. The Agricultural Revolution in Scotland. Glasgow; Burns, 1963. 317p.

Second Haney, Wava G. and Jane B. Knowles, eds. Women and Farming: Changing Roles, Changing Structures. Boulder, Colo.; Westview Press, 1988. 390p.

Third Hanf, Claus H., and Gerhard W. Schiefer, eds. Planning and Decision in Agribusiness: Principles and Experiences, A Case Study Approach to the

Use of Models in Decision Planning. Amsterdam and New York; Elsevier Science Publishing Co., 1983. 373p. (Development in Agricultural Economics, v.1).

Second Hansen, Gary E., ed. Agricultural and Rural Development in Indonesia. Boulder, Colo.; Westview Press, 1981. 312p.

Third Haque, Wahidul, et al. Towards a Theory of Rural Development. Bangkok; United Nations Asian Development Institute, August 1975. 102p.

Second Hardin, Charles M. The Politics of Agriculture. Glencoe, IL.; Interstate Printer and Publ., 1952. 282p.

Third Harl, Neil E. Farm Estate and Business Planning. 9th ed. Niles, Ill.; Century Communications, Inc., 1984. 394p.

Third Harris, Simon, Alan Swinbank, and Guy Wilkinson. The Food and Farm Policies of the European Community. New York; John Wiley and Sons, Inc., 1983. 354p.

Third Harrison, A. J. Economics and Land Use Planning. London; Croom Helm, 1977. 256p.

Third Harriss, John, ed. Rural Development: Theories of Peasant Economy and Agrarian Change: Anatomy of a Peasant Economy. London; Hutchinson, 1982. 409p.

Second Harrod, R. F. Towards a Dynamic Economics: Some Recent Developments of Economic Theory and Their Applications to Policy. London; Macmillan, 1948. 168p. (Reprinted by Greenwood Press, 1980)

Second Harsh, Stephen B., Larry J. Connor, and Gerald D. Schwab. Managing the Farm Business. Englewood Cliffs, N.J.; Prentice-Hall, 1981. 384p. Q

Third Hart, Keith. The Political Economy of West African Agriculture. Cambridge University Press, 1982. 256p.

Third Harvey, Andrew C. The Econometric Analysis of Time Series. Oxford; Philip Allan, 1981. 384p.

Third Harvey, Andrew C. Time Series Models. Oxford; Philip Allan Publishers; and New York; Wiley, 1981. 229p.

Second Hassan, Z. A. and H. B. Huff, eds. Agricultural Sector Models for Policy Analysis. Ottawa; Agriculture Canada, Commodity Markets Analysis Division, Marketing and Economics Branch, 1985. 242p.

Second Hassinger, E.W., and L.R. Whiting, eds. Rural Health Services: Organization, Delivery, and Use. Ames; Iowa State University Press, 1976. 308p.

Second Hathaway, D.E. Agriculture and the GATT: Rewriting the Rules. Washington, D.C.; Institute for International Economics, 1987. 157p.

Second Havens, A. Eugene, with Gregory Hooks, Patrick H. Mooney, and Max J. Pfeffer, eds. Studies in the Transformation of U.S. Agriculture. Boulder, Colo.; Westview Press, 1986. 319p.

Second Hawken, P. The Next Economy. North Ryde, NSW, Australia; Angus and Robertson, 1983. 215p. (Reprinted: New York; Holt, Reinhart and Winston, 1985.)

Third Hayami, Yujiro. Japanese Agriculture Under Siege: The Political Economy of Agricultural Policies. London; Macmillan, New York; St. Martin's Press, 1988. 145p.

First rank Hayami, Yujiro, and Vernon W. Ruttan. Agricultural Development: An International Perspective. Revised and expanded. Baltimore; Johns Hopkins University Press, 1984. 506p. (1st ed., 1971, 367p.) Q AAEA Classic

Second Hayami, Yujiro, Vernon W. Ruttan, and Herman M. Southworth, eds. Agricultural Growth in Japan, Taiwan, Korea and the Philippines. Honolulu; University Press of Hawaii for the East-West Center, 1979. 404p.

Third Hayenga, Marvin, et al. The U.S. Pork Sector: Changing Structure and Organization. Ames; Iowa State University Press, 1985. 172p.

Second Haynes, R. and R. Lanier, eds. Agriculture, Change and Human Values: Proceedings of a Multidisciplinary Conference. 2 vols. Gainesville, Fla.; University of Florida Press, 1982. 1176p.

Second Hazell, Peter, and Roger D. Norton. Mathematical Programming for Economic Analysis in Agriculture. New York; Macmillan, 1986. 432p.

Second Hazell, Peter, Carlos Pomareda, and Alberto Valdes, eds. Crop Insurance for Agricultural Development: Issues and Experience. Baltimore; Johns Hopkins University Press for the International Food Policy Research Institute, 1986. 322p.

Second Hazell, Peter, and A. Roell. Rural Growth Linkages: Household Expenditure Patterns in Malaysia and Nigeria. Washington, D. C.; International Food Policy Research Institute, 1983. 64p. (IFPRI Research Report no. 41)

Second Heady, Earl O. Agricultural Policy under Economic Development. Ames; Iowa State University Press, 1962. 682p. (Reissued 1965)

First rank Heady, Earl O. Economics of Agricultural Production and Resource Use. New York; Prentice-Hall, 1952. 850p. Q AAEA Classic

Second Heady, Earl O., ed. Economic Models and Quantitative Methods for Decisions and Planning in Agriculture. Ames; Iowa State University Press, 1971. 518p.

Second Heady, Earl O., and John Dillon. Agricultural Production Functions. Ames; Iowa State University Press, 1961. 667p.

Third Heady, Earl O., and L. G. Tweeten. Resource Demand and Structure of the Agricultural Industry. Ames; Iowa State University Press, 1963. 515p.

First rank Heady, Earl O., and Larry R. Whiting, eds. Externalities in the Transformation of Agriculture: Distribution of Benefits and Costs from Development. Ames; Iowa State University Press for Center for Agricultural and Rural Development, 1975. 341p.

First rank Heady, Earl O., and W. Candler. Linear Programming Methods. Ames; Iowa State College Press, 1958. 597p.

First rank Heady, Earl O., H. G. Diesslin, H. R. Jensen, and G. L. Johnson, eds. Agricultural Adjustment Problems in a Growing Economy. Ames, Iowa; Iowa State College Press, 1958.

Second Heady, Earl O., Howard C. Madsen, Kenneth J. Nicol, and Stanley H. Hargrove. Agricultural and Water Policies and the Environment: An Analysis of National Alternatives in Natural Resource Use, Food Supply Capacity and Environmental Quality. Ames, Iowa; Iowa State University, 1972. 295p. (Center for Agricultural and Rural Development Report 40T) Q

Third Healy, Robert G. Competition for Land in the American South: Agriculture, Human Settlement, and the Environment. Washington, D.C.; Conservation Foundation, 1985. 334p.

Third Hedlund, Stefan. Crisis in Soviet Agriculture. New York; St. Martin's Press, Inc., 1984. 256p.

Third — Hefford, R. K. Farm Policy in Australia. Brisbane; University of Queensland Press, 1985. 432p.

Second — Held, R. B. and D. W. Visser. Rural Land Uses and Planning: A Comparative Study of the Netherlands and the United States. Amsterdam; Elsevier Science Publ. Co., Inc., 1984. 360p.

Second — Helmberger, P., and S. Hoos. Cooperative Bargaining in Agriculture: Grower-Processor Markets for Fruits and Vegetables. Berkeley; University of California, Berkeley, Division of Agricultural Sciences, 1965. 234p. Q

Second — Henderson, J. M., and R. E. Quandt. Microeconomic Theory: A Mathematical Approach. 2d ed. New York; McGraw-Hill, 1980. 420p. (1st ed. 1958, 291p.).

Third — Herbert, David and R. Johnston, eds. Social Areas in Cities. London; Wiley, 1976. 2 vols. (Vol 2 of Spatial Perspectives on Problems and Policies)

Third — Herbst, John. Farm Management: Principles, Budgets, Plans. 5th rev. ed. Champaign, Ill.; Stipes Publ. Co., 1980. 288p. (Paper ed. Farm Management: Principles, Planning, Budgets, 1986.)

Third — Herdt, Robert W., and C. Capule. Adoption, Spread, and Production Impact of Modern Rice Varieties in Asia. Los Banos, Laguna, Philippines; International Rice Research Institute, 1983. 54p.

Third — Herring, Ronald J. Land to the Tiller: Political Economy of Agrarian Reform in South Asia. New Haven, Conn.; Yale University Press, 1983. 314p.

Third — Hewitt de Alcantara, Cynthia. Modernizing Mexican Agriculture: Socioeconomic Implications of Technological Change, 1940–1970. 5th ed. Mexico; Siglo Vientiuno Editores , 1985. 319p. (1st ed., Geneva: United Nations Research Institute for Social Development, 1976. 350p.) (UNRISD Studies on the Green Revolution)

Third — Hexem, Roger and Earl O. Heady. Water Production Functions for Irrigated Agriculture. Ames; Center for Agricultural and Rural Development, Iowa State University Press, 1978. 215p. Q

Second — Hey, John D. Uncertainty in Microeconomics. New York; New York University Press, 1979. 261p.

Third — Heyer, J., Pepe Roberts, and Gavin Williams, eds. Rural Development in Tropical Africa. London; Macmillan Press, 1981. 224p.

First rank — Hicks, John R. A Theory of Economic History. London; Oxford University Press, 1969. 181p.

Second — Hicks, John R. Surveys of Economic Theory. London; Macmillan, New York: St. Martin's Press, 1965, 1966, 1967. 3 vols.

Second — Hicks, John R. Value and Capital: An Inquiry Into Some Fundamental Principles of Economic Theory. 2d ed. Oxford; Clarendon Press, 1946. 340p.

First rank — Hicks, John R. The Theory of Wages. 2d ed. London; Macmillan, 1964. 388p. (1st ed.; 1932, 1948. 247p.)

Third — Higgins, Benjamin. Economic Development: Principles, Problems and Policies. Rev. ed. New York; Norton, 1968. 918p. (1st ed., 1959. 803p.)

Third — Hightower, Jim. Hard Tomatoes, Hard Times: The Failure of the Land Grant College Complex. Washington, D.C.; Agribusiness Accountability Project, 1972. 308p.

Second — Hildreth, R. J., Kathryn L. Lipton, Kenneth C. Clayton, and Carl C.

O'Connor, eds. Agricultural and Rural Areas Approaching the 21st Century: Challenges for Agricultural Economics. Ames; Iowa State University Press, 1987. 560p.

Third Hilf, Meinhard, Francis G. Jacobs, and E.U. Petersmann. The European Community and GATT. Deventer, the Netherlands; Kluwer, 1986. 398p.

Third Hill, Berkeley, and Derek Ray. Economics for Agriculture. New York; Macmillan, 1987. 320p.

Third Hill, Lowell, D., and Marvin R. Paulsen. Maize Production and Marketing in Argentina. Urbana, Ill.; University of Illinois, 1987. 39p. (Illinois Agricultural Experiment Station Bulletin No. 785) Q

Third Hill, P. Development Economics on Trial: The Anthropological Case for a Prosecution. Cambridge University Press, 1986. 198p.

Second Hillier, Frederick S., and Gerald J. Lieberman. Introduction to Operations Research. 4th ed. San Francisco; Holden-Day, 1986. 888p. (1st ed., 1967. 639p.)

Third Hinderink, Jan and J.J. Sterkenburg. Agricultural Commercialization and Government Policy in Africa. London, New York; KPI, 1987. 328 p. (Monogs. from the African Studies Centre, Leiden)

Third Hirschman, Albert O. Development Projects Observed. Washington, D. C.; Brookings Inst., 1967. 197p.

First rank Hirschman, Albert O. Essays in Trespassing: Economics to Politics and Beyond. Cambridge University Press, 1981. 310p.

First rank Hirschman, Albert O. The Strategy of Economic Development. New Haven; Yale University Press, 1958. 217p.

Third Hirschman, Albert O., ed. Toward a New Strategy for Development. New York; Pergamon Press, 1979. 365p.

Third Hoaglin, David C., et al. Data For Decisions: Information Stategies for Policymakers. Cambridge, Mass.; Abt Books, 1982. 318p.

Third Hogg, Robert V., and Allen T. Craig. Introduction to Mathematical Statistics. 4th ed. New York; Macmillan, 1978. 438p. (1st ed., 1959. 245p.)

Third Hollist, W. Ladd and F. LaMond Tullis, eds. Pursuing Food Security: Strategies and Obstacles in Africa, Asia, Latin America, and the Middle East. Boulder; L. Rienner, Publ., 1987. 357p.

Third Hoole, Francis W. Evaluation Research and Development Activities. Beverly Hills, Calif.; Sage Publications, 1978. 207p.

Second Hoos, Sidney, ed. Agricultural Marketing Boards: An International Perspective. Cambridge, Mass.; Ballinger Publ. Co., 1979. 367p.

Second Hoover, E.M. An Introduction to Regional Economics. 3d ed. New York; Knopf, 1984. 444p. (1st ed., 1971. 395p.)

Third Hopkins, Nicholas A. Agrarian Transformation in Egypt. Boulder, Colo.; Westview, 1987. 215p.

Third Hopkins, Raymond F., Donald J.Puchala, and Ross B. Talbot, eds. Food, Politics, and Agricultural Development: Case Studies in Public Policy of Rural Modernization. Boulder, Colo.; Westview Press, 1979. 311p.

Third Horan, Patrick M., and Charles M. Tolbert, II. The Organization of Work in Rural and Urban Labor Markets. Boulder, Colo.; Westview Press, 1984. 176p.

Second Hou, Chi-ming, and Tzong-shian Yu, eds. Agricultural Development in China, Japan, and Korea. Seattle; University of Washington Press, 1982. 892p.

Second Houck, James P. Elements of Agricultural Trade Policies. New York; Macmillan, 1986. 224p.

Third Howald, O., and E. Laur. Landwirtschaftliche Betriebslehre fur Bauerliche Verhaltnisse (Agricultural Management for Farming). 14th ed. Aarau, 1956. 379p.

Third Howard, Robert W. The Vanishing Land. New York; Villard Books, 1985. 318p.

Second Howell, John, ed. Borrowers and Lenders: Rural Financial Markets and Institutions in Developing Countries. London; Overseas Development Institute, 1980. 290p.

Third Hrubovcak, James, and Michael LeBlanc. Tax Policy and Agricultural Investment. Washington DC; U.S. Department of Agriculture, Economic Research Service, and Springfield, Vir.; NTIS, 1985. 14p. (USDA Technical Bulletin No. 1699) Q

Third Huang, Kuo S. U.S. Demand for Food: A Complete System of Price and Income Effects. Washington DC; U.S. Department of Agriculture, Economic Research Service, 1985. 51p. (USDA Technical Bulletin No. 1714) Q

Second Huddleston, Barbara, D. G. Johnson, Shlomo Reutlinger, and Alberto Valdes. International Finance for Food Security. Baltimore; Johns Hopkins Univ. Press, 1984. 100p.

Third Hunt, Diana. The Impending Crisis in Kenya: The Case for Land Reform. Aldershot, Hampshire and Brookfield, Vermont; Gower Publishing Company, 1984. 314p.

Third Hunter, Guy. Education for a Developing Region: A Study in East Africa. London; Greenwood Press, 1963, 1977. 119p.

Third Hunter, Guy. Modernizing Peasant Societies: A Comparative Study in Asia and Africa. London; New York, Oxford University Press for the Institute of Race Relations, 1969. 324p.

I

Third Iftikhar, Ahmed. Technological Change and Agrarian Structure: A Study of Bangladesh. Geneva; International Labour Office, 1981. 136p.

Third Ijere, Martin O. New Perspectives in Financing Nigerian Agriculture. Enugu, Nigeria; Fourth Dimension Publ., 1986. 130p.

Third Ilbery, Brian W. Agricultural Geography: A Social and Economic Analysis. Oxford University Press, 1986. 224p.

Third Imel, Blake, Michael R. Behr, and Peter G. Helmberger. Market Structure and Performance: The U. S. Food Processing Industries. Lexington, Mass.; Lexington Books, 1972. 115p. Q

Third India. Economic and Scientific Research Foundation. Agricultural Exports Strategy: Problems and Prospects. India; Radiant Pubs., 1986. 326p.

Third Innis, H. A. The Cod Fisheries: The History of an International Economy. New Haven, Conn.; Yale University Press; Toronto; Ryerson Press for the Carnegie Endowment for International Peace, Division of Economics and History, 1940. 520p.

Third International Association of Agricultural Economists. Policies, Planning, and Management in Agricultural Development; Papers and Reports of the 14th International Conference . . . Aug.–Sept. 1970. Oxford, Eng.; Oxford Institute of Agrarian Affairs, 1971. 616p.

Second International Food Policy Research Institute. Food Needs of Developing

Countries: Projections of Production and Consumption to 1990. Washington, D.C.; IFPRI, 1977. 157p. (IFPRI Research Report No. 3)

Second — International Labour Organization. Poverty and Landlessness in Rural Asia. Geneva, Switz.; ILO, 1977. 288p.

Third — International Livestock Centre for Africa. Small Ruminant Production in the Humid Tropics. Addis Ababa, Ethiopia; ILCA, 1979.

Third — International Rice Research Institute. Interface Between Agricultural Nutrition and Food Sciences. Los Banos, Philip.; IRRI and the United Nations Univ., 1979.

First rank — International Rice Research Institute. Economic Consequences of the New Rice Technology in Asia. Los Banos; IRRI, 1978. 402p.

First rank — Isard, W. Introduction to Regional Science. Englewood Cliffs, N.J.; Prentice-Hall, 1975. 506p.

Second — Isard, W., P. Liossatos, with Y. Kanemoto. Spatial Dynamics and Optimal Space-Time Development. New York; North-Holland, 1979. 434p.

Second — Isard, W., T.E. Smith, P. Isard, T.H. Tung, and M. Dacey. General Theory: Social, Political, Economic, and Regional, with Particular Reference to Decision-Making Analysis. Cambridge, Mass.; MIT Press, 1969. 1040p.

Second — Islam, Nural, ed. Agricultural Policy in Developing Countries: Proceedings of a Conference held by the International Economic Association at Bad Godesberg, West Germany (Aug. 26–Sept. 4, 1972) London: Macmillan, and New York; Wiley, 1974. 565p.

Third — Issert, J. The Legal Status of Agricultural Co-Operatives in European Countries. Trans. from French. Oxford; Plunkett Foundation, 1978. 112p.

J

Third — Jacobs, Everett M., ed. The Organization of Agriculture in the Soviet Union and Eastern Europe. Montclair, N.J.; Allanheld and Osmun, 1980, 1984. 500p. (Studies in East European and Soviet Russian Agrarian Policy: Vol. 2).

Third — Jaguaribe, H., A Ferrer, M. S. Wionczek and T. dos Santos. La Dependencia Politico-Economica de America Latina (The Political-Economic Dependency of Latin America). 12th ed. Mexico; Siglo Veintiuno, 1980. 293p. (1st ed., 1970)

Third — Jahnke, Hans E., D. Kirschke, and J. Lagemann. The Impact of Agricultural Research in Tropical Africa: A Study of the Collaboration Between the International Agricultural and National Research Systems. Washington, D.C.; World Bank, 1987. 175p. (CGIAR Study Paper no. 21)

Second — Jahr, Dale, J. W. Johnson, and R. C. Wimberly, eds. New Dimensions in Rural Policy: Building Upon Our Heritage. Washington, D. C.; U. S. Government Printing Office, Joint Economic Committee of Congress, 1986. 574p.

Third — Jain, L.C. with B. V. Krishnamurthy and P. M. Tripathi. Grass Without Roots: Rural Development Under Government Auspices. New Delhi and Beverly Hills, Calif.; Sage Publications, 1985. 240 p.

Second — Jamison, Dean T. and L. J. Lau. Farmer Education and Farm Efficiency. Baltimore; Johns Hopkins University Press, 1982. 320p.

Third — Jannuzi, F. Tomasson and James T. Peach. Agrarian Structure of Bangladesh: An Impediment to Development. Boulder, Colo.; Westview Press, 1980. 150p.

Second Jencks, C., M. Smith, H. Aclund, M.J. Bane, D. Cohen, H. Gintis, B. Heynes, and S. Michelson. Inequality: A Reassessment of the Effect of Family and Schooling in America. New York; Basic Books, 1972. 399p. (Reprinted by Harper and Row, 1973.)

Third Jeudwine, John W. The Foundation of Society and the Land. Rev. ed. Philadelphia; Ayer Publishers, 1975. 509p.

Third Johansen, Leif. A Multi-Sectoral Study of Economic Growth. 2d ed. Amsterdam; North-Holland, 1974, 274p. (1st ed., 1960. 177p.)

Third Johnson, Aaron C., Jr., Marvin B. Johnson, and Reuben C. Buse. Econometrics: Basic and Applied. New York; Macmillan Publishing Co., 1987. 480p. Q

Second Johnson, Arthur H. The Disappearance of the Small Landowner. Oxford; Clarendon Press, 1909. 164p. (Reprinted: Fairfield, N.J.; A. M. Kelly, 1979) (Ford Lectures, 1909)

First rank Johnson, D. Gale. Forward Prices for Agriculture. Chicago; University of Chicago Press, 1947. 259p. AAEA Classic

First rank Johnson, D. Gale. World Agriculture In Disarray. London; Macmillan; and New York; St. Martin's Press for the Trade Policy Research Centre, 1973. 304p.

Second Johnson, D. Gale. World Food Problems and Prospects. Washington, D. C.; American Enterprise Institute, 1975. 83p.

Second Johnson, D. Gale, and K. M. Brooks. Prospects for Soviet Agriculture in the 1980s. Bloomington; Indiana University Press, 1983. 224p.

Second Johnson, D. Gale, K. Hemmi, and P. Lardinois. Agricultural Policy and Trade: Adjusting Domestic Programs in an International Framework. New York University Press, 1986. 144p.

Third Johnson, D. Gale and Ronald D. Lee. Population Growth and Economic Development: Issues and Evidence. Madison; University of Wisconsin Press, 1987. 702p. (Working Group on Population Growth and Economic Development, Committee on Population, Commission on Behavioral and Social Sciences and Education, National Research Council).

Second Johnson, D. Gale, and J. Schnittker. U.S. Agriculture in a World Context: Policies and Approaches for the Next Decade. New York; Praeger, 1974. 260p.

Third Johnson, Donald E., L. R. Meiller, L. C. Miller, and G. F. Summers, eds. Needs Assessment: Theory and Methods. Ames; Iowa State University Press, 1987. 328p.

Second Johnson, E. A. J. The Organization of Space in Developing Countries. Cambridge, Mass.; Harvard University Press, 1970. 452p.

First rank Johnson, Glenn L., and C. L. Quance, eds. The Overproduction Trap in U. S. Agriculture. Baltimore; Johns Hopkins University Press, 1972. 211p.

Second Johnson, Glenn L., and A. Maunder, eds. Rural Change: The Challenge for Agricultural Economists. Westmead, Eng.; Grover; and Mountclair, N.J.; Allenheld, Osmun, 198l. 738p.

First rank Johnson, Glenn L., and S. H. Wittwer. Agricultural Technology Until 2030: Prospects, Priorities, and Policies. East Lansing; Michigan State University, Agricultural Experiment Station, 1984. 61p.

Third Johnson, Kenneth M. The Impact of Population Change on Business Activity in Rural America. Boulder, Colo.; Westview Press, 1985. 180p.

Second	Johnson, Paul R. The Economics of the Tobacco Industry. New York; Praeger, 1984. 157p.
First rank	Johnson, Stanley, Z. Hassan, and R. D. Green. Demand Systems Estimation: Methods and Applications. Ames; Iowa State University Press, 1984. 178p.
Third	Johnston, Bruce F. and W. C. Clark. Redesigning Rural Development: A Strategic Perspective. Baltimore, Md; Johns Hopkins University Press, 1982. 311p.
Second	Johnston, Bruce F., et al., eds. U.S.-Mexico Relations: Agriculture and Rural Development. Stanford, Calif.; Stanford University Press, 1987. 400p.
First rank	Johnston, Bruce F., and Peter Kilby. Agriculture and Structural Transformation: Economic Strategies in Late-Developing Countries. New York; Oxford University Press, 1975. 474p.
First rank	Johnston, J. Econometric Methods. 3d ed. New York; McGraw-Hill, 1984. 568p. (1st ed., 1963. 300p.)
Third	Jones, Gwyn E., and M. J. Rolls, eds. Progress in Rural Extension and Community Development. New York; John Wiley and Sons, 1982. 336p.
Third	Jones, Hywel G. An Introduction to Modern Theories of Economic Growth. New York; McGraw-Hill, 1976. 250p.
Second	Jones, James R., ed. East-West Agricultural Trade. Boulder, Colo.; Westview Press, 1986. 256p.
Second	Jones, W. O. Marketing Staple Food Crops in Tropical Africa. Ithaca; Cornell University Press, 1972. 293p.
Second	Jordan, Wayne R., ed. Water and Water Policy in World Food Supplies. College Station; Texas A & M University Press, 1987. 466p.
Third	Joshi, P.C. Institutional Aspects of Agricultural Development: India in the Asian Context. Riverdale, Maryland; Riverdale Co., 1987. 200p.
Second	Josling, Timothy E. International Dimensions of Agricultural and Food Policies. New York; Macmillan, 1985. 320p.
Third	Josling, Timothy E., B. Davey, A. McFarquhar, A. C. Hannah, and D. Hamway. Burdens and Benefits of Farm-Support Policies. London; Trade Policy Research Centre, 1972. 85p.
First rank	Judge, George G. and T. Takayama. Studies in Economic Planning over Space and Time. Amsterdam; North Holland Publ., and New York; Elsevier, 1973. 727p.
First rank	Judge, George G., et al. The Theory and Practice of Econometrics. 2d ed. New York; Wiley, 1985. 1019p. (1st ed., 1980. 793p.)
Second	Just, Richard E., D. L. Hueth, and A. Schmitz. Applied Welfare Economics and Public Policy. Englewood Cliffs, N.J.; Prentice-Hall, 1982. 491p.

K

First rank	Kadlec, John E. Farm Management: Decisions, Operation, Control. Englewood Cliffs, N.J.; Prentice-Hall, 1985. 429p. Q
Third	Kahlon, A. S., and M. V. George. Agricultural Marketing and Price Policies. New Delhi, India; Allied, 1985. 283p.
Third	Kahlon, A. S., and K. Singh. Managing Agricultural Finance: Theory and Practice. New Delhi, India; Allied, 1984. 344p.

Third Kahn, E. J., Jr. The Staffs of Life. Boston; Little, Brown and Co., 1985. 288p.

Second Kaldor, N. Strategic Factors in Economic Development. Ithaca, N.Y.; Cornell University, School of Industrial and Labor Relations, 1967. 83p.

Third Kamien, M. I., and N. L. Schwartz. Market Structure and Innovation. Cambridge University Press, 1982. 241p.

Third Kanon, D. D'Eveloppement ou Appauvissement. Paris; Economica, 1985. 188p.

Third Kanter, R. Moss. Commitment and Community. Cambridge, Mass.; Harvard University Press, 1972. 303p.

Third Kappelmann, Karl-Heinz. Der Agrarsektor als Wirtschaftsfaktor in der Bundesrepublik Deutschland. Peter Lang, Publ., 1983. 224p. (European University Studies Five: Vol. 440).

Third Karcz, Jerzy F. The Economics of Communist Agriculture: Selected Papers. Bloomington, Ind.; International Development Institute, 1979. 494p. (Studies in East European and Soviet Planning, Development, and Trade: No. 25).

Third Kay, Ronald D. Farm Management: Planning, Control, and Implementation. 2d ed. New York; McGraw-Hill Book Co., 1986. 401p. (1st ed., 1981. 370p.)

Third Kearl, Bryant, ed. Field Data Collection in the Social Sciences: Experiences in Africa and the Middle East. New York; Agricultural Development Council, 1976. 200p.

Third Kelejian, Harry H., and Wallace E. Oates. Introduction to Econometrics: Principles and Applications. 2d ed. New York; Harper and Row, 1981. 347p. (1st ed., 1974. 300p.)

Third Kellerman, Barbara, ed. Leadership: Multidisciplinary Perspectives. Englewoods Cliffs, N.J.; Prentice-Hall, 1984. 288p.

Second Kelley, Allen C., J. G. Williamson and R. J. Cheetham. Dualistic Economic Development: Theory and History. Chicago; University of Chicago Press, 1972. 399p.

Second Kelso, Maurice M., William E. Martin, and Lawrence E. Mack. Water Supplies and Economic Growth in an Arid Environment. Tucson; University of Arizona Press, 1973. 327p. Q

Second Kendrick, J. W., ed. International Comparisons of Productivity and Causes of the Slowdown. Cambridge, Mass.; Ballinger Publ., 1984.

Second Kendrick, J. W. and Beatrice N. Vaccara, eds. New Developments in Productivity Measurement. Chicago; University of Chicago Press, 1980. 717p.

Third Kennedy, E. and Bruce Cogill. Income and Nutritional Effects of the Commercialization of Agriculture in Southwestern Kenya. Washington, D.C.; International Food Policy Research Institute, 1987. 60p. (IFPRI Research Report 63)

Third Kennedy, Peter V. A Guide to Econometrics. 2d ed. Cambridge, Mass.; MIT Press, 1985. 238p. (1st ed., 1979. 175p.)

First rank Keynes, J. M. Scope and Method of Political Economy. 4th ed. Clifton, N.J.; A. M. Kelley, 1973. 382p. (Original ed., 1917)

Third Khan, Azizur Rahman, and Dharam Ghai. Collective Agriculture and Rural Development in Soviet Central Asia. New York; Macmillan, 1979. 192p.

Third Khan, Azizur Rahman, and E. Lee, eds. Poverty in Rural Asia. Bangkok;

International Labour Office, Asian Employment Programme, 1985. 276p.

Third Khusro, A.M. Economics of Land Reform and Farm Size in India. Madras, India; Macmillan, 1973. 162p.

Second Kilmer, Richard L., and W. J. Armbruster, eds. Economic Efficiency in Agricultural and Food Marketing. Ames; Iowa State University Press. 1987. 336p.

Second King, Leslie J. Central Place Theory. Beverly Hills, Calif.; Sage Publ., 1984. 96p.

Second King, R. Land Reform: A World Survey. Boulder, Colo.; Westview Press, 1977. 446p.

Third Kinsey, B.H. Agribusiness and Rural Enterprise. New York and London; Croom Helm Ltd, 1987. 228p.

Third Kitching, Gavin. Development and Underdevelopment in Historical Perspective: Populism, Nationalism, and Industrialization. Rev. ed. London and New York; Routledge, 1989. 196p. (1st ed., London and New York; Methuen, 1982)

Third Klein, L. and K. Ohkawa, eds. Economic Growth: The Japanese Experience Since the Meiji Era. Homewood, Ill.; Irwin, 1968. 424p.

Second Knapp, J.G. The Advance of American Cooperative Enterprise: 1920–1945. Danville, Ill.; Interstate, 1973. 646p.

Second Kneese, A.V., and C.L. Schultze. Pollution, Prices, and Public Policy. Washington, D.C.; Brookings Institute, 1975. 125p.

Second Knight, F. H. The Economic Organization. Chicago; University of Chicago Press, 1933.

Third Knudsen, O. and P. L. Scandizzo. Nutrition and Food Needs in Developing Countries. Washington, D.C.; World Bank, 1979. (World Bank Staff Working Paper No. 328)

Second Knutson, Ronald D., J. B. Penn, and W. T. Boehm. Agricultural and Food Policy. Englewood Cliffs, N.J.; Prentice-Hall, 1983. 387p.

Third Knutson, Ronald D., J. W. Richardson, D. A. Klinefelter, M. S. Paggi, and E. G. Smith. Policy Tools for U.S. Agriculture. College Station; Texas A and M University, 1986. 73p. (Agriculture and Food Policy Center, B-1548) Q

Third Kocher, J. E. Rural Development, Income Distribution, and Fertility Decline. New York; Population Council, 1973. 105p.

Third Koenigsberger, Otto, S. Groak, and N. Lichfield, eds. Review of Land Policies. New York; Pergamon Press, Inc., 1981. 200p.

Third Koetter, H. R. Involvement of the Rural Poor. Manila; Asian Development Bank, 1976.

Second Kolb, J.H. Emerging Rural Communities: Group Relations in Rural Society. Madison; University of Wisconsin Press, 1959. 212p.

Second König, Rene. The Community. New York; Schocken Books, 1968. E. Fitzgerald, trans. 218p.

Third Koo, A. Y. C. Land Market Distortion and Tenure Reform. Ames; Iowa State University Press, 1982. 137p.

Third Koo, Won W., ed. Transportation Models for Agricultural Products. Boulder, Colo.; Westview Press, 1985. 175p.

Third Korsching, Peter and Judith Gildner, eds. Interdependencies of Agriculture and Rural Communities in the Twenty-First Century. Ames, Iowa; North Central Regional Center for Rural Development, 1968. 237p.

Third Korten, D. C., and R. Klauss, eds. People-Centered Development: Contributions Toward Theory and Planning Frameworks. West Hartford, Conn.; Kumarian Press, 1984. 333p.

Third Kral, David M., and S. L. Hawkins, ed. Land Use Planning, Techniques and Policies. Madison, Wisc.; Soil Science Society of America, 1984. 123p.

Second Krueger, Anne O. and Vernon W. Ruttan. The Development Impact of Economic Assistance to LDC's. Minneapolis and St. Paul; University of Minnesota Economic Development Center, March 1983. 2 vols.

Second Krutilla, John V., and A. C. Fisher. The Economics of Natural Environments: Studies in the Valuation of Commodity and Amenity Resources. Rev. ed. Baltimore; Johns Hopkins University Press for Resources for the Future, 1985. 300p. (1st ed., 1975. 292p.)

First rank Kuhn, Thomas. Structure of Scientific Revolutions. 2d ed. Chicago; University of Chicago Press, 1970. 210p. (1st ed., 1962. 172p.)

Second Kunkel, J.H. Society and Economic Growth: A Behavioral Perspective of Social Change. New York; Oxford University Press, 1970. 368p.

L

Third La-Anyane, Seth. Economics of Agricultural Development in Tropical Africa. New York; Wiley and Sons, Inc., 1985. 150p.

First rank Labys, Walter, and C.W.J. Granger. Speculation, Hedging and Commodity Price Forecasts. Lexington, Mass.; Heath Lexington Books, 1970. 320p.

Second Lacy, William B., and L. Busch, eds. Biotechnology and Agricultural Cooperatives: Opportunities and Challenges. Lexington; Kentucky Agricultural Experiment Station, 1988. 119p.

Third Lal, D. The Poverty of "Development Economics." Rev. ed. Cambridge; Harvard University Press, 1985, 153p. (1st ed., London; Institute of Economic Affairs, 1983. 130p.)

Second Landsberg, H.H., L.L. Fischman, and J.L. Fisher. Resources in America's Future: Patterns of Requirements and Availabilities, 1960–2000. Baltimore; Johns Hopkins University Press for Resources for the Future, 1963. 1017p.

Second Langham, Max R., and Ralph H. Retzlaff, ed. Agricultural Sector Analysis in Asia. Singapore; Singapore University Press for the Agricultural Development Council, 1982. 420p.

Third Langoni, C. G. Distribuicao de Renda e Desenvolvimento Economico do Brasil (Income Distribution and Economic Development of Brazil). Rio de Janeiro; eda Expressao e Cultura, 1973. 315p.

Third Lappe, Frances M., and Joseph Collins. World Hunger: Twelve Myths. New York; Grove Press, 1986. 208p.

First rank Lardy, Nicholas R. Agriculture in China's Modern Economic Development. Cambridge University Press, 1983. 285p.

Second Lassey, William R. Planning in Rural Environments. New York; McGraw-Hill Book Co., 1977. 257p.

Third Law, Alton D. International Commodity Agreements: Setting, Performance, and Prospects. Lexington, Mass.; Lexington Books, 1975. 128p.

Third Lawrence, Peter, ed. World Recession and the Food Crisis in Africa. Boulder, Colo.; Westview Press, 1986. 320p.

Third Lea, David A. M., and D. P. Chaudhri, eds. Rural Development and the State: Contradictions and Dilemmas in Developing Countries. London and New York; Methuen, 1983. 351p.

Third Lee, Warren F., et al. Agricultural Finance. 8th ed. Ames; Iowa State University Press, 1988. 468p. (Primary author varies among editions.)

Second Leed, Theodore, and Gene A. German. Food Merchandising: Principles and Practices. 3d ed. New York; Lebhar-Friedman, 1985. 488p. (1st ed., New York; Chain-Store Age Books, 1973. 389p.)

Second Leftwich, Richard H. The Price System and Resource Allocation. 6th ed. Hindsdale, Ill.; Dryden Press, 1976. 433p.

Third Lehmann, D., ed. Peasants, Landlords, and Governments: Agrarian Reform in the Third World. New York; Holmes and Meier Publishers, 1974. 320p.

Second Leibenstein, H. Economic Backwardness and Economic Growth: Studies in the Theory of Economic Development. New York; Wiley, 1957. 295p.

Second Leistritz, F. Larry, and B. L. Ekstrom. Interdependencies of Agriculture and Rural Communities: An Annotated Bibliography. New York; Garland Publ., Inc., 1986. 200p.

Second Lele, Uma J. Food Grain Marketing in India: Private Performance and Public Policy. Ithaca, N.Y.; Cornell University Press, 1971. 264p.

Second Lele, Uma. The Design of Rural Development: Lessons from Africa. 2d ed. Baltimore; Johns Hopkins University Press for World Bank, 1979. 246p. (1st ed., 1975)

Second Leonard, David K. Reaching the Peasant Farmer: Organization Theory and Practice in Kenya. Chicago; University of Chicago Press, 1977. 297p.

Second Leontief, W. W. Essays in Economics: Theories and Theorizing. New York; Oxford University Press, 1966. 252p.

Second Leontief, W. W., et al. Studies in the Structure of the American Economy: Theoretical and Empirical Explorations in Input-Output Analysis. New York; Oxford University Press, 1953. 252p.

Third Lewis, J.P., and V. Kallab, eds. Development Strategies Reconsidered: U.S.-Third World Policy Perspective No. 5. New Brunswick, N.J.; Transaction Books for the Overseas Development Council, 1986.

Third Lewis, W. A. The Evolution of the International Economic Order. Princeton; Princeton University Press, 1978. 81p.

First rank Lewis, W. A. The Theory of Economic Growth. London; Allen and Unwin; and Homewood, Ill.; Richard D. Irwin, 1955. 453p. (Reprinted by New York; Harper Torchbooks, 1970)

Third Libecap, Gary D. Locking up the Range: Federal Land Controls and Grazing. San Francisco; Pacific Institute for Public Policy Research; and Cambridge, Mass.; Ballinger Pub. Co., 1981. 138p.

Third Lim, Edwin and Adrian Wood. China: Long-Term Issues and Options: The Report of a Mission Sent to China by the World Bank. Baltimore; Johns Hopkins University Press. 1985. 183p. (World Bank Rpt. No. 5206-CHA)

Third Lin, Sein, and W. Zaman. Land Policies in Developing Countries: Select Bibliography on Agrarian Reform: 1977–1983. Cambridge, Mass.; Lincoln Institute of Land Policy, 1983. 81p. (Monograph No. 83–6)

Third Lindblom, C.E. The Policy-Making Process. Englewood Cliffs, N.J.; Prentice-Hall, 1968. 122p.

Second	Lindholm, Richard, ed. Land Value Taxation: The "Progress and Poverty" Centenary. Madison; University of Wisconsin Press, 1982. 260p.
Third	Lippit, Victor D. Land Reform and Economic Development in China: A Study of Institutional Change and Development Finance. White Plains, New York; International Arts and Sciences Press, 1974. 183p.
Third	Lipson, F., and C. Batterton. A Report on Agricultural Cooperatives. Washington, D.C.; U.S. Federal Trade Commission, Bureau of Competition, 1975. 181p.
Second	Lipton, Michael. Why Poor People Stay Poor: Urban Bias in World Development. Cambridge, Mass.: Harvard University Press, 1976, 1977. 467p.
Third	Lipton, Michael. The Place of Agricultural Research in the Development of Sub-Saharan Africa. Washington, D. C.; CGIAR, World Bank; and Brighton, Eng.; Institute of Development Studies at the University of Sussex, 1985. 51p. (IDS Discussion Paper No. 202)
Third	Litan, Robert E., and William D. Nordhaus. Reforming Federal Regulation. New Haven; Yale University Press, 1983. 204p.
Second	Little, Ian M.D. Economic Development: Theory, Policy and International Relations. New York; Basic Books, 1982. 452p.
Third	Littrell, Donald W. The Theory and Practice of Community Development: A Guide for Practitioners. Columbia, Mo.; University of Missouri Press, 1971.
Third	Livingstone, I., and H. W. Ord. Agricultural Economics for Tropical Africa. London; Heinemann, 1981. 294p.
Second	Lluch, C., A.A. Powell, and R.R. Willaims, eds. Patterns in Household Demand and Savings. New York; Oxford University Press, for the World Bank, 1977. 280p.
Third	Long, Huey B., R. C. Anderson, and J. A. Blubaugh, eds. Approaches to Community Development. Iowa City, IA; National University Education Association and the American College Testing Program.
Third	Long, Larry. Migration and Residential Mobility in the United States. New York; Russell Sage Foundation; For the National Committee for Research on the 1980 Census, 1988. 397p. (The Population of the United States in the 1980s: A Census Monograph Series.)
Second	Long, Norman. Introduction to the Sociology of Rural Development. Boulder, Colo.; Westview Press, 1977. 221p.
Third	Lonsdale, Richard E., and Gyorgy Enyedi, eds. Rural Public Services: International Comparisons. Boulder, Colo.; Westview Press, 1984. 362p.
Third	Looney, J. W. Business Management for Farmers. St. Louis, Missouri; Doane Publ., 1983. 739p.
First rank	Losch, A. The Economics of Location. Trans. from the German 2d ed. New Haven; Yale University Press, 1954. 520p.
Third	Loudon, David L., and Albert J. Della Britta. Consumer Behavior: Concepts and Applications. 3d ed. New York; McGraw-Hill, 1988. 726p. (1st ed. 1979. 545p.)
Second	Lowe, Philip, et al. Countryside Conflicts: The Politics of Farming, Forestry and Conservation. Aldershot, Hants, Eng.; and Brookfield, Vermont; Gower/M. T. Smith, 1986. 378p.
First rank	Lucas, R., and T. Sargents, eds. Rational Expectations and Econometric Practice. Minneapolis; University of Minnesota Press, 1981. 689p.

Second Luloff, Albert E. and Louis E. Swanson, eds. American Rural Communities. Boulder, Colo.; Westview Press, 1988.

Third Lundsgaarde, Henry P., ed. Land Tenure in Oceania. Honolulu; University of Hawaii Press, 1974. 296p. (Association for Social Anthropology in Oceania Monographs: No. 2.)

Third Luz, Fabio. Seguros Agro Pecuarios. 2d ed. Rio de Janeiro; Ministerio da Agricultura ilr Servico de Economia Rural, 1949. 102p.

M

First rank Maass, A. and Anderson, R. L. And the Desert Shall Rejoice: Conflict, Growth and Justice in Arid Environments. Cambridge, Mass.; MIT Press, 1978. 447p.

Third Mabogunje, A. L. The Development Process: A Spatial Perspective. New York; Holmes and Meier, 1981. 383p.

Third MacBean, Alasdair I., and P.N. Snowden. International Institutions in Trade and Finance. London and Boston; Allen and Unwin, 1981. 255p.

Third MacDonald, M. Food, Stamps, and Income Maintenance. New York; Academic Press, 1977. 155p.

Third MacPherson, Stewart. Social Policy in the Third World: the Social Dilemmas of Underdevelopment. Totowa, N.J.; Allanheld, Osmun, 1982. 220p.

Second Madden, J.P. Economies of Size Studies: A Collection of Papers Presented August 3–4, 1983 at a Workshop at Purdue University in West Lafayette, Ind. Ames; Iowa State University Press for the Center for Agricultural and Rural Development, 1984. 220p.

Second Maddox, J.G., E.E. Liebhafsky, V.W. Henderson, and H.M. Hamlin. The Advancing South: Manpower Prospects and Problems. New York; Twentieth Century Fund, 1967. 276p.

Third Mahajan, V. S. Growth of Agriculture and Industry in India. New Delhi; Deep and Deep, 1983. 176p.

Second Maizels, A. (assisted by L.F. Campbell-Boross and P.B.D. Rayment). Exports and Economic Growth of Developing Countries. Cambridge; Cambridge University Press, 1968. 443p.

Third Makeham, J. P., and L. R. Malcolm. The Economics of Tropical Farm Management. Cambridge University Press, 1986. 202p.

Third Maki, W.R., and B.J.L. Berry, eds. Research and Education for Regional and Area Development. Ames; Iowa State University Press, 1966. 287p.

Third Malizia, Emil. Local Economic Development: A Guide to Practice. New York; Praeger, 1985. 243p.

First rank Malthus, T. R. Principles of Political Economy Considered with a View to Their Practical Application. 2d ed. London; William Pickering, 1836. 446p. (Latest reprint by Fairfield, N.J.; A. M. Kelley, 1986.)

Second Manchester, Alden C. The Public Role in the Dairy Economy: Why and How Governments Intervene in the Milk Business. Boulder, Colo.; Westview Press, 1983. 304p.

Second Manetsch, T. J., M. L. Hayenga, A. N. Halter, T. W. Carroll, M. H. Abkin, D. R. Byerlee, K-Y. Chong, G. Page, E. Kellogg, and G. L. Johnson. A Generalized Simulation Approach to Agricultural Sector Analysis with Special Reference to Nigeria. East Lansing; Michigan State University, Department of Agricultural Economics, 1971. 362p.

Third Mann, Harold H. Social Framework of Agriculture: India, Middle East, England. New York; A. M. Kelley, 1967. 501p.

Third Maos, Jacob. The Spatial Organization of New Land Settlement in Latin America. Boulder, Colo.; Westview Press, 1984. 170p.

Second Marcus, A. I. Agricultural Science and the Quest for Legitimacy: Farmers, Agricultural Colleges, and Experiment Stations. Ames; Iowa State University Press, 1985. 269p.

Second Marshall, F. Ray. Rural Workers in Rural Labor Markets. Salt Lake City, Utah: Olympus Publishing, 1974. 183p.

Second Marten, Gerald G., ed. Traditional Agriculture in Southeast Asia: A Human Ecology Perspective. Boulder, Colo.; Westview Press, 1986. 358p.

First rank Martin, Lee R., ed. A Survey of Agricultural Economics Literature. Minneapolis; University of Minnesota Press for the American Agricultural Economics Association, 1977–1981. 3 vols. (Vol. 4 due in 1991)

Third Martinez-Alier, Juan. Labourers and Landowners in Southern Spain. Totowa, N.J.; Rowman and Littlefield Publishers, 1971. 352p.

Second Marx, K. Capital: A Critique of Political Economy. New York; Modern Library, 1909–12. 3 vols. (1st German ed., 1867) Latest reprint by New York; Vintage Books, 1976–1981.

Second Mason, E.S. Economic Concentration and the Monopoly Problem. Cambridge, Mass.; Harvard University Press, 1957. 411p. (Reprinted in 1959)

Third Massey, Garth. Substance and Change: Lessons of Agropastoralism in Somalia. Boulder, Colo.; Westview Press, 1986. 300p.

Third Matthews, Alan. The Common Agricultural Policy and the Less Developed Countries. Dublin; Gill and Macmillan, 1985. 268p.

Second Matthews, W., ed. Outer Limits and Human Need: Resource and Environmental Issues of Development Strategies. Uppsala; Dag Hammarskjold Foundation, 1976. 102p.

Third Mauldon, Roger G. and Henry P. Schapper. Australian Farmers Under Stress in Prosperity and Recession. Perth; University of Western Australia Press, 1975. 244p.

First rank Maunder, Allen, and O. Kazushi, eds. Growth and Equity in Agricultural Development: Proceedings of the Eighteenth International Conference of Agricultural Economists. London; Gower Publ. Co., 1984. 619p.

Third Maunder, Allen, and G. P. Hirsch. Farm Amalgamation in Western Europe. London; Gower Publ. Co., 1978. 132p.

First rank Maunder, Allen, and Ulf Renborg, eds. Agriculture in a Turbulent World Economy; Important Research from the 19th International Conference of Agricultural Economists in Malaga, Spain. London; Gower, 1987. 820p.

Third Maunder, Allen, and Alberto Valdés, eds. Agriculture and Governments in an Interdependent World; Proceedings of the Twentieth International Conference of Agricultural Economists, Buenos Aires, August 1988. Aldershot, England; Dartmouth Publications, 1989. 903p.

Third Mazie, Sara Mills, ed. Population, Distribution, and Policy. Washington, D.C.; United States Commission on Population Growth and the American Future, 1972. 5 vols.

Second McAllister, Donald M. Evaluation in Environmental Planning: Assessing Environmental, Social, Economics and Political Trade-Offs. Cambridge, Mass.; MIT Press, 1980. 308p. (Reprinted in paperback, 1982.)

Second McCalla, Alex F., and T. E. Josling. Agricultural Policies and World Markets. New York; Macmillan Publ., 1985. 304 p.

First rank	McCalla, Alex F., and T. E. Josling, eds. Imperfect Markets in Agricultural Trade. Montclair, N.J.; Allanheld, Osmun and Co. Pubs., Inc., 1981. 250p.
Second	McCalla, Alex F., T. Kelley White, and Kenneth Clayton. Embargoes, Surplus Disposal, and U.S. Agriculture. Washington, D.C.; U.S. Department of Agriculture, Economic Research Service, 1986. various pagings, 300p. (USDA Agricultural Economics Report No. 564) Q
Second	McDowell, Robert E., and P.E. Hildebrand, eds. Integrated Crop and Animal Production: Making the Most of Resources Available to Small Farms in Developing Countries; A Bellagio Conference, 1978. New York; The Rockefeller Foundation, 1980. 78p.
Third	McGranahan, D.V., C. Richard-Proust, N.V. Sovani, and M. Subramanian. Contents and Measurement of Socioeconomic Development. New York; Praeger Publishers, 1972. 161p.
Third	McIver, J.P., and E.G. Carmines. Unidimensional Scaling. Beverly Hills, Calif.; Sage Publications, 1981. 96p.
Second	McKinnon, Ronald I. Money and Finance in Economic Growth and Development: Essays in Honor of Edward S. Shaw. New York; Dekker, 1976. 339p.
Third	McMahon, Joseph A. European Trade Policy in Agricultural Products. Dordrecht and Boston; Martinus Nijhoff, 1988. 358p.
Second	McPherson, W.W., ed. Economic Development of Tropical Agriculture: Theory, Policy, Strategy and Organization. Gainesville; University of Florida Press, 1968. 328p.
Second	Meade, J.E. A Neoclassical Theory of Economic Growth. 2d ed. London; Allen and Unwin, 1962. 185p. (1st ed., New York; Oxford University Press, 1961. 146p.)
Second	Meade, J.E. Efficiency, Equality, and Ownership of Property. London; Allen and Unwin, 1964. 92p. (Reissued: Cambridge; Harvard University Press, 1965)
Second	Meade, J.E. Principles of Political Economy: Vol. 2, The Growing Economy. London; Allen and Unwin; and Chicago; Aldine, 1968. 512p.
Second	Meadows, Dennis L. Dynamics of Commodity Production Cycles. Cambridge, Mass.; Wright-Allen, 1970. 104p.
Second	Meadows, Dennis L., and Donnella H. Meadows, eds. Toward Global Equilibrium: Collected Papers. Cambridge, Mass.; Wright-Allen Press, 1973. 358p.
Second	Meadows, Donnella H., Dennis L. Meadows, Jorgen Randers, and William W. Behrens, III. The Limits to Growth: A Report for the Club of Rome's Project on the Predicament of Mankind. 2d ed. New York; Universe Books, 1974. 205p. (1st ed., 1972. 205p.)
Third	Mehta, Bhoopal C. and Awadh Prasad. Agrarian Relations and Rural Exploitation. New Delhi; Ashish Publ. House, 1988. 268 p.
First rank	Meier, G.M., ed. Leading Issues in Economic Development. 3d ed. New York; Oxford University Press, 1976. 862p.
Third	Meier, R. L. Science and Economic Development: New Patterns of Living. 2d ed. Cambridge, Mass.; MIT Press, 1966. 266p. (1st ed., 1956)
Third	Meissner, H.H., ed. Poverty in the Affluent Society. Rev. ed. New York; Harper and Row, 1973. 289p. (1st ed., 1966. 251p.)
First rank	Mellor, John W. Economics of Agricultural Development. Ithaca, N.Y.; Cornell University Press, 1970. 418p. Q
First rank	Mellor, John W. The New Economics of Growth: A Strategy for India and

the Developing World. Ithaca, N.Y.; Cornell University Press, 1976. 335p.

First rank Mellor, John W., and G.M. Desai, eds. Agricultural Change and Rural Poverty on a Theme by Dharm Narain. Baltimore; Johns Hopkins University Press for International Food Policy Research Institute, 1985. 233p. (Reprinted by Oxford University Press, 1986)

Second Mellor, John W., C. L. Delgado, and M. J. Blackie, eds. Accelerating Food Production in Sub-Saharan Africa. Baltimore; Johns Hopkins University Press, 1987. 417p.

Third Melville, T. and M. Melville. Guatemala: The Politics of Land Ownership. New York; Free Press, 1971. 320p.

Third Mendras, Henri. Vanishing Peasant: Innovation and Change in French Agriculture. (Translated from the French by Jean Lerner) Cambridge, Mass.; MIT Press, 1970. 289p.

Third Mennes, L. B. M., J. Tinbergen, and J. G. Waardenberg. The Element of Space in Development Planning. Amsterdam: North-Holland, 1969. 341p.

Third Merillat, H. C. Land and the Constitution in India. New York; Columbia Univ. Press, 1970. 321p. (Reprint available from Books on Demand)

Second Mesarovic, M., and E. Pestel. Mankind at the Turning Point : The Second Report to the Club of Rome. New York; Dutton, 1974. 210p.

Third Mesarovic, M., D. Macko, and Y. Takahara. Theory of Hierarchical, Multi-level, Systems. New York; Academic Press, 1970. 294p.

Third Michman, Ronald D., and Stanley D. Sibley. Marketing Channels and Strategies. 2d ed. Columbus, Ohio; Grid Publ., 1980. 598p.

Second Miernyk, W.H., K.L. Shellhammer, D.M. Brown, R.L Coccari, C.I. Gallagher, and W.H. Wineman. Simulating Regional Economic Development: An Interindustry Analysis of the West Virginia Economy. Lexington, Mass.; Heath Lexington, 1970. 337p.

Second Mihran, G. A. Simulation: Statistical Foundations and Methodology. New York; Academic Press, 1972. 526p.

Second Milliken, George A. and Dallas E. Johnson. Analysis of Messy Data. New York; Van Nostrand Reinhold, 1984. 2 vols.

Third Minerbi, L., P. Nakamura, K. Nitz, and J. Yanai. Land Readjustment—The Japanese System: A Reconnaissance and a Digest. Boston, Mass.; Oelgeschlager, Gunn and Hain, Inc. in assoc. with the Lincoln Institute of Land Policy, 1986. 270p.

Third Mishan, E. J. Welfare Economics: An Assessment. Amsterdam; North-Holland; Atlantic Highlands, N.J.; Humanities Press, 1969. 83p.

Third Mitchell, Mark. Agriculture and Policy: Methodology for the Analysis of Developing Country Agricultural Sectors. London; Ithaca Press, 1985. 179p.

Second Mitra, A. Terms of Trade and Class Relations: An Essay in Political Economy. London; Frank Cass, 1977. 193p.

Third Moll, H.A.J. The Economics of Oil Palm. Wageningen, The Netherlands; PUDOC, 1987. 288p.

Third Montgomery, Douglas C., and Elizabeth A. Peck. Introduction to Linear Regression Analysis. New York; Wiley, 1982. 504p.

Second Montgomery, John D., ed. International Dimensions of Land Reform. Boulder, Colo.; Westview Press, 1984. 239p.

Second Moock, Joyce L. Understanding Africa's Rural Households and Farming Systems. Boulder, Colo.; Westview Press, 1986. 234p.

Third	Mood, Alexander M., Franklin A. Graybill, and Duane C. Boes. Introduction to the Theory of Statistics. 3d ed. New York; McGraw-Hill, 1974. 564p. (1st ed., 1950. 433p.)
Second	Mooney, Patrick H. My Own Boss? Class, Rationality, and the Family Farm. Boulder, Colo.; Westview Press, 1988. 306p.
Second	Moore, Henry L. Economic Cycles: Their Law and Cause. New York; Macmillan, 1914. 149p. (Reprinted 1967)
Third	Morawetz, David. Twenty-Five Years of Economic Development: 1950–1975. Washington, D.C.; World Bank, 1977. 126p.
Third	Moreland, William H. The Agrarian System of Moslem India. Cambridge, Eng.; Heffner and Sons, 1929, 296p. (Reprinted in Dehli; Oriental Books Reprint, 1968)
Second	Morgan, Dan. Merchants of Grain. Rev. ed. New York; Penguin Books, 1980. 519p. (1st ed., New York; Viking Press, 1979. 387p.)
Second	Morgenstern, O. On the Accuracy of Economic Observations. 2d ed. Princeton; Princeton University Press, 1973. 322p. (1st ed., 1950. 101p.)
Third	Moris, J. Managing Induced Rural Development. Bloomington, Ind.; International Development Institute, 1981. 190p.
Third	Morishima, M. The Theory of Economic Growth. Oxford; Clarendon Press, 1969. 314p.
Third	Morley, J.A. British Agricultural Co-Operatives. London; Hutchinson Benham, 1975. 168p.
Second	Moseman, Albert H. Building Agricultural Research Systems in the Developing Nations. New York; Agriculture Development Council, 1970. 137p.
Second	Mosher, A.T. Creating a Progressive Rural Structure: To Serve a Modern Agriculture. New York; Agricultural Development Council, 1969. 172p.
Second	Mosher, A.T. Getting Agriculture Moving: Essentials for Developmental Modernization. New York; Praeger, 1966. 191p.
Third	Mosher, A.T. Technical Cooperation in Latin-American Agriculture. Chicago; University of Chicago Press, 1957. 449p.
Second	Mosher, A.T. Thinking About Rural Development. New York; The Agricultural Development Council, 1976. 350p.
Third	Mosteller, F., and D. Moynihan, eds. On Equality of Educational Opportunity. New York; Random House, 1972. 570p.
Second	Moyer, D. D., and G. Wunderlich, eds. Transfer of Land Rights. Madison; University of Wisconsin, Department of Agricultural Economics; and Chicago; Farm Foundation, 1985. 178p.
Third	Moyer, Harriet, Daryl Heasley, and John Tait. Community Leadership Development: Present and Future. University Park, Penn.; Northeast Regional Center for Rural Development, 1986.
Third	Moyer, R., and S. Hollander, eds. Markets and Marketing in Developing Economies. Homewood, Ill.; Interscience Publ., 1968. 264p.
Second	Moynihan, Cornelius J. Introduction to the Law of Real Property: An Historical Background of the Common Law of Real Property and Its Modern Application. 2d ed. St. Paul, MN; West Publ. Co., 1988. 239p. (1st ed., 1962. 254p. Reprinted 1986)
Second	Mueller, D. Public Choice. Cambridge, Eng.; Cambridge University Press, 1979. 179p.
Third	Mueller, Willard F., ed. Proceedings of the Third National Symposium on

Cooperatives and the Law. Madison; University of Wisconsin, Center for Cooperatives, 1976. 205p. (1st Symposium: 1974)

Second Mueller, Willard F., Peter G. Helmberger, and Thomas W. Paterson. The Sunkist Case: A Study in Legal-Economic Analysis. Lexington Mass.; Lexington Books, 1987. 271p. Q

Second Mulkay, Michael J. Science and Sociology of Knowledge. London; G. Allen and Unwin, 1979. 132p.

Second Mundlak, Yair. Intersectoral Factor Mobility and Agricultural Growth. Washington, D.C.; International Food Policy Research Institute, 1979. 138p. (IFPRI Research Report No. 6) Q

Second Murdoch, William W. The Poverty of Nations: The Political Economy of Hunger and Population. Baltimore; Johns Hopkins University Press, 1980. 382p.

Third Murray, William G., et al. Farm Appraisal and Valuation. 6th ed. Ames; Iowa State University Press, 1983. 303p.

Third Musgrave, Richard A., and Peggy B. Musgrave. Public Finance in Theory and Practice. 4th ed. New York; McGraw Hill, 1984. 824p. (1st ed., 1973. 762p.)

Third Myers, James H., and William H. Reynolds. Consumer Behavior and Marketing Management. Boston; Houghton Mifflin, 1967. 336p.

Second Myint, Hla. The Economics of the Developing Countries. New York; Praeger, 1964. 192p.

First rank Myrdal, Gunnar. Against the Stream: Critical Essays in Economics. New York; Random House, 1973. 336p.

Second Myrdal, Gunnar. Objectivity in Social Research. Latrobe, Penn.; Archabby Press, 1969. 111p. (Reprinted in paperback by Middletown, Conn.; Wesleyan University Press, 1983, 117p.)

First rank Myrdal, Gunnar. Rich Lands and Poor: The Road to World Prosperity. New York; Harper, 1957. 168p. (Also issued as Economic Theory and Under-Developed Regions. London; Duckworth, 1957. 167p.)

N

Third Nachtigal, Paul A., ed. Rural Education: In Search of a Better Way. Boulder, Colo.; Westview Press, 1982. 326p.

Second Nadel, M. V. The Politics of Consumer Protection. Indianapolis, Ind.; Bobbs-Merrill, 1971. 257p.

Second Nair, Kusum. Transforming Traditionally: Land and Labor use in Agriculture in Asia and Africa. Riverdale, Maryland; Riverdale Co., 1983. 168p.

Third Nakajima, Chihiro. Subjective Equilibrium Theory of the Farm Household. Translation of his Noko Shutai Kinkoron. Amsterdam and New York; Elsevier Science Publ. Co., 1986. 302p.

Third Narajan, B. K. and D. V. Rao. Integrated Rural Development: An Approach to Command Areas. Bangalore, India; IBH Prakashana, 1983. 191p.

Second National Academy of Sciences (U.S.). The Impact of Science and Technology on Regional Economic Development. Washington, D. C.; National Academy of Science, 1969. 112p. (National Research Council Publication No. 1731)

First rank National Advisory Commission on Rural Poverty (U. S.). Rural Poverty in the United States. Washington, D.C.; U.S. Government Printing Office, 1968. 601p.

First rank National Advisory Commission on Rural Poverty, (U. S.). The People Left Behind. Washington, D.C.; Government Printing Office, 1967. 160p.

Third National Planning Association. U.S. Agriculture and Third World Economic Development: Critical Interdependency. Washington, D.C.; National Planning Assoc., 1987. 210p.

Second National Planning Association. State of American Agriculture. Washington, D.C.; The Association, 1984. 71p.

Second National Research Council (U. S.). World Food and Nutrition Study: Supporting Papers. Washington, D.C.; National Academy of Sciences, 1977. 5 vols.

Third National Research Council (U.S.). Conference on Agricultural Research Priorities for Economic Development in Africa. Washington, D.C.; National Academy of Sciences, 1968. 3 vols.

Third National Research Council (U.S.). Post-Harvest Food Losses in Developing Countries. Washington, D.C.; National Academy of Sciences, 1978. 206p.

Third National Research Council (U.S.). Productive Agriculture and a Quality Environment: Food Production, Living, Recreation, the Rural-Urban Interface. Washington, D.C.; National Academy of Sciences, 1974. 189p. (Paper edition available from Books on Demand.)

Third National Research Council (U.S.). The African Challenge: In Search of Appropriate Development Strategies. Nairobi; Heinemann, 1986. 182p.

Third Naylor, T.H., ed. The Design of Computer Simulation Experiments. Durham, N.C.; Duke University Press, 1969. 417p.

Third Neale, Walter C. Economic Change in Rural India: Land Tenure and Reform in Uttar Pradish, 1800–1955. New Haven; Yale University Press, 1962. 333p. (Reprinted by Associated Faculty Press, 1973. 352p.)

Third Nelson, A. G., W. F. Lee, and W. G. Murray. Agricultural Finance. 8th ed. Ames; Iowa State University Press, 1988. 468p. (Primary author varies among editions.)

First rank Nelson, Michael. The Development of Tropical Lands: Policy Issues in Latin America. Baltimore; Johns Hopkins University Press, 1973. 323p.

Second Nerlove, Marc. Distributed Lags and Demand Analysis. Washinton, D. C.; U. S. Department of Agriculture, 1958. 121p. (USDA Agricultural Handbook No. 141.) Q

First rank Nerlove, Marc. The Dynamics of Supply: Estimation of Farmers' Response to Price. Baltimore; Johns Hopkins University Press, 1958. 268p. (Reprinted in 1978 by AMS Press)

Third Nestel, B., ed. Agricultural Research for Development Potentials and Challenges in Asia. The Hague, Netherlands; ISNAR, 1983. 60p.

Third Neter, John, William Wasserman, and Michael H. Kutner. Applied Linear Regression Models. Rev. ed. Homewood, IL; R.D. Irwin, 1989. 667p. (1st ed., 1983. 547p.)

Third Neville-Rolfe, E. The Politics of Agriculture in the European Community. London; European Centre for Policy Studies, 1984. 547 p.

Third Newbery, David M. G. and Joseph E. Stiglitz. The Theory of Commodity Price Stabilization: A Study in the Economics of Risk. Oxford; Clarendon Press, 1981. 462p.

Second Newby, Howard, ed. International Perspectives in Rural Sociology. Chichester, Eng. and New York; Wiley, 1978. 220p.

Third Newell, A. and H. A. Simon. Human Problem Solving. Englewood Cliffs, N.J.; Prentice-Hall, 1972. 920p.

Second Nicholls, W.H. A Theoretical Analysis of Imperfect Competition With Special Applications in the Agricultural Industries. Ames; Iowa State College Press, 1941. 384p. AAEA Classic

Second Nicholls, W.H. Southern Tradition and Regional Progress. Chapel Hill; University of North Carolina Press, 1960. 202p. (Reissued: Westport, Conn.; Greenwood Press, 1976)

Third Niehoff, Arthur H, and K. L. Neff. Non-formal Education and the Rural Poor: Report of a Conference and Workshop. East Lansing; Michigan State University, Institute for International Studies, 1977. 248p.

Third Niehoff, Arthur H., ed. A Casebook of Social Change. Chicago; Aldine Publishing Co., 1966. 312p.

Third Nourse, H.O. Regional Economics: A Study in the Economic Structure, Stability and Growth of Regions. New York; McGraw-Hill, 1968. 247p.

Third Nunnally, Jum. Psychometric Theory. 2d ed. New York; McGraw-Hill, 1978. 701p. (1st ed., 1967. 640p.)

Second Nurkse, R. Problems of Capital Formation in Underdeveloped Countries, and Patterns of Trade and Development. New York; Oxford University Press, 1967. 226p.

O

Third Offer, Avner. Property and Politics, 1870–1914: Landownership, Law, Ideology and Urban Development in England. Cambridge University Press, 1981. 445p.

Third Ofori, Patrick E. Land in Africa: Its Administration, Law, Tenure and Use: A Select Bibliography. Nendeln, Liechtenstein; Kraus International Publications, 1978. 199p.

Second Ogburn, W.F. On Culture and Social Change, Selected Papers. Chicago; University of Chicago Press, 1964. 360p.

Third Oh, Heung Keun. Development of Food and Agricultural Statistics in Asia and Pacific Region, 1965–1987. Seoul; Korea Rural Economics Institute, 1988. 397p.

First rank Ohkawa, K., B. F. Johnston, and H. Kaneda, eds. Agriculture and Economic Growth: Japan's Experience. University of Tokyo Press, 1969; and Princeton University Press, 1970. 433p.

First rank Okun, A. M. Equality and Efficiency: The Big Tradeoff. Washington, D.C.; Brookings Institute, 1975. 124p.

Second Okun, A.M. The Political Economy of Prosperity. Washington, D.C.; Brookings Institute, 1970. 152p.

Second Okun, Bernard and Richard W. Richardson. Studies in Economic Development. New York; Holt, Rinehart, and Winston, 1961.

First rank Olson, Mancur. The Logic of Collective Action: Public Goods and the Theory of Groups. Cambridge, Mass.; Harvard University Press, 1965. 176p. (Reprinted in 1971, 186p.)

First rank Olson, Mancur. The Rise and Decline of Nations: Economic Growth, Stagflation, and Social Rigidities. New Haven, Conn.; Yale University Press, 1982. 273p.

Third Opie, John. The Law of the Land: Two Hundred Years of American Farmland Policy. Lincoln; University of Nebraska Press, 1987. 231p.

Second Orcutt, G. J., M. Greenberger, J. Korbel, and A. M. Rivlin. Microanalysis of Socio-Economic Systems: A Simulation Study. New York; Harper, 1961. 425p.

Third Organisation for Economic Co-operation and Development. Agricultural Trade With Developing Countries. Paris; OECD, 1984. 113p.

Third Organisation of Economic Co-operation and Development. The Implications of Different Means of Agricultural Income Support. Paris; OECD, 1983. 80p.

Third Organisation of Economic Co-operation and Development . The Instability of Agricultural Commodity Markets. Paris; OECD, 1980. 237p.

Third Organisation of Economic Co-operation and Development. Milk and Milk Products Balances In OECD Countries, 1974–1982. Paris; OECD, 1984. 173p.

Third Organisation for Economic Co-operation and Development. National Policies and Agricultural Trade. Paris; OECD, 1987. 333p.

Third Organisation for Economic Co-operation and Development. Problems of Agricultural Trade. Paris; OECD Publications and Information Center, 1982. 178p.

Third Organisation of Economic Co-operation and Development. Prospects for Agricultural Production and Trade in Eastern Europe: Bulgaria, Czechoslavakia, Romania, Vol. 2. Paris; OECD, 1982. 216p.

Second Organisation for Economic Co-operation and Development. The United States Agriculture and Food Act of 1981. Paris; OECD, 1982.

Third Orlove, Benjamin S. and Glynn Custred, eds. Land and Power in Latin America: Agrarian Economies and Social Process in the Andes. New York; Holmes and Meier, 1980. 258p.

Third Ortiz, Roxanne D. Roots of Resistance: Land Tenure in New Mexico, 1690–1980. University of California, Los Angeles, Chicano Studies Research Center, Pubns. Unit, 1980. 202p.

Third Osburn, Donald D., and Kenneth C. Schneeberger. Modern Agriculture Management. Reston, Virginia; Reston Publ. Co, 1978. 369p.

Third Oser, J. and Stanley Brue. The Evolution of Economic Thought. 4th ed. N. Y., San Diego; Harcourt Brace Jovanovich, 1988. 527p. (1st ed.: Oser only. New York; Harcourt, Brace and World, 1963. 399p.)

Third Osterud, Oyvind. Agrarian Structure and Peasant Politics in Scandinavia: A Comparative Study of Rural Response to Economic Change. Oslo; Universitetsforlaget, 1978. 278p.

Second Ostrom, V. The Intellectual Crisis in American Public Administration. 2d ed. University, Ala.; University of Alabama Press, 1989. (1st ed., 1973. 165p.)

Third Otalora, Hernando Gomez and Eduardo Wiesner Duran, eds. Lecturas sobre Desarrollo Economico Colombiano, en Honor de Alvaro Lopez Toro. Bogata; Fundacion para la Educacion Superior y el Desarrollo, 1974. 624p.

Third Ott, David J., Attiat F. Ott, and Jang H. Yoo. Macroeconomic Theory. New York: McGraw-Hill Book Company, 1975. 401p. (Reprinted by Lanham, Maryland; University Press of America, 1983.)

Third Ottoson, H.W., ed. Land Use Policy and Problems in the United States. Lincoln; University of Nebraska Press, 1963. 470p.

Third Ottoson, H. W. and E. M. Birch. Land and People in the Northern Plains Transition Area. Lincoln; Univ. of Nebraska, 1966. 362p. (Reprinted New York; Arno Press, 1979 and Ayer Company Publishers, Inc.)

Third Oxaal, I., T. Barnett, and D. Booth. Beyond the Sociology of Development: Economy and Society in Latin America and Africa. London and Boston; Routledge and Kegan Paul, 1975. 295p.

P

First rank Paarlberg, Don. Farm and Food Policy: Issues of the 1980s. Lincoln; University of Nebraska Press, 1980. 338p.

Third Paarlberg, Don. Toward a Well-Fed World. Ames; Iowa State University Press, 1988. 270p.

First rank Paarlberg, Robert L. Food Trade and Foreign Policy: India, the Soviet Union, and the United States. Ithaca, N.Y.; Cornell University Press, 1985. 266p.

Third Pacey, Arnold and Philip Payne, eds. Agricultural Development and Nutrition. London, Hutchinson; Boulder, Colo.; Westview Press, 1985. 255p.

Second Padfield, Harland and William E. Martin. Farmers, Workers and Machines: Technological and Social Change in Farm Industries of Arizona. Tucson; University of Arizona Press, 1965. 325p. Q

Third Page, Talbot. Conservation and Economic Efficiency: An Approach to Materials Policy. Baltimore; Johns Hopkins University Press for Resources for the Future, 1977. 266p.

Second Paige, Jeffery M. Agrarian Revolution: Social Movements and Export Agriculture in the Underdeveloped World. New York; Free Press, 1978. 435p.

Third Palmer, J.L., and J.A. Pechman, eds. Welfare in Rural Areas: The North Carolina-Iowa Income Maintenance Experiment. Washington, D. C.; Brookings Institution, 1978. 273p.

Third Palmer, Robin. Land and Racial Domination in Rhodesia. Los Angeles; University of California Press; and London; Heineman, 1977. 307p. (Perspective on Southern Africa: No. 24)

Third Panda, R. K. Agricultural Indebtedness and Institutional Finance, India. India; Ashish Publ., 1985. 180p.

Second Papi, G. U., and C. S. Nunn, eds. Economic Problems of Agriculture in Developed Societies. New York; St. Martin's Press, and London; Macmillan, 1969. 671p. (Reprinted: New York; Stockton, 1986)

Second Parker, William N. and Eric L. Jones, eds. European Peasants and Their Markets: Essays in Agrarian Economic History. Princeton, N.J.; Princeton University Press, 1975. 366p.

Third Parmar, B.D. Regional Development and Agricultural Wages. Delhi; Himalaya Publishing House, 1986. 243p.

Third Parpala, Oprea. Economii si politici agrare in Lume. Bucuresti; Editura Politica, 1982. 460p.

Third Pasour, E.C. U.S. Agricultural Policies: A Market Process Approach. Irvington-on-Hudson, N. Y.; Foundation for Economic Education, 1986. 184p.

Third Patricios, Nicholas N., ed. International Handbook on Land Use Planning. Westport, Conn.; Greenwood Press, 1986. 679p.

Third Paulino, L. A. Food in the Third World: Past Trends and Projection to 2000. Washington, D.C.; International Food Policy Research Institute, 1986. 76p. (IFPRI Research Report no. 52)

Second Pearse, Andrew C. Seeds of Plenty, Seeds of Want: Social and Economic Implications of the Green Revolution. Oxford; Clarendon Press; and New York; Oxford University Press, 1980. 262p.

Third	Pearson, Scott R., et al. Portuguese Agriculture in Transition. Ithaca, N.Y.; Cornell University Press, 1987. 283p.
Third	Peck, Ann E., ed. Selected Writings on Futures Markets: Explorations in Financial Futures Markets. Chicago; Board of Trade, 1985. 467p.
Third	Peck, Ann E., ed. Futures Markets: Their Economic Role. Washington, D.C.; American Enterprise Institute for Public Policy Research, 1985. 2 vols.
Second	Pederson, P. O. Urban-Regional Development in South America: A Process of Diffusion and Integration. The Hague and Paris; Mouton, 1975. 294p.
Third	Pedhazur, Elazar J. Multiple Regression in Behavioral Research. 2d ed. New York; Holt, Rinehart and Winston, 1982. 822p.
Third	Penson, John B., Jr., and David A. Lins. Agricultural Finance. Englewood Cliffs, N.J.; Prentice-Hall, 1980. 546p.
Third	Penson, John B., Jr., Rulon Pope, and M.L. Cook. Introduction to Agricultural Economics. Englewood Cliffs, N.J.; Prentice-Hall, 1986. 556p.
Second	Perelman, Michael. Farming for Profit in a Hungry World: Capital and the Crisis in Agriculture. Montclair, N.J.; Allanheld, Osmun and Co. Pubs., Inc., 1978. 250p.
Second	Perin, Constance. Everything in Its Place: Social Order and Land Use in America. Princeton University Press, 1977. 291p.
Second	Perloff, H.S., E.S. Dunn, Jr., E.E. Lampard, and R.F. Muth. Regions, Resources, and Economic Growth. Baltimore; Johns Hopkins University Press for Resources for the Future, 1960. 716p. (Reprinted: Lincoln; University of Nebraska Press, 1967)
Third	Perrie, Maureen. Agrarian Policy of the Russian Socialist Revolutionary Party. ; Cambridge University Press, 1977. 216p. (Soviet and Eastern European Studies)
Third	Petersen, Gary W. and Marvin T. Beatty, eds. Planning Future Land Uses. Madison, Wisc.; American Society of Agronomy, 1981. 71p. (ASA Special Publications Ser.)
First rank	Peterson, Trudy H. Farmers, Bureaucrats, and Middlemen: Historical Perspectives on American Agriculture. Washington, D.C.; Howard University Press, 1980. 357p.
Third	Peterson, Trudy H. Agricultural Exports, Farm Income, and the Eisenhower Administration. Lincoln; University of Nebraska Press, 1979. 222p.
Third	Peterson, W. H. The Great Farm Problem. Chicago; Regnery, 1959. 235p.
Third	Petras, J., ed. Critical Perspectives on Imperialism and Social Class in the Third World. New York; Monthly Review Press, 1978. 314p.
Third	Pfeifer, Karen. Agrarian Reform under State Capitalism in Algeria. Boulder, Colo.; Westview Press, 1985. 235p.
Third	Phelps, E.S. Golden Rules of Economic Growth: Studies of Efficient and Optimal Investment. New York; Norton, 1966. 189p.
Third	Phifer, Bryan and Fred List. Community Development: A New Dimension of Extension. Columbia, Mo.; University of Missouri, Extension Division, 1971.
Third	Phillips, W.G. The Agricultural Implement Industry in Canada: A Study in Competition. Toronto; University of Toronto Press, 1956. 208p.
Second	Phipps, Tim T., Pierre A. Crosson, and Kent Price, eds. Agriculture and the Environment. Washington, D.C.; National Center for Food and Agricultural Policy; and Resources for the Future, 1986. 298p.

First rank Pigou, A. C. The Economics of Welfare. 4th ed. London; Macmillan, 1932. 837p.

First rank Pimentel, David, and Carl W. Hall, eds. Food and Energy Resources. New York; Academic Press, 1984. 268p.

Third Pindyck, R., and D. Rubinfeld. Econometric Models and Economic Forecasts. 2d ed. New York; McGraw-Hill, 1981. 630p. (1st ed., 1976. 576p.)

First rank Pineiro, M., E. Trigo, and R. Florentino, eds. Technical Change and Social Conflict in Agriculture. Boulder, Colo.; Westview Press, 1983. 248p.

Second Pingali, Prabhu, Yves Bigot, and Hans Binswanger. Agricultural Mechanization and the Evolution of Farming Systems in Sub-Saharan Africa. Baltimore; Johns Hopkins University Press, 1987. 224p. AAEA Award Winner Q

First rank Pinstrup-Anderson, Per. Agricultural Research and Technology in Economic Development. London; Longman, Inc., 1982. 304p.

First rank Pinstrup-Anderson, Per, ed. Food Subsidies in Developing Countries: Costs, Benefits, and Policy Options. Baltimore; Johns Hopkins University Press for International Food Policy Research Institute, 1988. 374p.

First rank Pinstrup-Anderson, Per. Nutritional Consequences of Agricultural Projects: Conceptual Relationships and Assessment Approaches. Washington, D.C.; World Bank, 1981. 93p. (World Bank Staff Working Paper no. 456)

Third Pirtle, Thomas R. History of the Dairy Industry. Chicago; Mojonnier Bros., 1926. 645p. (Reprinted; Wilmington, Delaware; Scholarly Resources, Inc., 1973.)

Third Plant, Roger. Sugar and Modern Slavery: Haitian Migrant Labour and the Dominican Republic. London; Zed Press, 1986. 208p.

Second Platt, Rutherford H., and G. Macinko, eds. Beyond the Urban Fringe: Land-Use Issues of Nonmetropolitan America. Minneapolis; University of Minnesota Press, 1983. 431p.

Third Poats, Rutherford M. Technology for Developing Nations: New Directions for U. S. Technical Assistance. Washington, D.C.; Brookings Institute, 1972. 255p.

Third Poirot, Paul L., ed. The Farm Problem. Irvington-on-Hudson, N. Y.; Foundation for Economic Education, Inc., 1986. 152p.

Second Polanyi, K. The Great Transformation: The Political and Economic Origins of Our Time. New York; Rinehart, 1944. 305p. (Beacon Press paperback in 1957; Octagon, 1973.)

Third Pollard, S. The Idea of Progress: History and Society. London; Watts, 1968. 220p. (The New Thinkers Library No. 26) (Reprinted: Hammondsworth, Eng.; Penguin, 1971.)

Second Pomareda, Carlos. Financial Policies and Management of Agricultural Development Banks. Boulder, Colo.; Westview Press, 1984. 180p.

Second Pond, W. G., R. A. Merkel, L. D. McGilliard, and V. J. Rhodes, eds. Animal Agriculture: Research to Meet Human Needs in the 21st Century. Boulder, Colo.; Westview Press, 1980. 355p.

Third Pontecorvo, G., ed. The Management of Food Policy. New York; Arno Press for Columbia University, Graduate School of Business, 1976. 299p.

First rank Popper, K. R. The Logic of Scientific Discovery. New York; Basic Books, 1959. 479p.

Rank	Entry
First rank	Portes, A., and J. Walton. Labor, Class, and the International System. New York; Academic Press, 1981. 230p.
Third	Posner, R. Economic Analysis of Law. 3d ed. Boston; Little, Brown, 1986. 666p. (1st ed., 1972. 415p.)
Third	Poston, Richard W. Democracy Speaks Many Tongues: Community Development Around the World. New York; Harper and Row, 1962. 206p.
Third	Poston, Richard W. Small Town Renaissance: A Study of the Montana Study. New York; Harper and Brothers, 1950. 231p. (Reprinted: Westport, Conn.; Greenwood Press, 1971)
Third	Prasad, Ramayan. Agricultural Taxation and Economic Development. New Delhi; Deep and Deep Publications, 1987. 207p.
Third	Preston, L. E., and N. R. Collins. Studies in a Simulated Market. Berkeley: IBER Publications, 1966. 180p.
Third	Price, Kent A., ed. The Dilemmas of Choice. Washington, D.C.; National Center for Food and Agricultural Policy; and Resources for the Future, 1985. 248p.
Third	Provus, Malcolm. Discrepancy Evaluation for Educational Program Improvement and Assessment. Berkeley, Calif.; McCutchan, 1968. 380p.
Second	Purcell, Randall B. and Elizabeth Morrison, eds. U.S. Agriculture and Third World Development: The Critical Linkage. Boulder, Colo.; Lynne Rienner Publ., 1987. 258p.
Third	Purcell, Wayne. Agriculture Marketing: Systems, Coordination, Cash and Future Prices. Reston, Vir.; Reston Publishing Co, 1979. 472p.

R

Rank	Entry
Third	Rae, Alan N. Crop Management Economics. London and Granada; Brookfield Publishing Co., 1977. 525p. (Reprinted by London; Grosby Lockwood Staples, 1981)
Third	Rahman, Mushtaqur. Agrarian Egalitarianism, Land Tenures and Land Reforms in South Asia. Dubuque, Iowa; Kendall/Hunt Publ. Co., 1980. 200p.
Third	Rahmato, Dessalegn. Agrarian Reform in Ethiopia. Uppsala; Scandinavian Institute of African Studies, 1984. 105p. (Reprinted by Trenton, N.J.; Red Sea Press, 1985)
Third	Raj, K. N., ed. Essays on the Commercialization of Indian Agriculture. Oxford University Press, 1986. 375p.
Third	Rajapurohit, A. R., ed. Land Reforms in India. New Delhi; Ashish, 1984. 216p.
Third	Rao, Sudha V. Education and Rural Development. Beverly Hills, Calif.; Sage Publications, 1986. 336p.
Second	Raper, Arthur F. Rural Development in Action: The Comprehensive Experiment at Comilla, East Pakistan. Ithaca, N.Y.; Cornell University Press, 1970. 351p.
First rank	Rasmussen, Wayne D. and R. J. Hildreth. The USDA-Land Grant University in Transition. East Lansing; Michigan State University, Cooperative Extension Service, 1984.
Third	Rastyannikov, V. G. Agrarian Evolution in a Multiform Structure Society: Experience of Independent India. (Trans. from Russian). London, Boston; Routledge and Kigour, Methuen, Inc., 1981. 373p.
Third	Rau, A.F. Agricultural Policy and Trade Liberalization in the United States, 1934–1956: A Study of Conflicting Policies. Droz, Switzerland; Coronet Books, 1957. 160p.

Third Raunikar, Robert, ed. Food Demand and Consumption Behavior. Sponsored by S-119 Southern Regional Research Committee and the Farm Foundation. Athens; University of Georgia, 1977. 163p.

First rank Rausser, Gordon C., ed. New Directions in Econometric Modeling and Forecasting in U.S. Agriculture. New York; Elsevier-North Holland, 1982. 830p.

Second Rausser, Gordon C. and E. Hochman, eds. Dynamic of Agricultural Systems: Economic Prediction and Control. Amsterdam; North Holland Publ., 1979. 364p. Q

First rank Rausser, Gordon C. and K. R. Farrell, eds. Alternative Agricultural and Food Policies and the 1985 Farm Bill. Berkeley; Giannini Foundation, University of California, 1984. 425p.

Third Ravenhill, J., ed. Africa in Economic Crisis. New York; Columbia University Press, 1986. 359p.

Third Rawlins, N. Omri. Introduction to Agribusiness. Englewood Cliffs, N. J.; Prentice-Hall, Inc., 1980. 248p.

Second Rawls, J. The Theory of Justice. Cambridge, Mass.; Harvard University Press, 1971. 607p.

Second Rawski, Evelyn S. Agricultural Change and the Peasant Economy of South China. Cambridge, Mass.; Harvard University Press, 1972. 280p. (East Asian Ser: No. 66)

Third Ray, P.K. Agriculture Insurance: Principles and Organization and Application to Developing Countries. 2d ed. Oxford; Pergamon Press, 1981. 419p.

Third Ray, Susanta K., R. W. Cummings, Jr., and R. W. Herdt. Policy Planning for Agricultural Development. New Delhi, India; Tata and McGraw-Hill, 1979. 237p.

Third Reddy, D. Obul. Co-operative Agricultural Development Banks: A Case Study of Andhra Pradesh. Delhi, India; B. R. Publ. Corp., 1987. 429p.

Third Redfield, Robert. The Little Community: Viewpoints for the Study of a Human Whole. Chicago, Ill.; University of Chicago Press, 1955. 182p.

Second Redfield, Sarah E. Vanishing Farmland: A Legal Solution for the States. Cambridge, Mass.; Lexington Books, 1984. 224p.

Second Renne, R.R. Land Economics: Principles, Problems, and Policies in Utilizing Land Resources. Rev. ed. New York; Harper, 1958. 599p. (1st ed. 1947. 736p.)

First rank Reutlinger, Shlomo and Marcelo Selowski. Malnutrition and Poverty: Magnitude and Policy Options. Baltimore; Johns Hopkins Univ. Press, 1976. 82p. (World Bank Occ. Paper 23)

Second Reutlinger, Shlomo. Techniques for Project Appraisal Under Uncertainty. Baltimore; Johns Hopkins University Press, 1970. 95p.

First rank Reynolds, Lloyd G., ed. Agriculture in Development Theory. New Haven; Yale University Press, 1975. 510p.

Third Rhind, D., and R. Hudson. Land Use. London and New York; Methuen, Inc., 1980. 272p.

Second Richardson, Harry W. Regional Economics. Urbana; University of Illinois Press, 1979. 325p.

Third Richardson, Harry W. Regional Growth Theory. New York; Wiley, and London; Macmillan, 1973. 264p.

Second Riddell, Robert. Regional Development Policy: The Struggle for Rural Progress in Low-Income Nationals. Aldershot, Eng.; Gower, and New York; St. Martin's Press. 1985. 282p.

Second Riker, W.H. The Theory of Political Coalitions. New Haven; Yale University Press, 1962. 300p. (Reprinted Westport, Conn; Greenwood Press, 1984)

Third Ritson, Christopher. Agricultural Economics: Principles and Policy. New York; St. Martin's Press, Inc., 1977. 409p. (Reprinted by Boulder, Colo.; Westview Press, 1982).

Third Rivera, W. and S. Schram, eds. Agricultural Extension Worldwide: Issues, Practices and Emerging Priorities. London; Croom Helm, 1987. 294p.

First rank Robbins, L. An Essay on the Nature and Significance of Economic Science. 3d ed. London; Macmillan, 1932. 160p. (Reprinted by New York; New York University Press, 1984.)

Third Roberts, B., R. Finnegan, and D. Gallie, eds. New Approaches to Economic Life. Manchester; Manchester University Press, 1985. 566p.

Third Roberts, Colleen, ed. Agriculture Sector Symposium (8th, 1988 at World Bank): Trade, Aid and Policy Reform. Washington, D.C.; World Bank, 1988. 223p.

Third Roberts, Hayden. Community Development: Learning and Action. Toronto; University of Toronto Press, 1979. 201p.

Second Robinson, E. A. G., ed. Problems in Economic Development: Proceedings of a Conference Held by the International Economic Association. New York; St. Martin's Press, 1965. 625p.

Third Rochester, Anna. Lenin on the Agrarian Question. New York; International Pub., 1942. 224p.

Third Rock, V.P., ed. Policymakers and Model Builders: Cases and Concepts: Symposium on the Role of Economic Models in Policy Formation. New York; Gordon and Breach, 1969. 639p.

Second Rodefeld, Richard D., et. al. Change in Rural America: Causes, Consequences, and Alternatives. St. Louis; C.V. Mosby Co., 1978. 551p.

Third Rodney, W. How Europe Underdeveloped Africa. Washington, D.C.; Howard University Press, 1974. 288p.

Second Rogers, Everett M. Modernization Among Peasants; the Impact of Communication. New York; Holt, Rinehart and Winston, 1969. 429p.

Third Roling, N. G. Extension Science: Information Systems in Agricultural Development. Cambridge University Press, 1988. 233p.

Second Rosenblum, J. W., ed. Agriculture in the 21st Century. New York; John Wiley and Sons, 1983. 415p.

Third Rossi, Peter H., Howard E. Freeman, and Sonia R. Wright, eds. Evaluation. A Systematic Approach. 3d ed. Beverly Hills, Calif.; Sage, 1985. 423p. (1st ed., 1979. 336p.)

Second Rossmiller, G. E., ed. Agricultural Sector Planning: A General System Simulation Approach. East Lansing; Michigan State University, Department of Agricultural Economics, 1978. 430p.

Second Rostow, W. W. How It All Began: The Origins of Modern Economic Growth. New York; McGraw-Hill, 1975. 264p.

Second Rostow, W. W. The Process of Economic Growth. 2d ed. Oxford; Clarendon Press, 1960. 372p. (1st ed., 1952. 285p.)

First rank Rostow, W. W. The Stages of Economic Growth: A Non-Communist Manifesto. 2d ed. Cambridge; Cambridge University Press, 1971. 253p. (1st ed., 1952. 178p.)

Third — Rothenberg, J. The Measurement of Social Welfare. Englewood Cliffs, N.J.; Prentice-Hall, 1961. 357p.

Third — Rothman, J. Planning and Organizing for Social Change. New York; Columbia University Press, 1974. 628p.

First rank — Roumasset, James A., Jean-Marc Boussard, and Inderjit Singh, eds. Risk, Uncertainty and Agricultural Development. Laguna, Philippines; Southeast Asian Regional Center for Graduate Study and Research in Agriculture; and New York; Agricultural Development Council, 1979. 453p.

Second — Runge, C. Ford., ed. The Future of the North American Granary: Politics, Economics, and Resource Constraints in North American Agriculture. Ames; Iowa State University Press, 1985. 240p.

Second — Rural Appraisal Manual. 5th ed. Denver; American Society of Farm Managers and Rural Appraisers, 1979. 288p.

Third — Rural Housing Alliance. Low-Income Housing Programs for Rural America. 4th ed. Washington, D.C.; Rural Housing Alliance, 1973. 32p.

Third — Russel, E. John. A History of Agricultural Science in Great Britain: 1620–1954. London; Allen and Unwin, 1966. 493p.

Third — Russell, Robert R., and Maurice Wilkinson. Microeconomics: A Synthesis of Modern and Neoclassical Theory. New York; Wiley, 1979. 459p.

Second — Ruthenberg, H. Farming Systems in the Tropics. 3d ed. Oxford; Clarendon, 1980. 424p. (1st ed., 1971, 313p.)

First rank — Ruttan, Vernon W. Agricultural Research Policy. Minneapolis; University of Minnesota Press, 1982. 369p.

Second — Ruttan, Vernon W., and Carl Pray. Policy for Agricultural Research. Boulder, Colo.; Westview Press, 1987. 576p.

S

Third — Sahasraludhey, Sunil. The Peasant Movement Today. New Delhi; South Asia Bks., 1986. 224p.

Third — Sahu, Nirmal C. Economics of Forest Resources: Problems and Policies in a Regional Economy. Delhi, India; B. R. Publ. Corp., 1986. 360p. (Distributed by Apt Bks.)

Second — Saloutos, Theodore. The American Farmer and the New Deal. Ames, Iowa; Iowa State University Press, 1982. 327p.

Second — Saloutos, Theodore. Farmer Movements in the South, 1865–1933. Berkeley; University of California Press, 1960. 354p. (Reprinted Millwood, New York; Kraus, 1980) (University of California Publications in History, v.64)

First rank — Salter, Leonard A., Jr. A Critical Review of Research in Land Economics. Minneapolis; University of Minnesota Press, 1948. 258p. (Reprinted in 1967) AAEA Classic

Second — Salter, W. E. G. Productivity and Technical Change. Cambridge; At the University Press, 1969. 220p. (1st ed., 1960. 198p.) (Cambridge University Dept. of Applied Econ., Monograph 6)

Third — Sampath, R. K. Economic Efficiency in Indian Agriculture. Delhi; Macmillan Company of India, 1979. 191p.

First rank — Samuelson, Paul. Foundations of Economic Analysis. Cambridge; Harvard University Press, 1947. 447p.

First rank — Sanderson, Ezra D. The Rural Community: The Natural History of a Sociological Group. Boston; Ginn and Co., 1932. 723p.

Third Sanderson, Fred H. and S. Roy. Food Trends and Prospects in India. Washington, D.C.; Brookings Institution, 1979. 162p.

Second Sanderson, Steven E. The Transformation of Mexican Agriculture: International Structure and the Politics of Rural Change. Princeton; Princeton University Press, 1986. 324p.

Third Sanderson, Susan Walsh. Land Reform in Mexico: 1910–1980. Orlando, Fla.; Academic Press, 1984. 186p.

Third Sargent, M.J. Economics in Horticulture. London; Macmillan, 1973. 137p.

Second Sargent, Thomas J. Macroeconomic Theory. 2d ed. Boston; Academic Press, 1987. 510p. (1st ed., 1977)

Third Sarma, J.S. Agricultural Policy in India: Growth with Equity. Ottawa, Canada; Int. Develop. Research Centre, 1982. 94p.

Third Satin, Mark. New Age Politics: Healing Self and Society. Rev. ed. N.Y.; Dell Publ. Co., 1979. 349p. (1st ed., West Vancouver, British Columbia; Whitecap Books, 1978. 240p.)

Third Saunders, Robert J. and Jeremy J. Warford. Village Water Supply: Economics and Policy in the Developing World. Baltimore; Johns Hopkins University Press, 1976. 279p.

Second Scandizzo, Pasquale L. and Colin Bruce. Methodologies for Measuring Agricultural Price Intervention Effects. Washington, D.C.; World Bank, 1980. 96p. (World Bank Staff Working Paper, no. 394)

Second Scandizzo, Pasquale L., Peter Hazell and Jock Anderson. Risky Agricultural Markets: Price Forecasting and the Need for Intervention Policies. Boulder, Colo.; Westview Press, 1984. 142p. (A Westview Replica Ed.)

Second Scarf, Herbert E. and Terje Hansen. The Computation of Economic Equilibria. New Haven, Conn.; Yale University Press, 1973. 249p.

Second Scherer, Frederic M. Industrial Market Structure and Economic Performance. 2d ed. Boston; Houghton Mifflin, 1980. 632p. (1st ed., Chicago; Rand McNally, 1970. 574p.)

Third Scherer, Jacqueline. Contemporary Community: Sociological Illusion or Reality? London; Tavistock, 1972. 152p.

First rank Schertz, Lyle P. Another Revolution in U.S. Farming? Washington, D.C.; USDA, Economics, Statistics, and Cooperatives Service, 1979. 445p (USDA Agricultural Economic Report No. 441)

Third Schickele, R. Agricultural Policy: Farm Programs and National Welfare. New York; McGraw-Hill, 1954. 453p.

Third Schipper, L. Consumer Discretionary Behavior: A Comparative Study in Alternative Methods of Empirical Research. Amsterdam; North-Holland Publ. Co., 1964. 98p.

Second Schmid, A. A. Property, Power, and Public Choice: An Inquiry into Law and Economics. 2d ed. New York; Praeger, 1987. 332p. (1st ed., New York; Praeger, 1978. 316p.)

Second Schmitz, A., Alex F. McCalla, Donald O. Mitchell, and Colin Carter. Grain Export Cartels. Cambridge, Mass.; Ballinger, 1981. 298p. Q

Second Schmookler, J. Invention and Economic Growth. Cambridge; Harvard University Press, 1966. 332p.

Third Schneeberger, Kenneth C. and Donald D. Osburn. Financial Planning in Agriculture: A Key to Credit and Money Management. Danville, Ill.; Interstate Printers and Publishers, Inc., 1977. 80p.

Second Schneider, E. Pricing and Equilibrium. English version. New York; Macmillan, 1962. 375p. (Translated from the original German. London; William Hodge and Co., 1952. 327p.).

Third Schneider, H. K. Economic Man: The Anthropology of Economics. New York; Free Press, 1974. 278p.

Second Schnepf, Max, ed. Farmland, Food and the Future. Ankeny, Iowa; Soil Conservation Society of America, 1980. 214p.

Second Schran, Peter. The Development of Chinese Agriculture, 1950–1959. Urbana; University of Illinois Press, 1969. 238p.

Second Schuh, G. Edward, ed. Technology, Human Capital and the World Food Problem. St. Paul, Minn.; University of Minnesota Institute of Agriculture, 1986. 167p. (Minnesota Agr. Exp. Station Misc. Publ-37)

Second Schuh, G. Edward. The Agricultural Development of Brazil. New York; Praeger Publishers, 1970. 456p. (Benchmark Studies on Agricultural Development in Latin America, no. 6) Q

First rank Schuh, G. Edward, and Jennifer L. McCoy, eds. Food, Agriculture and Development in the Pacific Basin. Boulder, Colo.; Westview Press, 1986. 292p.

First rank Schultz, T. W. Agriculture in an Unstable Economy. New York; McGraw-Hill, 1945. 299p. AAEA Classic

First rank Schultz, T. W., ed. Distortions of Agricultural Incentives. Bloomington; Indiana University Press, 1978. 343p.

First rank Schultz, T. W. Economic Crisis in World Agriculture. Ann Arbor; University of Michigan Press, 1965. 114p.

First rank Schultz, T. W. The Economic Value of Education. New York; Columbia University Press, 1963. 92p.

First rank Schultz, T. W., ed. Economics of the Family: Marriage, Children and Human Capital. Chicago; University of Chicago Press, 1974. 584p. (Originally published as supplement to the *Journal of Political Economy*)

Second Schultz, T. W., ed. Food for the World. Chicago; University of Chicago Press, 1945. 352p. (Reprinted 1976)

First rank Schultz, T. W. Investment in Human Capital: The Role of Education and Research. New York; Free Press, 1971. 272p.

First rank Schultz, T. W. Transforming Traditional Agriculture. New Haven; Yale University Press, 1964. 212p. (Reprinted by Arno Press, 1976) AAEA Classic

First rank Schultz, T.W. The Economic Organization of Agriculture. New York; McGraw-Hill, 1953. 374p.

Second Schultz, T.W. Investing in People: The Economics of Population Quality. Berkeley; University of California Press, 1981. 173p.

Second Schultze, C. L. The Distribution of Farm Subsidies: Who Gets the Benefits? Washington, D. C.; Brookings Institution, 1971. 51p.

First rank Schumacher, E. F. Small Is Beautiful: Economics as if People Mattered. New York; Harper and Row, 1973. 290p. (Reissued, 1975. 305p.)

First rank Schumpeter, Joseph A. Capitalism, Socialism, and Democracy. 3d ed. New York; Harper, 1962. 431p. (1st ed., 1942. 381p.)

First rank Schumpeter, Joseph A. History of Economic Analysis. New York; Oxford University Press, 1954. 1260p.

Second Schutjer, W.A. and C.S. Stokes, eds. Rural Development and Human Fertility. New York; Macmillan Publ. Co., 1984. 318p.

Second Scott, A. Natural Resources: The Economics of Conservation. Toronto; University of Toronto Press, 1955. 184p.

First rank Scott, James C. The Moral Economy of the Peasant: Rebellion and Subsistence in Southern Asia. New Haven; Yale University Press, 1976. 246p.

Third Seddon, D., ed. Relations of Production: Marxist Approaches to Economic Anthropology. London; Frank Cass, 1978. 414p.

Third Seetharam, G. N. Strategy and Tactics of India's Agricultural Development: The Role of the State. Delhi; Ajanta Publ., 1984. 154p.

Third Seidman, Edward, ed. Handbook of Social Intervention. Beverly Hills, Calif.; Sage, 1983. 684p.

Second Seligson, Mitchell A. Peasants of Costa Rica and the Development of Agrarian Capitalism. Madison; University of Wisconsin Press, 1980. 220p.

Second Seligson, Mitchell A. Gap Between Rich and Poor: Contending Perspectives on the Political Economy of Development. Boulder, Colo.; Westview Press, 1984. 418p.

Second Selznick, Philip. T.V.A. and the Grass Roots: A Study in the Sociology of Formal Organization. New York; Harper and Row, 1966. (1st ed., Berkeley; University of California Press, 1949. 274p.)

Second Sen, Amartya K. Poverty and Famines: An Essay on Entitlement and Deprivation. Oxford, Eng.; Clarendon Press, 1981. 257p.

Second Sen, Amartya K. Employment, Technology and Development; A Study Prepared for the I.L.O. Oxford; Clarendon Press, 1975. 193p.

Second Sen, Bandhudas. The Green Revolution in India: A Perspective. New York; Wiley, 1974. 118p.

Third Sen, Chiranjib. Essays on the Transformation of India's Agrarian Economy. New York; Garland Publ., 1984. 285p. (Outstanding Dissertations in Economics Ser.) (Stanford Univ. Thesis, 1978).

Third Sender, J., and S. Smith. The Development of Capitalism in Africa. London; Methuen, 1986. 177p.

Third Sengupta, J. K., and K. A. Fox. Economic Analysis and Operations Research: Optimization Techniques in Quantitative Economic Models. Amsterdam; North Holland Publishing, 1969. 478p.

Second Shackle, G.L.S. Expectations in Economics. 2nd ed. Cambridge, Eng.; Cambridge University Press, 1952. 146p (1st ed., 1949; Reprinted 1978)

Third Shaffer, Ron. Community Economic Analysis: A How-to Manual. Ames; Iowa State University of Science and Technology, North Central Regional Center for Rural Development, 1984. 84p

Third Shah, A. K. Professional Management for the Cooperatives. Vikas, India; Advent Books, Incorporated, 1984. 350p.

Third Shand, R.T., ed. Technical Change in Asian Agriculture. Canberra; Australian National University Press, 1973. 319p.

Second Shand, R.T., ed. Agricultural Development in Asia. Canberra; Australian National University Press, 1969. 360p.

Second Shaner, Willis W., P.F. Philipp, and W.R. Schmehl. Farming Systems Research and Development: Guidelines for Developing Countries. Boulder, Colo.; Westview Press, 1982. 414p.

Third Shanin, Teodor, ed. Peasants and Peasant Societies: Selected Readings. 2d ed. Oxford; Blackwell, 1987. 497p.

Third Shanin, Teodor. The Awkward Class: Political Sociology of Peasantry in a Developing Society: Russia 1910–1925. Oxford; Clarendon Press, 1972. 253p.

Third Sharma, A. N. Economic Structure of Indian Agriculture. Bombay; Himalaya Publ. House., 1984. 554 p.

Third Sheddick, V. G. Land Tenure in Basutoland. New York; Johnson Reprint Corporation, 1970. 196p. (Repr. of 1954 ed.; London; H. M. Stationery Office)

Third Shenkin, Budd. Health Care for Migrant Workers: Policies and Politics. Cambridge, Mass.; Ballinger Publ. Co., 1974. 270p.

Third Shenoi, P. V. Agricultural Development in India: A New Strategy in Management. Delhi; Vikas Publishing House, 1975. 373p.

Second Shepherd, G. S. Agricultural Price Analysis. 5th ed. Ames; Iowa State University Press, 1963. 328p.

Second Shepherd, G. S. Farm Policy: New Directions. Ames; Iowa State University Press, 1964. 292p.

Second Shepherd, G. S., and G. A. Futrell. Marketing Farm Products: Economic Analysis. 7th ed. Ames; Iowa State University Press, 1982. 428 p.

Second Sher, J.P., ed. Education in Rural America: A Reassessment of Conventional Wisdom. Boulder, Colo.; Westview Press, 1977. 392p.

Third Sher, J.P., ed. Rural Education in Urbanized Nations: Issues aand Innovations. Boulder, Colo.; Westview Press, 1981. 346p.

Third Shideler, James H. Farm Crisis: 1919–1923. Berkeley; University of California Press, 1957. 345p. (Reprinted by Greenwood Press, 1957)

Second Shubik, M. Strategy and Market Structure: Competition, Oligopoly, and the Theory of Games. New York; Wiley, 1959. 387p.

Third Siamwalla, A. and S. Haykin. The World Rice Market: Structure, Conduct, and Performance. Washington,D.C.; IFPRI, 1983. 79p. (IFPRI Research Report No. 39).

Second Sicular, T., ed. Food Price Policy in Asia: A Comparative Study of Origins and Outcomes. Ithaca, N.Y.; Cornell University Press, 1989. 336p.

Third Silberberg, Eugene. The Structure of Economics: A Mathematical Analysis. New York; McGraw-Hill, 1978. 543p.

Third Silvers, Arthur and Pierre R. Crosson. Rural Development and Urban Bound Migration in Mexico. Baltimore, Maryland; Johns Hopkins University Press, 1980. 150p. (Resources for the Future Research Ser.: Paper R-17)

Second Simms, D. H. The Soil Conservation Service. New York; Praeger, 1970. 238p.

Second Simon, H. A. The Sciences of the Artificial. 2d ed. Cambridge, Mass.; MIT Press, 1981. 247p.

Third Simonsen, Roberto. Historia Economica do Brasil (1500/1820): Curso Professado na Escola Livre de Sociologia e Politica de Sao Paulo (Economic History of Brazil; 1500–1820). 7th ed. Sao Paulo: Companhia Editora Nacional, 1977. 475p.

Third Singelmann, Joachim. From Agriculture to Services: The Transformation of Industrial Employment. Beverly Hills; Sage Publications, 1978. 175p. (Sage Library of Social research; v. 69)

Third Singh, Gian. Economic Conditions of Agricultural Labourers and Marginal Farmers. New Delhi; B. R. Publ. Corp., 1986. 227p.

Third	Singh, J. P. The Role of Institutional Finance in Agriculture. New Delhi; Ashish Publ. House, 1986. 378p.
Third	Singh, Katar. Rural Development: Principles, Policies and Management. Beverly Hills, Calif., Sage Publ., 1986. 391p.
Third	Singh, Rem Babu. Geography of Rural Development: The Indian Micro-Level Experience. New Delhi; Inter-India Publications, 1986. 246p.
Third	Sinha, R. ed. The World Food Problem: Consensus and Conflict. Oxford, Eng.; Pergamon Press, 1978. 671p.
Third	Sisson, Charles A. Tax Burdens in American Agriculture: An Intersectoral Comparison. Ames; Iowa State University Press, 1982. 154p.
Second	Small Farm Viability Project. The Family Farm in California. Sacramento, Calif.; Small Farm Viability Project, 1977. 234p.
Third	Smethurst, Richard J. Agricultural Development and Tenancy Disputes in Japan, 1870–1940. Princeton; Princeton University Press, 1986. 472p.
Third	Smil, Vaclav, Paul Nachman and Thomas V. Long, II. Energy Analysis and Agriculture: An Application to U. S. Corn Production. Boulder, Colo.; Westview Press, 1983. 191p.
Second	Smith, Adam. An Inquiry into the Nature and Causes of the Wealth of Nations. Cannan ed. New York; Modern Library, 1937. 976p.
Third	Smith, Carol A., ed. Regional Analysis. Vol. 1: Economic Systems. New York; Academic Press, 1976.
Second	Smith, David M. The Geography of Social Well-Being in the United States: An Introduction to Territorial Social Indicators. New York; McGraw-Hill, 1973. 144p.
Third	Smith, Peter J. Agricultural Project Management: Monitoring and Control of Implementation. London and New York; Elsevier Applied Science Publishers, 1984. 190p.
Second	Smith, Stephen, C., and E.N. Castle, eds. Economics and Public Policy in Water Resource Development. Ames; Iowa State University Press, 1964. 463p.
Third	Smith, T. Lynn, and Paul E. Zopf, Jr. Demography: Principles and Methods. 2d ed. Port Washington, New York; Alfred Publ., 1976. 615p.
Second	Smith, Thomas C. The Agrarian Origins of Modern Japan. Stanford University Press, 1959. 250p. (Reprinted 1970)
Third	Smith, V. K. Scarcity and Growth Reconsidered. Baltimore; Johns Hopkins University Press, 1979. 298p.
First rank	Snedecor, George W., and William G. Cochran. Statistical Methods, 8th ed. Ames; Iowa State University Press, 1989. 503p.
Second	Snodgrass, Milton M. and Tim Wallace. Agriculture, Economics and Resource Management. 2d ed. Englewood Cliffs; Prentice Hall, Inc., 1980. 546p.
Third	Snyder, J. C., L. L. Nelson, and T. L. Guthrie. Profit Planning and Control, a Computer-Oriented System for Feed Industry Management. Chicago; American Feed Manufacturers Association, 1969. 291p.
Second	Sofranko, Andrew J. and James D. Williams, ed. Rebirth of Rural America: Rural Migration in the Midwest. Ames, Iowa; North Central Regional Center for Rural Development, Iowa State University, 1980. 215p.
Third	Solberg, Carl E. The Prairies and the Pampas: Agrarian Policy in Canada and Argentina, 1880–1930. Stanford University Press, 1987. 297p.

Third — Solimano, G. and L. Taylor, eds. Food Price Policies and Nutrition in Latin America. Tokyo; United National University Press, 1980. 170p.

Second — Solow, R. M. Capital Theory and the Rate of Return. Amsterdam; North-Holland, 1963. 98p.

Second — Solow, R.M. Growth Theory: An Exposition. Oxford; Oxford University Press. 1970. 109p. (Radcliffe Lectures, 1969) (Reprinted 1988)

Third — Somers, G. G., ed. Retraining the Unemployed. Madison; University of Wisconsin Press, 1968. 351p.

Second — Sorenson, Vernon L. International Trade Policy: Agriculture and Development. East Lansing; Michigan State University, 1975. 290p.

Second — Sorokin, Pitrim A., Carle C. Zimmerman and Charles J. Galpin, eds. A Systematic Source Book in Rural Sociology. Minneapolis; University of Minn. Press, 1930. 3 vols. (Reprint available)

Third — Sorokin, Pitrim A. Hunger as a Factor in Human Affairs. Gainesville; University Press of Florida, 1975. 319p.

Third — Sosnick, Stephen H. Hired Hands: Seasonal Farm Workers in the United States. Santa Barbara, California; McNally and Loftin, West Press, 1978. 453p.

Third — Southworth, Herman, ed. Farm Mechanization in East Asia. New York; The Agricultural Development Council, 1972. 433p.

First rank — Southworth, Herman M., and Bruce F. Johnston, eds. Agricultural Development and Economic Growth. Ithaca, N.Y.; Cornell University Press, 1967. 608p. (Reprinted in 1979) Q

Second — Southworth, Herman M., and M. Barnett, eds. Experience in Farm Mechanization in Southeast Asia. New York; Agricultural Development Council, 1974. 345p.

Second — Sowell, Thomas. The Economics and Politics of Race: An International Perspective. New York; Quill, 1985. 324p. (1st ed., New York; Morrow, 1983. 324p.)

Second — Spedding, C.R.W. An Introduction to Agricultural Systems. 2d ed. London, New York; Elsevier Science Publs., 1988. 189p. (1st ed., London; Applied Science Publishers, 1979. 169p.)

Second — Spengler, J. J., ed. Natural Resources and Economic Growth. Washington, D.C.; Resources for the Future, 1961. 306p.

Second — Spicer, Edward H., ed. Human Problems in Technological Change. New York; Russell Sage Foundation, 1952. 301p. (Reprinted 1963)

Third — Squire, Lyn and Herman G. van der Tak. Economic Analysis of Projects. Baltimore; Johns Hopkins University Press, 1975. 153p.

Third — Srinivasan, T.N. and Pranab K. Bardhan, eds. Rural Poverty in South Asia. New York; Columbia University Press, 1988. 565 p.

Third — Stanton, William J. Fundamentals of Marketing. 5th ed. New York; McGraw-Hill, 1978. 636p.

Second — Stavenhagen, Rodolfo, ed. Agrarian Problems and Peasant Movement in Latin America. Garden City, New York; Doubleday, 1970. 583p.

Third — Stavis, B. Making Green Revolution: The Politics of Agricultural Development in China. Ithaca, N.Y.; Cornell University Press, 1974. 274p.

Third — Steindl, J. Random Processes and the Growth of Firms: A Study of the Pareto Law. New York; Hafner; London; Griffin, 1965. 249p.

Third — Steiner, F. R. and Van Lier, H. N., eds. Land Conservation and Development: Examples of Land-Use Planning Projects and Programs. Amsterdam; Elsevier Science Publishing Company, Inc. 1984. 481p.

Third	Sterkenburg, J. J. Rural Development and Rural Development Studies: Cases From Africa and Asia. Amsterdam; Koninklijk Nederlands Aardrijkskundig Genootschap; Utrecht; Geografische Instituut. Rijksuniversitit Utrecht, 1987. 188 p. (Nederlandse Geografische Studies; 46)
First rank	Stevens, Robert D., ed. Tradition and Dynamics in Small Farm Agriculture: Economic Studies in Asia, Africa and Latin America. Ames; Iowa State University Press, 1977. 866p.
Third	Stevens, Robert D., and Cathy L. Jabara. Agricultural Development Principles: Economic Theory and Empirical Evidence. Baltimore; Johns Hopkins University Press, 1988. 478p.
Third	Stewart, I. G., and H. W. Ord, eds. African Primary Products and International Trade. Edinburgh; Edinburgh University Press, 1965. 218p.
Second	Stigler, G. J. The Theory of Price. 4th ed. New York; Macmillan, 1987. 371p. (Rev. ed., New York; Macmillan, 1952.)
Second	Stiglitz, J.E., and H. Uzawa, eds. Readings in the Modern Theory of Economic Growth. Cambridge, Mass.; MIT Press, 1969. 497p.
Second	Stone, R.D., D.A. Rowe, W.J. Corlett, R. Hurstfield, and M. Potter. The Measurement of Consumers' Expenditure and Behavior in the United Kingdom, 1920–38. vol. 1. Cambridge; University Press, 1954.
Third	Streeten, Paul, Shadid Burke, Mahbub Haq, Norman Hicks, and Frances Stewart. First Things First: Meeting Basic Needs in Developing Countries. New York; Oxford University Press, 1981. 206p.
Second	Streeten, Paul. What Price Food? Agricultural Price-Policies in Developing Countries. New York; St. Martin's Press, 1987. 127p. (Ithaca, N.Y.; Cornell Unversity Press paperback reprint, 1988)
Third	Strong, Ann L. Land Banking: European Reality, American Prospect. Baltimore; Johns Hopkins University Press, 1979. 312p.
Third	Stross, R.E. The Stubborn Earth: American Agriculturalists on Chinese Soil, 1898–1937. Berkeley, Calif.; University of Calif. Press, 1986. 272p.
Third	Struening, E. L. and M. Guttentag, eds. Handbook of Evaluation Research. Beverly Hills, Calif.; Sage, 1975. 2 vols.
Third	Subbarao, K. Rice Marketing System and Compulsory Levies in Andhra Pradesh: A Study of Public Intervention in Food-Grain Marketing, India. Bombay; Allied, 1978. 173p.
Third	Suchman, Edward A. Evaluative Research: Principles and Practice in Public Service and Social Action Programs. New York; Russell Sage Foundation, 1967. 186p.
Second	Summers, Gene F., ed. Technology and Social Change in Rural Areas; A Festschrift for Eugene A. Wilkening. Boulder, Colo., Westview Press, 1983. 266p.
First rank	Summers, Gene F. and Arne Selvik, eds. Non-Metropolitan Industrial Growth and Community Change. Lexington, Mass.; Lexington Books, 1979. 269p.
Second	Summers, Gene F., Leonard E. Bloomquist, Thomas A. Hirschl, and Ron E. Shaffer, eds. Community Economic Vitality: Major Trends and Selected Issues. Ames; Iowa State University, North Central Regional Center for Rural Development, 1988. 82p.
First rank	Summers, Gene F., S. D. Evans, F. Clemente, E. M. Beck, and J. Minkoff. Industrial Invasion of Nonmetropolitan America: A Quarter Century of Experience. New York; Praeger, 1976. 231p.

Second Summers, Gene F., et al, eds. Agriculture and Beyond: Rural Economic Development. Madison; College of Agricultural and Life Sciences, University of Wisc., 1987. 127 p.

Third Sumner, Daniel A., and Julian M. Alston. Removal of Price Supports and Supply Controls for U.S. Tobacco: An Economic Analysis of the Impact. Washington D.C.; National Planning Association, Food and Agriculture Committee Rep. No. 220, 1985. 64p. Q

Third Sundaram, I. S. Anti-Poverty Rural Development in India. New Delhi; D.K. Publications, 1984. 342p.

Second Sundquist, James L. Dispersing Population: What America Can Learn From Europe. Washington, D.C.; Brookings Institution, 1975. 290p.

Third Sundquist, James L., ed. On Fighting Poverty: Perspectives from Experience. New York; Basic Books, 1969. 256p.

Second Sundquist, James L., and D.W. Davis. Making Federalism Work: A Study of Program Coordination at the Community Level. Washington, D.C.; Brookings Institution, 1969. 293p.

Second Super, J.C. and T.C. Wright, eds. Food, Politics and Society in Latin America. Lincoln; University of Nebraska Press, 1985. 261p.

Third Suter, Robert C. The Appraisal of Farm Real Estate. 2d ed. Danville, Ill.; Interstate Printers and Publ., 1980. 671p.

Third Szymanski, A. The Logic of Imperialism. New York; Praeger Publishers, 1981. 598p.

T

Second Taeuber, Conrad and Irene B. Taeuber. The Changing Population of the United States. New York; John Wiley and Sons, 1958. 357p.

First rank Taeuber, Karl E., L.L. Bumpass, and J.A. Sweet, eds. Social Demography. New York; Academic Press, 1978. 336p.

Second Takayama, T., and G. G. Judge. Studies in Economic Planning over Space and Time. Amsterdam; North-Holland, 1973. 727p.

Third Talbot, R. B., and D. F. Hadwiger. The Policy Process in American Agriculture. San Francisco; Chandler, 1968. 378p.

Second Tang, Anthony M. and B. Stone. Food Production in the People's Republic of China. Washington, D.C.; International Food Policy and Research Institute, 1980. 2 vols. (IFPRI Research Report No.15)

Third Tang, Anthony M. An Analytical and Empirical Investigation of Agriculture in Mainland China, 1952–1980. Taipei, Taiwan; Chung-Hua Institute for Economic Research, 1984. 230p.

Third Tang, Chi-Yu. An Economic Study of Chinese Agriculture. New York; Garland, 1980. 514p.

Second Tannenbaum, Frank. The Mexican Agrarian Revolution. New York; Macmillan, 1929. 543p. (Reprinted Hamden, Conn.; Archon, 1968).

Third Tawney, R. H. Land and Labor in China. London; Allen and Unwin, 1932. 207p. (Reprinted by New York; Octagon, 1964; and M. E. Sharpe, Inc., 1978).

Second Taylor, Carl C. The Farmer's Movement, 1620 to 1920. New York; American Book Company, 1953. 519p. (Reprint by Greenwood Press, 1978)

Second Taylor, Carl C., et al. Rural Life in the United States. New York; Knopf, 1949. 549p. (Reprinted Westport, Conn.; Greenwood Press, 1972).

Second Taylor, Henry C., and Anne D. Taylor. The Story of Agricultural Economics in the United States, 1840–1932. Ames; Iowa State College Press, 1952. 1121 p. (Reprinted by Greenwood Press, 1974).

Third Taylor, Kit S. Sugar and the Underdevelopment of Northeastern Brazil, 1500–1970. Gainesville; University Presses of Florida, 1978. 167p.

First rank Taylor, Lance, ed. Models of Growth and Distribution for Brazil. New York; Oxford University Press, 1980. 355p.

Third Tendler, Judith. Agricultural Credit in Brazil. Part I–II. Washington, D.C.; U.S. Agency for International Development, 1962, 1970.

Second Tendler, Judith. Inside Foreign Aid. Baltimore; Johns Hopkins Press, 1975. 140p.

Second Theberge, James D. Economics of Trade and Development. New York; John Wiley, 1968. 545p.

Second Theil, Henri. Economic Forecasts and Policy. 2d rev. ed. Amsterdam; North-Holland Publishing, 1961. 567p.

Second Theil, Henri. Economics and Information Theory. Amsterdam; North-Holland, 1967. 488p.

Second Theil, Henri. Linear Aggregation of Economic Relations. Amsterdam; North-Holland, 1954. 205p.

First rank Theil, Henri. Principles of Econometrics. New York; Wiley, 1971. 736p.

Second Thiam, Tan Bock and Shao-Er Ong, eds. Readings in Asian Farm Management. Singapore; Singapore University Press, 1979. 350p.

Third Thimmaiah, G. and Abdul Aziz. Political Economy of Land Reforms. New Delhi; Ashish, 1983. 94p.

Third Thomas, Brinley. Migration and Economic Growth. A Study of Great Britain and the Atlantic Economy. 2d ed. Cambridge; Cambridge University Press for National Institute of Economic and Social Research, 1973. 498p. (1st ed. 1954, 362p.)

Third Thomas, Clive Y. The Rise of the Authoritarian State in Peripheral Societies. New York; Monthly Review Press, 1984. 157p.

First rank Thorbecke, Erik, ed. The Role of Agriculture in Economic Development. New York; Columbia University Press for the National Bureau of Economic Research, 1969. 480p. Q

Second Thorbecke, Erik, ed. Agricultural Sector Analysis and Models in Developing Countries. Rome; Food and Agriculture Organization, 1982. 415p. (Eng. and Fr.). (FAO Economic and Social Development Papers: No. 5)

Third Thorner, Daniel. The Agrarian Prospect in India. Five Lectures Delivered in 1955 at the Delhi School of Economics. 2d rev. ed. Bombay; Allied Publishers, 1976. 82p.

Third Thrall, R. M. et al., eds. Economic Modeling for Water Policy Evaluation. Amsterdam; North-Holland Publishing Co.; New York; Elsevier, 1976. 261p. (North-Holland/TIMS Studies in the Management Sciences, vol. 3) Q

First rank Thünen, J. H. Von. Von Thünen's Isolated State. Transl. C.M. Wartenberg. Oxford; Pergamon Press, 1966. 304p.

Second Thurow, L. C. Dangerous Currents: The State of Economics. New York; Random House, 1983. 247p. (New York; Vintage Books, 1984. 259p.)

Third Thurow, L. C., and R. E. B. Lucas. The American Distribution of Income: A Structural Problem. U. S. 92nd Congress, 2d Session, Joint Economic Committee Print. Washington, D.C.; U. S. Government Printing Office, 1972. 50p.

Third Timberlake, Michael, ed. Urbanization in the World-Economy. Orlando, Fla.; Academic Press, 1985. 387p.

Second Timmer, C. Peter. Getting Prices Right: The Scope and Limits of Agricultural Price Policy. Ithaca, N.Y.; Cornell University Press, 1986. 160p.

Second Timmer, C. Peter, ed. The Corn Economy of Indonesia. Ithaca, N.Y.; Cornell University Press, 1987. 302p.

First rank Timmer, C. Peter, Walter P. Falcon, and Scott R. Pearson. Food Policy Analysis. Baltimore; Johns Hopkins University Press, 1983. 301p. Q

Second Timmons, John R. and William G. Murray, eds. Land Problems and Policies. Ames; Iowa State University Press, 1950. 312p. (Reprinted by Ayer Company Publishers, Inc., 1972)

Second Tinbergen, J. Development Planning. K.D. Smith, translator. New York; McGraw-Hill, 1967. 256p.

Second Tinbergen, J. Income Distribution; Analysis and Policies. Amsterdam; North-Holland, 1975. 170p.

Second Tinbergen, J., Coordinator. Reshaping the International Order: A Report to the Club of Rome. New York; Dutton, 1976. 325p.

Second Tinbergen, J. and H. C. Bos. Mathematical Models of Economic Growth. New York; McGraw-Hill, 1962. 131p.

Third Tinker, I., M. B. Bransen, and M. Buvinic, eds. Women and World Development: Proceedings. . . . New York; Praeger, 1976. 228p.

Second Tintner, G. Econometrics. New York; Wiley, 1952. 370p.

Third Tiwary, J.K. Rural Development Administration: Perspectives and Prospects. Allahabad, India; Chugh Publications, 1984. 248 p.

First rank Todaro, Michael. Economic Development in the Third World. 4th ed. New York; Longman, 1989. 698p. (1st ed., Economic Development in the Third World: An Introduction to Problems and Policies in a Global Perspective. New York; Longman, 1977. 440p.)

Third Todaro, Michael, ed. The Struggle for Economic Development: Readings in Problems and Policies. New York; Longman, 1983. 409p.

Third Toennies, Ferdinand. Community and Society. Translated by C. Loomis. East Lansing; Michigan State University Press, 1957. (Reprinted by Transaction Books, 1988. 298p.)

First rank Tolley, G.S. and P.A. Zadrozny, eds. Trade, Agriculture, and Development. Cambridge, Mass.; Ballinger Publ., 1975. 218p.

Second Tolley, G.S., V. Thomas, and C.M. Wong. Agricultural Price Policies and the Developing Countries. Baltimore; Johns Hopkins University Press, 1982. 242p.

First rank Tomek, W.G. and K. L. Robinson. Agricultural Product Prices. 2d ed. Ithaca, N.Y.; Cornell University Press, 1981. 361p. (Original ed., 1972)

Third Tower, Edward, compiler. Agricultural Economics; Economics Reading Lists, Course Outlines, Exams and Problems. Durham, N.C.; Eno River Press, 1985. 184p. (Agriculture in Economic Development and Health Economics, Vol. 22)

First rank Toynbee, A. The Industrial Revolution. (Published in 1884 as Lectures on the Industrial Revolution in England.) Boston; Beacon Press, 1956. 139p.

Second Tullock, G. The Politics of Bureaucracy. Washington, D.C.; Public Affairs Press, 1965. 228p.

Second	Tuma, Elias H. Twenty-six Centuries of Agrarian Reform: A Comparative Analysis. Berkeley and Los Angeles; University of California Press and Near East Center, 1965. 309p.
First rank	Tweeten, Luther G. Foundations of Farm Policy. 2d ed. Lincoln; University of Nebraska Press, 1979. 567p.
Third	Tweeten, Luther and George L. Brinkman. Micropolitan Development: Theory and Practice of Greater Rural Economic Development. Ames; Iowa State University Press, 1976. 456p.

U

Third	Ulyanovsky, Rostislav. Agrarian India Between the World Wars: A Study of Colonial-Feudal Capitalism. Moscow; Progress Publishers, 1985. 294p. (Central Books, 1986).
Third	United Nations. Community Development and National Development: A Report. New York; United Nations Ad Hoc Group of Experts on Community Development, 1963. 78p.
First rank	United States Agricultural Policies for 1985 and Beyond. Tucson, Ariz.; University of Arizona and Resources for the Future, 1985.
Third	United States Congress. Public Policy and the Changing Structure of American Agriculture. Washington, D.C.; U.S. Gov't. Printing Office. 1978. 70 p.
Third	United States Congress. Joint Economic Committee. China Under the Four Modernizations: Selected Papers. Washington, D.C.; U.S. Gov't. Printing Office, 1982. 2 vols.
Third	United States Congress. Joint Economic Committee. China's Economy Looks Toward the Year 2000; Selected Papers. Washington, D.C.; U.S. Gov't. Printing Office, 1986. 2 vols.
Third	United States Congress. Office of Technology Assessment. A Review of U.S. Competitiveness in Agricultural Trade. Washington, D.C.; O.T.A. 1986. 101p.
Third	United States Congress. Office of Technology Assessment. Perspectives in Federal Retail Food Grading. Washington, D.C.; O.T.A. 1977. 87p.
First rank	United States Congress. Office of Technology Assessment. Technology, Public Policy, and the Changing Structure of American Agriculture. Washington, D.C.; O.T.A., 1986. 374p.
Third	United States Department of Agriculture. Community and Rural Development: National Extension Evaluation Project. Washington, D.C.; Agricultural Extension Service, USDA, 1980.
Second	United States Department of Agriculture. Development of Agriculture's Human Resources: A Report on Problems of Low-Income Farmers. Washington, D. C.; Soil Conservaion Service, 1955. 44p.
Third	United States Department of Agriculture. Revitalizing Rural America. Washington, D.C.; Agricultural Extension Service, 1986.
Third	United States Department of Agriculture. Economic Research Service. Agricultural-Food Policy Review: Perspectives for the 1980's. Washington, D.C.; USDA ERS, 1981. Q
Third	United States Department of Agriculture. Economics, Statistics and Cooperative Services. Looking Forward: Research Issues Facing Agriculture and Rural America. Washington,D.C.; ESCS, 1977. 444p.
Third	United States Department of Agriculture. Economics, Statistics and Coop-

erative Services. Small Farm Issues: Proceedings of the ESCS Small Farm Workshop. Washington,D.C.; ESCS, 1979. (ERS-60)

Third United States Department of Agriculture. Economics, Statistics and Cooperative Services. Structure Issues of American Agriculture. Washington D.C.; 1979. 305p. (USDA Agric. Econ. Rep. 438) Q

Second United States Department of Agriculture. Soil Conservation Service. A National Inventory of Soil and Water Conservation Needs. Washington, D.C.; U. S. Gov't Printing Office, 1958. 211p. (Revised in 1967)

Third United States Department of Commerce. Economic Development Administration. Regional Economic Development in the United States. (Papers prepared for the Organization for Economic Cooperation and Development). Washington, D. C.; 1967. 3 vols.

Second United States. General Accounting Office. Changing Character and Structure of American Agriculture: An Overview. Washington, D.C.; U.S. Gen. Accounting Off., 1978. 152p. (CED-78-178)

Third United States Senate. Committee on Agriculture, Nutrition and Forestry. Farm Structure: A Historical Perspective on Changes in the Number and Size of Farms. Washington, D.C.; , 1980. 379p.

Third United States Senate. Committee on Small Businesses. The Preservation and Control of Farm Land. Washington, D.C.; U.S. Gov't. Printing Office, 1979. 343p.

Second United States Senate. Select Committee on Nutrition and Human Needs. Dietary Goals for the United States. Washington, D.C.; U.S. Gov't. Printing Office, 1977. 79p. (Reprinted: Cambridge, Mass.; MIT Press; titled Eating in America). (2d ed. 1977. 83p.)

Third United States Water Resources Council. Water Resources Regions and Subregions for the National Assessment of Water and Related Land Resources. Washington, D.C.; U.S. Gov't Printing Office, 1970. 188p.

First rank University of Wisconsin. Institute for Research on Poverty. Rural Income Maintenance Experiment: Summary Report to the U.S. Department of Health, Education, and Welfare, and Office of Economic Opportunity. Madison; University of Wisconsin, 1976. 97p.

Third Uphoff, N.T., ed. Rural Development and Local Organization in Asia. Delhi, India; Macmillan India Lmtd., 1982. 1 vol.

Second Usher, Dan. The Measurement of Economic Growth. New York; Columbia University Press, 1980. 306p.

V

Second Valdés, Alberto, et al., eds. Economics and the Design of Small Farmer Technology. Ames; Iowa State University Press, 1979. 211p.

First rank Valdés, Alberto, ed. Food Security for Developing Countries. Boulder, Colo.; Westview Press, 1981. 351p.

Third Van Ginkel, Maarten and Douglas G. Tanner, eds. The Fifth Regional Wheat Workshop for Eastern, Central and Southern Africa and the Indian Ocean at Antsirabe, Madagascar, Oct. 1987. Mexico, D.F.; CIMMYT, 1987. 280p.

Third Van Young, Eric. Hacienda and Market in Eighteenth-Century Mexico: The Rural Economy of the Guadalajara Region, 1675–1820. Berkeley; University of California Press, 1981. 388p.

Third Vanek, J. Maximal Economic Growth: A Geometric Approach to Von

	Neumann's Growth Theory and the Turnpike Theorem. Ithaca, N.Y.; Cornell University Press, 1968. 122p.
First rank	Varian, H. Microeconomic Analysis. 2d ed. New York; Norton, 1984. 384p. (1st ed., 1978. 284p.)
Third	Venedikian, Harry M. and G. A. Warfield. Export-Import Financing. 2d ed. New York; Wiley, 1986. 456p.
Second	Vernon, R., ed. The Technology Factor in International Trade. New York; Columbia University Press, 1970. 493p.
Second	Vidich, Arthur J. and Joseph Bensman. Small Town in Mass Society. Princeton, N.J.; Princeton University Press, 1958. 329p. (Reprinted: Garden City, New York; Doubleday, 1960)
Second	Viner, J. International Trade and Economic Development: Lectures delivered at the National University of Brazil. Glencoe, Ill.; Free Press, 1952. 154p. (Reprinted: Oxford; Clarendon, 1964. 120p.)
Third	Vink, A. P. Land Use in Advancing Agriculture. New York; Springer-Verlag, 1975. 450p.
Second	Vogeler, Ingolf. The Myth of the Family Farm: Agribusiness Dominance of U. S. Agriculture. Boulder, Colo.; Westview Press, 1981. 352p.
Third	Von Oppen, M.; D. R. Raj,; P. Virinda and Sudhir Kumble, eds. Agricultural Markets in the Semi-Arid Tropics. Hyderabad, India; ICRISAT, 1985. 387p.
Second	Von Pischke, J.D., Dale W. Adams and Gordon Donald, eds. Rural Financial Markets in Developing Countries: Their Use and Abuse. Baltimore; Johns Hopkins University Press, 1983. 411p.
Third	Von Witzke, Harald, ed. Policy Coordination in World Agriculture. Kiel, Germany; Herbst, 1988. 245 p.

W

Third	Wadekin, K. Agrarian Policies in Communist Europe: A Critical Introduction. Totowa, N.J.; Allanheld, Osmun, 1982. 324p.
Third	Waldorf, William H. Demand for Manufactured Foods, Manufacturers' Services, and Farm Products in Food Manufacturing—A Statistical Analysis. Washington, D. C.; U. S. Department of Agriculture, 1964. 60p. (USDA Technical Bulletin 1317) Q
First rank	Walinsky, Louis J., ed. Agrarian Reforms as Unfinished Business: The Selected Papers of Wolf Ladejinsky. New York; Oxford University Press, 1977. 603p.
Second	Walker, Thomas W., ed. Nicaragua: The First Five Years. New York; Praeger Publ., 1985. 561p.
Third	Wallace, T. Dudley and J. Lew Silver. Econometrics: An Introduction. Reading, Mass.; Addison Wesley, 1988.
Second	Warner, Paul D. and James A. Christenson. The Cooperative Extension Service: A National Assessment. Boulder, Colo.; Westview Press, 1984. 195p.
Third	Warren, Roland L.. New Perspectives on the American Community: A Book of Readings. 4th ed. Homewood, Ill.; Dorsey, 1983. 434p. (3d ed., Chicago, Ill.; Rand McNally, 1977. 636p.)
First rank	Warren, Roland, L. The Community in America. Chicago; Rand-McNally, 1963. 347p. (3d ed. 1978, 448p.)
Second	Warren, Roland L. Social Change and Human Purpose: Toward Understanding and Action. Chicago; Rand McNally Co., 1977. 348p.

Third Warriner, D. Land Reform in Principle and Practice. Oxford; Clarendon Press, 1969. 457p.

Second Wasserstrom, R. and R. Wiles. Field Duty: U. S. Farm Workers and Pesticide Safety. Washington, D.C.; World Resources Institute, 1985. 78p. (Study/World Resources Institute; 3)

Third Watson, Andrew M. Agricultural Innovation in the Early Islamic World. Cambridge University Press, 1983. 260p. (Cambridge Studies in Islamic Civilization)

First rank Waugh, Frederick V. Demand and Price Analysis: Some Examples from Agriculture. Washington, D.C.; U.S. Department of Agriculture, 1964. 94p. (USDA Technical Bulletin 1316) AAEA Classic Q

Second Waugh, Frederick V. Selected Writings on Agricultural Policy and Economic Analysis. Martin E. Abel and James P. Houck, eds. Minneapolis; University of Minnesota Press, 1984. 466p.

Second Weber, Max. Types of Division of Labor. Repinted from The Theory of Social and Economic Organization. Transl. by A. M. Henderson and Talcott Parsons. 1st ed. Glencoe, Ill.; The Free Press, 1947. 436p.

Third Webster, C.C., and P. N. Wilson. Agriculture in the Tropics. 2nd ed. London and New York; Longman, 1988. 640p. (1st ed., 1966. 488p.)

Second Wennergren, E. Boyd, Morris Whitker, Charles Anholt. Agricultural Development in Bangladesh: Prospects for the Future. Boulder, Colo.; Westview Press, 1984. 373p.

Third Wetherill, Barrie G. Intermediate Statistical Methods. London and New York; Chapman and Hall, 1981. 390p.

Second Weyman, F. H. The Dynamics of the World Cocoa Market. Cambridge; M.I.T. Press, 1968. 253p. Q

First rank Wharton, Clifton R., ed. Subsistence Agriculture and Economic Development. University of Chicago; Aldine Publishing Co., 1969. 481p.

Second Whitehead, Alfred North. Science and the Modern World: Lowell Lectures, 1925. New York; Macmillan, 1925. (Reissued 1960) 304p. (Later eds. 1948,1954)

First rank Whiting, Larry R., ed. Communities Left Behind: Alternatives for Development. Ames, Iowa; Iowa State University Press, 1974. 151p.

Third Whyte, R. O. and P. Whyte. The Women of Rural Asia. Boulder, Colo.; Westview Press, 1982. 262p.

Second Whyte, W.F. and D. Boynton, eds. Higher-Yielding Human Systems for Agriculture. Ithaca, N.Y.; Cornell University Press, 1983. 342p.

Third Widstrand, Carl G., ed. Cooperatives and Rural Development in East Africa. Uppsala, Sweden; Scandinavian Institute of African Studies; New York, Africana Publ. Corp., 1970. 271 p.

Third Wigmore, John H. and D. B. Simmons. Notes on Land Tenure and Local Institutions in Old Japan. Washington, D. C.; University Publications of America, Inc., 1979. 270p.

Third Wilber, Charles, ed. The Political Economy of Development and Underdevelopment. 3d ed. New York; Random House, 1973. 434p. (3d ed., 1984. 595p.)

Second Wilcox, Walter W. Social Responsibility in Farm Leadership. Repr. of 1956 ed. Greenwood Press, 1976. 194p.

Second Wilcox, Walter W., W. W. Cochrane, and R. W. Herdt. Economics of American Agriculture. Englewood Cliffs, New York; Prentice-Hall, 1960. 538p. (3d ed. 1974. 504p.)

Third	Williams, D. B. Agriculture in the Australian Economy. Sydney; Sydney University Press, 1967. 422p. (2d ed., 1982)
Third	Williams, Robert G. Export Agriculture and the Crisis in Central America. Chapel Hill; University of North Carolina Press, 1986. 257 p.
Second	Williamson, Jeffrey G. and P. H. Lindert. American Inequality. New York; Academic Press, 1980. 362p.
Third	Williamson, Oliver E. Markets and Hierarchies; Analysis and Antitrust Implications: A Study in the Economics of Internal Organization. New York; Free Press, 1975. 286p. (Reprinted 1983)
Second	Wilson, William. The Declining Significance of Race: Blacks and Changing American Institutions. 2d ed. Chicago; University of Chicago Press, 1980. 243p. (1st ed., 1978. 204p.)
Third	Winter, J.Alan, J. Rabow, and M. Chesler. Vital Problems for American Society: Meanings and Means. New York; Random House Publ., 1968. 527p.
Third	Wionczek, M. S. Inversion y Tecnologia Extranjera en America Latina (Investment and Foreign Technology in Latin America). Mexico; Joaquin Mortiz, 1971. 189p.
First rank	Wold, Herman O.A., and L. Jureen. Demand Analysis: a Study in Econometrics. New York; Wiley, 1953. 358p.
Third	Wolfson, N. The Modern Corporation: Free Markets vs. Regulation. New York; The Free Press, and London; Collier-Macmillan, 1984. 191p.
Third	Wollman, N., and G. W. Bonem. The Outlook for Water: Quality and Quantity and National Growth. Baltimore; Johns Hopkins University Press, 1971. 286p.
Second	Wong, John, ed. Group Farming in Asia: Experiences and Potentials. Singapore; Singapore University Press, 1979. 296p.
Third	Wong, Lung-Fat. Agricultural Productivity in the Socialist Countries. Boulder, Colo.; Westview Press, 1986. 195p.
Second	Wonnacott, Thomas with John J. Wonnacott. Econometrics. 2d ed. New York; Wiley, 1979. 580p. (1st ed., Thomas Wonnacott, 1970. 445p.)
Third	Woolverton, Michael W. Computer Concepts for Agribusiness. Westport, Conn.; AVI Publishing Company, Inc., 1985. 311p.
Third	World Bank. Accelerated Development in Sub-Saharan Africa: An Agenda for Action. Washington, D.C.; World Bank, 1982. 198p.
Third	World Bank. Agricultural Research and Extension: An Evaluation of the World Bank's Experience. Washington, D. C.; World Bank, 1985. 110p.
Second	World Bank. The Assault on World Poverty; Problems of Rural Development, Education, and Health. Baltimore; Johns Hopkins University Press, 1975. 425p.
Third	World Bank. Brazil: A Review of Agricultural Policies. Washington D.C.; World Bank, Publications Department, 1982. 259p.
Third	World Bank. Financing Adjustment with Growth in Sub-Saharan Africa, 1986–1990. Washington, D. C., World Bank, 1986. 130p.
Third	World Bank. Poverty and Hunger: Issues and Options for Food Security in Developing Countries. Washington, D.C.; World Bank, 1986. 69p.
Third	World Commission on Environment and Development. Food Two Thousand: Global Policies for Sustainable Agriculture. London and N.J.; Zed Press, 1987. 131p.
Third	World Conference on Agrarian Reform and Rural Development Report.

Rome; Food and Agriculture Organization of the United Nations, 1979. 63p.

Second — Wortman, Sterling, and Ralph W. Cummings, Jr. To Feed This World, The Challenge and the Strategy. Baltimore; Johns Hopkins University Press, 1978. 440p.

Third — Wright, Deil S. Understanding Intergovernmental Relations. 2d ed. Monterey, Calif; Brooks/Cole Pubs., 1982. 532p. (1st ed., North Scituate, Mass.; Duxbury, 1978. 410p.)

Second — Wright, Erik Olin. Class Structure and Income Determination. New York; Academic Press, 1979. 271 p.

Third — Wright, Robert R. and Susan W. Wright. Land Use in a Nutshell. 2d ed. St. Paul; West Publishing Company, 1985. 356p. (1st ed., St. Paul; West Publishing, 1978. 316p.)

Y

Third — Yang, Martin M. Socio-Economic Results of Land Reform in Taiwan. Honolulu; University of Hawaii Press, 1970. 576p.

Third — Yang, Wei Y. Methods of Farm Management Investigations for Improving Farm Productivity. 2d ed. Rome; Food and Agriculture Organization of the U.N., 1965. 258p. (1st ed., 1958. 228p.) (FAO Agricultural Development Paper No. 64)

Third — Yates, Lamartine. Mexico's Agricultural Dilemma. Tucson, Ariz.; University of Arizona Press, 1981. 291p.

Second — Yotopoulos, Pan A. Allocative Efficiency in Economic Development: A Cross-Section Analysis of Epirus Farming. Athens; Center of Planning and Economic Research, 1967. 313p. (Research Monograph Series 18) Q

Second — Yotopoulos, Pan A., and Jeffrey B. Nugent. Economics of Development: Empirical Investigations. New York; Harper and Row, 1976. 478p.

Second — Yotopoulos, Pan A. Empirical Investigations in the Economics of Development. Tokyo; Keio-tsusin Co., 1984.

Second — Young, Frank W. Interdisciplinary Theories of Rural Development. Greenwich, CT; JAI Press, 1983. 235p.

Second — Young, Frank W. and Ruth C. Young. Comparative Studies of Community Growth. Morgantown, W. Va.; West Virginia University Press, 1973. 137p.

Z

Third — Zahlan, A. B. The Agricultural Sector of Sudan: Policy and System Studies. London; Ithaca Press, 1986. 423p. (Middle East Science Policy Studies: No. 6)

Second — Zarembka, Paul. Toward a Theory of Economic Development. San Francisco; Holden Day, 1972. 249p.

Second — Zellner, A. An Introduction to Bayesian Inference in Econometrics. New York; Wiley, 1971. 431p.

Third — Zellner, Richard A., and E. G. Carmines. Measurement in the Social Sciences: The Link between Theory and Data. New York; Cambridge University Press, 1980. 198p.

Second — Zietz, J. and A. Valdes. The Costs of Protectionism to Developing Countries: An Analysis for Selected Agricultural Products. Washington, D.C.; 1986. 98p. (World Bank Staff Working Paper No. 769)

Third Zurcher, Louis A., Jr. and Charles M. Bonjean, eds. Planned Social Intervention. Scranton, Penn.; Chandler, 1970. 505p.

Third Zusman, Pinhas, Abraham Melamed, and Itzhak Katzir. Possible Trade and Welfare Effects of EEC Tariff and "Reference Price" Policy on the European-Mediterranean Market for Winter Oranges. Berkeley; University of California, 1969. 41p. (Giannini Foundation Monograph Number 24) Q

C. Third World Core Monographs

The procedures described earlier in sections A and B apply to the Third World compilation and evaluation. It must be emphasized that all of the developed countries titles and Third World titles were offered to Third World reviewers so choices would be made from the most heavily cited titles.

Overseas scholars with extensive experience in teaching and research were asked to review and evaluate the lists. Additionally, persons from the developed world with extensive experience in Third World agricultural development evaluated the same titles. Logically, the titles should be basic to Third World needs, as well as to institutions in the developed world that offer agricultural economics development courses or research assistance for application in the Third World. As noted earlier, 44.8% of the titles are common to both lists, although the rankings are different.

The Third World list is manifestly a generic list of titles, which are not geographically limited or site-specific. Local or country materials were not included after the second review when it became clear that they were not going to serve the purposes of all or large portions of the Third World. Country or site-specific landmark volumes that serve as illustrative titles for other developing countries or regions are included and reviewers of lists were asked to accommodate this requirement. It must be assumed that local or country areas will always need local or regional material, a need not addressed in this project as being too specific and esoteric for worldwide application. Therefore, the numerous national development plans and the economic literature from developing countries have not been included unless they are exemplary and have wide application. There is some doubt that this generic but geographically localized literature will be used by other countries because of economic, national, or social variables. Reviewers were asked to score titles that should have wide application.

The same equation used in section B (p. 97) was used for ranking in the Third World list with this exception: Only two, not three, evaluation levels were allowed reviewers; therefore, only two numbers are possible with the second data element.

Very few of the Quality Publication Award documents made a final showing in the Third World list, although many of the AAEA Classics did. The 1,002 titles were also divided into three rankings levels. The second and third rankings constituted 40.7% and 43.1%, respectively, of the Third World list, and the first-ranked constituted 16.2%.

The Top Twenty Third World Monographs

The top-scoring monographs divided at a numerically distinctive position and are shown below. The Martin three-volume work achieved first rank, although it was not numerically as far in advance of the second through fifth rankings as it was in the developed countries list. The top five are the same in both lists, although titles ranked 2 and 3 swapped places, as did 4 and 5.

The Top Third World Monographs

1. Lee R. Martin, ed. *A Survey of Agricultural Economics Literature*. 3 vols. Minneapolis: University of Minnesota Press for the American Agricultural Economics Association, 1977–1981. 3 vols. (Vol. 4 due in 1992).
2. Herman M. Southworth and Bruce F. Johnston, eds. *Agricultural Development and Economic Growth*. Ithaca, N.Y.: Cornell University Press, 1967. 608p. Quality Award of AAEA.
3. Clifton R. Wharton, ed. *Subsistence Agriculture and Economic Development*. Chicago: University of Chicago, Aldine, 1969. 481p.
4. Yujiro Hayami and Vernon W. Ruttan. *Agricultural Development: An International Perspective*. Baltimore: Johns Hopkins University Press, 1971. 367p. (Revised and expanded in 1985, 506p.). AAEA Classic and Quality Publication Award.
5. Lloyd G. Reynolds, ed. *Agriculture in Development Theory*. New Haven, Conn.: Yale University Press, 1975. 510p.
6. Carl K. Eicher and John M. Staatz, eds. *Agricultural Development in the Third World*. Baltimore: Johns Hopkins University Press, 1984. 491p.
7. Theodore W. Schultz. *Transforming Traditional Agriculture*. New Haven, Conn.: Yale University Press, 1964. 212p. AAEA Classic.
8. Thomas M. Arndt, Dana G. Dalrymple, and Vernon Ruttan, eds. *Resource Allocation and Productivity in National and International Agricultural Research*. Minneapolis: University of Minnesota Press, 1977. 617p.
9. C. Peter Timmer, Walter P. Falcon, and Scott R. Pearson. *Food Policy Analysis*. Baltimore: Johns Hopkins University Press, 1983. 301p. Quality Publication Award of AAEA.
10. John W. Mellor. *Economics of Agricultural Development*. Ithaca, N.Y.: Cornell University Press, 1970. 418p. Quality Publication Award of AAEA.
11. John W. Mellor. *The New Economics of Growth: A Strategy for India and the Developing World*. Ithaca, N.Y.: Cornell University Press, 1976. 335p.
12. James A. Roumasset, Jean-Marc Boussard, and Inderjit Singh, eds. *Uncertainty and Agricultural Development*. Laguna, Philippines: Southeast Asian Regional Center

for Graduate Study and Research in Agriculture; and New York; Agricultural Development Council, 1979. 453p.

13–14. James K. Boyce and Robert E. Evenson. *National and International Agricultural Research and Extension Programs*. New York: Agricultural Development Council, 1975. 229p.

T. W. Schultz, ed. *Distortions of Agricultural Incentives*. Bloomington: Indiana University Press, 1978. 343p.

15–16. Hans P. Binswanger and Vernon W. Ruttan. *Induced Innovation: Technology, Institutions, and Development*. Baltimore: Johns Hopkins University Press, 1978. 423p. Quality Publication Award of AAEA.

Vernon W. Ruttan. *Agricultural Research Policy*. Minneapolis: University of Minnesota Press, 1982. 369p.

17–18–19–20. Hans P. Binswanger and Mark R. Rosenzweig. *Contractual Arrangements, Employment and Wages in Rural Labor Markets in Asia*. New Haven, Conn.: Yale University Press, 1984. 330p.

Bruce F. Johnston and Peter Kilby. *Agricultural and Structural Transformation: Economic Strategies in Late-Developing Countries*. New York: Oxford University Press, 1975. 474p.

Allen H. Maunder and Kazushi Ohkawa, eds. *Growth and Equity in Agricultural Development: Proceedings of the Eighteenth International Conference of Agricultural Economists*. London: Gower, 1984. 619p.

Don Paarlberg. *Farm and Food Policy: Issues of the 1980s*. Lincoln: University of Nebraska Press, 1980. 338p.

The Third World reviewers chose more recent works, dropping three pre-1970 titles from the developed countries list. Surprisingly, two remained from the 1960s. The two evaluating groups think similarly, but not identically. For example, the Binswanger and Ruttan volume moved from 6–8 in the developed countries list to 15–16 in the Third World; Ruttan's individual work fell from 11 to 15–16. The gainers were the second Mellor work, which went from 17–19 to 11; Timmer et al, from 16 to 9; and the Roumasset et al. from 20 to 12. Four different titles were introduced in the top twenty Third World group. The general subject matter and authors changed little, however.

Core List of Monographs for Third World Application, 1950–88, 1,002 titles

A

Third	Abdullah, T. A. and S. Ziedenstein. Village Women of Bangladesh: Prospects for Change. Oxford, England, Pergamon Press, 1982. 246p.
Third	Aboyade, O. Administering Food Producer Prices in Africa: Lessons from International Experiences. Washington, D.C.; International Food Policy Research Institute, 1985.
Second	Abrahamsen, M. A. Agricultural Cooperation in the United States. Plunkett Foundation for Co-op Studies, 1980. 224p.

Second Abramovitz, M., ed. Capital Formation and Economic Growth. Princeton, N.J.; Princeton University Press for National Bureau of Economic Research, 1959. 677p.

Second Adams, Dale W., Douglas H. Graham, and J.D. Von Pischke, eds. Undermining Rural Development with Cheap Credit. Boulder, Colo.; Westview Press, 1984. 318p.

Third Adams, F. Gerard and J. R. Behrman, eds. Econometric Modeling of World Commodity Policy. Lexington, Mass., Heath Publ., 1978. 223p.

First rank Adelman, I. and C. T. Morris. Economic Growth and Social Equity in Developing Countries. Stanford; Stanford University Press, 1973. 257p.

First rank Adelman, I. and E. Thorbecke, eds. The Theory and Design of Economic Development. Baltimore: Johns Hopkins University Press, 1967. 427p.

Second Adelman, I., and S. Robinson. Income Distribution Policy in Developing Countries: A Case Study of Korea. Stanford; Stanford University Press, 1978. 346p.

First rank Agarwala, A.N., and S.P. Singh, eds. The Economics of Underdevelopment. New York; Holt-Reinhardt, 1961. 510p.

Third Agency for International Development (U.S.) Workshop on Pastoralism and African Livestock Development. Washington, D.C.; Bureau for Program and Policy Coordination, Bureau for Africa and Office of Evaluation, 1980. 87p. (AID Program Evaluation Report No. 4.)

Second Agricultural Exports Strategy: Problems and Prospects. New Delhi; Radiant Publ., 1986. 349p.

First rank Ahmed, Iftikhar and Vernon W. Ruttan, eds. Generation and Diffusion of Agricultural Innovations: the Role of Institutional Factors. Aldershot, Hants, England; Brookfield, Vermont; Gower Publishing Company, 1988. 471p.

Third Ahmed, Raisuddin, and N. Rustagi. Agricultural Marketing and Price Incentives: A Comparative Study of African and Asian Countries. Washington, D.C.; International Food Policy Research Institute, 1985.

Second Ahsan, Syed M. Agricultural Insurance: A New Policy for Developing Countries. Brookfield, VT; Gower Publishing Company, 1985. 262p.

Third Ake, C. A Political Economy of Africa. London, Longmans, 1981. 196p.

Second Akoto, O. A. Public Policy and Agricultural Development in Africa. Brookfield, VT; Gower Publishing Company, 1988.

Second Alavi, Hamza, and Teodor Shanin, eds. Introduction to the Sociology of "Developing Societies." New York; Monthly Review Press, 1982. 474p.

Second Alberts, Tom. Agrarian Reform and Rural Poverty: A Case Study of Peru. Boulder, Colo.; Westview Press, 1983. 306p.

Second Alexander, M, ed. Agricultural Policy: A Limiting Factor in the Development Process. Washington, D.C., Inter-American Development Bank, 1975. 507p.

Second Alexandratos, Nikos, ed. World Agriculture: Towards 2000: An FAO Study. New York; New York University Press, 1988. 338p.

First rank Allen, G.R. Agricultural Marketing Policy. Oxford University Press, 1959. 336p.

Second Allison, Graham T. Land Policy in Developing Countries. Lincoln Institute of Land Policy, 1984. 72p.

Second Amacher, Ryan C., Robert D. Tollison, and Thomas D. Willett, eds. The Economic Approach to Public Policy. Ithaca, N.Y.; Cornell University Press, 1976. 528p.

Third Amann, V. F., ed. Agricultural Policy Issues in East Africa: Proceedings of the East African Agricultural Economics Society Conference, Nairobi, June 1971. Kampala, Uganda; Makerere University Printery, 1973. 341p.

Third Amin, Samir. Accumulation on a World Scale: A Critique of the Theory of Underdevelopment. Transl. from French by B. Pearce. New York, Monthly Review Press, 1974. 2 vols.

Third Amin, Samir. L'Afrique de l'ouest bloquee: L'economie politique de la colonisation (1880–1970). Paris; Les Editions de Minuit, 1971. 298p.

Third Amin, Samir. Trois Experiences Africaines de Developpement: Le Mali, la Guinee et le Ghana. Paris; Presses Universitaires de France, 1965. 233p.

First rank Amin, Samir. Unequal Development: An Essay on the Social Formations of Peripheral Capitalism. New York; Monthly Review Press, 1976. 440p. (Transl. of Le Developpement Inegal; Paris; Les Editions de Minuit, 1973.)

Third Amselle, J.-L., ed. Les Migrations Africaines: Reseaux et Processus Migratoires. Paris; Maspero, 1976. 126p.

Second Anderson, C. Arnold and M. J. Bowman, eds. Education and Economic Development. Chicago, Aldine Press, 1965. 436p.

Third Anderson, David, and R. Grove, eds. Conservation in Africa: People, Policies and Practice. Cambridge University Press, 1987. 355p.

Second Anderson, Jock R. and Peter B. R. Hazell, eds. Variability in Cereal Yields and Implications for Agricultural Research and Policy. Baltimore: Johns Hopkins University Press for the International Food Policy Research Institute, 1989. 384p.

Second Anderson, Jock, Robert W. Herdt, and Grant M Scobie. Science and Food: The CGIAR and its Partners. Washington, D.C., World Bank, 1988. 134p.

First rank Anderson, Jock, John Dillon, and J. Brian Hardaker. Agricultural Decision Analysis. Ames; Iowa State University Press, 1977. 344p.

Third Anderson, Kym and Rodney Tyers. Distortions in World Food Markets. Cambridge, England; Cambridge University Press, 1988.

First rank Anderson, Kym, Y. Hayami, and others. The Political Economy of Agricultural Protection: East Asia in International Perspective. Sydney, Australia, George Allen and Unwin, 1986. 185p.

Third Anderson, Teresa J., ed. Land Tenure and Agrarian Reform in Africa and the Near East: An Annotated Bibliography. Boston; G. K. Hall, 1976. 423p.

Second Andreou, Paris. Contemporary Issues in Agricultural and Economic Development of Developing Nations: Selected Readings in the Economic Development of Poor Countries. Nairobi; East African Lit. Bureau, 1977. 340p.

Second Anschel, Kurt R., Russell H. Brannon and Eldon D. Smith, eds. Agricultural Cooperatives and Markets in Developing Countries. New York, Praeger, 1969. 373p.

Third Anthony, Kenneth, B. F. Johnston, W. O. Jones, and V. Uchendu. Agricultural Change in Tropical Africa. Ithaca, N.Y.; Cornell University Press, 1979. 326p.

Third Are, L. A., ed. Socio-Economic Aspects of Rice Cultivation. Monrovia, Liberia; West Africa Rice Development Association, 1975. 216p. (Seminar Proceedings 3.)

Third Arhin, K., P. Hesp, and L. van der Laan, eds. Marketing Boards in Tropical Africa. London and Boston; Kegan Paul International, 1985. 208p.

Third Ariza-Nino, E. and C. Steedman, eds. Livestock and Meat Marketing in West Africa. Ann Arbor; University of Mich., Center for Research on Economic Development, 1979. 5 vols.

First rank Arndt, Thomas M., et al. Resource Allocation and Productivity in National and International Agricultural Research. Minneapolis; University of Minnesota Press, 1977. 617p.

Second Arrow, Kenneth J., and M. Kurz. Public Investment, the Rate of Return, and Optimal Fiscal Policy. Baltimore; Johns Hopkins University Press for Resources for the Future, 1970. 218p.

First rank Arrow, Kenneth J. Social Change and Individual Values. New York; John Wiley, 1951. 99p. (Second ed. New Haven, CT; Yale University Press, 1963. Reprinted in 1970. 124p.)

Third Artis, M.J. and A.R. Nobay, eds., Essays in Economic Analysis. London: Cambridge University Press, 1976. 282p.

Third Asefa, S., ed. World Food and Agriculture: Economic Problems and Issues. Kalamazoo, Mich.; Upjohn Institute, 1988. 144p.

Third Asian Development Bank. Agriculture in Asia: Its Performance and Prospects; The Role of ADB in Its Development. Manila, Philippines; Asian Development Bank, 1985.

Second Asian Development Bank. Asian Agricultural Survey, 1976; Rural Asia—Challenge and Opportunity. New York, Praeger, 1977. 489p.

First rank Asian Development Bank. Asian Agricultural Survey. Seattle; University of Washington Press, 1969. 795p.

Second Asian Productivity Organization. Cooperative Marketing of Farm Products in Asia: Reports of a Multi-Country Study Mission, 21st September–7th October 1981. Tokyo; Asian Productivity Organization, 1982. 182p.

Third Asian Productivity Organization. Productivity Measurement and Analysis: Asian Agriculture. Tokyo, Asian Prod. Organization, 1987. 834p.

First rank Askari, Hossein and Cummings, John T. Agricultural Supply Response: A Survey of the Econometric Evidence. New York; Praeger Publishers, 1976. 443p.

Third Astori, Danilo. La Agricultura en una Estrategia de Desarrollo Economico. Montevideo, Uruguay; Ediciones de la Banda Oriental, 1969. 132p.

Third Atkinson, Anthony B. and Stiglitz, J. Lectures on Public Economics. New York: McGraw-Hill, 1980 619p.

Third Attwood, D. W. and B. S. Baviskar, eds. Co-operatives and Rural Development. Oxford University Press, 1988. 320p.

Third Australian Bureau of Agricultural and Resource Economics. Japanese Agricultural Policies: A Time of Change. Canberra; Australian Government Publishing Service, 1988. 359p.

Third Axinn, N. W. and G. H. Axinn. Small Farms in Nepal. Kathmandu, Nepal; Rural Life Associates, 1983. 55p.

Third Ayuko, L. Organization, Structures and Ranches in Kenya. London; Overseas Development Institute, 1981. (ODI Pastoral Network Paper, No. 11b.)

B

Third Bachman, K. L. and L. A. Paulino. Rapid Food Production Growth in Selected Developing Countries. Washington, D.C.; International Food and Policy Research Institute, 1979. 98p. (IFPRI RR-11)

First rank	Bagchi, Amiya. The Political Economy of Underdevelopment. Cambridge and New York; Cambridge University Press, 1982. 280p.
Third	Balaam, David N. and M. J. Carey, eds. Food Politics: The Regional Conflict. Totawa, N. J.; Allanheld, Osmun, 1981. 246p.
First rank	Balassa, Bela. The Structure of Protection in Developing Countries. Baltimore, Johns Hopkins University Press, for the World Bank, 1971. 375p.
First rank	Balassa, Bela. Trade Prospects for Developing Countries. Homewood, Illinois; Richard D. Irwin, 1964. 450p.
Third	Baldwin, K. D. S. The Niger Agricultural Project: An Experiment in African Development. Cambridge, Mass.; Harvard University Press; and Oxford; B. Blackwell, 1957. 221p.
Third	Ban, S. H., P. Y. Moon, and D. H. Perkins. Rural Development (Series Studies in the Modernization of the Republic of Korea: 1945–1975). Cambridge, Mass., Harvard University Press, 1980. 468p. (Harvard East Asian Monog. No. 89)
Third	Bapna, S. L. Aggregate Supply Response of Crops in a Developing Region. New Delhi; Sultan and Chand, 1981. 164p.
First rank	Bardhan, Pranab K. Interlocking Factor Markets. London and Delhi; Macmillan, 1984.
First rank	Bardhan, Pranab K. Land, Labor, and Rural Poverty: Essays in Development Economics. New York; Columbia University Press, 1984. 288p.
First rank	Bardhan, Pranab K. The Political Economy of Development in India. Oxford and New York; Basil Blackwell, 1984. 118p.
Second	Barker, J. W. Agricultural Marketing. Oxford University Press, Inc. 1981. 226p..
Second	Barker, Jonathan, ed. The Politics of Agriculture in Tropical Africa. Beverly Hills, Calif.; Sage Publications, 1984. 320p.
First rank	Barker, Randolph, and Robert W. Herdt. The Rice Economy of Asia. Washington, DC; Resources for the Future. Baltimore; Johns Hopkins University Press, 1985. 324p.
Second	Barker, Randolph and Radha P. Sinha, eds. The Chinese Agricultural Economy. Boulder, Colo., Westview Press, 1983. 266p.
Third	Barlow, C. The Natural Rubber Industry: Its Development, Technology, and Economy in Malaysia. New York; Oxford University Press, 1978. 500p.
Third	Barnard, C. S. and J. S. Nix. Farm Planning and Control. Cambridge University Press, 1973. 549p. (2d ed. 1979, 600p.)
Third	Barnett, A. D. China's Economy in Global Perspective. Washington, D.C.; Brookings Institute, 1981. 752p.
Third	Barnett, Tony. The Gezira Scheme: An Illusion of Development. London and Totowa, N.J.; Cass, 1977. 192p.
Second	Barraclough, Solon L. Agrarian Structure in Latin America. Cambridge, Mass.; Lexington Books, 1973. 351p.
Third	Barry, Peter J., John A. Hopkin, and C. B. Baker. Financial Management in Agriculture. 4th ed. Danville, Ill.: Interstate, 1988. 500p. (1st ed.; 1973. 459p.)
Third	Barry, Peter J., ed. Risk Management in Agriculture. Ames, Iowa; Iowa State University Press, 1984. 282p.
Third	Bartsch, William H. Employment and Technology Choice in Asian Agriculture. New York; Praeger, 1977. 125p.

First rank Barwell, C. Farmer Training in East-Central and Southern Africa. Rome; Food and Agriculture Organization, 1975. 115p.

Second Basu, Subhas K. Commercial Banks and Agricultural Credit: A Study in Regional Disparity in India. Bombay; Allied, 1979. 201p.

Second Bates, Robert H. Essays on the Political Economy of Rural Africa. Cambridge University Press, 1983. 178p.

First rank Bates, Robert H. Markets and States in Tropical Africa: The Political Basis of Agricultural Policies. Berkeley; University of California Press, Bombay: Allied 1981. 178p.

Second Bates, Robert H. and M. F. Lofchie, eds. Agricultural Development in Africa: Issues of Public Policy. New York; Praeger, 1980. 451p.

Third Bauer, P. T. West African Trade: A Study of Competition, Oligopoly and Monopoly in a Changing Economy. Cambridge University Press, 1954. 450p. (Reprinted, with a new preface, by London; Routledge and Kegan Paul, 1963; and New York; A. M. Kelley, 1967.)

Second Baum, Kenneth H. and Lyle P. Schertz. Modeling Farm Decisions for Policy Analysis. Boulder, Colo.; Westview Press, 1983. 418p.

Second Bayliss-Smith, Tim., ed. Understanding Green Revolutions: Agrarian Change and Development Planning in South Asia. Wanmali, Sudhir. Cambridge University Press, 1984. 384p.

Second Beaumont, P. and Keith McLachlan, eds. Agricultural Development in the Middle East. New York; John Wiley and Sons, Inc., 1985. 349p.

Third Beckford, G. L. Persistent Poverty: Underdevelopment in Plantation Economies of the Third World. New York; Oxford University Press, 1972. 303p. (Reissued in abbreviated form: London: Zed Publ., 1983, 244p.)

Third Beckman, B. Organizing the Farmers: Cocoa Politics and National Development in Ghana. New York; Holmes and Meier; and Uppsala; Scandinavian Institute of African Studies, 1976. 299p.

Third Behrman, Jere R. Chile. New York; Columbia University Press for the National Bureau of Economic Research, 1976. 408p. (Foreign Trade Regimes and Economic Development).

Second Behrman, Jere R. Supply Response in Underdeveloped Agriculture: A Case Study of Four Major Annual Crops in Thailand, 1937–1963. Amsterdam; North Holland Publishers, 1968. 446p.

Second Beierlein, J. Principles of Agribusiness Management. Englewood Cliffs, N.J.; Prentice Hall, 1986. 441p.

Third Bell, C. P., Peter Hazell, and R. Slade. Project Evaluation in Regional Perspective: A Study of an Irrigation Project in Northwest Malaysia. Baltimore; Johns Hopkins University Press for World Bank, 1982. 326p.

Second Bellamy, Margot and Bruce Greenshields, eds. Agriculture and Economic Instability. Brookfield, Vermont: Gower Publishing Company, 1987. 381p. (I.A.A.E. Occasional Paper no. 4).

Third Beneria, Lourdes, ed. Women and Development: The Sexual Division of Labor in Rural Societies. Geneva, Switz., International Labour Office, 1982. 257p.

Third Benjamin, M. Investment Projects in Agriculture: Principles and Case Studies. Harlow, Essex and London; Longman, 1981. 297p. (Printed in paperback in 1985.)

Second Benor, D. and J. Q. Harrison. Agricultural Extension: The Training and Visit System. Washington, D.C.; The World Bank, 1977. 55p. (New ed. with Michael Baxter, 1984.)

Third Berardi, Gigi M., ed. World Food, Population, and Development. Totowa, N.J.; Rowman and Allanheld, 1985. 346p.

Second Berg, A. D. Malnutrition: What Can Be Done? Lessons from World Bank Experience. Baltimore, Johns Hopkins University Press, 1987. 139p.

Second Berg, A. D., N. S. Scrimshaw, and D. L. Call, eds. Nutrition, National Development, and Planning. Cambridge, Mass; MIT Press, 1973. 401p.

Second Berg, Robert J., and J. S. Whitaker, eds. Strategies for African Development. Berkeley; University of California Press, 1986. 603p.

Third Bergmann, D. R. L'agriculture francaise: perspectives, strategies et politiques a long terme. Paris; INRA, 1979.

Second Bergmann, Theodore. The Development Models of India, the Soviet Union and China. Assen, Van Gorcum, 1977. 255p. (Publications of European Society for Rural Sociology Ser.: No. 1).

Second Bernstein, Gail Lee. Haruko's World: A Japanese Farm Woman and Her Community. Stanford University Press, 1983. 199p.

Second Berry, R. Albert, and William Cline. Agrarian Structure and Productivity in Developing Countries. Baltimore; Johns Hopkins University Press, 1979. 248p.

Second Berry R. Albert, and R. Soligo, eds. Economic Policy and Income Distribution in Colombia. Boulder, Colo.; Westview Press, 1980. 269p.

Third Berry, S. S. Cocoa, Custom and Socio-Economic Change in Rural Western Nigeria. Oxford; Clarendon Press, 1975. 240p.

Second Berry, Wendell. The Gift of Good Land: Further Essays Cultural and Agricultural. Berkeley; North Point Press, 1981. 304p.

Second Bertrand, Trent. Thailand: Case Study of Agricultural Input and Output Pricing. Washington, D.C.; World Bank Publications Department, 1980. 134p. (Working Paper: No. 385).

Second Beteille, Andre. Studies in Agrarian Social Structure. Oxford University Press, 1974. 206p.

First rank Bhaduri, Amit. The Economic Structure of Backward Agriculture. New York; Academic Press, Inc., 1983. 151p.

Third Bhagwati, J. N., R. W. Jones, R. A. Mundell, and J. Vanek, eds. Trade Balance of Payments and Growth; Papers in International Economics in Honor of C. P. Kindleberger. Amsterdam; North-Holland Publ., 1971. 532p.

Third Bhalla, G. S., and G. K. Chadha. Green Revolution and the Small Peasant: A Study of Income Distribution Among Punjab Cultivators. New Delhi: Concept Pub. Co., 1983. 167p.

Third Bhalla, G. S., and Y. K. Alagh. Performance of Indian Agriculture: A Districtwise Study. New Delhi, India; Sterling, 1979. 239p.

Third Bharadqaj, K. Production Conditions in Indian Agriculture: A Study Based on Farm Management Surveys. New York; Cambridge University Press, 1974. 128p.

Third Biebuyck, D., ed. African Agrarian Systems. Oxford University Press, 1963. 407p.

Second Bingen, R. James. Food Production and Rural Development in the Sahel: Lessons from Maili's Operation Riz-Segou. Boulder, Colo., Westview Press, 1985. 167p.

First rank Binswanger, Hans P. The Economics of Tractors in South Asia: An Analytical Review. New York; Agricultural Development Council; and Hyderabad, India; International Crops Research Institute for the Semi-Arid Tropics, 1978. 96p.

First rank Binswanger, Hans P., Robert E. Evenson, Cecilia A. Florencio, and Benjamin N.F. White, eds. Rural Household Studies in Southeast Asia. Singapore; Singapore University Press, 1980. 369p.

First rank Binswanger, Hans P. and Mark R. Rosenweig. Contractual Arrangements, Employment and Wages in Rural Labor Markets: A Critical Review. New York; Agricultural Development Council, and Patancheru, India; International Crops Research Institute for the Semi-Arid Tropics, 1981. 69p.

First rank Binswanger, Hans P. and Mark R. Rosenzweig. Contractual Arrangements, Employment and Wages in Rural Labor Markets in Asia. New Haven; Yale University Press, 1984. 330p.

First rank Binswanger, Hans P. and Vernon W. Ruttan. Induced Innovation: Technology, Institutions and Development. Baltimore; Johns Hopkins University Press, 1978. 423p. Q

Second Binswanger, Hans P. and P. L. Scandizzo. Patterns of Agricultural Protection. Washington, D.C.; World Bank, 1983. (World Bank Report ARU15)

Second Bliss, C. J. and N. H. Stern. Palanpur: The Economy of an Indian Village. Oxford and New York; Oxford University Press, 1982. 340p.

Third Block, P. Land Tenure Issues in River Basin Development in Sub-Saharan Africa. Madison; University of Wisconsin, Land Tenure Center, 1986. 154p.

Third Booth, Anne and R. M. Sundrum. Labour Absorption in Agriculture: Theoretical Analysis and Empirical Investigation. New York, Oxford Univ. Press, 1985. 327p.

Third Booth, Anne, C. C. David, et al. Food Trade and Food Security in ASEAN and Australia. Kuala Lumpur; ASEAN-Australian Joint Research Project, 1986. 269p.

Second Bos, H. C. Money in Development: The Functions of Money in Equilibrium and Disequilibrium, with Special Reference to Developing Countries. Rotterdam; Rotterdam University Press, 1969. 183p.

Second Bose, S.C. Agrarian Bengal: Economy, Social Structure and Politics, 1919–47. South Asian Studies. New York; Cambridge University Press, 1986. 396p.

First rank Boserup, Ester. Conditions of Agricultural Growth: The Economics of Agrarian Change Under Population Pressure. Chicago; Aldine, 1965. 124p.

Second Boserup, Ester. Population and Technological Change; A Study of Long-Term Trends. Chicago: University of Chicago, 1981. 255p.

Third Bottcher, P. Untersuchungen und Beurteilung uber die Verwendungsmoglichkeit von Pappel-Kurzumtriebsholz zur Spanplattenherstellung. Braunschweig; Fraunhofer Institut fur Holzforschung, 1984.

First rank Boyce, James K., and Robert E. Evenson. National and International Agricultural Research and Extension Programs. New York; Agricultural Development Council, Inc., 1975. 229p.

Second Bradford, G.L., and F.B. Saunders, eds. Quantitative Techniques with Application to Rural Development Research. Lexington, Ky.; Southern Farm Management Research Committee, Farm Foundation, 1972. 197p.

Second — Bradnock, R.W. and M. Walker. Agricultural Change in South Asia. London; J. Murray, 1984. 64p.

Second — Braverman, Avishay; Choong Y. Ahn, and Jeffrey S. Hammer. Alternative Agricultural Pricing Policies in the Republic of Korea: Their Implications for Government Deficits, Income Distribution, and Balance of Payments. Washington, D.C.; World Bank Publications Department, 1983. 174p. (World Bank Staff Working Paper no. 621).

Second — Bray, Francesca. The Rice Economies: Technology and Development in Asian Societies. Oxford and New York; Blackwell, 1986. 254p.

Second — Breimyer, H.F. Economics of the Product Markets of Agriculture. Ames; Iowa State University Press, 1976. 208p.

Second — Brenner, Y. S. Agriculture and the Economic Development of Low Income Countries. Paris; Mouton De Gruyter, 1972. 254p. (Institute of Social Studies Paperbacks: No. 2).

Second — Bressler, Raymond G., Jr., and Richard A. King. Markets, Prices, and Interregional Trade. New York: Wiley, 1970. 426p. (Reprinted Raleigh, N.C.; Norman-Weather Printing Co., 1978)

Second — Broehl, Wayne G., Jr. The Village Entrepreneur: Change Agents in India's Rural Development. Cambridge, MA; Harvard University Press, 1978. 228p.

Third — Brokensha, D. W., D. M. Warren, and O. Werner, eds. Indigenous Knowledge Systems and Development. Lanham, Maryland and Washington, D.C.; University Press of America, 1980. 460p.

Second — Brown, Lester R. Man, Land and Food: Looking Ahead at World Food Needs. (World Food Supply Ser.). Salem, New Hamp; Ayer Company Pub., 1976. 153p. (Reprint of 1963 ed.)

Second — Brown, Maxwell L. Farm Budgets: From Farm Income Analysis to Agricultural Project Analysis. Baltimore, Md.; Johns Hopkins University Press, 1980. 160p. (World Bank Ser.)

Second — Brown, Murray, ed. The Theory and Empirical Measurement of Production. New York; Columbia University Press for the National Bureau of Economic Research, 1967.

Second — Brown, Murray. On the Theory and Measurement of Technical Change. Cambridge: At the University Press, 1968. 214p.

Third — Browne, Robert S and Robert J. Cummings. The Lagos Plan of Actions vs. the Berg Report: Contemporary Issues in African Economic Development. Lawrenceville, VA: Brunswick Publishing, 1985. 216 p.

Second — Browne, William P. and Don F. Hadwiger. World Food Policies: Toward Agricultural Interdependence. Boulder, Colo., Lynne Rienner Publ., 1986. 222p.

Third — Bryant, C., ed. Poverty Policy and Food Security in Southern Africa. Boulder, Colo.; Lynne Rienner; and London; Mansell, 1988. 291p.

Second — Buck, John L. Land Utilization in China: Statistics: China During the Interregnum (1911–1949), the Economy and Society. Edited by Ramon H. Myers. New York; Garland Publishing, Inc., 1981. 473p.

Third — Bundy, C. The Rise and Fall of the South African Peasantry. Berkeley; University of California Press, 1979. 276p.

Second — Buttel, Frederick H., and Howard Newby, eds. The Rural Sociology of the Advanced Societies: Critical Perspectives. Montclair, N.J.; Allanheld, Osmun and Co., 1980. 529p.

Third — Byerlee, D., C. K. Eicher, C. Liedholm, and D. S. C. Spencer. Rural

Employment in Tropical Africa: Summary of Findings. East Lansing; Michigan State University, Department of Agricultural Economics, Africa Rural Economy Program, 1977. 176p. (Working Paper No. 20.)

C

Third — Caballero, Jose M. and H. Maletta. Estilos de Desarrollo y Politicas Agroalimentarias — Tendencias y Dilemas en American Latina. (Expert Consultations on Styles of Development and Agricultural Policies in Latin America). Santiago, Chile, and Rome; CEPAL, FAO.; 1983.

Third — Caldwell, B. Beyond Positivism: Economic Methodology in the Twentieth Century. London and Boston: Allen and Unwin, 1982. 277p.

First rank — Caldwell, John C. African Rural-Urban Migration: The Movement to Ghana's Towns. New York; Columbia University Press, 1969. 257p.

Third — Caldwell, John C., N. O. Addo, S. K. Gaisie, A. Igun, and P. O. Olusanya, eds. Population Growth and Socio-Economic Change in West Africa. New York; Columbia University Press, 1975. 763p.

Third — Cantrelle, P., ed. Population in African Development, Vol. 1 of 2. Dolhain, Belgium; Ordina Editions for the International Union for the Scientific Study of Population, 1974.

Third — Cardoso, F. H. and E. Faletto. Dependency and Development in Latin America. Berkeley and Los Angeles; University of California Press, 1979. 227p.

Second — Carlson, Sune. A Study on the Pure Theory of Production. Clifton, N.J.; Augustus M. Kelley, 1965. 128p. (Reprint of 1939 ed.)

Third — Carnoy, M., in collaboration with J. Lobo, A. Toledo, and J. Velloso. Can Educational Policy Equalise Income Distribution in Latin America? Farnborough, United Kingdom; Saxon House, 1979. 110p.

Third — Carruthers, I. D., ed. Aid for the Development of Irrigation. Paris; Organization for Economic Cooperation and Development, 1983. 166p.

Third — Carruthers. I. D. and C. Clark. The Economics of Irrigation. 3d ed. Liverpool University Press, 1981. 300p.

Second — Carter, A. P., and A. Brody, eds. Applications of Input-Output Analysis. Amsterdam: North-Holland, 1972. 2 vols.

Second — Casley, D.J. and D. A. Lury. Data Collection in Developing Countries. 2d ed. New York; Clarendon Press, 1987. 225p. (First ed. New York; Oxford University Press, 1981. 244p.)

First rank — Castle, Emery N. and K. Hemmi. U.S.-Japanese Agricultural Trade Relations. Baltimore; Johns Hopkins University Press; and Washington, D.C.; Resources for the Future, 1982. 436p.

Second — Castle, Emery N., Manning H. Becker, and Gene A. Nelson. Farm Business Management. 3d ed. New York; Macmillan Publishing Co. Inc., 1986. 456p.

Third — Castro, Claudio de Moura, et al. A Educacao na America Latina: Um Estudo Comparativo de Custo e Eficiencia: Programa Eciel, Projeto Educacao e Desenvolvimento (Education in Latin America . . .). Rio de Janeiro: Editora da Fundacao Getulio Vargas, 1980. 225p. (Serie Educacao/FGV/IESAE No. 02)

Third — Cavallo, Domingo, and Yair Mundlak. Agriculture and Economic Growth in an Open Economy: The Case of Argentina. Washington, D. C.; International Food Policy Research Institute, 1982. 162p. (IFPRI Report 36) Q

Second	Center for Agricultural and Economic Adjustment, Iowa State University. Goals and Values in Agricultural Policy. Ames: Iowa State University Press, 1961. 364p.
Third	Center for Research on Economic Development, University of Michigan. Marketing, Price Policy and Storage of Food Grains in the Sahel: A Survey. Ann Arbor; University of Michigan, Center for Research on Economic Development, 1977. 2 vols. (Working Group on Marketing, Price Policy, and Storage of CILSS/Club du Sahel.)
Second	Centro Internacional de Agricultura Tropical (CIAT), ed. Cassava in Asia; Its Potential and Research Development Needs. Cali, Colombia; CIAT, 1986. 442p.
First rank	Chamberlin, E.H. The Theory of Monopolistic Competition. Eighth ed. Cambridge; Harvard University Press, 1962. 396p. (First ed: Cambridge, Mass.; Harvard Univ. Press, 1933. 213p.)
Third	Chambers, Robert. Managing Canal Irrigation: Practical Analysis for South Asia. New Delhi, India; Oxford and Cambridge University Presses, 1987. 279p.
Third	Chambers, Robert. Managing Rural Development: Ideas and Experience from East Africa. Uppsala, Sweden; Scandanavian Institute for African Studies, 1974. 215p.
Third	Chambers, Robert. Rural Development: Putting the Last First. London and New York; Longman, 1983. 246p.
Second	Chao, Kang. Agricultural Production in Communist China, 1945–1965. Madison: University of Wisconsin Press, 1970. 374p.
First rank	Chayanov, A. V. The Theory of Peasant Economy. (Translation of his Peasant Farm Organization; Moscow; Cooperative Publ. House, 1925.) Translated by D. Thorner, B. Kerblay, and R. E. F. Smith. Homewood, Ill.; Richard D. Irwin, 1966. 317p.
Third	Chekki, Dan A., ed. Community Development: Theory and Method of Planned Change. New Delhi, India; Vikas Press, 1979. 258p.
Second	Chen, Marty. Indian Women: A Study of Their Role in the Dairy Movement. New Delhi, India; Vikas Press, Inc., 1986. 248p.
Second	Chenery, Hollis, and M. Syrquin. Patterns of Development, 1950–1970. London, Oxford University Press, for the World Bank, 1975. 234p
Second	Chenery, Hollis, and T. N. Srinivasa, eds. Handbook of Development Economics. Amsterdam and New York; North-Holland Publ., 1988. (Vol. 9 in Handbooks in Economics)
First rank	Chenery, Hollis, et al. Redistribution With Growth: Policies to Improve Income Distribution in Developing Countries in the Context of Economic Growth. Oxford, England; published for the World Bank and Institute of Development Studies, University of Sussex, by Oxford University Press, 1974. 304p.
First rank	Chenery, Hollis. Structural Change and Development Policy. Oxford University Press for the World Bank, 1979. 526p.
Second	Cheung, Steven N. Theory of Share Tenancy: With Special Application to Asian Agriculture. Chicago; University of Chicago Press, 1969. 188p.
Second	Chiang, Alpha C. Fundamental Methods of Mathematical Economics. 3d ed. New York; McGraw-Hill, 1984. 788p. (lst ed: 1967, 690p.)
Third	Chilcote, R. and J. Edelstein. Latin America: The Struggle with Dependency and Beyond. New York; Wiley, 1974. 781p.
Second	Chilivumbo, Alifeyo. Migration and Uneven Rural Development in Africa: The Case of Zambia. University Press of America, 1986. 138p.

First rank — Chisholm, Anthony H. and Rodney Tyers, eds. Food Security: Theory, Policy and Perspectives from Asia and the Pacific Rim. Lexington, Mass.: Lexington Books, 1982. 359p.

Third — Chopra, R. N. Green Revolution in India: The Relevance of Administrative Support for Its Success. New Delhi, India; Intellectual Publ. House, 1985. 255p.

Third — Christ, C., et al., eds. Measurement in Economics: Studies in Mathematical Economics and Econometrics in Memory of Yehuda Greenfeld. Stanford, Calif; Stanford University Press, 1963. 319p.

First rank — Christenson, James A. and Jerry W. Robinson, Jr., eds. Community Development in America. Ames, Iowa; Iowa State University Press, 1980. 245p.

Third — Chuta, E., and C. Liedholm. Rural Non-Farm Employment: A Review of the State of the Art. East Lansing; Michigan State University, Department of Agricultural Economics, 1979. 96p. (Rural Development Paper, No. 4.)

Second — Cianferoni, Reginaldo. Guida allo Studio dell'Economia e Politica Agraria. (Guide to the Study of Agrarian Economy and Policies) Padova; CEDAM, 1978. 259p.

Second — Ciriacy-Wantrup, S. V. Resource Conservation: Economics and Policies. 3d ed. Berkeley: University of California Press, 1968. 395p. (1st ed., 1952, 395p.) AAEA classic.

Second — Clark, Colin, and M. Haswell. The Economics of Subsistence Agriculture. 4th ed. London, Macmillan, New York; St. Martins Press, 1970. 267p. (1st ed: 1964, 218p.)

First rank — Clark, Colin. Bioeconomic Modelling and Fisheries Management. New York; Wiley, 1985. 291p.

Second — Clark, Colin. The Conditions of Economic Progress. 3d ed. London; Macmillan, 1957. 720p. (1st ed. 1940, 504p.)

Third — Clayton, E. S. Agrarian Development in Peasant Economies: Some Lessons from Kenya. Oxford; Pergamon Press, 1964. 154p.

Third — Cleave, John H. African Farmers: Labour Use in the Development of Smallholder Agriculture. New York; Praeger, 1974. 253p.

Third — Cline, W. R. and A. Berry. Farm Size, Productivity and Technical Change. Washington, D.C., International Bank for Rural Development, 1976.

Third — Cline, W. R. and E. Delgado, eds. Economic Integration in Central America. Washington, D.C.; Brookings Institution, 1978. 712p.

Third — Cline, W. R. and S. Weintraub, eds. Economic Stabilization in Developing Countries. Washington, D.C.; Brookings Inst., 1981. 517p.

Third — Cockcroft, J. D., A. G. Frank and D. L. Johnson. Dependence and Underdevelopment: Latin America's Political Economy. Garden City, N.Y.; Doubleday Anchor, 1972. 448p.

Third — Cohen, J. M. Integrated Rural Development: The Ethiopian Experience and the Debate. Uppsala, Sweden; Scandanavian Institute for African Studies, 1987. 267p.

Third — Cohen, Ronald, ed. Satisfying Africa's Food Needs: Food Production and Commercialization in African Agriculture. Boulder, Colo., Lynne Rienner Publ., 1988. 244p.

First rank — Collinson, M.P. Farm Management in Peasant Agriculture: A Handbook for Rural Development Planning in Africa. New York; Praeger, 1972. 444p. (Reprinted Boulder, Colo.; Westview Press, 1983, 454p.)

Third Colman, David and Frederick Nixson. Economics of Change in Less Developed Countries. Oxford; Phillip Allan; Totowa, N.J.; Barnes and Noble Bks., 1986. 445p. (lst ed. New York; Wiley, 1978. 309p.)

Third Colman, David and Trevor Young. Principles of Agricultural Economics: Markets and Prices in Less Developed Countries. Cambridge and New York; Cambridge University Press, 1989. 323p.

Second Commins, S. K., M. Lofchie, and R. Payne, eds. Africa's Agrarian Crisis: The Roots of Famine. Boulder, Colo.; L. Rienner Publishers, 1986. 237p.

Second Commons, J. R. Institutional Economics: Its Place in Political Economy. New York; Macmillan, 1934. 921p. (Reissued by: Madison; Univ. of Wisconson Press, 1959.)

Second Contador, C. R., ed. Tecnologia e Desenvolvimento Agricola (Technology and Agricultural Development). Rio de Janeiro; Instituto de Pesquisas, 1975. 308p. (Instituto Monografia No. 17)

Third Cook, Paul and C. Kirkpatrick, eds. Privatisation in Less Developed Countries. Brighton, England, Wheatsheaf Book; N.Y., St. Martin's Press, 1988. 315p.

Second Coombs, P. H., and M. Ahmed. Attacking Rural Poverty; How Nonformal Education Can Help. International Council for Educational Development for the World Bank. Baltimore; Johns Hopkins University Press, 1974. 292p.

Second Coward, E. Walter Jr., ed. Irrigation and Agricultural Development in Asia: Perspectives from the Social Sciences. Ithaca, N.Y.; Cornell University Press, 1980. 369p.

Third Croll, E. Women and Rural Development in China: Production and Reproduction. Geneva; International Labour Office, 1985. 172p. (Women, Work and Development No. 11.)

Second Crosson, Pierre R., and S. Brubaker. Resources and Environmental Effects of U. S. Agriculture. Washington, D.C.: Resources for the Future, 1982. 255p.

Second Crosson, Pierre R., and Kenneth D. Frederick. The World Food Situation: Resource and Environmental Issues in the Developing Countries and the United States. Washington, D.C.; Resources for the Future, Inc., 1977. 230p.

Third Crotty, R. Cattle, Economics and Development. Farnborough, England; Commonwealth Agricultural Bureaux, 1980. 253p.

Third Cruise, O'Brien, R., ed. The Political Economy of Underdevelopment: Dependence in Senegal. Beverly Hills, Calif.; Sage, 1979. 277p.

Third Cruz de Schlesinger, L. and L. J. Ruiz. Mercadeo de Arroz en Colombia. Bogotá; Centro de Estudios sobre Desarrollo Económico, 1967.

Second Csaki, Csaba. Simulation and Systems Analysis in Agriculture. (Translation of his Szimeilacio Alkalmazasa a Mezogazdasagban, revised and enlarged). Amsterdam and New York, Elsevier Science Publ. Co., 1985. 262p. (Developments in Agricultural Economics, vol. 2).

Second Cukierman, A. Inflation, Stagflation, Relative Prices, and Imperfect Information. New York: Cambridge U. Press, 1984. 202p.

Second Cullen, Matthew and Sharon Woolery, eds. Second World Congress on Land Policy. Boston, Mass; Oelgeschlager, Gunn and Hain, Inc. in assoc. with Lincoln Institute of Land Policy, 1985. 320p.

Third Cummings, R. W., Jr., Robert W. Herdt, and S. K. Ray. Policy Planning for Agricultural Development. New Delhi, India; Tata and McGraw-Hill, 1979. 237p.

Third Curtis, Donald, Michael Hubbard, and Andrew Shepherd. Preventing Famine: Policies and Prospects for Africa. London and New York; Routledge, 1988. 250p.

D

Second Dahl, D.C., and J.M. Hammond. Market and Price Analysis: The Agricultural Industries. New York; McGraw-Hill, 1977. 323p.

Third Dahlberg, Kenneth A. Beyond the Green Revolution: The Ecology and Politics of Global Agricultural Development. New York, Plenum Press, 1979. 256p.

Second Dale, Peter F. Land Information Management: An Introduction with Special Reference to Cadastral Problems in Third World Countries. Oxford: Clarendon Press, 1988. 266p.

Third Dalby, D., and R. J. Harrison Church, eds. Drought in Africa. London; University of London, School of Oriental and African Studies, 1973. 124p. (Revised edition edited with F. Bezzaz; London; International African Institute, 1977, 200p.)

Second Dalrymple, Dana G. Development and Spread of High-Yielding Rice Varieties in Developing Countries. Washington, D.C.; Bureau of Science and Technology, Agency for International Development, 1986. 99p.

Second Dalrymple, Dana G. Development and Spread of High-Yielding Wheat Varieties in Developing Countries. Washington, D.C.; Bureau of Science and Technology, Agency for International Development, 1986. 99p.

Third Danda, Ajit K., ed. Studies on Rural Development: Experiences and Issues. New Delhi, Inter-India Publications, 1984. l07p.

Second Das, Arvind Ned. Agrarian Movements in India: Studies on 20th Century Bihar. London; F. Cass, 1982. 152p.

Second Dasgupta, Ajit K. Agriculture and Economic Development in India. New Delhi; Associated Pub. House, 1973. 117p.

Second Dauber, Roslyn, and Melinda Cain, eds. Women and Technological Change In Developing Countries. Boulder, CO; Westview Press for American Association for the Advancement of Science, 1981. 266p.

Second Davis, Irving F., ed. Selected Readings in Agricultural Credit. University of California Press for International Conference on Agricultural and Cooperative Credit, 1952. 582p.

Second Davis, Ted J., and Isabella A. Schirmer, eds. Sustainability Issues in Agricultural Development: Proceedings of the Seventh Agricultural Sector Symposium. Washington, D.C.; World Bank, 1987. 382p.

Second Dawson, Andrew H. The Land Problem in the Developed Economy. New York; St. Martin's Press, 1984. 280p.

Third Day, R. H., and A. Cigno, eds. Modelling Economic Change: The Recursive Programming Approach. Amsterdam; North-Holland Publ. Co., 1978. 447p.

Second de Haen, Hartwig, Glenn L. Johnson, and Stefan Tangermann, eds. Agriculture and International Relations: Analysis and Policy; Essays in Memory of Theodor Heidhus. New York; St. Martin's Press, 1985. 306p.

First rank de Janvry, Alain. The Agrarian Question and Reformism in Latin America. Baltimore; Johns Hopkins University Press, 1981. 311p.

Second de Janvry, Alain and Jean-Jacques Dethier. Technological Innovation in

Agriculture: The Political Economy of Its Rate and Basis. Washington, D.C., World Bank, 1985. 90p. (CGIAR Study Paper no. l)

First rank de Janvry, Alain, and K. Subbarao. Agricultural Price Policy and Income Distribution in India. Delhi, Oxford University Press, 1986. 113p.

Second De Wilde, John C., et al. Experiences with Agricultural Development in Tropical Africa. Vol. 1: The Synthesis; Vol. 2: The Case Studies. Baltimore; Johns Hopkins University Press, 1967. 264p. (World Bank Ser.)

Second De Wilde, John C. Agriculture, Marketing and Pricing in Sub-Saharan Africa. Los Angeles; African Studies Association, 1984. 129p.

Second Deaton, Angus and John Muellbauer. Economics and Consumer Behavior. Cambridge University Press, 1980. 450p. (Reprinted with corrections, 1983)

Second Deaton, Angus. Quality, Quantity, and Spatial Variation of Price: Estimated Price Elasticities from Cross-Sectional Data. Washington, D.C.; World Bank, 1987. 72p.

Second Dejene, Alemneh. Peasants, Agrarian Socialism and Rural Development in Ethiopia. Boulder, Colo.; Westview Press, 1986. 140p. (Special Studies on Africa).

Third Dernberger, R. F., ed. China's Development Experience in Comparative Perspective. Cambridge, Mass., Harvard University Press, 1980. 341p.

Second Desai, A.R., ed. Agrarian Struggles in Indian after Independence. Oxford University Press, 1986. 653p.

Third Desai, G. M., P. N. Chary, and S. C. Bandyopadhyay. Dynamics of Growth in Fertilizer Use at Micro Level. Ahmedabad, India; Indian Institute of Management, Center for Management in Agriculture, 1973. 175p.

Second Desai, Meghnad J. et al., eds. Agrarian Power and Agricultural Productivity in South Asia. Berkeley; University of California Press, 1984. 384p.

Third Desfosses, H., and J. Levesque, eds. Socialism in the Third World. New York; Praeger, 1975. 318p.

Second Devino, Gary T. Agribusiness Finance. Danville, Ill.; Interstate Printers and Publishers, Inc., 1981. 166p.

Third Devres, J. Assessment of the Agricultural Research Resources in the Sahel. Washington, D.C.; World Bank, 1984. 2 vols.

Second Dewan, M. L. Agriculture and Rural Development in India: A Case Study on the Dignity of Labour. New Delhi, India; Concept Publs., 1982. 240p.

Second Dewey, J. Logic: The Theory of Inquiry. New York: Holt, 1938. 546p.

Third Dias, R., G. E. Schuh and P. F. Warnken. Desenvolvimento da Agricultura Paulista (The Development of Paulista Agriculture). Sao Paulo; Instituto de Economia Agricola, 1972. 319p.

Third Diaz-Alejandro, C. F. Foreign Trade Regimes and Economic Development: Colombia. New York; Columbia University Press for the National Bureau of Economic Research, 1976. 281p.

First rank Dillman, Don A. and Daryl J. Hobbs, eds. Rural Society in the U.S.: Issues for the 1980's. Boulder, Colo.: Westview Press, 1982. 437p. (Rural Studies Series of the Rural Sociological Society)

First rank Dillon, John L. and Jack R. Anderson. The Analysis of Response in Crop and Livestock Production. 3d ed. Oxford and New York: Pergamon Press, 1989. 251p. (1st and 2d eds. by Dillon, 1968, 1977.)

Third Dillon, John L., and J. B. Hardaker. Farm Management Research for Small Farmer Development. Rome; Food and Agriculture Organization, 1980. 145p. (FAO Agriculture Services Bulletin, No. 41.)

First rank Dimarco, L. E., ed. International Economics and Development: Essays in Honor of Raul Prebisch. New York; Academic Press, 1972. 515p.

Second Dinham, Barbara and Colin Hines. Agribusiness in Africa. London; Earth Resources Research, 1983. 224p. (Reprinted Trenton, N.J.; Africa World Press, 1984)

Second Dobyns, H.F., P.L. Doughty and H.D. Lasswell, eds. Peasants, Power and Applied Social Change: Vicos as a Model. Beverly Hills, California; Sage Publications, 1971. 237p.

Third Dodge, D. Agricultural Policy and Performance in Zambia: History, Prospects, and Proposals for Change. Berkeley; University of California Press, 1977. 285p.

Second Doll, John P., V. J. Rhodes, and J. G. West. Economics of Agricultural Production, Markets, and Policy. Homewood, Ill.: Richard D. Irwin, 1968. 557p.

First rank Donald, Gordon. Credit for Small Farmers in Developing Countries. Boulder, Colo.; Westview Press, 1976. 286p.

Third Donnithorne, A. China's Economic System. New York; Praeger, 1967. 592p.

Third Doppler, W. The Economics of Pasture Improvement and Beef Production in Semi-Humid West Africa. Eschborn, West Germany; Deutsche Gesellschaft fur Technische Zusammenarbeit (German Agency for Technical Cooperation), 1980. 195p.

Second Dore, R.P. Land Reform in Japan. London, New York; Oxford University Press, 1959. 510p. (American Edition; New York; Shocken Books, 1985)

Second Dorfman, Robert and N.S. Dorfman, eds. Economics of the Environment: Selected Readings. New York; Norton, 1972. (2d ed., 1977. 494p.)

First rank Dorner, Peter, ed. Cooperative and Commune: Group Farming in the Economic Development of Agriculture. Madison, Wisc. University of Wisc., 1977. 392p.

Second Dorner, Peter, ed. Land Reform in Latin America: Issues and Cases. Madison, Wisc.; Land Tenure Center, University of Wisconsin, 1971. 276p.

Second Dorner, Peter. Land Reform and Economic Development. Harmondsworth, England; Penguin Books, 1972. 167p.

Second Douglass, Gordon K., ed. Agricultural Sustainability in a Changing World Order. Boulder, Colo.; Westview Press, 1984. 282p.

First rank Dovring, Folke. Land Economics. Boston, Mass.; Breton Publ., 1987. 532p.

Third Dozier, C. L. Land Development and Colonization in Latin America: Case Studies of Peru, Bolivia,and Mexico. New York; Praeger Publ., 1969. 229p.

Third Dubhashi, P. R. Policy and Performance: Agricultural and Rural Development in Post Independence India. Beverly Hills, Calif., Sage Publ., 1987. 320p.

Second Duggan, William R. Microeconomic Analysis of Southern African Agriculture. New York; Praeger Publishers, 1985. 272p.

Third Dumont, Rene. Types of Rural Economy; Studies in World Agriculture. Translation by Douglas Magnin, 1st English language ed. New York; Praeger, 1957. 555p.

Second Duncan, Kenneth, Ian Rutledge, and Colin Harding, eds. Land and Labour in Latin America: Essays on the Development of Agrarian Capitalism in the Nineteenth and Twentieth Centuries. Cambridge; Cambridge University Press, 1977. 535p.

Second Dunn, P. D. Appropriate Technology: Technology with a Human Face. New York, Schocken Books, 1979. 220p.

Third Du Sautoy, Peter. Community Development in Ghana. London; Oxford University Press, 1958. 209p.

E

Second Eashvaraiah, P. Political Dimensions of Land Reforms in India. New Delhi, India; Ashish, 1985. 136p.

Second Easter, K. W. ed. Irrigation Investment Technology and Management Strategies for Development. Boulder, Colo.: Westview Press, 1986. 270p.

Third Easter, K. W., J. A . Dixon, and M. Mgt. Hufschmidt, eds. Watershed Resources Management: An Integrated Framework with Studies from Asia and the Pacific. Boulder, Colo., Westview Press, 1986. 236p.

Second Easterlin, R. A., ed. Population and Economic Change in Developing Countries. Chicago; University of Chicago Press, 1980. 581p.

Second Eckhardt, Kenneth W., and David M. Erman. Social Research Methods: Perspective, Theory, and Analysis. New York; Random House, 1977. 410p.

Second Eckstein, A. China's Economic Revolution. New York, Praeger, 1977. 340p.

Third Eckstein, A. Quantitative Measures of China's Economic Output. Ann Arbor, Mich.; Univ of Michigan Press, 1980. 443p.

Second Edwards, Edgar O., ed. Employment in Developing Nations. New York; Columbia University Press, 1974. 428p.

Third Eicher, Carl K., and C. Liedholm, eds. Growth and Development of the Nigerian Economy. East Lansing; Michigan State University Press, 1970. 456p.

Third Eicher, Carl K., and Doyle C. Baker. Research on Agricultural Development in Sub-Saharan Africa: A Critical Survey. East Lansing; Michigan State University, Dept. of Agricultural Economics, 1982. 335p. (A revision of this work is in progress and will appear in 1992 in vol. 4 or 5 of the Lee Martin series: *A Survey of Agricultural Economics Literature*.)

First rank Eicher, Carl K., and J. Staatz, eds. Agricultural Development in the Third World. Baltimore; The Johns Hopkins University Press, 1984. 491p.

Second El Ghonemy, M.R., et al. Studies on Agrarian Reform and Rural Poverty. Rome: Food and Agriculture Organization of the United Nations, 1984. 104p.

Third Eldridge, P. J. The Politics of Foreign Aid in India. London; Wedenfeld and Nicholson, 1969. 289p. (New York; Shocken, 1970)

Second Ellickson, Robert C. and A. Dan Tarlock. Land Use Controls. Boston; Little, Brown and Company, 1981. 1239p.

Second Ellis, H. S., ed. The Economy of Brazil. Berkeley, University of California Press, 1969. 408p.

Third Ellis, H. S. and H. C. Wallich, eds. El Desarrollo Economico y America Latina (Economic Development and Latin America). Mexico City; Fondo de Cultura Economica, 1960, 1961. English edition—New York; St. Martin's Press, 1961.

Third Elz, Dieter. Agricultural Marketing Strategy and Pricing Policy. Washington, D.C.; World Bank, 1987. 148p.

Third Emmanuel, Arghiri, et al. Un Debat sur L'Echange Inegal: salires, sous-development, imperialisme. Paris; Maspero, 1969. 157p.

Third Ender, G. Food Security Policies of Six Asian Countries. Washington, D. C., Economics Research Service, USDA, 1983. 71p. (USDA Foreign Agric. Econ. Report No. 190)

Second Epp, Donald J. and John W. Malone, Jr. Introduction to Agricultural Economics. New York; Macmillan Publ. Co., 1981. 354p.

Third Essang, S. M., and O. Ogunfowora. Plantation Agriculture and Labour Use in Southern Nigeria. Ibadan, Nigeria; University of Ibadan, 1975. (University of Ibadan. Rural Development Paper, No. 15.)

Third Etienne, Gilbert. Rural Development in Asia: Meetings with Peasants. Translated by Arati Sharma. Rev. ed. New Delhi, Beverly Hills, Calif., Sage Publications, 1985. 276p.

Third European Economic Community. Food Security Policy: Examination of Recent Experience in Sub-Saharan Africa. Brussels; EEC, 1988. (Commission Staff Paper)

Second Evenson, Robert Eugene and Yoav Kislev. Agricultural Research and Productivity. New Haven, Conn., Yale University Press, 1975. 204p.

Third Evenson, Robert Eugene. The CGIAR Centers: Measures of Impact on National Research, Extension, and Productibility. Washington, D.C., World Bank and CGIAR, 1986.

Third Evenson, Robert Eugene. The International Agricultural Research Centers: Their Impact on Spending for National Agricultural Research and Extension. Washington, D.C.; World Bank, 1987. 73p. (CGIAR Study Paper, No. 22.)

F

Third Falcon, W. P. and G. F. Papanek, eds. Development Policy: The Pakistan Experience. Cambridge, Mass., Harvard University Press, 1971. 267p.

Third Falcon, W.P., et al. The Cassava Economy of Java. Stanford, Calif.; Stanford University Press, 1984. 212p.

Third FAO/AFAA Expert Consultation on Training in Agricultural and Food Marketing at University Level in Africa (Nairobi, 1975). Training in Agricultural and Food Marketing at University Level in Africa Report. Rome; Food and Agriculture Organization, 1976. 74p.

Third FAO/RED Workshop on the Effective Use of Marketing for the Development of Small Farmers in Asia. (Bangkok, 1976) Marketing for the Development of Small Farms in Asia. Rome; Food and Agriculture Organization, 1976. 86p.

Third FAO/UNFPA Expert Consultation on Land Resources for Populations of the Future (Rome, 1979) Report. Rome; Food and Agriculture Organization, 1980. 369p.

Third Farrington, J., F. Abeyratne, and G. J. Gill. Farm Power and Employment in Asia: Performance and Prospects. Bangkok, Agricultural Develop. Council for Agrarian Research and Development Council, Colombo, Sri Lanka, 1984.

Second Farris, Paul L., ed. Market Structure Research: Theory and Practice in Agricultural Economics. Ames; Iowa State University Press, 1964. 177p.

Third	Farvar, M.T., and J.P. Milton, eds. The Careless Technology: Ecology and International Development; the Record. Garden City, New York; Natural History Press, 1972. 1030p.
Second	Feder, Gershon, et al. Land Policies and Farm Productivity in Thailand. Baltimore; Johns Hopkins University Press, 1988. 165p.
First rank	Feeney, David A. The Political Economy of Productivity: Thai Agricultural Development, 1880–1975. Vancouver; University of British Columbia Press, 1981. 238p.
Third	Fei, John C. H., and G. Ranis. Development of the Labor Surplus Economy: Theory and Policy. Homewood, Ill.; Irwin, 1964. 324p.
Second	Fei, John C. H., G. Ranis and S. W. Y. Kuo. Growth with Equity—the Taiwan Case. New York; Oxford University Press, 1979. 422p.
First rank	Fennell, Rosemary. The Common Agricultural Policy of the European Community. Montclair, N.J.; Allenheld, Osmun, 1979. 243p. (2d ed. Oxford; Blackwell Scientific Publications, 1988. 227p.)
Second	Ferguson, Charles E. Microeconomic Theory. Homewood, Illinois; R. D. Irwin, 1961. 439 p. Later eds. written with J. P. Gould. (6th ed., 1986, by Gould and Edward P. Lazear. 640 p.)
Second	Ferguson, Charles. E. The Neoclassical Theory of Production and Distribution. Cambridge; At the University Press, 1969. 384p. (Reprinted with corrections 1975. 383p.)
Second	Fernon, B. Issues in World Farm Trade: Chaos or Cooperation. London; Trade Policy Research Centre, 1970. 143p.
Third	Fieldhouse, D.K. Black Africa, 1945–1980: Economic Decolonization and Arrested Development. London; Allen and Unwin, 1986. 260p.
Second	Fitchen, Janet. Poverty in Rural America: A Case Study. Boulder, CO; Westview Press, 1981. 257p. (Westview Special Studies in Contemporary Social Issues)
Third	Food and Agriculture Organization. African Agriculture: The Next 25 Years. Rome; Food and Agriculture Organization, 1986. 5 vols.
Third	Food and Agriculture Organization. Agricultural Development in Nigeria, 1965–1980. Rome; Food and Agriculture Organization, 1966. 512p.
Third	Food and Agriculture Organization. Agricultural Price Policies: Issues and Proposals. Rome, Food and Agriculture Organization, 1987. 210p. (FAO Economic and Social Development Series, no. 42.)
Third	Food and Agriculture Organization. Bibliography of Food Consumption Surveys. Rome; Food and Agriculture Organization, 1981. 85p. (FAO Food and Nutrition Paper, No. 18.)
Third	Food and Agriculture Organization. Bibliography on Land Settlement. Rome; Food and Agriculture Organization, 1976. 146p.
Second	Food and Agriculture Organization. Development Strategies for the Rural Poor. Rome; Food and Agriculture Organization, 1984. 117p.
Second	Food and Agriculture Organization. Economic Accounts for Agriculture: Production and Capital Formation. 2d issue. Rome; Food and Agriculture Organization, 1979. 319p.
Second	Food and Agriculture Organization. FAO Studies in Agricultural Economics and Statistics, 1952–1977: Selected Articles From the *Monthly Bulletin of Agricultural Economics and Statistics*. Rome; Food and Agriculture Organization, 1978. 442p. (FAO Economic and Social Development Series, no. 13; FAO Statistics Series, no. 20).
Second	Food and Agriculture Organization. Food Balance Sheets: 1979–1981 Average. Rome; Food and Agriculture Organization, 1984. 272p.

Third Food and Agriculture Organization. Perspective Study on Agricultural Development in the Sahelian Countries, 1975–1990. Vol. 1: Main Report; Vol. 2: Statistical Annex; Vol. 3: Summary and Conclusions. Rome; Food and Agriculture Organization, 1976.

First rank Food and Agriculture Organization. Review of Food Consumption Surveys 1988: Household Food Consumption By Economic Groups, Rome; Food and Agriculture Organization, 1988. 197p. (FAO Food and Nutrition Paper No. 44)

Third Food and Agriculture Organization. The Fifth World Survey. Rome; Food and Agriculture Organization, 1987. 75p.

Third Food and Agriculture Organization. The Pastoral Systems in the Sahel: Basic Socio-Demographic Data Connected with the Conservation and Development of Arid and Semi-Arid Rangelands. Rome; Food and Agriculture Organization, 1977.

First rank Food and Agriculture Organization. World Food Security: Selected Themes and Issues. Rome, 1985. 108p.

Third Food and Agriculture Organization, and the World Health Organization. Food and Nutrition Strategies in National Development. Geneva; World Health Organization, 1976. 64p. (FAO Nutrition Meetings Report Series, No. 56; and WHO Technical Report Series, No. 584.)

Second Foster, George M. Traditional Societies and Technological Change. New York; Harper and Row, 1973. 286p.

Third Foster, George M, T. Scudder, E. Colson, and R.V. Kemper, eds. Long-Term Field Research in Social Anthropology. New York; Academic Press, 1979. 358p.

Second Fox, Karl A., J. K. Sengupta, and E. Thorbecke. The Theory of Quantitative Economic Policy with Applications to Economic Growth and Stabilization. 2d ed. Amsterdam: North-Holland, 1973. 620p. (1st ed., 1966. 517p.)

Third Francioni, Manuel J. El Credito en la Produccion Agraria. Buenos Aires; El Ateneo, 1944. 430p.

Third Franke, R.W., and B.H. Chasin. Seeds of Famine: Ecological Destruction and the Development Dilemma in the West African Sahel. Montclair, N.J.; Allanheld and Osmun, 1980. 266p.

First rank Frankel, Francine R. India's Green Revolution: Economic Gains and Political Costs. Princeton University Press, 1971. 232p.

Second Freedman, Ronald, ed. Population: The Vital Revolution. Garden City, N.Y.; Basic Books, 1964. 274p.

First rank Friedman, M. A Theory of the Consumption Function. Princeton; Princeton University Press, 1957. 243p.

Second Friedman, M. Price Theory. Chicago: Aldine Publishing Co., 1976. 357p.

Third Fry, Maxwell J. Money, Interest, and Banking in Economic Development. Baltimore: Johns Hopkins University Press, 1988. 522 p.

Third Frykenberg, Robert E., ed. Land Tenure and Peasant in South Asia. New Delhi, India; Orient Longman, 1977. 312p.

Third Furtado, Celso. Analise do Modelo Brasileiro (Analysis of the Brazilian "Model") 7th ed. Rio de Janeiro; Civilizacao Brasileria, 1982. 122p. (1st edl., 1972)

Third Furtado, Celso. Dialetica do Desenvolvimento (The Dialectics of Development). 2d ed. Rio de Janeiro, Brazil; Eda Fundo de Cultura, 1968. 181p. (1st ed., 1964. 173p.)

Third Furtado, Celso. Economic Development of Latin America: Historical Background and Contemporary Problems. New York, Cambridge University Press, 1976. Translation of 2d ed of his Formacao Economica da America Latina, 1976. 317p.

Third Furtado, Celso. O Brasil Pos-Milagre (Brazil's Post-Miracle). 7th ed. Rio de Janeiro; Paz e Terra, 1982. 152p.

Second Furtado, Celso. Obstacles to Development in Latin America. New York, Doubleday, 1970. 204p.

Third Furtado, Celso. Subdesenvolvimento e Estagnocao na America Latina (Underdevelopment and Stagnation of Latin America). 3rd ed. Rio de Janeiro; Civilizacao Brasileira, 1968. 127p.

G

Second Gadalla, Saad M. Land Reform in Relation to Social Development, Egypt. Columbia; University of Missouri Press, 1962. 139p.

First rank Galbraith, John K. American Capitalism: The Concept of Countervailing Power. Rev. ed. Boston, Mass; Houghton Mifflin, 1956. 208p.

First rank Galbraith, John K. Economic Development. Cambridge, Massachusetts; Harvard University Press, 1964. 109p.

Second Gandhi, Ved P. Tax Burden on Indian Agriculture. Cambridge, Mass.; Harvard Law School, International Tax Program, 1966. 260p.

Third Gasser, W. R. Survey of Irrigation in Eight Asian Nations: India, Pakistan, Indonesia, Thailand, Bangladesh, South Korea, Philippines, and Sri Lanka. Washington, D.C., Economics and Statistics Service, USDA, 1981. 114p. (USDA Foreign Agricultural Economic Report No. 165.)

Second Gayoso, A. and W. W. McPherson. Effects of Changing Trade Systems in Latin America on U. S. Agricultural Exports. Gainesville; University of Florida, Institute of Food and Agricultural Sciences, 1971. 433p. (University of Florida Experiment Station Monograph Series No. 1)

Second Geary, Frank. Land Tenure and Unemployment. London; G. Allen and Unwin, 1925. 256p. (Reprinted New York; A. M. Kelley, 1969.)

Third Geertz, Clifford, ed. Old Societies and New States: The Quest for Modernity in Asia and Africa. Glencoe, Ill.; Free Press of Glencoe for Univ. of Chicago Committees for the Comparative Study of New Nations, 1963. 310p.

Second Gersovitz, Mark, Carlos F. Diaz-Alajandro, Gustav Ranis and Mark Rosenzweig. The Theory and Experience of Economic Development: Essays in Honor of Sir W. Arthur Lewis. London; George Allen and Unwin, 1982. 403p.

Second Ghai, Dharam and Lawrence Smith. Agricultural Prices, Policy and Equity in Sub-Saharan Africa. Boulder, Colo.; Lynne Rienner, 1987. 174p.

First rank Ghai, Dharam, Azizur R. Khan, Eddy Lee, and Samir Radwan, eds. Agrarian Systems and Rural Development. New York; Holmes and Meier Publ., Inc., 1979. 375p.

First rank Ghatak, Subrata, and Ken Ingersent. Agriculture and Economic Development. Baltimore; The Johns Hopkins University Press; Brighton; Wheatsheaf Books, 1984. 380p.

Second Ghose, Ajit Kumar, ed. Agrarian Reform in Contemporary Developing Countries. London; Croom Helm, and New York; St. Martin's Press, 1983. 364p.

Second Ghosh, Pradip K. ed. Development Policy and Planning: A Third World

Perspective. Westport, Ct.: Greenwood Press, 1984. 626p. (International Development Resource Books, No. 8).

First rank Ghosh, Pradip K. ed. Health, Food and Nutrition in Third World Development. Westport, Ct.: Greenwood Press, 1984. 617p. (International Development Resource Books, No. 6).

Second Giersch, H. International Economic Development and Resource Transfer; Workshop, 1978. Tubingen; J.C.B. Mohr, 1978. 619p.

First rank Gittinger, J. Price. Economic Analysis of Agricultural Projects. 2d ed., completely rev. & expanded. Baltimore; Johns Hopkins University Press for the International Bank for Reconstruction and Development, 1982. 505p.

First rank Gittinger, J. Price, Joanne Leslie and Caroline Hoisington. Food Policy: Integrating Supply, Distribution, and Consumption. Baltimore, Johns Hopkins University Press, 1987. 567p.

First rank Glaeser, Bernhard, ed. The Green Revolution Revisited. London; George Allen and Unwin; and New York; St. Martin's Press, 1987. 224p.

Third Glantz, M. H., ed. Drought and Hunger In Africa: Denying Famine a Future. Cambridge University Press, 1987. 457p.

Second Godelier, Maurice. Rationality and Irrationality in Economics. New York; Monthly Review Press, 1975. 326p.

Second Goldberg, Ray A. Agribusiness Management for Developing Countries: Southeast Asian Corn Systems and American and Japanese Trends Affecting It. New York; Ballinger Publishing Company. 1979. 672p.

Second Goldberg, Ray A., ed. Research in Domestic and International Agribusiness Management; A Research Manual, Vol. 1 (1980), Vol. 9 (1988). Greenwich, Conn.; Jai Press, Inc.

Second Goldberger, A. S. Econometric Theory. New York: Wiley, 1964. 399p.

Third Gomez, O. Hernando and Eduardo D. Wiesner, eds. Lecturas Sobre Desarrollo Economico Colombiano en Honor de Alvaro Lopez Toro. Bogota, Colombia; Fundacion para la Educacion Superior y el Desarrollo, 1974. 624p.

Third Gooneratne, W., ed. Labour Absorption in Rice-Based Agriculture: Case Studies from Southeast Asia. Bangkok, Thailand; Int. Labour Organization, ARTEP, 1982. 181p.

Third Goreaux, Louis-Marie. Income Elasticity of Demand for Food. Rome, Food and Agriculture Organization, and European Commission on Economics, 1959.

Third Graaf, J. de V. The Economics of Coffee. Wageningen, The Netherlands, PUDOC, 1986. 294p. (Economics of Crops in Developing Countries, No. l)

Second Graham, Norman A., and Keith L. Edwards. The Caribbean Basin to the Year 2000; Demographic, Economic, and Resource-Use Trends in Seventeen Countries: A Compendium of Statistics and Projections. Boulder, Colo.; Westview Press, 1984. 166p.

Second Gramlich, Edward M. Benefit-Cost Analysis of Government Programs. Englewood Cliffs, NJ; Prentice-Hall, 1981. 273p.

Third Gray, Cheryl W. Food Consumption Parameters for Brazil and their Application to Food Policy. Washington D.C.; International Food Policy Research Insititute, 1982. 78p. (IFPRI Research Report 32)

Third Gray, Jack and Gordon White, eds. China's New Development Strategy. London; Academic Press, 1982. 341p.

Second	Greenshields, Bruce L., and M.A. Bellamy, eds. Rural Development: Growth and Equity. International Association of Agricultural Economists' Proceedings. Aldershot, Hampshire and Brookfield, VT; Gower, 1983. 312p.
Third	Griffin, Keith and A. Saith. Growth and Equality in Rural China. Geneva, International Labour Organization, 1981. 166p.
First rank	Griffin, Keith. The Political Economy of Agrarian Change: An Essay on the Green Revolution. 2d ed. London; Macmillan, 1979. 268p. (1st ed. Cambridge, Mass.; Harvard Univeristy Press, 1974. 264p.)
Second	Grigg, David. Dynamics of Agricultural Change. New York; St. Martin's Press, 1982. 260p.
Second	Grigg, David. Introduction to Agricultural Geography. London, and Dover, N.H.; Hutchinson Education, 1984. 204p.
Second	Grigg, David. Population Growth and Agrarian Change: An Historical Perspective. New York; Cambridge University Press, 1980. 340p. (Cambridge Geographical Studies, 13)
Third	Griliches, Zvi and Michael D. Intriligator, eds. Handbook of Econometrics. Amsterdam; North-Holland Pub. Co.; and New York; Elsevier Science Pub. Co., 1983–1986. 3 vols. (Handbooks in Economics, bk. 2)
Second	Grindle, Merilee S. State and Countryside: Development Policy and Agrarian Politics in Latin America. Baltimore, Md.; Johns Hopkins University Press, 1985. 255p.
Second	Gudeman, Stephen. The Demise of a Rural Economy: From Subsistence to Capitalism in a Latin American Village. London and Boston; Routledge and K. Paul, 1978. 176p.
Third	Guillet, D. Agrarian Reform and Peasant Economy. Columbia; University of Missouri Press, 1979. 227p.
Second	Guru, D. D. Strategy of Agricultural Development. Patna, India; Nav-Vikas Prakashan, 1986. 256p.
Third	Gutelman, Michel. Reforme et Mystification Agraire en Amerique Latine: Le Cas du Mexique. Paris; Maspero, 1971. 259p. (Documents et recherches d'economie et socialisme, 5)
Third	Gutiérrez, A. N. and R. Hertford. Una Evaluación de la Intervención del gobierno en el Mercadeo de Arroz en Colombia. Cali, Colombia; Centro Internacional de Agricultura Tropical, 1974. (Technical Pamphlet No. 4)

H

Second	Hadwiger, Don F. Public Policy and Agricultural Technology: Adversity Despite Achievement. New York: Macmillan, 1987. 300p.
Second	Hagen, E. E. The Economics of Development. 3d ed. Homewood, Ill.; Irwin-Dorsey, 1980, 412p. (1st ed., 1960. 536p.)
First rank	Halcrow, Harold G. Economics of Agriculture. McGraw-Hill Book Co., 1980. 383p. Q
Third	Hall, A.E., G. H. Cannell, and H. W. Lawton, eds. Agriculture in Semi-Arid Environments. New York; Springer-Verlag, 1979. 340p.
First rank	Halter, A. N., and G. W. Dean. Decisions under Uncertainty with Research Applications. Cincinnati: South-West Publishing, 1971. 266p.
Second	Handelman, Howard. Struggle in the Andes: Peasant Political Mobilization in Peru. Austin; University of Texas Press, 1975. 321p.
Second	Hanf, Claus H., and Gerhard W. Schiefer, eds. Planning and Decision in Agribusiness: Principles and Experiences, A Case Study Approach to the

Use of Models in Decision Planning. Amsterdam and New York; Elsevier Science Publishing Co., 1983. 373p.

Third — Haque, Wahidul, et al. Towards a Theory of Rural Development. Bangkok: United Nations Asian Development Institute, 1975. 102p.

Second — Harbeson, John W. Nation-Building in Kenya: The Role of Land Reform. Chicago; Northwestern University Press, 1973. 421p.

Second — Harbison, Frederick H., and Charles A. Myers. Manpower and Education: Country Studies in Economics Development. New York; McGraw-Hill, 1965. 343p.

Second — Harrison, A. J. Economics and Land Use Planning. New York; Saint Martin's Press, Inc.; London; Croom Helm, 1977. 256p.

Second — Harrison, James Q., Jon A. Hitchings, and John A. Wall. India: Demand and Supply Prospects for Agriculture, Washington, D.C.; The World Bank, 1981. 133p.

Second — Harriss, Barbara. Transitional Trade and Rural Development: The Nature and Role of Agricultural Trade in a South Indian District. New Delhi, India; Vikas Publishing, 1981. 263p.

Second — Harriss, John and Mick Moore, eds. Development and the Rural-Urban Divide. London and Totowa, N.J.; F. Cass, 1984. 166p.

First rank — Harriss, John, ed. Rural Development: Theories of Peasant Economy and Agrarian Change; Anatomy of a Peasant Economy. London; Hutchinson, 1982. 409p.

Second — Harrod, R. F., and D. C. Hague, eds. International Trade Theory in a Developing World; Proceedings of a conference by the International Economic Association. London; MacMillan; New York; St. Martin's Press, 1963. 570p. (Reprinted 1965)

Second — Hart, Keith. The Political Economy of West African Agriculture. Cambridge University Press, 1982. 256p.

Third — Harvard University Business School. Colloquium on World Food Policy. Cambridge, Mass., Harvard University Business School, 1984.

Second — Harvey, Andrew C. The Econometric Analysis of Time Series. Oxford; Philip Allan, 1981. 384p.

Second — Harvey, Andrew C. Time Series Models. Oxford; Philip Allan Publishers, and New York; Wiley, 1981. 229p.

First rank — Hathaway, D.E. Agriculture and the GATT: Rewriting the Rules. Washington, D. C.; Institute for International Economics, 1987. 157p.

Second — Hayami, Yujiro. Japanese Agriculture Under Siege: The Political Economy of Agricultural Policies. New York; Macmillan, 1988. 145p.

Second — Hayami, Yujiro and M. Kikuchi. Asian Village Economy at the Crossroad: An Economic Approach to Institutional Change. Tokyo; Univ of Tokyo Press, 198l; Publ. in 1982 by Johns Hopkins University Press. 275p.

First rank — Hayami, Yujiro, and V. W. Ruttan. Agricultural Development: An International Perspective. Baltimore: Johns Hopkins University Press, 1971. 367p. (Revised and expanded, 1984. 506p.) Q AAEA Classic

Second — Hayami, Yujiro in assoc. with M. Akino, M. Shintani, and S. Yamada. A Century of Agricultural Growth in Japan: Its Relevance to Asian Development. Tokyo; University of Tokyo Press; Minneapolis; University of Minnesota Press, 1975. 248p.

Third — Hayami, Yujiro, M. Kikuchi, P. F. Moya, L. M. Bambo, and E. B. Marciano. Anatomy of a Peasant Economy: A Rice Village in the Philippines. Los Baños, Philippines; International Rice Research Institute, 1978. 149p.

First rank	Hayami, Yujiro, Vernon W. Ruttan and Herman M. Southworth, eds. Agricultural Growth in Japan, Taiwan, Korea and the Philippines. Honolulu; University Press of Hawaii for the East-West Center, 1979. 404p.
Second	Hazell, Peter and Roger D. Norton. Mathematical Programming for Economics Analysis in Agriculture. New York; Macmillan, 1986. 432p.
First rank	Hazell, Peter, Carlos Pomareda, and Alberto Valdés, eds. Crop Insurance for Agricultural Development: Issues and Experience. Baltimore; Johns Hopkins University Press for The International Food Policy Research Institute, 1986. 322p.
Second	Hazell, Peter and A. Roell. Rural Growth Linkages: Household Expenditure Patterns in Malaysia and Nigeria. Washington, D.C.; The International Food Policy Research Institute, 1983. 64p. (IFPRI Research Report No. 41)
Second	Headley, J.C., and J.N. Lewis. The Pesticide Problem: An Economic Approach to Public Policy. Baltimore; Johns Hopkins University Press for Resources for the Future, 1967. 141p.
Second	Heady, Earl O. Agricultural Policy under Economic Development. Ames: Iowa State University Press, 1962. 682p. (Reissued 1965)
Second	Heady, Earl O., ed. Economic Models and Quantitative Methods for Decisions and Planning in Agriculture. Ames: Iowa State University Press, 1971. 518p.
Third	Helleiner, G.K., ed. Agricultural Planning in East Africa. Nairobi; East African Publishing House, 1968. 183p.
First rank	Helmberger, P., and S. Hoos. Cooperative Bargaining in Agriculture: Grower-Processor Markets for Fruits and Vegetables. Berkeley; University of California, Division of Agricultural Sciences, 1965. 234p. Q
First rank	Henderson, J. M., and R. E. Quandt. Microeconomic Theory. 2d ed. New York: McGraw-Hill, 1980. 420p. (1st ed., 1958. 291p.)
First rank	Herdt, Robert W., and C. Capule. Adoption, Spread, and Production Impact of Modern Rice Varieties in Asia. Los Baños, Laguna, Philippines; International Rice Research Institute, 1983. 54p.
Second	Herring, Ronald J. Land to the Tiller: Political Economy of Agrarian Reform in South Asia. New Haven, Conn.; Yale University Press, 1983. 314p.
Second	Hewitt de Alcantara, Cynthia. Modernizing Mexican Agriculture: Socioeconomic Implications of Technological Change, 1940–1970. Geneva; United Nations Research Institute for Social Development, 1976. 350p. (UNRISD Studies on the Green Revolution) (5th ed. Mexico; Siglo Vientiuno Editores, 1985. 319p.)
Third	Heyer, J., Pepe Roberts, and W. M. Senga, eds. Agricultural Development in Kenya: An Economic Assessment. Nairobi; Oxford University Press, 1976. 371p.
First rank	Heyer, J., Pepe Roberts, and Gavin Williams, eds. Rural Development in Tropical Africa. London; Macmillan Press, 1981. 224p.
Second	Hicks, John R. Capital and Growth. New York; Oxford University Press, 1965. 343 p.
Second	Hicks, John R. A Theory of Economic History. London; Oxford University Press, 1969. 181p.
Second	Hicks, John R. Surveys of Economic Theory. London; MacMillan; New York; St. Martin's Press, 1965–1967. 3 vols.
Second	Hildreth, R. J., Kathryn L. Lipton, and Kenneth C.Clayton and Carl C. O'Connor, eds. Agricultural and Rural Areas Approaching the 21st Cen-

tury: Challenges for Agricultural Economics. Ames; Iowa State University Press, 1987. 560p.

Second Hilf, Meinhard, Francis G. Jacobs, and E-U. Petersmann, eds. The European Community and GATT. Deventer, the Netherlands; Boston; Kluwer, 1986. 398p. (Studies in Transnational Economic Law, vol. 4)

Second Hill, Berkeley and K. A. Ingersent. An Economic Analysis of Agriculture. Brookfield, Vermont; Gower Publishing Co., 1982. 355p.

Second Hill, Berkeley, and Derek Ray. Economics for Agriculture. New York; Macmillan, 1987. 320p.

Second Hill, Berkeley. Introduction to Economics for Students of Agriculture. New York; Pergamon Press, Inc., 1980. 346p.

Second Hill, Kim G., ed. Toward a New Strategy of Development. New York; Pergamon Press, 1979.

Second Hillier, Frederick S., and Gerald J. Lieberman. Introduction to Operations Research. San Francisco; Holden-Day, 1967. 639p. (4th ed., 1986, 888p.)

First rank Hillman, Jimmye S. and Robert A. Rothenberg. Agricultural Trade and Protection in Japan. Brookfield, Vermont; Gower Pub. Co., 1987. 90p. (Thames Essay Ser.: No. 50)

Third Hinderink, Jan and J. J. Sterkenburg. Agricultural Commercialization and Government Policy in Africa. London, New York; KPI, 1987. 328p. (Monogs. from the African Studies Centre, Leiden)

Third Hirashima, S. and M. Muqtada. Hired Labour and Rural Labour Markets in Asia: Studies Based on Farm-level Data. New Delhi, India; International Labour Organization, and ARTEP, 1986. 180p.

Third Hirschman, Albert O. Development Projects Observed. Washington, D.C.: Brookings Institution, 1967. 197 p.

First rank Hirschman, Albert O., ed. Essays in Trespassing: Economics to Politics and Beyond. Cambridge University Press, 1981. 310p.

First rank Hirschman, Albert O., ed. Latin American Issues: Essays and Comments. New York; Twentieth Century Fund, 1961. 201p.

Third Hirschman, Albert O. et al. Toward a New Strategy for Development: A Rothko Chapel Colloquium. New York; Pergamon Press, 1979. 365p.

Second Ho, Yhi-Min. Agricultural Development of Taiwan, 1903–1960. Nashville, Tenn.; Vanderbilt University Press, 1966. 172p.

Third Hoben, Allan. Land Tenure Among the Amhara of Ethiopia: The Dynamics of Cognatic Descent. Chicago; University of Chicago Press, 1973.

Third Hoefner, Jacob A. and P. J. Tsuchitani, eds. Animal Agriculture in China. Washington, D.C.; National Academy Press, 1980. 197p. (CSCPRC Report No. 11)

Third Hollist, W. Ladd and F. LaMond Tullis,eds. Pursuing Food Security: Strategies and Obstacles in Africa, Asia, Latin America, and the Middle East. Boulder; L. Rienner, Publ., 1987. 357p.

Third Homem de Melo, Fernando B. and E. R. Pelin. As Solucoes Energeticas e a Economia Brasileira (Energy Solutions and the Brazilian Economy). Sao Paulo; HUCITEC, 1984. 146p.

Third Hopkins, Nicholas S. Agrarian Transformation in Egypt. Boulder, Colo.; Westview, 1987. 225p.

Second Hopkins, Raymond F., Donald J. Puchala, and Ross B. Talbot, eds. Food, Politics, and Agricultural Development: Case Studies in Public Policy of Rural Modernization. Boulder, Colo.; Westview Press. 1979. 311p.

Second Hou, Chi-ming and Tzong-shian Yu, eds. Agricultural Development in China, Japan, and Korea. Seattle; University of Washington Press, 1983. 892p.

First rank Houck, James P. Elements of Agricultural Trade Policies. New York; Macmillan, 1986. 224p.

First rank Howell, John, ed. Borrowers and Lenders: Rural Financial Markets and Institutions in Developing Countries. London; Overseas Development Institute, 1980. 290p.

Second Howell, John, ed. Recurrent Costs and Agricultural Development. London; Overseas Development Institute, 1985. 223p.

Third Hsu, Robert C. Food for One Billion: China's Agriculture Since 1949. Boulder, CO; Westview Press, 1982. 156p.

First rank Hubbard, Michael. Agricultural Exports and Economic Growth: A Study of Botswana's Beef Industry. London; Routledge, 1980. 284p.

First rank Huddleston, Barbara, D. Gale Johnson, Shlomo Reutlinger, and Alberto Valdes, eds. International Finance for Food Security. Baltimore; Johns Hopkins University Press, 1984. 100p.

Second Hunt, Diana. The Impending Crisis in Kenya: The Case for Land Reform. Aldershot, Hampshire, and Brookfield, Vermont; Gower Publishing Company, 1984. 314p.

Second Hunt, Kenneth Edward, ed. Policies, Planning and Management for Agricultural Development. Conference Papers. Oxford Institute of Agrarian Affairs for the International Association of Agricultural Economists, 1971. 616p.

Second Hunter, Guy, ed. Agricultural Development and the Rural Poor: Declaration of Policy Guidelines for Action. London; Overseas Development Institute, 1978. 113p.

Second Hussain, A. and K. Tribe, eds. Paths of Development in Capitalist Agriculture: Readings from German Social Demoncracy 1891–99. London; Macmillan; Humanities Press, International, 1984. 198p.

Third Hyden, G. Efficiency Versus Distribution in East African Cooperatives: A Study in Organizational Conflicts. Nairobi; East African Literature Bureau, 1973. 254p.

Third Hyden, G. No Shortcuts to Progress: African Development Management in Perspective. London; Heinemann, 1983. 223p.

I

Third Idachaba, F. S. Agricultural Research Policy in Nigeria. Washington, D.C.; International Food Policy Research Institute for Tanzania, Ministry of Agriculture, 1980. 70p. (IFPRI Research Report, No. 17.)

Third Ijere, Martin O. New Perspectives in Financing Nigerian Agriculture. Enugu, Nigeria; Fourth Dimension Publ., 1986. 130p.

Second Ilbery, Brian W. Agricultural Geography: A Social and Economic Analysis. New York; Oxford University Press, 1986. 224p.

First rank Imel, B., M.R. Behr, and P.G. Helmberger. Market Structure and Performance: The U.S. Food Processing Industries. Lexington, Mass.; Heath Lexington Books, 1972. 115p. Q

Second Improved Vegetable Production in Asia. Taipei, Taiwan; Food and Fertilizer Technology Center for Asia and the Pacific Region, 1987. 207p. (FFTC Book Series No. 36).

Third Ingram, J. C. Economic Change in Thailand, 1850–1970. Stanford, Cal.;

Stanford University Press, 1971. 352p. (1st ed. title: Economic Change in Thailand since 1850. 1955. 254p.)

Third Institute d'Elevage et de Medecine Veterinaire des Pais Tropicaux. Elements for a Livestock Development Strategy in Sahel Countries. Alfort, France: Institute d'Elevage et de Medecine Veterinaire des Pais Tropicaux, 1980. 117p.

Third Inter-American Development Bank. Seminar on the Financing of Education in Latin America. Washington, D.C. and Mexico City; Inter-American Development Bank, 1978. 382p.

Third International Crops Research Institute for the Semi-Arid Tropics. Agricultural Markets in the Semi-Arid Tropics: Proceedings of the International Workshop. Andra Pradesh, Patancheru, India; ICRISAT, 1985. 387p.

Third International Crops Research Institute for the Semi-Arid Tropics. Socioeconomic Constraints to Development of Semi-Arid Tropical Agriculture: Proceedings. Andra Pradesh, Patancheru, India; ICRISAT, 1980. 435p.

Third International Food Policy Research Institute. Food Needs of Developing Countries: Projections of Production and Consumption to 1990. Washington, D.C., 1977. 157p. (IFPRI Research Report no. 3)

Third International Labour Organization. Employment Expansion in Asian Agriculture: A Comparative Analysis of South Asian Countries. Bangkok; I. L. O. Asian Employment Programme, 1980. 292p.

Third International Labour Organization. Mechanisation and Employment in Agriculture: Case Studies from Four Continents. Geneva, Switz.; ILO, 1973. 192p.

Third International Livestock Centre for Africa. Livestock Production in the Sub-Humid Zone of West Africa: A Regional Review. Addis Ababa, Ethiopia; ILCA, 1979. 184p.

Third International Livestock Centre for Africa. Small Ruminant Production in the Humid Tropics. Addis Ababa, Ethiopia; ILCA, 1979. 122p. (ILCA Systems Study No. 3)

Third International Rice Research Institute. Consequences of Small-Farm Mechanization. Los Baños, Philip.; IRRI, 1983. 184p.

First rank International Rice Research Institute. Economic Consequences of the New Rice Technology in Asia. Los Baños, Philippines; IRRI, 1978. 402p.

Third International Rice Research Institute. Irrigation Policy and Management in Southeast Asia. Los Baños, Philip., IRRI, 1978. 198p.

Third International Rice Research Institute. Rice Research Strategies for the Future. Los Baños, Philip.; IRRI, 1982. 553p.

Third International Rice Research Institute and the Chinese Academy of Agricultural Sciences. Rice Improvement in China and Other Asian Countries. Los Baños, Philip.; IRRI, 1980. 307p.

Second Intriligator, M.D., ed. Frontiers of Quantitative Knowledge. Amsterdam: North-Holland,1970–74. 2 vols. (Contributions to Economic Analysis, vols. 71 and 87)

Second Ishikawa, S. Economic Development in Asian Perspective. Tokyo, Japan; Kinokuniya Bookstore, 1967. 488p.

Second Ishikawa, S. Essays on Technology, Employment and Institutions in Economic Development: Comparative Asian Experience. Tokyo; Kinokuniya Publ., 1981. 466p.

First rank Islam, Nural, ed. Agricultural Policy in Developing Countries. New York; Wiley, 1974. 565p.

J

First rank Jaeger, William K. Agricultural Mechanization: The Economics of Animal Draft Power in West Africa. Boulder, Colo.; Westview, 1986. 199p.

Third Jaguaribe, H., A. Ferrer, M. S. Wionczek and T. dos Santos. La Dependencia Politico-Economica de America Latina (The Political Economic Dependency of Latin America). 12th ed. Mexico; Siglo Veintiuno, 1980. 293p. (1st ed., 1970)

Third Jain, S. Size Distribution of Income: A Compilation of Data. Washington, D.C., World Bank, 1975. 137p.

Third Jaiswal, P. L., ed. Rice Research in India. New Delhi; Indian Council of Agricultural Research, 1985. 726p.

Second Jamison, Dean T. and L. J. Lau. Farmer Education and Farm Efficiency. Baltimore; Johns Hopkins University Press, 1982. 320p. (World Bank Research Publication Ser.).

Second Jequier, Nicolas, ed. Appropriate Technology: Problems and Promises. Paris; Development Centre, Organ. for Economic Cooperation and Development, 1976. 344p.

Third Jodha, N.S., and V. S. Vyas. Conditions of Stability and Growth in Arid Agriculture. Vallabh Vidyanbagar, India, Agro-Economic Research Centre, Sardar Patel Univ., 1969. 127p.

First rank Johnson, D. Gale. World Agriculture In Disarray. London; Macmillan; and New York; St. Martin's Press for the Trade Policy Research Centre, 1973. 304p.

Second Johnson, D. Gale, and Karen M. Brooks. Prospects for Soviet Agriculture in the 1980s. Bloomington, Indiana; Indiana University Press, 1983. 224p.

Second Johnson, D. Gale, and G. E. Schuh, eds. The Role of Markets in the World Food Economy. Boulder, Colo., Westview Press, 1983. 326p.

First rank Johnson, D. Gale, Kenzo Hemmi, and Pierre Lardinois. Agricultural Policy and Trade: Adjusting Domestic Programs in an International Framework. New York; New York University Press, 1986. 144p.

Second Johnson, E.A.J. The Organization of Space in Developing Countries. Cambridge, Mass.; Harvard University Press, 1970. 452p.

Second Johnson, Glenn L., and A. Maunder, eds. Rural Change: The Challenge for Agricultural Economists. Westmead, England; Grover; and Montclair, N.J.; Allenheld, Osmun, 1981. 738p.

First rank Johnson, Glenn L., and C. L. Quance, eds. The Overproduction Trap in U. S. Agriculture. Baltimore: John Hopkins University Press, 1972. 211p.

First rank Johnson, Glenn L., and S. H. Wittwer. Agricultural Technology Until 2030: Prospects, Priorities, and Policies. East Lansing, MI; Michigan State University, Agricultural Experiment Station, 1984. 61p.

Third Johnson, H.G. Aspects of the Theory of Tariffs. Cambridge, Mass., Harvard University Press, 1972. 451p.

Second Johnson, H.G. U.S. Economic Policies Toward Less Developed Countries. Washington, D.C.; Brookings Institution, 1967. 279p.

Second Johnson, Paul R. The Economics of the Tobacco Industry. New York; Praeger, 1984. 157p.

First rank Johnson, Stanley, Zuhair Hassan and Richard D. Green. Demand Systems

Estimation: Methods and Applications. Ames, Iowa; Iowa State University Press, 1984. 178p.

First rank Johnston, Bruce F. and Peter Kilby. Agriculture and Structural Transformation: Economic Strategies in Late-Developing Countries. New York; Oxford University Press, 1975. 474p.

Second Johnston, Bruce F. and W. C. Clark. Redesigning Rural Development: A Strategic Perspective. Baltimore, Md., Johns Hopkins University Press, 1982. 311p.

First rank Johnston, Bruce F., et al, eds. U.S.-Mexico Relations: Agriculture and Rural Development. Stanford University Press, 1987. 400p.

First rank Jones, James R., ed. East-West Agricultural Trade. Boulder, Colo.; Westview Press, 1985. 256p.

Second Jones, Lawrence A., and D. Durand. Mortage Lending Experience in Agriculture. Princeton: Princeton University Press for the National Bureau of Economic Research., 1954. 233p.

Second Jones, Steve, P.C. Joshi, and M. Murmis, eds. Rural Poverty and Agrarian Reform. New Delhi, India; Allied Publ. for ENDA, Dakar, 1982. 384p.

First rank Jones, W.O. Marketing Staple Food Crops in Tropical Africa. Ithaca: Cornell University Press, 1972. 293p.

Second Jordan, Wayne R., ed. Water and Water Policy in World Food Supplies. College Station; Texas A & M University Press, 1987. 466p.

Second Joshi, P.C. Institutional Aspects of Agricultural Development: India in the Asian Context. Riverdale, Md.; Riverdale Co., 1987. 200p.

Third Joshi, P.C. Land Reforms in India: Trends and Perspectives. Bombay, India; Allied Publishers, 1975. 181p.

Second Josling, Timothy E., B. Davey, A. McFarquhar, A. C. Hannah, and D. Hamway. Burdens and Benefits of Farm-Support Policies. London; Trade Policy Research Centre, 1972. 85p.

First rank Josling, Timothy E. International Dimensions of Agricultural and Food Policies. New York; Macmillan, 1985. 320p.

Second Josling, Timothy E., T. Earley, and J. S. Hillman. Agricultural Protection: Domestic Policy and International Trade. Rome; Food and Agriculture Organization, 1973. (C 73/LIM/9)

Second Judge, George G. and Takayama, T. Studies in Economic Planning over Space and Time. Amsterdam; North Holland Publ., and New York; Elsevier, 1973. 727p.

First rank Judge, George G., et al. The Theory and Practice of Econometrics. 2d ed. New York; Wiley, 1985. 1019p. (1st ed., 1980. 793p.)

K

First rank Kadlec, John E. Farm Management: Decisions, Operation, Control. Englewood Cliffs, NJ; Prentice-Hall, 1985. 429p. Q

Second Kahlon, A. S. Agricultural Price Policy in India. New Dehli; Allied, 1983. 510p. (Distributed by South Asia Books)

Second Kahlon, A. S. and M. V. George. Agricultural Marketing and Price Policies. New Delhi; Allied, 1985. 283p. (Distributed by South Asia Books)

Second Kahlon, A. S. and K. Singh. Managing Agricultural Finance: Theory and Practice. New Dehli; Allied, 1985. 283p. (Distributed by South Asia Books)

Third Kamarck, A. M. The Tropics and Economic Development. Baltimore, Md; Johns Hopkins University Press, 1976. 113p.

Third Kanon, D. D'Eveloppement ou Appauvissement. Paris; Economica, 1985. 188p.

Third Kaynak, E., ed. World Food Marketing Systems. London; Butterworths, 1986. 333p.

Second Kay, Ronald D. Farm Management: Planning, Control and Implementation. New York; McGraw-Hill Book Co., 1981. 370p. (2d ed., 1986, 401p.)

Second Kearl, Bryant, ed. Field Data Collection in the Social Sciences: Experiences in Africa and the Middle East. New York; Agricultural Development Council, 1976. 200p.

Third Kelley, Allen C., and J. G. Williamson. Lessons from Japanese Development: An Analytical Economic History. Chicago, Ill.; University of Chicago Press, 1974. 285p.

Second Kelley, Allen C., J. G. Williamson, and R. J. Cheetham. Dualistic Economic Development: Theory and History. Chicago, Ill.; University of Chicago Press, 1972. 399p.

First rank Kendrick, John B. and Beatrice N. Vaccara, eds. New Developments in Productivity Measurement. Chicago; University of Chicago Press, 1980. 717p.

Third Kennedy, E. and Bruce Cogill. Income and Nutritional Effects of the Commercialization of Agriculture in Southwestern Kenya. Washington, D.C.; International Food Policy Research Institute, 1987. 60p. (Institute's Research Report 63)

Second Khusro, A.M. Economics of Land Reform and Farm Size in India. Madras, India; MacMillan, 1973. 162p.

First rank Kilmer, Richard L. and W. J. Armbruster, eds. Economic Efficiency in Agricultural and Food Marketing. Ames; Iowa State University Press, 1987. 336p.

Third Klein, M. A., ed. Peasants in Africa: Historical and Contemporary Perspectives. Beverly Hills, Calif.; Sage, 1980. 319p.

Second Klepper, Robert. The Economic Basis for Agrarian Protest Movements in the United States, 1870–1900. Salem, New Hamp.; Ayer Company Publishers, 1978. (Dissertations in American Economic History Ser.).

Third Knudsen, O. and P. L. Scandizzo. Nutrition and Food Needs in Developing Countries. Washington, D.C.; World Bank, 1979. 73p. (World Bank Staff Working Paper No. 328)

First rank Knutson, Ronald D., J. B. Penn, and W. T. Boehm. Agricultural and Food Policy. Englewood Cliffs, N. J.; Prentice-Hall, 1983. 387p.

Third Kocher, J. E. Rural Development, Income Distribution, and Fertility Decline. New York; Population Council, 1973. 105p. (Distributed by Bridgeport, Conn.; Key Book Service)

Second Koester, U. Policy Options for the Grain Economy of the European Community: Implications for Developing Countries. Washington, D.C.; International Food Policy Research Institute, 1982. 90p. (IFPRI Research Report No. 35)

First rank Kohls, R.L., and W.D. Downey. Marketing of Agricultural Products. 6th ed. London, New York; Macmillan, 1985. 624p.

Third Konczacki, Z. A. The Economics of Pastoralism: A Case Study of Sub-Saharan Africa. London; Cass, 1978. 185p.

Second Koo, A.Y.C. Land Market Distortion and Tenure Reform. Ames; Iowa State University Press, 1982. 137p.

Second	Koo, Won W., ed. Transportation Models for Agricultural Products. Boulder, Colo; Westview Press, 1985. 175p.
Third	Kraut, H., and H. D. Cremer, eds. Investigations into Health and Nutrition in East Africa. New York; Humanities Press; and Munchen; Weltforum Verlag, 1969. 342p.
First rank	Krueger, Anne O. Liberalization Attempts and Consequences. Cambridge, Mass.; Ballinger Pubs. Co., 1978. 310p.
Third	Krueger, Anne O. and Vernon W. Ruttan. The Development Impact of Economic Assistance to LDC's. Minneapolis and St. Paul; University of Minnesota Economic Development Center, March 1983. 2 vols.
Second	Krutilla, John V., and Anthony C. Fisher. The Economics of Natural Environments: Studies in the Valuation of Commodity and Amenity Resources. Rev. ed. Baltimore; Publ. for Resources for the Future, Inc., by Johns Hopkins University Press, 1985. 300p. (1st ed., 1975. 292p.)
Second	Kuhn, Thomas. Structure of Scientific Revolutions. 2d ed. University of Chicago Press, 1970. 210p. (1st ed., 1962. 172p.)
Third	Kuo, L.T.C. The Technical Transformation of Agriculture in Communist China. New York, Praeger, 1972. 266p.
Second	Kutcher, Gary P. and Pasquale L. Scandizzo. The Agricultural Economy of Northeast Brazil. Baltimore; Johns Hopkins University Press, 1982. 304p. (World Bank Research Publication Ser.).
Second	Kuznets, S. Economic Growth of Nations: Total Output and Production Structure. Cambridge, Mass.; Harvard University Press, 1971. 363p.
Third	Kuznets, S. Modern Economic Growth: Rate Structure and Spread. New Haven, Conn.; Yale University Press, 1966. 529p.

L

Second	La-Anyane, Seth. Economics of Agricultural Development in Tropical Africa. Wiley & Sons, Inc., 1985. 150p.
Third	Labys, Walter C., I. Nadiri and J. N. del Arco. Commodity Markets and Latin American Development: A Modeling Approach. New York; National Bureau of Economic Research, 1980. 280p.
Second	Land, Kenneth C., and Seymour Spilerman, eds. Social Indicator Models. New York, Russell Sage Foundation, 1975. 411p.
Third	Land Tenure Center. A Colloquium on Issues in African Land Tenure. Madison; University of Wisconsin, Land Tenure Center, 1985. 70p. (LTC Paper, No. 124.)
Second	Langham, Max R., and Ralph H. Retzlaff, ed. Agricultural Sector Analysis in Asia. Singapore; Singapore University Press for the Agricultural Development Council, 1982. 420p.
Third	Langoni, C. G. Distriuicao de Renda e Desenvolvimento Economico do Brasil (Income Distribution and Economic Development of Brazil). Rio de Janeiro; eda Expressao e Cultura, 1973. 315p.
Second	Lappe, Frances M., and Joseph Collins. Food First: Beyond the Myth of Scarcity. Revised and updated. New York; Ballantine Books, 1979. 619p. (1st ed.: Boston; Houghton, 1977. 466p.)
Second	Lardy, Nicholas R. Agriculture in China's Modern Economic Development. Cambridge University Press, 1983. 285p.
Third	Lateef, N. V. Crisis in the Sahel: A Case Study in Development Cooperation. Boulder, Colo.; Westview Press, 1980. 287p.

Third	Latham, M. C. Human Nutrition in Tropical Africa. Rome; Food and Agriculture Organization, 1980. 268p.
Second	Law, Alton D. International Commodity Agreements: Setting, Performance, and Prospects. Lexington, MA; Lexington Books, 1975. 128p.
Third	Lawani, Stephen M., F. M. Alluri, and E. N. Adimorah. Farming Systems in Africa: A Working Bibliography, 1930–1978. Boston; G. K. Hall, 1979. 251p.
Second	Lea, David A. M. and D. P. Chaudhri, eds. Rural Development and the State: Contradictions and Dilemmas in Developing Countries. London; New York; Methuen, 1983. 351p.
Second	Leach, Edmund. Pul Eliya, A Village in Ceylon: A Study of Land Tenure and Kinship. Cambridge; University Press, 1961. 343p. (Reprinted 1971)
Third	Lecaillon, J., C. Morrisson, H. Schneider, and E. Thorbecke. Economic Policies and Agricultural Performance of Low-Income Countries. Paris; Organisation for Economic Cooperation and Development, 1987. 208p.
Third	Lee, D.H.K. Climate and Economic Development in the Tropics. New York; Harper Bros. for the Council on Foreign Relations, 1957. 182p. (Reissued on Microfilm: Ann Arbor; University Microfilms, 1978)
Second	Lee, Delene W. and Jasper S. Lee. Agribusiness Procedures and Practices. New York; McGraw-Hill Book Co., 1980.
Third	Lee, R. Population, Food, and Rural Development. Oxford, England; Clarendon Press; and New York; Oxford University Press, 1988. 215p.
Second	Lee, T. H. Intersectoral Capital Flows in the Economic Development of Taiwan, 1895–1960. Ithaca, N.Y.; Cornell University Press, 1971. 197p.
Second	Lee, Warren F., W.G. Muray, and A.G. Nelson. Agricultural Finance. 8th ed. Ames; Iowa State University Press, 1988. 468p. (Primary author varies among editions)
Second	Leed, Theodore and Gene A. German. Food Merchandising: Principles and Practices. 3d ed. New York; Lebhar-Friedman, 1985. 488p. (1st ed., New York; Chain-Store Age Books, 1973. 389p.)
Third	Leff, N. H. Economic Policy-Making and Development in Brazil 1947–1964. New York; Wiley, 1968. 201p.
Second	Lehmann, D., ed. Peasants, Landlords, and Governments: Agrarian Reform in the Third World. New York; Holmes and Meier Publishers, 1974. 320p.
Second	Leibenstein, H. Economic Backwardness and Economic Growth: Studies in the Theory of Economic Development. New York; Wiley, 1957. 295p.
First rank	Lele, Uma J. Food Grain Marketing in India, Private Performance and Public Policy. Ithaca: Cornell University Press, 1971. 264p.
First rank	Lele, Uma J. The Design of Rural Development: Lessons from Africa. 2d ed. Baltimore; Johns Hopkins University Press for the World Bank, 1979. 246p.
First rank	Leonard, David K. Reaching the Peasant Farmer: Organization Theory and Practice in Kenya. Chicago; University of Chicago Press, 1977. 297p.
First rank	Leontief, W.W. Essays in Economics: Theories and Theorizing. New York; Oxford University Press, 1966. 252p.
Third	Lerner, D., and W. Schramm, eds. Communication and Change in the Developing Countries. Honolulu; University of Hawaii, East-West Center Press, 1976. 333p.

Third — Lewis, W. A. Aspects of Tropical Trade. Stockholm; Almqvist and Wicksell, 1969. 53p.

Third — Lewis, W. A. The Evolution of the International Economic Order. Princeton; Princeton University Press, 1978. 81p.

Third — Liedholm, C., and D. Mead. Small-Scale Industries in Developing Countries: Empirical Evidence and Policy Implications. East Lansing; Michigan State University, Department of Agricultural Economics, 1987. 141p. (International Development Paper, No. 9.)

Second — Lippit, Victor D. Land Reform and Economic Development in China: A Study of Institutional Change and Development Finance. White Plains, N.Y.; International Arts and Sciences Press, 1974. 183p.

Third — Lipton, Michael with Richard Longhurst. New Seeds and Poor People. London; Unwin Hyman, 1989. 473p.

First rank — Little, Ian. Economic Development: Theory, Policy and International Relations. New York; Basic Book, 1982. 452p.

Second — Little, Ian, T. Scitovsky and M. Scott. Industry and Trade in Some Developing Countries. London, New York; Oxford University Press for the OECD Development Centre, 1970. 512p.

Second — Livingstone, I. and H. W. Ord. Agricultural Economics for Tropical Africa. Portsmouth, N. Hampshire; Heinemann Educational Books, Inc., 1981. 294p.

Third — Lizano-Fait, E. La Integracion Economica Centro-Americana (The Economic Integration of Central America). Mexico; Fondo de Cultura Economica, 1975. 2 vols.

Second — Lo, Fu-chen, ed. Asia by the Year 2000. Kuala Lumpur, Asian Pacific Development Center, 1987.

Third — Lockwood, W. W., ed. The Economic Development of Japan: Growth and Structural Change, 1868–1938. Princeton, N.J.; Princeton University Press, 1954. 603p. (Expanded ed. 1968 and 1970, 686p.)

Third — Long, Frank A. and A. Oleson, eds. Appropriate Technology and Social Values: A Critical Appraisal. Cambridge, Mass., Ballinger, 1980. 215p.

Second — Long, Norman. Introduction to Sociology of Rural Development. Boulder, Colo.: Westview Press, 1977. 221p.

Second — Lundqvist, Lennart J. From Tenancy to Home Ownership: A Comparative Study of Tenure Conversions and Their Effects. London; Croom Helm Ltd.; Longwood Publishing Group, Inc., 1986. 288p.

Third — Luning, H. A. Economic Aspects of Low Labour-Income Farming. Wageningen, Netherlands; Centre for Agricultural Publications and Documentation, 1967. 144p. (Agricultural Research Report, No. 699.)

Third — Luz, Fabio. Seguros Agro Pecuarios. 2nd ed. Rio de Janeiro; Ministerio da Agricultura, Servico de Economia Rural, 1949. 102p.

M

Third — MacAndrews, C. and L.S. Chin, eds. Too Rapid Rural Development. Athens, Ohio; Ohio University Press, 1982. 370p.

Third — MacBean, Alasdair I. Export Instability and Economic Development. London; Allen and Unwin, 1966. 364p.

Second — MacBean, Alasdair I., and P.N. Snowden. International Institutions in Trade and Finance. London and Boston; Allen and Unwin, 1981. 255p.

Third — MacEwan, Arthur. Agricultural Development in Cuba. New York; St. Martin's Press, 1981.

Second MacPherson, Stewart. Social Policy in the Third World: The Social Dilemmas of Underdevelopment. Totowa, NJ; Allanheld, Osmun, 1982. 220p.

Second Madden, J.P. Economies of Size Studies: A Collection of Papers Presented August 3–4, 1983 at a Workshop at Purdue University in West Lafayette, Indiana. Ames; Iowa State University Press for the Center for Agricultural and Rural Development, 1984. 220p.

Second Mahajan, V. S. Growth of Agriculture and Industry in India. New Dehli, India; Deep and Deep, 1983. 176p.

Third Maital, Shlomo. Minds, Markets and Money: Psychological Foundations of Economic Behavior. New York; Basic Books, 1982. 310p.

Second Makeham, J. P. and L.R. Malcolm. The Economics of Tropical Farm Management. Cambridge University Press, 1986. 202p.

First rank Malthus, Thomas R. Principles of Political Economy Considered with a View to Their Practical Application. 2d ed. 446p. (Second edition first published in London, 1836, by William Pickering.) (Latest reprint by Fairfield, N. J.; A. M. Kelly, 1986)

Third Mancini, Luis Jacinto. . . . Las Reformas Agrarias de Post Guerra. Buenos Aires; Imprenta de la Universidad, 1943. 227p.

Third Mandal, G.C. and M.G. Ghosh. Economics of the Green Revolution: A Study in East India. Bombay, India; and New York; Asia Publs., 1976. 113p.

First rank Manetsch, T. J., M. L. Hayenga, A. N. Halter, T. W. Carroll, M. H. Abkin, D. R. Byerlee, K-Y. Chong, G. Page, E. Kellogg, and G. L. Johnson. A Generalized Simulation Approach to Agricultural Sector Analysis with Special Reference to Nigeria. East Lansing: Michigan State University, Department of Agricultural Economics, 1971. 362p.

Third Mann, C.K. and B. Huddelston. Food Policy: Framework for Analysis and Action. Bloomington, Ind., Indiana University Press, 1986.

Second Mann, Harold H. Social Framework of Agriculture: India, Middle East, England. New York; Augustus M. Kelley Publ., 1967. 501p.

Second Mansfield, Edwin, ed. Microeconomics Selected Readings. 5th ed. New York; W.W. Norton and Co., 1985. 606p. (1st ed: 1971. 528p.)

Second Maos, Jacob. The Spatial Organization of New Land Settlement in Latin America. Boulder; Westview Press. 1984. 170p.

Second Marten, Gerald G., ed. Traditional Agriculture in Southeast Asia: A Human Ecology Perspective. Boulder, Colo.; Westview Press, 1986. 358p.

First rank Martin, Lee R., ed. A Survey of Agricultural Economics Literature. Minneapolis; University of Minnesota Press for the American Agricultural Economics Association, 1977–1981. 3 vols. (Vol. 4 due in 1992)

First rank Marx, K. Capital: A Critique of Political Economy. New York; Modern Library, 1909–12. 3 vols. (1st German ed., 1867.)

Second Massey, Garth. Substance and Change: Lessons of Agropastoralism in Somalia. Boulder, Colo.; Westview Press, 1986. 300p.

First rank Maunder, Allen H. and Kazushi Ohkawa, eds. Growth and Equity in Agricultural Development; Proceedings of the Eighteenth International Conference of Agricultural Economists. London; Gower Publishing Company, 1984. 619p.

First rank Maunder, Allen H., and U. Renborg, eds. Agriculture in a Turbulent World Economy; Important Research from the Proceedings of the Nineteenth International Conference of Agricultural Economists in Malaga, Spain. London; Gower Publ., 1987. 820p.

First rank McCalla, Alex F. and Timothy E.Josling, eds. Imperfect Markets in Agricultural Trade. Mountclair, N.J.; Allanheld, Osmun and Co. Pubs., Inc., 1981. 250p.

Second McCalla, Alex F. and Timothy E. Josling. Agricultural Policies and World Markets. New York; Macmillan Publ., 1985. 304p.

First rank McDowell, Robert E. and P.E. Hildebrand. Integrated Crop and Animal Production: Making the Most of Resources Available to Small Farms in Developing Countries. New York; The Rockefeller Foundation, 1980. 78p.

Second McGranahan, D.V., C. Richard-Proust, N.V. Sovani, and M. Subramanian. Contents and Measurement of Socioeconomic Development. New York; Praeger Publishers, 1972. 161p.

Third McGreevey, W.P., ed. Third World Poverty: New Strategies for Measuring Development Progress. Lexington, Mass., Lexington Books, 1980. 215p.

Third McIntyre, J. Food Security in the Sahel: Variable Import Levy, Grain Reserves and Foreign Exchange Assistance. Washington, D.C.; International Food Policy Research Institute, 1981. 70p. (IFPRI Research Report 26.)

Third McKinnon, Ronald I. Money and Capital in Economic Development. Washington, D.C.; Brookings Institution, 1973. 184p.

Second McPherson, W.W., ed. Economic Development of Tropical Agriculture: Theory, Policy, Strategy and Organization. Gainesville: University of Florida Press, 1968. 328p.

Second Mears, L. A. The New Rice Economy of Indonesia. Yogyakarta, Indonesia; Gadjah Mada University Press, 1981. 605p.

Second Meier, G.M. and D. Seers, eds. Pioneers in Development. 2d ed. Oxford, England; Oxford University Press for the World Bank, 1987. 244p. (1st series, Oxford University Press, 1984. 372p.)

First rank Meier, G.M., ed. Leading Issues in Development Economics. 3d ed. New York; Oxford University Press, 1976. 862p.

First rank Mellor, John W. Economics of Agricultural Development. Ithaca, N.Y.; Cornell University Press, 1970. 418p.

First rank Mellor, John W. The New Economics of Growth: A Strategy for India and the Developing World. Ithaca, New York; Cornell University Press, 1976. 335p.

First rank Mellor, John W., and G. M. Desai, eds. Agricultural Change and Rural Poverty on a Theme by Dharm Narain. Baltimore; Johns Hopkins University Press for the International Food Policy Research Institute, 1985. 233p. (Reprinted by Oxford University Press, 1986)

First rank Mellor, John W., and R. Ahmed. Agricultural Price Policy for Developing Countries. Baltimore, Md.; Johns Hopkins University Press for IFPRI, 1988. 327p.

Second Mellor, John W., C. L. Delgado, and M. J. Blackie, eds. Accelerating Food Production in Sub-Saharan Africa. Baltimore; Johns Hopkins University Press, 1987. 417p.

Second Mellor, John W., T.F. Weaver, U.J. Lele, and S.R. Simon. Developing Rural India: Plan and Practice. Ithaca, N.Y.; Cornell University Press, 1968. 411p.

Second Melville, T. and M. Melville. Guatemala: The Politics of Land Ownership. New York; Free Press, 1971. 320p.

Third Miller, Larry. Agricultural Credit and Finance in Africa. New York; Rockefeller Foundation, 1977. 115p.

Second Milliken, George A. and Dallas E. Johnson. Analysis of Messy Data. New York; Van Nostrand Reinhold, 1984. 2 vols.

Third Mishan, E. J. Cost-Benefit Analysis. 3d ed. London and Boston; Allen and Unwin, 1982. 447p. (1st ed. New York; Praeger, 1976. 454p.)

Third Mishkin, F. S. A Rational Expectations Approach to Macroeconometrics. Chicago: University of Chicago Press, 1983. 172p.

Third Mitchell, Mark. Agriculture and Policy: Methodology for the Analysis of Developing Country Agricultural Sectors. London, Ithaca Press, 1985. 179p.

Second Moll, H.A.J. The Economics of Oil Palm. Wageningen, The Netherlands; PUDOC, 1987. 288p.

Third Monod, T., ed. Pastoralism in Tropical Africa. Oxford University Press for International African Institute, 1975. 502p.

Second Montgomery, John D., ed. International Dimensions of Land Reform. Boulder, CO; Westview Press, 1984. 239p.

First rank Moock, Joyce L. Understanding Africa's Rural Households and Farming Systems. Boulder, Colo.; Westview Press, 1986. 234p.

Third Moran, E. Developing the Amazon. Bloomington, Ind.; Indiana University Press, 1981. 292p.

Second Morawetz, David. The Andean Group: A Case Study in Economic Integration Among Developing Countries. Cambridge, Mass., M.I.T. Press, 1974. 171p.

Second Moris, J. Managing Induced Rural Development. Bloomington, Indiana; International Development Institute, 1981. 190p.

Second Morrissy, J. D. Agricultural Modernization through Production Contracting: The Role of the Fruit and Vegetable Processor in Mexico and Central America. New York; Praeger, 1974. 148p.

Third Mosher, A. T. Creating a Progressive Rural Structure. New York; Agricultural Development Council, 1969. 172p.

First rank Mosher, A. T. Getting Agriculture Moving: Essentials for Development and Modernization. New York; Praeger for Agricultural Development Council, 1966. 191p.

First rank Mosher, A. T. Thinking About Rural Development. New York; The Agricultural Development Council, 1976. 350p.

Second Mosher, A. T. Three Ways to Spur Agricultural Growth. New York, International Agric. Development Service, 1981. 61p.

Third Mosher, A. T. To Create a Modern Agriculture. New York; Agricultural Development Council, 1971. 162p.

Second Moss, Milton, ed. The Measurement of Economic and Social Performance. New York; National Bureau of Economic Research, 1973. 605p. (Studies in Income and Wealth, vol. 38)

Third Moyer, R., and S. Hollander, eds. Markets and Marketing in Developing Economies. Homewood, Ill.; Interscience Publ., 1968. 264p.

Second Murdoch, William W. The Poverty of Nations: The Policital Economy of Hunger and Population. Baltimore; Johns Hopkins University Press, 1980. 382p.

First rank Myint, Hla. The Economics of the Developing Countries. New York; Praeger, 1964. 192p.

First rank Myrdal, Gunnar. Rich Lands and Poor: The Road to World Prosperity. New York; Harper, 1957. 168p. (Reprinted as "Economic Theory and Underdeveloped Regions", 1971.)

First rank Myrdal, Gunnar. Against the Stream: Critical Essays in Economics. New York; Random House, 1973. 336p.

Second Myrdal, Gunnar. Asian Drama: An Enquiry into the Poverty of Nations. New York, Twentieth Century Fund, 1968. 3 vols.

N

Third Nair, Kusum. Transforming Traditionally: Land and Labor use in Agriculture in Asia and Africa. Riverdale, Md., Riverdale Co., 1983. 168p.

Second Nakajima, Chihiro. Subjective Equilibrium Theory of the Farm Household. Translation of his Noko Shutai Kinkoron. Amsterdam and New York, Elsevier Science Publ. Co., 1986. 302p.

Third Nash, Manning, ed. Essays On Economic Development and Cultural Change, in Honor of Bert F. Hoselitz. Chicago, Ill.; University of Chicago Press, 1977. 460p.

Second National Academy of Sciences (U.S.). World Food and Nutrition Study; Supporting Papers, Washington, D.C.: The Academy, 1977. 5 vols.

Third National Research Council (U.S.). Conference on Agricultural Research Priorities for Economic Development in Africa. Washington, D.C.; National Academy of Sciences, 1968. 3 vols.

Third National Research Council (U.S.). Post-Harvest Food Losses in Developing Countries. Washington; National Academy of Sciences, 1978. 206p.

Third National Research Council (U.S.). The African Challenge: In Search of Appropriate Development Strategies. Nairobi; Heinemann, 1986. 182p.

First rank Nelson, Michael. The Development of Tropical Lands: Policy Issues in Latin America. Baltimore, Md.; Johns Hopkins University Press. 1973. 323p.

Third Nelson, Richard R., T. P. Schultz and R. L. Slighton. Structural Change in a Developing Economy: Colombia's Problems and Prospects. Princeton, NJ; Princeton University Press, 1971. 322p.

Third Ness, Gayl D. and Hirofumi Ando. The Land is Shrinking: Population Planning in Asia. Baltimore, Md.; Johns Hopkins Univ Press, 1984. 225p.

Third Newby, Howard, ed. International Perspectives in Rural Sociology. Chichester, England and New York; Wiley, 1978. 220p.

Second Nicholls, W.H. and R. M. Paiva. Nine-nine Fazendas: Structure and Productivity of Brazilian Agriculture. Nashville, Tenn.; Vanberbilt University Center for Latin American Studies, 1965–1967. 2 vols.

Second Nobe, K.G. and R. K. Sampath, eds. Issues in Third World Development. Boulder, Colo.; Westview Press, 1983. 479p. (Westview Special Studies in Social, Political and Economic Development).

Third Norland, I, et. al., eds. Rice Societies: Asian Problems and Prospects. London; Curzon Press; and Riverdale, Maryland; Riverdale Publ., 1986. 321p.

Third Norton, R. D. and L. Solis. The Book of CHAC: Programming Studies for Mexican Agriculture. Baltimore; Johns Hopkins University Press for World Bank, 1983. 602p.

O

Second Ofori, Patrick E. Land in Africa: Its Administration, Law, Tenure and Use: A Select Bibliography. Nendeln, Liechtenstein; Kraus International Publications, 1987, 199p.

Second Ogura, Tokekazu. Can Japanese Agriculture Survive? A Historical and Comparative Approach. 3d ed. Tokyo; Agricultural Policy Research Center, 1980. 880p.

Third Oh, Heung Keun. Development of Food and Agricultural Statistics in Asia and Pacific Region, 1965–1987. Seoul; Korea Rural Economics Institute, 1988. 397p.

Third O'Hagan, James P., ed. Growth and Adjustment in National Agricultures: Four Case-Studies and an Overview. New York; Macmillan, 1978. 200p.

Third Ohkawa, K. Differential Structure and Agriculture: Essays on Dualistic Growth. Tokyo; Kinokuniya Bookstore Co. for the Hitotsubashi University, Institute of Economic Research, 1972. 298p. (Economic Research Series, no. 13.)

Second Ohkawa, K., and G. Ranis, eds. Japan and the Developing Countries. Oxford, England; and New York; Basil and Blackwell, 1985. 456p.

First rank Ohkawa, K., B. F. Johnston, and H. Kaneda, eds. Agriculture and Economic Growth: Japan's Experience. Tokyo; University of Tokyo Press, 1969; and Princeton, NJ; Princeton University Press, 1970. 433p.

Second Olson, Mancur. The Logic of Collective Action: Public Goods and the Theory of Groups. Cambridge, Mass.; Harvard University Press, 1965. 176p. (Reprinted 1971, 186p.)

Third Organisation for Economic Co-operation and Development. Agriculture in China: Prospects for Production and Trade. Paris; OECD, 1985. 84p.

Second Organisation for Economic Co-operation and Development. Agricultural Trade With Developing Countries. Paris; OECD 1984. 113p.

Second Organisation for Economic Co-operation and Development. Problems of Agricultural Trade. Paris; OECD Publications and Information Center, 1982. 178p.

Second Organisation for Economic Co-operation and Development. National Policies and Agricultural Trade. Paris, OECD, 1987. 333p.

Second Organisation of Economic Co-operation and Development . The Instability of Agricultural Commodity Markets. Paris; OECD, 1980. 237p.

Second Orlove, Benjamin S. and Glynn Custred, eds. Land and Power in Latin America: Agrarian Economies and Social Process in the Andes. New York; Holmes and Meier, 1980. 250p.

Second Osburn, Donald D., and Kenneth C. Schneeberger. Modern Agriculture Management. Reston, VA; Reston Pub. Co, 1978. 369p.

Third Oshima, H.T. Economic Growth in Monsoon Asia: A Comparative Study. Tokyo, Asian Productivity Organization, 1987. 371p.

Third Otalora, Hernando Gomez and Eduardo Wiesner Duran, eds. Lecturas sobre Desarrollo Economico Colombiano, en Honor de Alvaro Lopez Toro. Bogata; Fundacion para la Educacion Superior y el Desarrollo, 1974. 624p.

Third Oxaal, I., T. Barnett, and D. Booth. Beyond the Sociology of Development: Economy and Society in Latin America and Africa. London and Boston; Routledge and Kegan Paul, 1975. 295p.

P

First rank Paarlberg, Don. Farm and Food Policy: Issues of the 1980s. Lincoln; University of Nebraska Press, 1980. 338p.

Second Paarlberg, Robert L. Food, Trade and Foreign Policy: India, the Soviet Union and the United States. Ithaca, N.Y.; Cornell University Press, 1985. 266p.

Third Pacey, Arnold and Philip Payne, eds. Agricultural Development and Nutrition. London, Hutchinson; Boulder, Colo., Westview Press, 1985. 255p.

Third Page, H. J., and R. Lesthaeghe, eds. Child-Spacing in Tropical Africa: Tradition and Change. New York; Academic Press, 1981. 332p.

Second Paige, Jeffery M. Agrarian Revolution: Social Movements and Export Agriculture in the Underdeveloped World. New York; Free Press, 1978. 435p.

Third Palmer, Robin, and N. Parsons, eds. The Roots of Rural Poverty in Central and Southern Africa. London; Heinemann; and Berkeley; University of California Press, 1977. 430p.

Second Panayotou, T. Food Policy Analysis in Thailand. Bangkok and New York; Agricultural Development Council, 1985. 347p.

Second Panda, R. K. Agricultural Indebtedness and Institutional Finance; India. India; Ashish Publ., 1985. 180p.

Second Papi, Ugo and Charles S. Nunn, eds. Economic Problems of Agriculture in Industrial Societies: Proceedings of a Conference Held by the International Economic Association. New York; Saint Martin's Press, Inc., 1969. 671p. (Reprinted: New York; Stockton Publ., 1986)

Third Parsons, Kenneth H. Customary Land Tenure and Development of African Agriculture. Madison; University of Wisconsin, Land Tenure Center, 1971. 82p.

Third Pastore, A. C. A Resposta da Producao Agricola aos Precos no Brasil (The Response of Agricultural Production to Prices in Brazil). Sao Paulo; APEC Eda, 1973. 170p.

Third Paulino, L. A. Food in the Third World: Past Trends and Projection to 2000. Washington, D.C.; International Food Policy Research Institute, 1986. 76p. (IFPRI Researh Report-52).

Third Pearse, Andrew C. Seeds of Plenty, Seeds of Want: Social and Economic Implications of the Green Revolution. Oxford; Clarendon Press; and New York; Oxford University Press, 1980. 262p.

Third Pearson, Scott R., and J. Cownie. Commodity Exports and African Economic Development. Lexington, Mass.; Heath, 1974. 285p.

Second Pearson, Scott R., et al. Portugese Agriculture in Transition. Ithaca, N.Y.; Cornell University Press, 1987. 283p.

Third Pearson, Scott R., et al. Rice in West Africa: Policy and Economics. Stanford, Calif.; Stanford University Press, 1981. 482p.

Third Pearson, Scott R., T. Josling, and W. Falcon. Food Self-Reliance and Food Self-Sufficiency: Evaluating the Policy Options. Washington, D.C.; Aurora Associates.

Second Pedhazur, Elazar J. Multiple Regression in Behavioral Research. 2d ed. New York; Holt, Rinehart and Winston, 1982. 822p.

Third Peek, P. and G. Standing, eds. State Policies and Migration: Studies in Latin America and the Caribbean. London; Croom Helm, ILO, 1982. 403p.

Second Peleg, Kalman. Produce Handling, Packaging and Distribution. Westport, Conn.; A V I Publishing Company, Incorporated, 1985. 625p.

Second Penson, John B., Jr., Rulon Pope, and M.L. Cook. Introduction to Agricultural Economics. New York; Prentice-Hall, 1986. 556p.

Second Perkins, Dwight. Agricultural Development in China, 1368–1968. Chicago, Ill.; Aldine, 1969. 395p.

Second Perkins, Dwight, ed. China's Modern Economy in Historical Perspective. Stanford, Calif., Stanford University Press, 1975. 344p.

Third Perkins, Dwight, and S. Yusuf. Rural Development in China. Baltimore, Md.; Johns Hopkins University Press, 1984. 235p.

Second Peterson, Trudy, H. Farmers, Bureaucrats, and Middlemen: Historical Perspectives on American Agriculture. Washington, D.C.: Howard University Press, 1980. 357p.

Second Petras, J. and M. Zeithin, eds. Latin America: Reform or Revolution? A Reader. Greenwich, CT; Fawcett, 1968. 511p.

Third Phillips, J. Agriculture and Ecology in Africa: A Study of Actual and Potential Development South of the Sahara. London; Faber and Faber; and New York; Praeger, 1959. 423p.

First rank Pigou, A. C. The Economics of Welfare. 4th ed. London: Macmillan, 1962. 837p.

Second Pimentel, D. and C. W. Hall, eds. Food and Energy Resources. New York; Academic Press, 1984. 268p.

Third Pimentel, D. and C. W. Hall, eds. Food and Natural Resources. New York; Academic Press, 1989. 512p.

First rank Pineiro, M., E. Trigo, and R. Florentino, eds. Technical Change and Social Conflict in Agriculture. Boulder, Colo.; Westview Press, 1983. 248p.

First rank Pingali, Prabhu, Yves Bigot, and Hans Binswanger. Agricultural Mechanization and the Evolution of Farming Systems in Sub-Saharan Africa. Baltimore: Johns Hopkins University Press, 1987. 224p. AAEA Award Winner.

First rank Pinstrup-Andersen, Per, ed. Food Subsidies in Developing Countries: Costs, Benefits, and Policy Options. Baltimore, Md., Publ. for Int. Food Policy Research Inst. by Johns Hopkins University Press, 1988. 374p.

First rank Pinstrup-Andersen, Per. Nutritional Consequences of Agricultural Projects: Conceptual Relationships and Assessment Approaches. Washington, D.C.; World Bank, 1981. 93p. (World Bank Staff Working paper no. 456)

First rank Pinstrup-Andersen, Per. Agricultural Research and Technology in Economic Development. London; Longman, Inc., 1982. 304p.

Second Plato. Republic. New York; Modern Library, 1934.

Third Poleman, T.T. and D.K. Freebairn, eds. Food, Population, and Employment: The Impact of the Green Revolution. New York; Praeger, 1973. 272p.

Second Political Economy of Collectivized Agriculture: A Comparative Study of Communist and Non-Communist Systems. New York; Pergamon Press, Inc., 1979. 256p.

Second Pollard, S. The Idea of Progress: History and Society. London; Watts, 1968. 220p. (Reprinted Harmondsworth, England; Penguin, 1971.)

Second Pomareda, Carlos. Financial Policies and Management of Agricultural Development Banks. Boulder, CO; Westview Press, 1984. 180p.

Second Pontecorvo, G., ed., The Management of Food Policy. New York; Arno Press for Columbia University, Graduate School of Business, 1976. 299p.

Third Popkin, S. L. The Rational Peasant: The Political Economy of Rural Society in Vietnam. Berkeley; University of California Press, 1979. 306p.

Second Popper, Frank. The Politics of Land-Use Reform. Madison; University of Wisconsin Press, 1981. 338p.

Second Popper, K. R.. The Logic of Scientific Discovery. New York: Basic Books, 1959. 479p.

Second Prasad, Ramayan. Agricultural Taxation and Economic Development. New Delhi; Deep and Deep Publications, 1987. 207p.

Third Pratt, D. J., and M. D. Gwynne, eds. Rangeland Management and Ecology in East Africa. London; Hodder and Stoughton, 1977. 310p.

Third Prebisch, R. Change and Development: Latin America's Great Task. New York; Praeger, 1971. 293p.; and Washington, D.C.; Inter-American Development Bank, 1971. 235p.

Third Prebisch, R. El Mercado Comun Latinoamericano (The Latin American Common Market). New York; United Nations, 1959.

Third Preston, Samuel . Mortality Patterns in National Populations. New York, Academic Press, 1976. 201p.

Third Presvelan, C., and S. Spijkers-Zwart, eds. The Household, Women and Agricultural Development. Wageningen; J. Veenman and Zanen, 1980. 131p.

Third Psacharopoulos, G. and M. Woodhall. Education for Development: An Analysis of Investment Choices. New York; Oxford University Press, 1985. 337p.

Third Psacharopoulos,G., ed. The Political Economy of Poverty, Equity, and Growth: Country Perspectives. Washington, D.C., World Bank, 1988.

Second Purcal, J. T. Rice Economy: Employment and Income in Malaysia. Honolulu; EastWest Ctr; University of Hawaii Press, 1972. 262p.

R

Second Rae, Alan N. Crop Management Economics. London and Granada England; Brookfield Publishing Co., 1977. 544p. (Reprinted by Grosby Lockwood Staples, 1981)

Second Rahman, Mushtaqur. Agrarian Egalitarianism, Land Tenures and Land Reforms in South Asia. Iowa State University Research Foundation. Dubuque, Iowa; Kendall/Hunt Publishing Company, 1980. 200p.

Second Rahmato, Dessalegn. Agrarian Reform in Ethiopia. Uppsala; Scandinavian Institute of African Studies, 1984. 105p. (Reprinted by Trenton, N.J.; Red Sea Press, 1985.)

Second Raj, K. N., ed. Essays on the Commercialization of Indian Agriculture. Oxford University Press, Inc., 1986. 375p.

Second Ranis, Gustav, and T. P. Schultz, eds. The State of Development Economics: Progress and Perspectives. New York; Basil Blackwell, 1987.

Third Rao, C. H. H. Agricultural Production Functions, Costs, and Returns in India. Bombay; Asia Publ. House, 1965. 99p. (Delhi Institute of Economic Growth: Studies in Economic Growth, No. 5)

Second Rao, C. H. H. Technological Change and Distribution of Gains in Indian Agriculture. Delhi, Macmillan Co., 1975. 249p. (Studies in Economic Growth, No.17)

Third	Rao, C. H. H., S. K. Ray, and K. Subbarao. Unstable Agriculture and Droughts: Implications for Policy. New Delhi; Vikas, 1988. 192p.
Third	Rao, Vihendra K. R. V. Growth with Justice in Asian Agriculture: An Exercise in Policy Formulation. Geneva; UNRISD, 1974. 96p.
Second	Raper, Arthur F. Rural Development in Action: The Comprehensive Experiment at Commilla, East Pakistan. Ithaca; Cornell University Press, 1970. 351p.
Second	Rawski, Evelyn S. Agricultural Change and the Peasant Economy of South China. Cambridge; Harvard University Press, 1972. 280p.
Third	Rawski, T. G. Economic Growth and Employment in China. New York, Oxford; Oxford University Press, 1979. 194p.
Third	Ray, P. K. Agriculture Insurance: Principles and Organization and Application to Developing Countries. 2d ed. Oxford; Pergamon Press, 1981. 419p.
Second	Reddy, D. Obul. Co-operative Agricultural Development Banks: A Case Study of Andhra Pradesh. Paperback trade edition. Delhi, India; B.R. Publ. Corp., 1987. 429p.
First rank	Reutlinger, Shlomo and J. van H. Pellekaan. Poverty and Hunger: Issues and Options for Food Security in Developing Countries. Washington, D.C.; World Bank, 1986. 69p.
Second	Reutlinger, Shlomo and Marcelo Selowski. Malnutrition and Poverty: Magnitude and Policy Options. Baltimore, Md.; John Hopkins University Press, 1976. 82p. (World Bank Occ. Paper 23)
Third	Reynolds, C. W. The Mexican Economy: Twentieth Century Structure and Growth. New Haven, Conn.; Yale University Press, 1970.
First rank	Reynolds, Lloyd G., ed. Agriculture in Development Theories. New Haven; Yale University Press, 1975. 510p. 21
Second	Rice, E.B. and S. Bunyasi, eds. Agricultural Pricing and Trade Policy Seminar: Background Readings. Washington, D.C.; Economic Development Institute of the World Bank, 1986.
Third	Richards, Alan, ed. Food, States, and Peasants: Analyses of the Agrarian Question in the Middle East. Boulder, Colo.; Westview Press, 1986. 282p.
Third	Richards, P. Indigenous Agricultural Revolutuion: Ecology and Food Production in West Africa. London; Hutchinson, 1985. 192p.
Third	Riddell, Robert. Regional Development Policy: The Struggle for Rural Progress in Low-Income Nationals. Aldershot, England, Gower; New York, St. Martin's Press, 1985. 282p.
Third	Rimmer, Douglas, ed. Rural Transformation in Tropical Africa. Athens; Ohio University Press, 1988. 177p.
Second	Ritson, Christopher. Agricultural Economics: Principles and Policy. New York; Saint Martin's Press, Inc., 1977. (Reprinted in paperback, Boulder, Colo.; Westview Press, 1982)
Third	Rivera, W. and S. Schram, eds. Agricultural Extension Worldwide: Issues, Practices and Emerging Priorities. London; Croom Helm, 1987. 294p.
Second	Roberts, Colleen, ed. Agriculture Sector Symposium (8th, 1988 at World Bank): Trade, Aid and Policy Reform. Washington, D.C., World Bank, 1988. 223p.
Second	Robinson, E. A. G., ed. Problems in Economic Development: Proceedings of a Conference Held by the International Economic Assoc.. New York; St. Martin's Press, 1965. 625p.

Second — Robinson, J. Economic Heresies: Some Old-Fashioned Questions in Economic Theory. New York; Basic Books, 1971. 150p. (Reissued 1973)

Second — Robinson, Kenneth. Farm and Food Policies and Their Consequences. Englewood Cliffs, N.J.; Prentice-Hall, 1989. 294p.

Third — Robson, P. Economic Integration in Africa. London; Allen and Unwin, 1968. 320p.

Third — Roett, R., ed. Brazil in the Sixties. Nashville, Tenn; Vanderbilt University Press, 1972. 434p. Portuguese edition—Contador, ed., 1975.

First rank — Rogers, Everett M. and F. F. Shoemaker. Communication of Innovations. 2d ed. New York, The Free Press, 1971. 476p. (3d ed. published as Diffusion of Innovations, 1983. 453p.)

Third — Rogers, Everett M. Modernization Among Peasants; the Impact of Communication. New York; Holt, Rinehart and Winston, 1969. 429p.

Third — Rosberg, C. G., and T. G. Callaghy, eds. Socialism in Sub-Saharan Africa: A New Assessment. Berkeley; University of California Press, Institute of International Studies, 1979. 426p.

Third — Rosen, G. Peasant Society in a Changing Economy: Comparative Development in Southeast Asia and India. Urbana, Ill.; University of Illinois Press, 1975. 256p.

Third — Rosenberg, David, A., and Jean G. Rosenberg. Landless Peasants and Rural Poverty in Selected Asian Countries. Ithaca, New York; Cornell University, Rural Development Committee, Center for Int'l Studies, 1978. 108p. (Special Series on Landless and Nearlandlessness LNL2.)

Second — Rosenblum, J. W. ed. Agriculture in the 21st Century. New York; John Wiley and Sons, 1983. 415p.

Second — Rostow, W. W. The Stages of Economic Growth: A Non-Communist Manifesto. 2d ed. Cambridge University Press, 1971. 253p. (1st ed., 1952, 178p.)

First rank — Roumasset, James A., Jean-Marc Boussard, and Inderjit Singh, ed. Risk, Uncertainty and Agricultural Development. College, Laguna, Philippines: Southeast Asian Regional Center for Graduate Study and Research in Agriculture; and New York; Agricultural Development Council, 1979. 453p.

Third — Roy, P., F. B. Waisanen, E. M. Rogers, and UNESCO. The Impact of Communication on Rural Development: An Investigation in Costa Rica and India. Paris; UNESCO, and National Institute of Community Dev., 1969. 160p.

Second — Rudra, Ashok and P. K. Barhan. Agrarian Relations in West Bengal: Results of Two Surveys. Bombay; Somaiya Publ., 1983. 104p.

Third — Rukuni, Mandivanba and Carl K. Eicher. Food Security for Southern Africa. Harare, Zimbabwe; UZ/MSU Food Security Project, Dept. of Agricultural Economics and Extension, University of Zimbabwe, 1987. 406p.

First rank — Runge, C. Ford., ed. The Future of the North American Granary: Politics, Economics, and Resource Constraints in North American Agriculture. Ames, Iowa; Iowa State University Press, 1985. 240p.

Second — Russell, Robert R., and Maurice Wilkinson. Microeconomics: A Synthesis of Modern and Neoclassical Theory. New York; Wiley, 1979. 459p.

Third — Ruthenberg, H. Farming Systems in the Tropics. Oxford; Clarendon, 1971. 313p. (3d ed., 1980. 424p.)

Third — Ruthenberg, H. Smallholder Farming and Smallholder Development in Tanzania: Ten Case Studies. Munich; Weltforum Verlag, 1968. 360p.

First rank	Ruttan, Vernon W. Agricultural Research Policy. Minneapolis, Minn.; University of Minnesota Press, 1982. 369p.
Second	Ruttan, Vernon W. Agricultural Revolution in Southeast Asia: Impact on Grain Production and Trade. New York; The Asia Society, 1970. 2 vols.
Third	Ruttan, Vernon W. and Y. Hayami, eds. Induced Technological Change in Agriculture: Proceedings of a Workshop Developing a Framework for Assessing Future Changes in Agricultural Productivity held July 16–18, 1984. 1988.
First rank	Ruttan, Vernon W., and Carl Pray. Policy for Agricultural Research. Boulder, Colo.; Westview Press, 1987. 558p.
Third	Rweyemamu, J. F., ed. Industrialization and Income Distribution in Africa. Dakar, Senegal; Codesria, 1980. 227p.

S

Second	Sabot, R. H., ed. Migration and the Labor Market in Developing Countries. Boulder, CO; Westview Press, 1982. 254p.
Third	Sace, Alfredo. Programa Agrario del Aprismo. Lima; Ediciones Populares, 1946.
Second	Sahu, Nirmal C. Economics of Forest Resources: Problems and Policies in a Regional Economy. Delhi, India; B. R. Pub. Corp., 1986. 360p. (Distributed by Apt. Bks.)
Second	Saith, Ashwani. The Agrarian Question in Socialist Transitions. London; Totowa, N.J.; F. Cass, 1985.
Third	Salter, Leonard A., Jr. A Critical Review of Research in Land Economics. Minneapolis; University of Minnesota Press, 1948. 250p. (Reprinted in 1967). AAEA Classic
Third	Salter, Leonard A., Jr. A Critical Review of Research in Land Economics. Minneapolis; University of Minnesota Press, 1948. 258p. (Reprinted in 1967). AAEA Classic
First rank	Samuelson, Paul. Foundations of Economic Analysis. Cambridge; Harvard Univ. Press, 1947. 447p.
Third	Sanderson, Fred, H. and S. Roy. Food Trends and Prospects in India. Washington, D.C.; Brookings Institution, 1979. 162p.
Second	Sanderson, Steven E. The Transformation of Mexican Agriculture: International Structure and the Politics of Rural Change. Princeton, N.J.; Princeton University Press, 1986. 324p.
Third	Sandner, Gerhardt. La Colonizacion Agricola de Costa Rica (The Agricultural Colonization of Costa Rica) San Jose, Costa Rica; Instituto International de Ciencias de Agricolas, 1962–64. 2 vols.
Second	Sargent, Malcolm. Agricultural Co-Operation. Aldershot, Hampshire, England; Gower, 1982. 156p.
Third	Sarma, J.S. Agricultural Policy in India: Growth with Equity. Ottawa, Canada; Int. Develop. Research Centre, 1982. 94p.
Second	Saunders, Robert J. and Jeremy J. Warford. Village Water Supply: Economics and Policy in the Developing World. Baltimore; Johns Hopkins University Press, 1976. 279p.
Second	Savage, L. J.. The Foundations of Statistics. New York; Wiley, 1954. 294p. (Reissued 1972, New York; Dover)
Second	Scandizzo, Pasquale, L. Peter Hazell and Jock Anderson. Risky Agricultural Markets: Price Forcasting and the Need for Intervention Policies. Boulder, Col.; Westview Press, 1984. 150p.

Second Schmitz, A., Alex F. McCalla, Donald O. Mithcell, and Colin Carter. Grain Export Cartels. Cambridge, MA; Ballinger, 1981. 298p. Q

Third Schneider, H. K. Livestock and Equality in East Africa: The Economic Basis for Social Structure. Bloomington; Indiana University Press, 1979. 291p.

Second Schuh, G. Edward. The Agricultural Development of Brazil. New York, Praeger, 1970. 456p. (Also issued as O Desenvolvimento da Agricultura no Brasil. Rio de Janeiro, APEC Edia S.A., 1971) (Benchmark Studies on Agricultural Development in Latin America no. 6) Q

Third Schuh, G. Edward, ed. Technology, Human Capital and the World Food Problem. St. Paul, Minn.; University of Minn. Press, 1986. 167p. (Agr. Exp. Station Misc. Publ. 37)

First rank Schuh, G. Edward, and J.L. McCoy, eds. Food, Agriculture and Development in the Pacific Basin. Boulder, Colo.; Westview Press, 1986. 292p.

First rank Schultz, T. W. Economic Crisis in World Agriculture. Ann Arbor: University of Michigan Press, 1965. 114p.

First rank Schultz, T. W. The Economic Organization of Agriculture. New York: McGraw-Hill, 1953. 374p.

First rank Schultz, T. W. The Economic Value of Education. New York: Columbia University Press, 1963. 92p.

First rank Schultz, T. W.,ed. Distortions of Agricultural Incentives. Bloomington; Indiana University Press, 1978. 343p.

Second Schultz, T. W., ed. Economics of the Family: Marriage, Children and Human Capital. Chicago; University of Chicago Press, 1974. 584p.

First rank Schultz, T.W. Transforming Traditional Agriculture. New Haven, Conn; Yale Univ. Press, 1964. 212p. (Reprinted by Arno Press, 1976) AAEA Classic

First rank Schumpeter, Joseph A. History of Economic Analysis. New York: Oxford University Press, 1954. 1260p.

Third Schutjer, W.A. and C.S. Stokes, eds. Rural Development and Human Fertility. New York; Macmillan Publ. Co., 1984. 318p.

Second Scott, A. Natural Resources: The Economics of Conservation. Toronto; University of Toronto Press, 1955. 184p.

First rank Scott, James C. The Moral Economy of the Peasant: Rebellion and Subsistence in Southern Asia. New Haven; Yale University Press, 1976. 246p.

Second Seetharam, G. N. Strategy and Tactics of India's Agricultural Development: The Role of the State. Dehli, India; Ajanta Publ., 1984. 154p.

Second Seligson, Mitchell A. Gap Between Rich and Poor: Contending Perspectives on the Political Economy of Development. Boulder, Colo.; Westview Press, 1984. 418p.

Second Seligson, Mitchell A. Peasants of Costa Rica and the Development of Agrarian Capitalism. Madison, Wi.; University of Wisconsin Press, 1980. 220p.

Third Selowsky, M. Who Benefits from Government Expenditure? A Case Study of Colombia. New York, Oxford University Press, 1979. 186p.

Second Sen, Amartya K. Employment, Technology and Development: A Study Prepared for the ILO. Oxford, England; Clarendon Press, 1975. 193p.

Second Sen, Bandhudas. The Green Revolution in India: A Perspective. New York; Wiley, 1974. 118p.

Second Sen, Chiranjib. Essays on the Transformation of India's Agrarian Economy. New York; Garland Publ., 1984. 285p.

Third	Sender, J., and S. Smith. The Development of Capitalism in Africa. London; Methuen, 1986. 177p.
Second	Shah, A. K. Professional Management for the Cooperatives. Dehli, India; Vikas Publ. House, 1984. 350p.
Third	Shah, C.H. Agricultural Development in India: Policy and Problems; R. P. Nevatia Felicitation Volume. Bombay, India; Orient Longman, 1979. 688p.
Second	Shand, R.T., ed. Agricultural Development in Asia. Canberra, Australia; Australian National University Press, 1969. 360p.
Third	Shand, R. T., ed. Off-Farm Employment in the Development of Rural Asia: Papers Presented at a Conference Held in Chiang Mai, Thailand, 23 to 26 August 1983. Canberra; National Centre for Development Studies, Australian National University, 1986. 2 vols.
First rank	Shaner, Willis W., P.F. Philipp, and W.R. Schmehl. Farming Systems Research and Development: Guidelines for Developing Countries. Boulder, CO: Westview Press, 1982. 414p.
Second	Shanin, Teodor, ed. Peasants and Peasant Societies: Selected Readings. 2d ed. Oxford; Blackwell, 1987. 497p.
Second	Shannon, C. E., and Warren Weaver. The Mathematical Theory of Communications. Urbana; University of Illinois Press, 1949. (Reprinted 1969)
Second	Sharma, D.P. and V.V. Desai. Rural Economy in India. New Delhi, Vikas Publishing House, 1980.
Second	Shaw, R. Paul. Land Tenure and the Rural Exodus in Chile, Colombia, Costa Rica, and Peru. Gainesville; University Presses of Florida, 1976. 180p. (University of Florida Latin American Monographs: No. 19)
Third	Shaw, T. W., and K. A. Heard, eds. The Politics of Africa: Dependence and Development. New York; Africana Publishing Co. for Dalhousie University. 1979. 400p.
Third	Sheffield, J. R., ed. Education, Employment and Rural Development: Proceedings of a Conference Held at Kericho, Kenya. Nairobi; East African Publ. House, 1967. 499p.
Second	Siamwalla, A. and S. Haykin. The World Rice Market: Structure, Conduct, and Performance. Washington,D.C.; International Food Policy Research Inst., 1983. 79p. (IFPRI Research Report No. 39)
Third	Silberberg, Eugene. The Structure of Economics: A Mathematical Analysis. New York, McGraw-Hill, 1978. 543p.
Third	Simonsen, Roberto. Historia Economica do Brasil (1500/1820): Curso Professado na Escola Livre de Sociologia e Politica de Sao Paulo (Economic History of Brazil; 1500-1820). 7th ed. Sao Paulo: Companhia Editora Nacional, 1977. 475p.
Third	Simpson, J. The Economics of Livestock Systems in Developing Countries: Farm and Project Level Analysis. Boulder, Colo.; Westview Press, 1988. 297p.
Second	Singh, I.J., L. Squire, and J. Strauss, eds. Agricultural Household Models: Extension, Applications, and Policy. Baltimore, Md., Johns Hopkins University Press for the World Bank, 1986. 346p.
Second	Singh, I.J. Small Farmers and the Landless in South Asia. Washington, D.C.; World Bank, 1979. 194p. (World Bank Staff Paper No. 320)
Second	Singh, J. P. The Role of Institutional Finance in Agriculture. New Delhi, India; Ashish Publ. House, 1986. 378p.

Third Singh, Ram D. Economics of the Family and Farming Systems in Sub-Saharan Africa: Development Perspectives. Foreword by Theodore W. Schultz. Boulder, CO; Westview Press, 1988. 208p.

Second Singh, Rem Babu. Geography of Rural Development: The Indian Micro-Level Experience. New Delhi: Inter-India Publications, 1986. 246p.

Third Sinha, R., ed. The World Food Problem: Consensus and Conflict. Oxford, England; Pergamon Press, 1978. 671p.

Second Slater, Ken and Gordon Throup. Dairy Farm Business Management. 2d ed. Alexandria Bay, N.Y.; Diamond Farm Book Publishers, 1983. 192p.

First rank Smith, A. An Inquiry into the Nature and Causes of the Wealth of Nations. Cannan ed. New York; Modern Library, 1937. 976p.

Third Smith, A. K., and C. E. Welch, Jr., eds. Peasants in Africa. Waltham, Mass.; Crossroads Press, 1978. 130p.

Third Smith, Peter J. Agricultural Project Management: Monitoring and Control of Implementation. London, Elsevier Applied Science Publishers, 1984. 190p.

Third Smith, Peter J. Management in Agricultural and Rural Development. London and New York; Elsevier Applied Science, 1989. 250p.

Third Smith, T. Lynn, and Paul E. Zopf, Jr. Demography: Principles and Methods. 2d ed. Port Washington, N.Y.; Alfred Publ., 1976. 615p.

First rank Snedecor, George W., and William G. Cochran. Statistical Methods. 8th ed. Ames: Iowa State University Press, 1989. 503p.

Second Snodgrass, Milton M. and Tim Wallace. Agriculture, Economics and Resource Management. 2d ed. Englewood Cliffs, N.J.; Prentice-Hall, 1980. 546p.

First rank Solow, R.M. Growth Theory: An Exposition. Oxford; Oxford University Press, 1970. 109p. (Radcliffe Lectures 1969) (Reprinted 1988)

Third Sorokin, Pitrim A. Hunger as a Factor in Human Affairs. Gainesville, Fla.; University Press of Florida, 1975. 319p.

First rank Southworth, Herman M., and Bruce F. Johnston, eds. Agricultural Development and Economic Growth. Ithaca, New York; Cornell University Press, 1967. 623p. (Reprinted in 1979.) Q

Second Southworth, Herman M., and M. Barnett, eds. Experience in Farm Mechanization in Southeast Asia. New York, Agricultural Development Council, 1974. 345p.

Second Srinivasan, T.N. and Pranab K. Bardhan, eds. Rural Poverty in South Asia. New York; Columbia University Press, 1988. 565p.

Second Srivastava, G. C. Urbanization, Capital Formation and Labour Productivity in Agriculture. New Delhi, India; Radiant Publ., 1986. 205p.

First rank Stavenhagen, Rodolfo. Agrarian Problems and Peasant Movement in Latin America. Garden City, N.Y.: Doubleday, 1970. 583p.

Third Stavenhagen, Rodolfo. Las Clases Sociales en las Sociedades Agrarias (Social Classes in Agrarian Societies). Translated by J. A. Helman. New York; Doubleday Anchor, 1975. 266p.

Third Stavis, Benedict. Making Green Revolution: The Politics of Agricultural Development in China. Ithaca,N,Y.,Cornell University Press, 1974. 274p.

Third Stein, L. The Growth of East African Exports and their Effect on Economic Development. London; Croom Helm, 1979. 272p.

Third Sterkenburg, J. J. Rural Development and Rural Development Studies: Cases from Africa and Asia. Amsterdam; Koninklijk Nederlands Aardrijkskundig Genootschap; Utrecht: Geografische Instituut, Rijksuniversitfit Utrecht, 1987. 188p. (Nederlandse Geografische Studies; 46.)

Third Stevens, C. Food and and the Developing World: Four African Case Studies. New York; St. Martin's Press, 1979. 224p.

First rank Stevens, Robert D., and Cathy L. Jabara. Agricultural Development Principles: Economic Theory and Empirical Evidence. Baltimore; Johns Hopkins University Press, 1988. 478p.

First rank Stiglitz, J.E., and H. Uzawa, eds. Readings in the Modern Theory of Economic Growth. Cambridge, Mass.; MIT Press, 1969. 497p.

First rank Streeten, Paul. What Price Food? Agricultural Price Policies in Developing Countries. New York; St. Martin's Press, 1987. 127p. (Paperback ed. Ithaca, New York; Cornell University Press, 1988)

Third Streeten, Paul, Shadid Burke, Mahbub Haq, Norman Hicks, and Frances Stewart. First Things First: Meeting Basic Needs in Developing Countries. New York; Oxford University Press, 1981. 206p.

Second Subbarao, K. Rice Marketing System and Compulsory Levies in Andhra Pradesh: A Study of Public Intervention in Food-Grain Marketing, India. Bombay, India; Allied Publ., 1978. 173p.

Third Sundaram, I. S. Anti-Poverty Rural Development in India. New Delhi, D.K. Publications, 1984. 342p.

Second Super, J.C. and T.C. Wright, eds. Food, Politics and Society in Latin America. Lincoln, Nebr.; University of Nebraska Press, 1985. 261p.

Third Svejnar, J., and E. Thorbecke. Economic Policies and Agricultural Performance. The Case of Nepal, 1960–1982. Paris; Organization for Economic and Cooperative Development, 1986. 167p.

Second Symons, Leslie. Russian Agriculture: A Geographic Survey. London; Bell, 1972. 348p.

Third Szymanski, Albert. The Capitalist State and the Politics of Class. Cambridge, Mass.; Winthrop Publ., 1978. 333p.

Second Szymanski, Albert. The Logic of Imperialism. New York; Praeger Publishers, 1981. 598p.

T

Second Taeuber, Karl E., L.L. Bumpass, and J.A. Sweet, eds. Social Demography. New York: Academic Press, 1978. 336p.

Second Takashima, Masahiko, and Toshio Kuroyanagi. Nosei no Keizai Bunseki. (An Economic Analysis of Agricultural Administration). Tokyo: Meibun Shobo, Showa 56, 1981. 2 vols.

Third Tang, Anthony M. An Analytical and Empirical Investigation of Agriculture in Mainland China, 1952–1980. Taipei, Taiwan; Chung-Hua Institute for Economic Research, 1984. 230p.

Second Tang, Anthony M. and B. Stone. Food Production in the People's Republic of China. Washington, D.C.; International Food Policy and Research Institute, 1980. 2 vols. (IFPRI Res. Report No.15)

Second Tang, Chi-Yu. An Economic Study of Chinese Agriculture. New York; Garland Publ., Inc., 1980. 514p.

Third Tanzania. Ministry of Agriculture. The Agricultural Policy of Tanzania. Dar es Salaam; Government Printer, 1983. 35p.

Third Taylor, D. C., and T. H. Wickham. Irrigation Policy and the Management of Irrigation Systems in Southeast Asia. Los Baños, Philippines; International Rice Research Institute, 1978. 198p. (Reprinted by Bangkok; Agricultural Development Council, 1979.)

First rank — Taylor, Henry C., and Anne D. Taylor. The Story of Agricultural Economics in the United States, 1840–1932. Ames: Iowa State College Press, 1952. 1121p. (Reprinted in 1974 by Greenwood Press)

Second — Taylor, Kit S. Sugar and the Underdevelopment of Northeastern Brazil, 1500–1970. Gainesville; University Presses of Florida, 1978. 167p.

First rank — Theil, Henri. Economic Forecasts and Policy. 2d rev. ed. Amsterdam: North Holland Publishing, 1961. 567p.

Second — Thiam, Tan Bock and Shao-Er Ong, eds. Readings in Asian Farm Management. Singapore University Press, 1979. 350p.

Third — Thirtle, C. G., and V. W. Ruttan. The Role of Demand and Supply in the Generation and Diffusion of Technical Change. Chur, Switzerland and New York; Harwood Academic Publ., 1987. 173p.

Second — Thorbecke, Erik, ed. Agricultural Sector Analysis and Models in Developing Countries. (Eng. and Fr.) Rome; Food and Agriculture Organization, 1982. 415p. (FAO Economic and Social Development Papers: No. 5)

Third — Thorbecke, Erik and Jan Svejnar. Economic Policies and Agricultural Performance in Sri Lanka: 1960–1984. Paris; Development Centre of the Organisation for Economic Cooperation and Development, 1987. 120p.

Second — Thorner, Daniel. The Agrarian Prospect in India: Five Lectures Delivered in 1955 at the Dilhi School of Economics. 2d rev. ed. Bombay; Allied Publ., 1976.

First rank — Timmer, Peter C., ed. The Corn Economy of Indonesia. Ithaca, N.Y.; Cornell University Press, 1987. 302p.

First rank — Timmer, Peter C. Getting Prices Right: The Scope and Limits of Agricultural Price Policy. Ithaca, N.Y.; Cornell University Press, 1986. 160p.

First rank — Timmer, Peter C., Walter P. Falcon, and Scott R. Pearson. Food Policy Analysis. Baltimore; The Johns Hopkins University Press, 1983. 301p. Q

Third — Tinker, I., M. B. Bransen, and M. Buvinic, eds. Women and World Development: Proceedings. New York; Praeger, 1976. 228p.

Second — To Feed Ourselves: Proceedings of the First Eastern, Central and Southern Africa Regional Maize Workshop, Lusaka, Zambia, March 1985. Mexico, D. F.; International Maize and Wheat Improvement Center, 1986. 307p.

First rank — Todaro, M. Economic Development in the Third World. 4th ed. New York; Longmans, 1989. 698p. (1st ed., 1977, and others have different subtitles. 440p.)

Third — Todaro, M. Internal Migration in Developing Countries: A Review of Theory, Evidence, Methodology and Research Priorities. Geneva; International Labour Office, 1976. 106p.

Second — Tolley G.S., V. Thomas, and C.M. Wong. Agricultural Price Policies and the Developing Countries. Baltimore, Md.; Johns Hopkins University Press, 1982. 242p.

First rank — Tomek, W.G., and K.L Robinson. Agricultural Product Prices. Rev. ed. Ithaca; Cornell University Press, 1981. 361p. (Original ed., 1972)

Second — Tontz, R. L., ed. Foreign Agricultural Trade. Ames: Iowa State University Press, 1966. 500p.

Third — Tullis, F. LaMond and W. Ladd Hollist, eds. Food, the State, and International Political Economy: Dilemmas of Developing Countries. Lincoln and London; University of Nebraska Press, 1986. 351p.

First rank Tweeten, L.G. Foundations of Farm Policy. 2d ed. Lincoln: University of Nebraska Press, 1979. 567p.

U

Third United States. Department of Agriculture, Economic Research Service. Food Problems and Prospects in Sub-Saharan Africa: The Decade of the 1980's. Washington, D.C.; 1981. 293p. (USDA Foreign Agricultural Economic Report, No. 166.)

Second United States Congress. Office of Technology Assessment. A Review of U.S. Competitiveness in Agricultural Trade. Washington, D.C.; O.T.A., 1986. 101p.

First rank United States Congress. Office of Technology Assessment. Technology, Public Policy, and the Changing Structure of American Agriculture. Washington, D.C.; O.T.A., 1986. 374p.

Second Uphoff, N.T., ed. Rural Development and Local Organization in Asia. New Delhi, India; Macmillan India Lmtd., 1982. Vol. 1.

Third Upton, Martin. African Farm Management. Cambridge and New York; Cambridge University Press, 1987. 190p.

Third Urrutia, M. Winners and Losers in Colombia's Economic Growth of the 1970's. Washington; Oxford University Press for the World Bank, 1985. 142p.

V

Third Vakil, C.N. and C. H. Shah, eds. Agricultural Development of India; Policy and Problems. Bombay, Orient Longman, 1979. 688p.

Third Valdés, Alberto and J. Zietz, eds. Agricultural Protection in OECD Countries: Its Cost to Less Developed Countries. Washington, D.C.; International Food Policy Research Institute, 1980. 58p. (IFPRI Research Report No. 21)

First rank Valdés, Alberto, et al. Economics and the Design of Small Farmer Technology. Ames: Iowa State University Press, 1979. 211p.

First rank Valdés, Alberto, ed. Food Security for Developing Countries. Boulder, Colo.; Westview Press, 1981. 351p.

Third Van Binsbergen, W. M. J., and H. A. Meilink, eds. Migration and the Transformation of Modern African Society. Leiden, Netherlands; Afrika-Studiecentrum, African Perspectives, 1978. 178p.

Third Van Ginneken, W. Rural and Urban Income Inequalities in Indonesia, Mexico, Pakistan, Tanzania, and Tunisia. Geneva; International Labour Office, 1976. 67p.

Second Varian, H. Microeconomic Analysis. 2d ed. New York; W. W. Norton, 1984. 384p. (1st.ed., 1978. 284p.)

Third Veiga, A., ed. Ensaios Sobre Politica Agricola Brasileira (Essays on Brazilian Agricultural Policy). Sao Paulo; Governo do Estado de Sao Paulo, Secretatia de Agricultura, 1979. 294p.

Second Vink, A. P. Land Use in Advancing Agriculture. New York; Springer-Verlag, Inc., 1975. 450p.

Second Voll, Sarah P. A Plough in Field Arable: Western Agribusiness in Third World Agriculture. Hanover, N.H.; University Press of New England, 1980. 213p.

Second Von Oppen, M.; D. R. Raj, Virinda Kumble and P. Sudhir, eds. Agricultural Markets in the Semi-Arid Tropics. Hyderabad, India; International Center for Research in the Semi-Arid Tropics, 1985. 387p.

First rank Von Pischke, J.D., Dale W. Adams and Gordon Donald, eds. Rural Financial Markets in Developing Countries: Their Use and Abuse. Baltimore: The Johns Hopkins University Press, 1983. 411p.

Third Von Witzke, Harald, ed. Policy Coordination in World Agriculture. Kiel, Germany, Herbst, 1988. 245p. 49DM

W

Third Waggoner, G. R. and B. A. Waggoner. Education in Central America. Lawrence; University Press of Kansas, 1971. 180p.

Second Wald, H.P. Taxation of Agricultural Land in Underdeveloped Countries: A Survey and Guide to Policy. Cambridge, MA; Harvard Univ. Press 1959. 231p.

Third Walker, Kenneth R. Food Grain Procurement and Consumption in China. Cambridge University Press, 1984. 329p.

Second Walker, Thomas W., ed. Nicaragua: The First Five Years. New York; Praeger, 1985. 561p.

Second Ward, William B. Science and Rice in Indonesia. Oelgeschlager, Gunn and Hain, Inc., 1985. 160p.

Second Warley, Thorald K. Agriculture: The Cost of Joining the Common Market. London: Oxford University Press, 1967. 57p.

Second Warriner, D. Land Reform and Development in the Middle East. Greenwich, Conn.; Greenwood Press, 1976. 238p.

Second Warriner, D. Land Reform in Principle and Practice. Oxford: Clarendon Press, 1969. 457p.

First rank Waugh, Frederick V. Selected Writings on Agricultural Policy and Economic Analysis. Edited by Martin E. Abel and James P. Houck. Minneapolis, Minn.; University of Minnesota Press, 1984. 466p.

Third Webster, C.C., and P. N. Wilson. Agriculture in the Tropics. 2d ed. London, New York; Longman, 1980. 640p. (1st ed., 1966. 488p.)

Second Wennergren, E. Boyd, Morris Whitker, and Charles Anholt. Agricultural Development in Bangladesh: Prospects for the Future. Boulder, Co.; Westview Press, 1984. 373p.

First rank Weymar, F. H. The Dynamics of the World Cocoa Market. Cambridge; M.I.T. Press, 1968. 253p. Q

First rank Wharton, Clifton R., ed. Subsistence Agriculture and Economic Development. Chicago; University of Chicago, Aldine Publishing Co., 1969. 481p.

Third Whetham, E. H. Agricultural Marketing in Africa. Oxford University Press, 1972. 240p.

Third Whyte, R. O. and P. Whyte. The Women of Rural Asia. Boulder, Colo., Westview Press, 1982. 262p.

Third Whyte, W. F. and D. Boynton, eds. Higher Yielding Human Systems for Agriculture. Ithaca, N.Y.; Cornell University Press, 1983. 342p.

Third Wickizer, V. P., and M. K. Bennett. The Rice Economy of Monsoon Asia. Stanford, Cal.; Stanford University Press, 1941. 358p.

Third Widstrand, Carl G. African Co-operatives and Efficiency. Uppsala, Sweden; Scandanavian Institute for African Studies, 1972. 239p.

Second Widstrand, Carl G., ed. Cooperatives and Rural Development in East Africa. Uppsala, Sweden; Scandinavian Institute of African Studies; New York; Africana Publ. Corp., 1970. 271p.

Second — Williams, D., ed. Agriculture in the Australian Economy. 2d ed. Sydney Univ. Press, 1982. 422p. (1st ed., 1967. 349p.)

Second — Williams, Frederick. Reasoning with Statistics. 3d ed. New York: Holt, Rinehart and Winston, 1986. 214p. (1st. ed. 1968 182p.)

Second — Williamson, John. The Lending Policies of the International Monetary Fund. Washington, DC: Institute for International Economics, 1982. 72p. (Policy Analyses in International Economics, 1)

Third — Wionczek, M. S. Inversion y Tecnologia Extranjera en America Latina (Investment and Foreign Technology in Latin America). Mexico; Joaquin Mortiz, 1971. 189p.

Second — Wong, John, ed. Group Farming in Asia: Experiences and Potentials. Singapore; Singapore University Press, 1979. 296p.

Second — Wong, Lung-Fai. Agricultural Productivity in the Socialist Countries. Boulder, CO.; Westview Press, 1986. 195p.

Second — Wonnacott, Thomas and John J. Wonnacott. Econometrics. 2d ed. New York; Wiley, 1979. 580p. (1st ed., 1970. 445p.)

Third — Wood, L. J. Market Origins and Development in East Africa. Kampala; Makerere University, Department of Geography, 1974. 63p. (Makerere University Occasional Paper No. 57.)

Second — Woodruff, A. M., J. R. Brown and Sein Lin, eds. International Seminar on Land Taxation, Land Tenure and Land Reform in Developing Countries. West Hartford, Conn.; John C. Lincoln Institute of Land Policy, 1966. 598p.

Third — World Bank. Accelerated Development in Sub-Saharan Africa; An Agenda for Action. Washington,D.C.; World Bank, 1982. 198p.

Third — World Bank. Agricultural Research and Extension: An Evaluation of the World Bank's Experience. Washington,D.C.; World Bank, 1985. 110p.

Second — World Bank. The Assault on World Poverty; Problems of Rural Development, Education, and Health. Baltimore; Johns Hopkins University Press, 1975. 425p.

Third — World Bank. Ensuring Food Security in the Developing World: Issues and Options. Washington, D.C.; World Bank, 1985.

Third — World Bank. Poverty and Hunger: Issues and Options for Food Security in Developing Countries. Washington, D.C.; World Bank, 1986. 69p.

Third — World Bank. The Smallholder Dimension of Livestock Development: A Review of World Bank Experience. Washington, D.C.; World Bank, 1985. 2vols. (World Bank Report No. 5979.)

First rank — World Commission on Environment and Development. Food Two Thousand: Global Policies for Sustainable Agriculture. London and Totowa, N.Y.; Zed Press, 1987. 131p.

Second — Wortman, Sterling, and Ralph W. Cummings, Jr. To Feed This World: The Challenge and the Strategy. Baltimore; The Johns Hopkins University Press, 1978. 440p.

Second — Woube, Mengistu. Problems of Land Reform Implementation in Rural Ethiopia: A Case Study of Dejen and Wolmera Districts. Paperback ed. Uppsala; Dept. of Human Geography, Uppsala Univ., 1986. 174p.

Y

Third — Yang, Wei Y. Methods of Farm Management Investigations for Improving Farm Productivity. 2d ed. Rome; Food and Agriculture Organization of the U.N., 1965. 258p. (FAO Agricultural Development Paper No. 64) (Rev. ed., 1958. 228p.)

Second Yates, Lamartine. Mexico's Agricultural Dilemma. Tucson, Ariz.: University of Arizona Press, 1981. 291p.

First rank Yotopoulos, Pan A., and Jeffrey B. Nugent. Economics of Development; Empirical Investigations. New York: Harper and Row, 1976. 478p.

Second Yotopoulos, Pan A. Empirical Investigations in the Economics of Development. Tokyo; Keio-tsusin Co., 1984.

Second Young, Frank W. Interdisciplinary Theories of Rural Development. Greenwich, Conn.; JAI Press, 1983. 235p.

Third Young, Pauline V. Scientific Social Surveys and Research. 4th ed. Englewood Cliffs, N.J.; Prentice-Hall, 1966. 576p.

Z

Third Zachariah, K. C., and J. Conde. Migration in West Africa: Demographic Aspects. New York; Oxford University Press for the World Bank and Organization for Economic Cooperation and Development, 1980. 130p.

Second Zahlan, A. B. The Agricultural Sector of Sudan: Policy and System Studies. London; Ithaca Press, 1986. 423p. (Middle East Science Policy Studies: No. 6)

Second Zeller, Richard A., and E.G. Carmines. Measurement in the Social Sciences: The Link Between Theory and Data. New York; Cambridge University Press, 1980. 198p.

Second Zietz, J. and A. Valdés. The Costs of Protectionism to Developing Countries: An Analysis for Selected Agricultural Products. Washington, D.C.; World Bank, 1986. 98p. (World Bank Staff Working Paper No. 769)

Q = Quality Publication Award issued by the American Agricultural Economics Association.

AAEA Classic = Award winning Classic of the American Agricultural Economics Association.

D. The Nature of the Two Core Monograph Lists

Evaluators of titles were asked to determine those works which are considered useful or valuable in today's education and research needs. Concern was expressed for currency as well as historical significance. To achieve a balance, titles were included prior to the 1950 cut-off year to test the importance of early landmark works. It must be remembered that titles were extracted from citation lists of the literature of agricultural economics and rural sociology where a quantity of pre-1950 titles scored well in the citation counts. And thirteen of them rated high enough to appear in the core list for the Third World. These include the prime works of four pre-1900 authors: Malthus, Marx, Plato, and Adam Smith. These were also in the developed countries list, except Plato. The other nine early titles from the Third World list were published originally between 1925 and 1949: Chayanov, Colin Clark, John Dewey, Geary, Salter, Paul Samuelson, Shannon, Snedecor, and Wickizer.

These authors represent close ties with general economics and sociology, as do most of the early works in the developed countries list which has thrity-nine titles published before 1950. Nine of the thirteen Third World titles published before 1950 were also in the developed countries list, a great deal of unanimity of opinion on the classics. Of the thrity-nine pre-1950 titles in the developed countries list, all but two were reprinted, had succeeding editions, or are in print today. This is a positive correlation with the concepts of today's rural sociologists and agricultural economists as to what works are important. Two persons with pre-1950 imprints appear with two titles each; J. R. Commons and Ted W. Schultz.

E. The Hard Core Monographs

The evaluations and weighting of lists provided gradations of value on each title, both for the developed and developing countries literature. As mentioned earlier, both lists began with the same cadre of monographic titles and evolved into distinctive lists as the citation analysis proceeded and the evaluations of reviewers were tabulated. The titles that are included in both lists are the hard-core titles in agricultural economics and rural sociology.

The lists have 543 titles which are common to both; they break down in the categories shown in Table 19.

Table 19. Titles common in Third World and developed countries core lists

	Developed countries list	Third World list
First rank	103	155
Second rank	205	278
Third rank	235	110
Titles common to both	543	543

Of the 1,421 titles in the developed countries list, 38.2% are also in the Third World list; of the 1,002 titles in the Third World list, 54.2% are in the developed countries list. Judging from the rankings of these commonly held titles, the Third World reviewers tended to rank titles of greater significance than did their developed countries counterparts.

Because these 543 titles are the current highly rated monographs in agricultural economics and rural sociology, they have been pulled from the parent lists and presented below.

Monographs Appearing in Each Core Monograph List, 543 titles

	Rankings	
	Developed countries	Third World
Abramovitz, M., ed. Capital Formation and Economic Growth. Princeton, N.J.; Princeton University Press for National Bureau of Economic Research, 1959. 677p.	3	2
Adams, Dale W., Douglas H. Graham, and J.D. Von Pischke, eds. Undermining Rural Development with Cheap Credit. Boulder; Westview Press, 1984. 318p.	2	2
Adelman, I. and E. Thorbecke, eds. The Theory and Design of Economic Development. Baltimore; Johns Hopkins University Press, 1967. 427p.	1	1
Adelman, I. and C. T. Morris. Economic Growth and Social Equity in Developing Countries. Stanford; Stanford University Press, 1973. 257p.	1	1
Agarwala, A. N. and S. P. Singh, eds. The Economics of Underdevelopment. New York; Holt-Reinhardt, 1961. 510p.	1	1
Ahmed, Iftikhar, and Vernon W. Ruttan, eds. Generation and Diffusion of Agricultural Innovations: the Role of Institutional Factors. Aldershot, Hants, England and Brookfield, Vermont; Gower Publishing Co., 1988. 471p.	2	1
Ahsan, Syed M. Agricultural Insurance: A New Policy for Developing Countries. Brookfield, Vermont; Gower Publishing Co., 1985. 262p.	2	2
Akoto, O. A. Public Policy and Agricultural Development in Africa. Brookfield, Vermont; Gower Publishing Co, 1988.	2	2
Alavi, Hamza, and Teodor Shanin, eds. Introduction to the Sociology of "Developing Societies." New York; Monthly Review Press, 1982. 474p.	2	2
Alberts, Tom. Agrarian Reform and Rural Poverty: A Case Study of Peru. Boulder, Colo.; Westview Press, 1983. 306p.	2	2
Alexander, M., ed. Agricultural Policy: A Limiting Factor in the Development Process. Washington, D.C., Inter-American Development Bank, 1975. 507p.	2	2
Alexandratos, Nikos, ed. World Agriculture: Towards 2000: An FAO study. New York; New York University Press, 1988. 338p.	3	2
Allen, G. R. Agricultural Marketing Policy. Oxford University Press, 1959. 336p.	3	1
Amacher, Ryan C., Robert D. Tollison, and Thomas D. Willett, eds. The Economic Approach to Public Policy. Ithaca; Cornell University Press, 1976. 528p.	3	2
Amin, Samir. Accumulation on a World Scale: A Critique of the Theory of Underdevelopment. 2 vols. New York, Monthly Review Press, 1974. 666p. (Transl. from French by B. Pearce.)	2	3

	Rankings	
	Developed countries	Third World
Amin, Samir. Unequal Development: An Essay on the Social Formations of Peripheral Capitalism. New York; Monthly Review Press, 1976. 440p. (Transl. of Le Developpement inegal; Paris; Les Editions de Minuit, 1973.)	2	1
Anderson, C. Arnold and M. J. Bowman, eds. Education and Economic Development. Chicago; Aldine Press, 1965. 436p.	1	2
Anderson, Jock R., John L. Dillon, and J. Brian Hardaker. Agricultural Decision Analysis. Ames; Iowa State University Press, 1977. 344p.	2	1
Anderson, Kym and Rodney Tyers. Distortions in World Food Markets. Cambridge, England; Cambridge University Press, 1988.	3	3
Anderson, Kym, Y. Hayami, and others. The Political Economy of Agricultural Protection: East Asia in International Perspective. Sydney, Australia and Boston; George Allen and Unwin, 1986. 185p.	2	1
Andreou, Paris. Contemporary Issues in Agricultural and Economic Development of Developing Nations: Selected Reading in the Economic Development of Poor Countries. Nairobi; East African Lit. Bureau, 1977. 340p.	3	2
Anschel, Kurt R., Russell H. Brannon, and Eldon D. Smith, eds. Agricultural Cooperatives and Markets in Developing Countries. New York; Praeger, 1969. 373p.	2	2
Arndt, Thomas M., Dana G. Dalrymple, and Vernon Ruttan, eds. Resource Allocation and Productivity in National and International Agricultural Research. Minneapolis; University of Minnesota Press, 1977. 617p.	1	1
Arrow, Kenneth J. Social Choice and Individual Values. 2d ed. New Haven, Conn.; Yale University Press, 1963. 124p. (Reprinted in 1970. 1st ed. New York; John Wiley and Sons, 1951. 99p.)	1	1
Asian Productivity Organization. Productivity Measurement and Analysis: Asian Agriculture. Tokyo, Asian Prod. Organization, 1987. 834p.	3	3
Askari, Hossein, and John T. Cummings. Agricultural Supply Response: A Survey of the Econometric Evidence. New York; Praeger, 1976. 443p.	2	1
Astori, Danilo. La Agricultura en una Estrategia de Desarrollo Economico. Montevideo, Uruguay; Ediciones de la Banda Oriental, 1969. 132p.	3	3
Attwood, D. W. and B. S. Baviskar, eds. Co-operatives and Rural Development. Oxford University Press, 1988. 320p.	3	3
Bagchi, Amiya. The Political Economy of Underdevelopment. Cambridge and New York; Cambridge University Press, 1982. 280p.	2	1
Balassa, Bela. The Structure of Protection in Developing	1	1

	Rankings	
	Developed countries	Third World
Countries. Baltimore; Johns Hopkins University Press, for the World Bank, 1971. 375p.		
Balassa, Bela. Trade Prospects for Developing Countries. Homewood, Illinois: Richard D. Irwin, 1964. 450p.	2	1
Bardhan, Pranab K. The Political Economy of Development in India. Oxford and New York; Basil Blackwell, 1984. 118p.	2	1
Bardhan, Pranab K. Land, Labor, and Rural Poverty: Essays in Development Economics. New York; Columbia University Press, 1984. 252p.	1	1
Bardhan, Pranab K. Interlocking Factor Markets. London and Delhi: Macmillan, 1984.	2	1
Barker, J. W. Agricultural Marketing. Oxford University Press, 1981. 226p.	3	2
Barker, Jonathan, ed. The Politics of Agriculture in Tropical Africa. Beverly Hills: Sage Publications, 1984. 320p.	3	2
Barker, Randolph, and Robert W. Herdt. The Rice Economy of Asia. Washington, DC: Resources for the Future. Baltimore: Johns Hopkins University Press, 1985. 324p. Q	1	1
Barker, Randolph and Radha P. Sinha, eds. The Chinese Agricultural Economy. Boulder, Colo.; Westview Press, 1982. 266p.	2	2
Barnard, C. S. and J. S. Nix. Farm Planning and Control. 2d ed. Cambridge University Press, 1979. 600p. (1st ed. 1973, 543p.)	3	3
Barraclough, Solon L. Agrarian Structure in Latin America. Cambridge, Mass., Lexington Books, 1973. 351p.	2	2
Barry, Peter J., ed. Risk Management in Agriculture. Ames; Iowa State University Press, 1984. 282p.	1	3
Barry, Peter J., John A. Hopkin and C. B. Baker. Financial Management in Agriculture. 4th ed. Danville, Ill.: Interstate, 1988. 500p. (1st ed. 1973, 459p.) 3.	2	3
Bartsch, William H. Employment and Technology Choice in Asian Agriculture. New York, Praeger, 1977. 125p.	3	3
Bates, Robert H. Essays on the Political Economy of Rural Africa. Cambridge University Press, 1983. 178p.	3	2
Bates, Robert H. Markets and States in Tropical Africa: the Political Basis of Agricultural Policies. Berkeley; University of California Press, 1981. 178p.	2	1
Bates, Robert H., and M. F. Lofchie, eds. Agricultural Development in Africa: Issues of Public Policy. New York; Praeger, 1980. 451p.	3	2
Bauer, P. T. West African Trade: A Study of Competition, Oligopoly and Monopoly in a Changing Economy. Cambridge University Press, 1954. 450p. (Reprinted, with a new preface, by London; Routledge and Kegan Paul, 1963; and New York; A. M. Kelley, 1967.)	3	3

	Rankings	
	Developed countries	Third World
Baum, Kenneth H. and Lyle P. Schertz. Modeling Farm Decisions for Policy Analysis. Boulder, Colo.; Westview Press, 1983. 418p.	1	2
Bayliss-Smith, Tim, and Sudhir Wanmali, eds. Understanding Green Revolutions: Agrarian Change and Development Planning in South Asia. Cambridge University Press, 1984. 384p.	3	2
Beaumont, P., and Keith McLachlan, eds. Agricultural Development in the Middle East. Chichester, England and New York; John Wiley and Sons, 1985. 349p.	2	2
Beierlein, James G., Kenneth C. Schneeberger, and Donald D. Osburn. Principles of Agribusiness Management. Englewood Cliffs, N.J.; Prentice-Hall, 1986. 441p.	3	2
Benor, D., J. Q. Harrison, and Michael Baxter. Agricultural Extension: The Training and Visit System. New ed. Washington, D.C.; The World Bank, 1984. 85p. (1st ed. 1977, 55p.)	2	2
Berardi, Gigi M., ed. World Food, Population, and Development. Totowa, N.J.: Rowman and Allanheld, 1985. 346 p.	3	3
Berg, A. D. Malnutrition: What Can Be Done? Lessons from World Bank Experience. Baltimore; Johns Hopkins University Press for The World Bank, 1987. 139p.	2	2
Berg, A. D., N. S. Scrimshaw, and D. L. Call, eds. Nutrition, National Development, and Planning. Cambridge, Mass., MIT Press, 1973. 401p.	1	2
Bergmann, Theodor. The Development Models of India, the Soviet Union and China. Assen; Van Gorcum, 1977. 255p. (Publications of European Society for Rural Sociology Ser.: No. 1).	3	2
Bernstein, Gail Lee. Haruko's World: A Japanese Farm Woman and Her Community. Stanford University Press, 1983. 199p.	3	2
Berry, R. Albert, and William R. Cline. Agrarian Structure and Productivity in Developing Countries. Baltimore; Johns Hopkins University Press, 1979. 248p.	2	2
Berry, R. Albert, and R. Soligo, eds. Economic Policy and Income Distribution in Colombia. Boulder, Colo.; Westview Press, 1980. 269p.	2	2
Beteille, Andre. Studies in Agrarian Social Structure. Oxford University Press, 1974. 206p.	3	2
Bhaduri, Amit. The Economic Structure of Backward Agriculture. London and New York; Academic Press, Inc., 1983. 151p.	2	1
Bhagwati, J. N., R. W. Jones, R. A. Mundell, and J. Vanek, eds. Trade Balance of Payments and Growth; Papers in International Economics in Memory of C. P. Kindleberger. Amsterdam, North-Holland, 1971. 532p.	3	3
Biebuyck, D., ed. African Agrarian Systems. Oxford University Press, 1963. 407p.	3	3

	Rankings	
	Developed countries	Third World
Bingen, R. James. Food Production and Rural Development in the Sahel: Lessons from Mali's Operation Riz-Segou. Boulder, Colo., Westview Press, 1985. 167p.	2	2
Binswanger, Hans P., and P. L. Scandizzo. Patterns of Agricultural Protection. Washington, D.C.; World Bank, 1983 (World Bank Report ARU15).	1	2
Binswanger, Hans P., and Vernon W. Ruttan. Induced Innovation: Technology, Institutions, and Development. Baltimore; Johns Hopkins University Press, 1978. 423p. Q	1	1
Binswanger, Hans P., and Mark R. Rosenzweig. Contractual Arrangements, Employment and Wages in Rural Labor Markets in Asia. New Haven,Yale University Press, 1984. 330p.	1	1
Binswanger, Hans P. The Economics of Tractors in South Asia: An Analytical Review. New York; Agricultural Development Council; and Hyderabad, India; International Crops Research Institute for the Semi-Arid Tropics, 1978. 96p.	1	1
Binswanger, Hans P., Robert E. Evenson, Cecilia A. Florencio, and Benjamin N.F. White, eds. Rural Household Studies in Asia. Singapore: Singapore University Press, 1980. 369p.	1	1
Bliss, C. J. and N. H. Stern. Palanpur: The Economy of an Indian Village. Oxford and New York; Oxford University Press, 1982. 340p.	3	2
Booth, Anne and R. M. Sundrum. Labour Absorption in Agriculture: Theoretical Analysis and Empirical Investigations. New York; Oxford University Press, 1985. 327p.	3	3
Boserup, Ester. Conditions of Agricultural Growth: The Economics of Agrarian Change Under Population Pressure. Chicago; Aldine Publ. Co., 1965. 124p.	1	1
Boserup, Ester. Population and Technological Change: A Study of Long-term Trends. Chicago; University of Chicago Press, 1981. 255p.	3	2
Boyce, James K., and Robert E. Evenson. National and International Agricultural Research and Extension Programs. New York; Agricultural Development Council, Inc., 1975. 229p.	1	1
Bradnock, R.W., and M. Walker. Agricultural Change in South Asia. London; John Murray, 1984. 64p.	3	2
Bray, Francesca. The Rice Economies: Technology and Development in Asian Societies. Oxford and New York; Blackwell, 1986. 254p.	3	2
Breimyer, H.F. Economics of the Product Markets of Agriculture. Ames; Iowa State University Press, 1976. 208p.	2	2
Bressler, Raymond G., Jr., and R. A. King. Markets, Prices, and Interregional Trade. New York: Wiley, 1970. 426p. (Reprinted Raleigh, N.C.; Norman-Weathers Print. Co., 1978.)	1	2
Brown, David L., and John M. Wardwell, eds. New Directions in Urban-Rural Migration: The Population Turnaround in Rural America. Academic Press, Inc., 1980. 412p.	1	2

	Rankings	
	Developed countries	Third World
Brown, Lester R. Man, Land and Food: Looking Ahead at World Food Needs. New York; Ayer Company Publ., Inc., 1976. 153pp. (Reprint of 1963 ed.)	2	2
Brown, Murray., ed. The Theory and Empirical Analysis of Production. New York; Columbia University Press, for the National Bureau of Economic Research, 1967. 515p.	2	2
Brown, Murray. On the Theory and Measurement of Technical Change. Cambridge: At the University Press, 1968. 214p.	2	2
Browne, William P. and Don F. Hadwiger. World Food Policies: Toward Agricultural Interdependence. Boulder, Colo., Lynne Rienner Publ., 1986. 222p.	2	2
Buttel, Frederick H., and Howard Newby, eds. The Rural Sociology of the Advanced Societies: Critical Perspectives. Montclair, N.J.; Allanheld, Osmun and Co., 1980. 529p.	1	2
Caldwell, Bruce. Beyond Positivism: Economic Methodology in the Twentieth Century. London and Boston; Allen and Unwin, 1982. 277p.	2	3
Caldwell, John C. African Rural-Urban Migration: The Movement to Ghana's Towns. New York; Columbia University Press, 1969. 257p.	3	1
Carlson, Sune. A Study on the Pure Theory of Production. Clifton, N.J.; Augustus M. Kelley, 1956. 128p. (Reprint of 1939 ed.)	2	2
Carruthers, I. D., ed. Aid for the Development of Irrigation. Paris; Organization for Economic Cooperation and Development, 1983. 166p.	3	3
Carruthers. I. D., and C. Clark. The Economics of Irrigation. 3d ed. Liverpool Univ. Press, 1981. 300p.	3	3
Carter, A. P., and A. Brody, eds. Applications of Input-Output Analysis. Amsterdam: North-Holland, 1972. 2 vols.	2	2
Casley, Dennis J. Data Collection in Developing Countries. 2d ed. Oxford and New York; Clarendon Press, 1987. 225p. (1st ed. 1981, 244p.) T	2	2
Castle, Emery N., and K. Hemmi, eds. U.S.-Japanese Agricultural Trade Relations. Baltimore; Johns Hopkins University Press; and Washington, D.C.; Resources for the Future, 1982. 436p.	2	1
Castle, Emery N., Manning H. Becker, and A. Gene Nelson. Farm Business Management. 3d ed. Macmillan Publ. Co., Inc., 1986. 456p.	2	2
Chambers, Robert. Rural Development: Putting the Last 1 London and New York; Longman, 1983. 246p.	3	3
Chao, Kang. Agricultural Production in Communist China, 1945–1965. Madison; University of Wisconsin Press, 1970. 374p.	3	2
Chayanov, A. V. On the Theory of Peasant Economy. (Translation of his Peasant Farm Organization; Moscow; Cooperative	1	1

	Rankings	
	Developed countries	Third World
Publ. House, 1925.) Translated by D. Thorner, B. Kerblay, and R. E. F. Smith, with a forword by Teodor Shanin. Homewood, Ill.; Richard D. Irwin, 1966. 317p. (Reprinted by Madison; University of Wisconsin Press, 1986.)		
Chekki, Dan A., ed. Community Development: Theory and Method of Planned Change. New Delhi, India; Vikas Press, 1979. 258p.	3	3
Chenery, Hollis, and T. N. Srinivasa, eds. Handbook of Development Economics. Amsterdam and New York; North-Holland Publ., 1988–89. 2 vols.	2	2
Chenery, Hollis, and M. Syrquin. Patterns of Development, 1950–1970. London, Oxford University Press for the World Bank, 1975. 234p.	2	2
Chenery, Hollis, et al. Redistribution With Growth: Policies to Improve Income Distribution in Developing Countries in the Context of Economic Growth. Oxford, England; published for World Bank and Institute of Development Studies, University of Sussex, by Oxford University Press, 1974. 304p.	1	1
Chenery, Hollis. Structural Change and Development Policy. Oxford University Press for the World Bank, 1979. 526p.	1	1
Cheung, Steven N. Theory of Share Tenancy: With Special Application to Asian Agriculture and the First Phase of Taiwan Land Reform. University of Chicago Press, 1969. 188p.	1	2
Chisholm, Anthony H., and Rodney Tyers, eds. Food Security: Theory, Policy and Perspectives from Asia and the Pacific Rim. Lexington, Mass.; Lexington Books, 1982. 359p.	1	1
Christ, C., et al., eds. Measurement in Economics: Studies in Mathematical Economics and Econometrics in Memory of Yehuda Greenfeld. Stanford, Calif.; Stanford University Press, 1963. 319p.	3	3
Christenson, James A., and Jerry W. Robinson, Jr., eds. Community Development in America. Ames; Iowa State University Press, 1980. 245p.	1	1
Ciriacy-Wantrup, S. V. Resource Conservation: Economics and Policies. 3d ed. Berkeley; University of California Press. 1968. 395p. (1st ed. 1952) AAEA Classic	2	2
Clark, Colin, and M. Haswell. The Economics of Subsistence Agriculture. 4th ed. London; Macmillan; New York; St. Martin's Press, 1970. 267p. (1st ed. 1964, 218p.)	2	2
Clark, Colin W. Bioeconomic Modelling and Fisheries Management. New York; Wiley, 1985. 291p.	2	1
Clark, Colin W. The Conditions of Economic Progress. London: Macmillan, 3d ed., 1957. 720p. (1st ed. 1940, 504p.)	1	2
Cleave, John H. African Farmers: Labor Use in the Development of Smallholder Agriculture. New York: Praeger Publishers, 1974. 253p.	3	3
Cline, W. R. and A. Berry. Farm Size, Productivity and Techni-	3	3

	Rankings	
	Developed countries	Third World
cal Change. Washington,D.C., International Bank for Rural Development, 1976.		
Cohen, Ronald, ed. Satisfying Africa's Food Needs: Food Production and Commercialization in African Agriculture. Boulder, Colo.; Lynne Rienner Publ., 1988. 244p.	3	3
Collinson, M.P. Farm Management in Peasant Agriculture: A Handbook for Rural Development Planning in Africa. New York; Praeger, 1972. 444p. (Reprinted Boulder, Colo.; Westview Press, 1983, 454p.)	2	1
Commins, S. K., M. F. Lofchie, and R. Payne. Africa's Agrarian Crisis: The Roots of Famine. Boulder, Colo.; L. Rienner Publishing, 1986. 237p.	3	2
Commons, J.R. Institutional Economics: Its Place in Political Economy. New York: Macmillan, 1934. 921p. (Reissued: Madison; Univ. of Wisconsin Press, 1959.)	1	2
Cook, Paul and C. Kirkpatrick, eds. Privatisation in Less Developed Countries. Brighton, England; Wheatsheaf Book; and New York; St. Martin's Press, 1988. 315p.	3	3
Coombs, P.H., and M. Ahmed. Attacking Rural Poverty; How Nonformal Education Can Help. International Council for Educational Development for the World Bank. Baltimore; Johns Hopkins University Press, 1974. 292p.	3	2
Coward, E. Walter, Jr., ed. Irrigation and Agricultural Development in Asia: Perspectives from the Social Sciences. Ithaca,N.Y., Cornell University Press, 1980. 369p.	2	2
Crosson, Pierre R., and S. Brubaker. Resource and Environmental Effects of U. S. Agriculture. Washington, D.C.; Resources for the Future, 1982. 255p.	1	2
Crosson, Pierre R., and Kenneth D. Frederick. The World Food Situation: Resource and Environmental Issues in the Developing Countries and the United States. Washington, D.C.; Resources for the Future, Inc., 1977. 230p.	2	2
Cruz de Schlesinger, L. and L. J. Ruiz. Mercadeo de Arroz en Colombia. Bogotá; Centro de Estudios sobre Desarrollo Económico, 1967.	3	3
Csaki, Csaba. Simulation and Systems Analysis in Agriculture. (Translation of his Szimeilacio Alkalmazasa a Mezogazdasagban, revised and enlarged.) Amsterdam and New York, Elsevier Science Publ. Co., 1985. 262p.	2	2
Cukierman, A. Inflation, Stagflation, Relative Prices, and Imperfect Information. New York; Cambridge University Press, 1984. 202p.	2	2
Cullen, Matthew, and Sharon Woolery, eds. Second World Congress on Land Policy. Boston, Mass.; Oelgeschlager, Gunn and Hain, Inc. in association with Lincoln Institute of Land Policy, 1985. 320p.	3	2
Curtis, Donald, Michael Hubbard, and Andrew Shepherd. Pre-	3	3

	Rankings	
	Developed countries	Third World
venting Famine: Policies and Prospects for Africa. London and New York; Routledge, 1988. 250p.		
Dahl, Dale C., and J. M. Hammond. Market and Price Analysis: The Agricultural Industries. New York; McGraw-Hill, 1977. 323p.	3	2
Dahlberg, Kenneth A. Beyond the Green Revolution: The Ecology and Politics of Global Agricultural Development. New York; Plenum Press, 1979. 256p.	2	3
Dalrymple, Dana G. Development and Spread of High-Yielding Wheat Varieties in Developing Countries. Washington, D.C.; Bureau of Science and Technology, Agency for International Development, 1986. 99p.	3	2
Danda, Ajit K., ed. Studies on Rural Development: Experiences and Issues. New Delhi, Inter-India Publications, 1984. 107 p.	3	3
Dasgupta, Ajit K. Agriculture and Economic Development in India. New Dehli; Associated Publishing House, 1973. 117p.	3	2
Dauber, Roslyn, and Melinda Cain, eds. Women and Technological Change In Developing Countries. Boulder, Colo.; Westview Press for American Association for the Advancement of Science, 1981. 266p.	3	2
Davis, Ted J., and Isabella A. Schirmer, eds. Sustainability Issues in Agricultural Development: Proceedings of the Seventh Agricultural Sector Symposium. Washington, D.C.; World Bank, 1987. 382p.	3	2
Dawson, Andrew H. The Land Problem in the Developed Economy. New York; St. Martin's Press, 1984. 280p.	3	2
Day, R. H., and A. Cigno, eds. Modelling Economic Change: The Recursive Programming Approach. Amsterdam; North-Holland Publ. Co.; and New York; Elsevier, 1978. 447p.	1	3
de Haen, Hartwig, Glenn L. Johnson, and Stefan Tangermann, eds. Agriculture and International Relations: Analysis and Policy; Essays in Memory of Theodor Heidhus. New York; St. Martin's Press, 1985. 306p.	3	2
de Janvry, Alain and Jean-Jacques Dethier. Technological Innovation in Agriculture: The Political Economy of Its Rate and Basis. Washington, D.C., World Bank, 1985. 90 p. (CGIAR Study Paper no. 1)	1	2
de Janvry, Alain and K. Subbarao. Agricultural Price Policy and Income Distribution in India. Dehli; Oxford University Press, 1986. 113p.	2	1
de Janvry, Alain. The Agrarian Question and Reformism in Latin America. Baltimore; Johns Hopkins University Press, 1981. 311p.	1	1
De Wilde, John C. Agriculture, Marketing and Pricing in Sub-Saharan Africa. Los Angeles, Calif.; African Studies Association, 1984. 129p.	3	2
De Wilde, John C., et al. Experiences with Agricultural Devel-	3	2

	Rankings	
	Developed countries	Third World
opment in Tropical Africa. Vol. 1: The Synthesis; Vol. 2: The Case Studies. Baltimore; Johns Hopkins University Press, 1967. 264p. (World Bank Ser.)		
Deaton, Angus and John Muellbauer. Economics and Consumer Behavior. Cambridge University Press, 1980. 450p. (Reprinted with corrections in 1983.)	2	2
Dejene, Alemneh. Peasants, Agrarian Socialism and Rural Development in Ethiopia. Boulder, Colo.; Westview, 1986. 140p.	3	2
Dernberger, R. F., ed. China's Development Experience in Comparative Perspective. Cambridge, Mass., Harvard University Press, 1980. 341p.	3	3
Desai, A.R., ed. Agrarian Struggles in India after Independence. Oxford University Press, 1986. 653p.	3	2
Desai, Meghnad J., S. H. Rudolph, and A. Rudra, eds. Agrarian Power and Agricultural Productivity in South Asia. Berkeley; University of California Press, 1984. 384p.	3	2
Dewan, M. L. Agriculture and Rural Development in India: A Case Study on the Dignity of Labour. New Delhi, India; Concept Publs., 1982. 240p.	3	2
Dewey, J. Logic: The Theory of Inquiry. New York: Holt, 1938. 546p.	2	2
Dillman, Don A., and Daryl J. Hobbs, eds. Rural Society in the U.S.: Issues for the 1980's. Boulder, Colo.; Westview Press, 1982. 437p. (Rural Studies Series of the Rural Sociological Society)	1	1
Dillon, John L. and Jock R. Anderson. The Analysis of Response in Crop and Livestock Production. 3d ed. Oxford and New York; Pergamon Press, 1990. 251p. (1st and 2d ed. by Dillon, 1968, 1977.)	1	1
Dinham, Barbara, and Colin Hines. Agribusiness in Africa. London; Earth Resources Research, 1983. 224p. (Reprinted by Trenton, N.J.: Africa World Press, 1984).	3	2
Dobyns, H.F., P.L. Doughty and H.D. Lasswell, eds. Peasants, Power and Applied Social Change: Vicos as a Model. Beverly Hills, California: Sage Publications, 1971. 237p.	3	2
Doll, John P., V. J. Rhodes, and J. G. West. Economics of Agricultural Production, Markets, and Policy. Homewood, Ill.: Richard D. Irwin, 1968. 557p.	2	2
Donald, Gordon, ed. Credit for Small Farmers in Developing Countries. Boulder, Colo.; Westview Press, 1976. 286p.	1	1
Dore, R.P. Land Reform in Japan. American ed. New York; Shocken Books, 1985. (London, New York; Oxford University Press, 1959. 510p.)	3	2
Dorfman, Robert, and N.S. Dorfman, eds. Economics of the Environment: Selected Readings. 2d ed. New York; Norton, 1977. 494p. (1st ed. 1972)	3	2

	Rankings	
	Developed countries	Third World
Dorner, Peter, ed. Land Reform in Latin America: Issues and Cases. Madison, Wisc.; Land Tenure Center, University of Wisconsin, 1971. 276p.	1	2
Dorner, Peter. Land Reform and Economic Development. Harmondsworth; Penguin Books, 1972. 167p.	2	2
Douglass, Gordon K., ed. Agricultural Sustainability in a Changing World Order. Boulder, Colo.; Westview Press, 1984. 282p.	1	2
Dovring, Folke. Land Economics. Boston, Mass.; Breton Publ., 1987. 532p.	2	1
Duncan, Kenneth, Ian Rutledge and Colin Harding, eds. Land and Labour in Latin America: Essays on the Development of Agrarian Capitalism in the Nineteenth and Twentieth Centuries. Cambridge University Press, 1977. 535p.	2	2
Dunn, P. D. Appropriate Technology: Technology with a Human Face. New York; Schocken Books, 1979. 220p.	2	2
Eashvaraiah, P. Political Dimension of Land Reforms in India. New Dehli; Ashish, 1985. 136p.	3	2
Easter, K. W., ed. Irrigation Investment Technology and Management Strategies for Development. Boulder, Colo.; Westview Press, 1986. 270p. (Studies in Water Policy and Management, no. 9.)	2	2
Edwards, Edgar O., ed. Employment in Developing Nations: Report on a Ford Foundation Study. New York; Columbia University Press, 1974. 428p.	3	2
Eicher, Carl K., and Doyle C. Baker. Research on Agricultural Development in Sub-Saharan Africa: A Critical Survey. East Lansing; Michigan State University, Dept. of Agricultural Economics, 1982. 335p. (A revision of this work is in progress and will appear in 1992 in vol. 4 of the Lee Martin series: A Survey of Agricultural Economics Literature.)	3	3
Eicher, Carl K., and J. Staatz, eds. Agricultural Development in the Third World. Baltimore; Johns Hopkins University Press, 1984. 491p.	1	1
El Ghonemy, M.R., et al. Studies on Agrarian Reform and Rural Poverty. Rome; Food and Agriculture Organization of the United Nations, 1984. 104p.	2	2
Ellis, H. S. and H. C. Wallich, eds. El Desarrollo Economico y America Latina (Economic Development and Latin America). Mexico, BA; Fondo de Cultura Economica, 1960, 1961. English edition - New York; St. Martin's Press, 1961.	3	3
Elz, Dieter. Agricultural Marketing Strategy and Pricing Policy. Washington, D.C.; World Bank, 1987. 148p.	2	3
Epp, Donald J. and John W. Malone, Jr. Introduction to Agricultural Economics. New York; Macmillan, 1981. 354p.	3	2
Etienne, Gilbert. Rural Development in Asia: Meetings with Peasants. Translated by Arati Sharma. Rev. ed. New Delhi and Beverly Hills, Calif.; Sage Publications, 1985. 276p.	3	3

	Rankings	
	Developed countries	Third World
Evenson, Robert Eugene and Yoav Kislev. Agricultural Research and Productivity. New Haven, Conn.; Yale University Press, 1975. 204p.	2	2
Feder, Gershon, et al. Land Policies and Farm Productivity in Thailand. Baltimore: Johns Hopkins University Press, 1988. 165p.	3	2
Feeney, David A. The Political Economy of Productivity: Thai Agricultural Development, 1880–1975. Vancouver; University of British Columbia Press, 1981. 238p.	2	1
Fennell, Rosemary. The Common Agricultural Policy of the European Community. 2d ed. Oxford; Blackwell Scientific Publications, 1988. 227p. (1st ed. Montclair, N.J.; Allanheld, Osmun, 1979. 243p.)	2	1
Ferguson, Charles E., J.P. Gould, and Edward Lazear. Microeconomic Theory. 6th ed. Homewood, Ill.; R.D. Irwin, 1986. 640p. (1st ed. 1961, by Ferguson. 439p.)	3	2
Fitchen, Janet. Poverty in Rural America: A Case Study. Boulder, Colo.: Westview Press, 1981. 257p.	2	2
Food and Agriculture Organization. Review of Food Consumption Surveys 1988: Household Food Consumption By Economic Groups. Rome: FAO, 1988. 179p. (FAO Food and Nutrition Paper No. 44)	3	1
Food and Agriculture Organization. Agricultural Price Policies: Issues and Proposals. Rome, FAO, 1987. 210p. (FAO Economic and Social Development Series, no. 42.)	3	3
Food and Agriculture Organization. Economic Accounts for Agriculture: Production and Capital Formation. Rome, 2d issue, 1979. 319p.	2	2
Food and Agriculture Organization. World Food Security: Selected Themes and Issues. Rome, FAO, 1985. 108p.	3	1
Food and Agriculture Organization. Development Strategies for the Rural Poor. Rome, FAO, 1984. 117p.	2	2
Food and Agriculture Organization. African Agriculture: The Next 25 Years. Rome; Food and Agriculture Organization, 1986. 5 vols.	3	3
Food and Agriculture Organization. The Fifth World Food Survey. Rome; Food and Agriculture Organization, 1987. 75p.	3	3
Food and Agriculture Organization. Bibliography of Food Consumption Surveys. Rome; Food and Agriculture Organization, 1987. 49p. (FAO Food and Nutrition Paper, No. 18, Revision 2)	3	3
Food and Agriculture Organization. Food Balance Sheets: 1979–1981 Average. Rome: FAO, 1984. 272p.	3	2
Foster, George M. Traditional Societies and Technological Change. New York: Harper and Row, 1973. 286p.	2	2
Fox, Karl A., J. K. Sengupta, and E. Thorbecke. The Theory of Quantitative Economic Policy with Applications to Economic Growth and Stabilization. 2d ed. Amsterdam; North-Holland;	2	2

	Rankings	
	Developed countries	Third World
and New York; American Elsevier, 1973. 517p. (1st ed. Amsterdam; North-Holland, 1966. 517p.)		
Francioni, Manuel J. El Credito en la Produccion Agraria. Buenos Aires; El Ateneo, 1944. 430p.	3	3
Frankel, Francine R. India's Green Revolution: Economic Gains and Political Costs. Princeton University Press, 1971. 232p.	2	1
Friedman, M. A Theory of the Consumption Function. Princeton; Princeton University Press, 1957. 243p.	1	1
Furtado, Celso. Analise do Modelo Brasileiro (Analysis of the Brazilian "Model"). 7th ed. Rio de Janeiro; Civilizacao Brasileria, 1982. 122p. (1st ed., 1972)	3	3
Galbraith, John K. Economic Development. Cambridge; Harvard University Press, 1964. 109p.	2	1
Galbraith, John K. American Capitalism: The Concept of Countervailing Power. Rev. ed. Cambridge; Houghton Mifflin, 1956. 208p.	2	1
Gersovitz, Mark, Carlos F. Diaz-Alajandro, Gustav Ranis and Mark Rosenzweig. The Theory and Experience of Economic Development: Essays in Honor of Sir W. Arthur Lewis. London: George Allen and Unwin, 1982. 403p.	2	2
Ghai, Dharam and Lawrence Smith. Agricultural Prices, Policy and Equity in Sub-Saharan Africa. Boulder, Colo.; Lynne Rienner, 1987. 174p.	3	2
Ghai, Dharam, Azizur R. Khan, Eddy Lee, and Samir Radwan, eds. Agrarian Systems and Rural Development. New York; Holmes and Meier Publ., Inc., 1979. 375p.	2	1
Ghatak, Subrata, and Ken Ingersent. Agriculture and Economic Development. Baltimore: Johns Hopkins University Press, 1984. 380p.	2	1
Ghose, Ajit Kumar, ed. Agrarian Reform in Contemporary Developing Countries. London: Croom Helm, and New York: St. Martin's Press, 1983. 364p.	3	2
Ghosh, Pradip K., ed. Health, Food and Nutrition in Third World Development. Westport, Conn.; Greenwood Press, 1984. 617p. (International Development Resource Books, No. 6).	2	1
Ghosh, Pradip K., ed. Development Policy and Planning: A Third World Perspective. Westport, Conn.; Greenwood Press, 1984. 626p. (International Development Resource Books, No. 8)	3	2
Giersch, H. International Economic Development and Resource Transfer; Workshop 1978. Tubingen; J.C.B. Mohr, 1979. 619p.	3	2
Gittinger, J. Price, Joanne Leslie and C. Hoisington. Food Policy: Integrating Supply, Distribution, and Consumption. Baltimore; Johns Hopkins University Press, 1987. 567p.	2	1
Gittinger, J. Price. Economic Analysis of Agricultural Projects. 2d ed. Baltimore: Johns Hopkins University Press for the In-	1	1

	Rankings	
	Developed countries	Third World
ternational Bank for Reconstruction and Development, 1982. 505p.		
Glaeser, Bernhard, ed. The Green Revolution Revisited. London; Allen Unwin; and New York; St. Martin's Press, 1987. 224p.	2	1
Godelier, Maurice. Rationality and Irrationality in Economics. New York; Monthly Review Press, 1975. 326p.	3	2
Goldberg, Ray A., ed. Research in Domestic and International Agribusiness Management; Research Annual. Vol. 1 (1980) Vol. 9. (1988) Greenwich, Conn.; Jai Press, Incorporated.	2	2
Gomez, O. Hernando and Eduardo D. Wiesner, eds. Lecturas Sobre Desarrollo Economico Colombiano en Honor de Alvaro Lopez Toro. Bogota, Colombia; Fundacion para la Educacion Superior y el Desarrollo, 1974. 624p.	3	3
Graaf, J. de V. The Economics of Coffee. Wageningen, The Netherlands; PUDOC, 1986. 294 p. (Economics of Crops in Developing Countries, No. 1)	3	3
Graham, Norman A., and Keith L. Edwards. The Caribbean Basin to the Year 2000; Demographic, Economic, and Resource-Use Trends in Seventeen Countries: A Compendium of Statistics and Projections. Boulder, Colo.; Westview Press, 1984. 166p.	3	2
Gramlich, Edward M. Benefit-Cost Analysis of Government Programs. Englewood Cliffs, N.J.; Prentice-Hall, 1981. 273p.	3	2
Gray, Jack and Gordon White, eds. China's New Development Strategy. London; Academic Press, 1982. 341p.	3	3
Greenshields, Bruce L., and M.A. Bellamy. Rural Development: Growth and Equity. Oxford; International Association of Agricultural Economists; and Aldershot, Hampshire and Brookfield, Vermont; Gower Publishing Co., 1983. 312p.	2	2
Griffin, Keith. The Political Economy of Agrarian Change: An Essay on the Green Revolution. 2d ed. London; Macmillan, 1979. 268p. (1st ed. Cambridge, Mass.; Harvard University Press, 1974. 264p.)	1	1
Grigg, David. Dynamics of Agricultural Change. New York; St. Martin's Press, 1982. 260p.	2	2
Grigg, David. Introduction to Agricultural Geography. London and Dover, New Hamp.; Hutchinson Education, 1984. 204p.	2	2
Griliches, Zvi and Michael D. Intriligator, eds. Handbook of Econometrics. Amsterdam; North-Holland Pub. Co.; and New York; Elsevier Science Pub. Co., 1983–1986. 3 vols.	3	3
Grindle, Merilee S. State and Countryside: Development Policy and Agrarian Politics in Latin America. Baltimore; Johns Hopkins University Press, 1985. 255 p.	3	2
Gudeman, Stephen. The Demise of a Rural Economy: From Subsistence to Capitalism in a Latin American Village. London and Boston; Routledge and K. Paul, 1978. 176p.	2	2

	Rankings	
	Developed countries	Third World
Guillet, D. Agrarian Reform and Peasant Economy in Southern Peru. Columbia; University Missouri Press, 1979. 227p.	3	3
Gutiérrez, A. N. and R. Hertford. Una Evaluación de la Intervención del gobierno en el Mercadeo de Arroz en Colombia. Cali, Colombia; Centro Internacional de Agricultura Tropical, 1974. (Technical Pamphlet No. 4)	3	3
Hadwiger, Don F. Public Policy and Agricultural Technology: Adversity Despite Achievement. New York; Macmillan, 1987. 300p.	2	2
Hagen, E. E. The Economics of Development. 3d ed. Homewood, Ill.; Irwin-Dorsey, 1980. 412p. (1st ed., 1960. 536p.)	2	2
Halter, A. N., and G. W. Dean. Decisions under Uncertainty with Research Applications. Cincinnati: South-West Publishing, 1971. 266p.	2	1
Hanf, Claus H., and Gerhard W. Schiefer, eds. Planning and Decision in Agribusiness: Principles and Experiences, A Case Study Approach to the Use of Models in Decision Planning. Amsterdam and New York; Elsevier Science Publishing Co., 1983. 373p.	3	2
Haque, Wahidul, et al. Towards a Theory of Rural Development. Bangkok: United Nations Asian Development Institute, August 1975. 102p.	3	3
Harrison, A. J. Economics and Land Use Planning. London; Croom Helm, 1977. 256p.	3	2
Harriss, John, ed. Rural Development: Theories of Peasant Economy and Agrarian Change: Anatomy of a Peasant Economy. London: Hutchinson, 1982. 409p.	3	1
Hart, Keith. The Political Economy of West African Agriculture. Cambridge University Press, 1982. 256p.	3	2
Harvey, Andrew C. The Econometric Analysis of Time Series. Oxford: Philip Allan, 1981. 384p.	3	2
Harvey, Andrew C. Time Series Models. Oxford: Philip Allan Publishers; and New York; Wiley, 1981. 229p.	3	2
Hathaway, D.E. Agriculture and the GATT: Rewriting the Rules. Washington, D.C.; Institute for International Economics, 1987. 157p.	2	1
Hayami, Yujiro, and Vernon W. Ruttan. Agricultural Development: An International Perspective. Baltimore; Johns Hopkins University Press, 1971. 367p. (Revised and expanded in 1984, 506p.) Q AAEA Classic	1	1
Hayami, Yujiro, Vernon W. Ruttan, and Herman M. Southworth, eds. Agricultural Growth in Japan, Taiwan, Korea and the Philippines. Honolulu: University Press of Hawaii for the East-West Center, 1979. 404p.	2	1
Hayami, Yujiro. Japanese Agriculture Under Siege: The Political Economy of Agricultural Policies. London; Macmillan, New York; St. Martin's Press, 1988. 145p.	3	2
Hazell, Peter, and Roger D. Norton. Mathematical Programming	2	

	Rankings	
	Developed countries	Third World
for Economic Analysis in Agriculture. New York: Macmillan, 1986. 432p.		2
Hazell, Peter and A. Roell. Rural Growth Linkages: Household Expenditure Patterns in Malaysia and Nigeria. Washington, D.C.; The International Food Policy Research Institute, 1983. 64p. (IFPRI Research Report No. 41)	2	2
Hazell, Peter, Carlos Pomareda, and Alberto Valdes, eds. Crop Insurance for Agricultural Development: Issues and Experience. Baltimore; Johns Hopkins University Press for the International Food Policy Research Institute, 1986. 322p.	2	1
Heady, Earl O. Agricultural Policy under Economic Development. Ames: Iowa State University Press, 1962. 682p. (Reissued 1965)	2	2
Heady, Earl O., ed. Economic Models and Quantitative Methods for Decisions and Planning in Agriculture. Ames; Iowa State University Press, 1971. 518p.	2	2
Helmberger, P., and S. Hoos. Cooperative Bargaining in Agriculture: Grower-Processor Markets for Fruits and Vegetables. University of California, Berkeley, Division of Agricultural Sciences, 1965. 234p. Q	2	1
Henderson, J. M., and R. E. Quandt. Microeconomic Theory: A Mathematical Approach. 2d ed. New York; McGraw-Hill, 1980. 420p. (1st ed. 1958, 291p.)	2	1
Herdt, Robert W., and C. Capule. Adoption, Spread, and Production Impact of Modern Rice Varieties in Asia. Los Banos, Laguna, Philippines: International Rice Research Institute, 1983. 54p.	3	1
Herring, Ronald J. Land to the Tiller: Political Economy of Agrarian Reform in South Asia. Yale University Press, 1983. 314p.	3	2
Hewitt de Alcantara, Cynthia. Modernizing Mexican Agriculture: Socioeconomic Implications of Technological Change, 1940–1970. 5th ed. Mexico; Siglo Vientiuno Editores , 1985. 319p. (1st ed. Geneva; United Nations Research Institute for Social Development, 1976. 350p.) (UNRISD Studies on the Green Revolution)	3	2
Heyer, J., Pepe Roberts, and Gavin Williams, eds. Rural Development in Tropical Africa. London; Macmillan Press, 1981. 224p.	3	1
Hicks, John R. A Theory of Economic History. London: Oxford University Press, 1969. 181p.	1	2
Hicks, John R. Surveys of Economic Theory. London; MacMillan, New York: St. Martin's Press, 1965, 1966, 1967. 3 vols.	2	2
Hildreth, R. J., Kathryn L. Lipton, Kenneth C. Clayton, and Carl C. O'Connor, eds. Agricultural and Rural Areas Approaching the 21st Century: Challenges for Agricultural Economics. Ames; Iowa State University Press, 1987. 560p.	2	2

	Rankings	
	Developed countries	Third World
Hilf, Meinhard, Francis G. Jacobs, and E.U. Petersmann. The European Community and GATT. Deventer, the Netherlands: Kluwer, 1986. 398p.	3	2
Hill, Berkeley, and Derek Ray. Economics for Agriculture. New York: Macmillan, 1987. 320p.	3	2
Hillier, Frederick S., and Gerald J. Lieberman. Introduction to Operations Research. 4th ed. San Francisco; Holden-Day, 1986. 888p. (1st ed. 1967, 639p.)	2	2
Hinderink, Jan and J.J. Sterkenburg Agricultural Commercialization and Government Policy in Africa. London, New York, KPI, 1987. 328 p. (Monogs. from the African Studies Centre, Leiden)	3	3
Hirschman, Albert O. Development Projects Observed. Washington, D.C.; Brookings Inst., 1967. 197p.	3	3
Hirschman, Albert O. Essays in Trespassing: Economics to Politics and Beyond. Cambridge University Press, 1981. 310p.	1	1
Hirschman, Albert O., ed. Toward a New Strategy for Development. New York: Pergamon Press, 1979. 365p.	3	3
Hollist, W. Ladd and F. LaMond Tullis,eds. Pursuing Food Security: Strategies and Obstacles in Africa, Asia, Latin America, and the Middle East. Boulder, L. Rienner, Publ., 1987. 357p.	3	3
Hopkins, Nicholas A. Agrarian Transformation in Egypt. Boulder, Colo.; Westview, 1987. 215p.	3	3
Hopkins, Raymond F., Donald J.Puchala, and Ross B. Talbot, eds. Food, Politics, and Agricultural Development: Case Studies in Public Policy of Rural Modernization. Boulder, Colo.; Westview Press, 1979. 311p.	3	2
Hou, Chi-ming, and Tzong-shian Yu, eds. Agricultural Development in China, Japan, and Korea. Seattle; University of Washington Press, 1982. 892p.	2	2
Houck, James P. Elements of Agricultural Trade Policies. New York: Macmillan, 1986. 224p.	2	1
Howell, John, ed. Borrowers and Lenders: Rural Financial Markets and Institutions in Developing Countries. London: Overseas Development Institute, 1980. 290p.	2	1
Huddleston, Barbara, D. G. Johnson, Shlomo Reutlinger, and Alberto Valdes. International Finance for Food Security. Baltimore; Johns Hopkins Univ. Press, 1984. 100p.	2	1
Hunt, Diana. The Impending Crisis in Kenya: The Case for Land Reform. Aldershot, Hampshire and Brookfield, Vermont; Gower Publishing Company, 1984. 314p.	3	2
Ijere, Martin O. New Perspectives in Financing Nigerian Agriculture. Enugu, Nigeria; Fourth Dimension Publ., 1986. 130p.	3	3
Ilbery, Brian W. Agricultural Geography: A Social and Economic Analysis. Oxford University Press, 1986. 224p.	3	2
Imel, Blake, M.R. Behr, and P.G. Helmberger. Market Struc-	3	1

	Rankings	
	Developed countries	Third World
ture and Performance: The U.S. Food Processing Industries. Lexington, Mass.; Heath Lexington Books, 1972. 115p. Q		
International Food Policy Research Institute. Food Needs of Developing Countries: Projections of Production and Consumption to 1990. Washington, D.C., IFPRI, 1977. 157p. (IFPRI Research Report No. 3)	2	3
International Livestock Centre for Africa. Small Ruminant Production in the Humid Tropics. Addis Ababa, Ethiopia; ILCA, 1979.	3	3
International Rice Research Instituute. Economic Consequences of the New Rice Technology in Asia. Los Banos; IRRI, 1978. 402p.	1	1
Islam, Nural, ed. Agricultural Policy in Developing Countries: Proceedings of a Conference held by the International Economic Association at Bad Godesberg, West Germany (Aug. 26–Sept. 4, 1972). London; Macmillan, and New York; Wiley, 1974. 565p.	2	1
Jaguaribe, H., A Ferrer, M. S. Wionczek and T. dos Santos. La Dependencia Politico-Economica de America Latina (The Political Dependency of Latin America). 12th ed. Mexico; Siglo Veintiuno, 1980. 293p. (1st ed. 1970)	3	3
Jamison, Dean T. and L. J. Lau. Farmer Education and Farm Efficiency. Baltimore; Johns Hopkins University Press, 1982. 320p. (World Bank Research Publication Ser.)	2	2
Johnson, D. Gale, K. Hemmi, and P. Lardinois. Agricultural Policy and Trade: Adjusting Domestic Programs in an International Framework. New York University Press, 1986. 144p.	2	1
Johnson, D. Gale, and K. M. Brooks. Prospects for Soviet Agriculture in the 1980s. Bloomington; Indiana University Press, 1983. 224p.	2	2
Johnson, D. Gale. World Agriculture In Disarray. London; Macmillan; and New York; St. Martin's Press for the Trade Policy Research Centre, 1973. 304p.	1	1
Johnson, E.A.J. The Organization of Space in Developing Countries. Cambridge, Mass.; Harvard University Press, 1970. 452p.	2	2
Johnson, Glenn L., and C. L. Quance, eds. The Overproduction Trap in U. S. Agriculture. Baltimore; Johns Hopkins University Press, 1972. 211p.	1	1
Johnson, Glenn L., and A. Maunder, eds. Rural Change: The Challenge for Agricultural Economists. Westmead, England; Grover; and Mountclair, N.J.; Allenheld, Osmun, 1981. 738p.	2	2
Johnson, Glenn L., and S. H. Wittwer. Agricultural Technology Until 2030: Prospects, Priorities, and Policies. East Lansing; Michigan State University, Agricultural Experiment Station, 1984. 61p.	1	1
Johnson, Paul R. The Economics of the Tobacco Industry. New York; Praeger, 1984. 157p.	2	2

	Rankings	
	Developed countries	Third World
Johnson, Stanley, Zuhair Hassan and Richard D. Green. Demand Systems Estimation: Methods and Applications. Ames, Iowa; Iowa State University Press, 1984. 178p.	1	1
Johnston, Bruce F. and W. C. Clark. Redesigning Rural Development: A Strategic Perspective. Baltimore, Md; Johns Hopkins University Press, 1982. 311p.	3	2
Johnston, Bruce F., et al, eds. U.S.-Mexico Relations: Agriculture and Rural Development. Stanford University Press, 1987. 400p.	2	1
Johnston, Bruce F. and Peter Kilby. Agriculture and Structural Transformation: Economic Strategies in Late-Developing Countries. New York; Oxford University Press, 1975. 474p.	1	1
Jones, James R., ed. East-West Agricultural Trade. Boulder, Colo.; Westview Press, 1985. 256p.	2	1
Jones, W.O. Marketing Staple Food Crops in Tropical Africa. Ithaca: Cornell University Press, 1972. 293p.	2	1
Jordan, Wayne R., ed. Water and Water Policy in World Food Supplies. College Station; Texas A & M University Press, 1987. 466p.	2	2
Joshi, P.C. Institutional Aspects of Agricultural Development: India in the Asian Context. Riverdale, Maryland; Riverdale Co., 1987. 200p.	3	2
Josling, Timothy E. International Dimensions of Agricultural and Food Policies. New York: Macmillan, 1985. 320p.	2	1
Josling, Timothy E., B. Davey, A. McFarquhar, A. C. Hannah, and D. Hamway. Burdens and Benefits of Farm-Support Policies. London; Trade Policy Research Centre, 1972. 85p.	3	2
Judge, George G., et al. The Theory and Practice of Econometrics. 2d ed. New York; Wiley, 1985. 1019p. (1st ed. 1980, 793p.)	1	1
Kadlec, John E. Farm Management: Decisions, Operation, Control. Englewood Cliffs, N.J.; Prentice-Hall, 1985. 429p. Q	1	1
Kahlon, A. S., and M. V. George. Agricultural Marketing and Price Policies. New Delhi, India; Allied, 1985. 283p.	3	2
Kahlon, A. S. and K. Singh. Managing Agricultural Finance: Theory and Practice. New Dehli; Allied, 1985. 283p. (Distributed by South Asia Books)	3	2
Kanon, D. D'Eveloppement ou Appauvissement. Paris; Economica, 1985. 188p.	3	3
Kay, Ronald D. Farm Management: Planning, Control, and Implementation. 2d ed. New York; McGraw-Hill Book Co., 1986. 401p. (1st ed. 1981, 370p.)	3	2
Kearl, Bryant, ed. Field Data Collection in the Social Sciences: Experiences in Africa and the Middle East. New York; Agricultural Development Council, 1976. 200p.	3	2
Kelley, Allen C., J. G. Williamson and R. J. Cheetham. Dualistic Economic Development: Theory and History. Chicago; University of Chicago Press, 1972. 399p.	2	2

	Rankings	
	Developed countries	Third World
Kendrick, J. W. and Beatrice N. Vaccara, eds. New Developments in Productivity Measurement. Chicago: University of Chicago Press, 1980. 717p.	2	1
Kennedy, E. and Bruce Cogill. Income and Nutritional Effects of the Commercialization of Agriculture in Southwestern Kenya. Washington, D.C., International Food Policy Research Institute, 1987. 60 p. (IFPRI Research Report 63)	3	3
Khusro, A.M. Economics of Land Reform and Farm Size in India. Madras, India; MacMillan, 1973. 162p.	3	2
Kilmer, Richard L., and W. J. Armbruster, eds. Economic Efficiency in Agricultural and Food Marketing. Ames; Iowa State University Press. 1987. 336p.	2	1
Knudsen, O. and P. L. Scandizzo. Nutrition and Food Needs in Developing Countries. Washington, D.C.; World Bank, 1979. (World Bank Staff Working Paper No. 328)	3	3
Knutson, Ronald D., J. B. Penn, and W. T. Boehm. Agricultural and Food Policy. Englewood Cliffs, N.J.; Prentice-Hall, 1983. 387p.	2	1
Kocher, J. E. Rural Development, Income Distribution, and Fertility Decline. New York; Population Council, 1973. 105p.	3	3
Koo, A.Y.C. Land Market Distortion and Tenure Reform. Ames; Iowa State University Press, 1982. 137p.	3	2
Koo, Won W., ed. Transportation Models for Agricultural Products. Boulder, Colo.; Westview Press, 1985. 175p.	3	2
Krueger, Anne O. and Vernon W. Ruttan. The Development Impact of Economic Assistance to LDC's. Minneapolis and St. Paul: University of Minnesota Economic Development Center, March 1983. 2 vols.	2	3
Krutilla, John V., and Anthony C. Fisher. The Economics of Natural Environments: Studies in the Valuation of Commodity and Amenity Resources. Rev. ed. Baltimore; Johns Hopkins University Press for Resources for the Future, 1985. 300p. (1st ed. 1975, 292p.)	2	2
Kuhn, Thomas. Structure of Scientific Revolutions. 2d ed. University of Chicago Press, 1970, 210p. (1st ed. 1962, 172p.)	1	2
La-Anyane, Seth. Economics of Agricultural Development in Tropical Africa. New York; Wiley and Sons, Inc., 1985. 150p.	3	2
Langham, Max R., and Ralph H. Retzlaff, ed. Agricultural Sector Analysis in Asia. Singapore; Singapore University Press for the Agricultural Development Council, 1982. 420p.	2	2
Langoni, C. G. Distribuicao de Renda e Desenvolvimento Economico do Brasil (Income Distribution and Economic Development of Brazil). Rio de Janeiro; eda Expressao e Cultura, 1973. 315p.	3	3
Lardy, Nicholas R. Agriculture in China's Modern Economic Development. Cambridge University Press, 1983. 285p.	1	2
Law, Alton D. International Commodity Agreements: Setting,	3	2

	Rankings	
	Developed countries	Third World
Performance, and Prospects. Lexington, Mass.; Lexington Books, 1975. 128p.		
Lea, David A. M., and D. P. Chaudhri, eds. Rural Development and the State: Contradictions and Dilemmas in Developing Countries. London and New York: Methuen, 1983. 351p.	3	2
Lee, Warren F., et al. Agricultural Finance. 8th ed. Ames; Iowa State University Press, 1988. 468p. (Primary author varies among editions.)	3	2
Leed, Theodore, and Gene A. German. Food Merchandising: Principles and Practices. 3d ed. New York; Lebhar-Friedman, 1985. 488p. (1st ed. New York; Chain-Store Age Books, 1973. 389p.)	2	2
Lehmann, D., ed. Peasants, Landlords, and Governments:Agrarian Reform in the Third World. New York: Holmes and Meier Publishers, 1974. 320p.	3	2
Leibenstein, H. Economic Backwardness and Economic Growth: Studies in the Theory of Economic Development. New York: Wiley, 1957. 295p.	2	2
Lele, Uma J. Food Grain Marketing in India: Private Performance and Public Policy. Ithaca, New York; Cornell University Press, 1971. 264p.	2	1
Lele, Uma J. The Design of Rural Development: Lessons from Africa. 2d ed. Baltimore; Johns Hopkins University Press for the World Bank, 1979. 246p.	2	1
Leonard, David K. Reaching the Peasant Farmer: Organization Theory and Practice in Kenya. Chicago; University of Chicago Press, 1977. 297p.	2	1
Leontief, W. W. Essays in Economics: Theories and Theorizing. New York; Oxford University Press, 1966. 252p.	2	1
Lewis, W. A. The Evolution of the International Economic Order. Princeton; Princeton University Press, 1978. 81p.	3	3
Lippit, Victor D. Land Reform and Economic Development in China: A Study of Institutional Change and Development Finance. White Plains, New York; International Arts and Sciences Press, 1974. 183p.	3	2
Little, Ian. Economic Development: Theory, Policy and International Relations. New York: Basic Books, 1982. 452p.	2	1
Livingstone, I., and H. W. Ord. Agricultural Economics for Tropical Africa. London; Heinemann, 1981. 294p.	3	2
Long, Norman, Introduction to Sociology of Rural Development. Boulder, Colo.: Westview Press, 1977. 221p.	2	2
Luz, Fabio. Seguros Agro Pecuarios. 2d ed. Rio de Janeiro; Ministerio da Agricultura, Servico de Economia Rural, 1949. 102p.	3	3
MacBean, Alasdair I., and P.N. Snowden. International Institutions in Trade and Finance. London and Boston: Allen and Unwin, 1981. 255p.	3	2

	Rankings	
	Developed countries	Third World
MacPherson, Stewart. Social Policy in the Third World: the Social Dilemmas of Underdevelopment. Totowa, NJ: Allanheld, Osmun, 1982. 220p.	3	2
Madden, J.P. Economies of Size Studies: A Collection of Papers Presented August 3–4, 1983 at a Workshop at Purdue University in West Lafayette, Indiana. Ames: Iowa State University Press for the Center for Agricultural and Rural Development, 1984. 220p.	2	2
Mahajan, V. S. Growth of Agriculture and Industry in India. New Delhi; Deep and Deep, 1983. 176p.	3	2
Makeham, J. P., and L. R. Malcolm. The Economics of Tropical Farm Management. Cambridge University Press, 1986. 202p.	3	2
Malthus, T. R. Principles of Political Economy Considered with a View to Their Practical Application. 2d ed. London; William Pickering, 1836. 446p. (Latest reprint by Fairfield, N.J.; A. M. Kelley, 1986.)	1	1
Manetsch, T. J., M. L. Hayenga, A. N. Halter, T. W. Carroll, M. H. Abkin, D. R. Byerlee, K-Y. Chong, G. Page, E. Kellogg, and G. L. Johnson. A Generalized Simulation Approach to Agricultural Sector Analysis with Special Reference to Nigeria. East Lansing: Michigan State University, Department of Agricultural Economics, 1971. 362p.	2	1
Mann, Harold H. Social Framework of Agriculture: India, Middle East, England. New York; Augustus M. Kelley Publ., 1967. 501p.	3	2
Maos, Jacob. The Spatial Organization of New Land Settlement in Latin America. Boulder, Colo.; Westview Press, 1984. 170p.	3	2
Marten, Gerald G., ed. Traditional Agriculture in Southeast Asia: A Human Ecology Perspective. Boulder, Colo.; Westview Press, 1986. 358p.	2	2
Martin, Lee R., ed. A Survey of Agricultural Economics Literature. Minneapolis; University of Minnesota Press for the American Agricultural Economics Association, 1977–1981. 3 vols. (Vol. 4 due in 1992)	1	1
Marx, K. Capital: A Critique of Political Economy. New York: Modern Library, 1909–12. 3 vols. (1st German ed., 1867) Latest reprint by New York; Vintage Books, 1976–1981.	2	1
Massey, Garth. Substance and Change: Lessons of Agropastoralism in Somalia. Boulder, Colo.; Westview Press, 1986. 300p.	3	2
Maunder, Allen H., and U. Renborg, eds. Agriculture in a Turbulent World Economy; Important Research from the Proceedings of the Nineteenth International Conference of Agricultural Economists in Malaga, Spain. London; Gower Publ., 1987. 820p.	1	1
Maunder, Allen H., and Kazushi Ohkawa, eds. Growth and Eq-	1	1

	Rankings	
	Developed countries	Third World
uity in Agricultural Development: Proceedings of the Eighteenth International Conference of Agricultural Economists. London; Gower Publ. Co., 1984. 619p.		
McCalla, Alex F., and T. E. Josling, eds. Imperfect Markets in Agricultural Trade. Montclair, N.J.; Allanheld, Osmun and Co. Pubs., Inc., 1981. 250p.	1	1
McCalla, Alex F., and T. E. Josling. Agricultural Policies and World Markets. New York; Macmillan, 1985. 304 p.	2	2
McDowell, Robert E., and P.E. Hildebrand. Integrated Crop and Animal Production: Making the Most of Resources Available to Small Farms in Developing Countries. New York: The Rockefeller Foundation, 1980. 78p.	2	1
McGranahan, D.V., C. Richard-Proust, N.V. Sovani, and M. Subramanian. Contents and Measurement of Socioeconomic Development. New York: Praeger Publishers, 1972. 161p.	3	2
McPherson, W.W., ed. Economic Development of Tropical Agriculture: Theory, Policy, Strategy and Organization. Gainesville: University of Florida Press, 1968. 328p.	2	2
Meier, G.M., ed. Leading Issues in Economic Development. 3d ed. New York: Oxford University Press, 1976. 862p.	1	1
Mellor, John W., and G.M. Desai, eds. Agricultural Change and Rural Poverty on a Theme by Dharm Narain. Baltimore; Johns Hopkins University Press for International Food Policy Research Institute, 1985. 233p. (Reprinted by Oxford University Press, 1986.)	1	1
Mellor, John W. The New Economics of Growth: A Strategy for India and the Developing World. Ithaca, New York: Cornell University Press, 1976. 335p.	1	1
Mellor, John W. Economics of Agricultural Development. Ithaca, New York; Cornell University Press, 1970. 418p. Q	1	1
Mellor, John W., C. L. Delgado, and M. J. Blackie, eds. Accelerating Food Production in Sub-Saharan Africa. Baltimore; Johns Hopkins University Press, 1987. 417p.	2	2
Melville, T. and M. Melville. Guatemala: The Politics of Land Ownership. New York; Free Press, 1971. 320p.	3	2
Milliken, George A. and Dallas E. Johnson. Analysis of Messy Data. New York; Van Nostrand Reinhold, 1984. 2 vols.	2	2
Mitchell, Mark. Agriculture and Policy: Methodology for the Analysis of Developing Country Agricultural Sectors. London, Ithaca Press, 1985. 179 p.	3	3
Moll, H.A.J. The Economics of Oil Palm. Wageningen, The Netherlands, PUDOC, 1987. 288p.	3	2
Montgomery, John D., ed. International Dimensions of Land Reform. Boulder, Colo.; Westview Press, 1984. 239p.	2	2
Moock, Joyce L. Understanding Africa's Rural Households and Farming Systems. Boulder, Colo.: Westview Press, 1986. 234p.	2	1

	Rankings	
	Developed countries	Third World
Moris, J. Managing Induced Rural Development. Bloomington, Indiana; International Development Institute, 1981. 190p.	3	2
Mosher, A. T. Thinking About Rural Development. New York; The Agricultural Development Council, 1976. 350p.	2	1
Mosher, A. T. Getting Agriculture Moving: Essentials for Development and Modernization. New York; Praeger for Agricultural Development Council, 1966. 191p.	2	1
Mosher, A. T. Creating a Progressive Rural Structure. New York; Agricultural Development Council, 1969. 172p.	2	3
Moyer, R., and S. Hollander, eds. Markets and Marketing in Developing Economies. Homewood, Ill.; Interscience Publ., 1968. 264p.	3	3
Murdoch, William W. The Poverty of Nations: The Political Economy of Hunger and Population. Baltimore; Johns Hopkins University Press, 1980. 382p.	2	2
Myint, Hla. The Economics of the Developing Countries. New York; Praeger, 1964. 192p.	2	1
Myrdal, Gunnar. Against the Stream: Critical Essays in Economics. New York; Random House, 1973. 336p.	1	1
Myrdal, Gunnar. Rich Lands and Poor: The Road to World Prosperity. New York: Harper, 1957. 168p. (Also issued as Economic Theory and Under-Developed Regions. London; Duckworth, 1957. 167p.)	1	1
Nair, Kusum. Transforming Traditionally: Land and Labor use in Agriculture in Asia and Africa. Riverdale, Maryland; Riverdale Co., 1983. 168p.	2	3
Nakajima, Chihiro. Subjective Equilibrium Theory of the Farm Household. Translation of his Noko Shutai Kinkoron. Amsterdam and New York, Elsevier Science Publ. Co., 1986. 302p. (Developments in Agricultural Economics, vol. 3).	3	2
National Research Council (U.S.). The African Challenge: In Search of Appropriate Development Strategies. Nairobi; Heinemann, 1986. 182p.	3	3
National Research Council (U.S.). Post-Harvest Food Losses in Developing Countries. Washington; National Academy of Sciences, 1978. 206p.	3	3
National Research Council (U.S.). Conference on Agricultural Research Priorities for Economic Development in Africa. Washington, D.C.; National Academy of Sciences, 1968. 3 vols.	3	3
Nelson, Michael. The Development of Tropical Lands: Policy Issues in Latin America. Baltimore; Johns Hopkins University Press, 1973. 323p.	1	1
Newby, Howard, ed. International Perspectives in Rural Sociology. Chichester, England and New York: Wiley, 1978. 220p.	2	3
Ofori, Patrick E. Land in Africa: Its Administration, Law, Ten-	3	2

	Rankings	
	Developed countries	Third World
ure and Use: A Select Bibliography. Nendeln, Liechtenstein; Kraus International Publications, 1978. 199p.		
Oh, Heung Keun. Development of Food and Agricultural Statistics in Asia and Pacific Region, 1965–1987. Seoul, Korea Rural Economics Institute, 1988. 397p.	3	3
Ohkawa, K., B. F. Johnston, and H. Kaneda, eds. Agriculture and Economic Growth: Japan's Experience. University of Tokyo Press, 1969; and Princeton University Press, 1970. 433p.	1	1
Olson, Mancur. The Logic of Collective Action: Public Goods and the Theory of Groups. Cambridge, Mass.: Harvard University Press, 1965. 176p. (Reprinted in 1971, 186p.)	1	2
Organisation for Economic Co-operation and Development. Problems of Agricultural Trade. Paris: OECD Publications and Information Center, 1982. 178p.	3	2
Organisation for Economic Co-operation and Development. National Policies and Agricultural Trade. Paris, OECD, 1987. 333p.	3	2
Organisation for Economic Co-operation and Development. Agricultural Trade With Developing Countries. Paris; OECD, 1984. 113p.	3	2
Organisation for Economic Co-operation and Development . The Instability of Agricultural Commodity Markets. Paris; OECD, 1980. 237p.	3	2
Orlove, Benjamin S. and Glynn Custred, eds. Land and Power in Latin America: Agrarian Economies and Social Process in the Andes. New York; Holmes and Meier, 1980. 258p.	3	2
Osburn, Donald D., and Kenneth C. Schneeberger. Modern Agriculture Management. Reston, Virginia; Reston Publ. Co, 1978. 369p.	3	2
Oxaal, I., T. Barnett, and D. Booth. Beyond the Sociology of Development: Economy and Society in Latin America and Africa. London and Boston; Routledge and Kegan Paul, 1975. 295p.	3	3
Paarlberg, Don. Farm and Food Policy: Issues of the 1980s. Lincoln; University of Nebraska Press, 1980. 338p.	1	1
Paarlberg, Robert L. Food Trade and Foreign Policy: India, the Soviet Union, and the United States. Ithaca, New York: Cornell University Press, 1985. 266p.	1	2
Pacey, Arnold and Philip Payne, eds. Agricultural Development and Nutrition. London, Hutchinson; Boulder, Colo., Westview Press, 1985. 255p.	3	3
Paige, Jeffery M. Agrarian Revolution: Social Movements and Export Agriculture in the Underdeveloped World. New York; Free Press, 1978. 435p.	2	2
Panda, R. K. Agricultural Indebtedness and Institutional Finance, India. India; Ashish Publ., 1985. 180p.	3	2

	Rankings	
	Developed countries	Third World
Papi, Ugo and Charles S. Nunn, eds. Economic Problems of Agriculture in Developed Societies: Proceedings of a Conference Held by the International Economic Association. New York; Saint Martin's Press, and London; Macmillan, 1969. 671p. (Reprinted: New York; Stockton, 1986) (International Economic Assn. Ser.)	2	2
Paulino, L. A. Food in the Third World: Past Trends and Projection to 2000. Washington, D.C.; International Food Policy Research Institute, 1986. 76p. (IFPRI Research Report no. 52).	3	3
Pearse, Andrew C. Seeds of Plenty, Seeds of Want: Social and Economic Implications of the Green Revolution. Oxford; Clarendon Press; and New York; Oxford University Press, 1980. 262p.	2	3
Pearson, Scott R., et al. Portuguese Agriculture in Transition. Ithaca, New York; Cornell University Press, 1987. 283p.	3	2
Pedhazur, Elazar J. Multiple Regression in Behavioral Research. 2d ed. New York: Holt, Rinehart and Winston, 1982. 822p.	3	2
Penson, John B., Jr., Rulon Pope, and M.L. Cook. Introduction to Agricultural Economics. Englewood Cliffs, N.J.; Prentice-Hall, 1986. 556p.	3	2
Peterson, Trudy H. Farmers, Bureaucrats, and Middlemen: Historical Perspectives on American Agriculture. Washington, D.C.: Howard University Press, 1980. 357p.	1	2
Pigou, A. C. The Economics of Welfare. 4th ed. London: Macmillan, 1932. 837p.	1	1
Pimentel, D. and C. W. Hall, eds. Food and Energy Resources. New York; Academic Press, 1984. 268p.	1	2
Pineiro, M., E. Trigo, and R. Florentino, eds. Technical Change and Social Conflict in Agriculture. Boulder, Colo.; Westview Press, 1983. 248p.	1	1
Pingali, Prabhu, Yves Bigot, and Hans Binswanger. Agricultural Mechanization and the Evolution of Farming Systems in Sub-Saharan Africa. Baltimore: Johns Hopkins University Press, 1987. 224p. AAEA Award Winner Q	2	1
Pinstrup-Anderson, Per. Agricultural Research and Technology in Economic Development. London; Longman, Inc., 1982. 304p.	1	1
Pinstrup-Andersen, Per, ed. Food Subsidies in Developing Countries: Costs, Benefits, and Policy Options. Baltimore; Publ. for Int. Food Policy Research Inst. by Johns Hopkins University Press, 1988. 374p.	1	1
Pinstrup-Anderson, Per. Nutritional Consequences of Agricultural Projects: Conceptual Relationships and Assessment Approaches. Washington, D.C.; World Bank, 1981. 93p. (World Bank Staff Working Paper no. 456.)	1	1

	Rankings	
	Developed countries	Third World
Pollard, S. The Idea of Progress: History and Society. London: Watts, 1968. 220p. (The New Thinkers Library No. 26) (Reprinted: Hammondsworth, Eng.; Penguin, 1971.)	3	2
Pomareda, Carlos. Financial Policies and Management of Agricultural Development Banks. Boulder, Colo.; Westview Press, 1984. 180p.	2	2
Pontecorvo, G., ed. The Management of Food Policy. New York; Arno Press for Columbia University, Graduate School of Business, 1976. 299p.	3	2
Popper, K. R. The Logic of Scientific Discovery. New York; Basic Books, 1959. 479p.	1	2
Prasad, Ramayan. Agricultural Taxation and Economic Development. New Delhi; Deep and Deep Publications, 1987. 207p.	3	2
Rae, Alan N. Crop Management Economics. London and Granada; Brookfield Publishing Co., 1977. 525p. (Reprinted by London; Grosby Lockwood Staples, 1981).	3	2
Rahman, Mushtaqur. Agrarian Egalitarianism, Land Tenures and Land Reforms in South Asia. Paper ed. Dubuque, Iowa; Kendall/Hunt Publ. Co., 1980. 200p.	3	2
Rahmato, Dessalegn. Agrarian Reform in Ethiopia. Uppsala; Scandinavian Institute of African Studies, 1984. 105p. (Reprinted by Trenton, N.J.; Red Sea Press, 1985)	3	2
Raj, K. N., ed. Essays on the Commercialization of Indian Agriculture. Oxford University Press, 1986. 375p.	3	2
Raper, Arthur F. Rural Development in Action: The Comprehensive Experiment at Comilla, East Pakistan. Ithaca, New York; Cornell University Press, 1970. 351p.	2	2
Rawski, Evelyn S. Agricultural Change and the Peasant Economy of South China. Cambridge, Mass.; Harvard University Press, 1972. 280p. (East Asian Ser: No. 66)	2	2
Ray, P. K. Agriculture Insurance: Principles and Organization and Application to Developing Countries. 2d ed. Oxford; Pergamon Press, 1981. 419p.	3	3
Reddy, D. Obul. Co-operative Agricultural Development Banks: A Case Study of Andhra Pradesh. Delhi, India; B. R. Publ. Corp., 1987. 429p.	3	2
Reutlinger, Shlomo and Marcelo Selowski. Malnutrition and Poverty: Magnitude and Policy Options. Baltimore; John Hopkins Univ. Press, 1976. 82p. (World Bank Occasional Paper 23)	1	2
Reynolds, Lloyd G., ed. Agriculture in Development Theory. New Haven; Yale University Press, 1975. 510p.	1	1
Riddell, Robert. Regional Development Policy: The Struggle for Rural Progress in Low-Income Nationals. Aldershot, England; Gower, and New York; St. Martin's Press. 1985. 282p.	2	3
Ritson, Christopher. Agricultural Economics: Principles and Pol-	3	2

	Rankings	
	Developed countries	Third World
icy. New York; Saint Martin's Press, Inc., 1977. 409p. (Reprinted by Boulder, Colo.; Westview Press, 1982).		
Rivera, W. and S. Schram, eds. Agricultural Extension Worldwide: Issues, Practices and Emerging Priorities. London; Croom Helm, 1987. 294p.	3	3
Roberts, Colleen, ed. Agriculture Sector Symposium (8th, 1988 at World Bank): Trade, Aid and Policy Reform. Washington, D.C.; World Bank, 1988. 223p.	3	2
Robinson, E. A. G., ed. Problems in Economic Development: Proceedings of a Conference Held by the International Economic Association. New York; St. Martin's Press, 1965. 625p.	2	2
Rogers, Everett M. Modernization Among Peasants; the Impact of Communication. New York; Holt, Rinehart and Winston, 1969. 429p.	2	3
Rosenblum, J. W. ed. Agriculture in the 21st Century. New York; John Wiley and Sons, 1983. 415p.	2	2
Rostow, W. W. The Stages of Economic Growth: A Non-Communist Manifesto. 2d ed. Cambridge; Cambridge University Press, 1971. 253p. (1st ed. 1952, 178p.)	1	2
Roumasset, James A., Jean-Marc Boussard, and Inderjit Singh, eds. Risk, Uncertainty and Agricultural Development. Laguna, Philippines; Southeast Asian Regional Center for Graduate Study and Research in Agriculture; and New York; Agricultural Development Council, 1979. 453p.	1	1
Runge, C. Ford., ed. The Future of the North American Granary: Politics, Economics, and Resource Constraints in North American Agriculture. Ames; Iowa State University Press, 1985. 240p.	2	1
Ruthenberg, H. Farming Systems in the Tropics. 3d ed. Oxford; Clarendon, 1980, 424p. (1st ed. 1971, 313p.)	2	3
Ruttan, Vernon W. Agricultural Research Policy. Minneapolis; University of Minnesota Press, 1982. 369p.	1	1
Ruttan, Vernon W., and Carl Pray. Policy for Agricultural Research. Boulder, Colo.; Westview Press, 1987. 576p.	2	1
Sahu, Nirmal C. Economics of Forest Resources: Problems and Policies in a Regional Economy. Delhi, India; B. R. Publ. Corp., 1986. 360p. (Distributed by Apt. Bks.)	3	2
Salter, Leonard A., Jr. A Critical Review of Research in Land Economics. Minneapolis; University of Minnesota Press, 1948. 258p. (Reprinted in 1967). AAEA Classic	1	3
Samuelson, Paul. Foundations of Economic Analysis. Cambridge; Harvard University Press, 1947. 447p.	1	1
Sanderson, Fred H. and S. Roy. Food Trends and Prospects in India. Washington, D.C.; Brookings Institution, 1979. 162p.	3	3
Sanderson, Steven E. The Transformation of Mexican Agricul-	2	2

	Rankings	
	Developed countries	Third World
ture: International Structure and the Politics of Rural Change. Princeton University Press, 1986. 324p.		
Sarma, J.S. Agricultural Policy in India: Growth with Equity. Ottawa, Canada; Int. Develop. Research Centre, 1982. 94p.	3	3
Saunders, Robert J. and Jeremy J. Warford. Village Water Supply: Economics and Policy in the Developing World. Baltimore; Johns Hopkins University Press, 1976. 279p.	3	2
Scandizzo, Pasquale L., Peter Hazell and Jock Anderson. Risky Agricultural Markets: Price Forecasting and the Need for Intervention Policies. Boulder, Colo.; Westview Press, 1984. 142p.	2	2
Schmitz, A., Alex F. McCalla, Donald O. Mitchell, and Colin Carter. Grain Export Cartels. Cambridge, MA; Ballinger, 1981. 298p. Q	2	2
Schuh, G. Edward, ed. Technology, Human Capital and the World Food Problem. St. Paul, Minn.; University of Minn. Press, 1986. 167p. (Minnesota Agr. Exp. Station Misc. Publ. 37)	2	3
Schuh, G. Edward, and Jennifer L. McCoy, eds. Food, Agriculture and Development in the Pacific Basin. Boulder, Colo.; Westview Press, 1986. 292p.	1	1
Schuh, G. Edward. The Agricultural Development of Brazil. New York; Praeger Publishers, 1970. 456p. (Benchmark Studies on Agricultural Development in Latin America, no. 6) Q	2	2
Schultz, T. W., ed. Economics of the Family: Marriage, Children and Human Capital. Chicago; University of Chicago Press, 1974. 584p. (Originally published as supplement to the Journal of Political Economy)	1	2
Schultz, T. W., ed. Distortions of Agricultural Incentives. Bloomington; Indiana University Press, 1978. 343p.	1	1
Schultz, T. W. Economic Crisis in World Agriculture. Ann Arbor; University of Michigan Press, 1965. 114p.	1	1
Schultz, T. W. The Economic Organization of Agriculture. New York; McGraw-Hill, 1953. 374p.	1	1
Schultz, T. W. The Economic Value of Education. New York; Columbia University Press, 1963. 92p.	1	1
Schultz, T.W. Transforming Traditional Agriculture. New Haven, Conn; Yale Univ. Press, 1964. 212p. (Reprinted by Arno Press, 1976) AAEA Classic	1	1
Schumpeter, Joseph A. History of Economic Analysis. New York; Oxford University Press, 1954. 1260p.	1	1
Schutjer, W.A. and C.S. Stokes, eds. Rural Development and Human Fertility. New York; Macmillan Publ. Co., 1984. 318p.	2	3

	Rankings	
	Developed countries	Third World
Scott, A. Natural Resources: The Economics of Conservation. Toronto; University of Toronto Press, 1955. 184p.	2	2
Scott, James C. The Moral Economy of the Peasant: Rebellion and Subsistence in Southern Asia. New Haven; Yale University Press, 1976. 246p.	1	1
Seetharam, G. N. Strategy and Tactics of India's Agricultural Development: The Role of the State. Delhi; Ajanta Publ., 1984. 154p.	3	2
Seligson, Mitchell A. Gap Between Rich and Poor: Contending Perspectives on the Political Economy of Development. Boulder, Colo.; Westview Press, 1984. 418p.	2	2
Seligson, Mitchell A. Peasants of Costa Rica and the Development of Agrarian Capitalism. Madison; University of Wisconsin Press, 1980. 220p.	2	2
Sen, Amartya K. Employment, Technology and Development; A Study Prepared for the I.L.O. Oxford; Clarendon Press, 1975. 193p.	2	2
Sen, Bandhudas. The Green Revolution in India: A Perspective. New York, Wiley, 1974. 118p.	2	2
Sen, Chiranjib. Essays on the Transformation of India's Agrarian Economy. New York; Garland Publ., 1984. 285p. (Outstanding Dissertations in Economic Ser.) (Stanford Univ. Thesis, 1978).	3	2
Sender, J., and S. Smith. The Development of Capitalism in Africa. London; Methuen, 1986. 177p.	3	3
Shah, A. K. Professional Management for the Cooperatives. Vikas, India; Advent Books, Incorporated, 1984. 350p.	3	2
Shand, R.T., ed. Agricultural Development in Asia. Canberra; Australian National University Press, 1969. 360p.	2	2
Shaner, Willis W., P.F. Philipp, and W.R. Schmehl. Farming Systems Research and Development: Guidelines for Developing Countries. Boulder, Colo.; Westview Press, 1982. 414p.	2	1
Shanin, Teodor, ed. Peasants and Peasant Societies: Selected Readings. 2d ed. Oxford; Blackwell, 1987. 497p.	3	2
Siamwalla, A. and S. Haykin. The World Rice Market: Structure, Conduct, and Performance. Washington,D.C.; International Food Policy Research Institute, 1983. 79p. (IFPRI Research Report No. 39).	3	2
Silberberg, Eugene. The Structure of Economics: A Mathematical Analysis. New York, McGraw-Hill, 1978. 543p.	3	3
Singh, J. P. The Role of Institutional Finance in Agriculture. New Delhi; Ashish Publ. House, 1986. 378p.	3	2
Singh, Rem Babu. Geography of Rural Development: The Indian Micro-Level Experience. New Delhi: Inter-India Publications, 1986. 246p.	3	2

	Rankings	
	Developed countries	Third World
Sinha, R. ed. The World Food Problem: Consensus and Conflict. Oxford, England; Pergamon Press, 1978. 671p.	3	3
Smith, Peter J. Agricultural Project Management: Monitoring and Control of Implementation. London and New York, Elsevier Applied Science Publishers, 1984. 190p.	3	3
Smith, T. Lynn, and Paul E. Zopf, Jr. Demography: Principles and Methods. 2d ed. Port Washington, New York; Alfred Publ., 1976. 615p.	3	3
Snedecor, George W., and William G. Cochran. Statistical Methods, 8th ed. Ames; Iowa State University Press, 1989. 503p.	1	1
Snodgrass, Milton M. and Tim Wallace. Agriculture, Economics and Resource Management. 2d ed. Englewood Cliffs; Prentice-Hall, Inc., 1980. 546p.	2	2
Solow, R.M. Growth Theory: An Exposition. Oxford; Oxford University Press. 1970. 109p. (Radcliffe Lectures, 1969) (Reprinted 1988)	2	1
Sorokin, Pitrim A. Hunger as a Factor in Human Affairs. Gainesville; University Press of Florida, 1975. 319p.	3	3
Southworth, Herman M., and Bruce F. Johnston, eds. Agricultural Development and Economic Growth. Ithaca, New York; Cornell University Press, 1967. 608p. (Reprinted in 1979.) Q	1	1
Southworth, Herman M., and M. Barnett, eds. Experience in Farm Mechanization in Southeast Asia. New York; Agricultural Development Council, 1974. 345p.	2	2
Srinivasan, T.N. and Pranab K. Bardhan, eds. Rural Poverty in South Asia. New York, Columbia University Press, 1988. 565 p.	3	2
Stavenhagen, Rodolfo, ed. Agrarian Problems and Peasant Movement in Latin America. Garden City, New York; Doubleday, 1970. 583p.	2	1
Stavis, Benedict. Making Green Revolution: The Politics of Agricultural Development in China. Ithaca, New York; Cornell University Press, 1974. 274p.	3	3
Sterkenburg, J. J. Rural Development and Rural Development Studies: Cases From Africa and Asia. Amsterdam: Koninklijk Nederlands Aardrijkskundig Genootschap; Utrecht: Geografische Instituut. Rijksuniversitit Utrecht, 1987. 188p. (Nederlandse Geografische Studies; 46).	3	3
Stevens, Robert D., and Cathy L. Jabara. Agricultural Development Principles: Economic Theory and Empirical Evidence. Baltimore; Johns Hopkins University Press, 1988. 478p.	3	1
Stiglitz, J.E., and H. Uzawa, eds. Readings in the Modern Theory of Economic Growth. Cambridge, Mass.; MIT Press, 1969. 497p.	2	1
Streeten, Paul, Shadid Burke, Mahbub Haq, Norman Hicks, and	3	3

	Rankings	
	Developed countries	Third World
Frances Stewart. First Things First: Meeting Basic Needs in Developing Countries. New York; Oxford University Press, 1981. 206p.		
Streeten, Paul. What Price Food? Agricultural Price-Policies in Developing Countries. New York; St. Martin's Press, 1987. 127p. (Ithaca, N.Y.; Cornell Unversity Press paperback reprint, 1988)	2	1
Subbarao, K. Rice Marketing System and Compulsory Levies in Andhra Pradesh: A Study of Public Intervention in Food-Grain Marketing, India. Bombay; Allied, 1978. 173p.	3	2
Sundaram, I. S. Anti-Poverty Rural Development in India. New Delhi; D.K. Publications, 1984. 342p.	3	3
Super, J.C. and T.C. Wright, eds. Food, Politics and Society in Latin America. Lincoln; University of Nebraska Press, 1985. 261p.	2	2
Szymanski, Albert. The Logic of Imperialism. New York; Praeger Publishers, 1981. 598p.	3	2
Taeuber, Karl E., L.L. Bumpass, and J.A. Sweet, eds. Social Demography. New York; Academic Press, 1978. 336p.	1	2
Tang, Anthony M. An Analytical and Empirical Investigation of Agriculture in Mainland China, 1952–1980. Taipei, Taiwan; Chung-Hua Institute for Economic Research, 1984. 230p.	3	3
Tang, Anthony M. and B. Stone. Food Production in the People's Republic of China. Washington, D.C.; International Food Policy and Research Institute, 1980. 2 vols. (IFPRI Research Report No.15)	2	2
Tang, Chi-Yu. An Economic Study of Chinese Agriculture. New York; Garland Publ., Inc., 1980. 514p.	3	2
Taylor, Henry C., and Anne D. Taylor. The Story of Agricultural Economics in the United States, 1840–1932. Ames, Iowa State College Press, 1952. 1121 p. (Reprinted by Greenwood Press, 1974).	2	1
Taylor, Kit S. Sugar and the Underdevelopment of Northeastern Brazil, 1500–1970. Paper ed. Gainesville; University Presses of Florida, 1978. 167p.	3	2
Theil, Henri. Economic Forecasts and Policy. 2d rev. ed. Amsterdam; North Holland Publishing, 1961. 567p.	2	1
Thiam, Tan Bock and Shao-Er Ong, eds. Readings in Asian Farm Management. Singapore University Press, 1979. 350p.	2	2
Thorbecke, Erik, ed. Agricultural Sector Analysis and Models in Developing Countries. Rome; Food and Agriculture Organization, 1982. 415p. (English and French). (FAO Economic and Social Development Papers: No. 5).	2	2
Thorner, Daniel. The Agrarian Prospect in India. Five Lectures Delivered in 1955 at the Delhi School of Economics. 2d rev. ed. Bombay; Allied Publishers, 1976. 82p.	3	2
Timmer, C. Peter, Walter P. Falcon, and Scott R. Pearson. Food	1	1

	Rankings	
	Developed countries	Third World
Policy Analysis. Baltimore; Johns Hopkins University Press, 1983. 301p. Q		
Timmer, C. Peter. Getting Prices Right: The Scope and Limits of Agricultural Price Policy. Ithaca, New York; Cornell University Press, 1986. 160p.	2	1
Timmer, Peter C., ed. The Corn Economy of Indonesia. Ithaca, N.Y.; Cornell University Press, 1987. 302p.	2	1
Tinker, I., M. B. Bransen, and M. Buvinic, eds. Women and World Development: Proceedings.... New York; Praeger, 1976. 228p.	3	3
Todaro, Michael. Economic Development in the Third World. 4th ed. New York; Longmans, 1989. 698p. (1st ed. 1977, and others have different subtitles. 440p.)	1	1
Tolley, G.S., V. Thomas, and C.M. Wong. Agricultural Price Policies and the Developing Countries. Baltimore; Johns Hopkins University Press, 1982. 242p.	2	2
Tomek, W.G. and K. L. Robinson. Agricultural Product Prices. 2d ed. Ithaca, New York; Cornell University Press, 1981. 361p. (Original ed., 1972)	1	1
Tweeten, Luther. G. Foundations of Farm Policy. 2d ed. Lincoln: University of Nebraska Press, 1979. 567p.	1	1
Uphoff, N.T., ed. Rural Development and Local Organization in Asia. Delhi, India; Macmillan India Lmtd., 1982. 1 vol.	3	2
Valdés, Alberto, ed. Food Security for Developing Countries. Boulder, Colo.; Westview Press, 1981. 351p.	1	1
Valdés, Alberto, et al., eds. Economics and the Design of Small Farmer Technology. Ames; Iowa State University Press, 1979. 211p. + 2	2	1
Varian, H. Microeconomic Analysis. 2d ed. New York; W. W. Norton, 1984. 384p. (1st ed. 1978, 284p.)	1	2
Vink, A. P. Land Use in Advancing Agriculture. New York; Springer-Verlag, 1975. 450p. (Advanced Series in Agricultural Sciences, Vol. 1).	3	2
Von Oppen, M.; D. R. Raj,; P. Virinda and Sudhir Kumble, eds. Agricultural Markets in the Semi-Arid Tropics. Hyderabad, India; ICRISAT, 1985. 387p.	3	2
Von Pischke, J.D., Dale W. Adams and Gordon Donald, eds. Rural Financial Markets in Developing Countries: Their Use and Abuse. Baltimore; Johns Hopkins University Press, 1983. 411p.	2	1
Von Witzke, Harald, ed. Policy Coordination in World Agriculture. Kiel, Germany; Herbst, 1988. 245 p. 49DM	3	3
Walker, Thomas W., ed. Nicaragua: The First Five Years. New York; Praeger Publ., 1985. 561p.	2	2
Warriner, D. Land Reform in Principle and Practice. Oxford: Clarendon Press, 1969. 457p.	3	2

	Rankings	
	Developed countries	Third World
Waugh, Frederick V. Selected Writings on Agricultural Policy and Economic Analysis. Martin E. Abel and James P. Houck, eds. Minneapolis; University of Minnesota Press, 1984. 466p.	2	1
Webster, C.C., and P. N. Wilson. Agriculture in the Tropics. 2d ed. London and New York; Longman, 1988. 640p. (1st ed. 1966, 488p.)	3	3
Wennergren, E. Boyd, Morris Whitker, Charles Anholt. Agricultural Development in Bangladesh: Prospects for the Future. Boulder, Colo.; Westview Press, 1984. 373p.	2	2
Weyman, F. H. The Dynamics of the World Cocoa Market. Cambridge; M.I.T. Press, 1968. 253p. Q	2	1
Wharton, Clifton R., ed. Subsistence Agriculture and Economic Development. University of Chicago; Aldine Publishing Co., 1969. 481p.	1	1
Whyte, R. O. and P. Whyte. The Women of Rural Asia. Boulder, Colo.; Westview Press, 1982. 262p.	3	3
Whyte, W. F. and D. Boynton, eds. Higher Yielding Human Systems for Agriculture. Ithaca.,N.Y.; Cornell University Press, 1983. 342p.	2	3
Widstrand, Carl G., ed. Cooperatives and Rural Development in East Africa. Uppsala, Sweden; Scandinavian Institute of African Studies; New York, Africana Publ. Corp., 1970. 271 p.	3	2
Williams, D. B., ed. Agriculture in the Australian Economy. 2d ed. Sydney; Sydney University Press, 1982. (1st ed. 1967, 422p.)	3	2
Wionczek, Miguel. S. Inversion y Tecnologia Extranjera en America Latina (Investment and Foreign Technology in Latin America). Mexico; Joaquin Mortiz, 1971. 189p.	3	3
Wong, John, ed. Group Farming in Asia: Experiences and Potentials. Singapore; Singapore University Press, 1979. 296p.	2	2
Wong, Lung-Fat. Agricultural Productivity in the Socialist Countries. Boulder, Colo..; Westview Press, 1986. 195p.	3	2
Wonnacott, Thomas and John J. Wonnacott. Econometrics. 2d ed. New York; Wiley, 1979. 580p. (1st ed. 1970, 445p.)	2	2
World Bank. Accelerated Development in Sub-Saharan Africa: An Agenda for Action. Washington, D.C.; World Bank, 1982. 198p.	3	3
World Bank. Agricultural Research and Extension: An Evaluation of the World Bank's Experience. Washington, D.C.; World Bank, 1985. 110p.	3	3
World Bank. Poverty and Hunger: Issues and Options for Food Security in Developing Countries. Washington, D.C.; World Bank, 1986. 69p.	3	3
World Bank. The Assault on World Poverty; Problems of Rural Development, Education, and Health. Baltimore; Johns Hopkins University Press, 1975. 425p.	2	2

	Rankings	
	Developed countries	Third World
World Commission on Environment and Development. Food Two Thousand: Global Policies for Sustainable Agriculture. London and N.J.; Zed Press, 1987. 131p.	3	1
Wortman, Sterling, and Ralph W. Cummings, Jr. To Feed This World, The Challenge and the Strategy. Baltimore; Johns Hopkins University Press, 1978. 440p.	2	2
Yang, Wei Y. Methods of Farm Management Investigations for Improving Farm Productivity. 2d ed. Rome; Food and Agriculture Organization of the U.N., 1965. 258p. (FAO Agricultural Development Paper No. 64). (1st ed., 1958. 228p.)	3	3
Yates, Lamartine. Mexico's Agricultural Dilemma. Tucson, Arizona; University of Arizona Press, 1981. 291p.	3	2
Yotopoulos, Pan A., and Jeffrey B. Nugent. Economics of Development: Empirical Investigations. New York; Harper and Row, 1976. 478p.	2	1
Yotopoulos, Pan A. Empirical Investigations in the Economics of Development. Tokyo; Keio-tsusin Co., 1984.	2	2
Young, Frank W. Interdisciplinary Theories of Rural Development. Greenwich, CT: JAI Press, 1983. 235p.	2	2
Zahlan, A. B. The Agricultural Sector of Sudan: Policy and System Studies. London; Ithaca Press, 1986. 423p.	3	2
Zietz, J. and A. Valdes. The Costs of Protectionism to Developing Countries: An Analysis for Selected Agricultural Products. Washington, D.C.; 1986. 98p. (World Bank Staff Working Paper No. 769)	2	2

Q = Quality Publication Award of the American Agricultural Economics Association.

AAEA Classics = Award winning Classic of the American Agricultural Economics Association.

Two individuals are in this joint list six times each, as primary or secondary authors, or editors: Ted W. Schultz and Hans P. Bingswanger. Three people are represented as author or editor four times each: H. Chenery, B. Johnston, and J. Mellor.

F. Where Does the Core Come From?

The 1950–89 titles in the two complete master monographic lists are characterized in Table 20.

In the developed countries list, the publications come from thirty different countries, slightly greater in the Third World list. In the developed countries list, 46 commercial publishers were represented, 37 universities

Table 20. Characteristics of monograph lists (in percent)

	Developed countries list (N = 1420)	Third World list (N = 1002)
Place of publication		
United States	74.3	63.5
United Kingdom	13.2	14.6
India	3.0	5.5
Types of publishers		
Commercial presses	51.1	37.1
Universities	33.9	41.2
Governments (including the World Bank)	7.9	12.9
Independent organizations	7.1	8.8

Table 21. Publishers ranked by numbers of titles

	Developed countries list	Third World list
Westview Press	1	2
Johns Hopkins Univ. Press	2	1
Iowa State University Press	3	10
Oxford University Press	4	3
U.S. Government	5	
Macmillan	6	7
Wiley	7	11
Cambridge University Press	8	5
McGraw-Hill	9	
Praeger	10	8
North-Holland	11	
Prentice-Hall	12	
Cornell University Press	13	9
Academic Press	14	
World Bank[a]	15	4
Univ. of Chicago Press	16	14
Harvard University Press	17	12
Food & Agriculture Organization	18	6
International Food Policy and Research Institute		13
Pergamon		15

[a]The World Bank commissions many of its works to be published and sold by Johns Hopkins Univ. Press and Oxford Univ. Press. Representation in this table are those titles published directly by the World Bank.

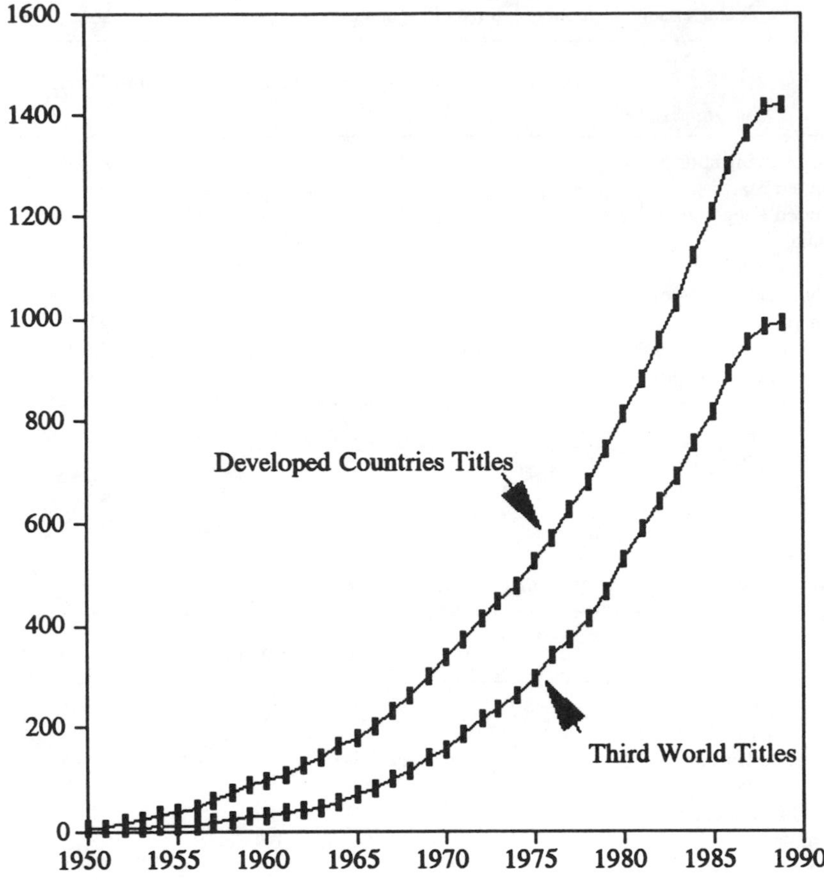

Figure 7. Publication years of core monographs.

were represented by presses or departmental publications, 29 governments or international govermental units such as the International Labour Organization (ILO) and FAO, and 26 independent organizations exemplified by the international agricultural research centers and Brookings Institution. The Third World list has 278 different publishers. These data demonstrate tremendous scope of publishers in the core literature. Publishers with the greatest numbers of titles in each list are ranked in Table 21.

The Johns Hopkins University Press has arrangements to handle the major works of at least three Washington, D.C., organizations represented in these core lists: International Food Policy and Research Institute, Resources for the Future, and the World Bank. Slightly over half of Johns Hopkins

University Press titles were identified as being "published for." With this in mind, the World Bank probably can be designated as the organization generating the greatest number of titles in the Third World list.

Figure 7 shows the time-spread of the titles in both monographic lists.

8. Measuring and Preserving Agricultural Economics and Rural Sociology Literature Collections

The agricultural sciences, along with most fields of knowledge, have created important storehouses of literature in their academic and research libraries. Storage of these historical materials and their retention for future use have become more than the concern of historians and librarians. The national and international scholarly communities have recently expressed concerns about dealing with the deterioration of literature collections. These interests come from several impulses.

Primary concern lies with the use of acidic paper in publishing within the past century, which speeds the process of paper deterioration. A book published in 1750 has a higher probability of surviving today's environments than does one published in 1950. To research and historical scholars, this means that the recorded activities of the past century will crumble in their hands. This is unacceptable to academic institutions that pride themselves on providing rich literature resources for their faculties. It is also unacceptable to society.

A second concern involves literature collections that receive little use. These collections require space and maintenance, making them the economic bane of many university administrators. The heavy use of microforms as a long-term storage medium for little-used library material has reduced the problem somewhat, and may also provide extended access to information in an economical manner. The quantity of filmed titles is only an infinitesimal portion of library collections, however. Microforms and other storage devices have provided increasing relief from the need to expand library storage and stack space. These alternatives and solutions to increasing expenditures are usually limitedly acceptable to prestigious research universities.

Finally, the sense that heritage literature may not be preserved is of increasing concern to scholars. This point has been brought home to many agricultural scientists who have observed the rapid and irreversible changes in agriculture and believe that these primary sources of information must be readily available.

Within the last decade, academic disciplines and administrations drawing together have begun to solve the problem. One of the fastest growing areas of library activity today is library collection evaluation and preservation. Preservation activities[1] have been organized at the international level by national library consortia and networks.[2] In the United States, national planning for funding and systematic coordination, began earnestly in 1986.[3] The agricultural sciences will be swept up in this process and it behooves agriculturalists and librarians to prepare carefully for this financial investment.

A. U.S. Agricultural Literature Collection Evaluation and Preservation

Evaluation of Agricultural Collections

Earlier chapters have outlined some of the evaluation tools available to libraries to test the strengths and weaknesses of their collections. The agricultural literature evaluation techniques are the same as those used in other science disciplines. The reader is referred to a 1985 article, which summarizes the methods and issues in collection evaluation today.[4] Collection evaluation is important in library management, in order to measure the merits of a collection, its uniqueness, and potential national, local, or regional significance.

Evaluation and rating tools have evolved through active investigation; they still remain rather simplistic in what they can reveal or measure. This is not because the methodologies and expertise are deficient. The reason is that the returns have been minimal and often disregarded by library administrators. Only now is the problem pressing enough so that solutions must be found. Statistical techniques are being used to understand the problem, but the methods often lack adequate definition and focus. Distinctions be-

1. The International Federation of Library Associations and Institutions has developed a Core Programme on Preservation and Conservation, and established a National Preservation Programme Office at the Library of Congress, Washington, D.C. The first issue of its *International Preservation News* appeared in September 1987.

2. The Research Libraries Group, Inc. (RLG) issued *RLG Preservation Manual* in 1983, and carries a summary of its national preservation activities in its *News* 20 (Fall 1989).

3. In 1986, the Commission on Preservation and Access was established with primary sponsorship by the Council of Library Resources. The goals are to foster and support systematic collaboration among all U.S. libraries to ensure the preservation of the human record, and to assist in promoting adequate funding for this immense task. March 1987 brochure, *The Commission on Preservation and Access*.

4. Martin Faigel, "Methods and Issues in Collection Evaluation Today," *Library Acquisitions: Practice and Theory* 9 (1985): 21–35.

tween collections or institutions can not adequately be drawn without more definitive, thoughtful, labor-intensive and costly efforts.

One of the primary uses of measurement tools in the coming battle for preservation will be to determine which materials deserve preservation and where the best investments can be made. This conservation movement should generate more absolute and useful evaluation tools in order to justify the increasing monies which will be invested.

Published guides give some assistance in determining the strengths of agricultural collections, although not in a very authoritative manner. One example is the guide to the collections policies of the National Agricultural Library.[5] Similar narrative descriptions are recorded in an online consortium database that allows for some machine correlations, but which has very limited representation from agricultural libraries.[6] And there are several published guides to collections identifying subject strengths in U.S. library collections.[7] Guides to specific subject collections, usually centered on a person or a donor, also exist although there are few in agriculture.

Without renewed interest and commensurate investment for evaluation of research and academic library collections in the agricultural sciences, the preservation work will be more haphazard and expensive than it should be.

Preservation of Agricultural Collections

The current planning for the preservation of agricultural collections follows closely that of past efforts in other disciplines. Items that are easy to microfilm, or in recent years put onto optical disks, are handled in the United States through joint efforts by the state land-grant university libraries in conjunction with the National Agricultural Library. Although some random titles were filmed earlier, not until 1975 did the concerted efforts of these institutions come together to film the agricultural, forestry, and extension publications of the land-grants which resulted in worthy preservation of over 2,000,000 pages.[8] Commendable as this effort has been, a wealth of

5. National Agricultural Library, *Collection Development Policy of the National Agricultural Library* (Beltsville, Md.: USDA National Agricultural Library, September 1988), 53p.

6. The Research Libraries Group, Inc., maintains an online register of collection levels of many of its members (termed a *Conspectus*) using the Library of Congress classification system as the schematic. Also see Anthony W. Ferguson, Joan Grant, and Joel S. Rutstein, "The RLG Conspectus: Its Uses and Benefits," *College and Research Libraries* 49(3) (May 1988): 197–206.

7. Perhaps the most valuable is *Subject Collections: A Guide to Special Book Collections and Subject Emphases . . .*, which is in its 6th ed., 1985, in two volumes. It is compiled by Lee Ash and William G. Miller, and published by R. R. Bowker, N.Y.

8. "Cooperative Microfilming of State Land-Grant Agricultural Publications: A Status Report, 1982." *Agricultural Libraries Information Notes* 8(9) (September 1982): 1–2. In June 1984 only four states (Alaska, Hawaii, Ohio, Wyoming) and Puerto Rico had not done full filming of their

material in need of preservation has not yet been realistically evaluated or preserved in the agricultural sciences. These fall roughly into three organizational categories:

(1) Serial or journal publications not the direct responsibility of the land-grant system or the federal government. This category includes major regional or national newspapers; journals of societies and commercial presses; and national, international, and state government documents. Select titles have been filmed or preserved by libraries and by some commercial firms such as University Microfilm International, and by a few journal publishers. Neverless, this immense body of crumbling pages remains with little attention.
(2) The U.S. government serials and journals, as well as monographic titles, constitute a good 25% of agricultural literature prior to 1980 on a title basis and probably close to 35% on a page count.
(3) Perhaps the most difficult major group is that of published books from commercial and university presses. The core of this genre is identified title by title in Chapter 7 for agricultural economics and rural sociology. The remaining monographs from this extensive study are provided in this chapter as historically significant titles worthy of preservation consideration.

Preservation of agriculture literature may be observed from different points of view and groupings. Regardless of the approach, several principles need to be agreed upon before a major impact on agricultural literature preservation can be realized. First among these principles is the agreement that cooperation for such an undertaking must be fostered among the land-grant and agricultural libraries of the United States. The preservation job is vast, difficult, and expensive. It will require the best of planning and long-range efforts. The task must include cooperative efforts with state libraries, such as the exemplary work of the Wisconsin Historical Society Library and the New York State Library.

A second principle maintains that responsibilities must be affixed with publishers of the literature and their assistance obtained, probably in conjunction with libraries.

Third, cooperation implies cooperative funding and mutually acceptable aims that are part of the planning and financial process.

There is little doubt that with current technology and funding only a relatively small percentage of agricultural literature will be preserved in a permanent manner. It will be better to have a valuable, minor portion preserved than to try to preserve every piece of paper, much of which is of questionable valuable.

And finally, determination of what is the most valuable, the core, or

---

publications from the land-grant inception to 1969 which are the dates covered by most land-grant filming.

historically worthy of preservation must be made. Money and effort must be concentrated on these determinations to attain goals for perservation.

B. Historically Significant Monographs in Agricultural Economics and Rural Sociology

The following compilation is an adjunct to the basic core lists in Chapter 7. This list contains older titles cited in the twenty-four peer reviewed volumes or other citation lists published between 1949 and 1988. These monographs were not considered appropriate for the core list of *currently* valuable titles in Chapter 7; instead they constitute a beginning list of historically important monographs. As part of the heritage literature of agricultural economics and rural sociology, they are as significant as the titles in the Chapter 7 lists. No subject specialists or historians evaluated the list.

This compilation must be viewed with two basic understandings. In the first place, citation analysis techniques based on numbers of times cited were used to separate out the less valuable titles. Second, numerous titles were excluded from the list based on one or more of the following criteria:

(1) Short monographs, fifty pages or fewer, which were cited only once, are excluded.
(2) Federal and state documents of brief pagination and with a highly specialized focus are not included.
(3) Early or all editions are not cited. This does not mean that the earlier edition is historically unimportant. One citation serves as an alert to all editions.
(4) Select esoteric works, particularly with limited geographic scope, are excluded.
(5) Local geographic materials not in a national or international context are excluded.

It is accurate to assume that these titles, along with those in Chapter 7, constitute most of the vital historical titles in this discipline. It is *not* a fair assumption that this list includes all of the most valuable pre-1960 titles in agricultural economics and rural sociology, however. This list must be viewed as a basic compilation from which to proceed to a more complete listing.

Historically Significant Monographs

A

Aaron, H.J. Who Pays the Property Tax? A New View. Washington, D.C.; Brookings Institution, 1975. 110p.

Abrahamsen, M.A., and C.L. Scroggs, eds. Agricultural Cooperation: Selected Readings. Minneapolis; University of Minnesota Press, 1957. 576p.

Abrams, Charles. Revolution in Land. New York; Harper and Brothers, 1939. 820p.

Abramovitz, M. Resources and Output Trends in the United State since 1870. New York, National Bureau of Economic Research, 1956. 23p. (Its Occasional Paper No. 52)

Acerbo, Giacomo. Storia ed Ordinamento del Credito Agrario Nei Diversi Paesi. Piacenza; Federazione Italiana Dei Consorzi Agrari, 1929. 635p.

Ackerman, Joseph, and Marshall Harris. Family Farm Policy. University of Chicago Press, 1947. 469p.

Adas, M. The Burma Delta Economic Development and Social Change on an Asian Rice Frontier: 1850–1941. Madison; University of Wisconsin Press, 1974.

Adams, Edward F. The Modern Farmer in His Business Relations. San Francisco, Calif.; N.J. Stone Co., 1899. 662p.

Adams, R.L., and W.W. Bedford. Everyday Farm Laws. Danville, Ill.; Interstate Printers and Publishers, 1949. 272p.

Adelman, I. Theories of Economic Growth and Development. Stanford; Stanford University Press, 1961.

Aereboe, Friedrich. Agrarpolitik; ein lehrbuch. Berlin; Parey, 1928. 619p.

Aereboe, Friedrich. Die Bewirtschaftung von Landgutern und Grundstucken. Berlin, 1917. 655p. (2d ed., 1928. 535p.)

Aereboe, Friedrich. Buchfuhrung. Anleitung fur den Praktischen Landwirt. 2d ed. Berlin; Druck von Gerbr. Unger, 1898–1901. 2 vols.

Aereboe, Friedrich. Die Taxation von Landgutern. Berlin. 1912. 542p.

Ahmad, N. A New Economic Geography of Bangladesh. New Delhi, India; Vikas Publishing House. 1976. 249p. American Institute of Banking. Agricultural Credit. New York; American Bankers Association, 1954. Various paging.

Alberici, A., and M. Baravelli. Savings Banks and Savings Facilities in African Countries. Milan, Italy; Cassa di Risparmio delle Provincie Lombarde, 1973. 131p. (Credit Markets of Africa, No. 7.)

Amstutuz, A. E. Computer Simulation of Competitive Market Response. Cambridge; M.I.T. Press, 1967. Anderson, Bruce. The Farmer Seeks Jeffersonian Democracy. Baltimore, Md.; King, Brothers, Inc., Printers, 1943. 279p.

Anderson, Charles H. The Sociology of Survival: Social Problems of Growth. Homewood, Ill.; Dorsey Press, 1976. 299p. Anderson, E. Per Capita Consumption of Foods, United States, 1909–39. Washington, D.C.; USDA, Bureau of Agricultural Economics, 1941. (Mimeo)

Anderson, R. S., P. R. Brass, E. Levy, and B. M. Morris, eds. Science, Politics and the Agricultural Revolution in Asia. Boulder, Colo.; Westview Press, 1982. 512p.

Andreae, B. Betriebsformen in der Landwirtschaft. Stuttgart; Ulmer, 1964. 426p.

Aoki, M. Optimization of Stochastic Systems. New York; Academic Press, 1967. 354p.

App, Frank. Farm Economics, Management and Distribution. 2d ed., rev. Philadelphia; J.B. Lippincott, 1938. 700p.

Armbruster, Walter J., Dennis R. Henderson, and Ronald D. Knutson, eds. Federal Marketing Programs in Agriculture: Issues and Options. Danville, Ill.; Interstate Printers and Publishers, Inc., 1983. 326p.

Arrow, K., S. Karlin, and P. Suppes, eds. Mathematical Methods in the Social Sciences; Proceedings of 1959 Symposium. Stanford; Stanford University Press, 1959. 365p.

Asher, Percy H. National Self-Sufficiency. London, New York; T. Nelson and Sons, Ltd., 1938. 188p.

Asian Productivity Organization. Farm Mechanization in Asia. Tokyo; Asian Prod. Organization, 1983. 510p.

Asian Productivity Organization. Grain Legumes Production in Asia. Tokyo; Asian Prod. Organization, 1982. 550p.

Asmis, W. Landwirtschaftliche Absatzkunde. Berlin; Parey, 1931. 299p.

Association of Land-Grant Colleges and Universities. Committe on Postwar Agricultural Policy. Postwar Agricultural Policy Report. Berkeley, Calif.; The Association, 1944. 61p.

Astori, Danilo. La Agricultura en una Estrategia de Desarrollo Economico. Montevideo, Uruguay; Ediciones de la Banda Oriental, 1969. 132p.

Atkeson, Thomas C., and Mary Meek Atkeson. Pioneering in Agriculture: One Hundred Years of American Farming and Farm Leadership. New York; Orange Judd Publishing Co., Inc., 1937. 222p.

Aubert, J. Guide Comptable, Fiscal and Social de l'agriculture. Bruxelles; L'Avenir, 1948. 152p.

Australian Ministry of Post-War Reconstruction. Farm Management and Elementary Agricultural Economics, by R.B. McMillan and K.O. Campbell. Melbourne; McMillan, R.Band, and K.O. Campbell, 1947. 313p.

Ayres, C. E. The Theory of Economic Progress; a Study of the Fundamentals of Economic Development and Cultural Change. Chapel Hill, N.C.; University of North Carolina Press, 1944. 317p. (3d ed. Kalamazoo, MI; New Issues Press, Western Michigan University, 1978. 324p)

Ayres, Leonard P. The Economics of Recovery. New York; Macmillan, 1933. 189p.

B

Bacon, L.B., and F.C. Schloemer. World Trade in Agricultural Products: Its Growth, Its Crisis, and the New Trade Policies. Rome; FAO, 1940. 1102p.

Baer, J.B., and O.G. Saxon. Commodity Exchanges and Futures Trading; principles and operating methods. New York; Harper, 1949. 324p.

Baer, W. and I. Kerstenetzky, eds. Inflation and Growth in Latin America. Homewood, Ill.; Irwin, 1964. 542p. (5)

Bailey, Liberty H. Cyclopedia of American Agriculture. New York; Macmillan, 1907–09. 4 vol.

Bailey, Liberty H. The Harvest of the Year to the Tiller of the Soil. New York; Macmillan Co., 1927. 209p.

Baldwin, Bird T. Farm Children: An Investigation of Rural Life in Selected Areas of Iowa. Iowa Child Welfare Research Station. New York, London; D. Appleton and Company, 1930. 337p.

Baligh, H. H. and L. E. Richartz. Vertical Market Structures. Boston; Allyn and Bacon, 1967.

Ball, Carleton R. Federal, State, and Local Administrative Relationships in Agriculture. Berkeley, Calif.; University of California Press, 1938. 2 vols.

Bandini, Mario. Manuale di Economia e Politica Agraria. Bologna; Edizioni Agricole, 1954. 343p.

Bandini, Mario and Giuseppe Guerrieri. Istituzioni di Economica e Polictica Agraria. Bologna; Edizioni Agricole, 1968. 516p.

Bandini, Mario and C. Vanzetti. Economia e Politica Agraria. Lezioni per le Facolta di Economia e Commercio. Bologna; Edagricole, 1967. 410p.

Bardhan, Pranab K., and T. N. Srinivasan, eds. Poverty and Income Distribution in India. Calcutta; Statistical Publishing Society, 1974. 553p.

Bardhan, Pranab K., A. Viadyanathan, Y. Alagh, G. S. Bhalla, and A. L. Bhadem, eds. Labour Absorption in Indian Agriculture, Some Exploratory Investigations. Bangkok, Thailand; International Labour Office, 1978. 216p.

Barlow, C., S. Jayasuriya, and E. C. Price. Evaluating Technology for New Farming Systems: Case Studies from Philippine Rice Farms. Los Banos, Philippines; IRRI, 1983. 110p.

Barou, Noah. Co-operative Insurance. London; P.S. King, 1936. 391p.

Bartelli et al. editors. Soil Surveys and Land Use Planning. Madison, Wisconisn; Soil Science Society of America and American Society of Agronomy, 1966. 196p.

Basiuk, T.L. Organizatsiio Socialisticheskogo Sel'Skokhoziastevennogo Proizvodstva. (Organization of Social Agricultural Production). Moscow. Rev. ed., 1947. 768p.

Bates, Thomas H., and Andrew Schmitz. A Spatial Equilibrium Analysis of the World Sugar Economy. Berkeley; University of California, Giannini Foundation Monograph Number 23, 1969. 42p. Q

Bautista, R. M. and S. Naya, eds. Energy and Structural Change in the Asia-Pacific Region: Papers and Proceedings of the Thirteenth Pacific Trade and Development Conference. Manila; Philippine Institute for Development Studies (PIDS) and ADB, 1984. 532p. (1)

Beale, Calvin L. The Revival of Population Growth in Nonmetropolitan America. Washington, D.C.; USDA, Economics, Statistics, and Cooperatives Service, 1977. 15p. (Its ERS-605).

Beals, Carleton. American Earth: The Biography of a Nation. Philadelphia, New York; J.B. Lippincott Co., 1939. 500p.

Beattie, Bruce B., Emery N. Castle, William G. Brown, and Wade Griffin. Economic Consequences of Interbasin Water Transfer. Corvallis; Oregon State University, 1971. 82p. (College of Agriculture Tech. Bull. No. 116) Q

Beauchamp, Joan. Agriculture in Soviet Russia. London; V. Gollancz, Ltd., 1931. 126p.

Beeler, M.N. Marketing Purebred Livestock. New York; Macmillan, 1929. 393p.

Belshaw, Horace. The Provision of Credit with Special Reference to Agriculture. Cambridge, England; W. Heffer and Sons, Ltd., 1931. 326p.

Benedict, M. R., and O. C. Stine. The Agricultural Commodity Programs. New York; Twentieth Century Fund, 1956. 510p.

Benedict, M. R. Can We Solve the Farm Problem? New York; Twentieth Century Fund, 1955. 601p.

Beneke, Raymond R. Managing the Farm Business. New York; Wiley, 1955. 464p.

Benjamin, Earl W., and Howard C. Pierce. Marketing Poultry Products. 3d ed. New York; J. Wiley and Sons, Inc., Ltd., 1937, 401p.

Bennett, M.K. International Commodity Stockpiling as An Economic Stabilizer. Stanford; Stanford University Press, 1949. 205p.

Benson, Ezra T. Freedom to Farm. Garden City; Doubleday, 1960. 239p.

Benton, Alva H. An Introduction to the Marketing of Farm Products. Chicago, New York, A.W. Shaw Co., 1926. 427p.

Bergman, Theodor. Farm Policies in Socialist Countries. Translated by Lux Furtmuller. Lexington, Mass.; Lexington Books, 1975. 289.

Bernal, E. A. The Role of Landlords in Philippine Agriculture Development. Los Banos, University of the Philippines, College of Agriculutre, 1967.

Bernard, Francios. ...Les Systemes de Culture; les Speculations Agricoles. Montpellier; C. Coulet, 1898. 392p.

Bernhardt, Joshua. The Sugar Industry and the Federal Government: A Thirty Year Record, 1917–47. Washington, D.C.; Sugar Statistics Service, 1949. 344p.

Beyer, G.H., and J.H. Rose. Farm Housing. New York; Wiley for the Social Science Research Council, 1957. 194p.

Bhagwati, J. N. and T. N. Srinivasan. Foreign Trade Regimes and Economic Development: India. New York; Columbia Univ. Press, 1975. 261p. Publ. for National Bureau of Economic Research.

Bienen, H., and V. P. Diejomaoh, eds. The Political Economy of Income Distribution in Nigeria. New York; Holmes and Meier, 1981. 520p.

Black, D. The Theory of Committees and Elections. Cambridge; Cambridge University Press, 1958. 241p.

Black, John D. Parity, Parity, Parity. Cambridge, Mass.; Harvard University Press, 1942. 369p.

Black, John D., M. Clawson, Charles R. Sayre, and W.W. Wilcox. Farm Management. New York; Macmillan, 1947. 1073p.

Black, John D., et al. Research Method and Procedure in Agricultural Economics. New York Social Science Research Council, 1948. 2 vols.

Black, John D. Introduction to Economics for Agriculture. New York; Macmillan, 1953. 726p.

Black, John D. Introduction to Production Economics. New York; Henry Holt, 1926. 975p. (2)

Black, John D., ed. Research in Agricultural Credit—Scope and Method. New York; Social Science Research Council, 1931. 201p.

Black, John D., and M. E. Kiefer. Future Food and Agriculture Policy. New York; McGraw-Hill, 1948. 348p.

Black, John D. Agricultural Reform in the United States. New York, 1929. 511p.

Black, John D. The Dairy Industry and the A.A.A. Washington, D.C.; The Brookings Institute, 1935. 520p.

Black, John D. Food Enough. Lancaster, PA; Jaques Cattell Press, 1943. 269p.

Blackeslee, LeRoy. Post World War II Government Policy Impacts on the U.S. Wheat Sector. Pullman, Wash.; Washington State University, 1980. 52p. (College of Agriculture Res. Center Tech. Bulletin No. 93) Q

Blackwell, Roger D., James F. Engel, and David T. Kollat. Cases in Consumer Behavior. New York; Holt, Rinehart and Winston, 1969. 431p.

Blohm, G. Angewandte Landwirtschaftliche Betriebslehre. Stuttgart; Ulmer, 1948. 360p. (4th ed. 1964, 441p.)

Blyn, G. Agricultural Trends in India, 1891–1947: Output, Availability and Productivity. Philadelphia; University of Pennsylvania Press, 1966. 370p.

Bogart, Ernest L. Economic History of American Agriculture. New York, Chicago; Longmans, Green and Co., 1923. 173p.

Boss, Andrew. Farm Management. Chicago, New York; Lyons and Carnahan, 1914. 237p. (Revised edition, 1923, 277p.)

Boulding, Kenneth E. A Reconstruction of Economics. New York; Wiley, 1950. 340p.

Bowman, Isaiah. Limits of Land Settlement; a Report on Present-Day Possibilities. New York; Council on Foreign Relations, 1937. 380p.

Bowring, James R., Herman M. Southworth, and Frederick V. Waugh. Marketing Policies for Agriculture. Englewood Cliffs, NJ; Prentice-Hall, 1960. 270p.

Boyazoglu, Alexander J. Agricultural Credit. London; P.S. King and Son, Ltd., 1932. 267p.

Boyle, James E. Farm Relief; a Brief on the McNary-Haugen Plan. Garden City, N.Y.; Doubleday, Doran and Company, Inc., 1928. 281p.

Boyle, James E. Marketing of Agricultural Products. New York; McGraw-Hill, 1925. 479p.

Boyle, James E. Agricultural Economics. Philadelphia; J.B. Lippincott, 1921. 448p.

Boyte, Harry C. Community is Possible. New York; Harper and Row, 1984.

Bradford, L. A., and G. L. Johnson. Farm Management Analysis. New York; Wiley, 1953. 438p.

Brandt, K. The Reconstruction of World Agriculture. New York; W. W. Norton Co, 1945. 416p.

Brannon, Russel H. The Agricultural Development of Uruguay: Problems of Government Policy. New York, Praeger, 1968. 366p.

Branton, J.H. Vital Agriculture in Great Britain, Denmark and the Argentine. Bedford, England; Rush and Warwick, 1938. 86p.

Braverman, Harry. Labor and Monopoly Capital: The Degradation of Work in the Twentieth Century. New York; Monthly Review Press, 1974.

Brayne, F. L. Socrates in an Indian Village. Oxford; Oxford University Press, 1929. 130p.

Brentano. L. Agrarpolitik; ein Lehrbuch. 2d ed. Stuttgart und Berlin; J. G. Cotta'sche Buchhandlung Nachfolger, 1925. 294p.

Bressler, R. G. Economies of Scale in the Operation of Country Milk Plants with special reference to New England. Boston; New England Agricultural Experiment Stations and the United States Department of Agriuclture, 1942. 92p.

Brett, E. A. Colonization and Underdevelopment in East Africa: The Politics of Economic Change, 1919–1939. London; Heineman; and New York; NOK Publ., 1973. 330p.

Brewster, Kingman, James S.Y. Ivins., and Percy W. Phillips. Taxation under the A.A.A. (Agricultural Adjustment Administration). New York; Baker, Voorhis and Co., 1934. 341p.

Brinkmann, Theodor. Die danische Landwirtschaft. Jena; Fischer, 1908. 197p.

Brinkmann, Theodor. Economics of the Farm Business. Berkeley, Calif.; University of California Press, 1935. 172p.

Brizi, A. Economica Agraria: Sunti Raccolti alle Lezioni nella Facolta Agraria de (Napoli) per gli studenti. Citta di Castello; Macri, 1944. 306p. (2d. ed., 1950. 339p.)

Brooks, Thomas Joseph. Markets and Rural Economics: Science of Commerce and Distribution. An Investigation of Agricultural Production and the Economics of Distribution. New York; The Shakespeare Press, 1914. 397p.

Brunner, Edmund de, and J.H. Kolb. Rural Social Trends. New York, London; McGraw-Hill Book Company, Inc., 1933. 386p.

Buchanan, J. M. and G. Tullock. The Calculus of Consent: Logical Foundations of Constitutional Democracy. Ann Arbor; University of Michigan Press, 1962.

Buchenberger, Adolf. Agrarwesen und Agrarpolitik. Leipzig; C. F. Winter, 1892–93. 2 vols.

Buchwald, N., and R. Bishop. From Peasant to Collective Farmer. New York; International Publishers, 1933. 101p.

Buck, John Lossing. Land Utilization In China . . . 1929–1933. Shanghai; The Commerce Press, 1937. 2 vols.

Buechel, F.A. The Commerce of Agriculture, a Survey of Agricultural Resources. New York; John Wiley; and London; Chapman and Hall, 1926. 439p.

Bulgakov, S. Kapitalizm i Zemledeliie (Capitalism and Agriculture). St. Petersburg, 1900. 2 vols.

Bunting, A. H., ed. Change in Agriculture. New York; Praeger, 1970. 813p.

Burby, William E. Handbook of the Law of Real Property. 3d ed. St. Paul, MN; West Pub. Co., 1965.

Burr, Walter. Small Towns, an Estimate of Their Trade and Culture. New York; Macmillan, 1929. 267p.

Busch, W. Die Landbauzonen im Deutschen Lebensraum. Stuttgart, 1936. 189p.

Busch, W. Landwirtschaftliche Betriebslehre. Essen, 1958. 331p.

Butterfield, Kenyon. Chapters in Rural Progress. Chicago; University of Chicago Press, 1908. 251p. (2)

Butterworth, J.E., ed. Commission on Rural Education and the War: Rural Schools for Tomorrow. Washington, D.C.; National Education Association of the U.S., Dept. of Rural Education Yearbook, 1945. 152p.

Butz, Earl L. The Production Credit System for Farmers. Washington, D.C.; Brookings Institution, 1944. 104p.

C

Caisse Centrale de Reassurance des Mutuelles Agricoles de l'Afrique du Nord. Atlas de la Mutualite Agricole en Afrique du Nord; Auurances, Credit [et] Cooperation, 1907–1947. Algeria; Baconnier, 1948. 130p.

Calkins, Peter H. The New Decision Making Environment in Chinese Agriculture. Ames; Iowa State University Press, 1980. 28p. (International Studies in Economics Monog. No. 14)

Callison, Charles S. Land-to-the-Tiller in the Mekong Delta: Economic, Social and Political Effects of Land Reform in Four Villages of South Vietnam. Lanham, Mass.; University Press of America, 1983. 418p.

Campbell, Persia C. American Agricultural Policy. London; P.S. King and Son, 1933. 304p.

Canaletti Gaudenti, Alberto. . . . La Socializzazione Agraria nell'U.R.S.S. Roma; Capriotti, 1944 150p.

Capstick, Margaret. The Economics of Agriculture. New York; St. Martin's Press, 1970. 163p.

Carey, Lee J., editor. Community Development as a Process. Columbia; University of Missouri Press, 1970.

Carrier, Lyman. The Beginnings of Agriculture in America. New York and London; McGraw-Hill Co., Inc., 1923. 323p.

Carver, Thomas N. Elements of Rural Economics. Boston; Ginn and Co., 1924. 266p.

Carver, Thomas N. Principles of Rural Economics. Boston; Ginn and Co., 1911. 386p. (New edition 1932, 401p.)

Carver, Thomas N., comp. Selected Readings in Rural Economics. Boston, New York; Ginn and Company, 1916. 974p.

Cary, Lee J., ed. Directory: Community Development Education and Training Programs Throughout the World. Columbia, MO; Community Development Society, 1976. 303p.

Cassels, J. M. A Study of Fluid Milk Prices. Cambridge; Harvard University Press, 1937. 303p.

Caudill, H.M. Night Comes to the Cumberlands: A Biography of a Depressed Area. Boston; Little, Brown, 1963. 394p.

Cauley, Troy Jesse. Agrarianism: A Program for Farmers. Chapel Hill; The University of North Carolina Press, 1935. 211p.

Center for Agricultural and Economic Adjustment, Iowa State University. Farmers in the Market Place. Ames; Iowa State University Press, 1964.

Center for Agriculture and Economic Adjustment, Iowa State University. Food: One Tool in International Economic Development. Ames; Iowa State University Press, 1962. 419p.

Center for Agricultural and Economic Adjustment, Iowa State University. Labor Mobility and Population in Agriculture. Ames; Iowa State University Press, 1961. 231p.

Chang, K. Y., ed. Perspectives on Development in Mainland China. Boulder, Colo.; Westview Press, 1985. 447p.

Chang, Pei-kang. Agriculture and Industrialization. Cambridge; Harvard University Press, 1949. 270p.

Chayanov, A. V. Oeuvres Choisies de A. V. Cajanov. Translated by B. Kerblay. East Ardsley, Wakefield, Eng.; S. R. Publishers; New York; Johnson Reprint Corp., 1967. 8 vols.

Chayanov, A.V. Osnovnye Idei i Metodty Raboty Obshestvennoi Agronomii. (Principal Ideas and Working Methods of Social Agronomy). Moscow, 1918.

Chayanov, A.V., and V.R. Kratinov. Metodyi Taksatsionnykh Ischislenni v Sel'skom Khoziaistve (Methods of Appraisal in Agriculture). Moscow, 1927. 136p.

Chen, Han-seng. Landlord and Peasant in China; a Study of the Agrarian Crisis in South China. New York; International Publishers, 1936. 144p.

Cheng, C. Y. China's Economic Development: Growth and Structural Change. Boulder, Colo., Westview Press, 1982. 535p.

Cheng, S. H. The Rice Industry of Burma 1852–1940. Singapore; University of Malaya Press, 1968. 307p.

Chernichovsky, D. and O. A. Meesook. Patterns of Food Consumption and Nutrition in Indonesia. Washington, D.C., World Bank, 1984. 72p. (World Bank Staff Working Paper No. 670)

Chesnutt, Samuel L. The Rural South: Background, Problems, Outlook. Montgomery, Ala.; Dixie Book Company, Inc., 1939. 466p.

Chisholm, Michael. Rural Settlement and Land Use: An Essay in Location. 3d ed. London; Hutchinson, 1979. 189p.

Christenson, R. M. The Brannan Plan; farm politics and policy. Ann Arbor; University of Michigan Press, 1959. 207p.

Christiansen, Martin K., Coordinator. Speaking of Trade: Its Effect on Agriculture. St. Paul; Agricultural Extension Service, University of Minnesota, 1978. 106p. Q

Christy, F.T., Jr., and A. Scott. The Common Wealth in Ocean Fisheries: Some Problems of Growth and Economic Allocation. Baltimore; Johns Hopkins Univerisity Press for Resources for the Future, 1965. 281p.

Clark, Colin. Population Growth and Land Use. London; Macmillan, 1967. 406p. (2d ed 1977. 415p.)

Clark, F.E., and L.D.H. Weld. Marketing Agricultural Products in the United States. New York, 1932. 672p.

Clark, H.F. Life Earnings in Selected Occupations in the United States. New York; Harper, 1937. 408p.

Clawson, Marion. Methods of Measuring the Demand for and Value of Outdoor Recreation. Washington, D.C.; Resources for the Future, 1959. 36p. Q

Clawson, Marion. Uncle Sam's Acres. New York; Dodd, Mead, 1951. 414p.

Clemen, Rudolf Alexander. The American Livestock and Meat Industry. New York; The Ronald Press Company, 1923. 872p.

Clower, R. W., G. Dalton, M. Harwitz, and A. A. Walters. Growth Without Development: An Economic Survey of Liberia. Evanston, Ill., Northwestern University Press, 1966. 385p.

Cohen, K. J. Theory of the Firm: Resource Allocation in a Market Economy. Englewood Cliffs, NJ; Prentice-Hall, 1965.

Cohen, Ruth L. The Economics of Agriculture. London; Nisbet & Co. ltd., 1940. 202p. (New edition: New York; Pitman, 1949. 216p.)

Cole, William E., and Hugh Price Crowe. Recent Trends in Rural Planning. New York; Prentice-Hall, Inc., 1937. 579p.

Coles, Robert. Children of Crisis: A Study of Courage and Fear. Boston; Little, Brown, and Co., 1967. 401p.

Comish, Newel H. Cooperative Marketing of Agricultural Products. New York, London; D. Appleton and Co., 1929. 479p.

Confederazione Fascista dei Lavaratori dell' Agricoltura. La Charte du Travail et L'agricultura. Rome; Soc. an. "Arte della Stamp", 1937. 374p.
Conference on Economic Policy for American Agriculture, 1931. Report of Proceedings. 2d ed. University of Chicago Press, 1932. 2 vols.
Connor, L.R. Statistics in Theory and Practice. London; Sir I. Pitman and Sons, Ltd., 1932. 371p.
Constandse, A.K. and E.W. Hofstee. Rural Sociology in Action. Rome; Food and Agriculture Organization of the United Nations, 1964. 64p. (F.A.O. Agricultural Development Paper no.79)
Copodo, Michel. Du Prix de Roviont au Produit not on Agriculturo: Ossei d'uno Theorie de la Production. Paris; Contro National d'information Economique, 1946. 416p.
Coppock, John O. North Atlantic Policy: The Agricultural Gap. New York; Twentieth Century Fund, 1963. 270p.
Coppock, John T. An Agricultural Atlas of England and Wales. London; Faber and Faber, 1964. 255p.
Correa, Hector. The Economics of Human Resources. Amsterdam; North-Holland, 1963. 262p. (1967. 264p.) (Reprinted: Westport, Conn.; Greenwood Press, 1982. 262p.)
Cosnier, Henri Charles. . . . L'Ouest Africain Francais, Ses Ressources Agricoles, Son Organisation Economique. Paris; E. Larose, 1921. 253p.
Cotiler, J. and R. R. Fagen, eds. Latin America and the United States: The Changing Political Realities. Stanford, Calif.; Stanford University Press, 1974. 417p.
Coulson, A. Tanzania: A Political Economy. Oxford University Press, 1982. 394p.
Cournot, Antoine. Researches into the Mathematical Principles of the Theory of Wealth. Translated by N.T. Bacon. London and New York; Mcmillan co., 1897. 213p. (1st ed. in French, 1838.) (Latest reprint by Irving Fischer. New York; A.M. Kelley, 1971. 213p.)
Coutu, A. J. and R. A. King. The Agricultural Development of Peru. New York, Praeger Publ., 1969. 183p. (Praeger Special Studies in International Economics and Development).
Cowan, C. D., ed. The Economic Development of Southeast Asia—Studies in Economic History and Political Economy. New York; Praeger, 1964. 192p.
Coward, Raymond T. and Richard K. Kerckhoff. The Rural Elderly: Program Planning Guidelines. Ames, Iowa; North Central Regional Center For Rural Development, Iowa State University, 1978. 81p.
Cox, Alonzo Bettis. Cotton Markets and Cotton Merchandising. 2d ed. rev. Jan. 1949. Austin, T.X.; Hemphill, 1949. 183p.
Crabb, A.R. The Hybrid Corn Makers: Prophets of Plenty. New Brunswick; Rutgers University Press, 1947. 331p.
Croll, E. Women in Rural Development—The People's Republic of China. Geneva, Switzerland; ILO, 1979. 61p.
Crowther, Samuel. America Self-Contained. Garden City, N.Y.; Doubleday, Doran and Co., Inc., 1933. 340p.
Csizmadia, E. Socialist Agriculutre in Hungary. Collets (UK) and State Mutual Books, 1977. 180p.
Cummings, Richard O. The American and His Food. Chicago, Ill.; University of Chicago Press. 1940. 267p.
Cussler, Margaret, and M. L. Q. DeGive. Twixt the Cup and the Lip. Washington, D.C.; Consortium Press, 1971.

D

Daggett, Stuart. Principles of Inland Transportation. 4th ed. New York; Harper, 1955. 788p.

Dagli, V., ed. A Regional Profile of Indian Agriculture. Bombay; Voral and Co., Publishers, 1975. 311p.

Dahlinger, Charles W. The New Agrarianism; a Survey of the Prevalent Spirit of Social Unrest, and a Consideration of the Consequent Campaign for the Adjustment of Agriculture with Industry and Commerce. New York and London; G. P. Putnam's Sons, 1913. 249p.

Dalton, George, ed. Tribal and Peasant Economies: An Economic Survey of Economic Anthropology. New York; Natural History Press, 1967. 35p.

Davenport, Arthur C. The American Livestock Market: How it Functions. Chicago; Drovers Journal Print, 1922. 174p.

Davie, Lynn and Associates. Community Resource Development: A Description Based on the Analysis of 52 Case Studies Using the Shared Process Evaluation System. Toronto; Lynn Davie and Associates, 1979.

Davis, Harold T. The Theory of Econometrics. Bloomington, IN; Principia Press, 1941. 482p.

Davis, H. R. and M. Guttentag, editors. Handbook of Evaluation Research, Vol. 1. Beverly Hills, Calif.; Sage, 1975.

Davis, I.R., Jr., ed. Selected Readings in Agricultural Credit for use of International Conference on Agricultural and Cooperative Credit; August 4–September 12, 1952. Berkeley, Calif.; University of California, 1952. 582p.

Davis, J.S. On Agricultural Policy, 1926–1938. Stanford, Calif.; Stanford University Press, California Food Research Institute, 1939. 494p.

Davis, J.S. Wheat and the A.A.A. Washington, D.C.; Brookings Institution, 1935. 468p.

Davis, John H. and Ray A. Goldberg. A Concept of Agribusiness. Boston; Division of Research Graduate School of Business Administration, Harvard Univeristy, 1957. 136p.

Davis, Robert K., and S.H. Hanke. Pricing and Efficiency in Water Resource Management. Report to the National Water Commission. Washington, D.C.; George Washington University, National Resources Policy Center, 1971. 273p. (U.S. Department of Commerce, NTIS No. PB 209 083)

Dawber, Mark A. Rebuilding Rural America. New York; Friendship Press, 1937. 210p.

Dawson, C.A., and Eva R. Younge. Pioneering in the Prairie Provinces: The Social Side of the Settlement Process. Toronto; Macmillan of Canada, Ltd., 1940. 338p.

Day, R. H., and I. J. Singh. Economic Development as an Adaptive Process: The Green Revolution in the Indian Punjab. London; Cambridge University Press, 1977. 326p.

Day, R. Recursive Programming and Production Response. Amsterdam; North-Holland, 1963. 226p.

De Neufville, Judith I. Social Indicators and Public Policy: Interaction Processes of Design and Application. New York; Elsevier Scientific Publ., 1975. 311p.

Dean, J. Managerial Economics. Englewood Cliffs, N.J.; Prentice-Hall, 1951. 621p.

Deavers, Kenneth L., and David L. Brown. Social and Economic Trends in Rural America. Washington, D.C., Economics, Statistics, and Cooperatives Services, USDA, 1979. A White House Rural Development Background Paper. (5)

Degon, Madeleine. . . . Le Credit Agricole: Sources, Formes, Caracteres, Fonctionnement en France, et dans les Principaux Pays. Paris; Librairie du Recueil Sirey, 1939. 278p.

Derman, W., and L. Derman. Serfs, Peasants, and Socialists—A Former Serf Village in the Republic of Guinea. Berkeley; University of California Press, 1973. 282p.

Desai, G. M. and G. Singh. Growth of Fertilizer Use in Districts of India: Performance and Policy Implications. CMA Monograph No. 41. Ahmedabad, India; Indian Institute of Management, Center for Management in Agriculture, 1973.

Desai, Meghnad J. The Computer Simulation of the California Dairy Industry. Berkeley, Calif.; Giannini Foundation Special Report, 1968.

Deutsch, M. The Resolution of Conflict. New Haven, Conn.; Yale University Press, 1973.

Dies, E.J. Titans of the Soil: Great Builders of Agriculture. Chapel Hill; University of North Carolina Press, 1942. 213p.

Dietze, Constantin von. Grundzuge der Agrarpolitik. Hamburg and Berlin; Parey, 1967. 291p.

Digby, M. Agricultural Co-operation in the Commonwealth. 3d ed. Oxford; Blackwell, 1970. 272p.

Dipman, Carl William. How to Sell Fruits and Vegetables. New York; The Progessive Grocer, 1936. 200p.

Dixey, Roger N., ed. International Explorations of Agricultural Economics: A Tribute to the Inspiration of Leonard Knight Elmhirst. Ames; Iowa State University Press, 1964. 306p.

Dobson, W. D. and E. M. Babb. An Analysis of Alternative Price Structures and Intermarket Competition in Federal Order Milk Markets. West Lafayett; Purdue University, Agricultural Experimental Station, 1970. 34p. (Purdue University Agric. Exp. Station Research Bulletin 870) Q

Donald, R. James, and Levi A. Powell. The Food and Fiber System—How It Works. Washington, D.C.; U.S. Department of Agriculture, Economic Research Service, 1975. 47p. (USDA Agricultural Information Bull. 383) Q

Donaldson, G.F., and J.P.G. Webster. An Operating Procedure for Simulating Farm Planning-Monte Carlo Method. Ashford, Kent; Wye College, Department of Economics, 1968. 30p.

Douglas, F.C.R. Land-Value Rating: Theory and Practice. London; L. and V.Woolf at the Hogarth Press, 1936. 76p.

Dovring, F. Land and Labor in Europe in the Twentieth Century; a Comparative Survey of Recent Agrarian History. With a chapter on Land Reform as a Propaganda Theme by K. Dovring. 3d ed. The Hague; Nijhoff, 1965. 511p.

Dowell, Austin A. The American Farmer and the Export Market. Minneapolis; University of Minneapolis Press, 1934. 269p.

Dragoni, C. Economia Agraria. Milan; University of Hoepli, 1932. 794p.

Dubov, Irving, ed. Contemporary Agricultural Marketing. Knoxville; University of Tennessee Press, 1968. 270p.

Duckman, A.N. and G.B. Masefield. Farming Systems of the World. London; Chatto and Windus, 1970. 542p.

Duerr, W.A. Fundamentals of Forestry Economics. New York; McGraw-Hill, 1960. 579p.

Duggan, I. W., and R. U. Battles. Financing the Farm Business. New York; Wiley, 1950. 354p.

Dummeier, E.F., and Richard B. Heflebower. Economics with Applications to Agriculture. 2d ed. New York; McGraw-Hill Book Company, 1940. 752p.

Dumont, Rene. African Agricultural Development; Reflections on the Major Lines of Advance and the Barriers to Progress. New York; Food and Agricultural Organization, 1966.

Dunn, E.S., Jr. The Location of Agricultural Production. Gainesville; University of Florida Press, 1954. 115p.

Durrenberger, E. Paul. Agricultural Production and Household Budgets in a Shan Peasant Village in Northwest Thailand: A Quantitative Description. Athens; Ohio University Center for International Studies, 1978. 142p. (Papers in International Studies: Southeast Asia; No. 49).

Durtschi, E. Landwirtschaftliche Marktlehre. Frauenfeld; Huber, 1961. 237p.

Duryee, William B. A Living from the Land. New York, London; Whittlesey House, McGraw-Hill Book company, Inc., 1934. 189p.

E

Eckaus, Richard S., editor. Appropriate Technologies for Developing Countries. Washington, D.C.; National Academy of Sciences, 1977. 140p.

Eckaus, Richard S. and K. S. Parikh. Planning for Growth: Multisectoral, Intertemporal Models Applied to India. Cambridge, Mass.; MIT Press, 1968. 208p.

Eckaus, Richard S. and P. N. Rosenstein-Rodan, eds. Analysis of Development Problems. Studies of the Chilean Economy. Amsterdam; North Holland Publ., 1973. 430p.

Eckstein, A. China's Economic Development: The Interplay of Scarcity and Ideology. Ann Arbor; University of Michigan Press, 1975. 399p.

Eckstein, A., W. Galenson, T. C. Liu, eds. Economic Trends in Communist China. Chicago; Aldine, 1968. 757p.

Eckstein, S., G. Donald, D. Horton, and T. Carroll. Land Reform in Latin America: Bolivia, Chile, Mexico, Peru and Venezuela. Washington, D.C., 1978. 40p. (World Bank Staff Working Paper No. 275.)

Eddy, Edward D. Labor and Land Use on Mixed Farms in the Pastoral Zone of Niger. Ann Arbor; University of Michigan, Center for Research on Economic Development, 1979. 493p. (Cornell Thesis in 1979; 481 leaves)

Edwards, Corwin D. Maintaining Competition. New York; McGraw Hill, 1949. 337p.

Edwards, J. A., K. C. Gibbs, L. J. Guedry, and H. H. Stoevener. The Demand for Non-Unique Outdoor Recreational Services: Methodological Issues. Corvallis; Oregon Experimental Station, 1976. 60p. (Oregon Agric. Exp. Station Tech. Bulletin No. 133) Q

Eliot, Clara. The Farmer's Campaign for Credit. New York, London; D. Appleton and Co., 1927. 312p.

Elliot, F. F. Types of Farming in the United States. Washington, D.C.; U.S. Department of Commerce, Census Bureau, US Government Printing Office, 1933. 225p.

Ellis, H. S. and H. C. Wallich, eds. El Desarrollo Economico y America Latina (Economic Development and Latin America). Mexico, BA; Fondo de Cultura Economica, 1960, 1961. English edition—New York; St. Martin's Press, 1961.

Ellis, H.S., and L.A. Metzler, eds. Readings in the Theory of International Trade, selected by a committe of the American Economic Assn. Philadelphia; Blakiston, 1950. 637p.

Ellison, Thomas. The Cotton Trade of Great Britain. Including a History of the Liverpool Cotton Market and of the Liverpool Cotton Brokers' Association. London; E. Wilson, 1886. 355p.

Ellul, J. The Technological Society. Trans. from French by J. Wilkinson. New York; Vintage Books, 1964. 449p. (Reprinted by New York; Knopf, 1970.)

Elvin, M. The Pattern of the Chinese Past: A Social and Economic Interpretation. Stanford, Calif.; Stanford University, 1973. 346p.

Ely, Richard T., and G.S. Wehrwein. Land Economics. New York; Macmillan, 1940. 512p.

Emel'ianov, I.V. Economic Theory of Cooperation Economic Structure of Cooperative Organizations . . . Washington, D.C.; Edwards Brother, Inc., 1942. 269p.

Engberg, R.C. Industrial Prosperity and the Farmer. New York; Macmillan, 1927. 286p.

Engelbrecht, T.H. Die Landbauzonen der Aussertropischenlander; auf Grund der Statischen Quellenwerke Dargestellt. Berlin; 1893–99. 3 vols.

Ensminger, Douglas, ed. Food Enough or Starvation for Millions. New Delhi; Tata McGraw-Hill, 1977. 562p.

Ensminger, Douglas. Rural India in Transition. New Delhi; All India Panchayat Parishad, 1972. 115p.

Erdei, Ferenc. Mezogazdasag es szovetkezet. Budapest; Akadeniai Kiado, 1959. 382p.

Erdman, H. E. American Produce Markets. Boston, 1928. 449p.

Evangelou, P. Livestock Development in Kenya's Maasailand: Pastoralists' Transistion to a Market Economy. Boulder, Colo.; Westview Press, 1984. 309p.

Extension Committee on Organization and Policy. Community Resource Development. Washington, D.C.; U.S. Department of Agriculture, Cooperative Extension Service, 1966.

Ezekial, Mordecai, and Louis H. Bean. Economic Bases for the Agricultural Adjustment Act. Washington, D.C.; U.S.Department of Agriculture, 1933. 67p.

Ezekiel, Mordecai, ed. Towards World Prosperity, Through Industrial and Agricultural Development and Expansion. New York, London; Harper and Brothers, 1947. 455p.

Ezekiel, Mordecai. New York; Harcourt, Brace and Co., 1936. 326p.

F

Fairchild, George Thompson. Rural Wealth and Welfare: Economic Principles Illustrated and Applied in Farm Life. New York, London; Macmillan, 1900. 381p.

Fallers, Lloyd. Inequality: Social Stratification Reconsidered. Chicago; University of Chicago Press, 1973. 330p.

FAO/UNFPA Expert Consultation on Land Resources for Populations of the Future (Rome, 1977) Rome; Food and Agriculture Organizatoin, 1978. 88p.

Farm Foundation. Turning the Searchlight on Farm Policy. Chicago, 1952.

Farmer, B. H., ed. Green Revolution? Technology and Change in Rice-Growing Areas of Tamil Nadu and Sri Lanka. Boulder, Colo.; Westview Press, 1977. 429p.

Fay, I.G. Notes on Extension in Agricuture. London; Asia Publishing House, 1962. 204p.

Federal Reserve System. Agricultural Adjustment and Income. Washington, DC; Board of Governors, 1945. (Postwar Economic Studies No 2)

Fellner, W. Competition among the Few: Oligopoly and Similar Market Structures. New York; Knopf, 1949. 328p.

Fellows, I. F. Budgeting: Tool of Research and Extension in Agricultural Economics. Storrs; Agricultural Experiment Station, University of connecticut, 1960. 45p.

Ferber, Robert, ed. Consumption and Income Distribution in Latin America: Selected Topics. Washington, D.C., for ECIEL by Organization of American States, 1980. 484p.

Ferguson, D.C., ed. A Conceptual Framework for the Evaluation of Livestock Production Development Projects and Programs In Sub-Saharan West Africa. Ann Arbor; University of Michigan, Center For Research on Economic Development, 1976. 183p.

Fienup, D. F., R. H. Brannon, and F. A. Fender. The Agricultural Development of Argentina: A Policy and Development Perspective. New York; Praeger, 1969. 437p.
Filley, Horace Clyde. Cooperation in Agriculture. New York; J. Wiley and Sons; London; Chapman and Hall, 1929. 468p.
Fillmore, Eva. A. Farm Children; an Investigation of Rural Life in Selected Areas of Iowa. Iowa Child Welfare Research Station. New York, London; D. Appleton and Co., 1930. 337p.
Finch, Vernor C., and O.E. Baker. Geography of the World's Agriculture. Washington, D.C.; Government Printing Office, 1917. 149p.
Finck von Finckenstein, Hans W. Der Aufbau der Agrarwirtschaft. Basel; Verlag fur Recht und Gesellschaft, 1942. 236p.
Fine, J. C. and R. G. Lattimore, eds. Livestock in Asia: Issues and Policies. Ottawa, Canada, International Develop. and Research Centre, 1982.
Finney, D. J. An Introduction to Statistical Science in Agriculture. 2d ed. Edinburgh; Oliver and Boyd, 1962. 216p.
Fishel, W., ed. Resource Allocation in Agricultural Research. Minneapolis, MN; Univ of Minn. Press, 1971. 391p. (2)
Fisher, L.H. The Harvest Labor Market in California. Cambridge, Mass.; Harvard University Press, 1953. 183p.
Fitzgerald, E.V.K. The State and Economic Development in Peru Since 1968. Cambridge, England; Cambridge University Press, 1976. 127p.
Flanders, M.J. and A. Razin, eds. Development in an Inflationary World. New York; Academic Press, 1981. 492p.
Food and Agriculture Organization. Agricultural Commodities: Projections for 1975 and 1985. Rome; Food and Agriculture Organization, 1967. 2 vols.
Food and Agriculture Organization. Agricultural Credit in Asia: Report of the FAO Regional Seminar on Agricultural Credit for Small Farmers, Bangkok, 1974. Rome, Food and Agriculture Organ.,1975. 84p.
Food and Agriculture Organization. Approaches to Agricultural Development in the Light of World Economic Change. Rome; Food and Agriculture Organization, 1974. 1 vol.
Food and Agricultural Organization. General Guidelines to the Analysis of Agricultural Production Projects. Rome; Food and Agriculture Organization, 1971.
Food and Argicultural Organization. Population and Agricultural Development: Selected Relationships and Possible Planning Uses, No. 6: Economic-Demographic Interactions in Agricultural Development—The Case of Rural-to-Urban Migration. Rome; F.A.O., 1978. 171p. (Development Documents: No. 52)
Food and Agriculture Organization. Regional Food Plan for Africa. Rome; Food and Agriculture Organization, 1978. 86p.
Food and Agriculture Organization. Survey of Rural Cooperatives in Countries in Southeast Asia (with References to Australia and New Zealand). Washington, D.C., 1949. 96p.
Forster, G. W. Farm Organization and Management. 3d ed. New York; Prentice-Hall, 1953. 430p.
Forster, G. W. and M. C. Leager. Elements of Agricultural Economics. New York; Prentice-Hall, 1950. 441p.
Fowke, Vernon C. Canadian Agricultural Policy; the Historical Pattern. Toronto; University of Toronto Press, 1946. 304p.
Francioni, Manuel J. El Credito en la Produccion Agraria. Buenos Aires; El Ateneo, 1944. 430p.

Franda, Marcus F. West Bengal and the Federalizing Process in India. 1968. Princeton, NJ; Princeton University Press, 1968. 257p.

Frauendorfer, S. von. Agrarwirtschaftliche Forschung und Agrarpolitik in Italien. Berlin; Parey, 1942. 307p.

Fraser, Wilber John. Profitable Farming and Life Management. Danville, Ill.; The Interstates Printers and Publishers, 1937. 416p.

Frederick, A. L, and Dennis R. Henderson, eds. Public Choices for a Changing Agriculture. Published by the North Central Public Policy Education Committee, 1987. 48p. (North Central Regional Publication No. 266) Q

Frey, Thomas L., and Robert H. Behrens. Lending to Agricultural Enterprises. Boston, Mass.; Bankers Publishing Co., 1981. 475p.

Friedrich, K.H. Farm Management Data Collection and Analysis: An Electronic Data Processing Storage and Retrieval System. Rome; Food and Agriculture Organization, 1977. 260p.

Fukumot, Kwao. Nihon Nogyo Ni Okeru Shihonka-teki Keiei Hatten No Ryakuzu (General Survey of the Development of Capitalistic Management of Japanese Agriculture). Tokyo; Kaihosha, 1949. 234p.

Fuller, V. Labor Relations in Agriculture: West Coast Bargaining Systems. Berkeley; University of California, Institute of Industrial Relations, 1955. 46p.

Furtado, Celso. A Economia Brasileira: Contribucao a Analise do Seu Desenvolvimento. Rio de Janeiro; Editora A Noite, 1954. 246p.

G

Galarza, E. Spiders in the House and Workers in the Field. Notre Dame, Ind.; University of Notre Dame Press, 1970. 306p.

Galbraith, John K. Inequality in Agriculture; Problem and Program. Ontario Agricultural College, Department of Agricultural Economics, 1956. (Morrison Memorial Lecture)

Gammans, Leonard David. Report on Co-operation in India and Europe. Singapore; Printed at the Government Printing Office by V.C.G. Gatrell, Acting Government Printer, 1933. 314p.

Garcia, M. and P. Pinstrup-Anderson. The Pilot Food Price Subsidy Scheme in the Philippines: Its Impact on Income, Food Consumption and Nutritional Status. Washington, D.C.; International Food Policy and Research Institute, 1987. (IFPRI Research Report No. 651)

Garlock, F. L. Effect of the Seasonality of Agriculture on Iowa Banking. Washington, D.C.; USDA, Bureau of Agricultural Economics, 1932. 20p.

Garrigou-Lagrange, Andre. Production Agricole et Economie Rurale. Paris; Librairie Generale De Droit et de Jurisprudence, 1939. 211p.

Gee, Wilson. American Farm Policy. New York; W.W. Horton and Co., 1934. 146p.

Gee, Wilson. The Place of Agriculture in American Life. New York; Macmillan, 1930. 217p.

Gee, Wilson. The Social Economics of Agriculture. Revised ed. New York; Macmillan, 1942. 720p.

Gemmill, G. T. and Carl K. Eicher. A Framework for Research on the Economics of Farm Mechanization in Developing Countries. East Lansing; Michigan State University, Department of Agricultural Economics, 1973. 67p. (African Rural Employment Paper No. 6.)

George, Henry. Protection or Free Trade: An Examination of the Tariff Question, with Especial Regard to the Interests of Labor. Garden City, N.Y.; Doubleday, Doran and Company, Inc., 1931. 335p.

George, Henry. Progress and Poverty: An Inquiry into the Cause of Industrial Depression and of Increase of Want with Increase of Wealth. Latest printing: New York; Robert Schalkenbach Foundation, 1971. 599p. (First published in 1879.)

Gibson, W.L., Jr., R.J. Hildreth, and G. Wunderlich, eds. Methods for Land Economics Research. Lincoln; University of Nebraska Press, 1966.

Gillette, John M. Constructive Rural Sociology. New ed. New York; Macmillan Co., 1916. 301p.

Gillette, John M. Rural Sociology. New York; Macmillan, 1936. 778p.

Ginzberg, E. Human Resources: The Wealth of a Nation. New York; Simon and Schuster, 1958. 183p.

Goldberger, A. S. Impact Multipliers and Dynamic Properties of the Klein-Goldberger Model. Amsterdam; North-Holland, 1959. 138p.

Goldstein, Benjamin F. Marketing: A Farmer's Problem. New York; Macmillan, 1928. 330p.

Golob, Eugene O. The Meline Tariff: French Agriculture and Nationalist Economic Policy. New York; Columbia University Press, 1944. 266p. (Reprinted by A M S Press, 1968. (Studies in History Economics and Public Law: No. 506.)

Goltz, Theodor, freiherr von der. Agrarwesen und Agrarpolitik. 2d ed. Jena; G. Fischer, 1904. 330p.

Goltz, Theodor, freiherr von der. Landwirtschaftliche Buchfuhrung. 10th ed. Revised by Seelhorst. Berlin; P. Parey, 1910. 210p.

Goltz, Theodor, freiherr von der. Landwirtschaftliche Taxationslehre. 3d ed. Berlin; P. Parey, 1903. 670p.

Gordon, David L. Employment and Development of Small Enterprises: Sector Policy Paper. Washington, D.C.; World Bank, 1978. 93p. T

Graf, Truman F., and Robert E. Jacobson. Resolving Grade B Milk Conversion and Low Class 1 Utilization Pricing and Pooling Problems. Madison; University of Wisconsin, College of Agriculture and Life Sciences, 1973. 77p. (Research Report 2503) Q

Graham, Edward H. Natural Principles of Land Use. London, New York; Oxford University Press, 1944. 274p.

Gras, N.S.B. A History of Agriculture in Europe and America. 2d ed. New York; 1940. 496p.

Gratto, Charles P., Everett E. Peterson, James G. Kendrick, Otto Doering, Richard Barrows, and Larry Libby. Perspectives on Tomorrow: Food-Population-Resources: The Issues and the Options. 1978. (North Central Regional Publ. No. 53)Q

Gray, Lewis C. Introduction to Agricultural Economics. New York; Macmillan, 1929. 556p.

Graziadei, Antonio. Elementi di Economia Agraria. Rome; Edizioni dell'Atenso, 1946. 221p.

Great Britain. Ministry of Agriculture and Fisheries. Wages and Conditions of Employment in Agriculture. London; H.M. Stationery Office, 1919. 2 vols.

Green, F.E. A History of the English Agricultural Labourer, 1870–1920. London; P.S. King and Son, 1927. 356p.

Griffin, Keith, ed. Institutional Reform and Economic Development in the Chinese Countryside. Hong Kong, Macmillian Press, Ltd., 1984. 336p.

Griswold, A. W. Farming and Democracy. New York; Harcourt, Brace, 1948. 227p.

Grunwald, J. and P. Musgrove. Natural Resources in Latin American Development. Baltimore, Md., Johns Hopkins University Press, 1970.

Guimei, Mokbel. Le Credit Agricole et l'Egypte. Origine et Developpement du Credit Agricole Dans les Principaux Pays. La Loi Egyptionne no 23 de 1927. Paris; Editions et Publications Contemporaines, P. Bossuet, 1931. 301p.

Gupta, A. P. Marketing of Agricultural Produce in India. Bombay, India; Vora and Co. Publ., 1975. 264p.

H

Haberler, G., ed. Readings in Business Cycle Theory, selected by a committe of the American Economic Association. Philadelphia; Blakiston, 1944. 494p.
Hagood, Margaret J. Mothers of the South: Portraiture of the White Tenant Farm Woman. Chapell Hill; University of North Carolina Press, 1939. 252p.
Hahn, Werner G. The Politics of Soviet Agriculture: 1960–1970. Johns Hopkins University Press, 1972. 320p.
Hainisch, Michael. Die Landflucht, Ihr Wesen und Ihre Bekampfung im Rahmen einer Agrarreform. Jena; G.Fischer, 1924. 371p.
Hainsworth, G.B., ed. Village-Level Modernization in Southeast Asia. Vancouver, British Columbia; University of British Columbia Press, 1982. (3)
Halcrow, Harold G., J. Ackerman, M. Harris, C.L. Stewart, and J.F. Timmons. Modern Land Policy. Urbana; University of Ill. Press, 1960. 449p.
Hale, William Jay. Farmward March: Chemurgy Takes Command. New York; Coward-McCann, Inc., 1939. 222p.
Hall, Alfred D. Reconstruction and the Land; an Approach to Farming in the National Interest. London; Macmillan, 1942. 286p.
Hamberg, D. Models of Economic Growth. New York; Harper, 1971. 246p.
Hanau, A., M. Rolfes, H. Wilbrandt and E. Woermann, eds. Friedrich Aereboe: Würdigung und Auswahl aus seinen Werken aus Anlass der 100. Wiederkehr seines Geburtstages. Hamburg and Berlin, 1965. 365p.
Hare, H.R. Farm Business Management. Toronto; The Hyerson Press, 1946. 450p.
Hargreaves, James. Farm Politics; Old Problems in a New World. Montreal; Renouf Publishing Company, 1942. 102p.
Harmston, F. K. The Community as an Economic System. Ames; Iowa State University Press, 1983. 333p.
Harris, Seymour Edwin, 1897–, ed. The New Economics: Keynes' Influence on Theory and Public Policy. 1st ed. New York; A.A. Knopf, 1947. 686p.
Hasan, P. Korea: Problems and Issues in a Rapidly Growing Economy. Baltimore; Johns Hopkins University Press for the World Bank, 1976. 277p.
Haseyama, T. A. Hirata, and T. Yaragihara, eds. Two Decades of Asian Development and Outlook for the 1980's. Tokyo, Institute of Developing Economies, 1983. 384p. (Its IDE Symposium Proceedings No. 8) (2)
Hathaway, D.E., J.A. Beegle, and W.K. Bryant. The People of Rural America: A 1960 Census Monograph. Washington, D.C.; U.S. Bureau of the Census, 1968. 289p.
Hathaway, D.E. Government and Agriculture. New York; Macmillan, 1963. 412p.
Haveman, R.H. Water Resource Investment and the Public Interest: An Analysis of Federal Expenditures in Ten Southern States. Nashville; Vanderbilt University Press, 1965. 199p.
Hawley, A.H. The Changing Shape of Metropolitan America: Deconcentration Since 1926. Glencoe, Ill.; Free Press, 1956. 177p.
Hawthorn, Horace B. The Sociology of Rural Life. New York, London; The Century Co., 1926. 517p.
Hayek, F.A. von. The Road to Serfdom. Chicago; University of Chicago Press, 1944. 248p.
Haythorne, George V. Labor in Canadian Agriculture. Cambridge, Mass.; Harvard University Press, Harvard Studies in Labor in Agriculture, 1960. 122p.
Haythorne, George V. Land and Labour; a Social Survey of Agriculture and the Farm

Labour Market in Central Canada. Toronto. Published for McGill University by the Oxford University Press, 1941. 568p.

Hazari, R.K. The Economics of Estate Farming: A Plan for Agro-Industry. Bombay; Indian Society of Agricultural Economics, 1954. 73p.

Heady, Earl O., G. L. Johnson, and L. S. Hardin, eds. Resource Productivity, Returns to Scale, and Farm Size. Ames; Iowa State College Press, 1956. 208p.

Heady, Earl O., and H. R. Jensen. Farm Management Economics. New York; Prentice-Hall, 1954. 645p.

Heaton, J. E. The Agricultural Development of Venezuela. New York; Praeger, 1969. 320p.

Helleiner, Gerald K. Peasant Agriculture, Government and Economic Growth in Nigeria. Homewood; Irwin, 1966. 600p.

Henderson, J. M., and A. O. Krueger. National Growth and Economic Change in the Upper Midwest. Minneapolis; University of Minnesota Press, 1965. 231p.

Henzler, R. Die Genossenschaft eine Fördernde Betriebswissenschaft. Essen, 1957. 228p.

Herrick, Myron T., and R. Ingalls. Rural Credits, Land and Cooperative. New York, London; D.Appleton and Co., 1928. 519p.

Hertz, Friedrich O. Dic Agrarischen Fragen im Verhaltnis Zum Socialismus. Vienna; L. Rosner, 1899. 141p.

Hicks, John R. The Crisis in Keynesian Economics. Oxford, Basil Blackwell, 1974. 85p.

Higby, Annette; Harmon Hoff and Eugene Severns. FHA Farm Loan Handbook. National Clearinghouse for Legal Services Incorporated, 1981. 157p.

Hildebrand, B. Die National-okonomie der Gegenwart und Zukunft und Andere Gesammelte Schriften. Jena; Gustav Fischer, 1922. (Mostly written between 1848 and 1864.)

Hildreth, C., and F. G. Jarrett. A Statistical Study of Livestock Production and Marketing. New York; Wiley, 1955. 156p.

Hill, Brian E. and K. A. Ingersent. An Economic Analysis of Agriculture. London; Heinemann Educational Books, 1977. 296p.

Hill, H., and G. Moffett. No Harvest for the Reaper: The Story of the Migratory Agricultural Worker in the United States. New York; National Association for the Advancement of Colored People, 1960. 45p.

Hirshleifer, J., J.C. De Haven, and J.W. Milliman. Water Supply: Economics, Technology, and Policy. Chicago, University of Chicago Press, 1960. 378p.

Hjelm, Lennart. Don Jordbruksekonomiska Kostnadsuberudingem Innebord Och Grundorut Sattningerar. Lund, Berlingaka Boktryckoriet, 1948. 170p.

Hoffer, Charles H. Introduction to Rural Sociology. Rev. ed. New York; Farrar and Rinehart, Inc., 1936. 500p.

Hoffman, A.C. Large-Scale Organization in the Food Industries. U.S. 76th Congress, 3d Session, Temporary National Economic Committee, Monograph No. 35, Committee print, 1940. 174p.

Hofstee, E. W. Rural Life and Rural Welfare in the Netherlands. The Hague, 1957. 364p.

Hoglund, C. R., G. L. Johnson, C. A. Lassiter, and L. D. McGilliard, eds. Nutritional and Economic Aspects of Feed Utilization by Dairy Cows. Ames; Iowa State College Press, 1959. 287p.

Holmes, Clarence Leroy. Economics of Farm Organization and Management. Boston, New York; D.C. Heath and Company, 1928. 422p.

Holmes, Roy H. Rural Sociology: The Family-Farm Institution. 1st ed. New York, London; McGraw-Hill Book Company, Inc., 1932. 416p.

Holt, Alan J. Wheat Farms of Victoria; A Sociological Survey. Melbourne; The School of Agriculture, University of Melbourne, 1946. 179p.

Honandle, Beth Walter. Capacity Building (Management Improvement) for Local Governments: An Annotated Bibliography. Washington, D.C.; USGPO, U.S. Department of Agriculture, Economic Statistics Service, 1981. 78p. (RDRR-28)

Hong, W. and L. Krause. Trade and Growth of the Advanced Developing Countries in the Pacific Basin. Seoul; Korea Development Institute Press, 1981. 620p.

Hooker, A.A. The International Grain Trade. 2d ed. London; Sir I. Pitman and Sons, Ltd., 1939. 168p.

Hoon, K. L. Land Utilization and Rural Economy in Korea. New York; Greenwood Press, 1969. 302p.

Hooper, S.G. The Finance of Farming in Great Britain. London; Europea Publications, 1955. 247p.

Hoover, E. M. The Location of Economic Activity. New York; McGraw-Hill, 1948. 310p.

Hopkins, Raymond F. and D.J. Puchala, eds. The Global Political Economy of Food. Madison; University of Wisconsin Press, 1978. 339p. (Reprint of contents of Summer 1978 issue of *International Organization.*)

Horner, J.T. Agricultural Marketing. Rev. ed. New York; J. Wiley & Sons, 1925. 249p.

Horowitz, I. L., ed. Masses in Latin America. New York; Oxford University Press, 1970. 608p.

Horton, D.C. Patterns of Farm Financial Structure. National Bureau of Economic Research. Princeton; Princeton University Press, 1957. 185p.

Houck, James P., and J. S. Mann. An Analysis of Domestic and Foreign Demand for U.S. Soybeans and Soybean Products. St. Paul; Univ. of Minnesota, 1968. 59p. (Univ. of Minnesota Agric. Exp. Stn. Tech. Bull. 256) Q

Houthakker, H.S. Economic Policy for the Farm Sector. Washington, D.C.; American Enterprise Institute for Public Policy Research, 1967. 65p.

Hoveland, C. S., ed. Crop Quality, Storage, and Utilization. Madison, Wisc.; American Society of Agronomy, 1980.

Howard, H. Landwirtschaftliche Buchfuhrung. 2d ed. Leipzig, 1923. 123p.

Howard, Louise E. Labour in Agriculture; an International Survey. London; Oxford Univeristy Press, H. Milford, 1935. 339p.

Howell, H. B. Better Farm Accounting with Separate Depreciation Schedule for Continuous Use. 4th ed. Ames; Iowa State University Press, 1980. 48p. (2d ed. 1947. 40p.)

Hu, T. C. Integer Programming and Network Flows. Reading, Mass.; Addison-Wesley, 1969. 452p.

Hubbard, Leonard E. The Economics of Soviet Agriculture. London; Macmillan, 1939. 315p.

Huffman, R.E. Irrigation Development and Public Water Policy. New York; Ronald Press, 1953. 336p.

Hunt, Robert L. Farm Management in the South. Danville, Ill.; The Interstate Publisher and Printer, 1942. 566p.

Hunter, D.J., ed. Food Goals, Future Structural Changes, and Agricultural Policy: A National Basebook. Ames; Iowa State University Press, 1969. 325p.

Hurlburt, V. L. On the Theory of Evaluating Farmland by the Income Approach. Washington, D.C.; USDA, Agricultural Research Service, 1959. 34p.

I

Imperial Conference on Agricultural Cooperation, 2d. Report of Proceedings Held on July 18, 19, and 20, 1936. London; P.S. King and Sons, Ltd., 1938. 250p.

India. National Planning Committee. Land Policy, Agricultural Labour and Insurance; Report of the Sub-Committee. Chairman, K.T. Shah; Secretary, Radha Kamal Mukerjee; ed. by K.T. Shah. Bombay; Vora, 1948. 176p.

Indian Society of Agricultural Economics. Agrarian Reforms in Western Countries. Bombay; Vora and Co. Publ., Ltd., 1946. 122p.

Indian Society of Agricultural Economics. Comparative Experience of Agricultural Development in Developing Countries of Asia and South-East since World War II. Bombay, the Society, 1972. 434p.

Institute of Pacific Relations. Agrarian China: Selected Source Materials from Chinese Authors, Compiled and Translated. Chicago, Ill.; University of Chicago Press, 1938. 258p.

Institute of Farm Management and Agricultural, Economic Technical and Economic Changes in Danish Farming. 40 Years of Farm Records, 1917–1957. Copenhagen, 1959.

International Institute of Agriculture. Agricultural Problems in Their International Aspect. Rome; International Institute of Agriculture, 1926. 662p.

International Institute of Agriculture. . . . Etude metodologique et statistique sur les recensements de la population agricole, les salaires de la main d'oeuvre rurale et les courants d'emigration dans les differents etats. Rome; Officina Poligrafica Italiana, 1912. 150p.

International Labour Office. The Representation and Organisation of Agricultural Workers. Geneva; Impr. du Journal de Geneve, 1928. 210p.

International Labour Organization. Growth, Employment and Equity: A Comprehensive Strategy for the Sudan, 1975. Geneva; I. L. O., 1976. 2 vols.

International Rice Research Institute. Changes in Rice Farming in Selected Areas of Asia. Los Banos, Philippines, 1975. 377p.

Irimajiri, Koshu. Nihon Nomin Keizai-shi Kenkyu (Studies in the History of Economy of Japanese Farmers). Tokyo; Kamakura Kunko, 1949. 456p.

Ishikawa, S. Agricultural Development Strategies in Asia: Case Studies of the Philippines and Thailand. Manila; Asian Development Bank, 1970. 128p.

Ishaque, Hafiz S.M. Rural Bengal: Her Needs and Requirements. Sirajganj; Printed at the Nur-e-elahi Press, 1938. 183p.

Islam, M.M. Development Strategy of Bangladesh. New York; Pergamon Press, 1978 109p.

J

Jacks, G.V., and R.O. Whyte. Vanishing Lands: A World Survey of Soil Erosion. New York; Doubleday, Doran and Co., Inc., 1939. 332p.

James, H. Land Planning in the United States for the City, State, and Nation. New York; Macmillan, 1926, 427p

James, William E. Asian Agriculture in Transition: Key Policy Issues. Manila; Asian Development Bank, 1983. 93p. (ADB Staff Paper No. 19)

Jasdanwalla, A. Marketing Efficiency in Indian Agriculture. Bombay; Allied Publishers, 1966. 132p.

Jasny, Naum. The Socialized Agriculture of the U.S.S.R.: Plans and Performance. Stanford, Calif.; Stanford University Press, 1949. 837p.

Jensen, E. Danish Agriculture: Its Economics and Development, a description and economic analysis centering on the free trade epoch 1870–1930. Copenhagen; J.H. Schultz, 1937. 417p.

Jessness, Oscar B., ed. Readings on Agricultural Policy. Philadelphia; Blakiston for the American Farm Economics Association, 1949. 470p.

Jessness, Oscar B. The Co-operative Marketing of Farm Products. Philadelphia; J.B. Lippincott, 1923. 292p.

Jewett, A.L. and E.C. Voorhies. Agricultural Cooperatives: Strength in Unity. Edited by Agricultural Council of California. Danville, Ill.; Interstate, 1963. 139p.

Jha, Kumar K. Agricultural Finance in Nepal. New Delhi; Heritage, 1978. 241p.

Johl, S. S., and M. S. Mudahar. The Dynamics of Institutional Change and Rural Development in Punjab, India. Ithaca, N.Y.; Rural Development Committee, Center for International Studies, Cornell Univ., 1974. 171p.

Johl, S. S., and A. S. Kahlon. Application of Programming Techniques to Indian Farming Conditions. Ludhiana; Punjab Agricultural University, 1967. 98p.

Johnson, D. Gale. Trade and Agriculture: A Study of Inconsistant Policies. New York; Wiley, 1950. 198p.

Johnson, G. L., A. Halter, H. R. Jensen, and D. Thomas, eds. A Study of Managerial Processes of Midwestern Farmers. Ames; Iowa State University Press, 1961. 221p.

Johnson, Julia and Glenna Dunning, eds. Land Planning in National Parks and Forests: A Selective Bibliography. C P L Bibliographies, 1977. 68p.

Johnston, Bruce F. The Staple Food Economies of Western Tropical Africa. Stanford, Calif.; Stanford University Press, 1958. 305p. (Reprinted in 1963.)

Jones, E. L. editor. Agriculture and Economic Growth in England; 1650–1815. London; Methuen, 1967. 195p.

Josling, Timothy E. Agriculture and Britain's Trade Policy Dilemma. London; Trade Policy Research Centre, 1970.

Josling, Timothy E. Problems and Prospects for U.S. Agriculture in World Markets. Washington, D.C.; National Planning Association,1981. 59p. (Committee on Changing International Realities); (NPA Report No. 183)

Joubert, Henri. Le Warrantage des Produits Agricoles. Paris; Rousseau et cie, 1933. 213p.

Jouzier, Etienne. . . . Economie Rurale. Paris; J.B. Bailliere et fils, 1920. 550p.

Joyce, Charles L., ed. Towards a Rational U.S. Policy on River Basin Development in the Sahel; Proceedings of a Colloquium. Washington, D.C.; Agency for International Development, 1978. 335p.

K

Kahn, Si. How People Get Power: Organizing Opressed Communities for Action. New York; McGraw-Hill, 1970. 128p.

Kantor, H.S., C.S. Cronemeyer, and F.L. Hauser. Problems Involved in Applying a Federal Minimum Wage to Agricultural Workers. Washington, D.C.; U.S. Department of Labor, 1960. 2 vols.

Kawada, S. Nogyo Keiznaigaku (Agricultural Economics). Tokyo; 1927. 13p.

Kawanishi, O. Noson Mondai Kenkyu (Studies on Rural Problems). 1926. 416p.

Keatinge, Gerald Francis. Rural Economy in the Bombay Deccan. London, New York, Bombay, Calcutta; Longmans, Green and Company, 1912. 212p.

Keith, Robert G. Conquest and Agrarian Change. (Historical Studies: No. 93). Cambridge, Mass.; Harvard University Press, 1976. 176p.

Kelsey, Lincoln D. and Cannon C. Hearne. Cooperative Extension Work. Ithaca, N.Y.; Comstock Pub. Co., 1949. 424p. (3d ed., 1963. 490p.)

Kelsey, Rayner W. Relief and its Antecedents. Haverford, PA; Pennsylvania History Press. 1929. 36p.

Kemper, Max. Marxismus und Landwirtschaft. Krefeld; A. Hontges, 1929. 119p.

Kendrick, J.W., ed. Output, Input and Productivity Measurement, National Bureau of Economic Research. Princeton, NJ; Princeton University Press, 1961. 506p.

Kenen, P.B. and R. Lawrence, eds. The Open Economy: Essays on International Trade and Finance. New York; Columbia Univ. Press, 1968. 391p. (3)

Kenyon, Damid E., and Samuel Evans. Short-term Soybean Acreage Projection Model Including Price and Policy Impacts. Blacksburg; Virginia Polytechnic Institute and State University, 1975. 74p. (Res. Div. Bull. 106) Q

Kerridge, E. The Agricultural Revolution. London; Allen & Unwin, 1967. 428p.

Keynes, John M. The General Theory of Employment, Interest and Money. New York; Harcourt, Brace and Company, 1936. 403p.

Keynes, John M. Essays in Persuasion. New York; Harcourt Brace and Co., 1932. 376p.

Khan, M. H. The Role of Agriculture in Economic Development: A Case Study of Pakistan. Wageningen, Holland; Agricultural Univ., Centre for Agricultural Publ. and Documentation, 1966. 161p.

Khan, M.H. The Economics of the Green Revolution in Pakistan. New York; Praeger, 1975. 229p.

Kile, Orville M. The New Agriculture. New York; Macmillan, 1932. 218p.

Kim, K. S., and M. Roemer. Growth and Structural Transformation. (Studies in the Modernization of the Republic of Korea: 1945–1975). Cambridge, Mass.; Harvard Univ., 1979. 195p. (Harvard East Asian Monograph No. 86)

King, Richard A., ed. Interregional Competition Research Methods. Raliegh, N.C.; North Carolina State University, Agricultural Policy Institute, 1963. 204p.

Kirk, John Henry. Agriculture and the Trade Cycle, Their Mutual Relations, With Special Reference to the Period 1926–1931. London; P.S. King and Son, Ltd., 1933. 272p.

Kirkpatrick, Ellis L. The Farmer's Standard of Living. New York, London; The Century Co., 1929. 299p.

Kishida, Y., ed. Agricultural Mechanization in Southeast Asia. Tokyo; Farm Machinery Industrial Research Corp., 1971. 2 vols.

Kleijnen, J. P. C. Statistical Techniques in Simulation, Parts 1 and 2. New York; Marcel Dekker, 1974–75. 2 vols. (775p.)

Klein, L.R. An Introduction to Econometrics. Englewood Cliffs, N.J.; Prentice-Hall, 1962. 280p.

Knapp, J.G. The Rise of American Cooperative Enterprise: 1620–1920. Danville, Ill.; Interstate, 1969. 532p.

Kneese, A.V. The Economics of Regional Water Quality Management. Baltimore; Johns Hopkins University Press for Resources for the Future, 1964. 214p.

Kneese, A.V. Water Pollution: Economic Aspects and Research Needs. Washington, D.C.; Resources for the Future, 1962. 107p.

Knight, Frank H. Freedom and Reform; Essays in Economics and Social Philosophy. New York, London; Harper and Brothers, 1947. 409p.

Knight, P.T. Brazilian Agricultural Technology and Trade: A Study of Five Commodities. New York; Praeger, 1971. 223p.

Knipovich, B. Sel'skokhozristvennoe Raionirovanie (Agricultural Production Regions). Moscow; 1925. 192p.

Kolesnyev, S. G. Organizatsiia Sotsialisticheskizh Seloskozhozistvennyz Prediriatii (Organization of Socialist Agricultural Businesses). Moscow, 1957. 632p.

Koopmans, T. C., ed. Statistical Inference in Dynamic Economic Models. New York; Wiley, 1950. 438p.

Koopmans, T. C. Linear Regression Anaylsis in Economic Time Series. Haarlem; Haarlem Press, 1937. 150p.

Kreitlow, B.W. Rural Education: Community Backgrounds. New York; Harper, 1954. 411p.

Krzymovski, R. Geschichte der Deutschen Landwirtschaft. Stuttgart, 1939. 164p.

Krzymovski, R. Philosophie der Landwirtschaftslehre. Stuttgart, 1919. 164p.

Kuvshinov, I.A. Ekonomika Sotsialistichekogo Sel'skogo Khoziaistva (Economics of Socialist Agriculture). Moscow; Gos. Izd- vo Selkhozlit-ry, 1957. 400p. (2d ed. 1959. 429p.)

L

Labys, Walter. C., ed. Quantitative Models of Commodity Markets. Cambridge, Mass.; Ballinger Publ., 1975. 404p.

Ladd, E.C., Jr. Ideology in America: Change and Response in a City, a Suburb, and a Small Town. Ithaca, N.Y.; Cornell University Press, 1969.

Ladd, G. W. Agricultural Bargaining Power. Ames; Iowa State University Press, 1964. 163p.

Lal, Prem Chand. Reconstruction and Education in Rural India in the Light of the Programme Carried on at Sriniketan, the Institute of Rural Reconstruction. London; G. Allen and Unwin, Ltd., 1932. 262p.

Lamartine, Yates P. Food Production in Western Europe: An Economic Survey of Agriculture in Six Countries. London, New York; Longmans, Green and Co., 1940 572p.

Lamartine, Yates Paul. Food, Land and Manpower in Western Europe. London; Macmillan and NewYork; St. Martin's, 1960. 294p.

Langoni, C. G. Distriuicao de Renda e Desenvolvimento Economico do Brasil (Income Distribution and Economic Development of Brazil). Rio de Janeiro; eda Expressao e Cultura, 1973. 315p.

Larmer, Ernest M. Financing the Livestock Industry. New York; Macmillan, 1926. 327p.

Lasley, Floyd A., and C. N. Shaw. Economic Aspects of Dairying in the Northeast. Washington, D.C.; U.S. Department of Agriculture, Economic Research Service, 1970. 55p. (USDA Agri. Econ. Rep. No. 188.)

Latil, Marc. L'évolution du Revenu Agricole; les Agriculteurs Devant les Exigences de la Croissance Économique et des Luttes Sociales. Paris; A. Colin, 1956. 378p.

Laur, E. F. Landwirtschaftliche Betriebslehre für bäuerliche Verhältnisse. 10th ed. Aarau, 1938. 392p.

Laur, E. F. Volkwirtschaftliche Grundlagen der Wirschaftslehre des Landbaus und der Bauernpolitik. 4th ed. Aarau, 1946. 112p.

Leclerg, E. L., W. H. Leonard and A. G. Clark. Field Plot Technique. 2d ed. Minneapolis, MN; Burgess, 1962. 373p.

Lee, Mabel D. The Economic History of China, with Special Reference to Agriculture. New York, 1921. 463p.

Lewis, O. Village Life in Northern India. N.Y.; Vantage Books, 1958. 384p.

Liashchenko, Petr I. Sotsial'naia Ekonomiia Sel'skogo Khoziaisva. Moscow and Leningrad; Gosudarstvennoe Izdatel'stvo, 1930. 2 vols.

Likert, Rensis and Jane Gibson Likert. New Ways of Managing Conflict. New York; McGraw-Hill, 1976. 375p.

Lim, D., ed. Further Readings in Malaysian Economic Development. Kuala Lumpur, Malaysia; Oxford University Press, 1983. 309p.

Lin, Tung-Hai. Development of the Agrarian Movement and Agrarian Legislation in China, 1912–1930. Gordon Press Publishers, 1976.

Lindstrom, David E. American Farmers' and Rural Organizations; ed by Herbert McNee Hamlin. Champaign, Ill; Garrard Press, 1948. 457p.

Lipton, Michael, J. Connell, B. Dasgupta, and R. Laishley. Migration from Rural

Areas: The Evidence from Village Studies. Delhi; Oxford University Press, 1976. 228p.

List, F. National System of Political Economy. Trans. G.A. Matile. New York; Garland, 1974. 497p. (Reprinted from 1856 edition, Philadelphia; Lippincott.)

Livermore, Shaw. Early American Land Companies; Their Influence on Corporate Development. New York; Octagon Books, 1968. 327p. (Columbia University Thesis, 1938)

Lockwood, B., P.K. Mukherjee, and R. T. Shand. The High-Yielding Varieties Programme in India. New Delhi; Planning Commission, Gov't of India Programme Evaluation Organisation, 1971. 2 vols.

Loomis, Ralph A. and Glen T. Barton. Productivity of Agriculture, United States, 1870–1958. Washington, D.C.; U.S. Dept. of Agric., 1961. 63p. (USDA Tech. Bul. No. 1238)

Lundberg, E. Studies in the Theory of Economic Expansion. London; King, 1937. 265p. (2d ed. Kelley and Millman, 1954. 265p.)

Lundquist, G.A. Principles of Rural Sociology. Boston and New York; Ginn and Co., 1927. 484p.

Luz, Fabio. Seguros Agro Pecuarios. 2d ed. Rio de Janeiro; Ministerio da Agricultura ilr Servico de Economia Rural, 1949. 102p.

Lydall, H. The Structure of Earnings. Oxford; Clarendon Press, 1968. 394p.

M

Maass, A., M. M. Hufschmidt, R. Dorfman, H. A. Thomas, J., S. A. Marglin, and G. M. Fair. Design of Water-Resource Systems. Cambridge; Harvard University Press, 1962. 620p.

MacArthur, R. H. and J. H. Connell. The Biology of Populations. New York; Wiely, 1966. 200p.

MacGibbon, Duncan A. The Canadian Grain Trade. Toronto; Macmillan of Canada, Ltd., 1932. 503p.

MacGillivray, J.H., and R.A. Stevens. Agricultural Labor and Its Effective Use. Palo Alto, Calif.; National Press, 1964. 107p.

Mackintosh, William A. Economic Problems of the Prairie Provinces. Toronto; Macmillan, 1935. 308p.

Mackintosh, William A. . . . Agricultural Cooperation in Western Canada. Kingston; Queen's University; Toronto; The Ryerson Press, 1924. 173p.

Macklin, Theodore. Efficient Marketing for Agriculture, Its Services, Methods and Agencies. New York, 1921. 418p.

Madden, J. Patrick and Marion D. Yoder. Program Evaluation: Food Stamps and Commodity Distribution in Rural Areas of Central Pennsylvania. University Park, PA; Pennsylvania State University Agricultural Experiment Station, 1972. 119p. (Agricultural Ex. Station Bulletin No. 780) Q

Maklin, Theodore. Making the Most of Agriculture; Efficient Marketing, Profitable Farming, Worth-while Living. Boston and New York; Ginn and Co., 1927. 542p.

Maital, Shlomo. Minds, Markets and Money: Psychological Foundations of Economic Behavior. New York; Basic Books, 1982. 310p.

Majka, Linda C. & Majka, Theo J. Farm-Workers, Agribusiness, and the State. Philadelphia; Temple University Press, 1982. 320p.

Makarov, N. P. Krestiaonskoe Khozianistvo i ego Evoliutsiia (The Peasant Farm and Its Development), Moscow, 1920. 2 vols.

Mallart y Cuto, Jose. Organizacion Cientifica del Trabajo Agricola. 1st ed. Barcelona; Salvat Editores, s.a., 1934. 237p.

Mancini, Luis Jacinto. . . . Las Reformas Agrarias de Post Guerra. Buenos Aires; Imprenta de la Universidad, 1943. 227p.
Manetsch, T. J., F. A. Ramos, and S. C. Lenchner. Computer Simulation of a Program for Modernizing Cotton Production in Northeast Brazil. East Lansing, MI; Michigan State University, Systems Science Program, 1968. (Working Paper 3)
Mangus, A.R. Rural Regions of the United States. Washington, D.C.; Federal Works Agency, Works Projects Administration, 1940. 230p.
Marenghi, E. Lezioni di Contabilitá Agraria. Milano, 1922. 366p.
Markham, J.W. The Fertilizer Industry: Study of the Imperfect Market. Nashville; Vanderbilt University Press, 1958. 249p.
Marshall, F. Ray. Labor in the South. Cambridge, Mass.; Harvard University Press, 1967. 406p.
Marszalkowicz, Teresa. Funkeja Produkcji Rolniczej. Warsaw; Panstwowe Wydawn Ekonomiczne, 1965. 315p.
Martin, A. Economics and Agriculture. London; Routledge & Kegan Paul, 1958. 169p.
Martin-Leake, Hugh. Land Tenure and Agricultural Production in the Tropics: Being a discussion on the Influence of the Land Policy on Development in Tropical Countries. Cambridge, England; W. Heffer and Sons, Ltd., 1927. 139p.
Maslov, P. Agrarnyi Vopros v Rossii (The Agrarian Problem in Russia). 3d ed. Moscow, 1906. 462p.
Mayer, Joseph. Social Science Principles in the Light of Scientific Method, with Particular Application to Modern Economic Thought. Durham, N.C.; Duke University Press, 1941. 573p.
McBride, G. The Land Systems of Mexico. New York; American Geographical Society, 1923. 204p. T.
McBride, George M. Land Systems of Mexico. New York; Octagon Books, 1971. 204p. Repr. of 1923 ed.
McBride, J. Vanishing Bracero: Valley Revolution. San Antonio, Texas; Naylor, 1963. 83 leaves.
McCallum, John. Unequal Beginnings: Agriculture and Economic Development in Quebec and Ontario Until 1870. Toronto; University of Toronto Press, 1980. 148p.
McConnell, Charles M. The Rural Billion. New York; Friendship Press, 1931. 171p.
McCrone, G. The Economics of Subsidizing Agriculture; a Study of British Policy. Toronto; University of Toronto Press, 1962. 189p.
McKean, R.N. Efficiency in Government through Systems Analysis with Emphasis on Water Resources Development. New York; Wiley, 1958. 336p.
McLoughlin, P. F. M., ed. African Food Production Systems: Cases and Theory. Baltimore; Johns Hopkins University Press, 1970. 318p.
McRae, S. G. and C. P. Burnham. Land Evaluation. Oxford; Clarendon Press, 1981. 239p.
McWilliams, Carey. Ill Fares the Land; Migrants and Migratory Labor in the United States. Boston; Little, Brown and Co., 1942. 419p.
Mead, E. Federal Reclamation: What It Should Include. Washington, D.C.; Government Printing Office, 1926. 42p.
Mears, L. A., M. H. Agabin, T. L. Anden, and R. C. Marquez. The Rice Economy of the Philippines. Quezon City; University of the Philippines Press, 1974. 435p.
Meek, Charles K. Land Law and Custom in the Colonies. 2d ed. London; Cumberlege, 1949. 337p.
Meier, R. C., W. T. Newell, and H. L. Pazer. Simulation in Business and Economics. Englewood Cliffs, N.J.; Prentice-Hall, 1969. 369p.

Menzel, Bernhard. Die Sozialen Lasten der Deutschen Landwirtschaft. Greifswald; L. Bamberg, 1930. 93p.

Menzies, M.W. Poverty in Canada: Its Nature, Significance, and Implications for Public Policy. Winnipeg; Manitoba Pool Elevators, 1965. 39p.

Meyer, Konrad, ed. Gefuge und Ordnung der Deutschen Landwirtschaft. Berlin; Reichsnahrstand verlags-ges m.b.h., 1939. 752p.

Meyer, Lothar M. B. Wirtschaftslehre des Landbaues. Neudamm; J. Neumann, 1928. 336p.

Mighell, Ronald L., and J.D. Black. Interregional Competition in Agriculture, with Special Reference to Dairy Farming in the Lake States and New England. Cambridge; Harvard University Press, 1951. 320p.

Miller, C. J. editor. Marketing and Economic Development. Lincoln; University of Nebraska, 1967. 422p.

Miller, Larry. Selling in Agribusiness. Jasper S. Lee, editor. New York; McGraw-Hill Book Co, 1979. 136p. (Career Preparation for Agriculture-Agribusiness Ser.)

Minlos, B. Das Dorf in Republikanischen Spanien. Moscow; Internationales Agrarinstitut, 1939. 97p.

Mishan, E.J. The Costs of Economic Growth. New York; Praeger, 1967. 190p.

Montgomery, Robert H. The Cooperative Pattern in Cotton. New York; Macmillan, 1929. 335p.

Moore, H.L. Forecasting the Yield and Price of Cotton. New York; Macmillan, 1917. 173p.

Moore, H.L. Snythetic Economics. New York; Macmillan, 1929. 186p.

Moore, J.R., and R.G. Walsh, eds. Market Structure of the Agricultural Industries: Some Case Studies. Ames; Iowa State University Press, 1966. 412p.

Morelle, W., L. Hesser, and E. Melichar. Merchant and Dealer Credit in Agriculture. Washington, D.C.; Board of Governors of the Federal Reserve System, 1966. 70p.

Morgan, Ora, ed. Agricultural Systems of Middle Europe: A Symposium. New York; Macmillan, 1933. 405p. (Reprinted by ASM Press, 1972)

Morgan, T., G. W. Betz, and N. K. Choudhry. Readings in Economic Development. Belmont, Calif.; Wadsworth, 1963. 431p.

Morin, A. The Organizability of Farm Labor in the United States. Cambridge; Harvard University Press, 1952. 102p. (Harvard Studies in Labor in Agriculture, No. 2-HL)

Morman, J.B. Thc Principles of Rural Credits. New York; Macmillan, 1915. 296p.

Mortenson, W.P. Modern Marketing of Farm Product. Danville, Ill.; Interstate, 1963. 277p.

Mortenson, W. P. A Study of Egg Handling in Wisconsin. Madison; University of Wisconsin, Dept. Agr. Econ., 1959. 25p.

Morton, J. E. On the Evolution of Manpower Statistics. Kalamazoo, Mich.; Upjohn Institute, 1969. 113p.

Moszczenski, Stephen. Rachunkowość Gospodarstw Wiejskich. Warsaw, 1947. 460p.

Mott, F.D., and M.I. Roemer Rural Health and Medical Care. New York; McGraw-Hill, 1948. 608p.

Mourse, E.O. Legal Status of Agricultural Co-operation. New York; Macmillan, 1927. 555p.

Mubyarto, ed. Growth and Equity in Indonesian Agricultural Development. Jakarta, Indonesia; Yayasan Agro Ekonomika, 1982.

Mudd, S. editor. The Population Crisis and the Use of World Resources. The Hague; Junk, 1964. 562p. (World Academy of Art and Science 2).

Mueller, Wilard F. and L. Garoian. Changes in the Market Structure of Grocery Retailing. Madison; University of Wisconsin Press, 1961. 215p.
Mukerji, Nitya Gopal. Handbook of Indian Agriculture. 3d ed., rev. Calcutta; Thacker, Spink and Co., 1915. 620p.
Mukherjee, B.B. Co-operation and Rural Welfare in India. Calcutta and Simla; Thacker Spink and Co., 1929. 198p.
Mukherjee, P. K. Economics Surveys in Under-Developed Countries. 2d ed. Bombay; Asia Publishing House, 1960.
Mundlak, Yair. Long-Term Projections of Supply and Demand for Agricultural Products in Israel. Jerusalem; Faculty of Agriculture, The Hebrew University, 1964. 2 vols.
Murray, William G., and A. G. Nelson. Agricultural Finance. 4th ed. Ames; Iowa State University Press, 1960. 486p. (5th ed. 1967. 561p.)
Myers, Robin. Louisiana Story, 1964: The Sugar System and the Plantation Workers. New York; National Advisory Committee on Farm Labor, 1964. 40p.
Myrick, Herbert. Rural Credits System for the United States, Prepared at the Request of the Rural Credits Committee of the Farm Bloc of the United States Senate. New York; Orange Judd Publishing Company, 1922. 240p.

N

Nagle, J.C. Agricultural Trade Policies. Lexington, Mass.; Lexington Books, 1976. 171p.
Narain, D. The Impact of Price Movements on Areas Under Selected Crops in India, 1900–1939. Cambridge, Eng.; Cambridge University Press, 1965. 234p.
Nash, Michael J. Crop Conservation and Storage in Cool Temperate Climates. Pergamon Press, Incorporated, 1978. 393p. (2d ed. 1985. 286p.)
National Advisory Committee on Farm Labor. Farm Labor Organizing, 1905–1967: A Brief History. New York; National Advisory Committe on Farm Labor, 1967. 68p.
National Conference on Land Utilization. (Chicago, 1931). Proceedings . . . Called by the Secretary of Agriculture and the Executive Committee of the Association of Land-Grant Colleges and Universities. Washington, D.C.; United States Government Printing Office, 1932. 251p.
National Industrial Conference Board. The Agricultural Problem in the United States. New York; National Industrial Conference Board, 1926. 157p.
National Workshop on Agricultural Marketing: Marketing Efficiency in a Changing Economy. Washington, D.C.; U.S.Department of Agriculture, Agric. Marketing Service, 1955. (AMS-20)
Neetz, R. E. et al. Agricultural Statistics of Eastern Europe and the Soviet Union 1950–66. Washington, D.C.; United States Department of Agriculture, Economic Research Service, 1969. 110p. (ERS-Foreign 252).
Nicholls, W.H. The Importance of an Agricultural Surplus in Underdeveloped Countries. J.S. McLean Memorial Lecture. Ontario; Agricultural College, Department of Agricultural Economics, 1962. 55p.
Nicholls, W.H. Price Policies in the Cigarette Industry: A Study of "Concerted Action" and Its Social Control, 1911–50. Nashville; Vanderbilt University Press, 1951. 444p.
Nicholson, Heather Johnson. Distant Hunger: Agriculture, Food, and Human Values. West Lafayette, Ind.; Purdue Unversity, 1979.
Nicholson, Joseph Shield. The Relations of Rents, Wages and Profits in Agriculture, and Their Bearing on Rural Depopulation. London; S.Sonnenschein and Co., Ltd. New York; C. Scribner's Sons, 1906. 176p.
Nicol, K.J., S. Sriplung, and E. O. Heady, eds. Agricultural Development Planning in Thailand. Ames; Iowa State University Press, 1982. 326p.

Nisbet, R. History of the Idea of Progress. New York; Basic Books, 1980. 370p.
Noble, M.C.S., Jr., and H.A. Dawson. Handbook on Rural Education: Factual Data on Rural Education, Its Social and Economic Backgrounds. New York; National Education Association of the U.S., Department of Rural Education, 1961. 168p.
Nordin, J. A., G. G. Judge, and O. Wahby. Application of Econometric Procedures to the Demands for Agricultural Products. Ames; Iowa State College, 1954. (Iowa State College Research Bulletin 410)
North Carolina State University. Agricultural Policy Institute. Problems of Chronically Depressed Rural Areas. Raliegh, N.C.; Agricultural Policy Institute, 1965. 235p. (API Series 19)
Norton, H. S. Modern Transportation Economics. Columbus, Ohio; Merrill, 1963. 463p. (2d ed. 1971. 470p.)
Norton, L. J. Financing Agriculture. Danville, Ill.; Interstate, 1938. (Revised ed. 1948. 434p.)
Nourse, E.G., ed. Agricultural Economics: A Selection of Materials in which Economic Principles are Applied to the Practice of Agriculture. Chicago; University of Chicago Press, 1916. 896p.
Nourse, E.G. American Agriculture and the European Market. New York; McGraw-Hill, 1924. 333p.
Nourse, E.G., and J.G. Knapp. The Cooperative Marketing of Livestock. Washington, D.C.; Brookings Institution, 1931. 486p.
Nulty, L. The Green Revolution in West Pakistan: Implications for Technological Change. New York, Praeger, 1972. 150p.

O

O'Brien, C. Agricultural Economics. London, 1929. 195p.
O'Donovan, John. The Economic History of Livestock in Ireland. Dublin and Cork; Cork University Press; London, New York; Longmans, Green and Co., Ltd., 1940. 460p.
Ogden, Jean, and Jess Ogden. Small Communities in Action: Stories in Citizen Programs at Work. New York; Harper and Row, 1946. 244p.
Ogden, Jean, and Jess Ogden. These Things We Tried: A Five-Year Experiment in Community Development. Charlottesville, VA; University of Virginia, 1947. 432p.
Ohlin, B. Interregional and International Trade. Cambridge, Mass., Harvard Univ., Press, 1933. 617p. (Revised ed., 1967. 324p.)
Oi, W. Y., and A. P. Hunter, Jr. Economics of Private Truck Transportation. Dubuque, Iowa; William C. Brown, 1965. 365p.
Ojala, E. Agriculture and Economic Progress. London; Oxford University Press, 1952. 220p.
Oram, P.A., J. Zapata, G. Alibaruho, and S. Roy. Investment and Input Requirements for Accelerating Food Production in Low-Income Countries by 1990. Washington, D.C.; Int. Food Policy and Research Inst., 1979. 179p. (IFPRI Research Report No. 10) (2)
Orden, D., D. Greene, T. Roe, and G. E. Schuh. Policies Affecting the Food and Agricultural Sector in Peru, 1970–1982: An Evaluation and Recommendation. Washington, D.C.; U.S. AID, 1982.
Organisation for Economic Co-operation and Development. Agriculture in the Planning and Management of Peri-Urban Areas, Vol.II. (Document Ser.) Paris; Organization for Economic Cooperation and Development, 1979.
Organisation for Economic Co-operation and Development. The Energy Problem and

the Agro-Food Sector. Paris; Organisation for Economic Cooperation & Development, 1982. 83p.
Organisation for Economic Co-operation and Development. Low Incomes in Agriculture: Problems and Policies. Paris, 1964. 515p. (Agricultural Policy Reports)
Organisation for Economic Co-operation and Development. Study of Trends in World Supply and Demand of Major Agricultural Commodities: Report by the Secretary-General. Paris; OECD, 1976. 349p.
Orwin, C.S., and W.R. Peel. The Tenure of Agricultural Land. New York; Cambridge University Press, 1925. 76p.
Orwin, C.S. Farming Costs. Being a new edition of The Determination of Farming Cost, 1917. Oxford; Clarendon Press, 1921. 141p.
Oshima, H.T. The Significance of Off-farm Employment and Incomes in Post-War East Asian Growth. Manila; Asian Development Bank, 1984. 71p. (Asian Dev. Bank Economic Staff Paper No. 21).
Ostrolenk, Bernhard. The Surplus Farmer. New York, London; Harper and Brothers, 1932. 135p.
Owen, L.A. The Russian Peasant Movement, 1906–1917. London; P.S. King, 1937. 267p.
Oxford University. Agricultural Economics Research Institute. Country Planning; a Study of Rural Problems. London; Oxford University Press, 1944. 288p.

P

Padberg, D.I. Economics of Food Retailing. Ithaca, N.Y.; Cornell University Food Distribution Program, 1968. 292p.
Pal, B. N. Principles of Agricultural Economics. Allahada, India; Kitab Mahal, 1959. 751p.
Papanek, G, et al. The Indonesian Economy. New York; Praeger, 1980. 438p. (3)
Parker, R.C., P.W. Jaynes, and L. Stratton. Economic Report on the Baking Industry. Report of the U.S. Federal Trade Commission. Washington, D.C.; U.S. Gov't Printing Office, 1967. 120p.
Parsons, K.H. The Owner Cultivator in a Progressive Agriculture; and F.A.O. Land Tenure Study. Rome; Food and Agriculture Organization of the United Nation, 1958. 66p. (F.A.O. Agricultural Studies no.39)
Parsons, K.H., R. J. Penn, and P.M. Raup, eds. Land Tenure; Proc. of the Int. Conf. on Land Tenure and Related Problems in World Agriculture. Madison; University of Wisconsin Press, 1956. 739p.
Parsons, Talcott. The Structure of Social Action. New York; McGraw-Hill, 1937. 817p. (2d ed. New York; Free Press Paperback, 1968. 2 vols.)
Patel, A.D. Indian Agricultural Economics. Bombay; D.P. Raraporavala Sons and Co., 1937. 324p.
Pearson, Frank A., and Kenneth R. Bennett. Statistical Methods Applied to Agricultural Economics. New York; J. Wiley and Sons, Inc. and London; Chapman and Hall, Ltd., 1942. 443p.
Pearson, K. The Grammar of Science. 1st ed., 1892. Latest; London; J.M. Dent and Sons, 1937.
Pedley, William H. Labour on the Land: A Study of the Developments Between the Two Great Wars. Westminster; P.S. King and Staples, 1942. 190p.
Pelzer, Karl J. Pioneer Settlement in the Asiatic Tropics: Studies in Land Utilization and Agricultural Colonization in Southeastern Asia. New York; American Geographical Society, 1948. 288p.

Perkins, Brian B. and Dale E. Hathaway. Movement of Labor Between Farm and Nonfarm Jobs. East Lansing; Michigan Agric. Exp. Station, 1966. 48p. (Michigan Agr. Exp. Station Research Bulletin 13)

Petersen, Asmus. Grundlagen zu einer Reichsbonitierung der Landwirtschaftlichen Kulturböden Deutschlands. Berlin, 1934. 151p.

Petersen, Asmus. Thünens Isolierter Staat: Die Landwirtschaft als Glied der Volkswirtschaft. Berlin, 1944. 199p.

Petrini, F. Landsbygdssociologi. Stockholm, 1961. 128p.

Phelan, John, editor. Readings in Rural Sociology. New York; Macmillan, 1920. 632p.

Plattner, S., ed. Formal Methods in Economic Anthropology. Washington, D.C.; American Anthropological Association, 1975. 215p.

Poe, Clarence. How Farmers Co-operate and Double Profits. New York; Orange Judd Co., 1915. 244p.

Poka-Pivny, Adalbert de. Documentation Relative au credit agricole international. Pour l'Institut international d'agriculture. Rome; Impr. de l'Institut international d'agriculture, 1930. 273p.

Polanyi, K. The Great Transformation: The Political and Economic Origins of Our Time. New York; Rinehart, 1944. 305p. (Beacon Press paperback in 1957; Octagon, 1973.)

Post-Harvest Food Crop Conservation: Association of Consulting Scientists Symposium on Post-Harvest Food Crop Conservation, Harrogate, 13–15 November, 1979. London; Pergamon Press, Inc., 1980. 138p.

Poston, Richard W. Action Now! A Citizen's Guide to Better Communities. Carbondale, Ill.; Southern Illinois University Press, 1976. 257p.

Poston, Richard W. Democracy is You: A Guide to Citizen Action. New York; Harper and Row, 1953.

Powell, G. Harold. Cooperation in Agriculture. New York; Macmillan, 1921. 327p.

Pratt, Edwin A. Agricultural Organisation. London; P.S. King and Son, 1912. 259p.

Predohl, A. Aussenwirtschaft, Weltwirtschaft, Handelspolitik und Wahrungspolitik. Gottingen, 1949. 354p.

Prentice, E. Parmalee. Hunger and History: The Influence of Hunger on Human History. New York, London; Harper and Brothers, 1939. 269p.

Price, Roger. The Modernization of Rural France: Communications Networks and Agricultrual Market Structures in Nineteenth Century France. New York; St Martin's Press, Inc, 1938. 560p. (Reprinted 1982)

Probyn, John W., ed. Systems of Land Tenure in Various Countries. London, New York; Cassells, Petter and Galpin, 1881. 534p. (Reprinted; Ayer Company Publishers, Inc., 1975)

Prothero, Rowland E. English Farming Past and Present. London; Ayer Company Publishers, Inc., 1917. 519p. (Reprinted: 6th ed 1961. 559p.)

Psacharopoulos, G. Returns to Education: An International Comparison. New York, Elsevier Publ., 1973. 216p.

Purcal, John T. Rice Economy: A Case-Study of Four Villages in West Malaysia. Kuala Lumpur, University of Malaysia Press, 1971. 248p.

Q

Quaintance, Hadly W. . . . The Influence of Farm Machinery on Production and Labor. New York; Published for the Association by the Macmillan Co., 1904. 106p.

Queuille, Henri. . . . Le Drame Agricole, un Aspect de la Crise Economique. Paris; Hachette, 1932. 191p.

R

Raiffa, H. A., and R. S. Schlaifer. Applied Statistical Decision Theory. Boston; Harvard University, 1961. 356p.

Ramaswamy, Tumkur N. Economic Stabilisation of Indian Agriculture. Benares; Nand Kishore and Bros, 1946. 176p.

Ramblyn, Lewis R. Inequality: A Portrait of Rural America. Washington, D.C.; Rural Evaluation Assoc., 1973. 59p.

Ramos, J.R. Labor and Development in Latin America. New York; Columbia University Press, 1970. 281p.

Randall, Alan and John R. Stoll. Economic Surplus and Benefit-Cost Analysis. Lexington; Dept. of Agric. Econ., University of Kentucky, 1980. 39p. (AER Rep. No. 35) Q

Rao, B. P. The Economics of Agricultural Credit: Use in Southern Brazil. India; Andhra University Press, 1973. 111p.

Rao, T. S. Guide to Methods and Procedures of Rural Credit Surveys. Rome; Food and Agriculture Organization of the United Nations, 1962. 107p. (F.A.O. Agricultural Development Paper no. 73)

Raper, Arthur F. Preface to Peasantry. Chapel Hill; University of North Carolina, 1936. 423p.

Rassmussen, P. N. Studies in International Relations. Amsterdam, Holland; North-Holland Publs., 1956.

Redclift, M. Agrarian Reform and Peasant Organization on the Ecuadorian Coast. London; Athlone Press for the Institute of Latin America, 1978. 186p.

Reeves, F.W., ed. Education for Rural America: Conference on Education in Rural Communities. Chicago; University of Chicago Press, 1945. 314p.

Renshaw, E.F. Toward Responsible Government: An Economic Appraisal of Federal Investment in Water Resource Programs. Chicago; Idyia Press, 1957. 164p.

Report on the Agro-Ecological Zones Project: Results for Southeast Asia, Vol. 4. (World Soil Resources Reports: No. 48-4) Rome; Food-Ag Organisation, 1980. 40p.

Research and Education for Regional and Area Development. Ames; Iowa State University Press, 1966. 287p.

Rhoades, Elmer L. Introductory Readings in Marketing. Commodity Characteristics and Marketing Functions. Chicago, New York; A.W.Shaw Company, 1927. 752p.

Ribich, T. I. Education and Poverty. Washington, D.C.; Brookings Institution, 1968. 163p.

Ricci, Umberto. . . . Les Bases Theoriques de la Statistique Agricole Internationale. Rome; Impr. de l'Institut International d'Agriculture, 1914. 314p.

Richardson, Gerald. A B C of Coopertives; a Handbook for Consumers and Producers. London, New York; Longmans, Green and Co, 1940. 263p.

Ridker, R., and H. Lubell, eds. Employment and Unemployment Problems of the Near East amd South Asia. Delhi; Vikas Publ., 1971. 2 vols.

Rindfuss, Ronald R., and James A. Sweet. Postwar Fertility Trends and Differentials in the United States. New York; Academic Press, 1977. 225p. (Studies in Populations)

Rippy, M., ed. Cultural Changes in Brazil. Indianapolis, IN; Ball State Univ., 1970. (2)

Rivkin, Malcolm D. Area Development for National Growth: A Turkish Precedent. New York; Praeger, 1965. 234p.

Roberts, E. F. The Law and the Preservation of Agruicultural Land. Ithaca, New York; Cornell University, Northeast Regional Center for Rural Development, 1982. 145p.

Robinson, E.A.G. and J.E. Vaizey, eds. The Economics of Education; Proceedings of a Conference held by the International Economic Association. New York; St. Martins Press, 1966. 781p.

Robinson, J. The Economics of Imperfect Competition. London; Macmillan, 1933. 352p.

Robinson, Jerry W., Jr. A Conflict Management Training Program: A Leaders' Guide for Extension Professionals. Ithaca, New York; Cornell University, Northeast Regional Center of Rural Development, 1978. Various paging

Rogers, Arthur G. The Business Side of Agriculture. London; Methuen and Co., 1904. 163p.

Rogers, Everett M. and Rabel Burdge. Social Change in Rural Societies. 2d ed. New York; Appleton-Century-Crofts, 1972. 472p. (3d ed. New York; Prentice-Hall, 1988. 395p.)

Rogers, G.B., and L.A. Voss, eds. Readings on Egg Pricing. College of Agriculture, University of Missouri, 1971. 271p.

Rollins, George W. The Struggle of the Cattleman, Sheepman and Settler for Control of Lands in Wyoming, 1867–1910. Reprinted by Ayer Company Publishers, Inc., 1979. 379p.

Roscher, Wilhelm. Natiónalokonomik des Ackerbaues und der Verwandten Urproduktionen. 3d ed., edited by Heinrich Dade. Stuttgart; J. G. Cotta, 1903. 864p.

Rosenberg, Morris. Logic of Survey Analysis. New York; Basic Books, 1968. 283p. T

Ross, E.J. Belgian Rural Cooperation: A Study in Social Adjustment. Milwaukee; The Bruce Publishing Co., 1940. 194p.

Rossi-Doris, Manlio. Note di Economia e Politica Agraria. Roma; Edizioni Italiane, 1949. 377p.

Roy, E. P. Collective Bargining in Agriculture. Danville, Ill.; Interstate, 1970. 280p.

Roy, E. P. Contract Farming and Economic Integration. 2d ed. Danville, Ill.; Interstate, 1972. 661p.

Royal Institute of International Affairs. Agrarian Problems from the Baltic to the Aegean: Discussion of a Peasant Programme. London; The Royal Institute of International Affairs, 1944. 96p.

Rudra, A. and Pranab K. Bardhan. Agrarian Relations in West Bengal. Bombay, India; Somaiya Publ., 1983. 104p.

Rungeling, B., L. H. Smith, V. W. Briggs, Jr., and J. Adams. Employment, Income and Welfare in the Rural South. New York; Praeger, 1977. 355p.

Ruttan, Vernon W. The Economic Demand for Irrigated Acreage: New Methodology and Some Preliminary Projections, 1954–1980. Baltimore; Johns Hopkins University Press for Resources for the Future, 1965. 139p. Q

Ruttan, Vernon W. Growth Stage Theories, Dual Economy Models, and Agricultural Development Policy. J.S. McLean Visiting Professor Lecture, University of Guelph, Department of Agricultural Economics, 1968. (Univ. of Guelph Publ. No. AE 1968/2)

S

Sace, Alfredo. Programa Agrario del Aprismo. Lima; Ediciones Populares, 1946.

Saha, K.B. Economics of Rural Bengal. Calcutta; Chuckervertty, Chatterjee and Co., Ltd., 1930. 296p.

Sahota, G. S. Fertilizer and Economic Development. New York; Praeger, 1967. 240p. (2)

Sakurai, Toyo. Nogyo Kakumei to Kyodo Keiei (Agricultural Revolution and Co-operative Management). Tokyo; Shiryosha, 1949. 236p.

Salas, Rafael M. More Than the Grains; Participatory management in the Philippine Rice Sufficiency Program, 1967–1969. International Specialized Book Services, 1985. 245p.

Salzman, P. C., ed. When Nomads Settle: Processes of Sedentarization as Adaptation and Response. New York; Praeger, 1980. 184p.

Sampson, Anthony. The Seven Sisters: The Great Oil Companies and the World They Shaped. New York; Bantam Books, 1976. 395p.

Samuelson, Paul. Collected Scientific Papers of Paul Samuelson. Cambridge, Mass; M.I.T. Press, 1966. 5 vols.

Sandee, J. A Demonstration Planning Model for India. Bombay; Asia Publishing House, 1960. 59p.

Sanders, Irwin T. The Community. 3d ed. New York; Ronald Press, 1975.

Sarfalvi, B. Land Utilization in Eastern Europe. Budapest; Akademiai Kidao, 1967. 88p.

Sato, Shosuke. History of the Land Question in the United States. (Johns Hopkins University. Studies in the Social Sciences). Baltimore, Johns Hopkins University; A M S Press, Inc., 1978. 181p.

Schafer, Joseph. The Social History of American Agriculture. New York; Macmillan, 1936. 302p.

Scheftel, Yetta. The Taxation of Land Value: A Study of Certain Discriminatory Taxes on Land. Boston, New York; Houghton Mifflin Company, 1916. 389p.

Schell, Orville. Modern Meat. Random House, 1984. 337p.

Schiff, Ashley L. Fire and Water: Scientific Heresy in the Forest Service. Cambridge, Mass.; Harvard University Press, 1962. 225p.

Schiller, O.M. Co-operation and Intergration in Agricultural Production. Concepts and Pratical Application, an International Synopsis. Bombay; Asia Publishing House, 1969. 230p.

Schmidt, Carl T. American Farmers in the World Crisis. New York; Oxford University Press, 1941. 345p.

Schmidt, H., et al. Long-Term Development of Supply and Demand for Agricultural Products in the Federal Republic of Germany. IFO-Institut fur Wirschaftsforschung, Munich, Germany, 1967. 259p.

Schmitz, A., and D. L. Bawden. The World Wheat Economy: An Empirical Analysis. Berkeley; California Agr. Exp. Sta., 1973. 81p. (Giannini Foundation Monograph 32)

Schneidau, R.E., and L.A. Duewer. Symposium: Vertical Coordination in the Pork Industry. Westport, Conn.; AVI Publishing, 1972. 277p.

Schoff, L.H. A National Agricultural Policy for All of the People in the United States. New York; Harper for Columbia University Seminar on Rural Life, 1950. 153p.

Schonfeld, L. Landwirtschaftliche Buchfuhrung mit Einschluss der Bewertung und Betriebskalkulation. Vienna, 1931. 208p.

Schuessler, Karl. Analyzing Social Data: A Statistical Orientation. Boston; Houghton-Mifflin, 1971. 476p.

Schultz, Henry. The Theory and Measurement of Demand. Chicago; University of Chicago Press, 1938. 817p.

Schultz, T. W. Redirecting Farm Policy. New York; Macmillan, 1943. 75p.

Schumpeter, Joseph A. Theorie der wirtschaftlichen Entwicklung. Translated in 1926 as "The Theory of Economic Development," by R. Opie. New York; Oxford University Press, 1911. (Reprinted 1961; also published by Harvard University Press, 1934.)

Scott, Gregory J. Markets, Myths and Middlemen: A Study of Potato Marketing in Central Peru. Lima, Peru; International Potato Center, 1985. 184p.

Seedorf, W., and P. Hesse. Grundriss der Landwirtschaftlichen Marktlehre fur Landwirte, volkswrite, Kaufleute, Verwaltungsbeamte, Landwritschaftliche Schullen und Studierende. Berlin; P. Parey, 1932. 351p.

Seers, D., ed. Cuba: The Economic and Social Revolution. Chapel Hill, N.C.; University of North Carolina, 1964. 432p. (1)
Seifert, W. W., and N. W. Kamrany. A Framework for Evaluating Long-Term Strategies for the Development of the Sahel-Sudan Region. Vol. 1: Summary Report: Project Objectives, Methodologies and Major Findings. Cambridge, Mass.; MIT, Center for Policy Alternatives, 1974.
Selltiz, C., M. Jabada. M. Deutsch, and S. W. Cook. Research Methods in Social Relations. Revised edition. New York; Holt, Rinehart, and Winston, 1965,c 1959. 622p.
Sen, Sachin. The Tenure of Agricultural Land. Calcutta; The Politics Club, 1937. 202p.
Sering, M., H. Niehaus, and F. Schlomer. Deutsche Agrarpolitik auf geschichtlicher und landeskundlicher Grundlage. Leipzig; H. Buske, 1934. 194p.
Sering, M. International Price Movements and the Condition of Agriculture in Non-Tropical Countries. Translated by Carles E. Stangeland. Berlin; Reichsdruckerei, 1927. 134p.
Serpieri, Arrigo. Istituzioni de Economia Agraria. Bologna; Edizioni Agricole, 1946. 718p.
Settegast, Hermann. Die Landwirtschaft und Ihr Betrieb. 3d ed. Breslau; Wihelm Gottl. Korn, 1885. 607p.
Sharp, P.F. The Agrarian Revolt in Western Canada; a Survey Showing American Parallels. Minneapolis; University of Minnesota Press, 1948. 204p.
Shaw, R. D'A. The Impact of the Green Revolution on Jobs. Washington, D.C., Overseas Development Council, 1970.
Sheldon, William D. Populism in the Old Dominion; Virgina Farm Politics, 1885–1900. Princeton, NJ; Princeton University Press, 1935. 182p.
Shen, T. H. Agricultural Development in Taiwan Since World War II. Ithaca, New York; Cornell University Press, 1964. 399p.
Shepherd, G.S. Agricultural Price Policy. Ames, Iowa; Collegiate Press, 1945. 361p. (2d ed. Iowa State Universtiy Press, 1947. 440p.)
Shoup, C. The Fiscal System of Venezuela. Baltimore; Johns Hopkins Press, 1959. 491p.
Shover, John L. First Majority—Last Minority: The Transforming of Rural Life in America. New York; Praeger Publishers, 1981. 388p. T
Shumway, C. Richard, Gordong A. King, Harold O. Carter, and Gerald W. Dean. Regional Resource Use for Agricultural Production in California, 1961–65 and 1980. Berkeley; University of California, 1970. 118p. (Giannini Foundation Monograph 25) Q
Sigurdson, J. Rural Industrialization in China. Cambridge, Mass.; Harvard University Press, 1977. 281p.
Silcock, Thomas H. The Economic Development of Thai Agriculture. Ithaca, New York; Cornell University Press, 1970. 250p.
Silcock, Thomas H. Thailand: Social and Economic Studies in Development. Canberra, Australia; Australia National University Press, 1967. 334p.
Simons, Algie M. The American Farmer. Chicago; C.H. Kerr and Co., 1903. 208p.
Simpson, John A. The Militant Voice of Agriculture. Oklahoma City; John A. Simpson, 1934. 206p.
Singer, H. W. and S. J. Maxwell. Development Through Food Aid: Twenty Years' Experience. Hague, Netherlands; World Food Programme Report on the Netherlands Gov't. Seminar on Food Aid, 1983.
Singh, Baljit. Whither Agriculture in India? A Study of the Re-organisation of Agricultural Planning in India. Agra, India; N.R. Agrawal, 1946. 346p.

Singh, Tarlok. Poverty and Social Change; a Study in the Economic Reorganization of Indian Rural Society. London; Longmans, Green and Co., Ltd., 1945. 200p.
Skalweit, August. Agrarpolitik. 2d ed. Berlin & Leipzig; W. de Gruyter & Co., 1924. 507p.
Skvortsov, A.I. Khoziaistiennye Raiony Ivropeiskoi Rossii. (Type of Farming Regions in European Russia). St. Petersburg, 1914. 2 vols.
Slocum, W. L. Agricultural Sociology: A Study of Sociological Aspects of American Farm Life. New York; Harper & Brothers, 1962. 532p.
Smith, Bruce. Rural Crime Control. New York; Institute of Public Administration, Columbia University, 1933. 306p.
Smith, G.H. et al. Conservation of Natural Resources. 3d ed. New York; Wiley, 1965. 533p.
Smith, L.P.F. The Evolution of Agricultural Cooperation. Oxford; Blackwell, 1961. 216p.
Smith, M. Estellie, ed. Those Who Live From the Sea: A Study in Maritime Anthropology. St. Paul, West Publishing Co., 1977. 276p.
Smith, M. G. and C. F. Christian. Adjustments in Agriculture—a National Basebook. Ames, Iowa State University Press, 1961. 376p.
Smith, William C. The Business of Farming. Cincinnati; Stewart and Kidd Co., 1914. 292p.
Smith-Gordon, Lionel. Co-operation for Farmers. London; Williams and Norgats, 1918. 247p.
Solo, R.A. and E.M. Rogers. Inducing Technological Change for Economic Growth and Development. East Lansing; Michigan State University Press, 1972. 238p.
Solow, Barbara L. Land Question and the Irish Economy, 1870–1903. Cambridge, Mass.; Harvard University Press, 1971. 247p. (Economics Studies: No. 139)
Sonka, Steven and Earl O. Heady. American Farm-Size Structure in Relation to Income and Employment Opportunities of Farms, Rural Communities, and Other Sectors. Ames; Iowa State University, 1974. 102p. (Center for Agricultural and Rural Development, Report 48) Q
Sorel, G. The Illusions of Progress. J. and C. Stanley, translators. Berkeley; University of California Press, 1969. 222p. (1st ed., 1908.)
Sorenson, Vernon L., ed. Agricultural Market Analysis: Development, Performance, Process. Michigan State University, Bureau of Business and Economic Research, 1964. 344p.
Sorkin, A. L. American Indians and Federal Aid. Washington, D.C.; Brookings Institution, 1971. 231p.
Soth, Lauren. Farm Touble. Princeton, N.J.; Princeton University Press, 1957. 221 p. (Reprint ed., 1975; Greenwood Press)
Spaull, Hebe, and D.H. Kay. The Co-operative Movement at Home and Abroad. London; Macmillan, 1947. 191p.
Spiegel, Henry W. Land Tenure Policies at Home and Abroad. Chapel Hill; The University of North Carolina Press, 1941. 171p.
Spitze, R. G. F. and M. A. Martin, editors. Analysis of Food and Agricultural Policies for the Eighties. Champaign, Ill.; University of Illinois, 1980. 163p. (University of Illinois. Agricultural Experiment Station. Bulletin 764) (North Central Regional Research Publ. No. 271) Q
Spring, Joel H. Education and the Rise of the Corporate State. Boston; Beacon Press, 1972. 206p.
Staples, Melville H., ed. The Challenge of Agriculture; the Story of the United Farmers of Ontario. Toronto; G.N. Morgan, 1921. 197p.

Steel, W. F. Small-Scale Employment and Production in Developing Countries: Evidence from Ghana. New York, Praeger, 1977. 235p.

Steen, Herman. Cooperative Marketing: The Golden Rule in Agriculture. Garden City, N.Y.; Doubleday, Page and Co., 1923. 366p.

Steiner, P. O. Public Expenditure Budgeting. Washington, Brookings Institution, 1969. 117p.

Stevens, I. M. R., and R. L. Fox. Improving Livestock Marketing Efficiency—A Study of Nine Cooperative Livestock Markets in Ohio, Indiana, and Michigan. Washington, D.C.; USDA, Farmer Cooperative Service, 1958. 42p.

Stevens, R., H. Alavi, and P. Bertoci, eds. Rural Development in Bangladesh and Pakistan. Honolulu; University of Hawaii Press, 1976. 399p.

Stewart, Paul W., and J.F. Dawhurst. Does Distribution Cost Too Much? A Review of the Costs Involved in Current Marketing Methods and a Program for Improvement; the Factual Findings. New York; The Twentieth Century Funds, 1939. 403p.

Stigler, G.J., and K.E. Boulding, eds. Readings in Price Theory. Chicago; Irwin, 1952. 568p.

Stinson, Thomas F., Lloyd D. Bender, and Stanley W. Voelker. Northern Great Plains Coal Mining Regional Impacts. Washington, D.C.; U.S. Dept. of Agriculture, Economics Research Service, 1982. (USDA Agricultural Information Bulletin No. 452) Q

Stoddard, Ellwyn R. Mexican-Americans. New York; Random House, 1973. 269p.

Stoevner, Herbert, Joe Stevens, Howard Horton, Adam Sokoloski, Loys Parrish, and Emery Castle. Multi-Disciplinary Study of Water Quality Relationships: A Case of Yaquina Bay, Oregon. Corvaliis; Agricultural Experiment Station Oregon State University, 1972. Q

Stokey, Edith and Richard Zeckhauser. A Primer for Policy Analysis. New York; W.W. Norton and Co., 1978. 356p.

Strong, Ann L. Private Property and the Public Interest: The Brandywine Experience. Baltimore; Johns Hopkins University Press, 1975. 206p.

Studenskii, G. A. Ocherki Sel'sko-khoziaistvennoi Ekonomii. Moscow; Izdanie Tsentrosoiuza, 1925. 383p.

Subramaniam, C. The New Strategy in Indian Agriculture. New Delhi, India; Vikas Publ. House, 1979. 91p.

Swackhamer, G. L., and R. J. Doll. Financing Modern Agriculture: Banking's Problems and Challenges. Kansas City, MO; Federal Reserve Bank of Kansas City, 1969 78p.

Sworling, B.C. International Control of Sugar, 1918–41. Stanford, Calif.; Stanford University Press, 1949. 69p.

Szymanski, Albert. The Capitalist State and the Politics of Class. Cambridge, Mass.; Winthrop Publ., 1978. 333p.

T

Taeuber, Conrad, ed. America in the Seventies: Some Social Indicators. Philadelphia; The Annals of the American Academy of Political and Social Science, 1978. (Vol 435)

Tang, Anthony M. Economic Development in the Southern Piedmont, 1860–1950: Its Impact on Agriculture. Chapel Hill; University of North Carolina Press, 1958. 256p.

Taylor, Carl C., Douglas Ensminger, Helen Johnson, and Jean Joyce. India's Roots of Democracy. Bombay; Orient Longmans, 1965. 694p.

Taylor, Henry C. Agricultural Economics. New York; Macmillan Co., 1919. 439p.

Taylor, Henry C. Introduction to the Study of Agricultural Economics. New York; Macmillan, 1905. 327p.

Taylor, Henry C. Outlines of Agricultural Economics. New York; Macmillan, 1925. 614p. (Revised ed. 1931)

Taylor, Henry C. World Trade in Agricultural Products. New York; Macmillan Co., 1943. 286p.

Taylor, L. and A. R. Jones. Rual Life and Urbanized Society. New York; Oxford University Press, 1964. 493p.

Teele, R.P. The Economics of Land Reclamation in the United States. Chicago; Shaw, 1927. 337p.

Teggart, F.J., ed. The Idea of Progress: A Collection of Readings. Berkeley; University of California Press, 1929. (Revised edition 1949. 457p.)

Terray, E. Marxism and Primitive Societies. Part 2: Historical Materialism and Segmentary Linear-Based Societies. New York; Monthly Review Press, 1972. 186p. (Translated by M. Klopper.)

Thomsen, Frederick L. Agricultural Marketing. New York; McGraw-Hill, 1951. 483p.

Thorner, D., B. Kerblay, and R. E. F. Smith, eds. The Theory of Peasant Economy. Homewood, Ill.; Irwin, 1925.

Thrall, R.M., C. H. Coombs, and R. L. Davis, eds. Decision Processes. New York; Wiely. 1954. 332p.

Till, T. E. Rural Industrialization and Southern Rural Poverty: Patterns of Labor Demand in Southern Nonmetropolitan Labor Markets and Their Impact on Local Poverty. Austin; University of Texas, Center for the Study of Human Resources, 1974. 37p. (Center for the Study of Human Resources. Working Paper; 74-4)

Timmons, John F., J.C. O'Byrne, and R.K. Frevert, eds. Iowa's Water Resources: Sources, Uses, and Laws. Ames; Iowa State College Press, 1956. 225p.

Tinbergen, J. Statistical Testing of Business Cycle Theories. Geneva; League of Nations, 1939. 2 vols.

Tobata, Seiichi. Nikon Nogyo no Terkai Katei (Evolutionary Process of Japan's Agriculture) Tokyo, 1947.

Tolley, G.S., and F.E. Riggs, eds. Economics of Watershed Planning. Ames; Iowa State University Press, 1961. 339p.

Tostlebe, A. S. The Growth of Physical Capital in Agriculture, 1870–1950. New York; National Bureau of Economic Research, 1954. 92p. (Occas. Pap. 44)

Tracy, M. Agriculture in Western Europe. London; Jonathan Cape, 1964. 415p. (3d ed. New York; Harvester Wheatsheaf, 1989. 382p.)

Trant, G. I., D. L. MacFarlane, and L. A. Fischer. Trade Liberalization and Canadian Agriculture. Toronto; University of Toronto Press, 1968. 119p.

Troelston, E. S. The Principles of Farm Finance. St. Louis; Educational Publishers, 1951. 397p.

Truman, David. The Governmental Process. New York; Alfred Knopf Inc., 1951. 554p. (2d ed.; The Governmental Process; Political Interests and Public Opinion. 1971. 544p.)

Tschizaka, K. Nogyo Keizaigaku Koyo (Outline of Agricultural Economics). Tokyo, 1929. 255p.

Tsuji, H. Comparison of Rice Policies Between Thailand, Taiwan, and Japan. Kyoto, Japan; Kyoto University Press, 1982.

Tuck, R. H. An Introduction to the Principles of Agricultural Economics. London; Longmans, Green, 1961. 260p.

Turner, F.J. The Frontier in American History. New York; Holt. 1920. 375p.

Tweeten, Luther G., et al., eds. Structure of Agriculture and Information Needs Regarding Small Farms. Washington, D.C.; National Rural Center, 1980. Various paging.

U

United Nations. Dept. of Economic Affairs. Land Reform: Defects in Agrarian Structure as Obstacles to Economic Development. New York; U.N., 1951. 101p.

United Nations. Economic Commission for Latin America. Development Problems in Latin America. Austin, Texas; Univ. of Texas Press, 1970. 318p.

United States Advisory Commission on Intergovernmental Relations. Urban and Rural America: Policies for Future Growth-A Commission Report. Washington, D.C.; U.S. Government Printing Office, 1968. 186p.

United States Agency for International Development (USAID). Design and Evaluation of Aid-Assisted Projects. Washington, D.C.; The U.S. Agency for International Development, 1980.

United States. Bureau of Labor Statistics. Productivity in Agriculture: 1909–1942. Washington, D.C., 1943 20p.

United States. Bureau of the Census. Farms and Farm People: Population, Income, and Housing Characteristics, by Economic Class of Farm. A Special Cooperative Study, USDA and Census Bureau, 1953.

United States. Bureau of the Census. Agriculture Census. Cash Rent, Paid, or Payable, by Cash Tenants and By Part Owners Renting on a Cash Basis. Washington, D.C.; Government Printing Office, 1944. 135p.

United States. Bureau of the Census. Fifteenth Census of the United States: 1930. Census of Agriculture. Large-Scale Farming in the United States, 1929. Washington, D.C.; United States Government Printing Office, 1933. 106p.

United States. Bureau of the Census. United States Census of Agriculture: 1945. Special Report. Farm Work Power. Washington, D.C.; United States Government Printing Office, 1949. 62p.

United States Congress. Joint Economic Committee, 85th Congress, 1st Session. Policy for Commercial Agriculture: Its Relation to Economic Growth and Stability. Washington, D.C.; U.S. Government Printing Office, 1957. 864p.

United States Congress. Joint Economic Committee. An Economic Profile of Mainland China; Studies Prepared for the Joint Economic Committee. Washington, D.C.; U.S. Government Printing Office, 1967. 2 vols.

United States Congress. Joint Economic Committee. Prices and Profits of Leading Retail Food Chains, 1970–74: Hearings before the Joint Economic Committee. 95th Congress, 1st Session. Washington, D.C.; U.S. Gov't Printing Office, 1978. 268p.

United States Congress. Special Committee on Postwar Economic Policy and Planning. Postwar Agricultural Policies. Tenth Report, 79th Congress, 2d Session. Washington, D.C.; Government Printing Office, 1946. (House Report 2728)

United States. Department of Agriculture. Milk Pricing Advisory Committee. Milk Pricing Policy and Procedures. Washington, D.C.; 1973. 2 parts.

United States. Department of Agriculture. Development of Agriculture's Resources: A Report on Problems of Low-Income Farmers. Washington, D.C.; USDA, 1955.

United States. Department of Agriculture. Evaluation of Economic and Social Consequences of Cooperative Extension Programs. Washington, D.C.; SEA-Extension (January), 1980. 188p.

United States. Department of Agriculture. Farm Policy in the Years Ahead. Report of National Agricultural Advisory Commission. Washington, D.C.; USDA, 1964.

United States. Department of Agriculture. Economic Research Service. Economic Development Division. Characteristics of U.S. Rural Areas with Noncommuting Population. U.S. 92d Congress, 2d Session, U.S. Senate Committee on Agriculture and Forestry, Committee Print, 1972.

United States. Department of Agriculture. Office of Energy. Fuel Ethanol and Agriculture: An Economic Assessment. (U.S.D.A. Agricultural Economic Report No. 562) Washington, D.C., 1986.

United States Department of Health, Education, and Welfare. Rural Income Maintenance Experiment: A Social Experiment in Negative Income Taxation. Summary Report. Sponsored by the Office of Economic Opportunity and the Department of Health, Education, and Welfare. 1976.

United States Department of Health, Education, and Welfare. Toward a Social Report. Washington, D.C.; U.S. Gov't Printing Office, 1969. 101p.

United States Department of Health, Education, and Welfare. Highlights of Ten-State Nutrition Survey, 1968–1970. Atlanta, Georgia; National Center for Disease Control, 1972.

United States Department of Health, Education, and Welfare. Office of Education. Report of the Task Force on Rural Education. 1969. (E.R.I.C. ED 051 921).

United States Forest Service. An Assessment of the Forest and Range Land Situation in the United States. Washington,D.C.; U.S. Gov't. Printing Office, 1980. 631p.

United States House of Representatives. Committee on Agriculture, 83th Congress, 2d Session. Long-Range Farm Program. Washington, D.C.; U.S. Gov't Printing Office, 1954.

United States House of Representatives. Committee on Agriculture. Farm Credit Legislation. Hearing Before the Committee on Agriculture, House of Representatives, Seventy-Sixth Congress. . . . To Reduce Permanently the Interest Rates on Federal Land Bank and Land Bank Commissioner Loans . . . To Provide for the Adjustment and Refinancing of Farm-Mortgage Debts; to Limit the Institution of Foreclosure Proceedings and The Taking of Deficiency Judgments; and For Other Purposes. Washington, D.C.; United States Government Printing Office, 1940. 515p.

United States House of Representatives. Committee on Agriculture, 80th Congress, 2d Session. Long-Range Agricultural Policy. Washington, D.C.; Government Printing Office, 1948.

United States House of Representatives. Committee on Agriculture, 83th Congress, 2d Session. Long-Range Farm Program. Washington, D.C.; Government Printing Office, 1954.

United States House of Representatives. Special Committee on Postwar Economic Policy and Planning. Postwar Agricultural Policies. Tenth Report, 79th Congress, 2d Session, House Report 2728. Washington, D.C.; Government Printing Office, 1946.

United States. National Resources Board Land Planning Committee. Supplementary Report. . . . Washington, D.C.; 1935–1942. various pagings (Reprinted: New York; Arno, 1972).

United States President. Carter Admin. Small Community and Rural Development Policy. Washington,D.C.; GPO, 1979. 42p.

United States Senate. 87th Congress, 2d session. Policies, Standards, and Procedures in the Formulation, Evaluation, and Review of Plans for Use and Development of Water and Related Land Resources. Senate Document 97. Washington, D.C.; Government Printing Office, 1962.

United States Senate. Committee on Agriculture and Forestry. Marketing Alternatives for Agriculture: Is There a Better Way? U.S. 94th Congress, 2d Session. Washington, D.C.; U.S. Gov't Printing Office, 1976. 109p.

United States Senate. Committee on Agriculture, Nutrition, and Forestry. National Conference on Nonmetropolitan Community Service Research. Washington, D.C.; U.S. Gov't Printing Office, 1977.

United States Water Resources Council. The Nation's Water Resources: The First National Assessment. Washington, D.C.; U.S. Gov't Printing Office, 1968. Various pagings.

United States. Federal Trade Commission. Agricultural Income Inquiry. Washington, D.C.; United States Government Printing Office, 1938.

United States. National Resources Board. Land Planning Committee. Supplementary Report. Washington, D.C.; 1935–1942. various pagings (Reprinted: New York; Arno, 1972).

United States. National Resources Committee. Structure of the American Economy, Part I, Basic Characteristics. Washington, D.C.; U.S. Government Printing Office, 1939. 2 vols.

United States. National Resources Planning Board. Industrial Location and National Resources. Washington, D.C.; U.S. Printing Office, 1942. 360p.

United States. Tariff Commission. Wheat and Wheat Products. Report of the United States Tariff Commission to the President of the United States. Differences in Costs of Production of Wheat, Wheat Flour, and Wheat Mill Feed in the United States and in Canada, as Ascertained Pursuant to the Provisions of Section 315 of Title III of the Tariff Act of 1922 . . . Washington, D.C.; Government Printing Office, 1924. 71p.

United States. Tariff Commission. Sugar. Report to the President of the United States. Differences in Costs of Production of Sugar in the United States and Cuba, as Ascertained Pursuant to the Provisions of Section 315 of Title III of the Tariff Act of 1922. Washington, D.C.; United States Government Printing Office, 1926. 218p.

United States. Water Resource Policy Commission. A Water Policy for the American People. Washington, D.C.; Government Printing Office, 1950. 3 vols.

Upton, Martin. Agricultural Production Economics and Resource-use. London; Oxford University Press, 1976. 357p.

Uri, Pierre, et al. A Future for European Agriculture. Paris; The Atlantic Institute. 1970. 75p.

Urushihara, Yasushi. Nogyo Keizaigaku no Taikci. (System of Agricultural Economics). Tokyo; Bunshindo, 1978. 239p.

Usher, Albert P. The History of the Grain Trade in France, 1400–1710. Cambridge, Mass.; Harvard University Press, 1913. 425p.

V

Vaizey, J. The Economics of Education. London; Faber and Faber, 1962. 165p.

Van de Watering, Hylke, et al. Peru: Long-Term Projections of Demand for and Supply of Agricultural Commodities through 1980. Universidad Agria, Programa de Investigaciones para el Desarrallo, La Molina, Peru. Published by Israel Program for Scientific Translations, 1969. 195p.

Van Hekken, P. M. and H. U. E. Thoden van Velzen. Land Scarcity and Rural Inequality in Tanzania: Some Case Studies from Rungwe District. (Communications: No. 3) The Hague; Mouton De Gruyter, 1972. 127p.

Vaughan, L. M., and L. S. Hardin. Farm Work Simplification. New York; Wiley, 1949. 145p.

Veblen, T. The Instinct of Workmanship and the State of the Industrial Arts. New York; B. H. Henback, 1918. 355p. (Reprinted by Kelley)

Venezian, E.L. and W.K. Gamble. The Agricultural Development of Mexico: Its Structure and Growth since 1950. New York; Praeger Publ., 1969. 281p.

Vincent, W. H. editor. Economics and Management in Agriculture. Englewood Cliffs, NJ; Prentice-Hall, 1962. 452p.

Virenque, P. H., et al. Long-Term Development of Supply and Demand for Agricultural Products in Belgium, 1970–75. Antwerp, Belgium; Universitaire Faculteiten St. Ignatus, SESO-Studiecentrum voor Economisch en Sociaal Onderzoek, 1967.

Vogt, P.L. Introduction to Rural Economics. New York; Appleton, 1925. 377p.

W

Wachter, S. M. Latin American Inflation: The Stucturalist-Monetarist Debate. Lexington, Mass.; Lexington Books, 1976. 165p.

Wadham, S.M., and G.L. Wood. Land Utilization in Australia. Melbourne, London; Melbourne University Press and Oxford University Press, 1939. 360p.

Waite, W.C, and H.C. Trelogan. Agricultural Market Prices. 2d ed. New York; Wiley, 1951. 440p.

Walker, F. A. Land and Its Rent. Boston; Little, Brown, 1883. 232p. (Reprinted in 1981, Hyperion Press)

Wallace, Henry A. Agricultural Prices. Des Moines, Iowa; Wallace Publishing Company, 1920. 224p.

Wallace, Henry A. Our Debt and Duty to the Farmer. New York, London; The Century Co., 1925. 232p.

Wallace, Henry A. The Wheat Situation; A Report to the President. Washington, D.C.; United States Department of Agriculture, 1923.

Wallace, Luther T., Daryl Hobbs, and Raymond D. Vlasin, eds. Selected Perspectives for Community Resource Development. Raleigh, N.C.; North Carolina State University, Agricultural Policy Institute, 1969. 388p.

Wallerstein, Immanuel. The Modern World System: Capitalist Agriculture and the Origins of the European World Economy in the 16th Century. New York; Academic Press, Inc., 1974.

Ward, Michael et al. Co-Operation Between Co-Operatives: A Case Study of Agricultural Co-Operative in the North East of the Republic of Ireland. (Pub by Plunkett Foundation). New York; State Mutual Bk, 1982. 245p.

Ward, Ronald W. The Economics of Florida's FCOJ Imports and Exports: An Econometric Study. Tallahasse; Florida Dept. of Citrus, 1976. (Florida Dept. of Citrus, Econ. Res. Dept. Rep. 76-1) Q

Waring, P. Alston, and Walter M. Teller. Roots in the Earth: The Small Farmer Looks Ahead. New York, London; Harper and Brothers, 1943. 202p.

Warkov, Seymour, ed. Energy Policy in the United States: Social and Behavioral Dimensions. New York; Praeger Publ., 1978. 239p.

Warley, Thorald K. editor. Agricultural Producers and Their Markets. Oxford; Blackwell, 1967. 595p.

Warren, George F. Farm Management. New York; Macmillan, 1913. 590p.

Warren, George F., and F.A. Pearson. The Agricultural Situation: Economic Effects of Fluctuating Prices. New York; J. Wiley and Sons, 1924. 306p.

Warriner, D. Economics of Peasant Farming. 2d ed. London; Frank Cass, 1964. 208p.

Watestradt, F. Die Wirtschaftslehre des Landbaues. Stuttgart; E. Ulmer, 1912. 539p.

Wayland, S.R., E. de S. Brunner, and F.W. Cyr, eds. Farmers of the Future: Prospects and Policies for Establishing a New Generation on the Land. New York; Columbia University Teachers College, Bureau of Publications, 1953. 85p.

Weatherford, W.D., Jr. Geographic Differentials of Agricultural Wages in the United States. Cambridge, Mass.; Harvard University Press, Harvard Studies in Labor in Agriculture, 1957. 99p.

Weber, A. Theory of the Location of Industries. C. J. Friedrich, trans. Chicago; University of Chicago Press, 1929. 256p. (Originally published, 1909.)

Wellman, Harry R. Methods of Research in Agricultural Economics. Washington, D.C.; Farm Credit Administration, Cooperative Research and Service Division, 1939. 92p.

Westergaard, H.L. Contributions to the History of Statistics. London, 1932. 280p.

Westermeier, N. Die Landwirtschaftliche Betriebseinrichtung in Lehre und Beispiel Dargestellt. Berlin, 1906. 226p.

Whetham, E. H. The Economic Background to Agricultural Policy. Cambridge; University Press, 1960. 147p.

Whetham, E. H., and J. I. Currie, eds. Readings in the Applied Economics of Africa. Cambridge University Press, 1967. 2 vols.

White, Henry F. The Farmer and Economic Progress. Siloam Springs, Arkansas; The John Brown University Press, 1946. 424p.

Wilcox, C. A. A Charter for World Trade. New York; Macmillan, 1949. 333p.

Willcox, O.W. Reshaping Agriculture. New York; W.W. Norton and Co., 1934. 157p.

Williams, Anne S., R. C. Youmans, and D. M. Sorenson. Providing Public Services: Leadership and Organizational Considerations. Corvallis, Ore.; Western Rural Development Center, Oregon State University, 1975. (Its Special Report 1)

Williams, D.B. Agricultural Extension: Farm Extension Services in Australia, Britain and the United States of America. Carlton; Melbourne University Press, 1968. 218p.

Williams, D. B. editor. Agriculture in the Australian Economy. London; Architectural Press, 1967. 349p.

Williams, S. W., D. A. Vose, C. E. French, H. L. Cook, and A. C. Manchester. Organization and Competition in the Midwest Dairy Industries. Ames; Iowa State University Press, 1970. 339p.

Wills, Walter J. Introduction to Agricultural Sales. Reston, Virginia; Reston Publishing Company, Inc., 1983. 275p.

Wilson, C.M. The Landscape of Rural Poverty: Corn Bread and Creek Water. New York; H. Holt and Co., 1940. 309p.

Wionczek, M. S. Inversion y Tecnologia Extranjera en America Latina (Investment and Foreign Technology in Latin America). Mexico; Joaquin Mortiz, 1971. 189p.

Wiser, William H., and Charlotte V. Wiser. Behind Mud Walls, 1930–1960. Berkeley; University of California Press, 1963. 249p. (Revised ed. 1971. 287p.)

Witt, Lawrence W., and C. Eicher. The Effects of U.S. Agricultural Surplus Disposal Programs on Recipient Countries. East Lansing; Michigan State University, 1964.

Wolff, Henry W. Co-operation in Agriculture. London; P.S. King and Son, 1914. 378p.

Wood, Neal. John Locke and Agrarian Capitalism. Berkely; University of California Press, 1984. 184p.

Wrench, Guy Theodore. The Restoration of the Peasantries, with Especial Reference to That of India. London; The C.W. Daniel Co., Ltd., 1939. 147p.

Y

Yajuma, T., ed. Studies in the Structure of Farm Product Markets. Sapporo, Japan; Hokkaido University. 1960.

Yen, Y. C. et al. Rural Reconstruction and Development: A Manual for Field Workers. New York; Praeger, 1967. 426p.

Yoder, Fred R. Introducton to Agricultural Economics. New York; Thomas Y. Crowell Co., 1938. 494p.

Z

Zahler, Helene Sara. Eastern Workingmen and National Land Policy, 1829–1908. New York; Columbia University Press, 1941. 246p.

Zimmermann, Erich Walter. World Resources and Industries: A Functional Appraisal of the Availability of Agricultural and Industrial Resources. New York, London; Harper and Br, 1933. 842p. (Revised edition 1951. 832p.)

footnotes to chapter 8

9. Agricultural Economics and International Agricultural Development Informal Papers for Scholarly Research

A genre of literature common in the economics field has appeared in agricultural economics in recent years. This type of publication is characterized by brief length and informal physical presentation. Such papers are usually not peer-reviewed, and are intended to put forth ideas, proposals, and data to elicit comments from fellow researchers and scientists. These publications are issued by institutes, university departments or colleges, government research and analysis agencies, and select international groups. The readers are researchers; the publications are rarely used by undergraduate students.

These series are usually known as *Working Papers* or *Discussion Papers*, but in some cases they take more formal titles such as *Occasional Papers*. Citations to these working documents are becoming more and more commonplace in research work, and cause a great deal of work for librarians who must locate and acquire the more valuable ones for library research collections. A list of these titles was compiled because of the growing prominence of this genre of literature in agricultural economics and international agricultural development.

Compilation was made from a variety of sources, a major portion being done by Samuel Demas and the Collections Development staff of Mann Library in conjunction with the faculty at Cornell University. The size has been doubled and expanded to reflect the bibliographic work and records encountered in the preparation of this book. In addition, use was made of a 1981 list of serials of the Giannini Foundation of Agricultural Economics Library, University of California, Berkeley[1] and the 1988 annual source lists in *World Agricultural Economics and Rural Sociology*, and *Rural Development Abstracts*.

1. Grace Dote, compiler and ed., *Selected Serials List of the Giannini Foundation Library* (Berkeley, Calif.; Giannini Foundation, March 1982), 47p. The Giannini Library issued a related publication in 1989: *Some Sources of Information in Obtaining Ephemeral Materials . . .*, 7 leaves.

Scope and Reasons for Inclusion

This is a selective list of informal paper series built around the following points:

(1) More formal publications, more widely distributed, and usually of greater substance are *not* included, such as report series and bulletins common to agricultural experiment stations. Although some series titles will thus be omitted, these are few and readily identifiable from standard bibliographic sources.
(2) Titles are of recent age; this is a functional list.
(3) This is not a core list, but is devised to cover the total informal working paper literature of most value to researchers in agricultural economics.
(4) Economic series are not included unless they have heavy emphasis on agricultural topics or trade, or are widely cited by agricultural economists for theories or their continuing substantive contents. Two commercial firms have announced the availability of working papers in economics on microforms; they are Microforms International, a subsidiary of Pergamon Press, and University Microfilm International. Few agricultural titles are included in their offerings; general economics is their aim.
(5) Titles in this list usually provide analysis of situations or data; but they are not statistical publications.
(6) Subject coverage tends to follow the patterns used for determination of journals and monographs in previous chapters. Emphases are on advanced work, agricultural economics, and international development related to agriculture. Therefore, series that concentrate on national or state problems tend not to be included, unless known to be cited by scholarly agricultural economists.

Major Current Working Papers for Agricultural Economics and International Agricultural Development

Ahmadu Bello University (Zaria, Nigeria). Institute for Agricultural Research.
Samaru Miscellaneous Paper.
Arizona. University. Department of Agricultural Economics.
Working Papers.
Asian Development Bank.
Economic Staff Paper.
Australia. Bureau of Agricultural Economics.
Discussion Paper.
Occasional Paper.
Australian National University, Canberra. Centre for Resource and Environmental Studies.
Working Papers.
Australian National University, Canberra. National Centre for Development Studies.
Rural Development Working Paper.
Working Papers in Trade and Development.
Belgium. Institut Economique Agricole, Brussels.
Notes.

Bielefeld. Universitat. Forschungsschwerpunkt Entwicklungssoziologie.
  Arbeitspapiere.
Birbeck College, University of London.
  Discussion Papers in Economics.
Botswana. Ministry of Agriculture. Agricultural Technology Improvement Project (ATIP).
  ATIP Working Paper.
Bremen. University. Sudan Economy Research Group.
  Discussion Papers.
California. University, Berkeley. Berkeley Roundtable on International Economics (BRIE).
  BRIE Working Papers.
California. University, Berkeley. Department of Agricultural and Resource Economics.
  Working Paper.
California. University, Berkeley. Department of Economics.
  Working Papers.
California. University, Davis. Department of Agricultural Economics.
  Working Paper Series.
California. University, Davis. Research Program in Applied Macroeconomics and Macropolicy.
  Working Paper Series.
California. University, Riverside. Resources and Environmental Economics and Public Policy Group.
  Working Paper Series.
Cambridge University. Agricultural Economics Unit.
  Occasional Papers.
Canada. Agriculture Canada. Commodity Markets Analysis Division.
  Working Paper.
Canada. Agriculture Canada. Marketing and Economics Branch.
  Working Paper.
  Economic Working Papers.
Canada. Agriculture Canada. Policy Branch.
  Working paper.
Central Bank of Ceylon.
  Occasional Papers.
Clemson University. Department of Agricultural Economics and Rural Sociology.
  Working Paper.
Colorado State University. Department of Agricultural & Natural Resources Economics.
  Working Papers.
Columbia University. Center for the Study of Futures Markets.
  Working Paper Series.
Cornell University. Department of Agricultural Economics.
  Staff Paper.
Exeter. University (England).
  Agricultural Economics Discussion Paper.
Florida. University. Food and Resource Economics Department.
  Staff Paper.
France. Institut National de la Recherche Agronomique. Station d'Economie Rurale. (E.N.S.A.M.).
  Serie Notes et Documents.

Ghana. University. Institute of Statistical, Social and Economic Research.
Discussion Papers.
Göttingen. Universitat. Institute fur Agrarokonomie.
Working Paper.
Guelph. University. Department of Agricultural Economics and Business.
Working Paper Series.
Harvard Institute for International Development.
Development Discussion Papers.
Harvard University. Institute of Economic Research.
Discussion Papers.
Hebrew University, Rehovoth, Israel. Center for Agricultural Economics Research.
Working Paper.
Ibadan University, Nigeria. Institute of African Studies.
Occasional Publication.
Illinois. University. Department of Agricultural Eocnomics.
Staff Papers (in two sub-series).
India. Centre for Women's Development Studies, New Delhi.
Occasional Paper.
Indian Institute of Management, Ahmedabad.
Working Paper.
Inter-American Development Bank, Washington, D.C.
Working Paper.
International Agricultural Trade Research Consortium. (Financed by USDA Economic Research Service and Foreign Agricultural Service; Agriculture Canada and Participating Institutions).
Working Papers.
International Food Policy Research Institute, Washington, D.C.
Working Papers on Commercialization of Agriculture and Nutrition.
International Institute for Applied Systems Analysis (IIASA), Vienna.
Working Papers.
International Institute of Tropical Agriculture, Ibadan, Nigeria. Agricultural Economics.
Discussion Paper.
International Labour Office, Geneva. World Employment Programme Research.
Working Paper.
International Livestock Centre for Africa, Addis Ababa, Ethiopia. Livestock Policy Unit (LPU).
LPU Working Paper.
International Maize and Wheat Improvement Center, Mexico, D.F. CIMMYT Economics Program.
Working Paper.
International Monetary Fund, Washington, D.C.
IMF Working Paper.
Staff Paper.
International Rice Research Institute (IRRI), Los Baños, Phillipines. Department of Agricultural Economics.
IRRI Research Papers.
International Service for National Agricultural Research (ISNAR), The Hague.
Working Papers.
International Wheat Council, London.
Secretariat Paper.

Iowa State University. Department of Agricultural Economics.
Card Staff Paper.
Card Working Paper Series.
Israel. Center for Agricultural Economic Research, Rehovoth.
Working Paper.
Japan. International Development Center of Japan (IDCJ), Tokyo.
IDCJ Working Paper Series.
Johannes Kepler Universitat Linz. Institut fur Volkswirtschaftslehre.
Arbeitspapier.
Kentucky. University. Department of Agricultural Economics.
Staff Papers.
Kiel. Universitat. Institut fur Agrarpolitik und Marktlehre.
Diskussionsbeitrage.
Lincoln College, University of Canterbury. Agribusiness and Economics Research Unit.
Discussion Paper.
Lincoln College, University of Canterbury. Agricultural Economics Research Unit. Discussion Paper.
Manchester. University.
Manchester Papers on Development.
Manchester. University. Department of Agricultural Economics and Farm Management.
Manchester Working Papers in Agricultural Economics.
Manitoba. University. Department of Agricultural Economics and Farm Management.
Occasional (or Paper) Series.
Maryland. University. Department of Agricultural and Resource Economics (AREC).
AREC Working Paper.
Massachusetts. University. Department of Agricultural and Resource Economics, Amherst.
Staff Paper (in two sub-series).
Massey University. Department of Agricultural Economics and Farm Management.
Agricultural Strategy Paper.
Discussion Papers.
Technical Discussion Paper.
McGill University. Center for Developing Area Studies (CDAS).
CDAS Discussion Paper Series.
McMaster University. Department of Economics.
Working Paper.
Michigan State University (MSU).
MSU International Development Papers.
Michigan State University. Department of Agricultural Economics. African Rural Economy/Employment Program.
Staff Paper.
Working Papers.
Michigan State University. Office of Women in International Development.
Working Paper.
Michigan. University. Center for Research on Economic Development.
Discussion Paper.
Minnesota. University. Department of Agricultural and Applied Economics.
Staff Papers Series.
Mississippi Agricultural and Forestry Experiment Station. Department of Agricultrual Economics.
Staff Paper.

Missouri. University. Department of Agricultural Economics.
Agricultural Economics Working Paper.
Nairobi. University (Kenya). Institute for Development Studies.
Discussion Paper.
Working Paper.
Naples. Universita. Centro di Specializzazione e Richerche Economico-Agrarie per il Mezzagiorno.
Estratto.
National Bureau of Economic Research, Inc. Cambridge, Mass.
Working Paper Series.
Technical Working Paper Series.
Nebraska. University. Department of Agricultural Economics.
Staff Paper.
Netherlands. Institute of Social Studies, The Hague. Dairy Aid and Development.
Working Paper.
New Mexico State University. Department of Agricultural Economics and Agriclutural Business.
Staff Report Series.
Newcastle upon Tyne. University. Department of Agricultural Economics and Agricultural Marketing.
Discussion papers.
North Carolina State University. Department of Economics and Business.
Faculty Working Paper.
North Central Regional Research Group. Studies on the Organization and Control of the U.S. Food System.
Working Papers.
North Dakota State University. Dept. of Agricultural Economics.
Staff Paper Series.
Notre Dame. University. Department of Economics.
Working Paper Series.
Ohio State University. Department of Agricultural Economics and Rural Sociology.
Economics and Sociology Occasional Paper.
Open University, U.K. Development Policy and Practice (DPP).
DPP Working Paper.
Organization for Economic Cooperation and Development. Development Centre.
Occasional Paper.
Overseas Development Council (U.K.), London.
Development Paper.
Occasional Paper.
ODI/IIMI Irrigation Management Network Paper.
Palm Oil Research Institute, Kuala Lumpur, Malaysia.
Occasional Paper.
Pennsylvania State University. Department of Agricultural Economics and Rural Sociology.
Staff Paper.
Philippines. University. School of Economics, Manila.
Discussion Paper.
Plunkett Foundation for Cooperative Studies, London.
Occasional Papers.
Purdue. University. Department of Agricultural Economics.
Staff Papers.

Queen's University, Ontario. Institute for Economic Research.
  Discussion Papers.
Queensland. University. Department of Agriculture.
  Agricultural Economics Discussion Papers Series.
Reading. University. Centre for Agricultural Strategy (CAS).
  CAS Paper.
South Dakota State University.
  Economic Staff Paper Series.
Sussex. University. Institute of Development Studies (IDS).
  IDS Discussion Papers.
Swedish University of Agricultural Sciences, Uppsala. International Rural Development Centre.
  Issue Paper.
  Working Paper.
Sydney. University. Department of Agricultural Economics. Agricultural Economics Research.
  Miscellaneous Papers.
Tel-Aviv. University. Foerder Institute for Economics Research.
  Working Paper.
Tennessee. University. Department of Agricultural Economics and Rural Sociology.
  Staff Paper.
Texas A & M University. Agricultural and Food Policy Center (AFPC).
  AFPC Staff Report.
Texas A & M University. Department of Agricultural Economics and Rural Sociology.
  Faculty Paper Series.
Texas. University. El Paso. Center for Inter-American and Border Studies.
  Border Issues and Public Policy Working Paper Series.
Toronto. University. Department of Economics.
  Working Paper.
Toronto. University. Development Studies Programme.
  Working Paper.
United Nations University, Helsinki. World Institute for Development Economics Research (WIDER).
  WIDER Working Papers.
United States. Agency for International Development (AID).
  AID Discussion Papers.
United States. Bureau of the Census.
  Working Paper.
United States. Department of Agriculture. Economic Research Service.
  Staff Report.
University of Southern California. Department of Economics. Modeling Research Group (MRG).
  MRG Working Paper.
Utrecht. State University. Department of Geography of Developing Countries.
  Diskussiestukken.
Washington. State University. Department of Agricultural Economics.
  Staff Paper.
West Africa Rice Development Association, Monrovia, Liberia.
  Occasional Paper.
Western Ontario. University. Centre for the Study of International Economic Relations.
  Working Paper.

Wisconsin. University, Madison. Center for Demography and Ecology (CDE).
CDE Working Paper.
Wisconsin. University, Madison. Department of Agricultural Economics.
Staff Paper.
Wisconsin. University, Madison. Land Tenure Center (LTC).
LTC Paper.
World Bank, Washington, D.C.
Staff Commodity Papers.
World Bank Discussion Paper
World Bank Staff Working Paper.
World Bank. Development Research Department.
Discussion Paper.
World Food Programme, Rome.
Occasional Paper.
Wye College. University of London. Centre for European Agricultural Studies.
Occasional Papers.
Wye College. University of London. Department of Agricultural Economics.
Discussion Paper in Agricultural Policy.
Yale University. Economic Growth Center.
Center Discussion Paper.
Zimbabwe. University, Harrare. Department of Agricultural Economics and Extension.
Working Paper.
Zimbabwe. University, Harrare. Department of Land Management.
Working Paper.

10. Reference Update

One of the more trying tasks in agricultural economics and rural development is to keep up with the reference or working tools that appear in a continuous stream, such as handbooks, guides, cumulative indexes of long-term value, authoritative histories, data collections, and analyses of data covering major periods of time, countries or commodities, and extensive or very valuable bibliographies. These are not books to be read from cover to cover or used as a reading adjunct to a class. They provide reference points to be used for authoritative data, citations, sources of information, or general background.

The most recent major compilation of reference tools for agricultural economics and rural sociology was in 1981, in *Guide to Sources for Agricultural and Biological Research*, edited by J. Richard Blanchard and Lois Farrell (735 pages). This immense work serves as the basic guide to the literature of the agricultural sciences. It was sponsored by the USDA's National Agricultural Library, and published by the University of California Press. The book's Chapter H, compiled by Catherine Blizzard, is on social sciences and has the following subdivisions, all of which are covered in this book on the literature of agricultural economics and rural sociology and in this chapter:

Agricultural Economics
Agricultural Geography
Agricultural History
Agricultural Biography
Agricultural Legislation
Land Reform
Agricultural Development
Rural Sociology
Agricultural Education

The H chapter cites 445 reference or background items. Each reference is annotated and sequentially numbered. The reader is referred to Blanchard and Farrell's *Guide* for the continuing and historically important reference tools, particularly as they apply to U.S. agricultural economics and rural sociology although select worldwide titles are included. This chapter is a supplement to and an update on the *Guide*'s chapter H on social sciences.

A few citations to works earlier than 1980 are included here when they appeared to be of value to this writer. In many cases these were omitted from Blanchard and Farrell's *Guide* because of space considerations. Some titles have been updated and the successor edition noted (reference by H number is made back to the related item in chapter H). When a title is a direct successor, the reader should consult Blanchard and Farrell for the complete annotation. The inclusion of titles in this list is a bit more restrictive than in Blanchard and Farrell, because some of the important titles are in the core monograph lists in Chapter 7 of this book. In this list, there is a distinct bias toward U.S. agriculture, although the major new tools for the Third World are also included. As with any compilation of this type, some items may have been overlooked.

Two major developments have occurred in agricultural bibliography since the preparation of the Blanchard and Farrell's *Guide* which do not apply exclusively to agricultural economics and rural sociology. These are of such importance that they must be mentioned.

The first major development is the significant series begun by the National Agricultural Library in 1978: *USDA Bibliographies and Literature of Agriculture (BLA-)*. The series publishes compilations from USDA organizations and individuals, although others have contributed some of the bibliographic works. The majority of the ninety-three titles published in the first eleven years were the work of NAL staff members. The subjects range over all of agriculture; these are representative titles:

Relationship of Birds and Spruce Budworms: A Literature Review and Annotated Bibliography . . . (Sept. 1982, 37p. *BLA*-23)
The Protection of Stone Fruits, Exclusive of Cherries, 1979–March 1985; Citations from AGRICOLA . . . (Aug. 1985, 89p. *BLA*-40)
Agricultural Databases Directory . . . (Oct. 1985, 174p. + indexes. *BLA*-42)
World List of Poultry Serials . . . (Aug. 1989, 182p. *BLA*-76)
Promoting Nutrition Through Education: A Resource Guide . . . (Sept. 1989, 97p. *BLA*-89)

The National Agricultural Library, Reference Branch, has provided a short title, keyword index to various NAL publications, including the *BLA* series. There are no dates, authors, or annotations, however. The publication is *Keyword Index to Quick Bibliographies, Bibliographies and Literature of Agriculture, Special Reference Briefs, Agri-topics, Pathfinders, Search Tips, Fact Sheets, Miscellaneous Information Center Issuances* (Beltsville, Md.; National Agricultural Library, 1989, supplement 1990).

The second major development since 1981 was the introduction of bibliographic citations stored on compact disks (CD). This has spurred scholarship. These systems include search and retrieval software operated on a microcomputer, so that the heavy cost of machine-time and telecommunications to query remotely stored databases has been negated. The storage capacity is vast and the software sufficiently simple to be used with little instruction. Although not perfect in all aspects, this storage and retrieval system has made bibliographic and research searching infinitely more palatable and inexpensive.

The three primary agricultural citation databases (AGRICOLA, CABI Abstracts, and AGRIS) are all available on CD for variant prices per citation stored. Not all of these databases cover the full time period of available machine-readable citations, but the years of citations stored on CD are growing rapidly. These services all provide updating on a regular basis; one is available from more than one commercial vendor with different search software.

Reference Update on Sources in Agricultural Economics and Rural Sociology

ACCIS Guide to United Nations Information Sources on Food and Agriculture. Compiled by the Advisory Committee for the Co-ordination of Information Systems (ACCIS). Rome: Food and Agriculture Organization, 1987. 124p. (ACCIS Guides to United Nations Information Sources no. 1).

Agricultural Chartbook. 1985+. Annual. (1986 ed. as *USDA Agricultural Handbook* no. 663, handbook nos. different each issue.) Washington, D.C.: U. S. Department of Agriculture, Economic Research Service. 1986 ed., 110p.

Agricultural Policy and Development in West Africa. [1974–82]. Annotated Bibliography. *Vol. 1: General* (30p.); *Vol. 2: Gambia and Senegal* (51p.); *Vol. 3: Benin, Central Africa Republic, Chad, Congo, Gabon, Guinea-Bissau, Mauritania, Togo* (51p.); *Vol. 4: Ghana, Liberia and Sierra Leone* (85p.); *Vol. 5: Nigeria* (174p.); *Vol. 6: Cameroon and Ivory Coast* (82p.); *Vol. 7: Mali, Niger and Upper Volta* (84p.). Farnham Royal, England, Commonwealth Agricultural Bureaux, 1983–87. Printed from CAB Abstracting Services. Approximately 1,200 citations.

American Society of Farm Managers and Rural Appraisers. *Membership Directory*. Denver, Colo.: 1929+.

Amols, George, and Kaiser Wilson. *Agricultural Finance Statistics, 1960–1983*. Washington, D.C.: U.S. Dept. of Agriculture, 1984. 53p. (USDA Statistical Bulletin no. 706).

Barnard, Charles H., and John Jones. *Farm Real Estate Values in the United States by Counties, 1850–1982*. Washington, D.C.: U.S. Dept. of Agriculture, Economic Research Service, 1987. 111p. (USDA Statistical Bulletin no. 751)

Borst, Alan, Karen J. Spatz, and Kristeen Kaiser. *Directory of U. S. Agricultural Cooperative Exporters*. Washington, D.C.: U.S. Dept. of Agriculture, Agricultural Cooperative Service, 1988. 48p. (USDA Agricultural Cooperative Service Report no. 21)

Broadbent, K. P. *A Chinese/English Dictionary of China's Rural Economy*. Farnham Royal, Eng.: Commonwealth Agricultural Bureaux, 1978. 406p.

Bunch, Karen, compiler. *Food, Consumption, Prices, and Expenditures, 1963–83*. Washington, D.C.: U.S. Dept. of Agriculture, Economic Research Service, 1984. 108p. (USDA Statistical Bulletin no. 713).

Cavusgil, S. Tamer, and John R. Nevin, eds. *International Marketing: An Annotated Bibliography*. Chicago: American Marketing Association, 1983. 139p.

Centro de Documentacion Economica para America Latina (CEDEAL). *Resúmenes Analíticos en Economía Agrícola Latinoamericana (Abstracts on Latin American Agricultural Economics)*. Cali, Colombia: Centro Internacional de Agricultura Tropical, 1976–81. 6 vols., each approximately 275p. Includes a list of keywords used.

Chicago Board of Trade. *Commodity Futures Trading: Bibliography*. 1966+. Annual. Cumulative through 1983. [H020]

Commission of the European Communities. *The Agricultural Situation in the Community*. 1975+. Annual. Brussels: Commission of the European Communities.

Commission of the European Communities. *Agriculture: Statistical Yearbook. Agriculture: Annuaire Statistique*. 1986+. Luxembourg: Office des Publications Officielles des Communautes Europeennes.

Commonwealth Secretariat. *Training for Agricultural Development: A Directory of Commonwealth Resources*. 3d ed. London, Commonwealth Secretariat Pub., 1989. 273p. An unusual document listing the forty-five countries of the Commonwealth with their general education and higher degree programs as well some training opportunities from 381 institutions. Most information is standard for directories although the breakdown of degrees offered is extensive. Includes veterinary and fisheries sciences as well as all aspects of agriculture. Very limited printing; out of print within six months of publication.

Congressional Information Service. *Current National Statistical Compendiums on Microfiche*. Bethesda, Md.: Congressional Information Service, 1986+. Annual updates. Microfiched annual statistical abstracts and yearbooks from 160 countries, with new titles and countries yearly. Continental subsets available; full service about $1,000 per year.

Coyle, Barry, Robert G. Chambers, and Andrew Schmitz. *Economic Gains From Agricultural Trade: A Review and Bibliography*. Washington, D.C.: U.S. Dept. of Agriculture, Economic Research Service, 1986. 48p., including forty-one citations and twenty-seven pages of explantory text. (USDA Bibliographies and Literature of Agriculture no. 48)

Daberkow, Stan G., and Leslie A. Whitener. *Agricultural Labor Data Sources: An Update*. Washington, D.C.: U. S. Dept. of Agriculture. Economic Research Service, 1986. 25p. (USDA Agricultural Handbook no. 658). Covers U.S. federal sources only. The 208 citations are limited to journal literature with a few reports; primarily 1975 through 1987.

Darnay, Brigitte T., and John Nimchuk. *Newsletters Directory*, 3d ed. Detroit: Gale Research Co., 1987. 1162p. Has approximately 350 entries for agricultural sciences.

Dearing, J. A. *A Selective Annotated Bibliography of Fishery Statistical Publications*. Rome: Food and Agriculture Organization, June 1988. 219p. (FAO Fisheries Circular no. 813) Includes references to publication sources from 100 countries, 13 international organizations, and 24 national censuses or surveys. Based on publications available in the FAO David Lubin Memorial Library.

Economic Survey of Europe in 1986–87. 1987+. Annual. New York: United Nations-Secretariat, Economic Commission for Europe. 358p. in 1987.

Eichborn, Reinhard von. *Cambridge-Eichborn German Dictionary: Economics, Law, Administration, Business, General*, 2 vols. A Glossary of Terms in English, French, Spanish, and Arabic. Cambridge: Cambridge University Press, 1983.

Emerson, Robert D., and Anita L. Battiste. *U.S. Agriculture and Foreign Workers: An Annotated Bibliography*. Washington, D.C.: U.S. Dept. of Agriculture, Economic Research Service, Dec. 1988. 112p. (USDA Bibliographies and Literature of Agriculture No. 73) Approximately 1,000 citations, primarily from the 1970s and 1980s.

Evalds, Victoria K. *Union List of African Censuses, Development Plans and Statistical Abstracts*. New York: Hans Zell, 1985. 232p.

Fenton, Thomas, and Mary J. Heffron, compilers and editors. *Food, Hunger, Agribusiness: A Directory of Resources*. Maryknoll, N.Y.: Orbis Books, 1987. 131p.

Fisher, Rita C., Julia C. Peterson, John W. Beecher, Jane S. Johnson, and Carol Boast. *Agricultural Information Resource Centers: A World Directory, 1990*. Urbana, Ill.: IAALD/CTA, 1990. 641p. Has 3,971 worldwide entries; first updating in thirty years. [A342]

Food and Agriculture Organization. *Agricultural Credit*. Rome: FAO, 1983. 371p. (FAO: GIP: Terminology Bulletin).

Food and Agricultural Organization. *Bibliography of Food and Agricultural Marketing in the Developing Countries*. Rome: FAO, 1982. 120p. Publications in West European languages with summary contents. [H088]

Food and Agriculture Organization. Documentation Centre. *Agricultural Credit: Annotated Bibliography, Author and Subject Index. No. 1–4, 1967–1985*. Rome: FAO. Each updating about 50p. [H023]

Frank, Nathalie D., and John V. Ganly. *Data Sources For Business and Market Analysis*. 3d ed. Metuchen, N.J.: Scarecrow Press, 1983. 470p. [H002]

Garkey, Janet, and Wen S. Chern. *Handbook of Agricultural Statistical Data*. Supported by the Statistical Reporting Service, USDA, and the Economic and Statistics Committee, American Agricultural Economics Association. Washington, D.C.: U.S. Department of Agriculture, Statistical Reporting Service, 1986. 139p.

Ghosh, Pradip, K., ed. *Health, Food and Nutrition in Third World Development*. Westport, Conn. and London: Greenwood Press, 1984. Prepared under the auspices of the Center for Interational Development, University of Maryland, College Park, and the World Academy of Development and Cooperation, Washington, D.C. 618p. (International Development Resource Books no. 6) One of a series of twenty resource books dealing with Third World development. Includes lists of recent books, information sources, and bibliographies.

Gunston, C. A., and C. M. Corner. *Gunston and Corner's German-English Glossary of Financial and Economic Terms*, 8th ed. Frankfurt-am-Main: F. Knapp, 1983. 918p. [H105]

Harriss, Barbara. *Marketing in the Semi-Arid Tropics of West Africa: A Partially Annotated and Indexed Bibliography and List of Common Abbreviations, Addresses and a French-English Technical Glossary*. Andhra Pradesh, India: International Crops Research Institute for the Semi-Arid Tropics, 1982. 225p.

Ingalshe, Gene. *Cooperative Facts*. Washington, D.C.: U.S. Dept. of Agriculture, Economics, Statistics, and Cooperatives Service, 1987. 23p. (USDA Agricultural Cooperative Service Cooperative Information Report no. 2). [H182]

Ingalshe, Gene. *Farmer Cooperative Publications*. Washington, D.C.: U.S. Dept. of Agriculture, Agricultural Cooperative Service. Rev. Dec. 1988. Revised every two or three years. 37p. (USDA Agricultural Cooperative Service Cooperative Information Report no. 4). [H059]

Institute of Cultural Affairs International, ed. Directory of Rural Development Projects; Project Descriptions Prepared for the International Exposition of Rural Development. 1st ed. Munich; K. G. Saur, 1985. 515 p. Part II is One Page Project Descriptions divided into seven areas: Sub-Saharan; Eastern and Western Europe; Carribean, Central and South America; North Africa and the Middle East; North America; South Asian Sub-Continent; Oceania, East, and Southeast Asia. Other parts are indexes of sponsors, subjects, and titles, plus a conclusion section. An interesting compilation of about 250 projects, but not very authoritatively done or complete.

Institute of Developing Economies. (Ajia Keizai Kenkyosho). *One Hundred Years of Agricultural Statistics in Japan*. Tokyo: Institute of Developing Economies, 1969. 270p.

International Marketing Data and Statistics, 1st ed. 1975–76+. London: Euromonitor Publications. Vol. 11 in 1986–87.

International Trade Centre, Geneva. *A Guide to the World's Foreign Trade Statistics: A Directory of the Foreign Trade Statistical Serials Published by International Organizations, Governmental Bodies, and Selected Semi-Official Agencies, with detailed Bibliographical Notes and Practical Advice to Aid Researchers and Documentalists*. Geneva: International Trade Centre, UNCTAD/GATT, 1977. 155p.

Jones, John, and Charles H. Barnard. *Farm Real Estate: Historical Series Data, 1950–85*. Washington, D.C.: U.S. Dept. of Agriculture, 1985. 51p. (USDA Statistical Bulletin no. 738)

Kahlia, D. R., and Mahendra Jain. *Statistical Sources on Indian Agriculture*. New Delhi: Marwah, 1978. 279p.

Kendall, Maurice G., and William R. Buckland. *A Dictionary of Statistical Terms*, 5th ed. Prepared for the International Statistical Institute. Burnt Mill, Harlow, Essex, Eng.: Longmans Scientific and Technical; and New York: Wiley, 1989. 268p[H159]

Kraenzle, Charles A., and Celestine C. Adams. *Cooperative Historical Statistics*. Washington, D.C.: U.S. Dept. of Agriculture, Agricultural Cooperative Service, 1987. 78p. (USDA Agricultural Cooperative Service, CIR 1) Provides time series data on marketing, farm supply, and related service cooperatives from 1863 to 1985. Revised every two or three years.

Kravis, Irving B., Alan Heston, and Robert Summers. *World Product and Income: International Comparisons of Real Gross Product*. Produced by the Statistical Office of the United Nations and the World Bank, in collaboration with Alicia R. Civitello. Baltimore: Published for the World Bank by Johns Hopkins University Press, 1982. 388p.

Kriesberg, Martin. *International Organizations and Agricultural Development*. Rev. ed. Washington, D.C.: U.S. Dept. of Agriculture, Economic Research Service, 1984. 137p. (Foreign Agricultural Economic Report no. 131). [A328]

Langley, James A., and Suchada Langley. *State-Level Wheat Statistics, 1949–88*. Washington, D.C.: U.S. Department of Agriculture, Economic Research Service, 1989. 86p. (USDA Statistical Bulletin, no. 779).

Langley, James A., and Letricia M. Womack. *State-Level Feed Grain Statistics, 1949–86*. Washington, D.C.: U.S. Department of Agriculture, Economic Research Service, 1987. 171p. (USDA Statistical Bulletin no. 757).

Laws Relating to Agriculture. Vol. 1 (1884–1971), Gilman G. Udell, compiler. Vol. 2 (1971–81), Gerald P. Walsh, Jr., compiler. Washington, D.C.: U.S. Government Printing Office, 1971, 1985. [H292]

Mackie, Arthur B., Stephen W. Hiemstra, and Stacey L. Rosen. *World Food Grain Trade, 1962–83: Barley, Corn, Rye, Oats, and Other Cereals*. Washington, D.C.: U.S. Department of Agriculture, Economic Research Service, 1987. 145p. (USDA Statistical Bulletin no. 755).

Mackie, Arthur B., Stephen W. Hiemstra, and Stacey L. Rosen. *World Food Grain Trade, 1962–83: Wheat, Rice, and Wheat Flour*. Washington, D.C.: U.S. Department of Agriculture, Economic Research Service, 1987. 89p. (USDA Statistical Bulletin no. 734).

Manheim, Jarol B., and Allison Ondrasik. *Datamap 1988: Index of Published Tables of Statistical Data*. Phoenix, Ariz.: Oryx Press, 1988. 838p. Indexes twenty-eight statistical compilations, such as the USDA's *Agricultural Statistics*.

Marketing Information: A Professional Reference Guide. 1982+. Biennial. Atlanta: College of Business Administration, Georgia State University.

Nicholas, David. *Commodities Futures Trading: A Guide to Information Sources and Computerized Services*. London and New York: Mansell, 1985. 144p. [H154]

O'Brien, Jacqueline Wasserman, and Steven R. Wasserman, eds. *Statistics Sources: A Subject Guide to Data on Industrial, Business, Social, Education, Financial, and Other Topics for the United States and Internationally*, 2 vols., 14th ed. Detroit: Gale Research, 1991. 3524p.

Organisation for Economic Cooperation and Development (OECD). *Development Cooperation, 1972 Review*. Paris: OECD, 1973+. Annual. Issued earlier under slightly variant titles; 1987 issue was titled *Report*. 1988 ed., 268p. Issues before 1985 available on microfiche.

Owen, Wyn F., and Larry R. Cross, eds. *Guide to Graduate Study in Economics, Agricultural Economics, and Doctoral Degrees in Business and Administration in the United States of America and Canada*, 8th ed. Boulder, Colo.: Prepared for the American Economic Association and the American Agricultural Economics Association by the Economics Institute, University of Colorado, 1989. 518p. [H120]

Padilla, Martine. *Les Cent Premiers Groupes Agro-Industriels Mondiaux. Top One Hundred Agro-Industrial Groups in the World,* 3d ed. Montpéllier, France: Institut Agronomique Meditérranéen, 1983. 479p.

Pardey, Philip G., and Johannes Roseboom. *ISNAR Agricultural Research Indicator Series: A Global Database on National Agricultural Research Systems*. Cambridge, Eng., and New York: Cambridge University Press, 1989. 547p. Primarily covers personnel and expenditures for 154 countries. Bibliographic and information sources are extensive. ISNAR is International Services for National Agricultural Research.

Peters, G. H., with the assistance of K. R. Clark. *Agriculture*. Published for the Royal Statistical Society and the Economic and Social Research Council. London and New York: Chapman and Hall, 1988. 209p. (*Reviews of United Kingdom Statistical Sources*, vol. 23; series edited by W. F. Maunder).

Pratt, Brian, and Jo Boyden, eds. *The Field Directors' Handbook: An Oxfam Manual for Development Workers*, 4th ed. Oxford and New York: Published for Oxfam by Oxford University Press, 1985. 512p.

Roberts, Gerald, consulting ed. *Guide to World Commodity Markets*. 4th ed. London and New York: Kogan Page & Nichols, 1985. 409p.

Sable, Martin H. *Mexican and Mexican-American Labor in the United States: An International Bibliography*. New York: Haworth Press, 1986. 3,000 citations.

Shapiro, Irving J. *Dictionary of Marketing Terms*, 4th ed. Totowa, N.J.: Littlefield, Adams, 1981. 276p.

Technical Centre for Agricultural and Rural Cooperation. *Tropical Agriculture: Information Sources. Vol. I: European Community; Vol. II: ACP Countries*. Wageningen, The Netherlands: CTA, 1987–88. Vol. 1, 185p.; vol. 2, 355p. The first volume lists institutes of nine EEC countries, with four indexes to the alphabetical listing. Vol. 2 lists 337 libraries and documentation centers in developing countries with basic information. Main topics of interest and coverge are accessed by a keyword index. Services and collection sizes are provided.

Timms, Dan, and Mathew Shane. *World Agricultural Trade Shares, 1962–1985*. Washington, D.C.: U.S. Dept. Agriculture, Economic Research Service, 1987. 300p. (USDA Statistical Bulletin no. 760).

United Nations. Economic and Social Commission for Asia and the Pacific. *Agricultural Statistics for Asia and the Pacific, 1985*. Bangkok, 1986. 63p. Previous ed. 1979.

United Nations, and Commission of the European Communities. *World Comparisons of Purchasing Power and Real Product for 1980; Phase IV of the International Comparison Project*. New York: United Nations, Eurostat, 1986+.

United States. Bureau of the Census. Agriculture Division. *1987 Census of Agriculture* (AC87). Divided into five publishing categories:

Advance Reports, in fifty-six parts. Covers each county or equivalent. Issued in 1988.
Vol. 1: *Geographic Area Series*, (A1–56) in fifty-six parts. Issued in 1989–91.
Vol. 2: *Subject Series*, (S1–6).
- Part 1: *Agricultural Atlas of the United States* (1990, 199p.)
- Part 2: *Coverage Evaluation* (1990, Various paging)
- Part 3: *Ranking of States and Counties* (1990, 99p.)
- Part 4: *History*
- Part 5: *Government Payments and Market Value of Agricultural Products Sold* (1990, 449p.)
- Part 6: *ZIP Code Tabulations of Selected Items* (1990, 629p.)

Vol. 3: *Related Surveys*
- Part 1: *The Farm and Ranch Irrigation Survey, 1988*. (1990, 114p.)
- Part 2: *Agricultural Economics and Land Ownership Survey* (1990)

Vol. 4: *Census of Horticultural Specialties*

Titles without dates are scheduled to appear in 1991. The Bureau of the Census offers the *Advance Reports* on a flexible diskette; all data is available on computer tapes; data for conterminous U.S. and Puerto Rico are available on CD-ROM; national and state level data from the 1987 Census are available online. The Bureau has issued a guide, *Census of Agriculture, 1987 on CD-ROM; Technical Documentation* (1990, various paging totally 88p.). A commercial source also has issued the 1982 Census on CD-ROM. [H179]

United States. Department of Agriculture. Economic Research Service. *Agricultural-Food Policy Review: U.S. Agricultural Policies in a Changing World*. Washington, D.C.: Nov. 1989. 401p. (USDA Agricultural Economic Report no. 620). Background information for debating the "omnibus agricultural and rural development legislation to take effect when the 1985 Act expires in 1990."

United States. Department of Agriculture. Economic Research Service. *Major Statistical Series of the U.S. Department of Agriculture*. Washington, D.C.: 1987–90. (USDA Agriculture Handbook no. 671). Updates 1970 ed. with same title and issued as USDA Agricultural Handbook no. 365. Issued in twelve booklets:

(1) *Agricultural Prices, Expenditures, Farm Employment, and Wages* (April 1990, 23p.)
(2) *Agricultural Production and Efficiency*, by James H. Hauver. (October 1989, 35p.)
(3) *Farm Income*. (November 1988, 45p.)
(4) *Agricultural Marketing Costs and Charges*, by Harry H. Houp. (July 1987, 35p.)
(5) *Consumption and Utilization of Agricultural Products*, Harry H. Houp and Karen Bunch. (October 1989, 34p.)
(6) *Land Values and Land Use*, by Charles H. Barnard and Roger Hexem. (August 1988, 19p.)
(7) *Crop and Livestock Estimates*. (June 1989, 29p.)
(8) *Farmer Cooperatives*, by Ralph M. Richardson. (September 1988, 12p.)
(9) *Market News*. (May 1989, 32p.)
(10) *International Agricultural Statistics*, by Stephen R. Milmoe. (October 1987, 21p.)
(11) *The Balance Sheet*, by Kenneth Erickson et al. (May 1989, 13p.)
(12) *Costs of Production*, by Robert G. McElroy. (September 1987, 15p.)

United States. Department of Agriculture. Statistical Reporting Service. *Scope and Methods of the Statistical Reporting Service*. Washington, D.C.: September 1983. 140p. (USDA Miscellaneous Publication no. 1308)

United States. Department of Agriculture. Office of Rural Development Policy. Rural Resources Guide: A Directory of Public and Private Assistance for Small Communities. Washington, D.C.; For sale by Supt. of Documents, U.S. Gov't. Printing Office, 1985. 475 p. Divided into Community Facilities, Services, General Community Improvement, and Natural Resources. Has a chapter on Information/Research/ Liaison, another on Multipurpose Foundations, plus a listing of Regional and State Contacts, and a general index. Covers U.S. only.

United States. Economics, Statistics, and Cooperatives Service. *Economics of Agriculture; Reports and Publications Issued or Sponsored by U.S. Department of Agriculture's Economics, Statistics, and Cooperatives Service*. April 1961–Sept. 1965–83. Washington, D.C.: 1969–84. Partially superseded by *Reports from USDA's Economics Agencies: Agriculture Economics*.

United States. Foreign Agricultural Service. *Food and Agricultural Export Directory*. Washington, D.C.: 1969.

United States, State Agricultural Data. 1987 ed. Compiled by Letricia M. Womack and Larry G. Traub. Washington, D.C.: U.S. Dept. of Agriculture, Economic Research Service, 1987. 103p. (USDA Agriculture Information Bulletin no. 512). Issued yearly with varying compilers. Agricultural Information Bulletin no. changes yearly.

United States. World Agricultural Outlook Board. *Major Crop Areas and Climatic Profiles*. Washington, D.C.: 1987. 159p. (USDA Agricultural Handbook no. 664).

Vernon, R., ed. *Directory of Research Workers in Agricultural and Allied Sciences*. Exeter, Eng.: CAB International, 1989. 490p. Covers twenty-nine CABI countries and three dependent territories.

World Agricultural Statistics, 1985. Rome: Food and Agricultural Organization, 1985. 94p. Issued irregularly. (FAO Statistical Pocketbook).

World Commodity Outlook: Food, Feedstuffs and Beverages. 1983+. Annual. London: Economist Intelligence Unit.

World Commodity Outlook: Industrial Raw Materials. 1983+. Annual. London: Economist Intelligence Unit.

World Development Report. 1978+. Annual. New York: Oxford University for the World Bank, 1983+. 1978–82 published by the World Bank. Issues average 200–240p.

World Indices of Agricultural and Food Production, 1976–85. Washington, D.C.: U. S. Department of Agriculture, Economic Research Service, 1986. 160p. (USDA Statistical Bulletin no. 744). Revised yearly.

World Tables, 1976+ . . . from the Data Files of the World Bank. Annual. Baltimore and London: Johns Hopkins University Press for the World Bank, 1988–89 ed. 653p. Recent annual data available on diskette and tapes. (1976–84 issued irregularly).

Yokoyama, Kevin M., Kulavit Wanitprapha, Stuart T. Nakamoto and PingSun Leung. *U.S. Import Statistics for Animal Related Commodities, 1981–1986.* New Brunswick, N.J., and Oxford, Eng.: Transaction Books, 1988. 310p.

Yokoyama, Kevin M., Kulavit Wanitprapha, Stuart T. Nakamoto, PingSun Leung, and John C. Roecklein. *U.S. Import Statistics for Agricultural Commodities, 1981–1986.* New Brunswick, N.J. and Oxford, Eng.: Transaction Books, 1988. 879p.

Appendix A. Languages in AGRICOLA/CABI Databases

Citations in CABI and AGRICOLA, by language (1984–87)

	Russian		Japanese		Spanish		German		French		English		All languages[a]	
	CABI	AGRICOLA	CABI	AGRICOLA	CABI	AGRICOLA	CABI	AGRICOLA	CABI	AGRICOLA	CABI	AGRICOLA	CABI	AGRICOLA
1984 No.	8,318	19,870	2,[illegible]0	2,527	3,037	3,867	7,564	11,527	5,322	11,168	90,245	150,806	131,752	174,198
Percent	6.3%	11.4%	[illegible].5%	1.5%	2.3%	2.2%	5.7%	6.6%	4.0%	6.4%	68.5%	86.6%	100.0%	100.0%
1985 No.	7,923	4,890	2,[illegible]75	1,151	2,928	1,750	7,182	4,999	4,618	4,979	87,322	88,687	126,225	93,549
Percent	6.3%	5.2%	[illegible].6%	1.2%	2.3%	1.9%	5.7%	5.3%	3.7%	5.3%	69.2%	94.8%	100.0%	100.0%
1986 No.	6,883	4,417	1,7[illegible]6	890	2,414	1,538	6,721	3,622	4,686	4,314	85,843	83,637	120,795	87,412
Percent	5.7%	5.1%	[illegible].4%	1.0%	2.0%	1.8%	5.6%	4.1%	3.9%	4.9%	71.1%	95.7%	100.0%	100.0%
1987 No.	5,647	3,121	1,6[illegible]2	168	1,955	1,016	5,811	1,805	3,917	3,173	81,574	73,168	111,440	75,287
Percent	5.1%	4.1%	[illegible].4%	0.2%	1.8%	1.3%	5.2%	2.4%	3.5%	4.2%	73.2%	97.2%	100.0%	100.0%
Total no.	28,771	32,298	7,4[illegible]3	4,736	10,334	8,171	27,278	21,953	18,543	23,634	344,984	396,298	490,212	430,446
Average no.	7,193	8,075	1,8[illegible]1	1,184	2,584	2,043	6,820	5,488	4,636	5,909	86,246	99,075	122,553	107,612
Percent	5.9%	7.5%	[illegible].5%	1.1%	2.1%	1.9%	5.6%	5.1%	3.8%	5.5%	70.4%	92.1%	100.0%	100.0%

Citations pertaining to agricultural economics and rural sociology in CABI and AGRICOLA, by language (1984–87)

	Russian		Japanese		Spanish		German		French		English		All languages	
	CABI	AGRICOLA	CABI	AGRICOLA	CABI	AGRICOLA	CABI	AGRICOLA	CABI	AGRICOLA	CABI	AGRICOLA	CABI	AGRICOLA
1984 No.	271	664	[illegible]	87	223	172	783	512	675	567	6,017	9,150	9,844	12,316
Percent	3%	5%	[illegible]%	1%	2%	1%	8%	4%	7%	5%	61%	74%	100%	100%
1985 No.	294	199	[illegible]	66	221	100	693	213	581	246	6,144	6,007	9,514	7,936
Percent	3%	3%	[illegible]%	1%	2%	1%	7%	3%	6%	3%	65%	76%	100%	100%
1986 No.	263	136	[illegible]	25	191	115	743	167	524	228	5,917	5,579	9,109	7,373
Percent	3%	2%	[illegible]%	0%	2%	2%	8%	2%	6%	3%	65%	76%	100%	100%
1987 No.	252	120	2[illegible]	22	206	58	739	68	388	127	5,748	5,092	8,697	6,474
Percent	2.9%	1.9%	0.3%	0.3%	2.4%	0.9%	8.5%	1.1%	4.5%	2.0%	66.1%	78.7%	100.0%	100.0%
Total no.	1,080	1,119	6[illegible]	200	841	445	2,958	960	2,168	1,168	23,826	25,828	37,164	34,099
Average no.	270	280	15	50	210	111	740	240	542	292	5,957	6,457	9,291	8,525
Percent	2.9%	3.3%	0.[illegible]%	0.6%	2.3%	1.3%	8.0%	2.8%	5.8%	3.4%	64.1%	75.7%	100.0%	100.0%

[a]Some citations list more than one language. Thus, the sum of the citations by language may exceed the "total" articles and is not useful in calculating the remaining citations to articles in languages not represented in this table.

Appendix B. American Agricultural Economics Association Classic Book List

This list was created in 1987 by Dr. Dale W Adams, book review editor of the *American Journal of Agricultural Economics*. It was compiled by asking for book nominations and then voting on those titles by the fifty to sixty elected Fellows of the American Agricultural Economics Association. These titles received the greatest number of votes, but were closely followed by forty additional titles. The books are currently being reviewed again, from an historical perspective, in the book review section of the *American Journal of Agricultural Economics*.

Benedict, M. R. *Farm Policies of the United States, 1790–1950*. New York: Twentieth Century Fund, 1953. 548p.

Ciriacy-Wantrup, S. V. *Resource Conservation: Economics and Policies*. Los Angeles and Berkeley: University of California Press, 1952. 395p. 3d ed., 1968, 395p.

Cochrane, Willard W. *Farm Prices: Myth and Reality*. Minneapolis: University of Minnesota Press, 1958. 189p. Repr. 1974.

Ezekiel, Mordecai, and Karl A. Fox. *Methods of Correlation and Regression Analysis, Linear and Curvilinear*. New York: Wiley, 1959. 548p. Repr. 1963.

Galbraith, John K. *The New Industrial State*. Boston: Houghton Mifflin, 1967. 427p. 4th ed., 1985, 438p.

Hayami, Yujiro, and Vernon W. Ruttan. *Agricultural Development: An International Perspective*. Baltimore: Johns Hopkins University Press, 1971. 367p. Rev. ed., 1984, 506p.

Heady, Earl O. *Economics of Agricultural Production and Resource Use*. New York: Prentice-Hall, 1952. 850p.

Johnson, D. Gale. *Forward Prices for Agriculture*. Chicago: University of Chicago Press, 1947. 259p. Repr. 1976.

Nicholls, W. H. *A Theoretical Analysis of Imperfect Competition with Special Applications in the Agricultural Industries*. Ames, Iowa: Iowa State College Press, 1941. 384p.

Salter, Leonard A., Jr. *A Critical Review of Research in Land Economics*. Minneapolis: University of Minnesota Press, 1948. 258p. Repr. 1967.

Schultz, T. W. *Agriculture in an Unstable Economy*. New York: McGraw-Hill, 1945. 299p.

Schultz, T. W. *Transforming Traditional Agriculture*. Chicago: University of Chicago Press, 1964. 212p. Repr. 1976.

Waugh, Frederick V. *Demand and Price Analysis: Some Examples from Agriculture*. Washington, D.C.: U.S. Department of Agriculture, 1964. (USDA Technical Bulletin no. 1316). 94p.

Index

Authors and titles in the core lists of journals (pp. 78–83), primary numbered report series (pp. 87–91), the core monograph lists (pp. 100–173, 175–228, 230–64), the historically significant monographs (pp. 272–314), and Appendix B are not included in this index.

Library of Congress Cataloging-in-Publication

Olsen, Wallace C.
  Agricultural economics and rural sociology : the contemporary core literature / Wallace C. Olsen.
    p. cm. — (Literature of the agricultural sciences)
  Includes bibliographical references and index.
  ISBN 0-8014-2677-4 (alk. paper)
  1. Agriculture—Economic aspects. 2. Sociology, Rural. 3. Agriculture—Economic aspects—Developing countries. 4. Developing countries—Rural conditions. I. Title. II. Series.
HD1415.047 1991
338.1—dc20 91-55261